P9-DBO-597

encyclopedia of
SCIENCE

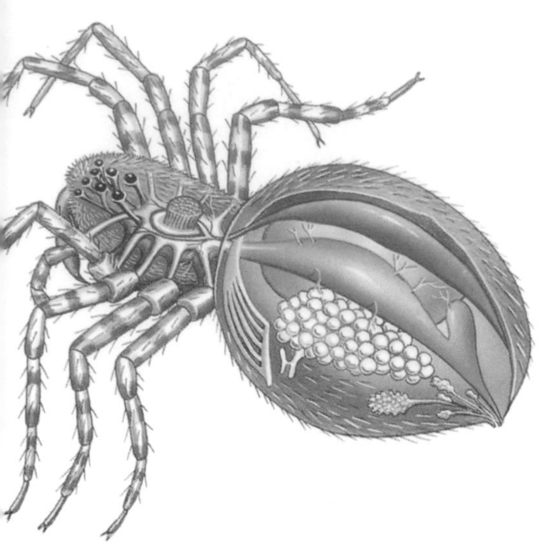

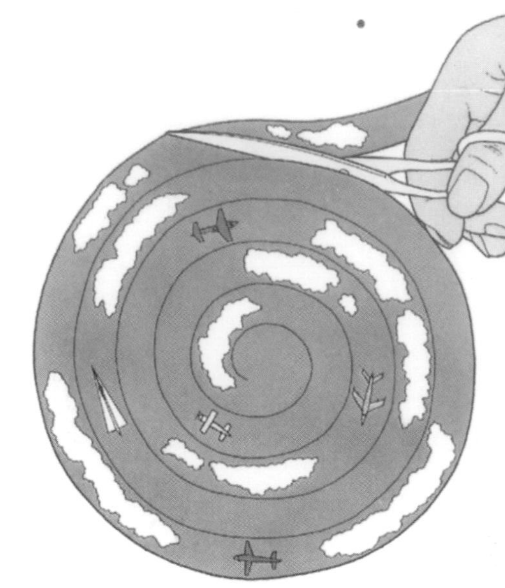

This edition produced in 1994 for
Shooting Star Press Inc
230 Fifth Avenue
Suite 1212
New York, NY 10001

Designed and produced by
Aladdin Books Ltd
28 Percy Street
London W1

Printed in the Czech Republic

ISBN 1-56924-066-3

Some of the material in this book was previously published in the Hands On Science series

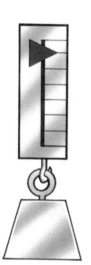

CONTENTS

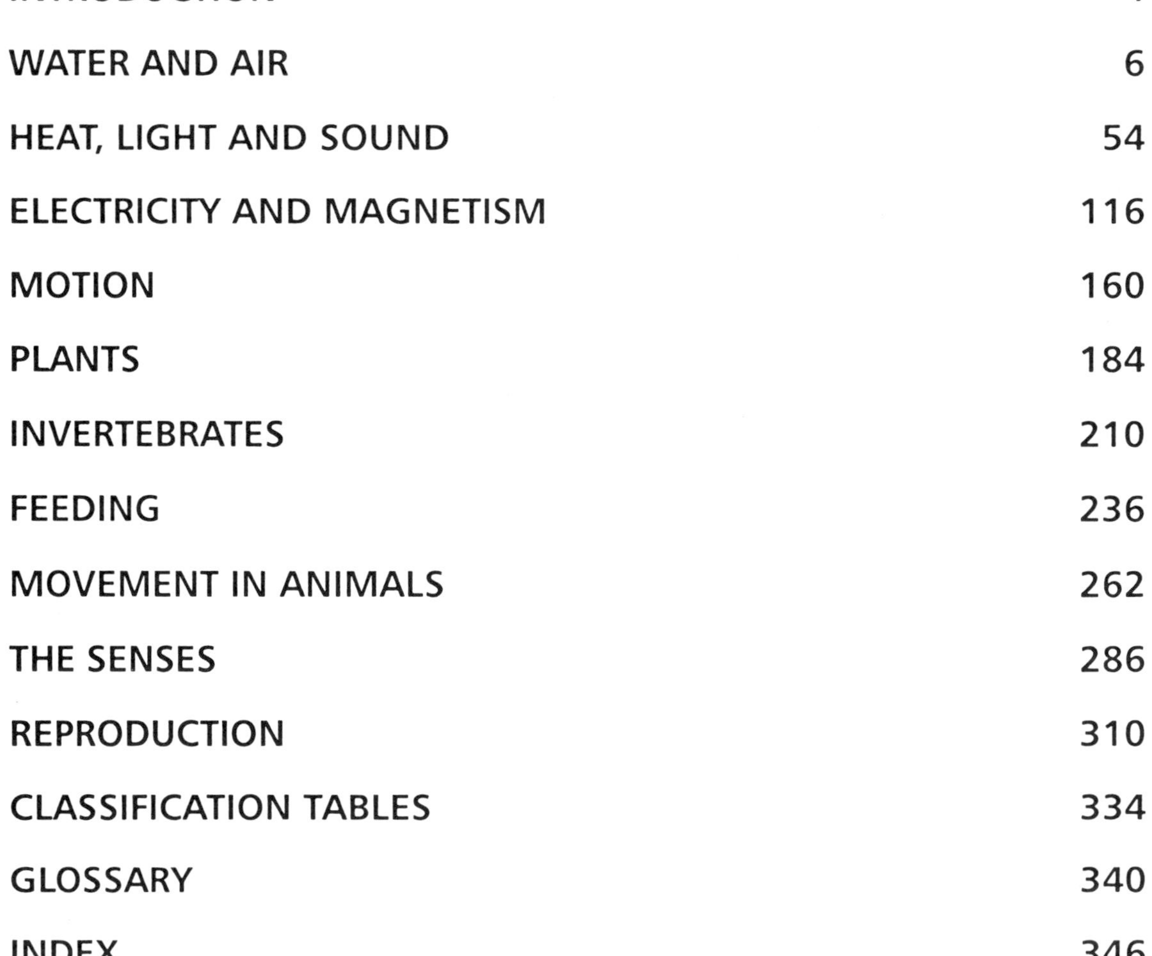

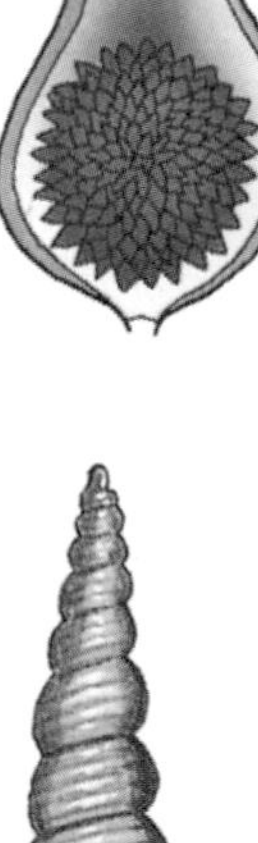

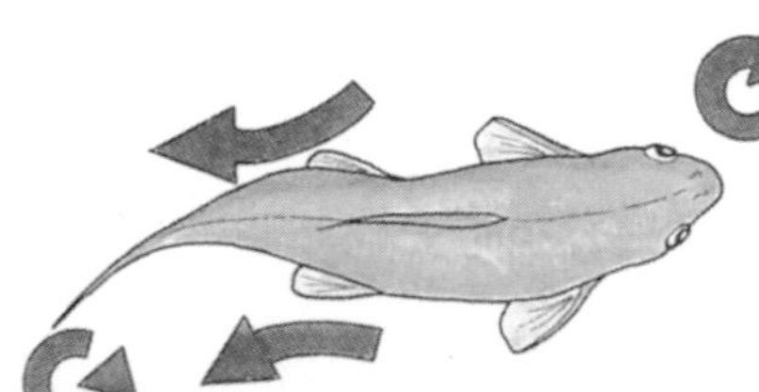

encyclopedia of
SCIENCE

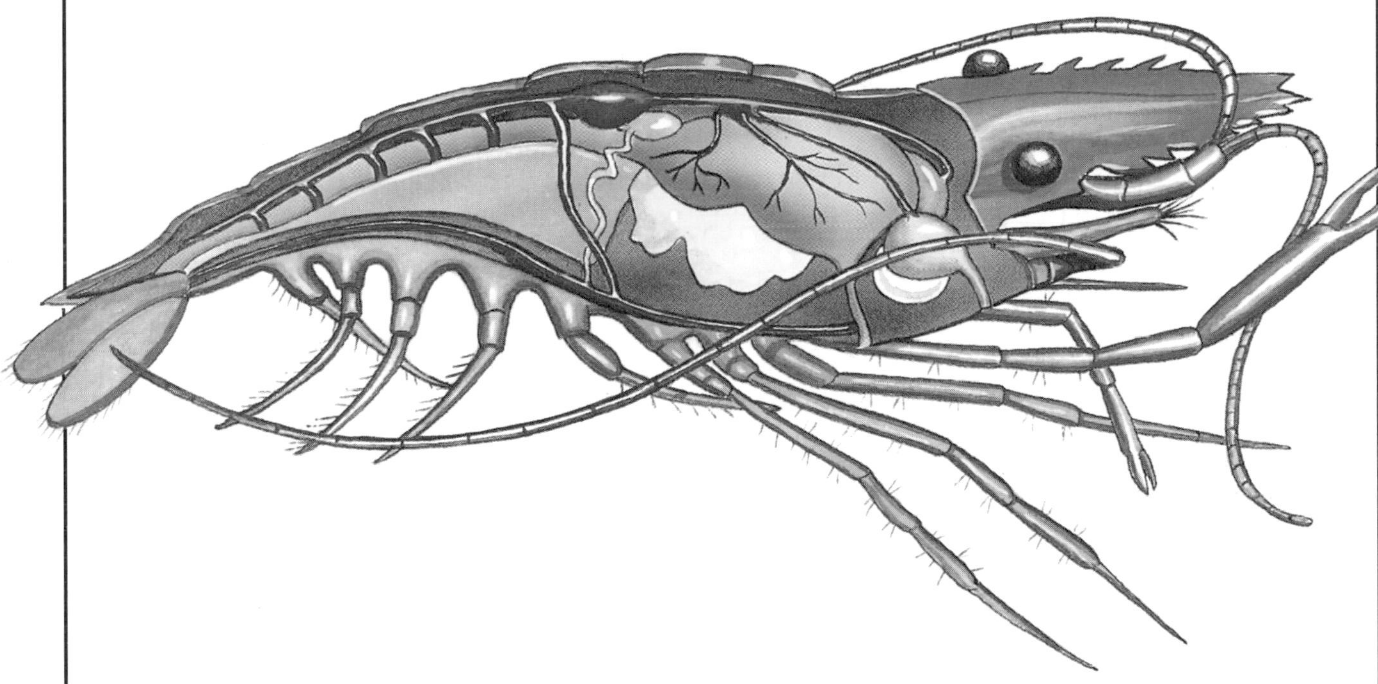

Written by
Neil Ardley, Dr Jeffrey Bates, William Hemsley, Peter Lafferty,
Steve Parker, Clint Twist and Kathryn Whyman

Illustrated by
Neil Bullpit, Richard Hull, Aziz Khan, Ian Moores,
Alex Pang, Zolfaghari and Creative Hands

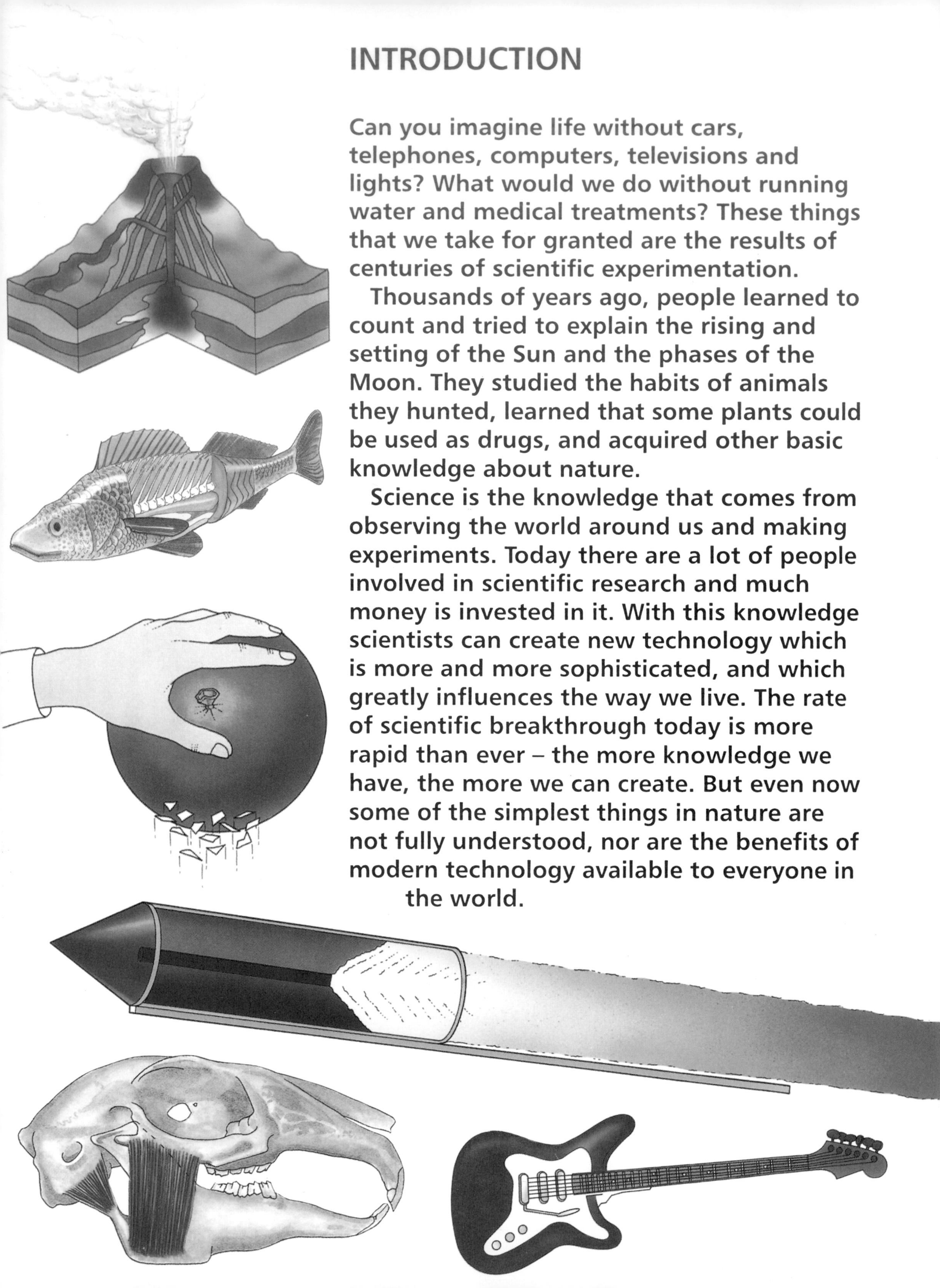

INTRODUCTION

Can you imagine life without cars, telephones, computers, televisions and lights? What would we do without running water and medical treatments? These things that we take for granted are the results of centuries of scientific experimentation.

Thousands of years ago, people learned to count and tried to explain the rising and setting of the Sun and the phases of the Moon. They studied the habits of animals they hunted, learned that some plants could be used as drugs, and acquired other basic knowledge about nature.

Science is the knowledge that comes from observing the world around us and making experiments. Today there are a lot of people involved in scientific research and much money is invested in it. With this knowledge scientists can create new technology which is more and more sophisticated, and which greatly influences the way we live. The rate of scientific breakthrough today is more rapid than ever – the more knowledge we have, the more we can create. But even now some of the simplest things in nature are not fully understood, nor are the benefits of modern technology available to everyone in the world.

This encyclopedia introduces the reader to scientific experimentation and the ways in which scientists look at the world. It concentrates on the two main areas of science – the physical and living worlds. Topics begin by looking at the properties of natural phenomena such as water and air, heat, light and sound, and end with their larger scale uses in the world of technology. The complex forces involved in movement, electricity and magnetism are then explored in the following chapters.

Simple experiments using everyday materials are suggested and illustrated with diagrams, and ideas and questions thrown up for discussion. Experiments include how to make a parachute, a telescope, and a water gauge and how to test your reflexes.

The second half of the book looks at living things; plants to insects and large mammals. It explains the different ways in which species feed, reproduce and move.

Easy-to-follow classification tables for the living world, a diagram of human body systems and a periodic table at the back of the book are provided for quick reference, together with a comprehensive glossary and an easy-to-access index.

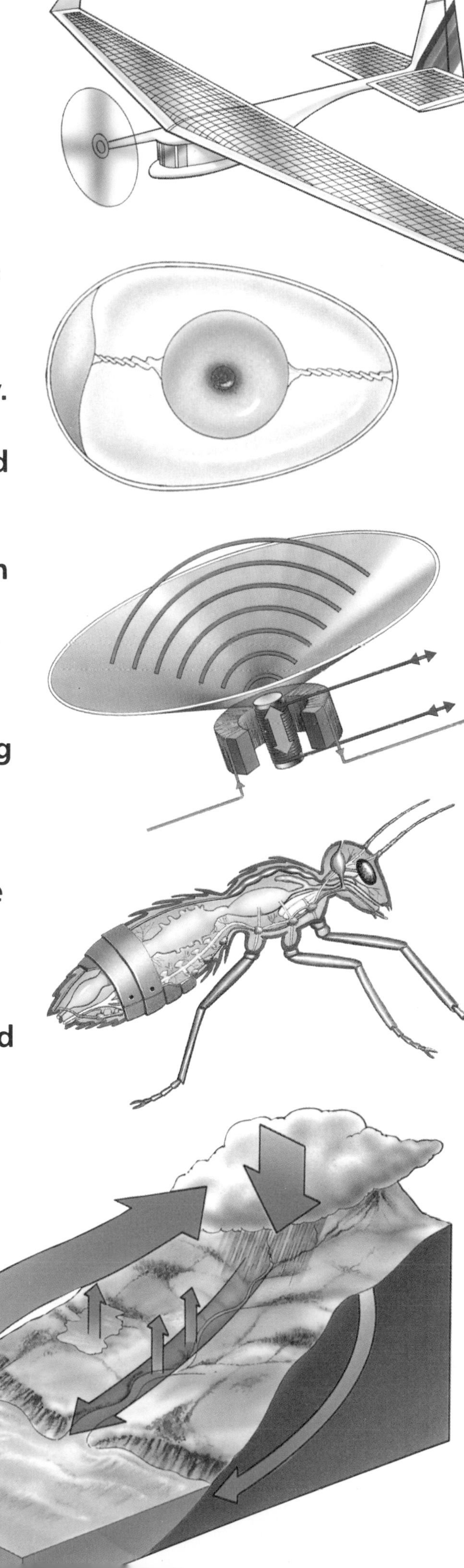

encyclopedia of science

WATER AND AIR

CONTENTS

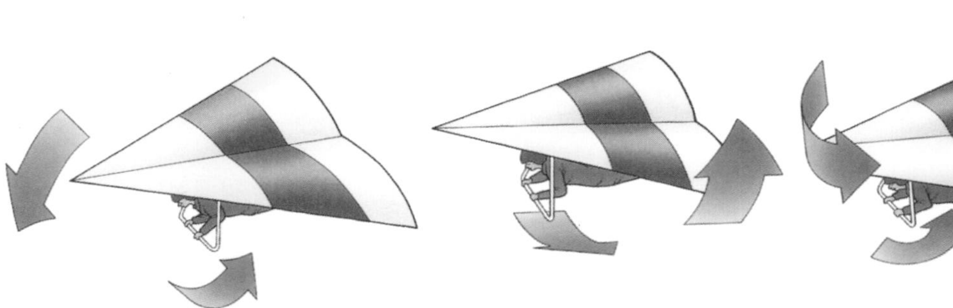

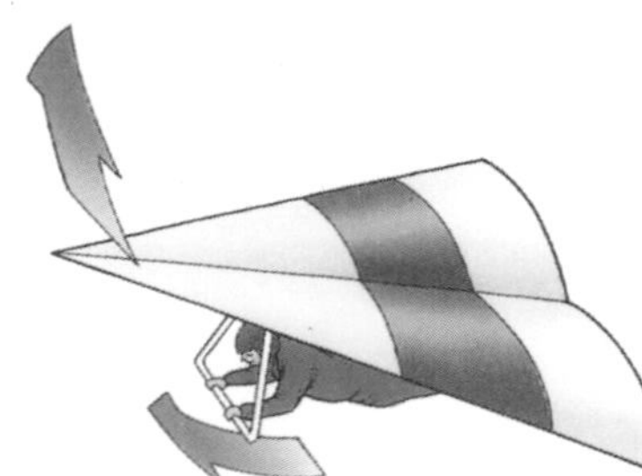

INTRODUCTION

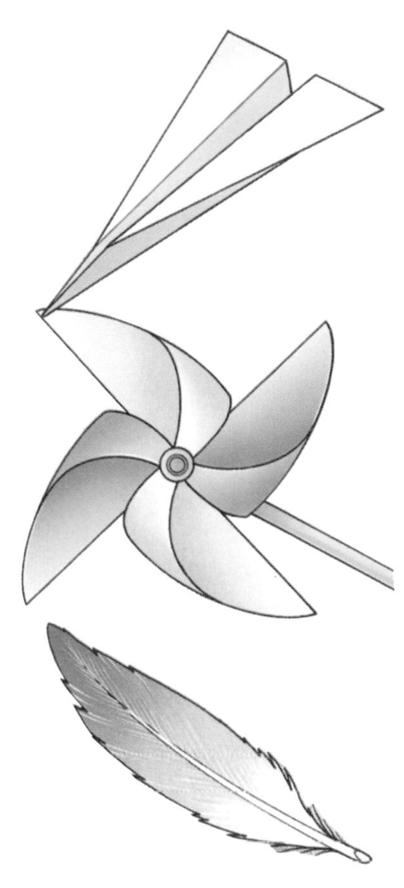

Water and air are two natural phenomena essential for life. Water is the most abundant substance on the planet, and the seas cover over 70 percent of the Earth's surface. But without rain, which comes from the air in the Earth's atmosphere, life would be impossible. The atmosphere, which extends 500 miles into space, provides us with air to breathe, and acts as a warm blanket for Earth, producing the right conditions for life. Air is all around us. We cannot see it, but it is not empty space. It is actually a rich mixture of many gases, including oxygen, that we breathe. Air movement is a source of power used to generate electricity.

This first section looks at the unusual and beautiful properties of water, how we can control its flow, and how we use it as a source of energy. It also explains what air is, what causes winds and hurricanes, what air pressure is and how things travel through air.

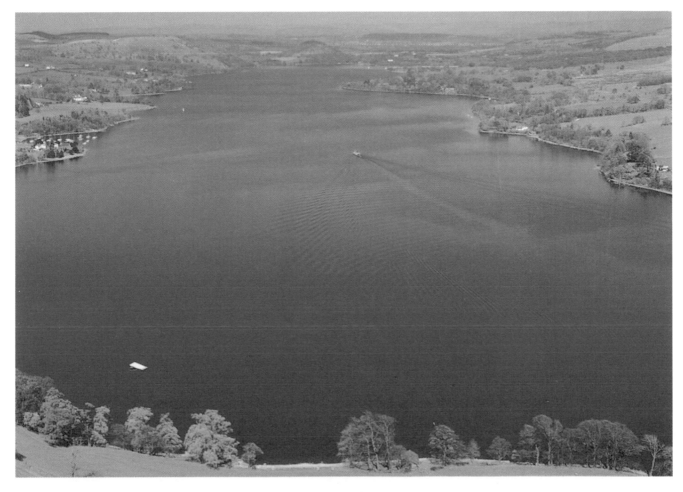

RAIN

Water is constantly moving through the atmosphere. Invisible water vapor rises into the air, then falls as rain. Rain provides all the useful water which we need on the Earth. Without rain there would be no drinking water, grass, trees or crops. Water is essential to all living things.

RAIN CYCLE

Most of the water that falls as rain starts out in the sea. The heat of the Sun causes tiny particles of water (which are called molecules) to drift away from the surface into the air. This process, which is known as evaporation, also occurs on lakes and rivers. The water molecules are carried by winds and gradually rise, often helped by mountains. As they rise, the molecules cool and form clouds. When sufficient water has gathered in a particular cloud, it falls as rain. Once the water is on the ground, it flows back toward the sea.

▲ The water in each raindrop may have traveled hundreds of miles before finally falling back to earth.

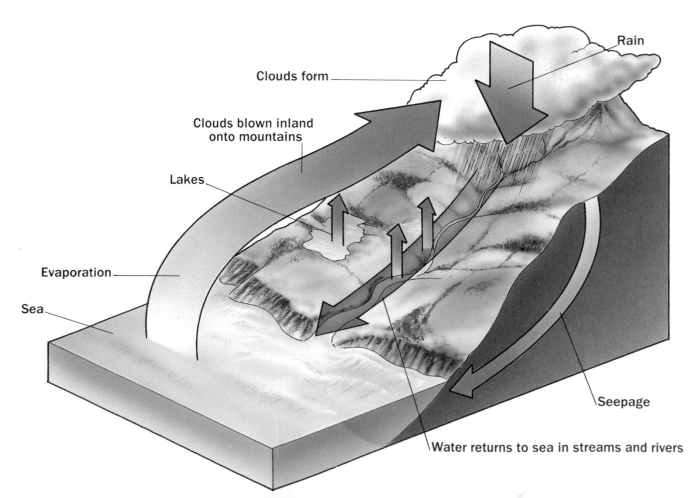

Rain
Clouds form
Clouds blown inland onto mountains
Lakes
Evaporation
Sea
Seepage
Water returns to sea in streams and rivers

ARTIFICIAL RAIN

The amount of rain that falls on a particular region depends on a number of factors. The most important are the distance from the sea and the direction of the wind. Some regions have a regular pattern of rainfall, in others it can vary enormously from year to year. In parts of the world where there is insufficient rainfall to grow crops, farmers often spray their fields with water. Providing additional water to crops is called irrigation, and is common in hot countries. Spraying is a very useful form of irrigation, but it can be wasteful because a lot of water is lost to the atmosphere.

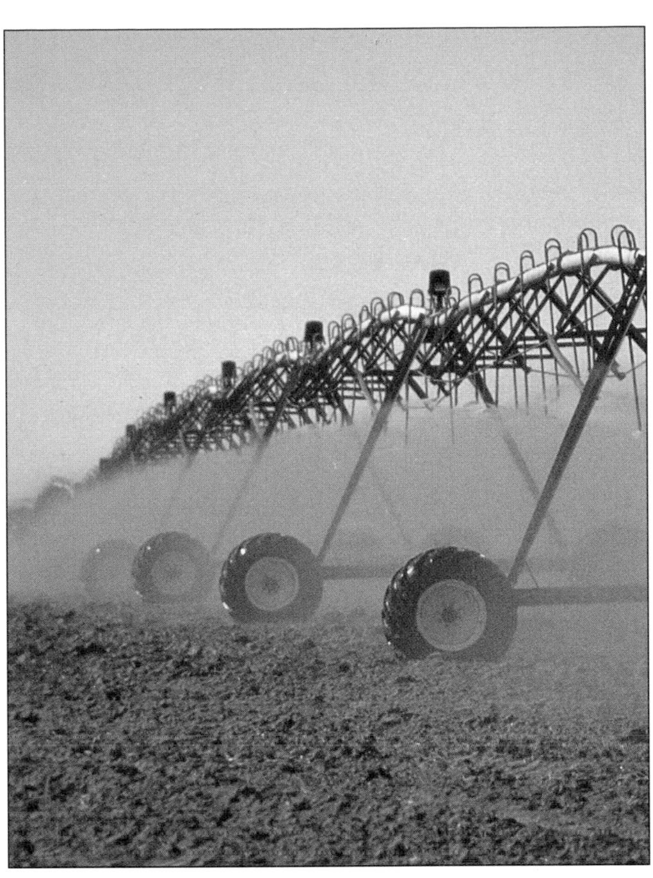

► Irrigation can enable crops to grow even in the middle of a desert. Without irrigation, much less food would grow.

MAKE A RAIN GAUGE

Rainfall is measured using a rain gauge. You can make one from the top of a detergent bottle and a metal can, as shown in the diagram.

Place your rain gauge in the open, away from buildings and trees. Dig a hole or use stones to prevent it from being blown over.

At the same time each week, measure the amount of water that has been collected. Make a chart showing the weekly totals.

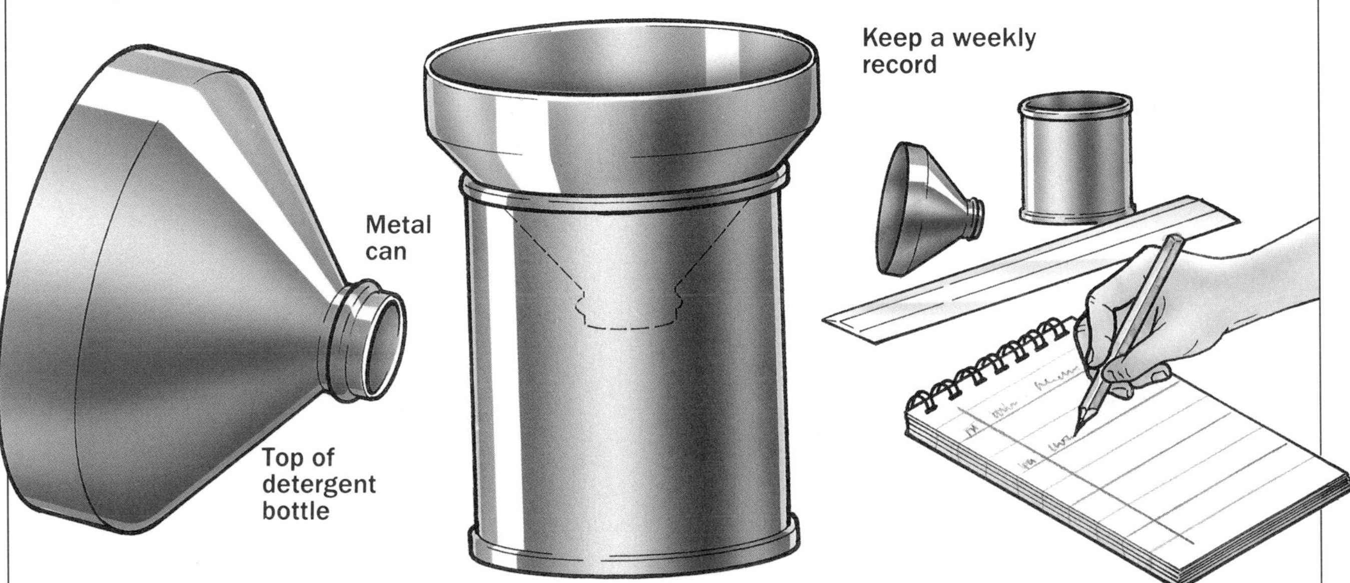

WATER – SOLID, LIQUID AND GAS

Water is a very unusual substance because we often see it in all three physical states. As a liquid it flows in rivers and pipes, and as a vapor it floats with the air. When it is cold enough, water freezes into solid ice. The difference between the states is the amount of energy in the water molecules.

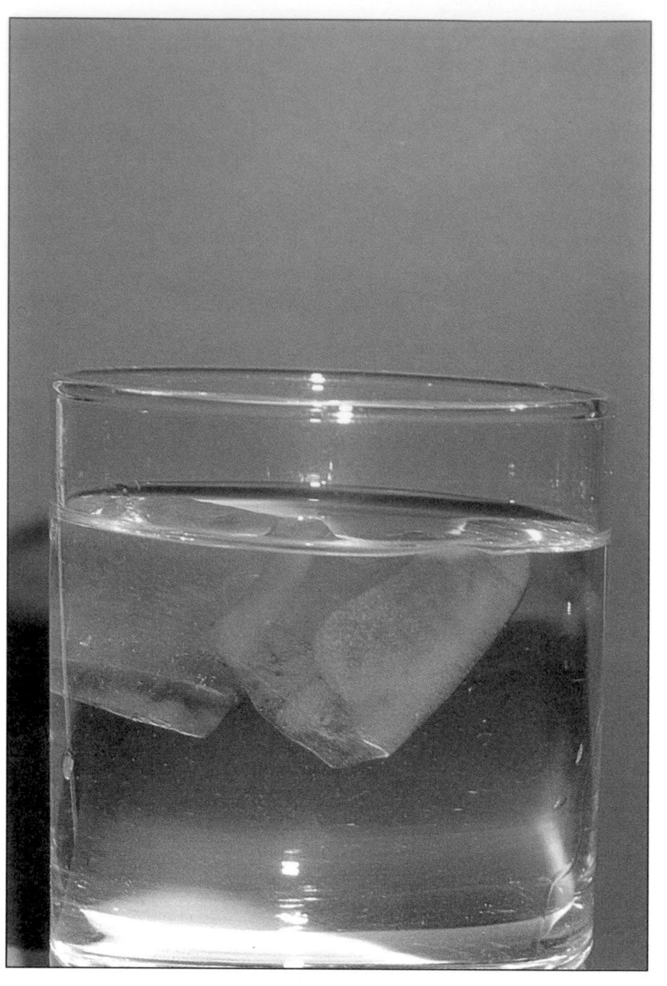

▲ The three states of water – solid ice floats in liquid water, and the air contains invisible water vapor.

WHAT'S HAPPENING?

All matter is composed of atoms or molecules held together by powerful forces. In solids, the molecules have little energy and stay together in a rigid structure. The water molecules in ice only have enough energy to vibrate very slightly. In a liquid, the molecules have enough energy to overcome part of the force holding them together. The molecules in liquid water are still held together, but are able to move freely in relation to each other. In a vapor or gas, the molecules have enough energy to completely overcome the force between them. The separate water molecules that make up water vapor can easily mix into the air. Water vapor given off by boiling water is usually called steam.

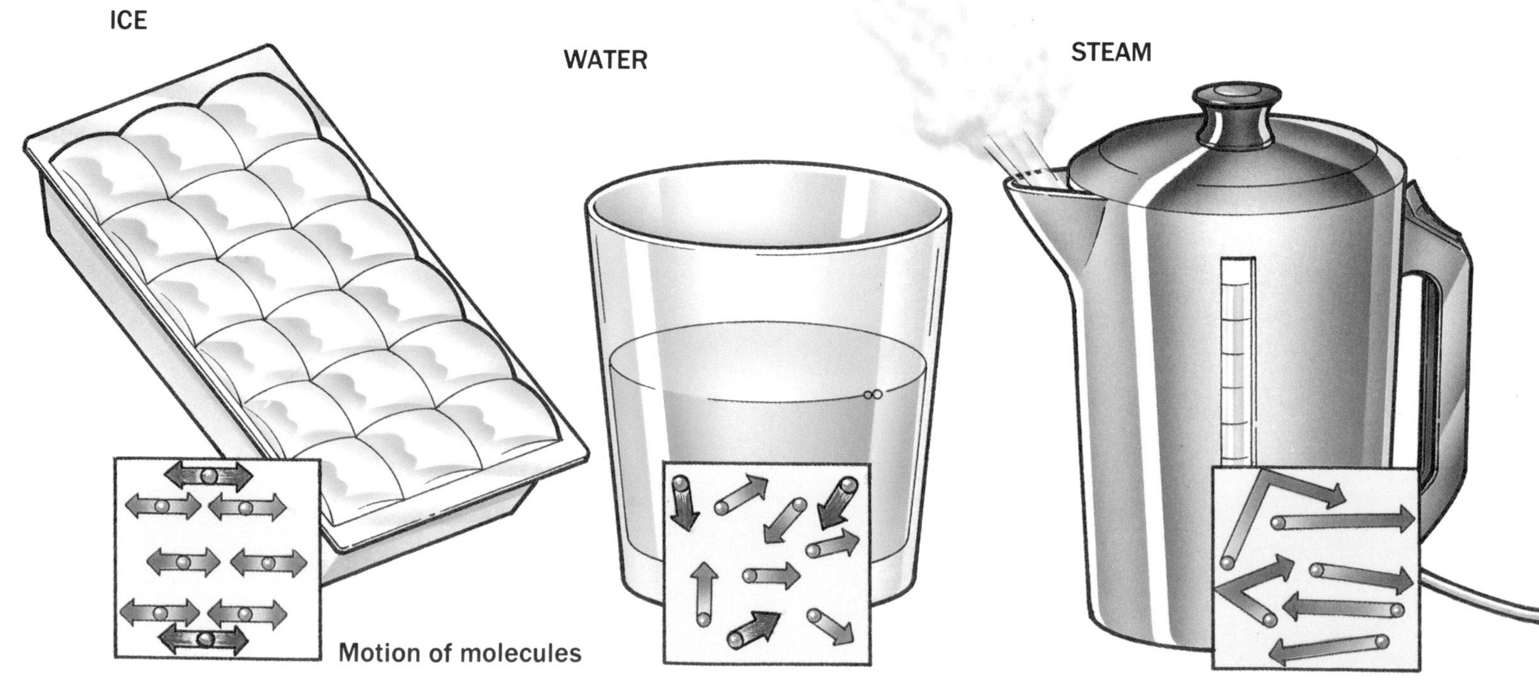

EVAPORATION

Evaporation occurs when a molecule of liquid water receives enough energy from the sun to break away from the surface. The energy arrives in the form of heat, but during evaporation the temperature of the liquid remains constant. The extra energy is carried away by the evaporating molecules. Boiling is a special form of evaporation in which there is another source of heat. In nature boiling often occurs near volcanoes. When a liquid boils, all the molecules have enough heat energy to break away from each other. This is why boiling water and steam are so dangerous – they contain enough heat energy to cause serious burns.

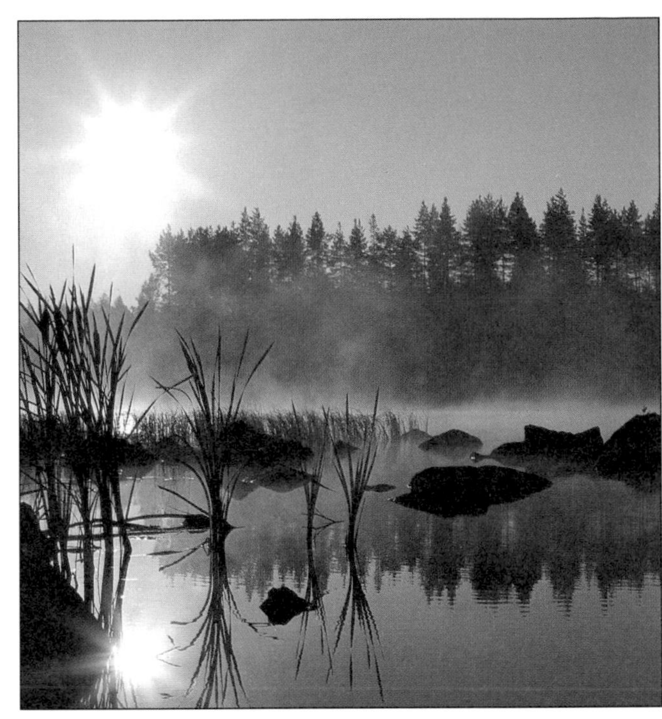

▲ Every water surface is constantly losing water by evaporation. Above the surface of lakes this can sometimes be seen as a thin mist.

EVAPORATION PROJECT

Place the same amount of water in a small bottle and a shallow bowl. Leave them in a room for a day or two, then check what has happened. The bowl will have lost more of its water.

If possible, repeat the experiment in a sunny place, a shady place, and inside the refrigerator. You will find that temperature also affects the rate at which water evaporates from the bowl.

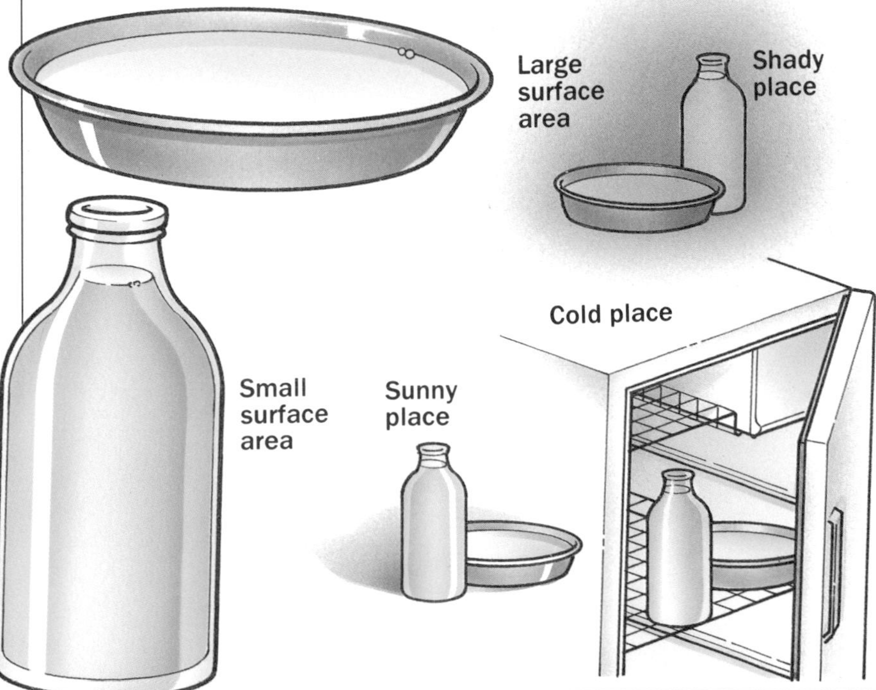

QUIZ

Clothes dry because the water evaporates. Clothes dry quickest when hung on a line in the sun. Why does spreading the clothes on a line make them dry faster than if they were rolled up in a ball? Remember that more water evaporates from a large surface than from a small one.

CLOUDS AND CONDENSATION

Condensation is the process by which water vapor turns back into a liquid state. This happens when the water molecules lose heat energy and condense. Condensation is almost the exact opposite of evaporation. The difference is that water vapor can condense on any cold surface or object.

CLOUD FORMATION

Warm air can hold more water vapor than cold air. As warm air rises, it cools and the water molecules condense onto tiny specks of dust. These minute droplets of water fall very slowly toward earth, only to be swept back up by warm rising air which contains more water vapor. As the process is repeated, the water droplets begin to form a cloud which we can see from the ground. If the cloud moves into colder air, the droplets get bigger as more water molecules condense. When the droplets are too heavy to remain in the cloud, they fall as rain.

Large clouds may be hundreds of yards thick, and contain thousands of gallons of water. ▲

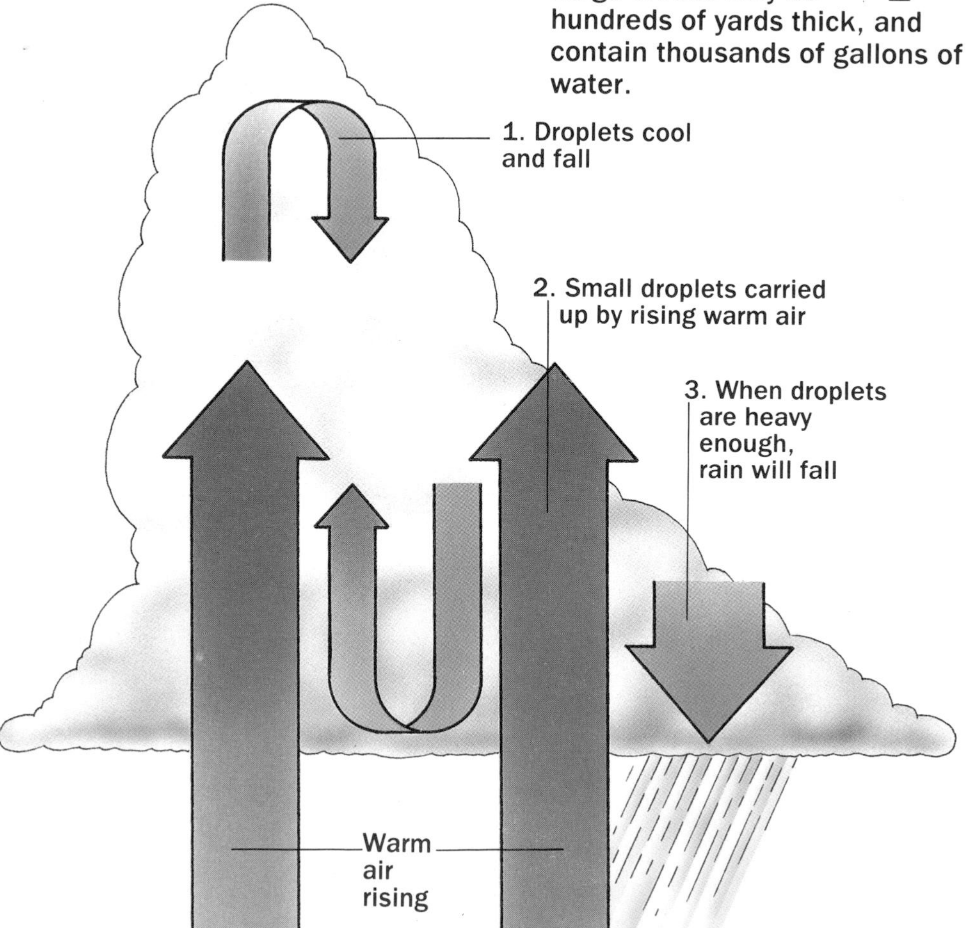
1. Droplets cool and fall
2. Small droplets carried up by rising warm air
3. When droplets are heavy enough, rain will fall
Warm air rising

CONDENSING

Put a clean dry glass in the freezer of a refrigerator, and leave it for about 20 minutes. When you take it out of the freezer, a fine mist of water droplets will appear. This is formed by water vapor in the air condensing on the cold glass. Place a saucer over a hot drink for a minute, then lift it up. Water vapor that would normally escape into the atmosphere has condensed into droplets on the bottom of the saucer.

FOG

Fog is really a cloud that has formed close to the ground. When a region of damp air comes into contact with a cooler land surface, some of the water vapor condenses into tiny droplets. These are small enough to remain suspended in the air and obscure our vision.

▲ Fog usually forms during the night when the ground cools. In the morning, the sun's heat soon evaporates fog.

QUIZ

When we breathe out, we are exhaling water vapor into the air. Normally this water vapor remains invisible, but on cold days our breath can be seen. Why is this, and where does the water go eventually? Remember that we can see clouds because they consist of tiny water droplets.

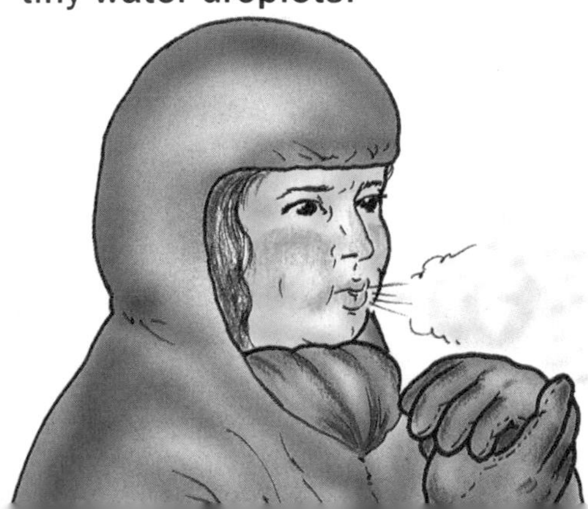

SALTWATER SEAS

Nearly all the water on Earth is seawater. In fact, the seas and oceans of the world contain 97 percent of our planet's water. Seawater is water that has various things dissolved in it, chiefly the substance that we call salt. Rainwater contains no dissolved salt, and is therefore called freshwater.

SOLUTIONS

When certain solid substances are placed in water, they gradually break up and become mixed in with the water – they dissolve. The type of mixture that is formed is known as a solution, and water is said to be a solvent.The substance that dissolves is known as a solute. Dry salt is made up of atoms arranged into small crystals. When salt is added to water, the water molecules break up the salt crystals. The particles making up the salt dissolve throughout the water. If all the water evaporates, the salt will be left behind. This is how salt flats are created over millions of years.

▲ The Earth is a saltwater world. The oceans cover about 70% of our planet's surface.

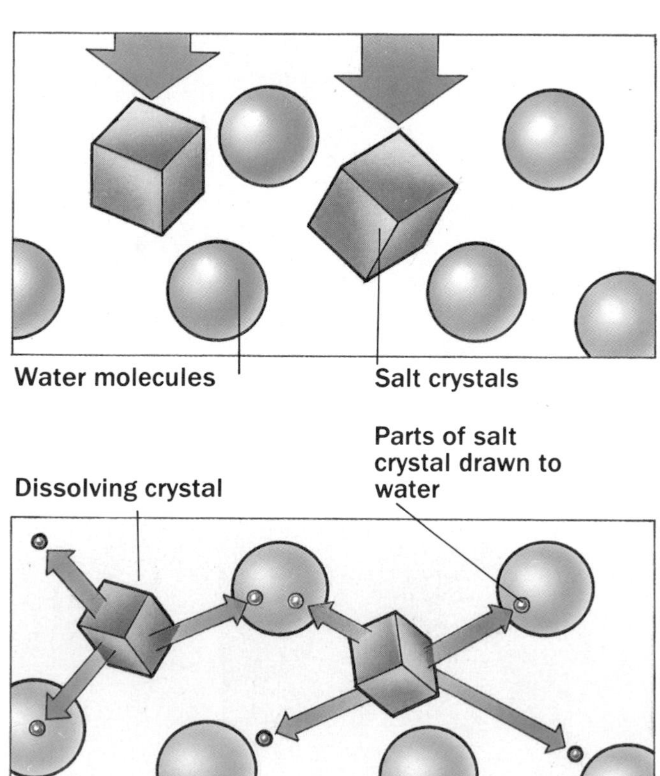

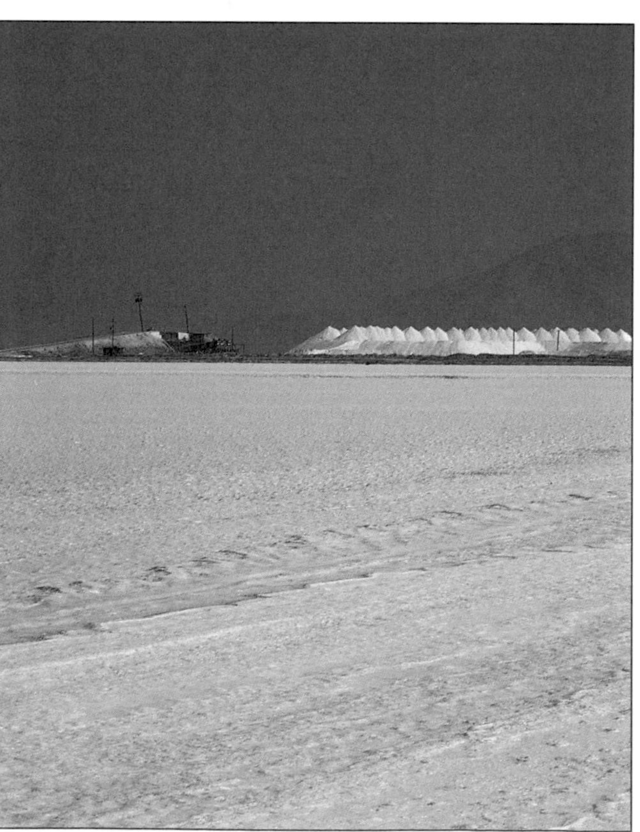

▼ These salt flats were created millions of years ago by a saltwater sea.

THE USEFUL SOLVENT

Many other liquids, like alcohol and gasoline, also act as solvents. But water is the most useful solvent because it is harmless to living things. Many flavored drinks are solutions. Tea leaves do not dissolve in water, but some of their flavor does and this makes a refreshing drink. Instant coffee is coffee that has been specially treated so that it dissolves completely. Colored materials can also be dissolved in water to make paints and inks. When the water evaporates, the color is left behind. Many useful chemicals also dissolve in water. Farmers and gardeners often apply fertilizer or weedkiller as a solution in water. Plants absorb water from the ground, and in doing so they also absorb anything that is dissolved in the water.

△ Children use different color paints which have been dissolved in water. These are called "watercolors."

WHAT IS SOLUBLE?

Test different substances to see which are soluble in water. Use clean water each time. Stirring the water speeds up the dissolving process.

Some substances only partly dissolve so you can use water to separate a soluble substance from an Insoluble one, like salt and sand (insoluble).

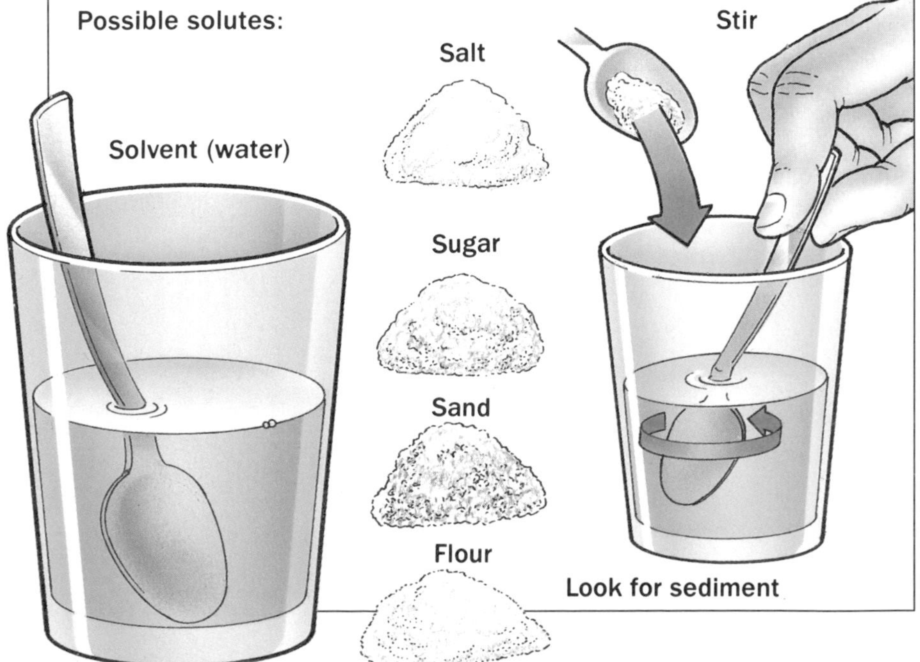

QUIZ

Water molecules are constantly evaporating from the sea, leaving the salt behind. But the sea does not get any saltier. Can you work out why not? Remember that the seas gain as much water as is lost to the air through evaporation.

ICE

Most of the world's ice is located permanently around the North and South Poles. These two regions are very cold because they receive very little energy from the sun. Water can only remain in liquid form above 32 degrees Fahrenheit (32°F), below that temperature it turns into solid ice.

FREEZE/THAW

As water cools, its molecules lose energy. At 32°F, the energy possessed by the molecules falls and the molecules stop moving freely. They become fixed in an arrangement called a crystal. When water molecules form an ice crystal or a snowflake, the average distance between them increases slightly. This increase means that water expands when it freezes. Above 32°F, the molecules gain enough energy to move freely again, and the ice melts. Over many years, through repeated freezing and melting, water can easily break up large rocks into small stones.

▲ Icicles form when dripping water freezes. Each drop makes the icicle longer.

▼ Water expands with force when it freezes. The force is strong enough to shatter rock or burst metal water pipes.

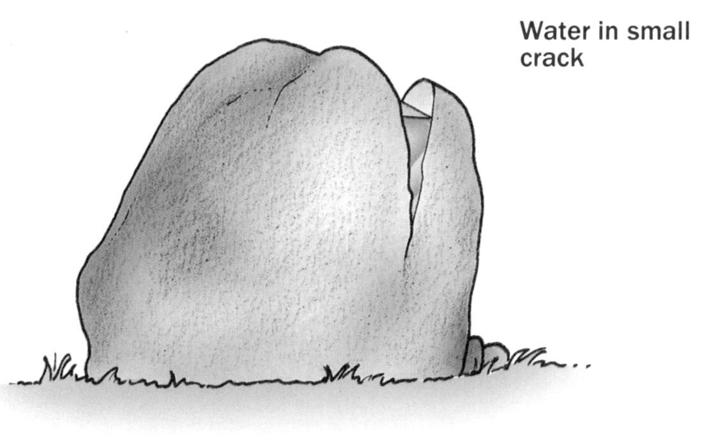

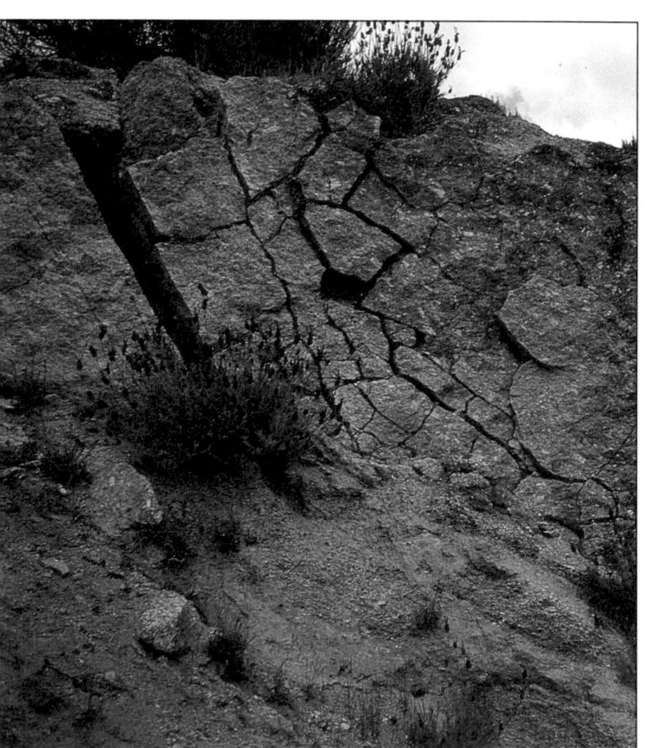

HAIL

Water often freezes high in the atmosphere. In winter it often falls to earth without melting, as ice crystals that we call snowflakes. Hail occurs when water droplets are swirled by the wind between layers of warm and cold air. The droplets alternately freeze and then partially melt many times before finally falling to earth. A hailstone is made up of layers like an onion.

▲ Sometimes hailstones fall together with rain. Updrafts take raindrops upward into the cold air, where they freeze. Then they fall to where they pick up a layer of water on them and are then blown upward again.

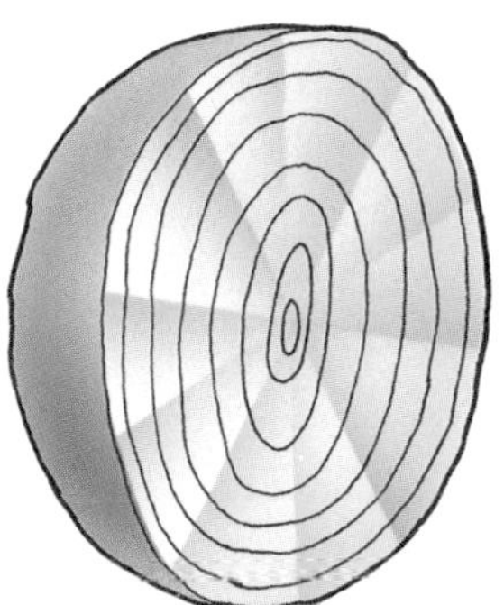

EXPANSION PROJECT

You can demonstrate how ice expands by using a small plastic container. Chose one that has a tight-fitting top.

Make a hole in the top, and plug it with plastic wrap. Fill the container to the brim and put on the top.

Put the container in the freezer overnight. As the water freezes, the expansion forces out the plug.

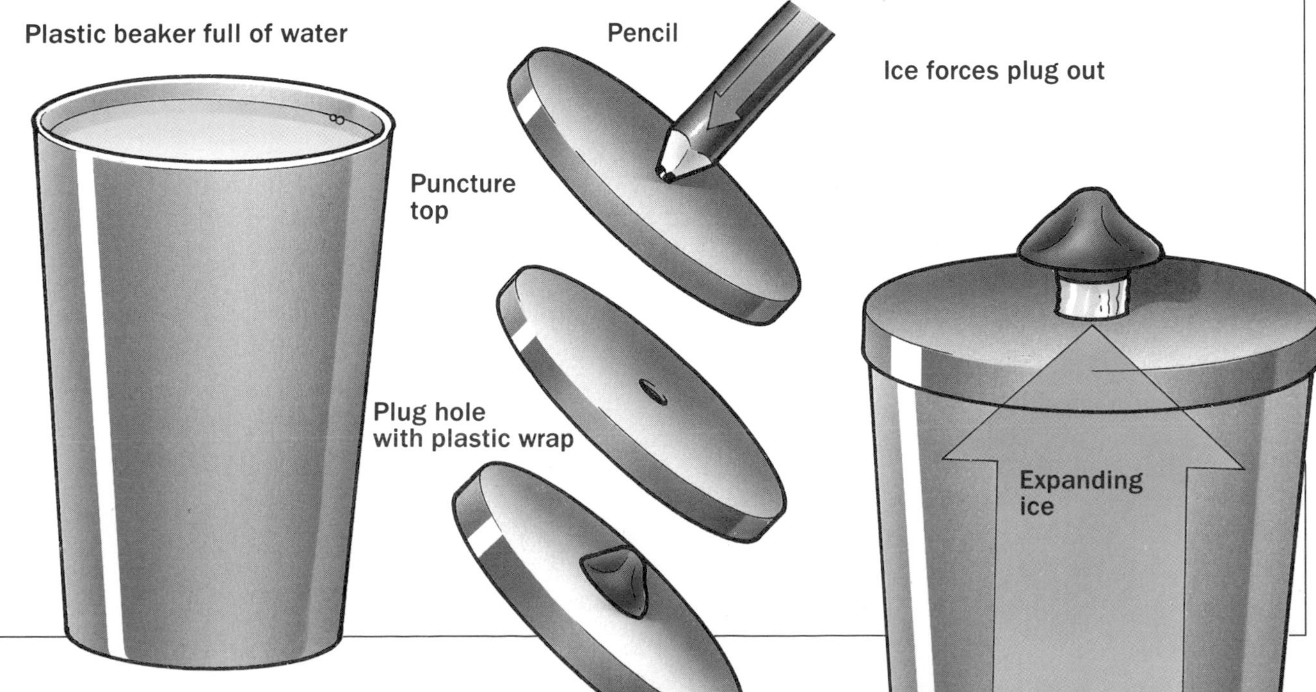

FLOATING

Some things, like a steel ball, sink through water just like they fall through air. Others start to sink then stop – they float. Most kinds of wood float. Ice floats in water because it expands when it freezes. This means that ice is less *dense* than water. Most woods are less dense than water.

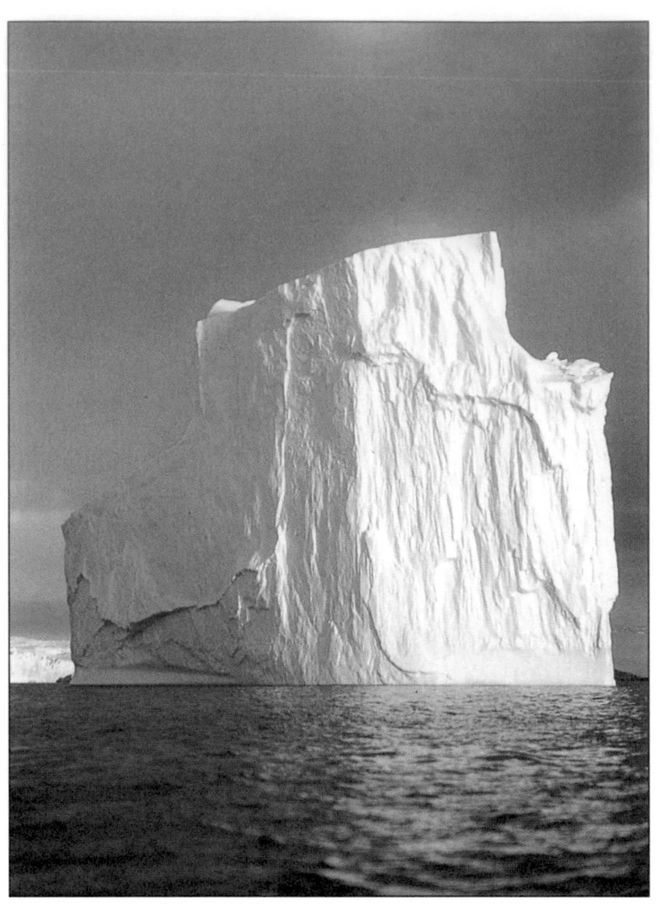

▲ Ice is 10% less dense than water. For this reason, 90% of the volume of an iceberg is below the surface.

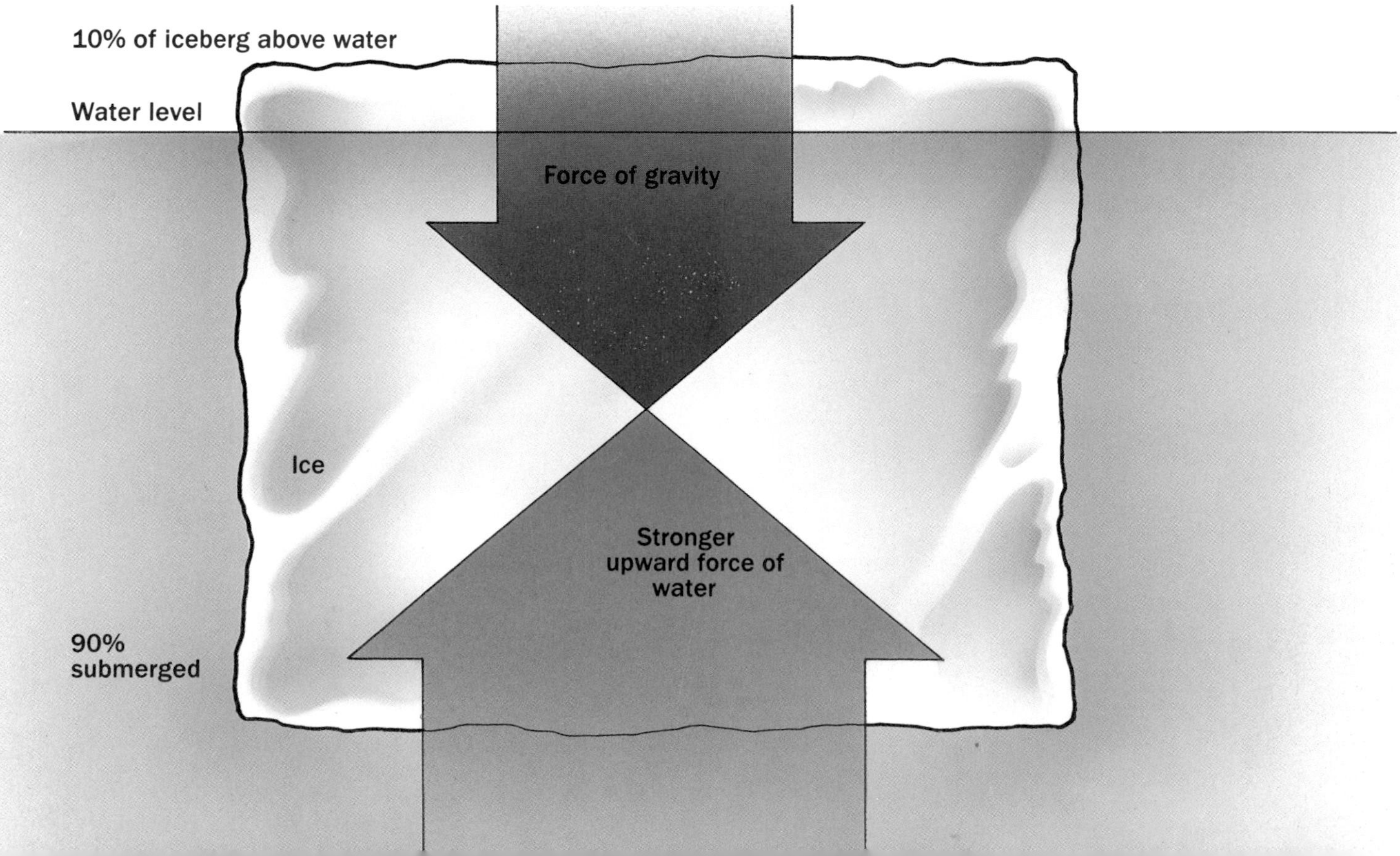

DENSITY

Everything is subject to the downward pulling force of the Earth, which is known as gravity. It is the force of gravity acting upon an object that gives it the property of weight. When an object is placed in water, the liquid exerts an upward force on it. If the upward force is enough to equal the force of gravity, the object will float. The amount of the upward force depends on the density of the object. Density is the ratio between the weight of an object and its volume. Substances that have a density lower than that of water, float. Those that have a density greater than water, sink.

10% of iceberg above water

Water level

Force of gravity

Ice

Stronger upward force of water

90% submerged

STEEL SHIPS

Steel is about eight times more dense than water, and a piece of solid steel will sink straight to the bottom. Air, on the other hand, is very much less dense than water. Steel ships float because the heavy steel hull contains a large volume of air. The density of the ship is the combined density of the steel and the air that it encloses. As long as this is less than the density of water, the ship will float. When the ship is loaded with passengers or cargo, its density increases and it floats lower in the water. If the ship is overloaded, the sides may drop below the surface of the water. When this happens, the ship will fill with water and sink.

MODERN OCEAN LINER

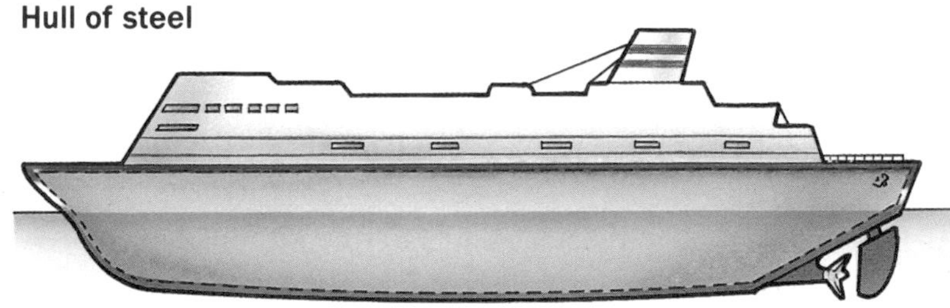
Hull of steel
Hollow areas enable liner to float

► For many years people thought that steel ships were impossible because a solid mass of steel does not float.

WHAT FLOATS?

Test as many objects as you can to see whether they float. All the solid objects that float have a density less than that of water.

A metal dish will also float in water. Try it, then load the dish with stones and watch what happens when the water comes over the sides.

Drop into water
Try the experiment with other things

QUIZ

The human body floats, largely because of the air in our lungs. Why do you think divers carry weights? What does carrying a weight do to the diver's density? What must the diver do to surface again?

SURFACE TENSION

Any large area of water forms a flat, even surface. But a single drop of water has a curved surface. This curvature occurs because the molecules in the layer of water at the surface behave differently from the rest. The result is known as surface tension, and it makes water behave as if it had a thin, elastic skin.

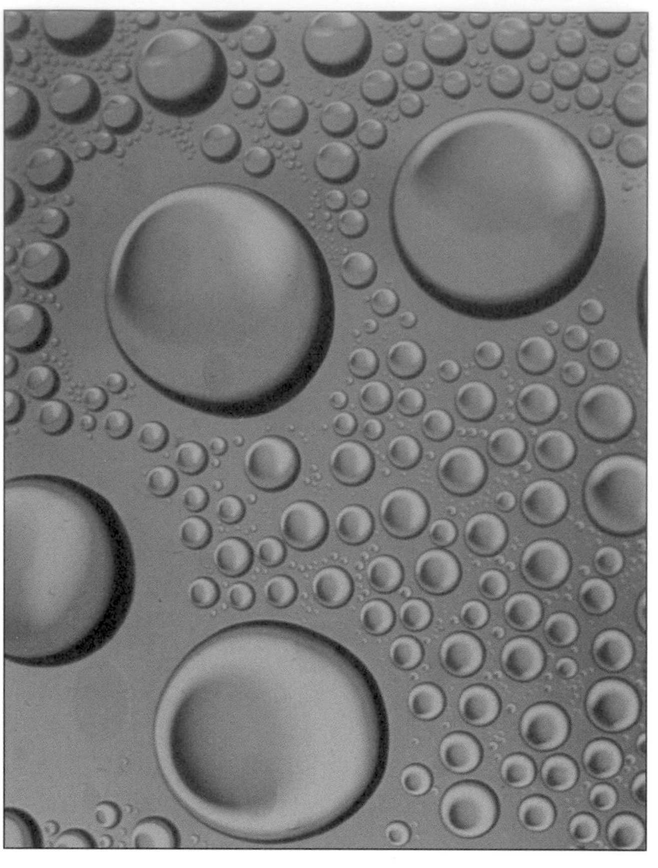

▲ Surface tension makes a single drop of water try and pull itself into the shape of a sphere.

WALKING ON WATER

This "skin" that covers water is not very strong, and heavy objects pass straight through it. However, some insects, like the water skater, are so light in weight they can actually walk on the skin without breaking the surface. This is not the same as floating. The water skater can walk on water because the force of gravity acting on it is not enough to overcome the forces that create surface tension.

▼ If you look closely, you can see the tiny depressions in the surface layer caused by the insect's weight.

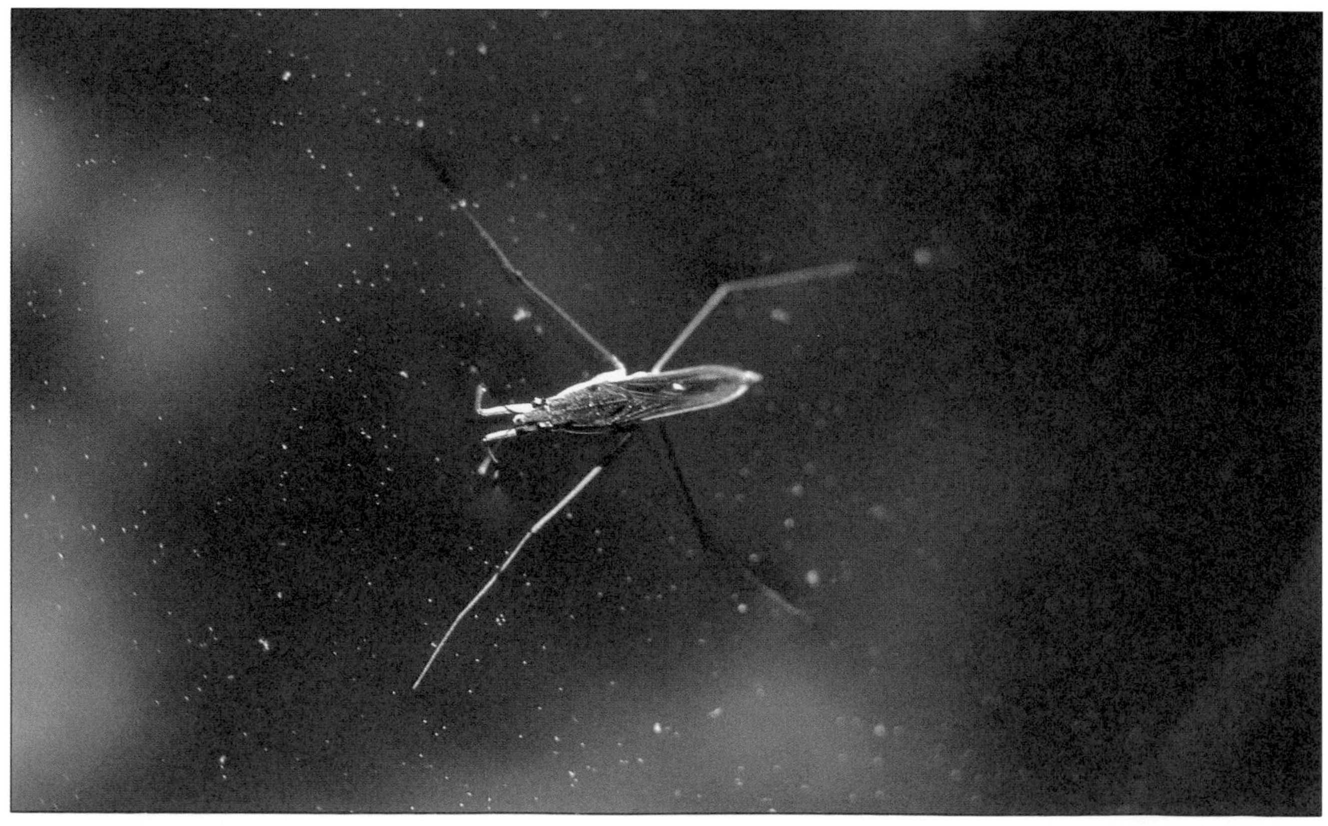

MENISCUS

All molecules in liquid water are subject to the forces between them. In the surface layer, there is no force from above. As a result, the sideways and inward forces act more strongly. This is why a drop of water pulls itself into a curved shape.

In a container, the surface layer is known as a meniscus. If the container is not full, the meniscus will curve upward slightly at the sides in a concave shape. The pulling force between molecules of glass and molecules of water is stronger than the force between the water molecules. If the container is filled above the brim, a convex meniscus forms because surface tension holds the water in.

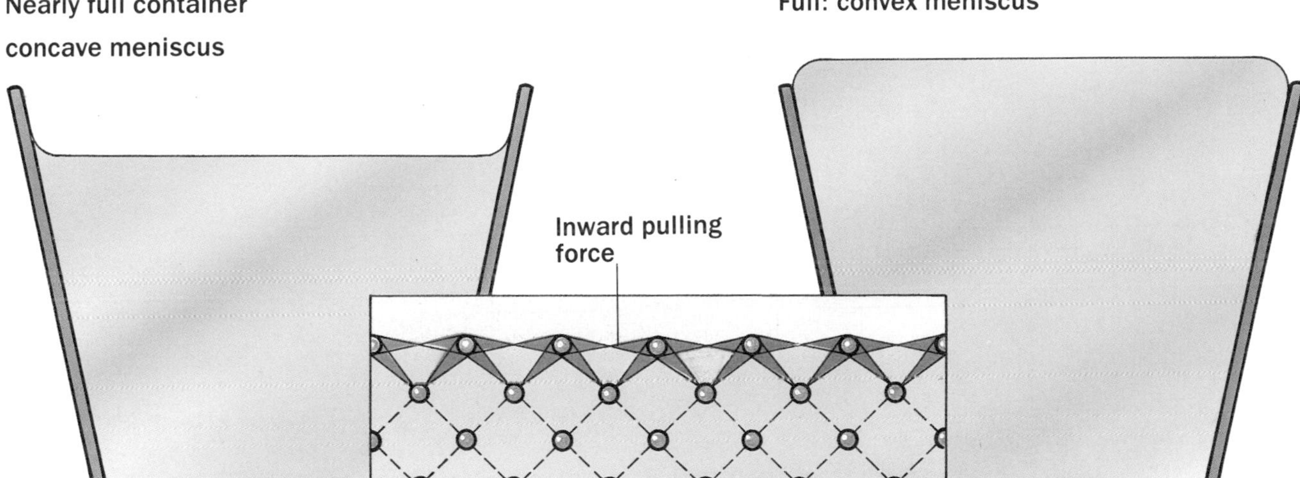

FLOAT A NEEDLE

Steel sinks, but with care you can float a clean needle in a bowl of water. This is because the surface tension is sufficient to support it.

If you have difficulty, try floating the needle with a small piece of paper towel underneath. When the towel sinks, the needle will float.

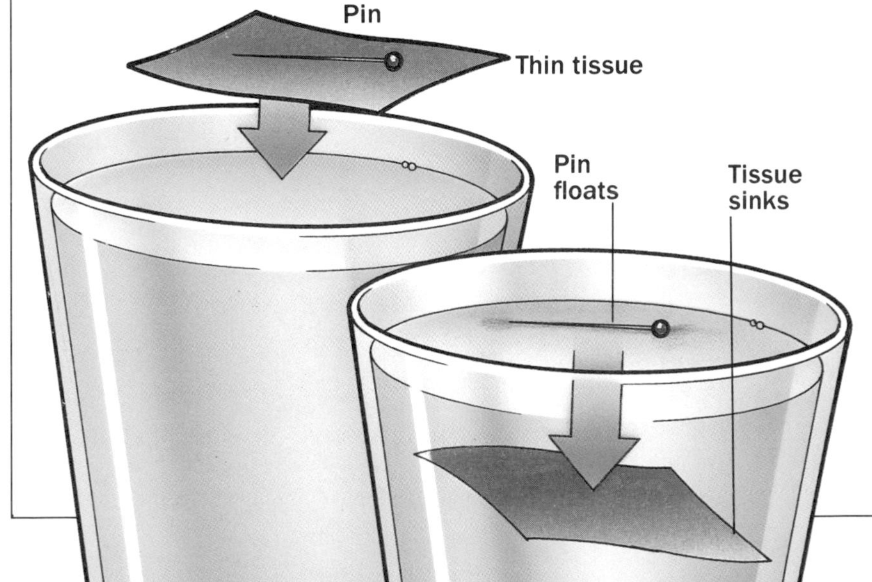

QUIZ

Water will rise up a very narrow tube by itself. This effect is known as capillary action. Can you explain how surface tension causes this? Think about the shape of the meniscus which curves upward.

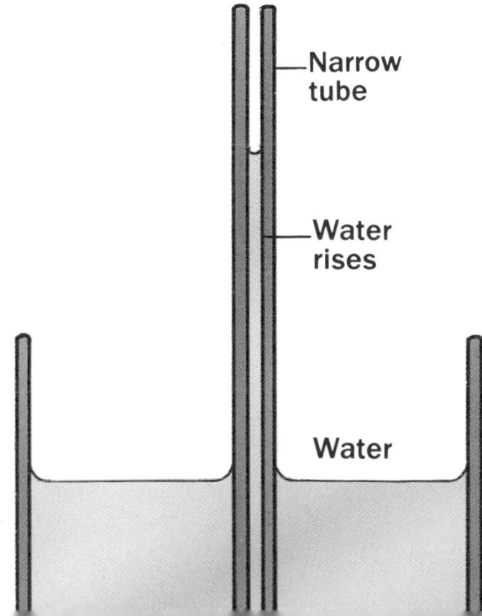

WATER LEVEL

Under the influence of gravity, water usually moves downward. If placed on a permeable surface, one that allows water to pass through it, the water soaks in. On an impermeable surface, water cannot pass through and so follows any downward slope until it cannot flow any further.

WATER TABLE

Some types of rock are permeable like a sponge. Others are completely impermeable. When rain falls onto permeable rock, it soaks in until it meets a layer of impermeable rock. The level of water inside an area of permeable rock is known as the water table. In hilly country, the water table is often above the level of the valley floor. If the hills contain both types of rock, the downward movement of the water will make it flow onto the surface where the two rock layers meet. This outflow is known as a spring, and many streams start out in this way.

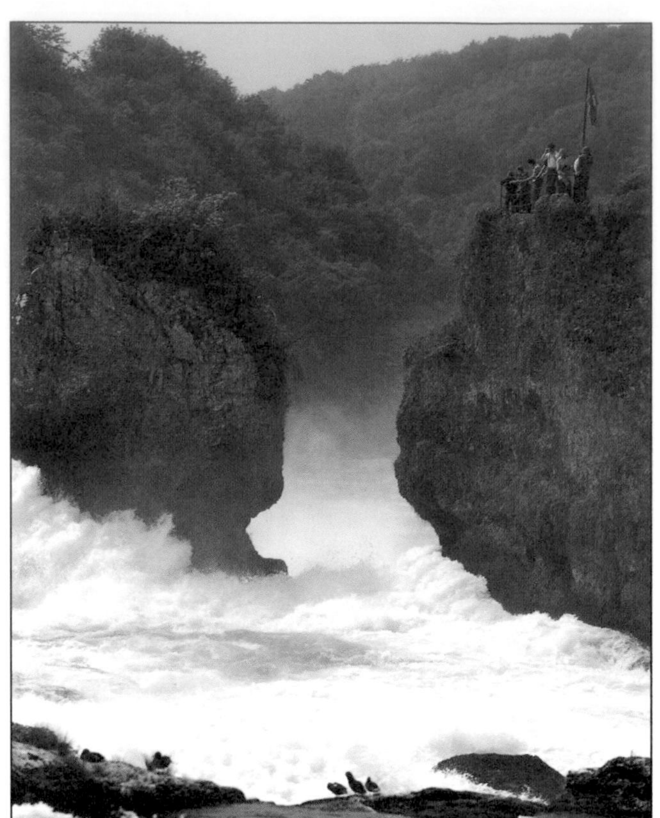

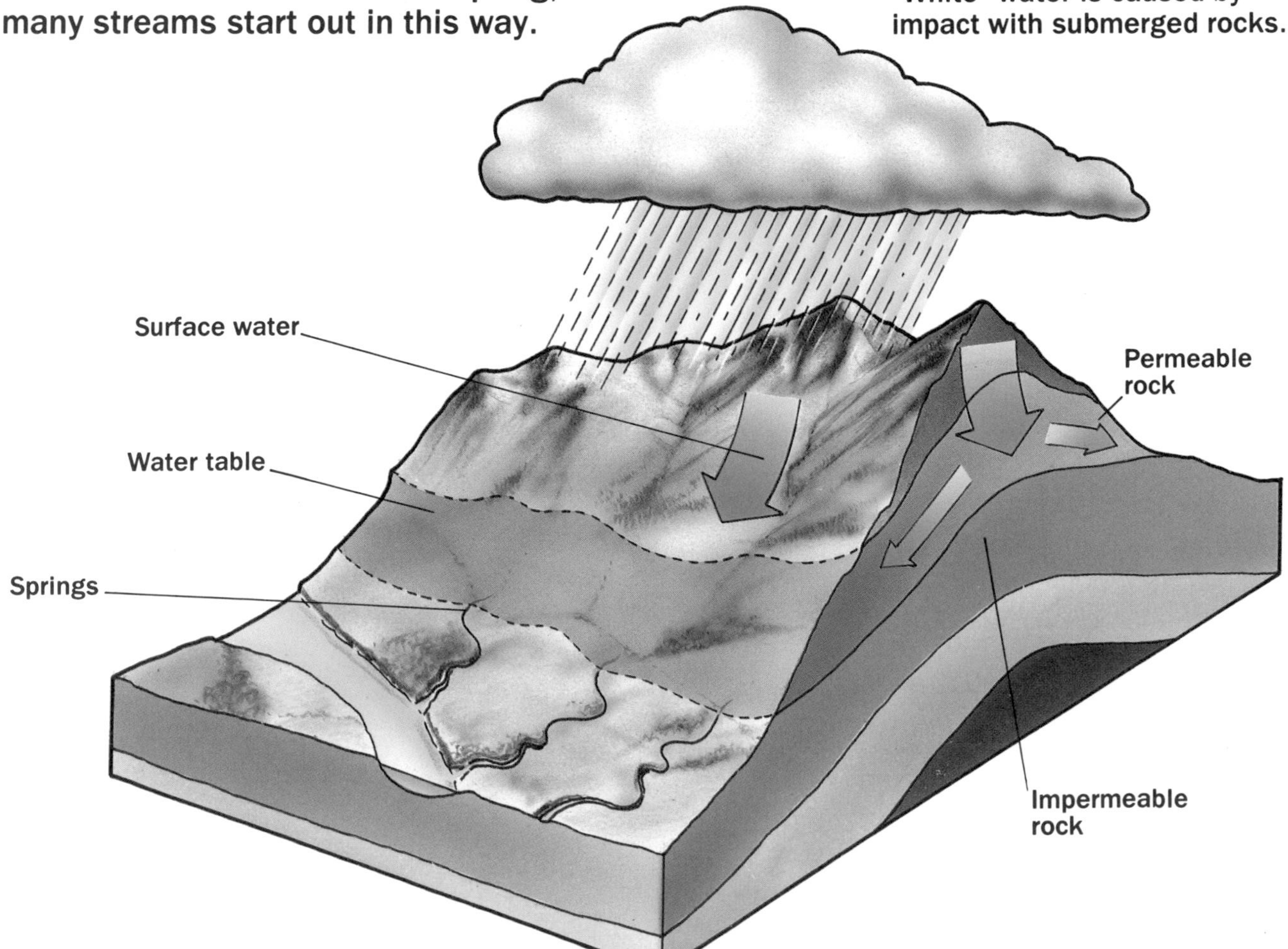

▲ The steeper the slope, the faster the flow of water. "White" water is caused by impact with submerged rocks.

Surface water

Permeable rock

Water table

Springs

Impermeable rock

ARTESIAN WELLS

In most places, the water table is below the surface of the ground. When a hole is drilled down through the rock, water will be found at the depth of the water table. Sometimes the water comes gushing up the hole, creating an artesian well.

Water flows up an artesian well of its own accord because it is trying to get back to the level of the water table. Artesian wells can be drilled wherever a layer of permeable rock has been folded below the water table by a layer of impermeable rock.

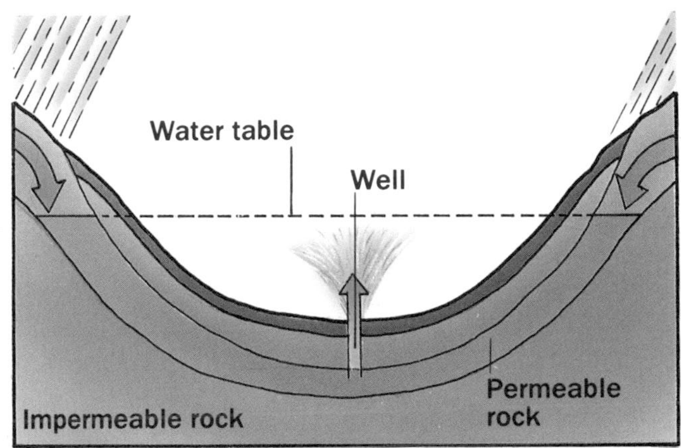

◀ An artesian well is a natural fountain. The water will rise in the air almost to the level of the surrounding water table.

WATER LEVEL PROJECT

You can demonstrate the effect of an artesian well by using some sticky tape to connect some "bendy" straws to a detergent bottle as shown in the diagram. As long as the open end of the straw remains above the water level in the bottle, nothing happens. When the end of the straw is lowered below the water level in the bottle, water will start to flow. The two water surfaces (in the bottle and in the straw) are connected by the water between them. Water will flow out of the straw until the two surfaces have reached the same level.

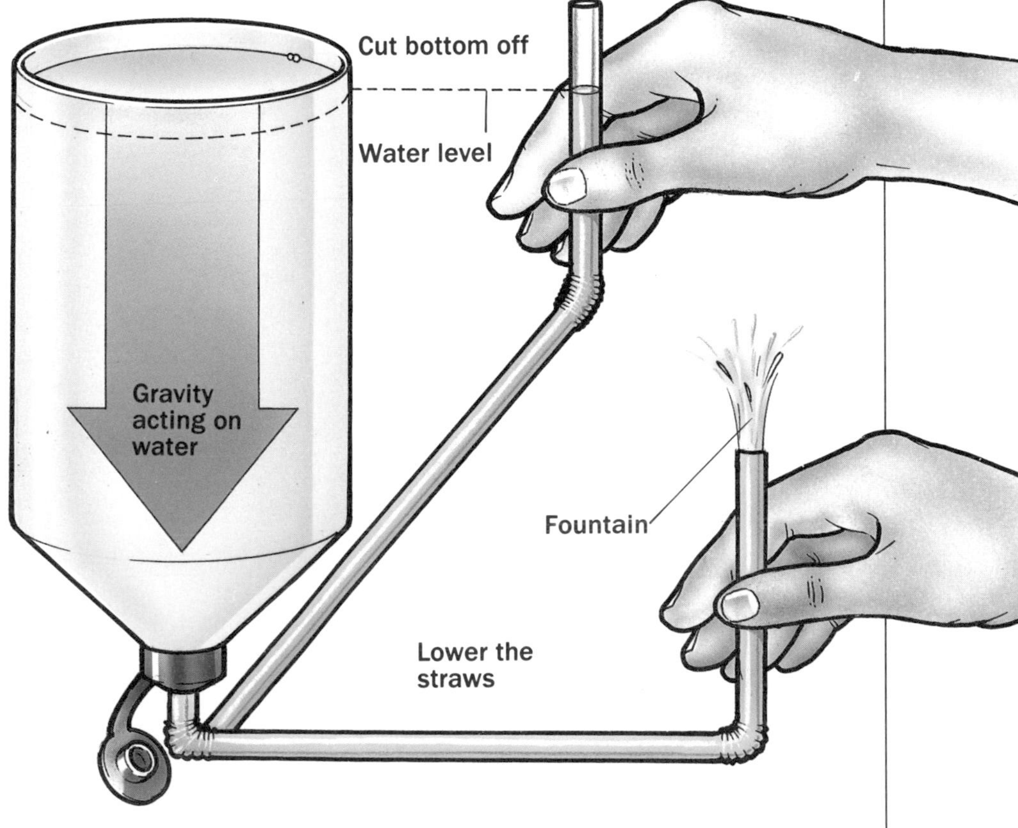

To raise water above the water table, it must be lifted out of the ground. A bucket well lifts one bucket at a time, but there is no flow. By using a pump, water can be made to flow uphill against the force of gravity. Water will also flow uphill in a siphon, but only if it eventually flows to a lower level.

▲ A bucket well is one of the simplest machines. It is reliable – but very slow and inefficient.

PUMPS

A simple pump consists of a cylinder fitted with two valves and a piston. The valves in a pump allow water (or air) to flow in one direction only. When the piston is pulled out (the upstroke), it creates a vacuum which sucks water into the cylinder through the inlet valve. When the piston is pushed in (the downstroke), the water is forced through the outlet valve. The one-way action of the valves ensures that air cannot get into the cylinder on the upstroke, and prevents the water from going back through the inlet valve on the downstroke.

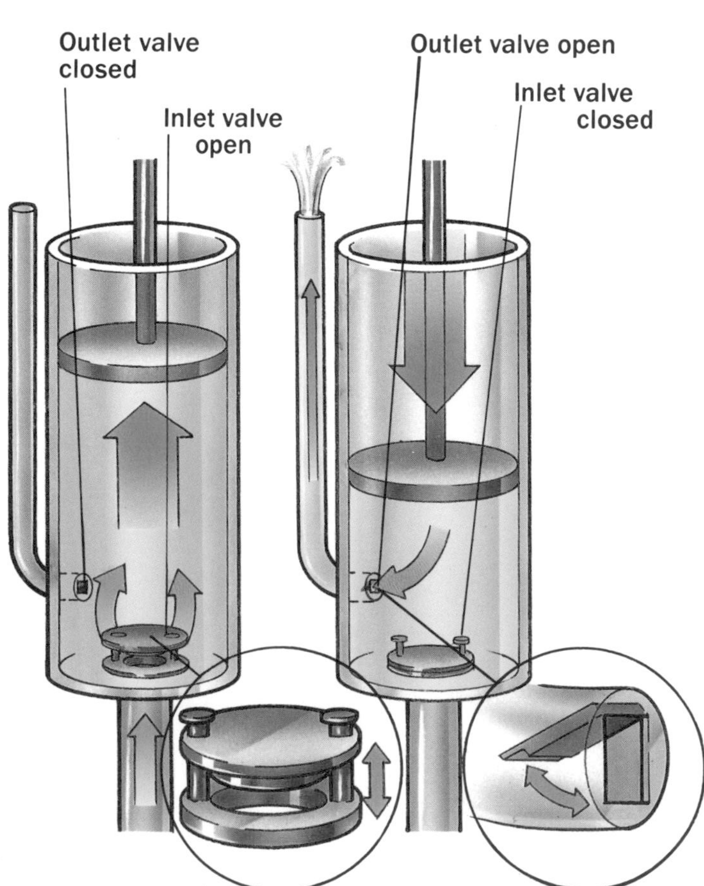

▼ Without constant pumping out, mines dug below the water table would soon become completely flooded.

SIPHONS

Water will flow uphill along a tube if the outflow is below the original water level. When this occurs, the tube is known as a siphon. A siphon works because the weight of the air exerts a force on the surface of the water. As long as the outflow is below the water level, this force is sufficient to move the water along the tube. If the outflow is raised above the water level, even very slightly, the flow will stop. In order for a siphon to function, the tube must be completely full of liquid. With water, it is safe to start a siphon by sucking the water along the tube. With other liquids, the tube must be filled by immersing it, and then sealing the ends.

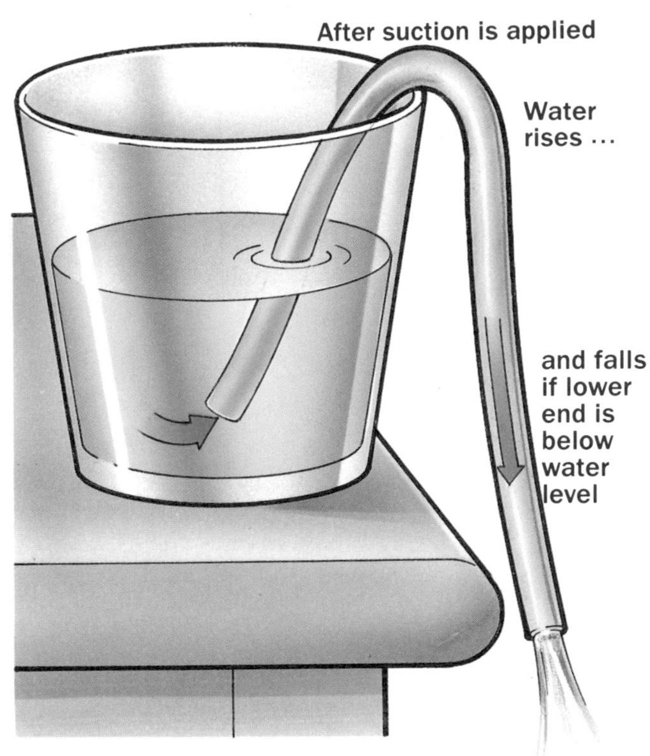

MAKE A SIPHON

You can make a series of siphons with two lengths of plastic tubing or a number of "bendy" straws connected together. Use one siphon to fill a container while the other siphon empties it.

If you are using transparent tubing, very briefly lift the inflow end out of the water and let a small amount of air into the tube. Watch what happens as the air bubble is carried along the tube.

QUIZ

Usually the water table is below the surface of the ground, and pumps have to be used to bring the water to the surface. Why would you need a pump to bring the water to the surface? Can you explain why a siphon cannot be used to lift water out of the ground? Think about the levels of the ends of a siphon tube.

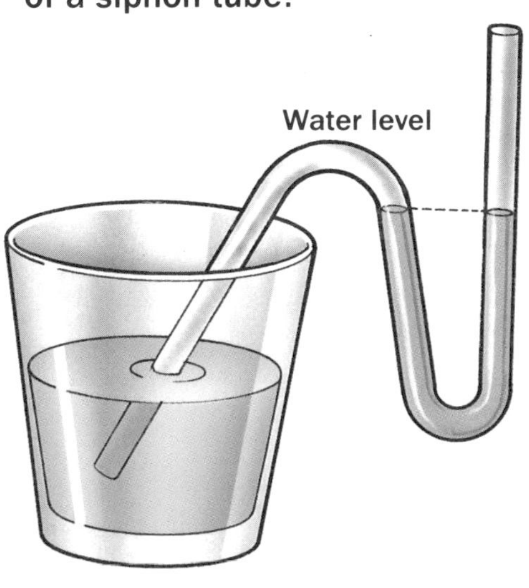

UNDER PRESSURE

When water moves slowly, it is a calm, flowing liquid. But when it is under pressure, it can be a powerful force. Think of the difference between water running calmly from a faucet and the same flow as it squirts from the jet of a hose. Or imagine water running in a wide river or over a narrow waterfall.

HIGH PRESSURE

Any force applied to water is transmitted through it, either as movement or pressure. If water can move it will, and increased force means faster movement. The speed at which water moves down a pipe depends on the pressure behind it. If the outlet of the pipe is reduced in size, the speed of the water coming out of the pipe increases. Because the pressure is the same along the pipe, the same amount of water flows through the wide pipe and the narrow outlet. For this to happen, the water has to move faster through the outlet.

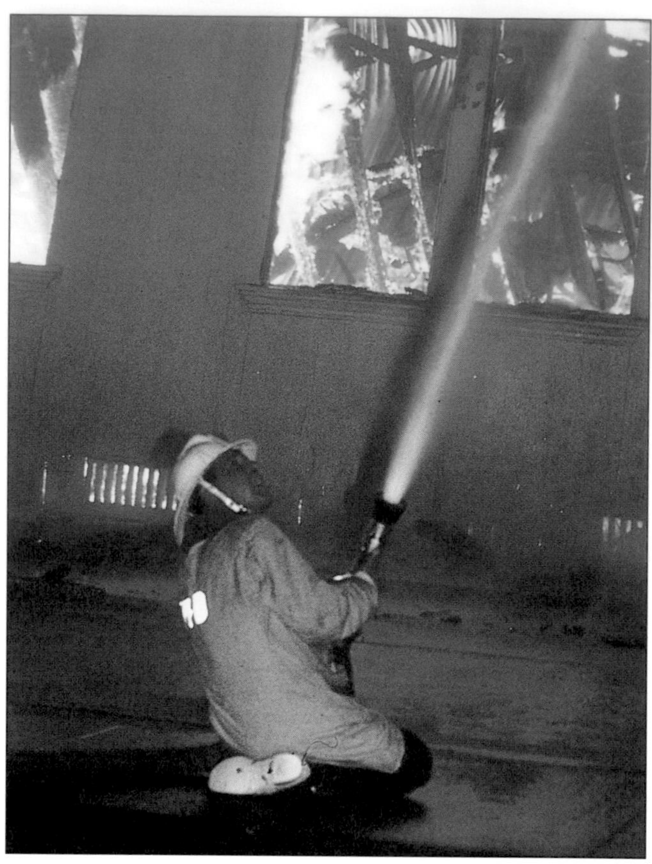

▲ Fire hoses deliver water from a safe distance and to the tops of buildings.

▼ A high pressure water jet carries tremendous force. Water can blast ingrained dirt from stone and brick.

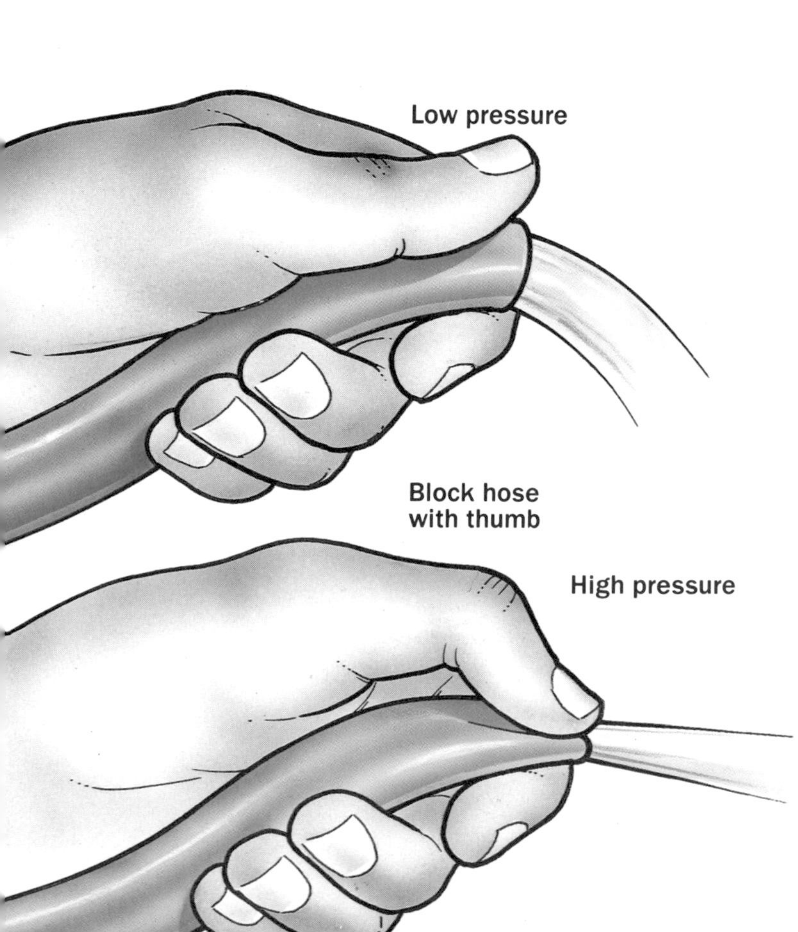

BREAKING THE SURFACE

Hitting the surface of water at high speed can be the same as hitting a brick wall. The faster something moves, the more force it carries with it. When something strikes water, a lot of the force is transmitted back into it because water does not compress.

Divers use their hands to break the surface of water so that it flows around them, and little force is transmitted. Test this by alternately slapping and chopping a bowl of water with your hand. A "belly flop" into a pool can really hurt.

▼ More than one attempt at the water speed record has ended in disaster when the boat has crashed at speed.

LOOKING AT PRESSURE

Use a detergent bottle to examine how the pressure of a water jet varies. Changes in both pressure and size of opening affect the jet.

Without a nozzle in place, it requires great force to make the water travel any distance. But the bottle's contents empty very quickly.

With the nozzle on, the water comes out of the bottle at high pressure and travels farther. The jet contains a much smaller volume of water.

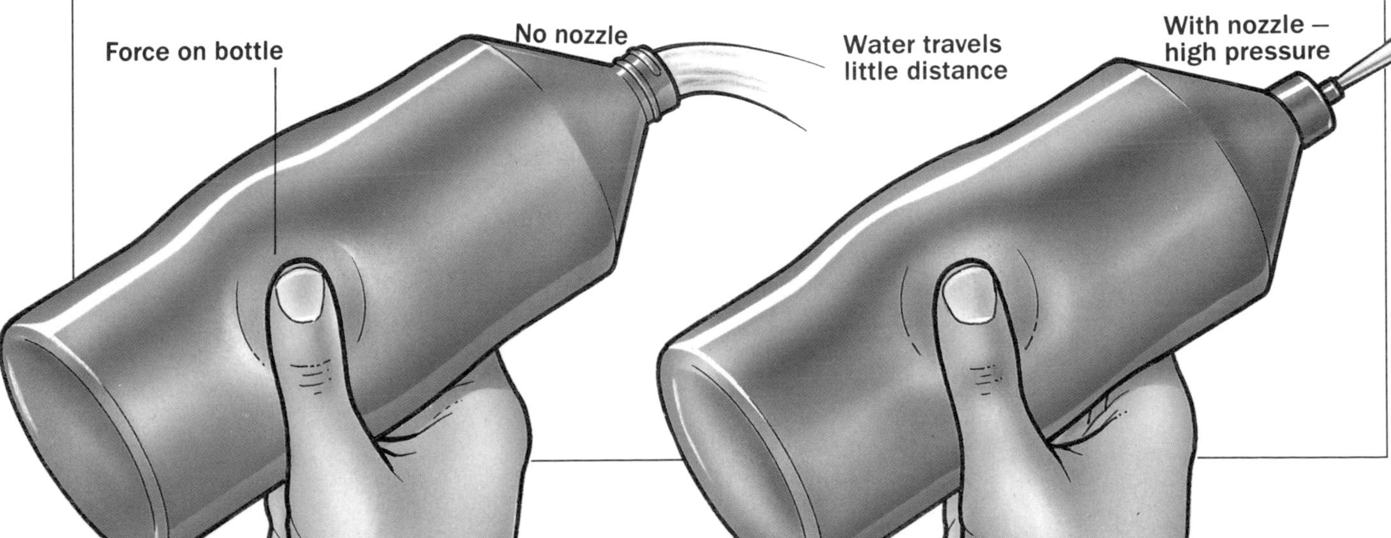

DAMS FOR WATER SUPPLY

The water that comes out of the faucet originally fell to earth as rain. But it does not rain every day. In order to ensure a regular supply to the faucet, water is often stored in artificial lakes called reservoirs. Many reservoirs are formed by building a wall or dam across a river valley, causing the river to flood.

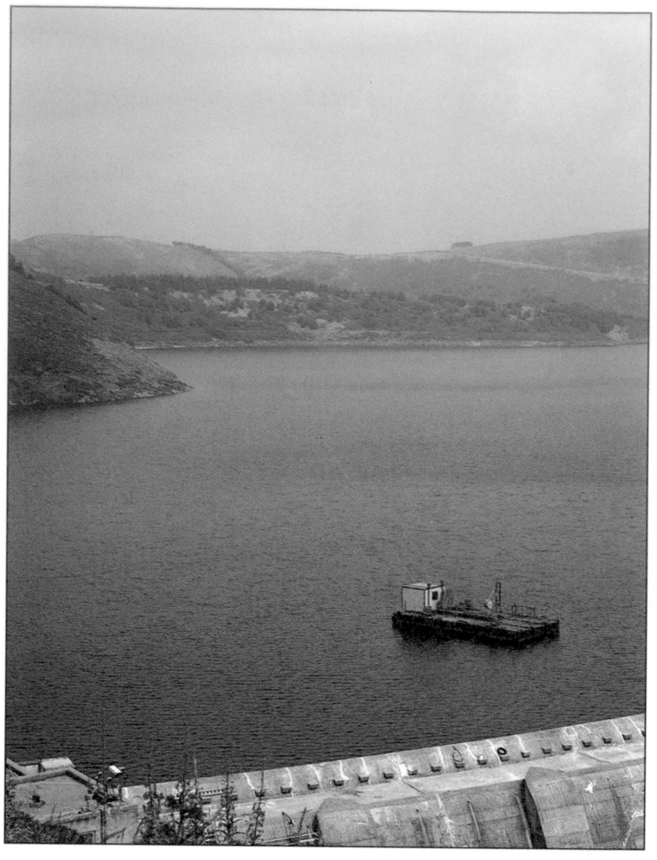

▲ If a reservoir is not constantly filled with rainwater from streams and rivers, it will soon run dry.

DEPTH AND PRESSURE

Water does not require any external force to create pressure: its own weight is enough. A solid object exerts pressure downward because of the force of gravity. But a liquid, like water, exerts pressure in all directions. Near the surface, the pressure is not very great. But water pressure increases with depth, as the weight of the water above increases. Dams have to be much thicker at the base in order to withstand the increased water pressure. Some modern dams are built of concrete, but many are built of earth and gravel with a central core of waterproof clay.

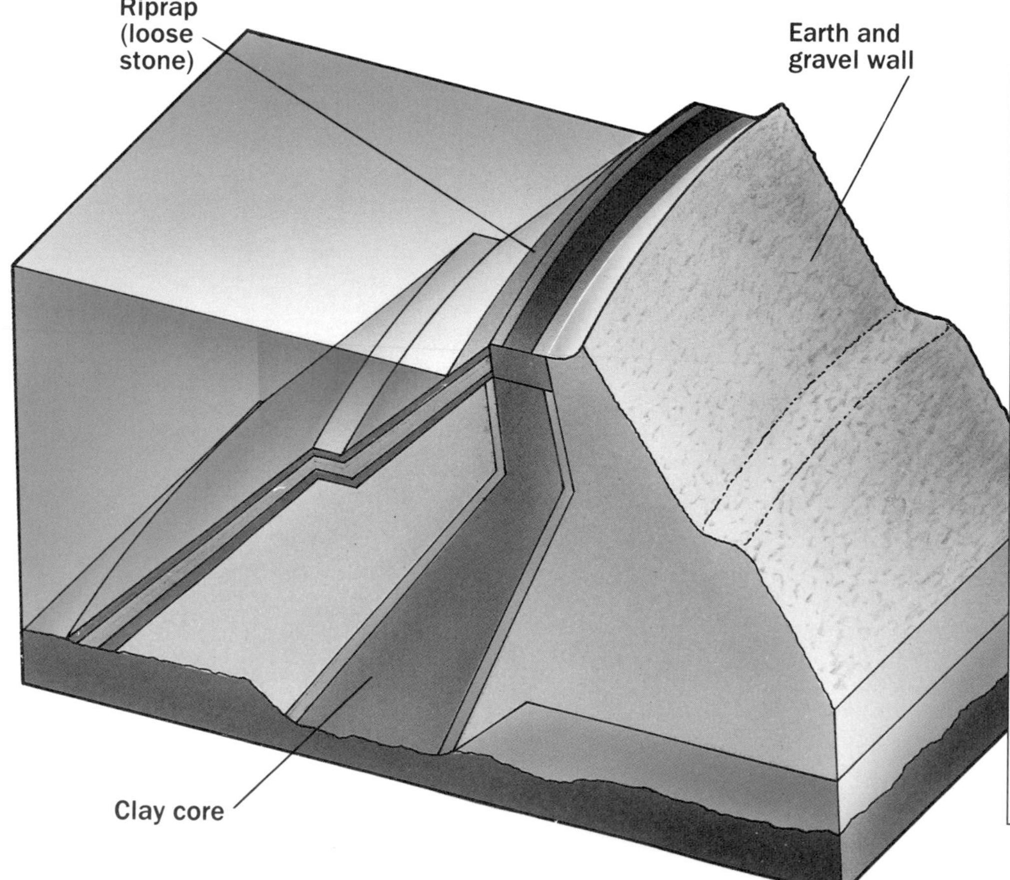

PRESSURE PROJECT

You can demonstrate the fact that water pressure increases with depth by using a detergent bottle. Make a series of equal sized holes down the side of the bottle, then fill it with water. The stream of water that comes out of the lowest hole travels the greatest distance. The water pressure is greatest at the bottom of the container, and therefore exerts the most force. The stream of water from the highest hole travels the least distance.

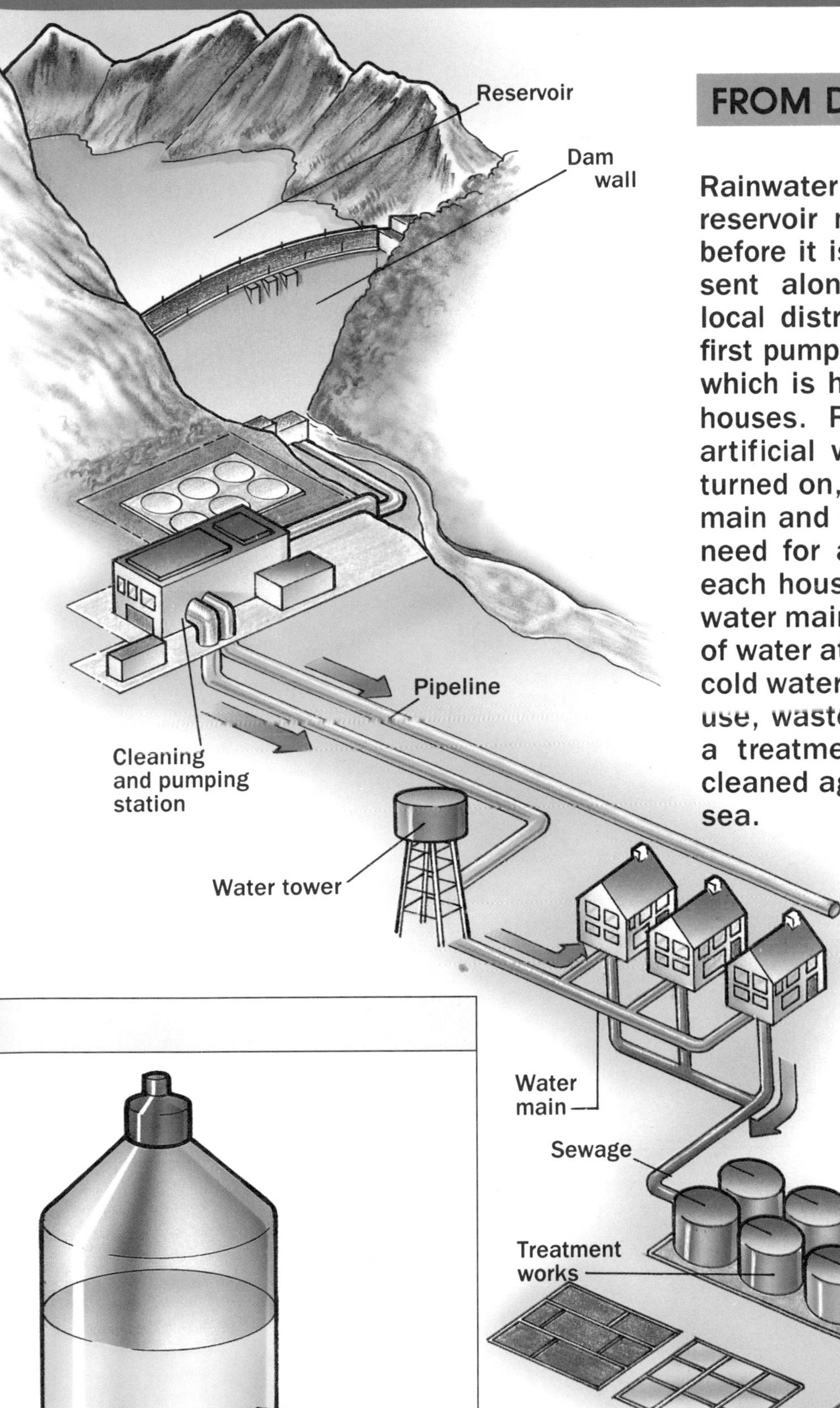

FROM DAM TO FAUCET

Rainwater that has collected in a reservoir must be cleaned and purified before it is safe to drink. Clean water is sent along underground pipelines for local distribution. In many places, it is first pumped to the top of a water tower which is higher than all the surrounding houses. Raising the water creates an artificial water table. When a faucet is turned on, water will flow from the water main and up into the house, without the need for a pump. The pipes leading to each house are much narrower than the water main, and this increases the speed of water at the faucet. The water from the cold water faucet shows this effect. After use, waste water is carried by sewers to a treatment works. Here the water is cleaned again before flowing back to the sea.

WHERE?

A turbine, a machine with blades like a windmill, is used to generate electricity. The water pressure behind a dam can be used as a source of energy to spin around the blades of a turbine. Why would a higher dam allow you to generate more power at the turbine?

DAMS FOR POWER

Moving water contains a considerable amount of energy that can be used to drive machines. Some of the earliest machines were waterwheels, which were often used to turn millstones and grind corn. The modern equivalent is the turbine, which uses water power to generate electricity.

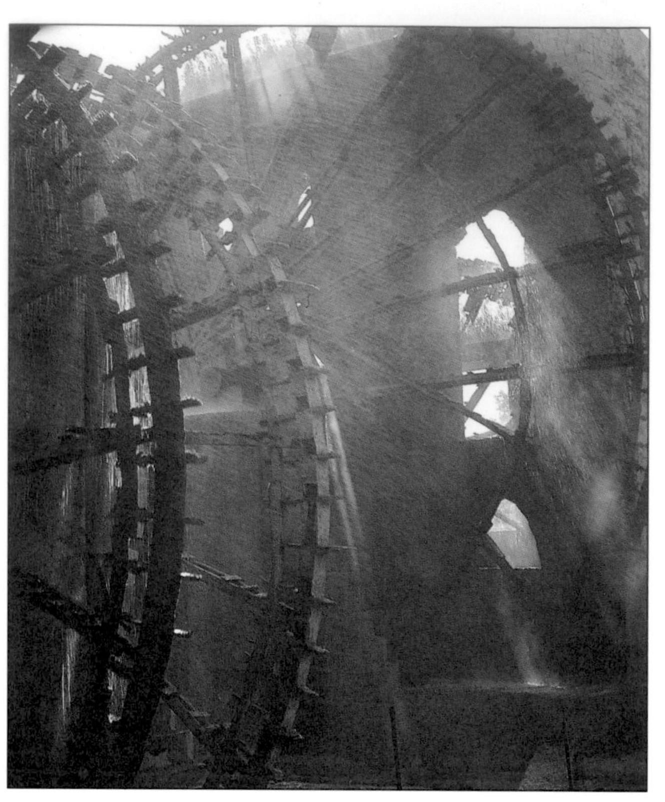

▲ A waterwheel converts the energy in the flow of water into circular motion. Water power was also used in many early factories.

HYDRO-ELECTRICITY

Electricity generated by water power is known as hydro-electricity ("hydro" is the Greek word for water). Hydro-electric power stations are cheap to run, because their fuel (water) comes free of charge. Water is stored behind a dam in order to provide a constant supply. At the base of the dam, the water is allowed to flow through a series of tunnels to the turbines. The amount of water entering the tunnels can be controlled by sluice gates. The tunnels narrow near the far end, so that water is moving as quickly as possible when it reaches the turbines. Each turbine is attached to an electricity generator in the power house in front of the dam. The electric current produced is then carried by cables to the pylons carrying the power supply.

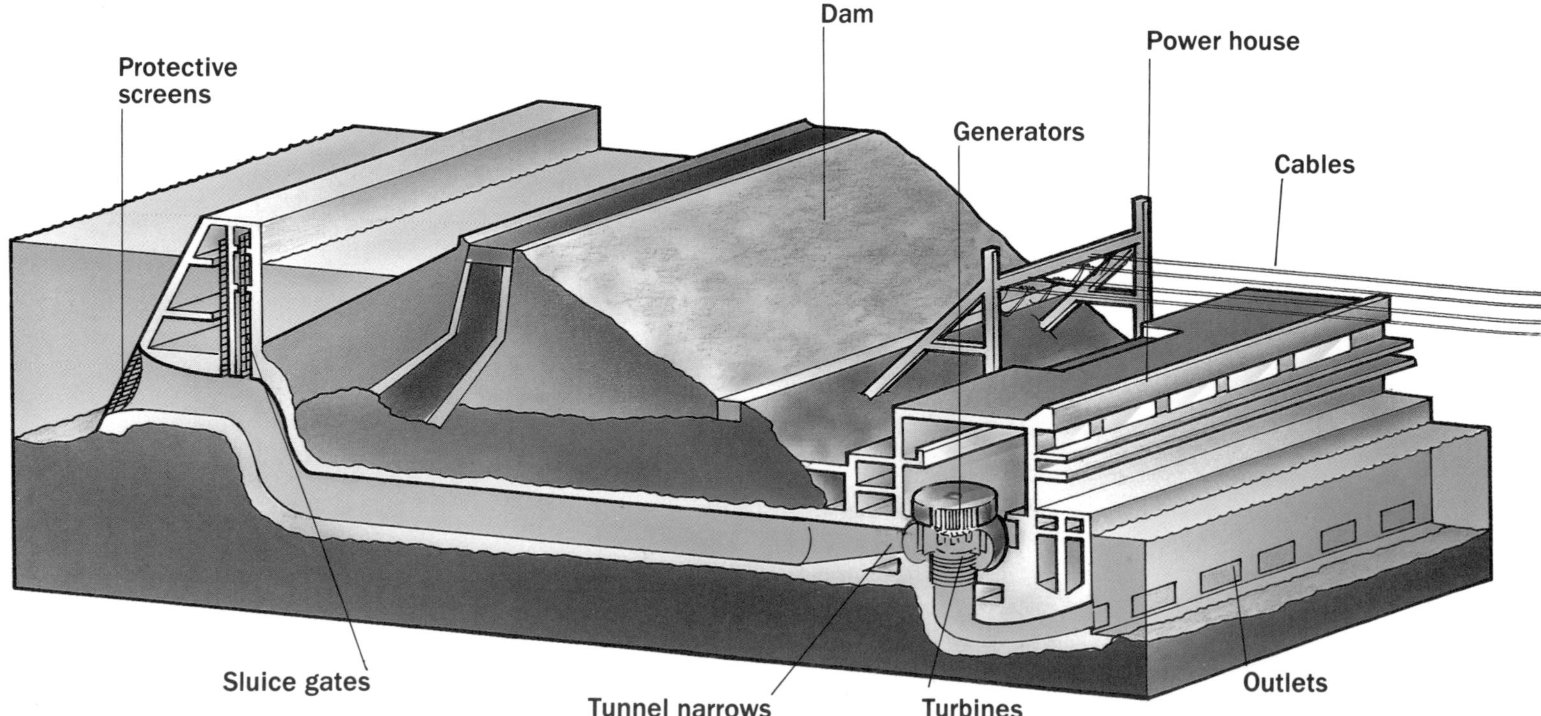

MAKE A WATER TURBINE

You can make a simple turbine using the top part of a detergent bottle. Make a series of cuts around the side as shown in the diagram. Fold the flaps so that they slope like the sails of a windmill. Try and fold each flap at the same angle. Place your turbine over the pointed end of a pencil so it can turn easily, and hold it under a faucet of running water. The greater the force of the water out of the faucet, the faster your turbine will spin.

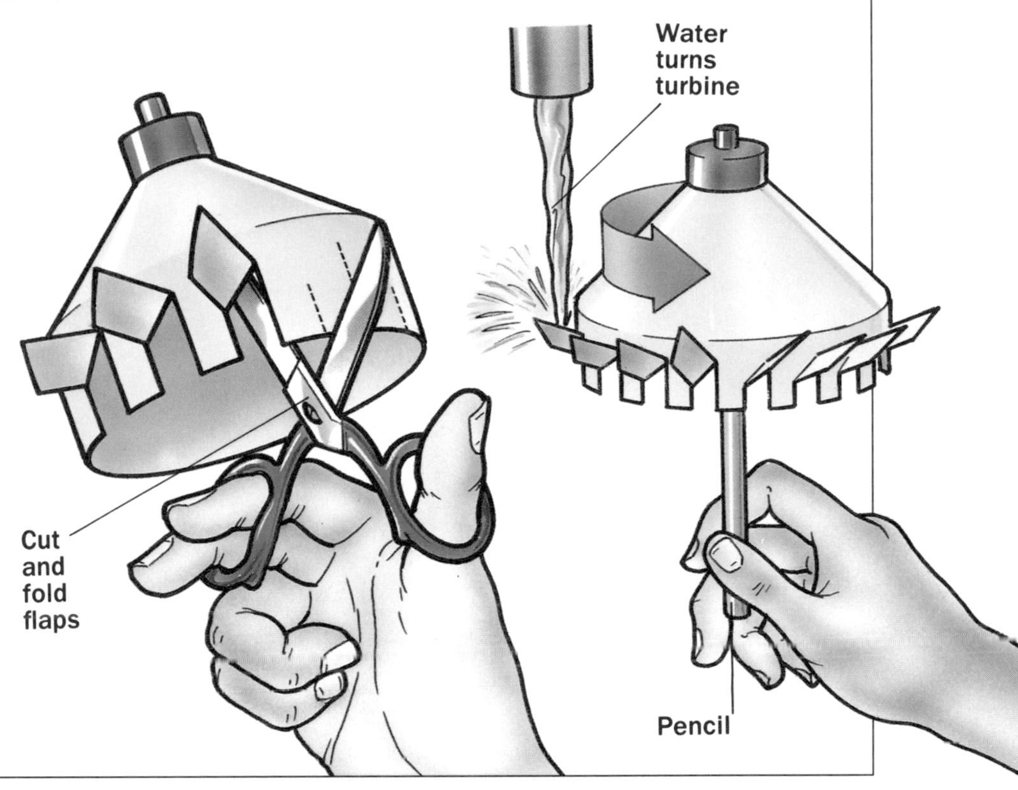

▶ Modern turbines are among the largest machines built, and weigh thousands of tons.

GENERATOR

A modern turbine is completely immersed in the flow of water. The water arrives at great speed and is forced through the curved blades of the turbine in order to get out. The movement of the water turns the turbine. A shaft connects the turbine to a generator. As the magnets inside the generator rotate they create an electric current in the coils.

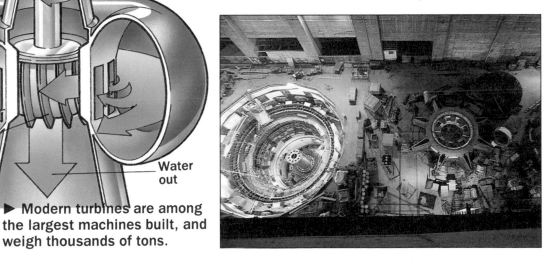

Although we do not notice it, the air above us is really quite heavy, and exerts a pressure on the Earth. However, the pressure of the air is not the same all over. The differences in air pressure are caused by differences in temperature. Cold areas tend to have high pressure. Warm areas have low pressure.

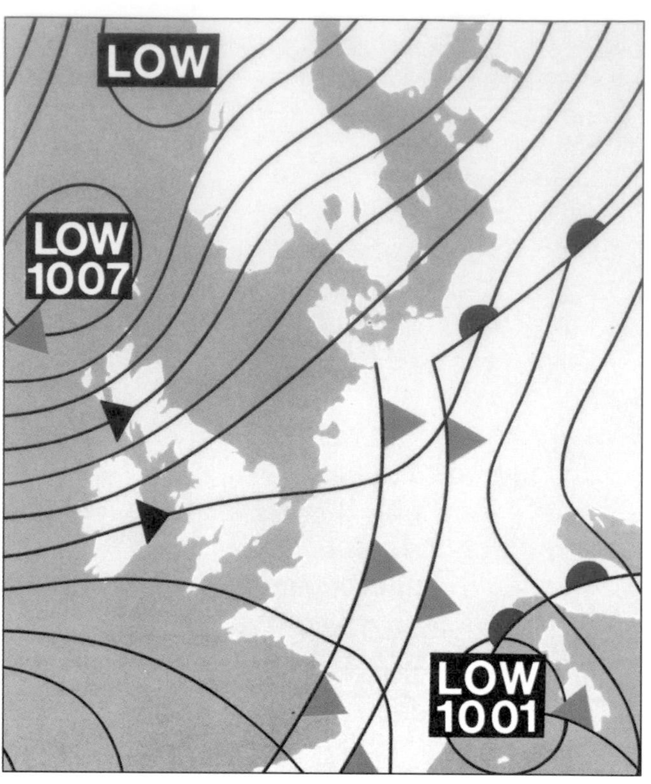

▲ A weather map has lines called isobars drawn on it. They join places with equal air pressure. When the isobars are close together, the winds will be very strong.

WHAT ARE WINDS?

Warm air is lighter and less dense than cold air. Because of this, warm air rises, leaving behind an area of low pressure, called a depression. Cold air sinks downwards in the atmosphere, creating an area of high pressure, called an anticyclone. Winds are caused by air flowing from areas of high pressure to areas of low pressure. The situation is complicated by the rotation of the Earth. This causes winds to blow outwards from the center of an anticyclone in a circular clockwise movement in the northern hemisphere, and in a counterclockwise direction in the southern hemisphere.

WORLD WIND PATTERNS

Where the Earth is hottest – at the Equator – air rises and creates a low pressure region called the doldrums. The air that rises from the doldrums travels away from the Equator and falls when it cools. This creates areas of high pressure known as the horse latitudes. The air that falls in the horse latitudes travels towards the Equator, causing winds called the trade winds. In addition, there is also falling air in the Arctic and Antarctic because these areas are so cold. This creates high pressure areas at the poles, with winds blowing toward the Equator. These winds are called the polar winds. In between the polar winds and the trade winds, there is a belt of winds called the westerlies. These blow from the horse latitudes to the poles.

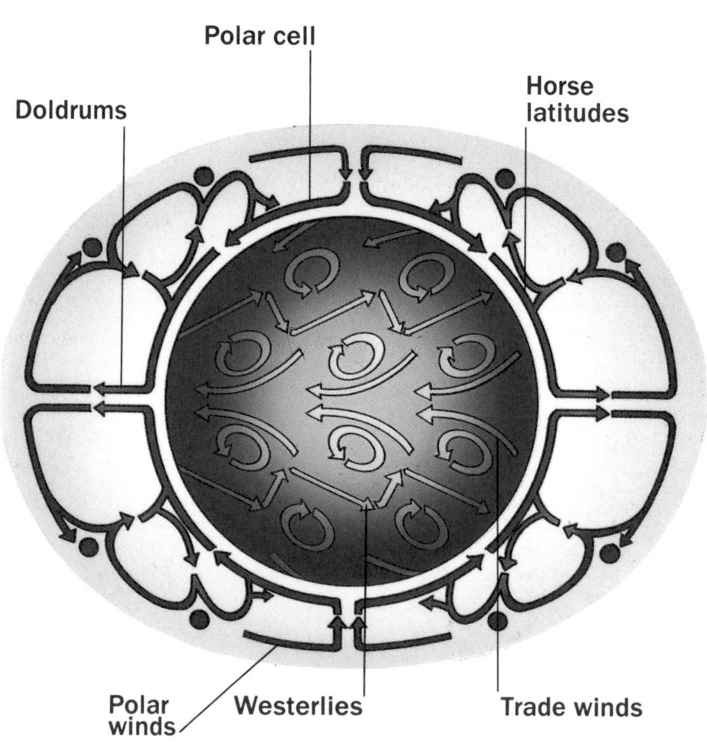

GIANT STORMS

Violent storms of whirling wind and rain can start over the seas near the Equator. These storms are called hurricanes when they take place over the Atlantic Ocean, cyclones in the Indian Ocean and typhoons in the Pacific Ocean. Cyclones and hurricanes are very strong winds circling round an area of low pressure. Some cyklones may be 300 miles (500 km) across, with winds blowing at more than 120 mph (200 km/h). A tornado is a funnel shaped storm that is usually about 300 ft (100 m) across. The air in its centre whirls around at over 360 mph (600 km/h). The low pressure in the center of a tornado can make buildings explode like pricked balloons.

► A tornado, or "twister," can suck up everything in its path and cause terrible damage.

MAKE A WIND VANE

Make the vane by taping triangular pieces of cardboard to the ends of a strong plastic drinking straw.

Attach the vane to a rubber-topped pencil using a pin through the center of the straw. Make sure it can turn freely.

Use modeling clay to hold a cardboard tube to a wooden base. Place clay inside the tube to hold the pencil steady.

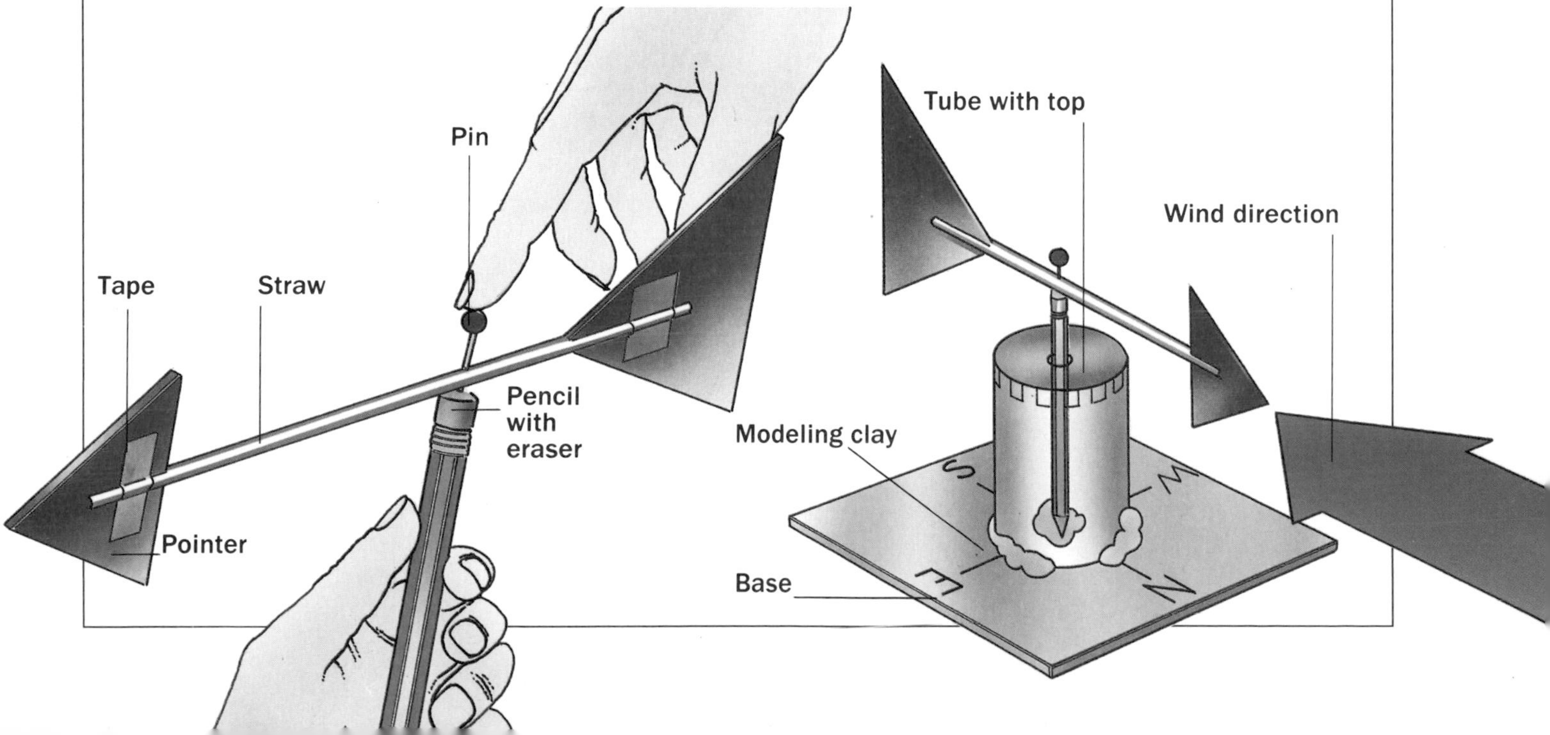

Pin
Tape
Straw
Pencil with eraser
Pointer
Tube with top
Wind direction
Modeling clay
Base
S
W
E
N

WIND POWER

The windmill is an ancient source of power. In the year 650, the Persians used windmills to grind corn. By 1200 windmills in Europe pumped water, ground corn and drove machinery. Today windmills make electricity without producing pollution.

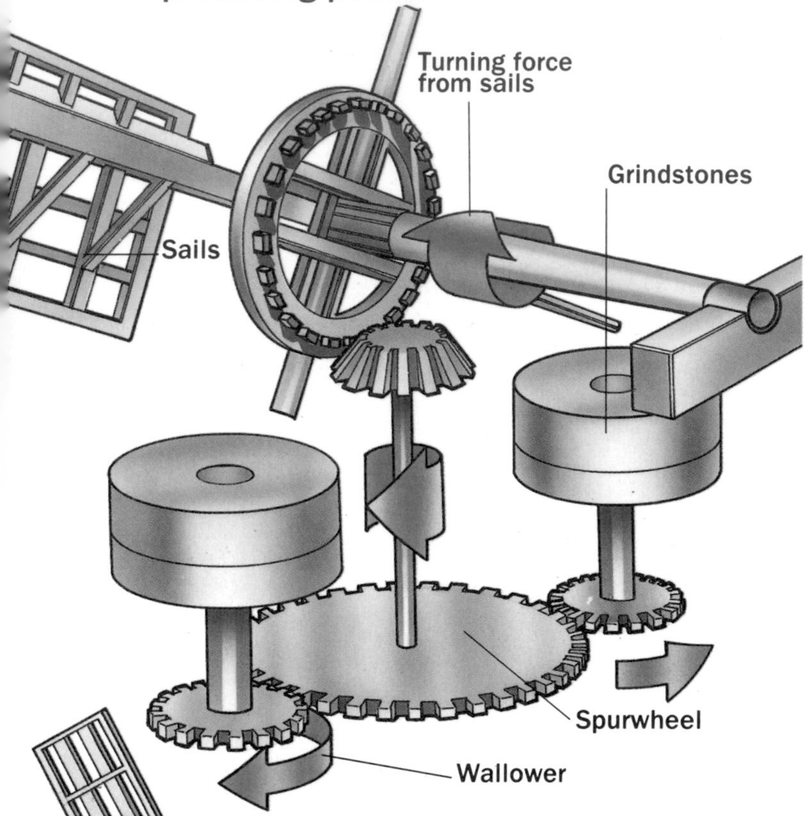

Turning force from sails

Grindstones

Sails

Spurwheel

Wallower

Mill rotates to face wind

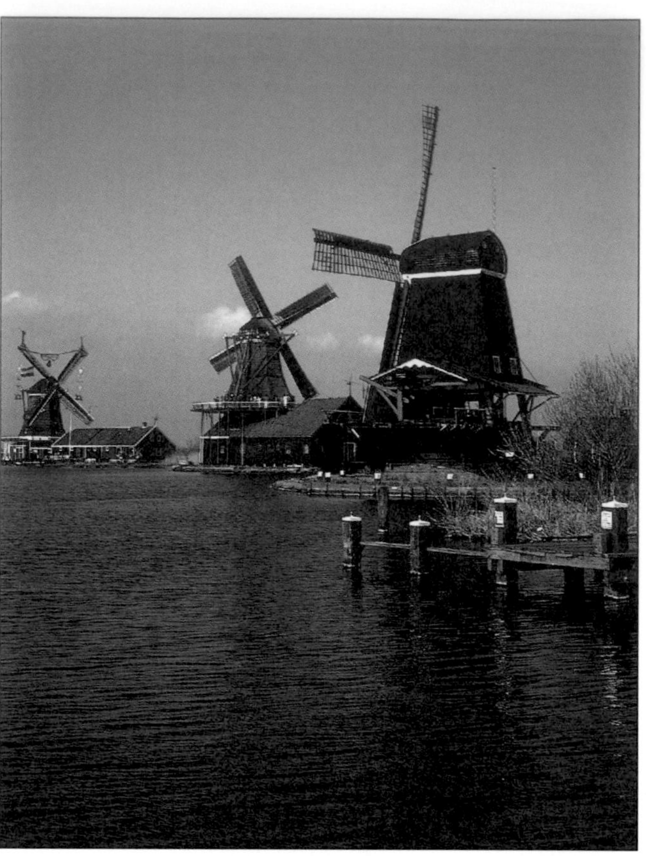

▲ Windmills are used to pump water from the low-lying areas in the Netherlands. The largest Dutch windmill, in Maasland, has sails measuring 29 m (95 ft) from tip to tip.

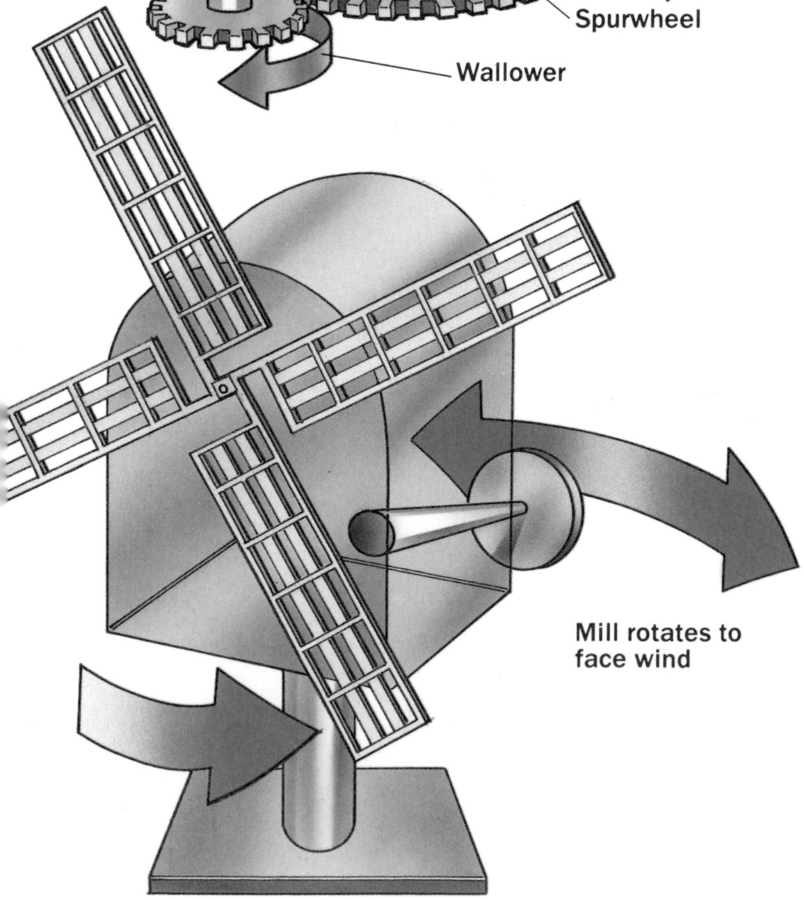

THE WINDMILL

There are two types of traditional windmill. The first type is the post mill, which is turned by hand around a post to face into the wind. The second type is the tower mill which has a revolving turret on top of a tall tower. There is a device, called a fantail, attached to the turret which keeps the sails pointing into the wind. The angle of the wooden sails can be adjusted to extract as much power as possible from the wind. Inside the windmill, the sails turn a drivewheel. The drivewheel is connected to the grindstones, using gears and cogs. The moving grindstones press against two upper fixed stones. The grain is fed to the stones through hoppers in the upper grindstones.

MODERN WINDMILLS

There are several different designs for a large, wind-driven electric generator. Some designs look like large versions of the normal windmill. Often, there are only two giant blades, shaped like the propellers of an airplane. Another design consists of two flexible metal strips connected to an upright pole at the top and bottom. This design catches the wind whatever direction it is blowing in.

▲ Rows of windmills are used to generate electricity in a remote area.

◀ Windmills can be designed with many blades to catch the wind efficiently.

MAKE A WINDMILL AND HAMMER

To make a simple windmill, cut a thin cardboard square about two-thirds of the way along the diagonals. Fold the corners into the center as shown in the diagram. Push a pin through the center and into one end of the stick. Push the straw through holes in the box as shown and insert the stick. Cut a cam and a hammer from the thick cardboard. Attach the cam to the end of the stick. Fix the hammer to the side of the box, using a paper fastener. Face your windmill into the wind.

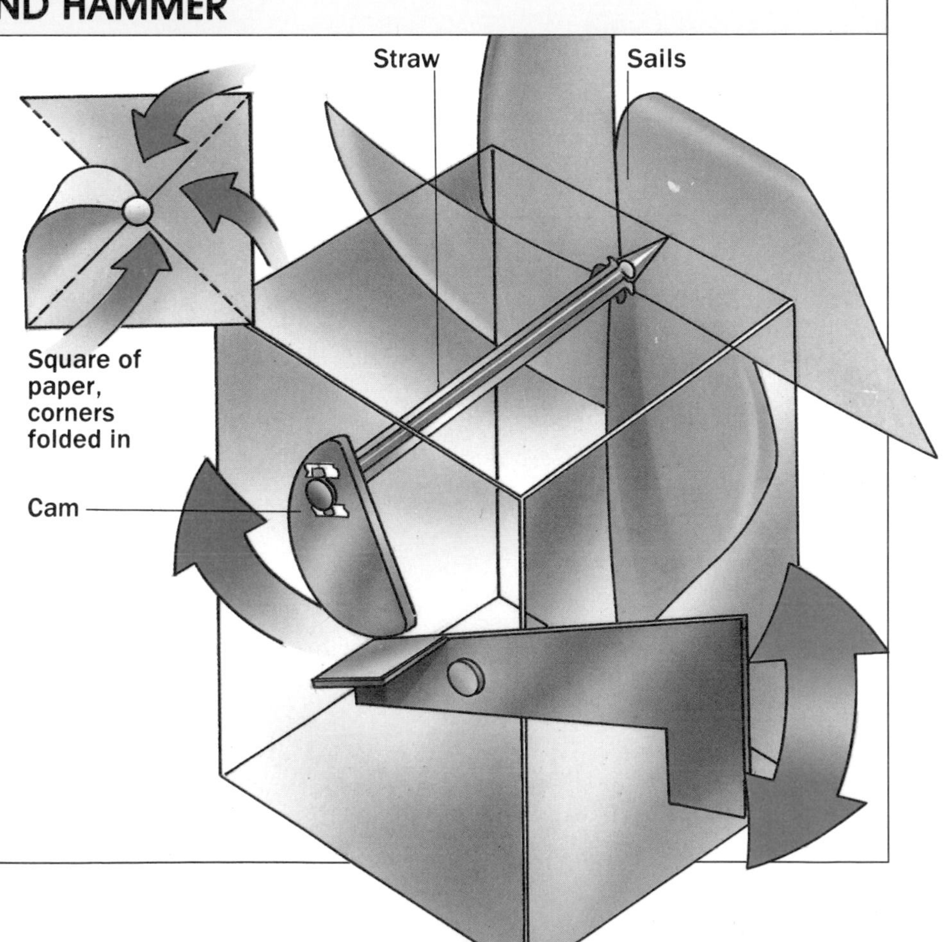

USING WINDS

About 5,000 years ago, the Egyptians invented the sail and used the wind to push their boats along. For many centuries, sailing ships ruled the seas. However, after the first boat powered by a steam engine was built in 1783 by the Marquis de Jouffroy d'Abbans, sailing ships became less important.

▲ Birds like this eagle can soar to great heights without flapping their wings. They are lifted by air currents.

HOW SAILS WORK

A sailboat can move in any direction, no matter where the wind comes from. This is possible because the sail can catch the wind at any angle. When the wind is directly behind the boat, the sail is held at right angles to the wind. To move in other directions, the sail is held at different angles so that part of the force on the sail pushes the boat in the direction it wants to travel. To move into the wind, the sail is held edge-on to it. Water resistance on the keel of the boat, called the heeling force, helps the sail move the boat in the right direction.

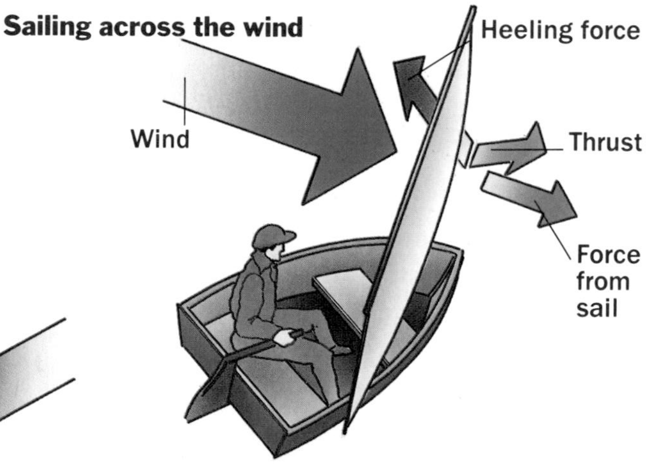

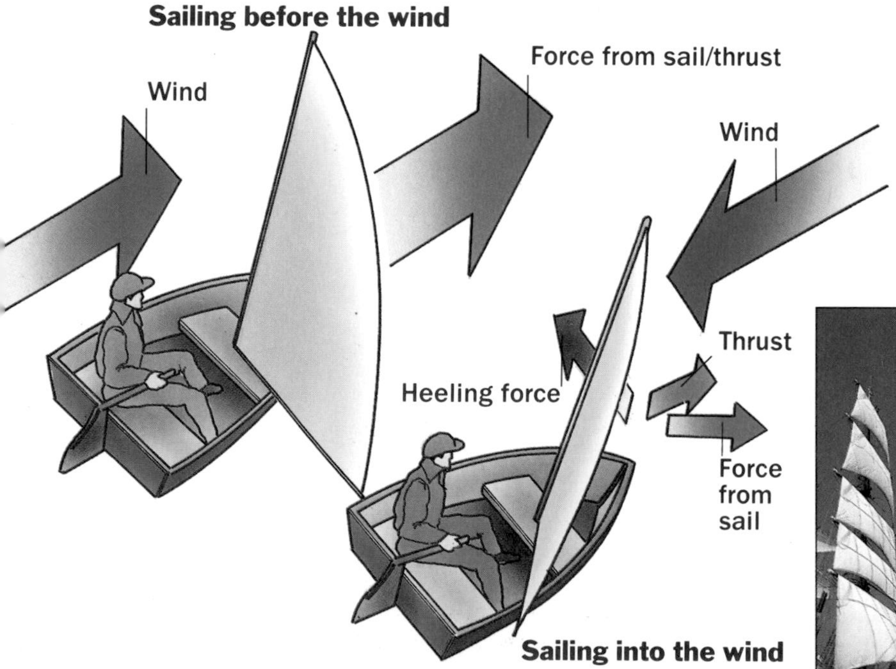

Sailing across the wind

Wind

Heeling force

Thrust

Force from sail

Sailing before the wind

Wind

Force from sail/thrust

Wind

Thrust

Heeling force

Force from sail

Sailing into the wind

► By changing the position of the sails, boats can sail before and into the wind and can easily change direction.

MEASURING THE WIND

The strengths of winds are described using a scale called the Beaufort scale. This scale was developed in 1805 by a British admiral, Francis Beaufort. Wind strength is measured on a scale of 0 to 12. On the Beaufort scale, a calm day is indicated by 0, a gentle breeze is 3, a strong breeze is 6, a strong gale is 9, and a hurricane is 12. To measure wind speed exactly an instrument called an anemometer is used. Some anemometers can measure the direction and the speed of the wind at the same time. They look like small airplanes placed on top of a pole. Other anemometers look like whirling cups on the top of a high post.

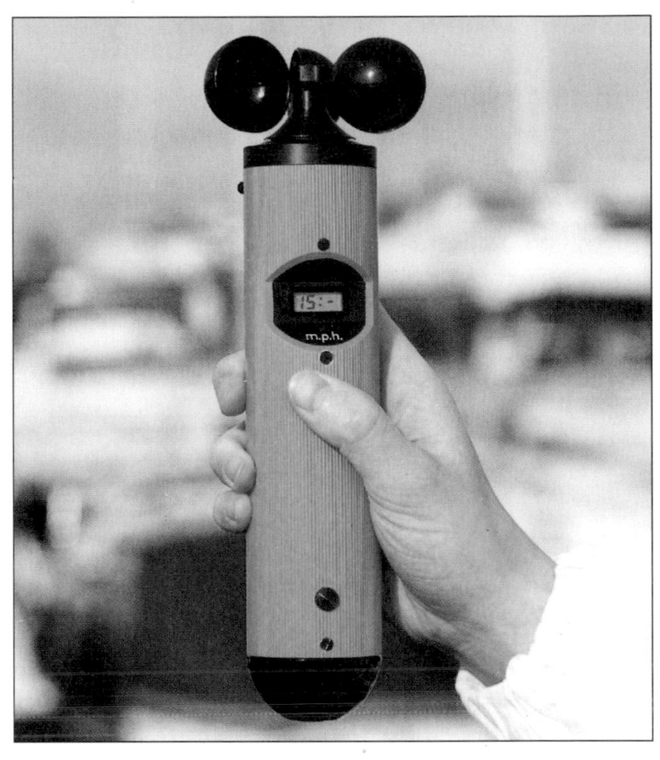

▲ A rotating cup anemometer is used at airports and weather stations. The wind speed is measured by turning the trimming wheel.

MAKE YOUR OWN WIND METER

Fix cardboard disks to strong drinking straws. The straws should be taped together at right angles and fixed to the top of a tube so they can turn easily.

Fix a cardboard paddle wheel to the side of the tube and a cardboard tag to one straw. Make a reference mark on the tube, and number each paddle on the wheel.

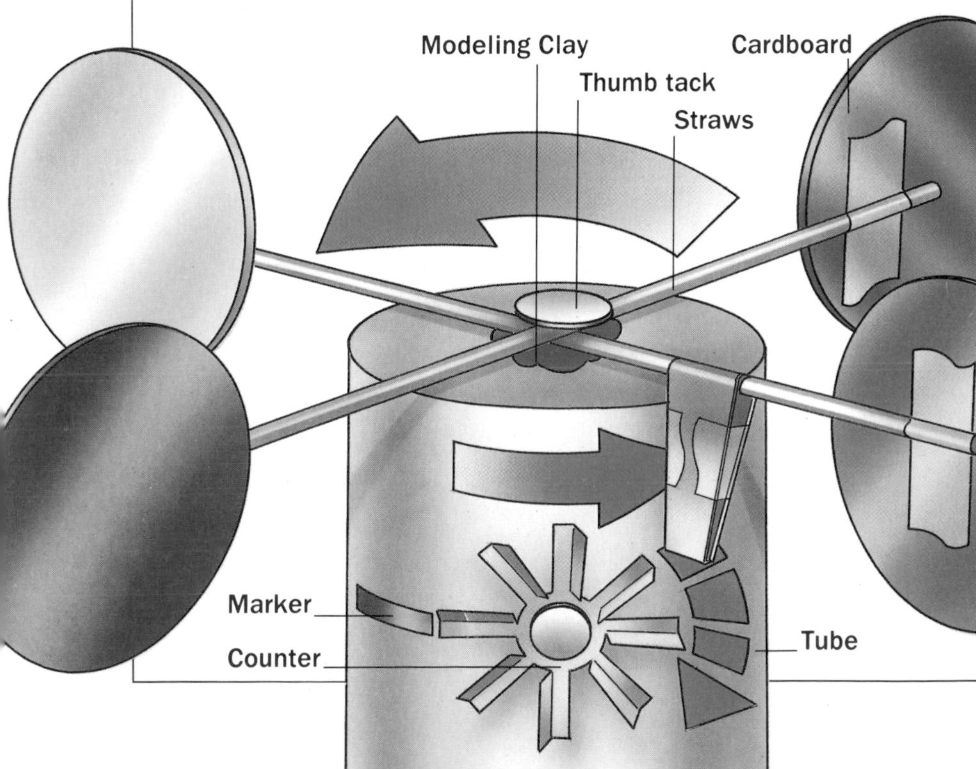

QUIZ

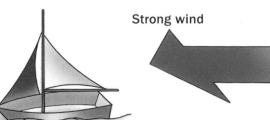

Why do sailing boats use smaller sails in very strong winds? Do you think that the force produced by the wind on the sails depends upon the size of the sails? What else does the wind force depend upon?

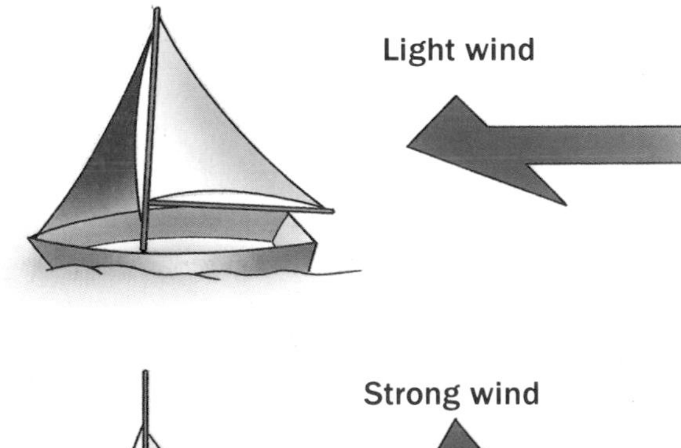

USING AIRSTREAMS

We can produce airstreams easily using fans. These airstreams can be controlled and put to work. They can be taken from one place to another using pipes. So, sometimes airstreams are used to control machinery in industry. They are also used to sort out garbage, and to hold hovercraft off the ground.

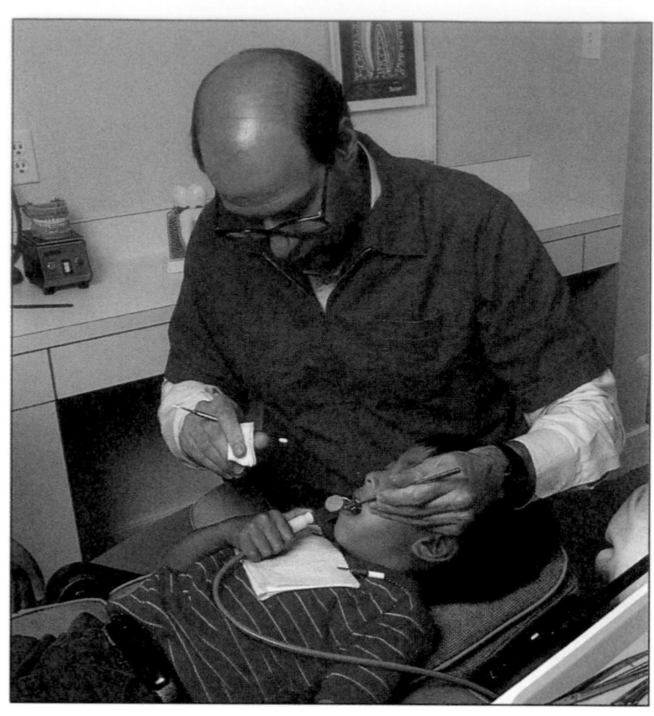

▲ A dentist uses streams of air to suck away waste liquids and keep the patient's mouth clear.

SORTING GARBAGE

At your local garbage disposal site, the trash is carefully sorted. Some types of garbage are valuable. They can be recycled and used again. Paper, for example, can be shredded and made into paper towels, newspaper and flowerpots. Other waste can be burnt to produce heat energy. Airstreams are used to separate the different types of garbage. The garbage is carried from the tip by a conveyor belt. At the end of the conveyor belt it is dropped into a strong upward current of air. As the garbage falls, the air current carries the lightest material, like paper and cardboard, upwards to be collected for reuse.

FLOATING ON AIR

The hovercraft is called an air-cushion vehicle as it rides on a cushion of air. The air cushion is held in place by a kind of flexible skirt around the base of the craft. A powerful fan forces air into the skirt. The air cannot escape and it lifts the craft off the ground. The hovercraft is driven forward by large propellers at the back. These spin in the air like aircraft propellers. The hull of the hovercraft does not touch the ground as it skims along. This means that it can be used over land, water or swamp. For this reason, hovercraft have been used by explorers in South America and Africa. Hovercraft can travel faster than ships, but they can only be used in calm seas as they overturn easily.

▼ The hovercraft is used in country, like swampland, where normal vehicles cannot go, and for short sea journeys.

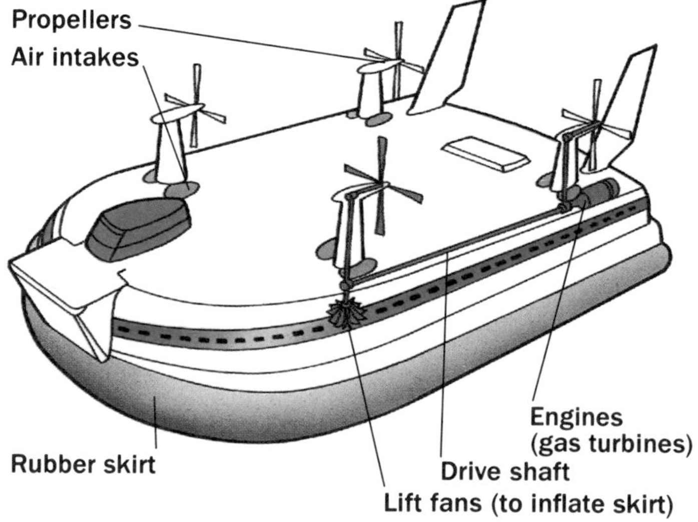

PAINTING WITH AIR

Streams of air can be used for painting. The first step is to obtain a supply of high-pressure air. This is done with an air compressor, a machine that pumps air into a sealed tank until the pressure builds up. Air, or spray, painting is done with a spray gun. This is attached to the compressed air tank, and to a small container of paint. When the trigger on the spray gun is pressed, air squirts out of a nozzle on the gun. The air flow draws paint from the container and carries it to the object being painted. A spray gun can paint an object in minutes.

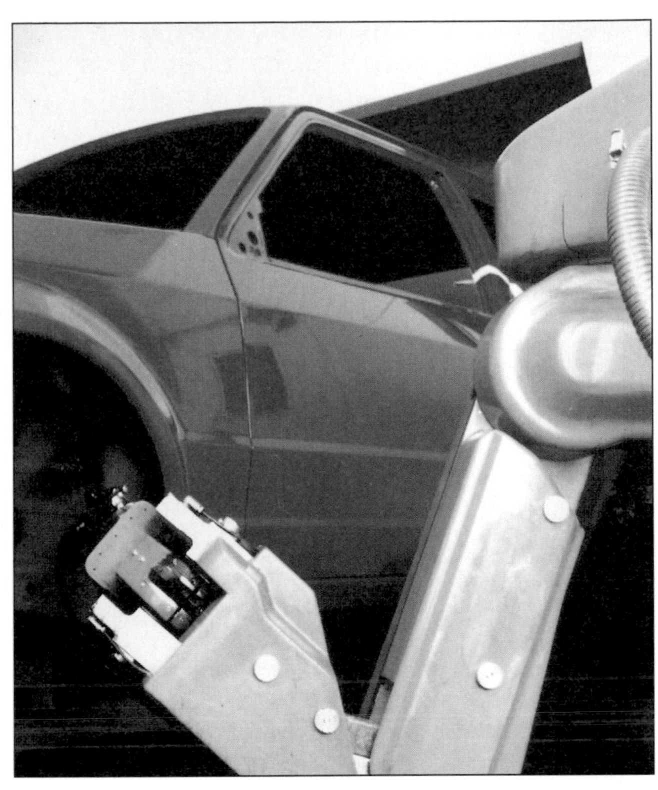

► Spray painting is used in industry because it produces a smooth surface. It is easy for robot painters to use spray guns.

MAKE A SPRAY GUN

A spray gun can be made with a drinking straw and a plastic pen tube. Fix the pen tube to the straw so that when you blow into the tube, the air stream flows across the top of the straw.

The flow of air across the straw reduces the air pressure in the straw. This draws the paint up the straw and into the air stream. What is the effect of blowing harder into the pen tube?

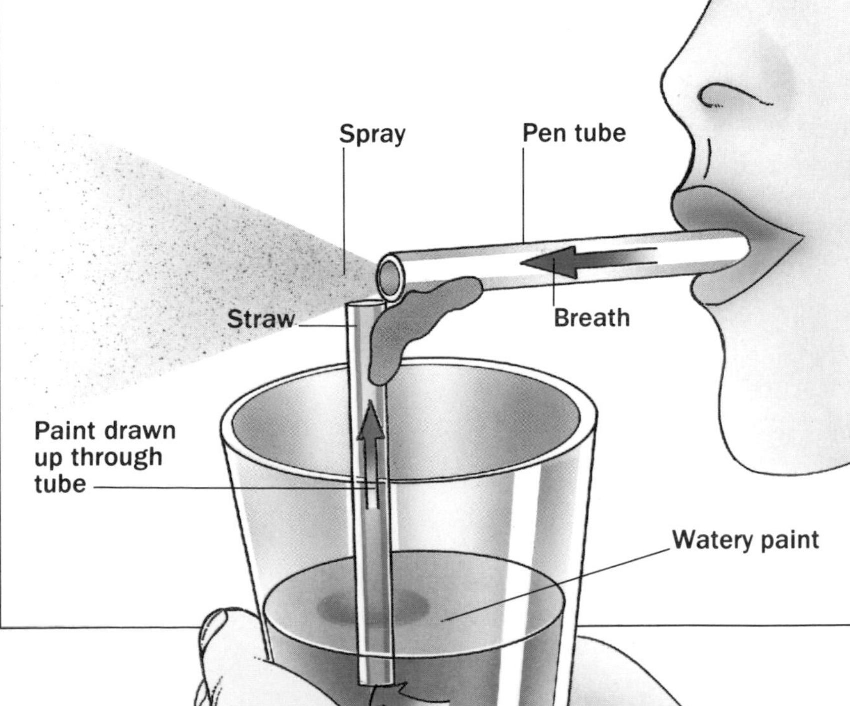

WHAT HAPPENS?

If there is a light breeze, what happens if a mixture of corn and chaff are thrown up into the air? The same effect can be seen if you blow on a mixture of corn and chaff held on your hand. This process is called winnowing. It was used by farmers in ancient times to separate corn from unwanted chaff.

If there was no air, all objects would fall at the same rate. Light objects would reach the ground side-by-side with heavy objects released at the same time from the same height. However, falling through air is different. Light objects can sometimes fall very slowly. This is why a parachutist can land safely.

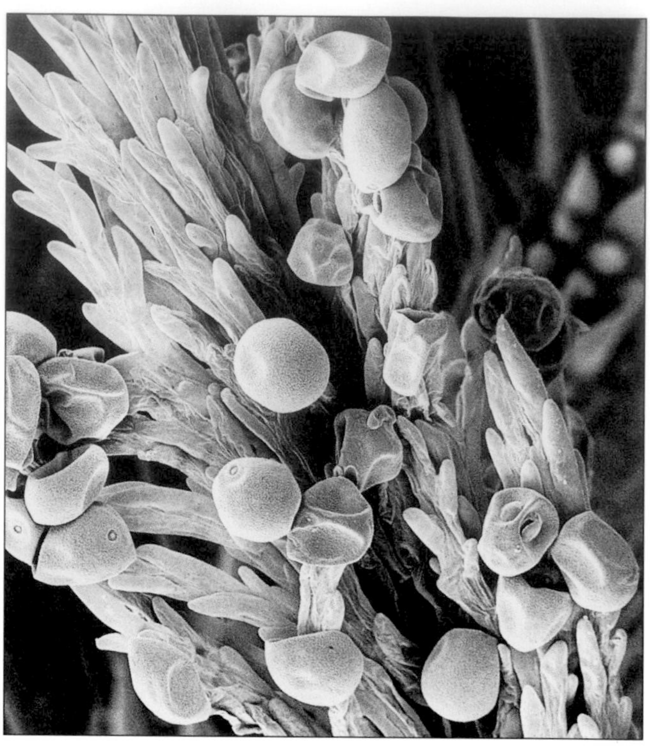

▲ Pollen (magnified many times in this photograph) falls to the ground unless carried upwards by air currents.

FALLING

When something falls through the air, the air slows its fall. There is air resistance, or "drag," on the object. Eventually, the drag slowing a falling object becomes as strong as the pull of gravity which is trying to speed it up. When this happens the speed of the object stays the same. It is said to be moving at its terminal speed. Objects with different shapes have different terminal speeds because the drag is different for different shapes. A person falling with a parachute has a slow terminal speed because the parachute creates lots of drag and so slows his or her fall.

▼ The flying squirrel, which lives in Africa, can glide 90 m (300 ft) from one tree to another.

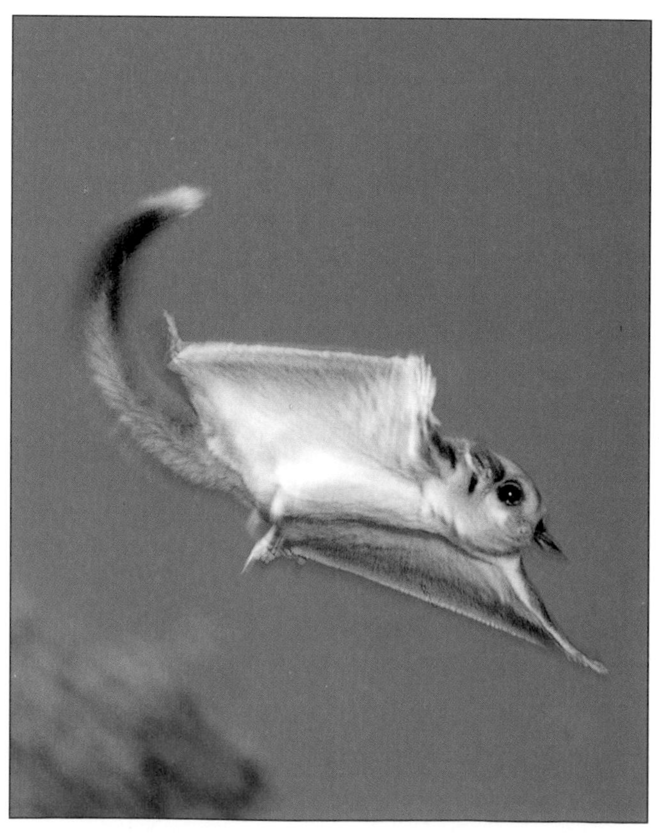

GLIDING THROUGH THE AIR

There are squirrels, lizards, frogs and fish that are skilled gliders. There is even a flying snake which can glide through the air. These animals have folds of skin on each side of their bodies, or on their feet, which they stretch out to form gliding wings. The wings act like parachutes and slow their fall when they leap from high in the treetops. The flying lemur, from the island of Madagascar, is almost helpless on the ground, but it can glide for up to 440 ft (135 m) when it extends the flaps that stretch between its arms and legs. The flying frog has folds of skin between its toes which it extends to make four tiny parachutes. Flying fishes extend fins on the sides of their bodies, and can glide more than 100 yards across the surface of the sea.

FLOATING ON THE AIR

Many living things are able to float on the air. They can do this because they are very light. They also have a large surface area, like a parachute. This means that they can easily float long distances in the air. A dandelion seed may be carried more than 6 miles (10 km) by the wind before landing. Some seeds, such as maple or sycamore seeds, have wings that spin as the seed falls. This helps the seed stay airborne longer.

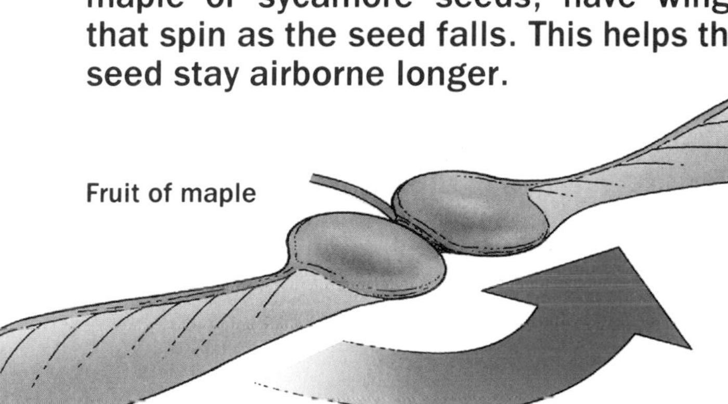

▲ A small spider can be carried thousands of miles by its silken parachute. Small spiders have even been found in the air thousands of feet above the Earth's surface.

MAKE A PARACHUTE

Get a square of light cloth, such as an old handkerchief. Cut a circle from the cloth. Tie lengths of string through holes around its edges.

Tie the other ends of the strings to a matchbox with a small weight inside. Cut a hole in the center of the cloth, to let the air flow through it.

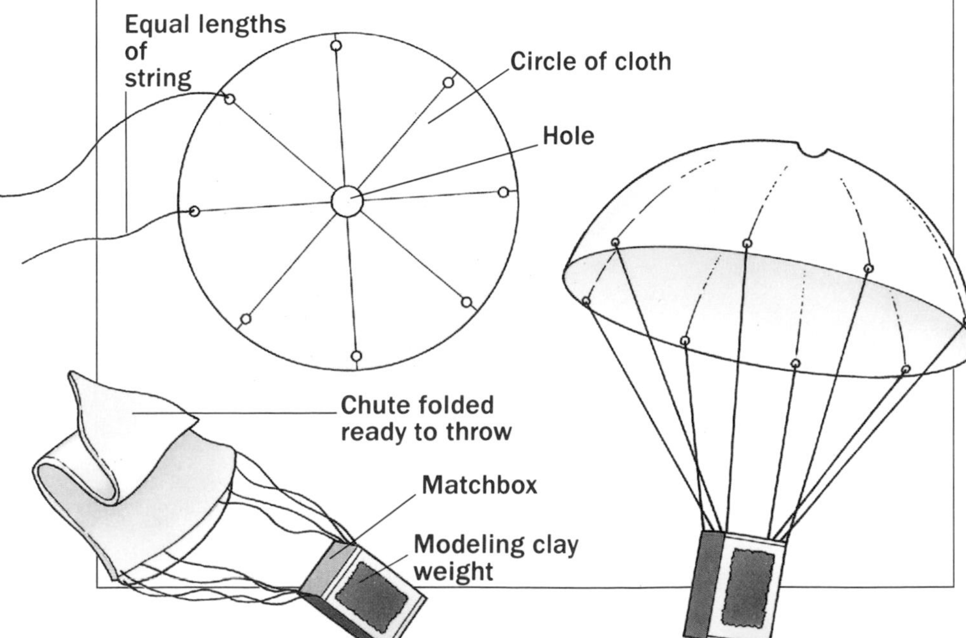

WHY?

Why does a dandelion seed have a fluffy head? Why does it need a sudden puff of wind to break the seeds free from the plant? Why are heavier seeds, such as sycamore, elm or pine cones, different?

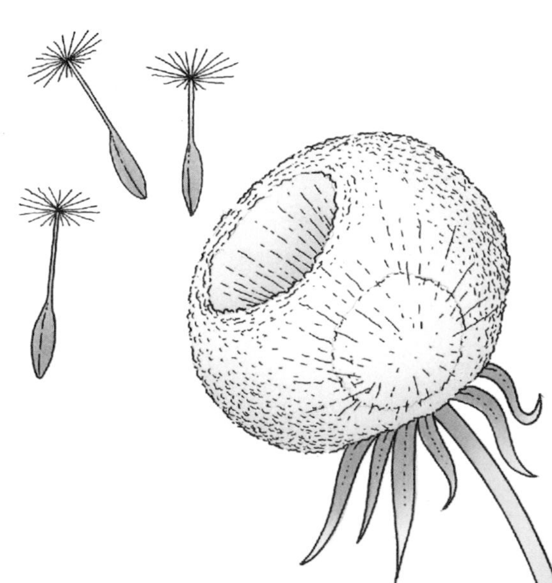

LIGHTER THAN AIR

Balloons and blimps float in the air like boats float in water. They are able to do this because their weight is supported by an upwards force called an upthrust, or lift force. The upthrust force is caused by the air pushing on the bottom of the balloon, just like water pushing against the bottom of a floating boat.

▲ A hot air balloon rises because the warm air inside it is less dense than the surrounding air. This produces a large upthrust force.

EXPANDING AIR

Most things expand, or get bigger, when they are heated. If you heat air in a flexible container, such as a balloon, the air will expand, stretching the balloon. This expansion makes the air in the balloon less dense than the surrounding air. It still weighs the same as it did when cold, but it takes up more space. Because it is taking up more space, it feels a greater upthrust force from the air around it. If the balloon was heated even more, the upthrust might increase sufficiently to lift the balloon from the ground. This is how a hot air balloon rises in the air.

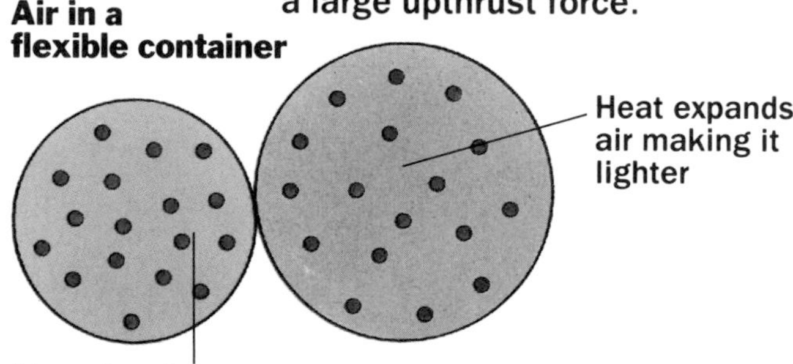

LIGHTER GASES

Some gases, such as helium, are naturally less dense than air. A balloon filled with these gases does not have to be heated to cause lift. In a modern blimp, the lift is provided by a large bag, called the envelope, containing helium. Inside the envelope are small compartments, called ballonets, containing air.

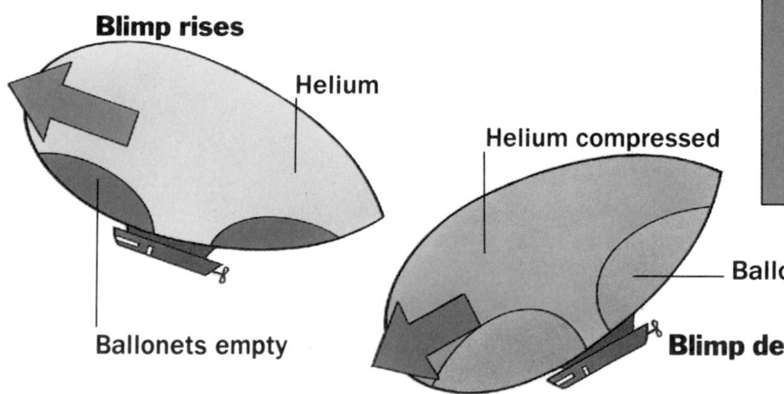

Pumping air out of the ballonets decreases the blimp's weight and the blimp rises. Pumping air into the ballonets increases the ship's weight and the ship falls. A blimp also has propellers that drive it through the air.

▲ The propellers, tail fins and rudder on a blimp can be turned to maneuver the blimp when it is moving.

THE HOT AIR SCREW

Draw a spiral and aircraft on a circle of cardboard. Cut along the spiral and pull it out a little to make a spiral or coil.

Stand a sharpened pencil on a radiator using modeling clay. Place the coil on the pencil. Watch it turn around.

The coil turns because heated air is rising from the radiator. The current of heated air twists the coil like a propeller.

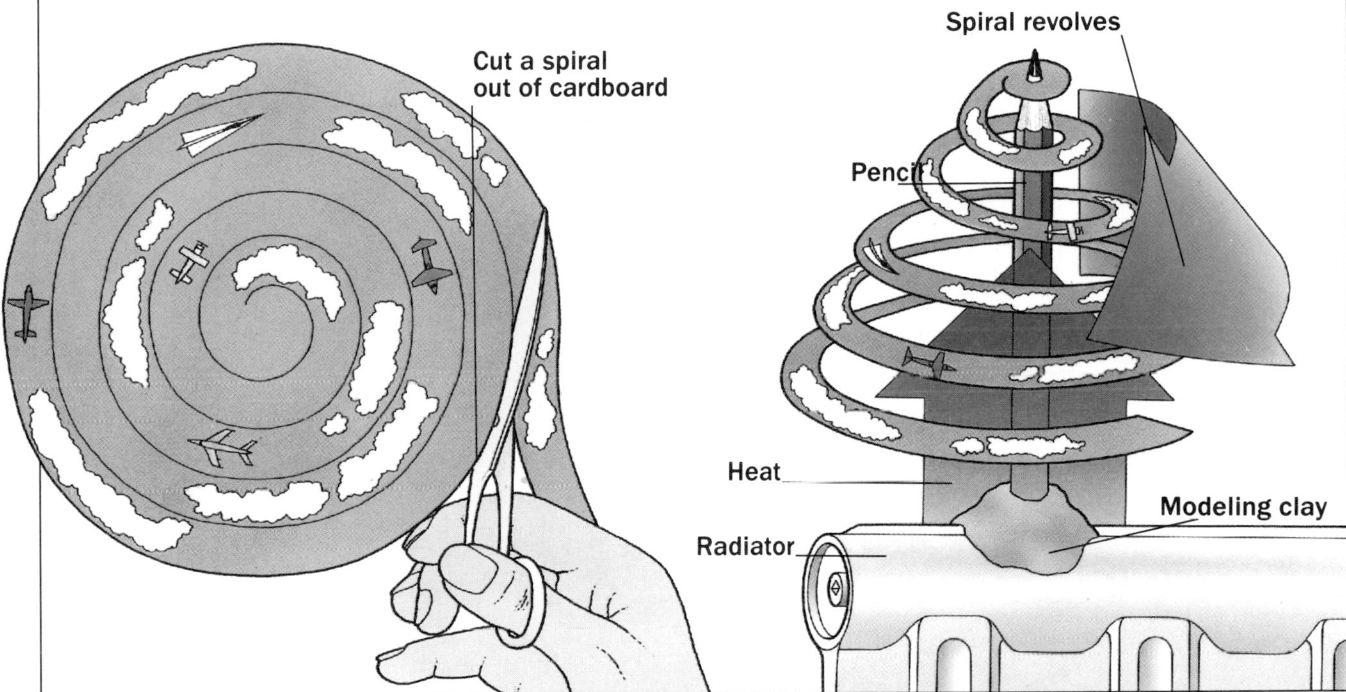

WHAT HAPPENS?

What happens when an inflated balloon is placed in a warm oven or cupboard and left for half an hour? What happens when the balloon is placed in a refrigerator and left for the same time? Make your experiment more precise by measuring the size around the balloon before placing it in the cupboard or refrigerator and again after taking it out. Does the size of the balloon depend on how long it is in the cupboard or refrigerator or warm oven?

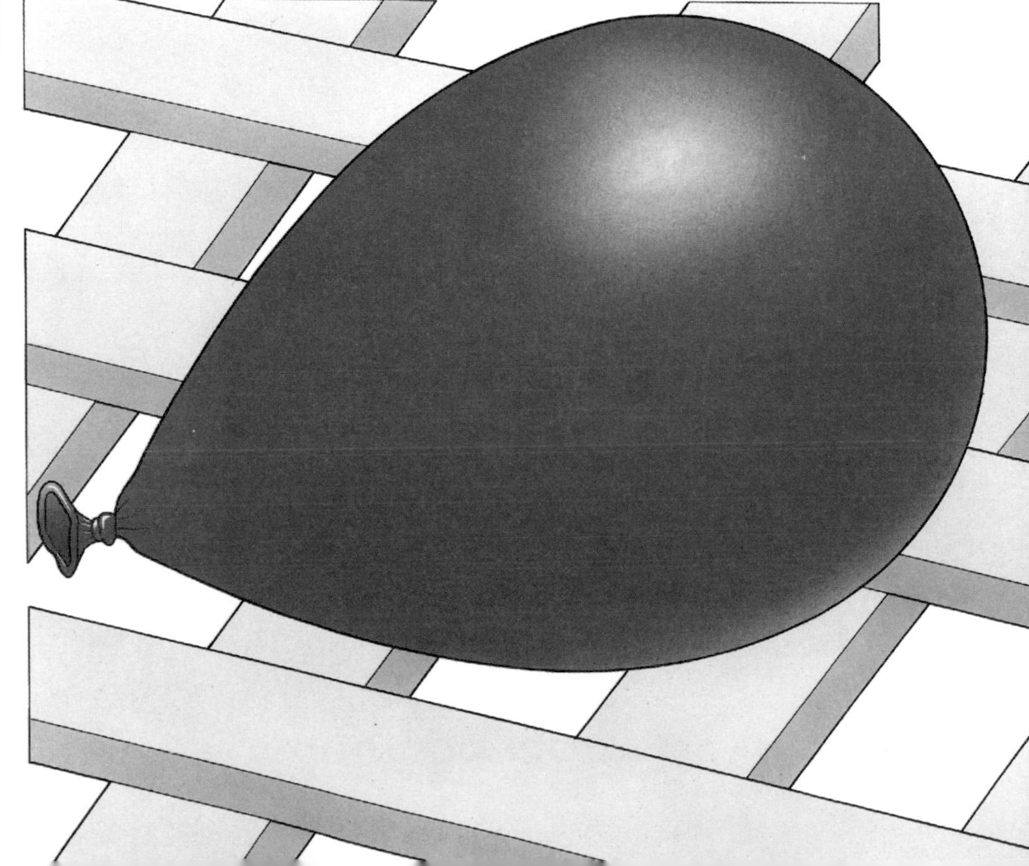

There are many different kinds of flying machines, or aircraft. Some are huge, like the jumbo jet, and some are tiny, like the hang glider. But they all rely on wings to lift them up and keep them aloft. The wings provide an upward force, called "lift," that balances the weight of the aircraft and keeps it in the air.

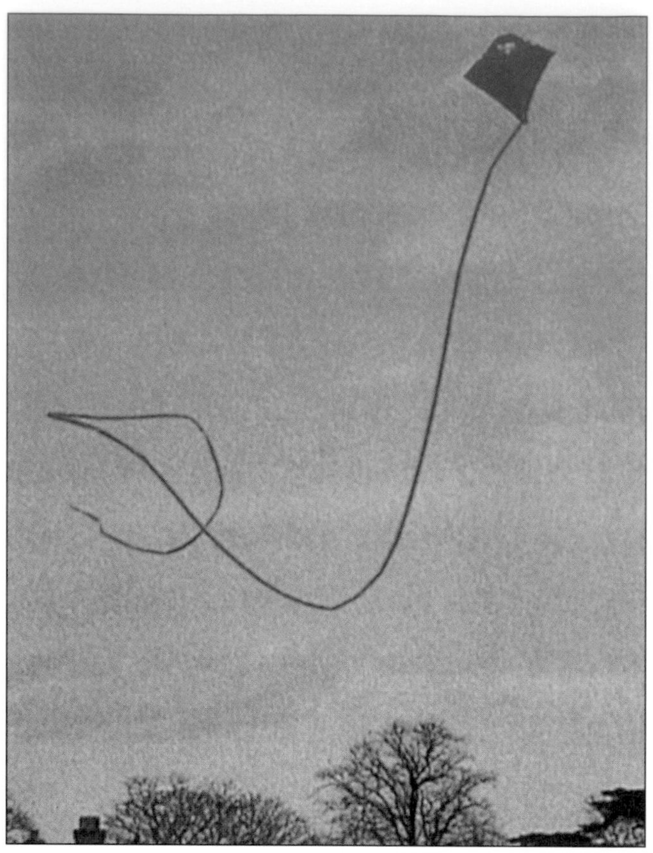

▲ A kite flies steadily in the sky when all the forces acting on it are balanced. The pull on the string is balanced by the wind.

FLYING WITHOUT POWER

Kites and gliders fly without engine power. They use the forces created by flowing air to provide lift. The wind blows against the kite, which is held at an angle to the wind by the string. The kite deflects the wind downward. As this happens, a reaction force is created on the kite, lifting it up. A hang glider gets its lift in a different way. The triangular glider wing fills with air as the wind blows across it. The wing becomes rounded on top. The air flow around the curved wing produces a force that lifts the glider. A fixed-wing glider like the Space Shuttle also gets its lift from the airflow around its carefully designed wings.

GETTING LIFT

The cross-section of an aircraft wing is a special shape called an airfoil. The airfoil is curved on top and almost flat on the bottom. As the air blows over the wing, or the aircraft moves through the air, the air divides to pass around the wing. The air that passes along the top of the wing moves faster than the air that passes underneath. This is because the air flowing over the top of the wing has further to go, owing to the curved surface of the wing. Fast-moving air has a lower pressure than slow-moving air, so the pressure on the top of the wing is less than the pressure on the bottom. This difference in pressure creates the upwards force called lift. If the aircraft is moving fast enough, the lift is strong enough to support the aircraft.

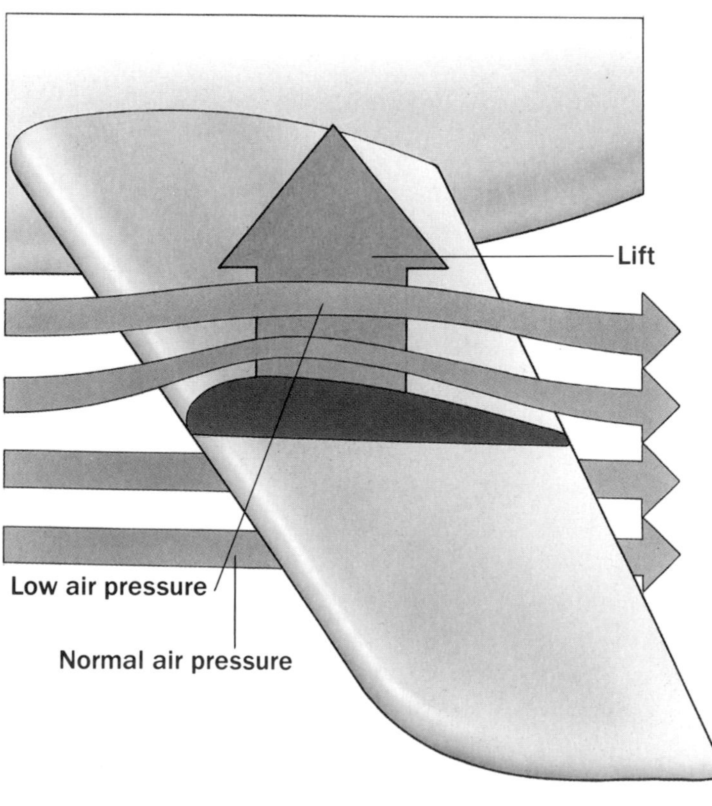

BIRD LIFT

Birds do more than just flap their wings in order to fly. They also twist the wings, and adjust the angles of the feathers. On the downbeat, the edges of the wing feathers overlap slightly so that no air can pass through them and the wing pushes against the air. On the upbeat, the feathers twist apart so that air can pass through. At the same time, the tips of the wings move in a circle. A forward push of the wingtips on the downstroke propels the bird through the air.

▲ The photograph shows feathers on a bird's wing.

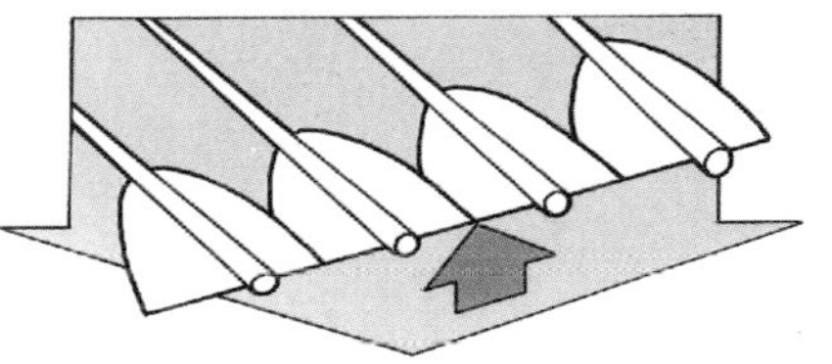

Air resistance closes feathers

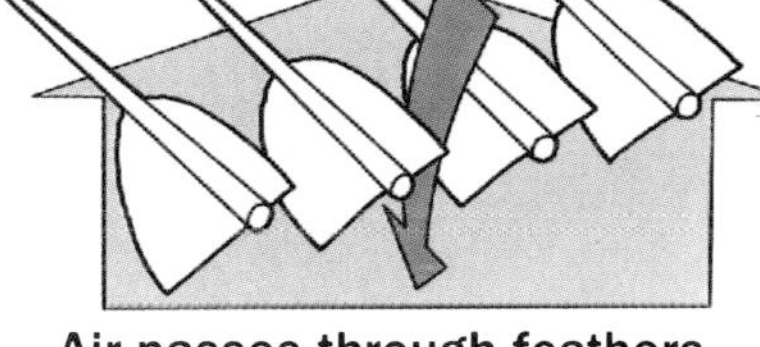

Air passes through feathers

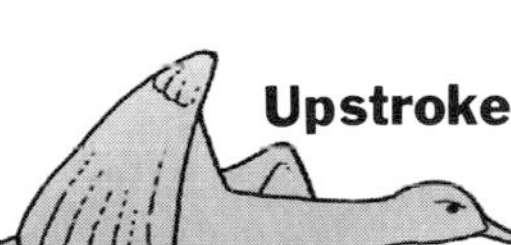

FAST AIR, LOW PRESSURE

You can see the effect of fast-moving air with a strip of paper. Hold one end of the paper near your mouth and blow. The paper will move upwards and flutter, because the air blowing over its top surface has less pressure than the air beneath it and so has the effect of lifting the paper. Cut small flaps in the end of the strip. Bend one flap down and blow. What happens? Place a small disk of cardboard on a table and see if you can lift it slightly by blowing over the top of it.

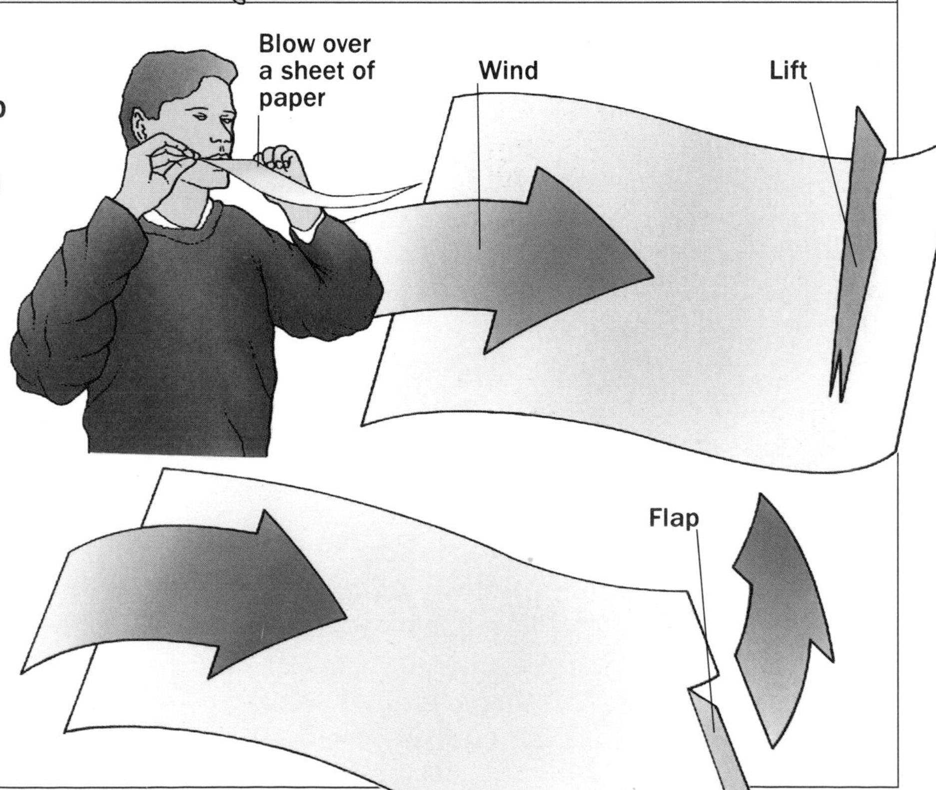

USING LIFT

The curved airfoil is put to many different uses. The paradise tree snake from Southeast Asia turns its body into an airfoil when it glides down from a high tree. Throwing sticks and boomerangs, used by some hunting people, are shaped like airfoils to help them fly long distances through the air.

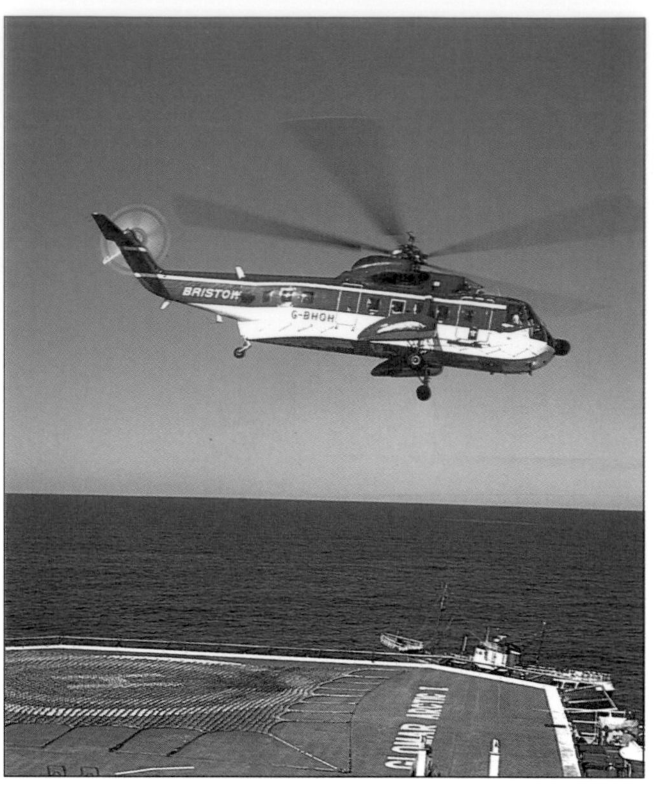

▲ The angle of a helicopter's blades can be altered to make it move straight up, or forward or backwards. To hover, the speed of the rotors is adjusted.

THE HELICOPTER

The helicopter looks very different from other aircraft. Yet, it too gets its lift from airfoils. The whirling rotors have an airfoil shape like the wings of a fixed-wing plane. The difference is that, while a fixed-wing craft has to speed through the air before its wings can lift it up, the rotors of a helicopter produce lift without the craft moving forward. The lift is produced by the airflow over the airfoil-shaped blades as they spin. The airflow around the spinning rotor blades causes low pressure above the blades, which lifts the helicopter.

WING SHAPES

Aircraft have different shapes of wings. A slow-flying glider or light aircraft has long straight wings, which produce high lift at slow speeds. An airliner has swept-back wings which cause less air resistance, or drag, at high speed. However, lift is also reduced so high speeds are needed to take off. A supersonic aircraft, such as Concorde or the Space Shuttle, has dart-shaped or delta wings. This shape reduces drag and helps control the craft at faster-than-sound speeds.

Many aircraft wing shapes have been designed to copy the very effective wing shapes of birds. The long, thin wings of a condor, for example, allows it to soar for hours in search of prey. A hawk has swept-back wings to increase its speed and to allow it to make a sudden dive.

▲ Bats have wings made of skin stretched between thin bones. They are fast and agile fliers.

THE BOOMERANG

The boomerang is a V-shaped throwing stick used for hunting by the Australian aborigines. A boomerang is shaped like an airfoil. Its top surface is rounded and the bottom surface is flat. When the boomerang is thrown, it spins as it moves toward the target. Because of its airfoil shape, the boomerang is lifted as it spins through the air. If the boomerang misses its target, the lift gradually turns the boomerang in a circle so that it returns to the thrower.

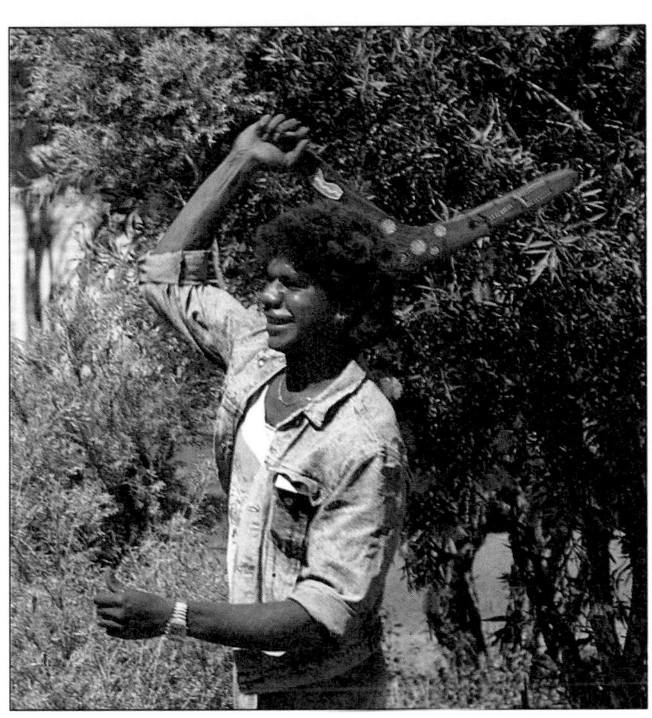

► Some Australian Aborigines can expertly throw a boomerang to kill game 500 feet away.

MAKE AN AIR-POWERED HELICOPTER

Make two rotor blades by taping a paper strip to two plastic drinking straws. The upper surface of the paper should be curved. Bend one end of the straw so that it points to one side.

Cut two holes in opposite sides of a cardboard tube, sealed at one end. Fix the rotor blades into the holes, using tape. Fix another rotor across the top of the tube.

Blow up a balloon and connect the neck of the balloon to the cardboard tube. When the balloon is released, air will flow through the straws and turn the rotors.

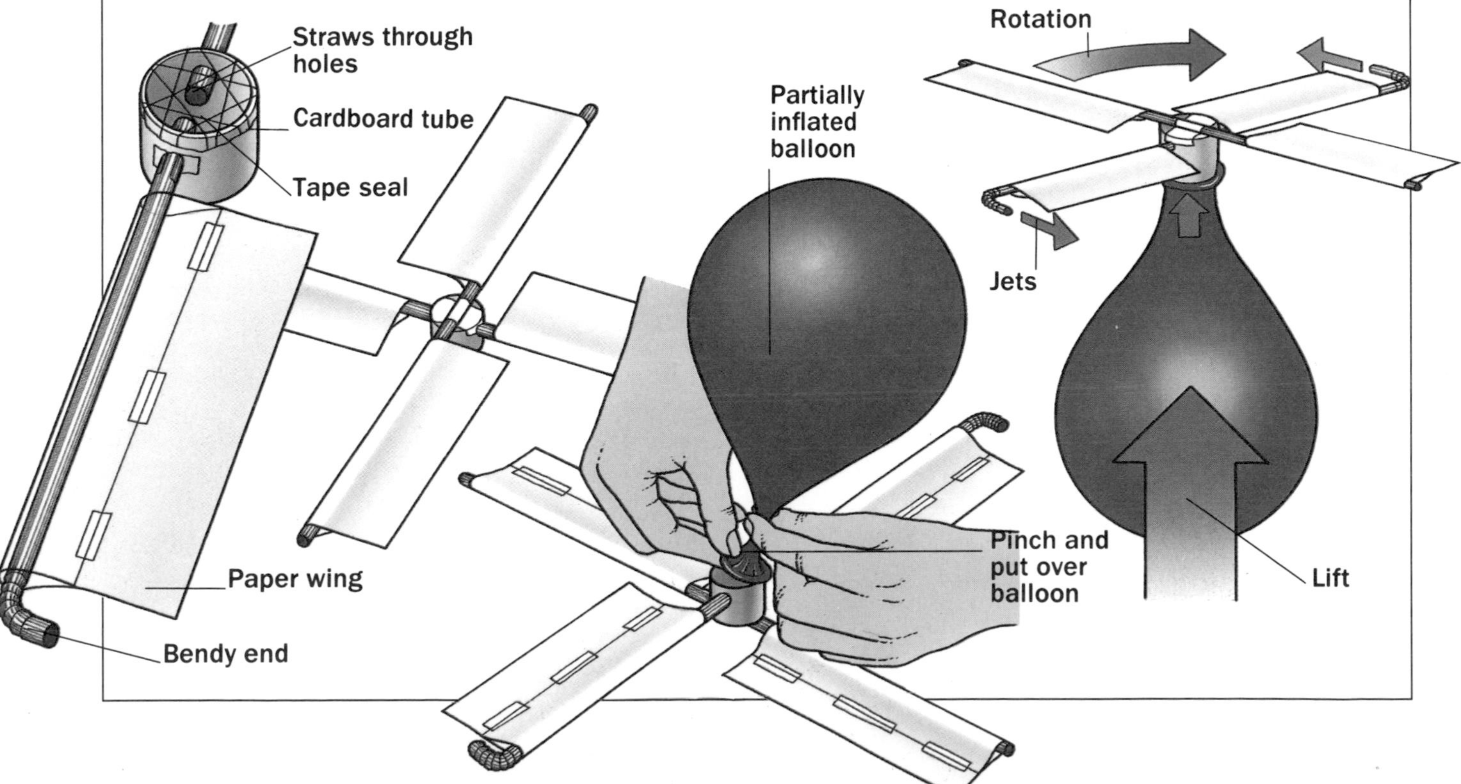

MOVING THROUGH THE AIR

An aircraft moves through the air because of the forward force, called the thrust, provided by its engines. Sometimes the engine turns a propeller which pushes air backward as it spins, resulting in a forward thrust on the craft. Other aircraft have jet engines which eject a stream of hot gas to produce the thrust.

CONTROLLING AN AIRCRAFT

Flaps on the wings and tail are used to steer an aircraft, and to change its height. Flaps on the back edge of the main wings are called ailerons. These are operated by the pilot moving the control column, or stick, to left or right. The ailerons are connected so that when one goes up, the other goes down. The flaps on the back edge of the tail wings are called elevators. They are also worked by moving the control column. The elevators make the plane climb or dive. The rudder is a flap on the back of the tail. The rudder is used with the ailerons to make a turn.

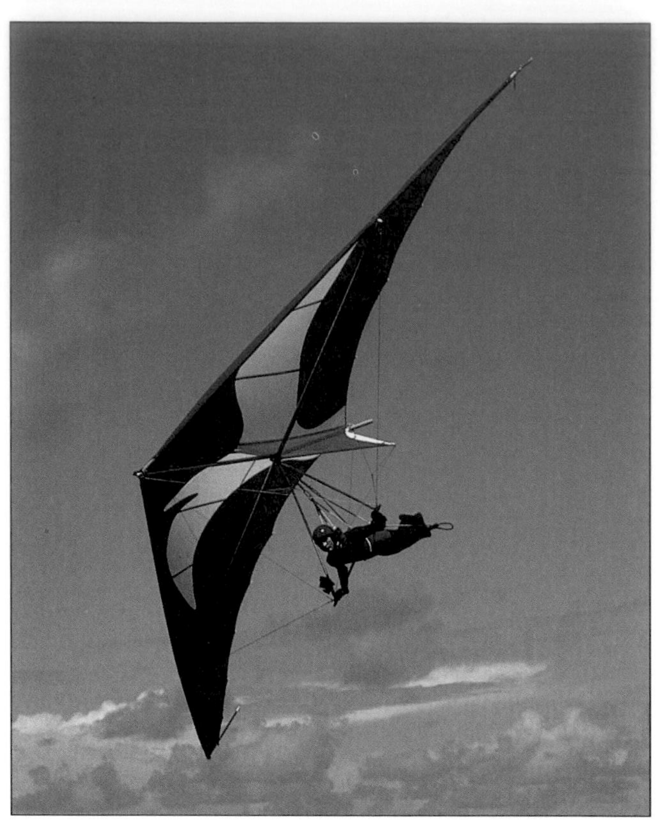

▲ The direction or height of a hang-glider is altered by changing the position of its wings.

HOW TO STEER

To descend, the pilot of a plane pushes the control column forward. This lowers the elevators on the tail and deflects the airflow so that the tail rises and the nose dips. To climb, a plane pilot pulls the column back. To roll an airplane, the column is moved to one side. This raises one aileron and lowers the other. The wing with the lowered aileron rises and the other wing drops. To turn a plane, the pilot presses the foot pedals to turn the rudder to one side. At the same time, the control column is moved to one side to raise and lower the ailerons.

The controls are different but the effect is the same on a hang glider. The pilot moves the control bar to one side to turn. It is moved forward to climb and backward to dive.

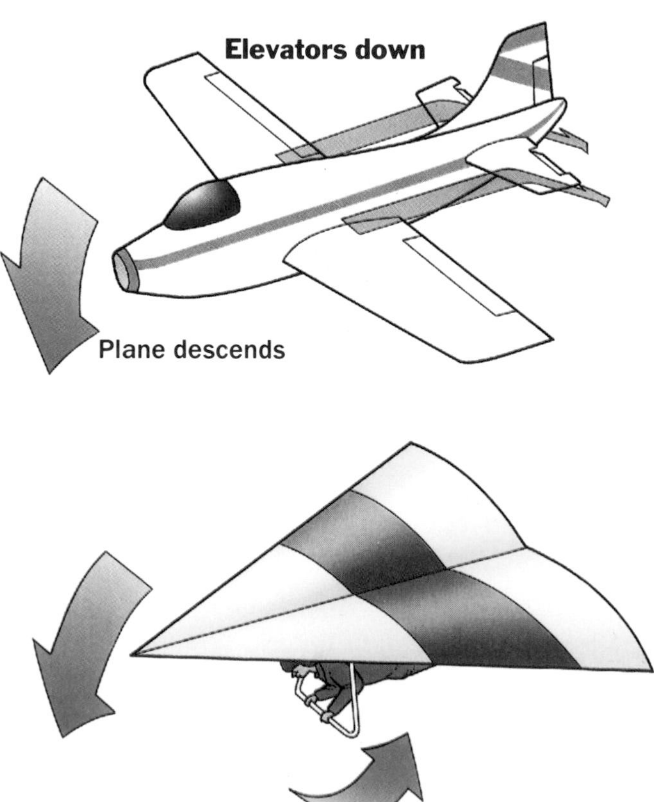

MAKE A SUPER PLANE

Start with a rectangular sheet of paper. Fold it down the center lengthwise. Fold the front edges back twice, to form a triangular shape. Fold the triangular wings out from the body to make the shape shown. This plane should fly well,but to improve its performance, tear a slot at the back and fold it upwards to form a tail. You can make the plane do aerobatics by tearing flaps on the back of the wings. Experiment with the flaps in different positions. How can you make the plane dive, turn, or even loop the loop? How can you make it glide the farthest?

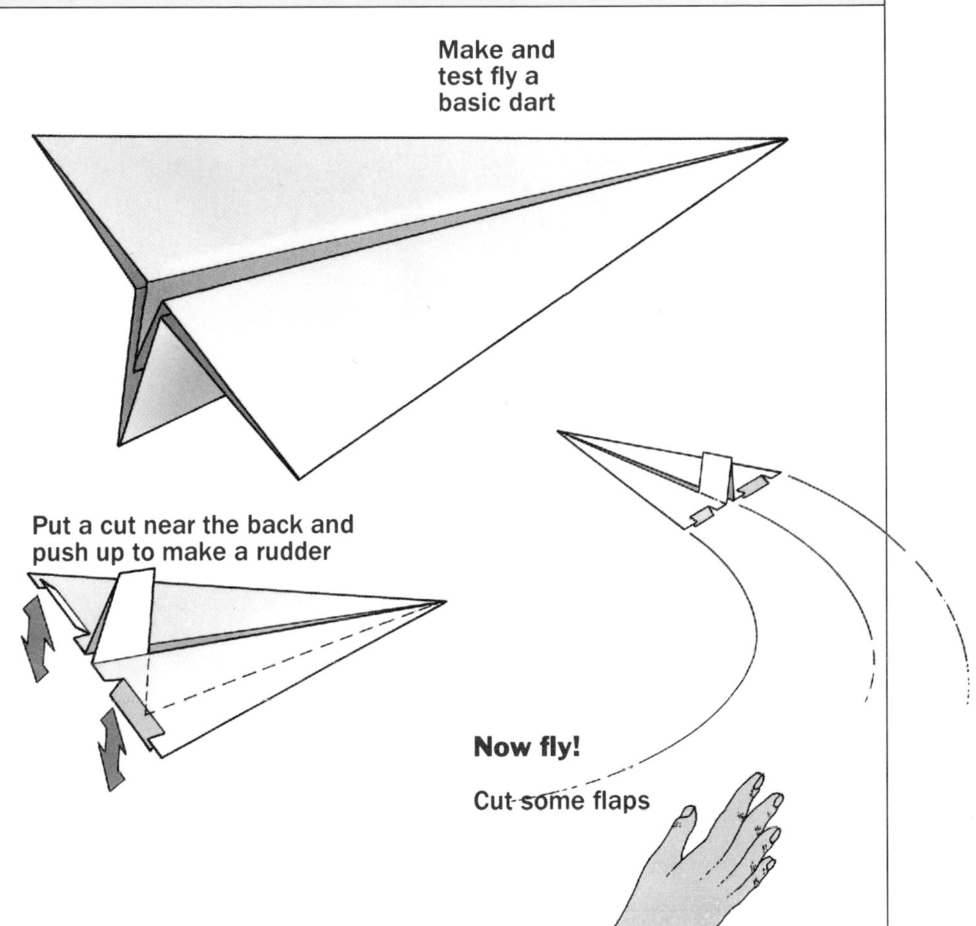

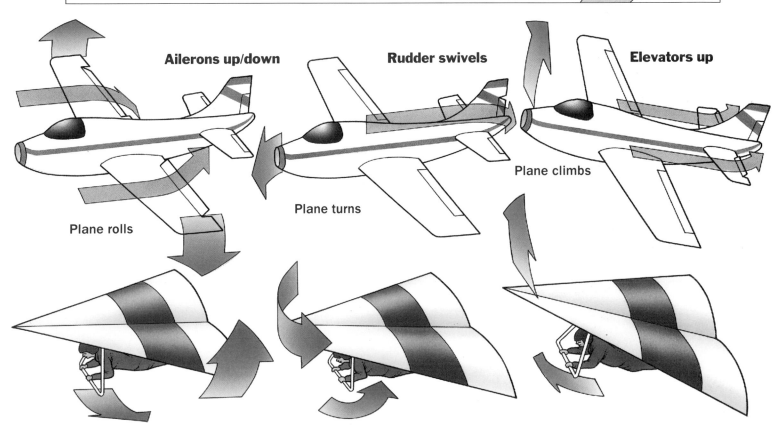

Make and test fly a basic dart
Put a cut near the back and push up to make a rudder
Now fly!
Cut some flaps

Ailerons up/down

Plane rolls

Rudder swivels

Plane turns

Elevators up

Plane climbs

A fan is used to blow air along, to create a breeze on a hot day, for example. As the blades of the fan turn, they create forces that blow the air forward. But the forces created by the turning blades can be used in other ways. They can pull an aircraft or ship along, and turn machinery, such as electric generators.

THE PROPELLER

Propellers consist of blades attached to a hub which turns. The blades are shaped like airfoils so that when they turn there is less pressure on the curved front surface. This creates a suction force which drags the ship or aircraft forward. Also, as the propeller turns, the blades strike the water or air and push it backward. This produces a forward force, called the reaction force. The reaction force and the suction drive the ship or plane forward. In some propellers, the angle, or pitch, of the blades can be adjusted. At high pitch, the propeller drives the craft forward at speed. The blades can be "feathered" so that they produce little drag when not turning.

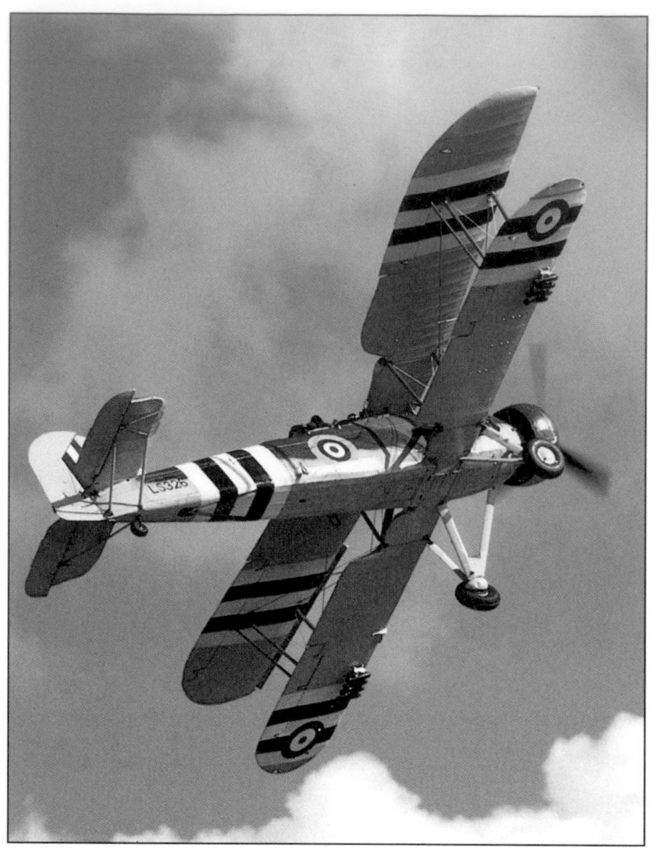

▲ The propeller engine is not as powerful or economical as the jet engine. Nevertheless, it is still used on some aircraft.

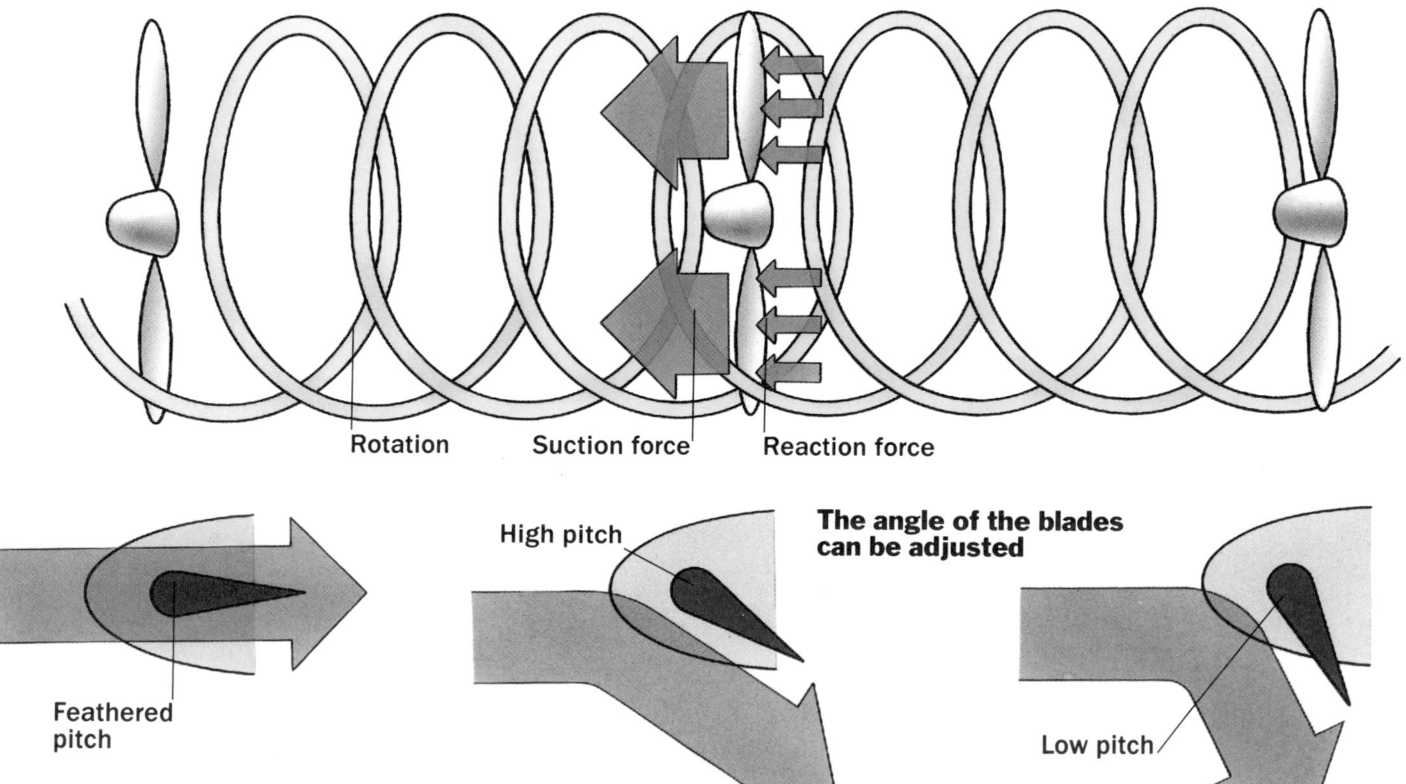

The angle of the blades can be adjusted

THE TURBINE

Turbines are a type of engine used to turn electric generators in power stations, ships propellers, and machines in factories. Jet engines which power most large aircraft are a kind of turbine. Inside a turbine, there are two sets of blades. High-pressure steam, water or gas flows over blades, like the blades of a fan or propeller. As the steam, water or gas flows past the blades, it makes them turn. Some are fixed to the shaft and others attached to the casing. This rotation turns the ship's propeller or the electric generator.

► Inside a giant turbine used to produce electricity. The blades can be seen. In most power stations, the turbines are turned by steam.

MAKE A PROPELLER-DRIVEN BOAT

Make a propeller by attaching paper blades to the ends of a strong drinking straw. Make sure one side of the blades is curved and the other side is flat, as can be seen in the illustration on the right. Use sticky tape to fix a small cardboard tube to the side of a light, plastic bottle. At the other end of the bottle, attach a bent paper clip. Push a bent paper clip through the center of the straw and join the clips with a rubber band as shown. Attach lollipop sticks to the sides of the bottle, using drinking straws and tape. Wind the propeller to twist the rubber band, and release.

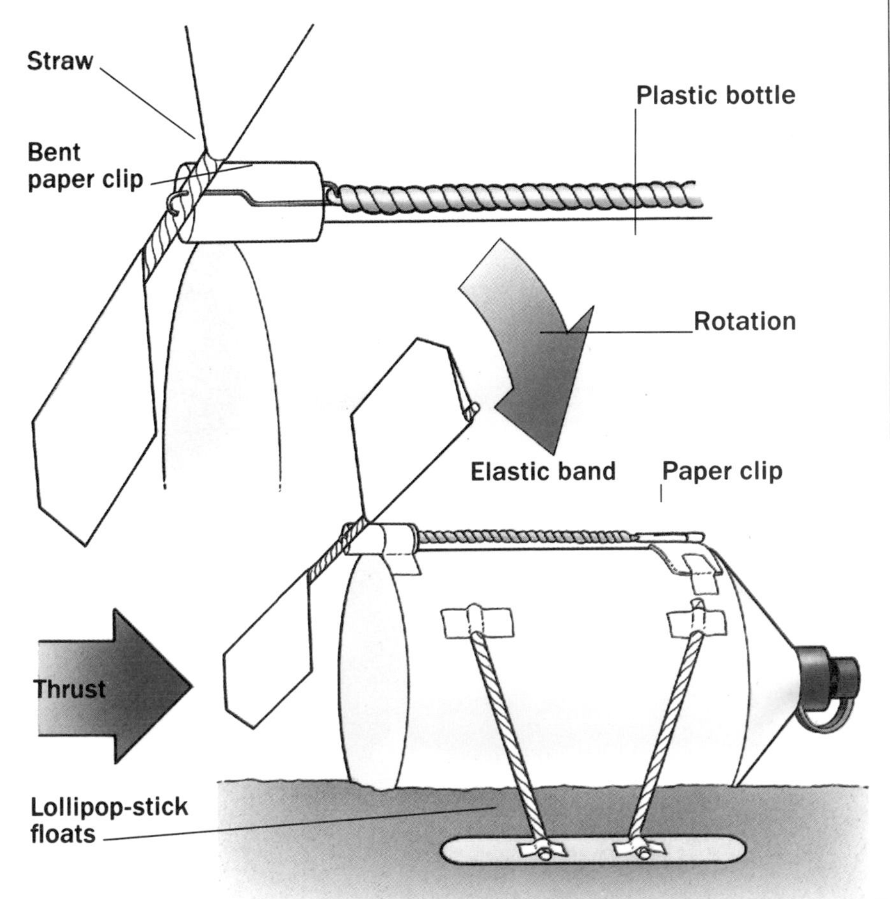

Jets and rockets are engines which push aircraft along, rather than pull them through the air using a propeller. In both a jet engine and in a rocket, a stream of hot gases flows from the rear of the engine. As the gases stream out, a thrust or push is developed which drives the engine forward.

THE JET ENGINE

In a jet engine, a fuel such as kerosene is burnt in a combustion chamber. The hot gases escaping from the combustion chamber pass out the rear of the engine, driving the engine forward. As the gases pass out of the engine, they go through a turbine, causing the turbine blades to turn. The blades of the turbine are attached to a shaft. The shaft is connected to another turbine-like device, called a compressor, at the front of the engine. As the compressor is turned by the turbine, the air needed to burn the fuel is drawn into the engines at the front. The compressor squashes, or compresses, the air and forces it at high pressure into the combustion chamber where it burns fiercely.

▲ The jet engine is used in most airliners and military fighters. The photograph shows a side-view of the air-intake and compressor found at the front of a jet engine.

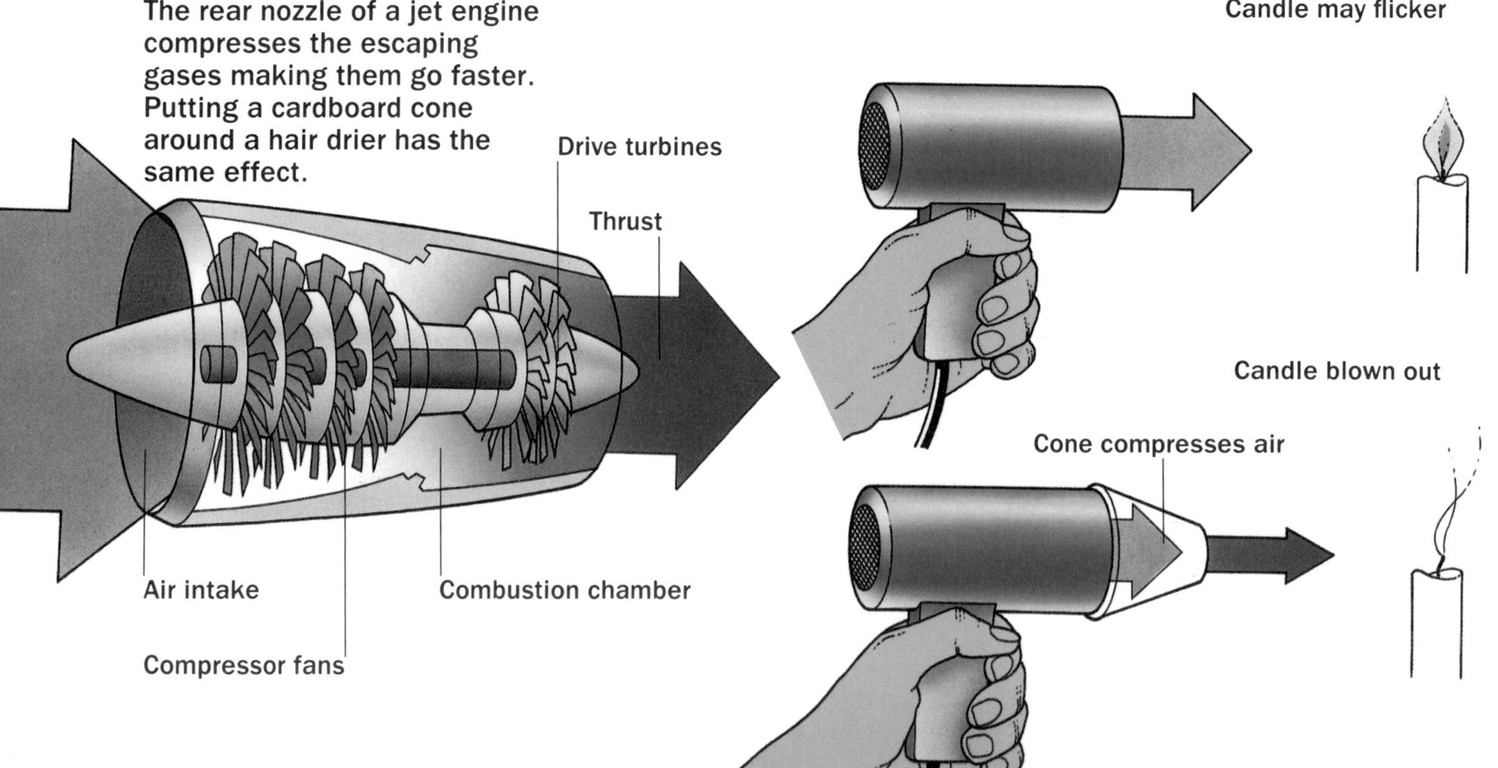

The rear nozzle of a jet engine compresses the escaping gases making them go faster. Putting a cardboard cone around a hair drier has the same effect.

ROCKETS

The simplest kind of rocket is the firework rocket. Inside the rocket, the explosive fuel burns violently. The gases produced escape from the back of the rocket. Many different fuels are used in space rockets. The most energy-packed is hydrogen. Hydrogen was used to fuel the giant Apollo spacecraft which sent people to the Moon. The oxygen needed to burn the hydrogen is carried in tanks aboard the rocket.

▲ An Ariane rocket takes off at the launch site at Kouru in French Guyana. Rockets work in space because they do not need air to burn their fuel.

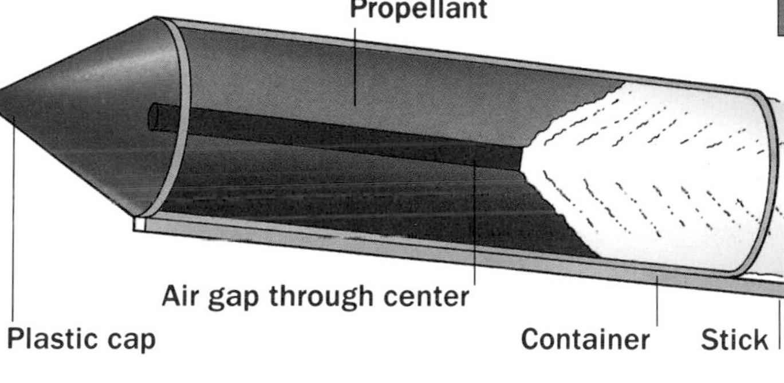

BALLOON ROCKET

Blow up a long, thin balloon. Put a small tube of cardboard in the neck of the balloon to form a nozzle like on a rocket engine.

Thread string through a drinking straw, and stretch the string across a room. Fix the ends of the string to the walls with adhesive tape.

Fix the drinking straw to the side of the balloon with tape. Hold the balloon at one end of the room and let go of the nozzle.

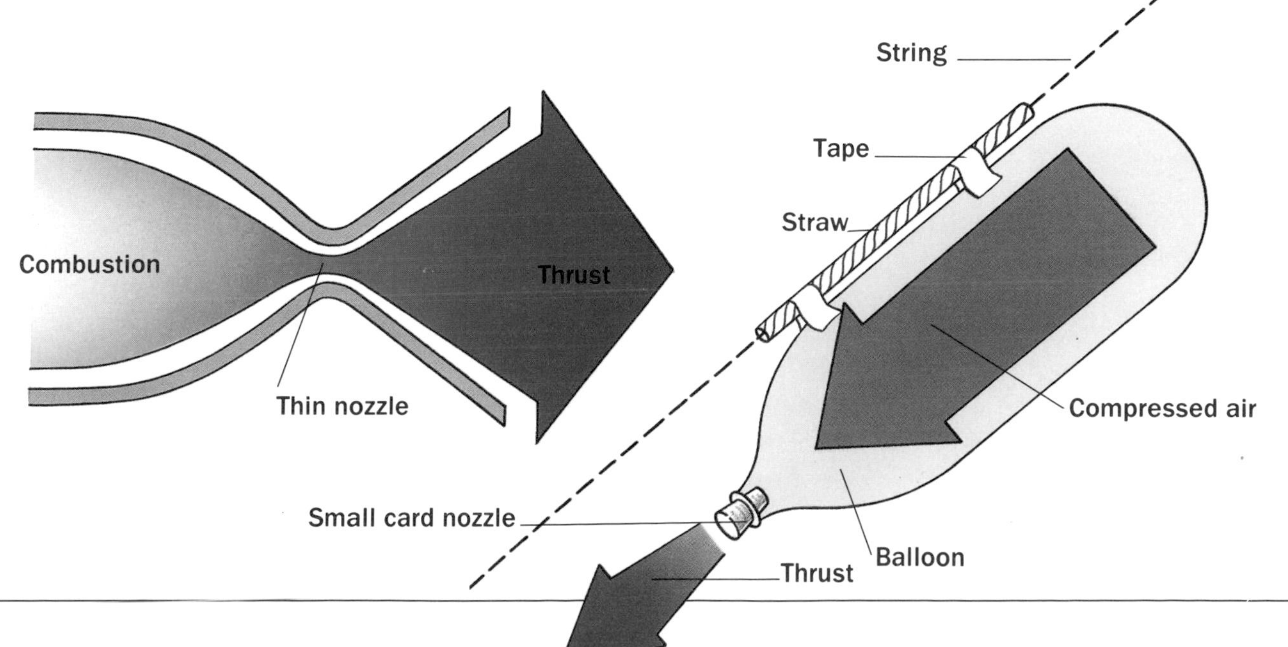

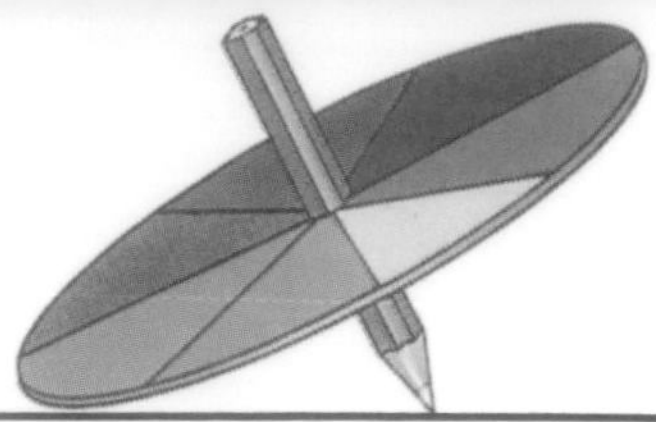

encyclopedia of science

HEAT, LIGHT AND SOUND

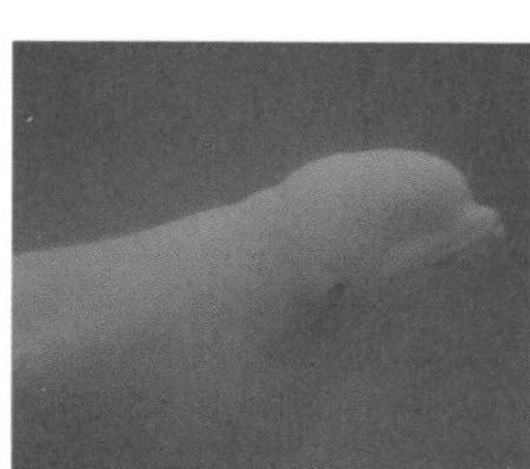

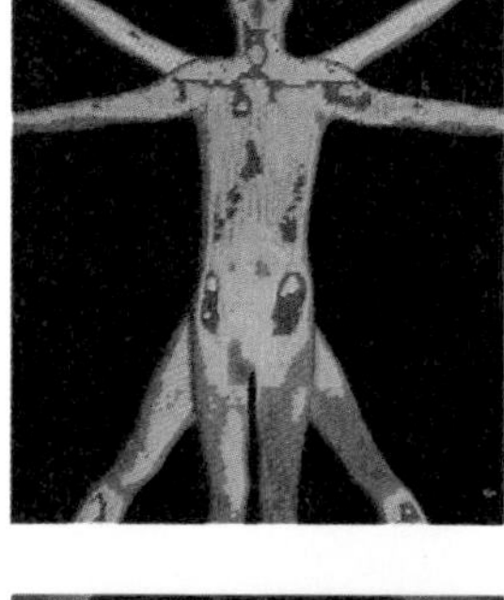

CONTENTS

INTRODUCTION

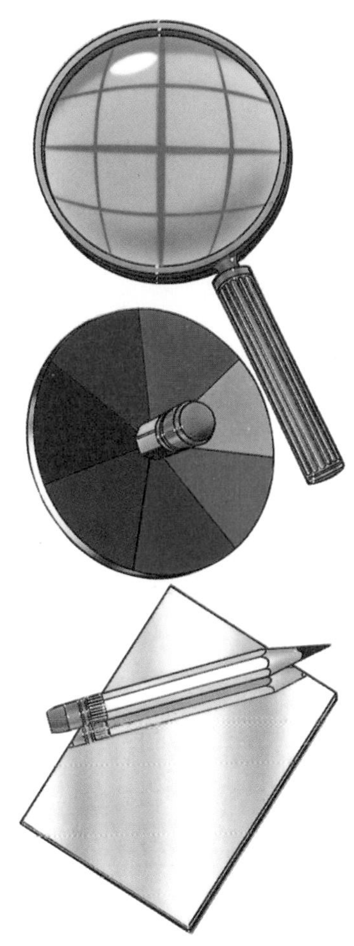

Heat, light and sound are all forms of energy. We respond to them directly with our sense organs and they affect us profoundly. Degrees of heat determine whether things live or die, light makes the world visible to us, and sound helps us to communicate.

Heat, one of the most important forms of energy, warms our homes and food, runs our machinery and is used in many chemical processes.

Without sunlight there would be no life on Earth at all. Plants use sunlight to grow and to make food. All the food we eat comes from plants, or animals that eat plants.

Every sound we hear is produced by vibrations of an object. We use sound in many diverse ways; for example, for ships to gauge depth of water, and for leisure activities such as singing and dancing. Today storing sounds, such as musical recordings on compact disk, is very big business.

Here we discuss where heat, light and sound come from, and how we use them.

HEAT ENERGY

Nothing can happen without energy, so it is lucky for us that energy comes in many forms. Heat is one form of energy. This is shown when a hot-air balloon rises in the sky. Heat energy makes the air in the balloon expand and so become less dense than the surrounding air. The balloon then floats.

MOVING MOLECULES

A hot object has energy because the tiny particles it is made of (atoms and molecules) are moving. If we touch the object, we feel the movement of the molecules as warmth or heat. In a solid, there are strong forces attracting each molecule to its neighbors, and so the molecules cannot move far. However, they are able to vibrate rapidly. In a liquid, the atoms and molecules can move more than in solids because the force between molecules is less strong. This is why a liquid can flow. In a gas, the force between molecules is weak and they can move freely. They bounce off the sides of their container.

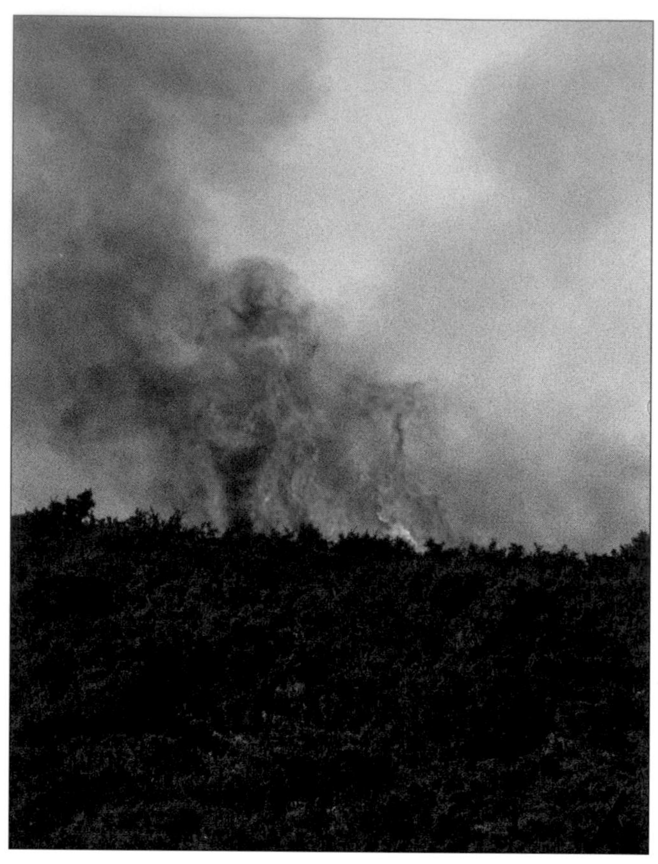

△ A forest fire shows the power of uncontrolled heat. It causes great destruction, and its energy lifts vast amounts of smoke and ash into the air.

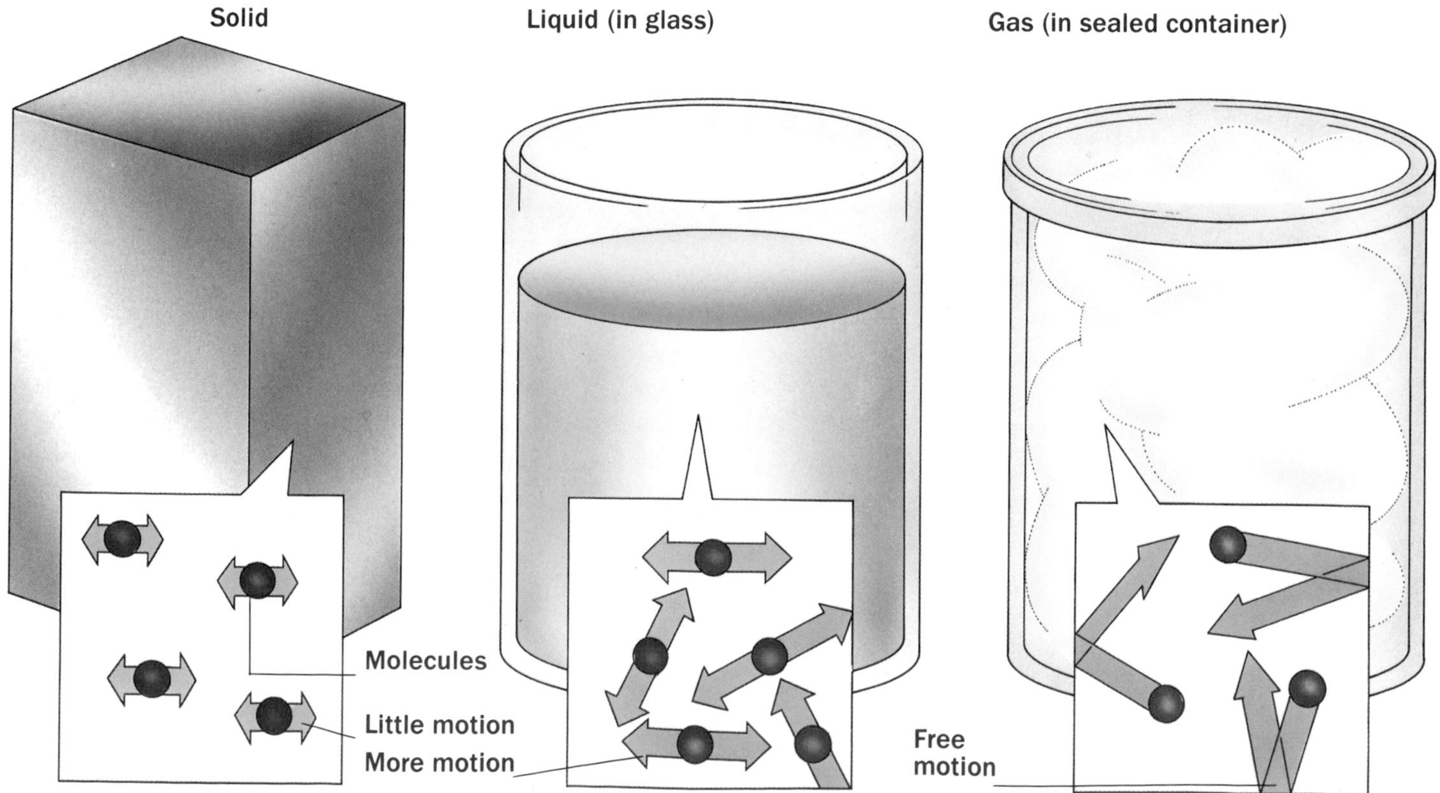

CHANGING ENERGY

There are many different forms of energy, including heat, light, electrical, sound, chemical, nuclear, stored (or potential) and movement (or kinetic) energy. Whatever its form, energy can be used to do work, such as lifting a weight. The units used to measure energy and work are called joules. A person who lifts a weight of an apple through a distance of 1 meter does 1 joule of work and at the same time uses at least one joule of energy.

One form of energy can be converted into a different form. For example, electrical energy can be converted into heat energy by an electric heater, or into kinetic energy by an electric motor.

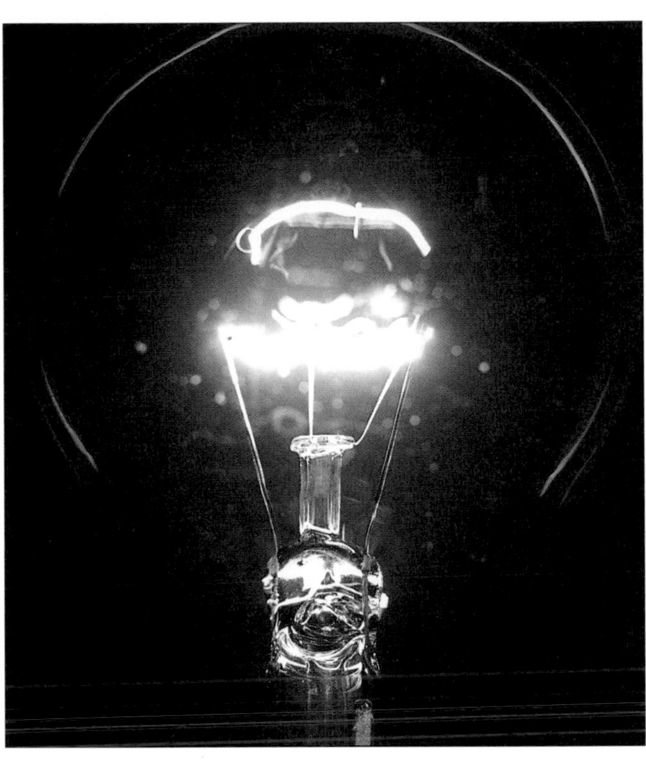

△ Electricity produces heat and light in the filament of an electric lamp. The power of a lamp is measured in watts. A 100-watt lamp uses 100 joules of energy each second.

HOT SHOT

You can convert kinetic (or movement) energy to heat by shaking small metal balls in a cardboard tube. First measure the temperature of the balls using a thermometer. Then shake the balls vigorously. Measure the temperature again. It rises because the balls take up some of the energy of shaking.

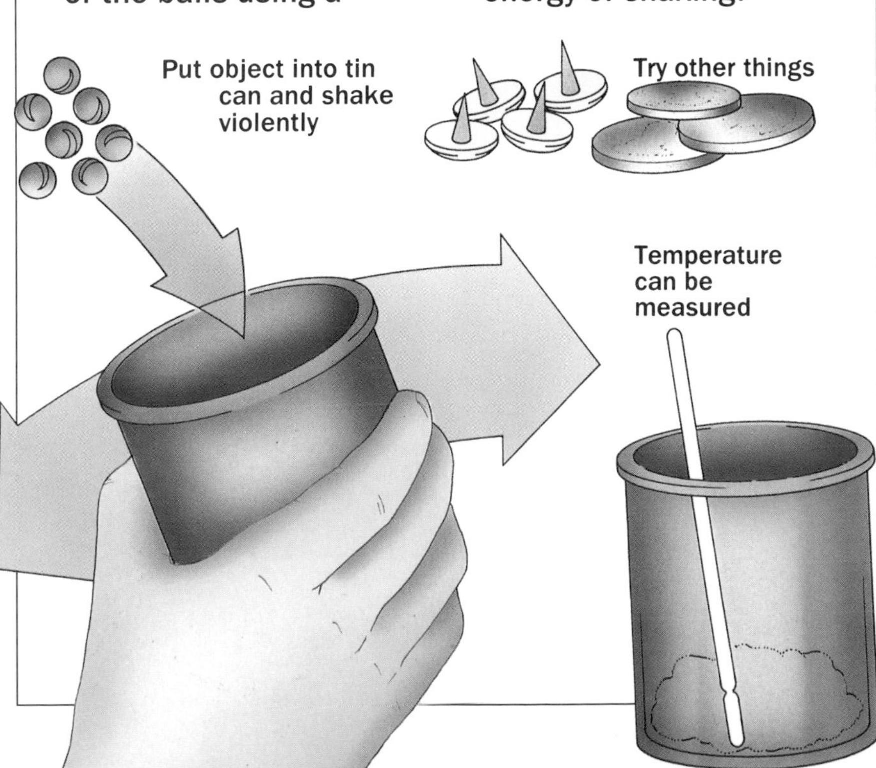
Put object into tin can and shake violently
Try other things
Temperature can be measured

QUIZ

A bicycle pump gets hot as it pumps. Energy squeezes air molecules into a small space. Why does the temperature increase? The energy is converted to heat.

There is a difference between heat and temperature. The heat of an object is the total amount of energy it has because its molecules are moving. Moving molecules have kinetic energy. The temperature of the object indicates how fast the molecules are moving. The faster they move, the higher the temperature.

TEMPERATURE SCALES

There are three common temperature scales: Celsius (which is the same thing as centigrade), Fahrenheit and kelvin. On the Celsius scale, the temperature of freezing water is 0°C, and the temperature of boiling water is 100°C. On the Fahrenheit scale, freezing water is 32°F and boiling water is 212°F. Zero degrees in the kelvin scale is taken as the lowest possible temperature, called absolute zero, which is -273.15°C (-459.67°F). The size of a degree in the kelvin scale is the same as in the Celsius scale. So freezing water is 273.15 K.

△ An iceberg contains more heat than a cup of boiling water. Even though it is freezing, it is large and so its total energy is enormous.

▽ The hottest place on Earth is Al'Aziziyah in Libya. On September 13, 1922, a temperature of 58°C (136.4°F) was recorded.

THERMOMETERS

There are many different kinds of thermometers. The simplest kind contains a liquid, such as mercury, which expands when heated. The expanding liquid moves up a thin glass tube marked with a scale. Other thermometers, called thermocouples, use metal strips that produce small amounts of electricity when heated. Another kind is a resistance thermometer. An electric current flowing through the thermometer varies as the temperature changes. A pyrometer compares the color of a hot object with that of an electrically-heated wire.

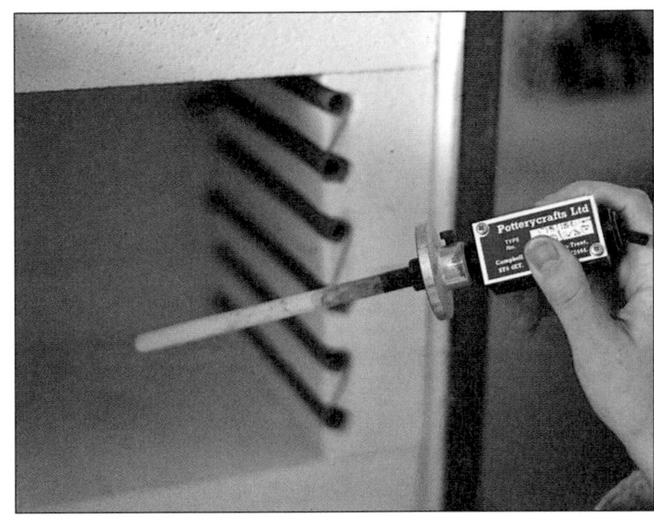

△ A pyrometer can be used to measure the very high temperature of a kiln.

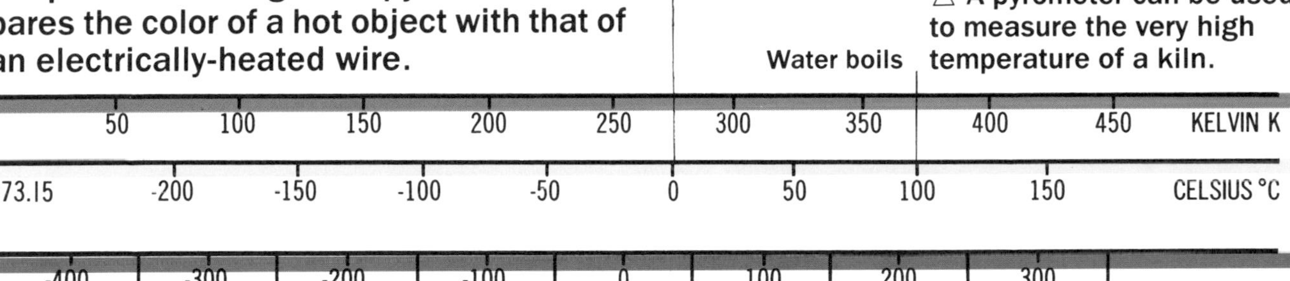

MAKE AN AIR THERMOMETER

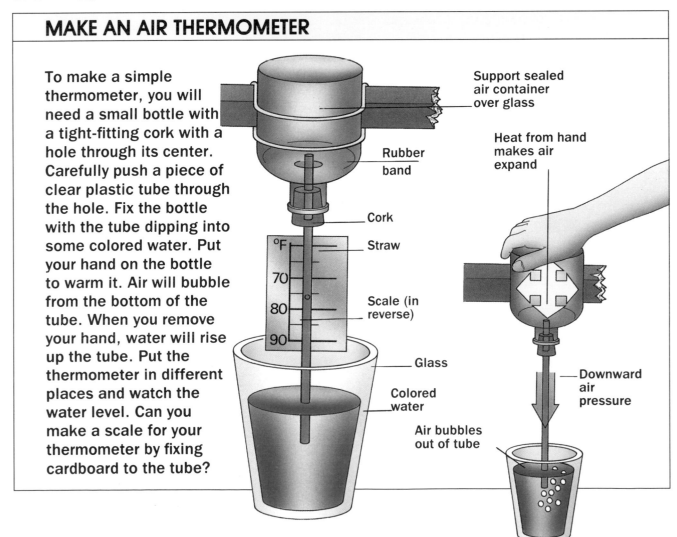

To make a simple thermometer, you will need a small bottle with a tight-fitting cork with a hole through its center. Carefully push a piece of clear plastic tube through the hole. Fix the bottle with the tube dipping into some colored water. Put your hand on the bottle to warm it. Air will bubble from the bottom of the tube. When you remove your hand, water will rise up the tube. Put the thermometer in different places and watch the water level. Can you make a scale for your thermometer by fixing cardboard to the tube?

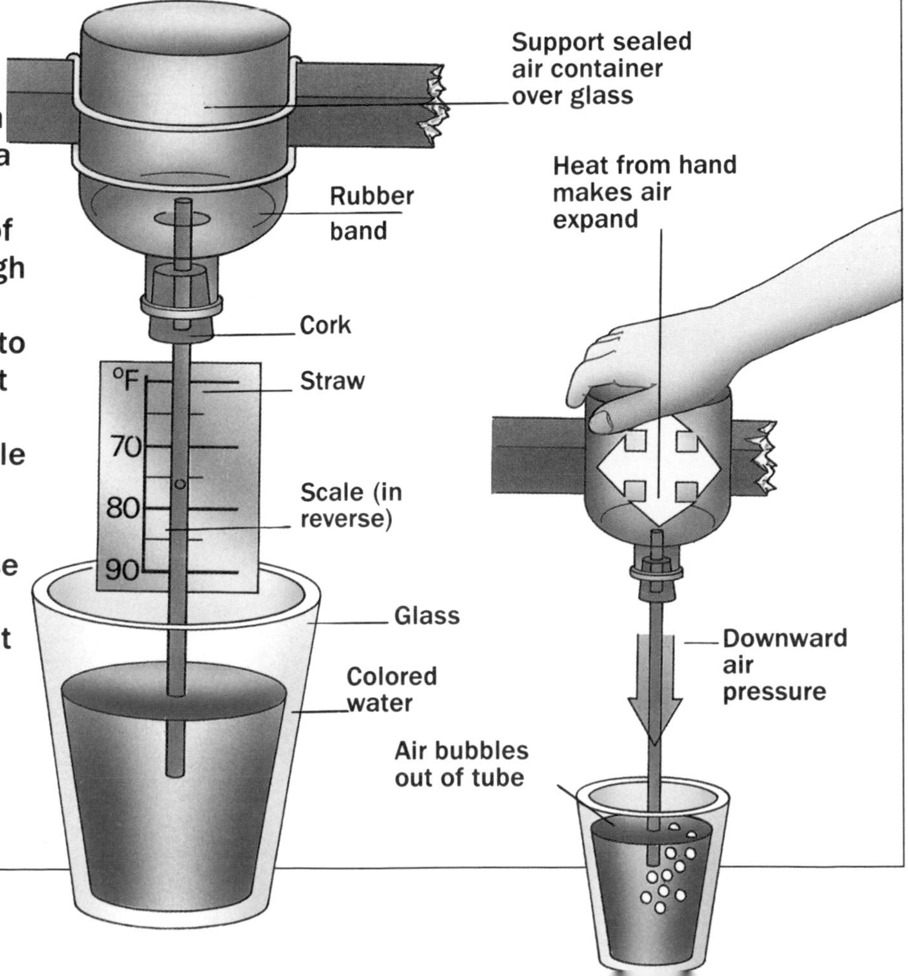

Support sealed air container over glass

Rubber band

Cork

Straw

°F 70 80 90

Scale (in reverse)

Glass

Colored water

Heat from hand makes air expand

Downward air pressure

Air bubbles out of tube

The lowest temperatures on Earth occur in Antarctica. On July 21, 1983, the Soviet research station at Vostok recorded a temperature of -89.2°C (-128.6°F). The coldest place in the Solar System is Pluto. Its average temperature is -382°F. In outer space, away from any star, even lower temperatures occur: about -454°F.

▽ At absolute zero, an object has no heat energy. But even just above absolute zero, its molecules start to vibrate, and it does have heat energy.

HOW LOW CAN YOU GO?

As an object gets colder, its molecules move less and less quickly. If it were possible to continue the cooling process, the molecules would eventually become completely still. The temperature at which movement of molecules stops is called absolute zero (equal to -459.67°F, -273.15°C or 0 K). But at very low temperatures, it is extremely difficult to remove heat from an object. It is impossible to reach absolute zero exactly.

Rising energy

Rising temperature

0 K (absolute zero)

3 K

LOW TEMPERATURE GASES

Many gases can be cooled until they become liquids. Oxygen and nitrogen can be liquified in this way. Liquid hydrogen and helium are produced in a two-stage cooling process in which they are compressed, cooled and then allowed to expand through a small nozzle to obtain further cooling. When a gas expands rapidly, it cools down. Liquid gases are very cold and can be used for a number of purposes. For example, they can be used in medicine to freeze some living tissues very quickly. The tissues are then not damaged by the freezing. Making gases into liquids can also be a way of storing them – for example, to use as rocket fuel.

▽ Liquid hydrogen and oxygen are used to power space rockets. The hydrogen burns with the oxygen in the combustion chamber of the rocket motor.

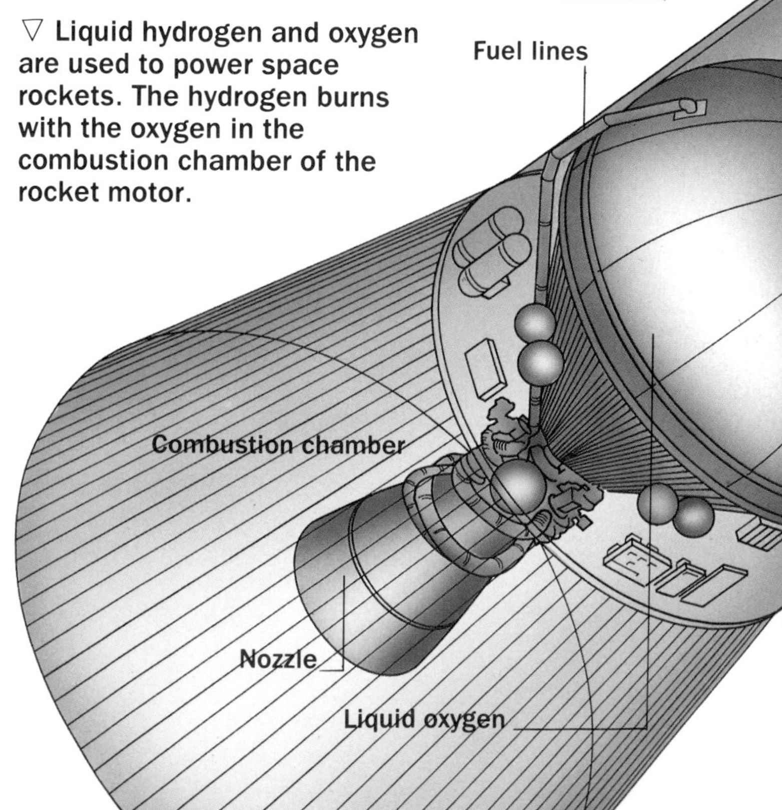

SUPERFLUIDS AND CONDUCTORS

At temperatures near to absolute zero, some materials behave in strange ways. Certain metals, such as lead and mercury, lose their resistance to the passage of an electric current. They become superconductors. If an electric current starts to move through a superconductor, it keeps on flowing forever. Liquid helium also behaves strangely near absolute zero. It is a superfluid, and can flow uphill. If an empty cup is placed in a bowl of superfluid helium, the liquid climbs up the sides and fills the cup. If the bowl becomes empty, the liquid flows out of the cup and back into the bowl.

△ Superconductors can carry large currents and are used to make the very powerful magnets needed for particle accelerators.

Liquid hydrogen

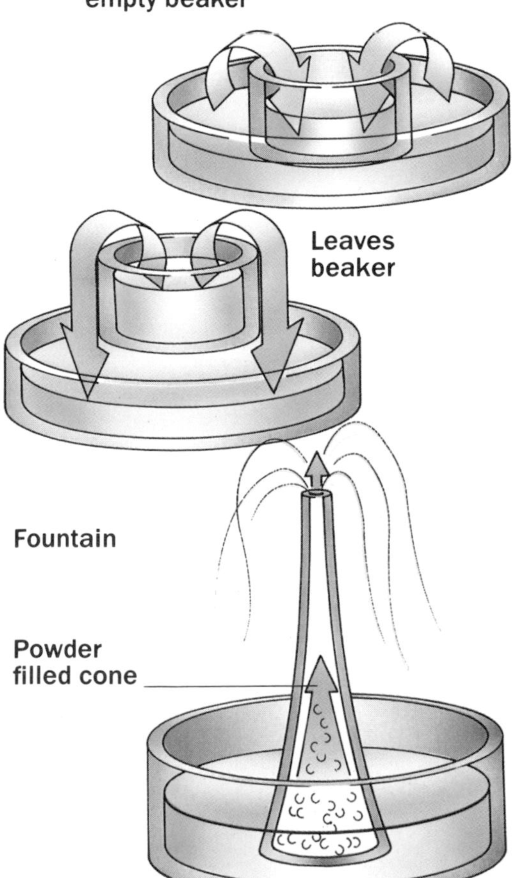

▷ Superfluid helium crawls into an empty container, and then flows out again. If the helium is put into a powder-filled cone, it makes a fountain when flowing upward through the nozzle.

AT HIGH TEMPERATURES

The highest temperature of all time occurred about 15,000 million years ago, during the enormous explosion that began the Universe. This produced temperatures of at least 10 billion degrees. On Earth, temperatures are much lower. The hottest flame burns at about 9,032°F.

△ The highest man-made temperatures are those that occur at the center of a nuclear bomb blast, where they can reach as high as 300-400 million degrees.

INSIDE THE STARS

The Sun is a star, and at its center the temperature is 15 million degrees. In the center of a star, matter is converted into energy by the process of nuclear fusion, in which small atoms join to make larger ones. The energy flows outward through the radiative layer as radiation. In the convective layer, currents of hot material carry the heat. The photosphere is a thin, relatively cool outer layer which glows – the Sun's photosphere is at 10,832°F. The outermost layer, the chromosphere, is a region with giant flames that leap thousands of miles into space.

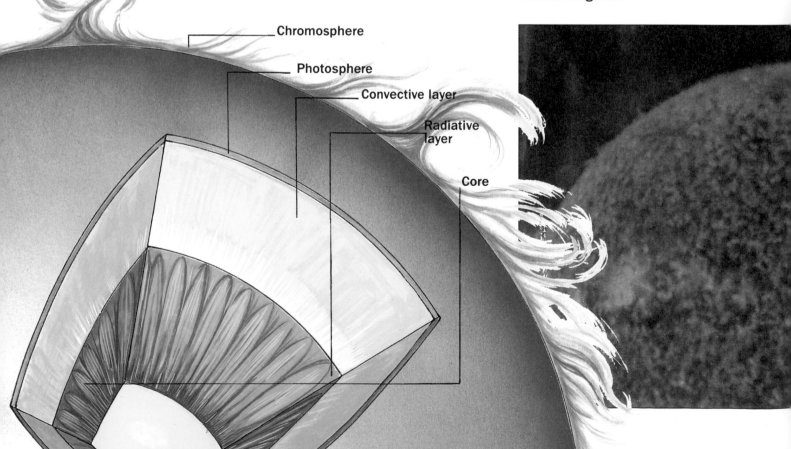

Chromosphere
Photosphere
Convective layer
Radiative layer
Core

INSIDE THE EARTH

The surface of the Earth is a thin layer of rock called the crust. It is about 5 mi thick under the sea and about 25 mi thick on land. Below the crust is a layer of liquid rock (magma) about 1,800 mi thick. This layer – called the mantle – has a temperature of 2,732-5,400°F. The molten rock sometimes flows through cracks in the crust or out of volcanoes, as lava. Beneath the mantle lies the outer core, composed of liquid metal at a temperature of 7,053°F. Finally, right at the center, is a ball of solid metal 1,700 mi across. Its temperature reaches as much as 7,200°F.

▽ Red-hot lava flows like a river from an erupting volcano. This molten rock has a temperature of up to 1,800°F.

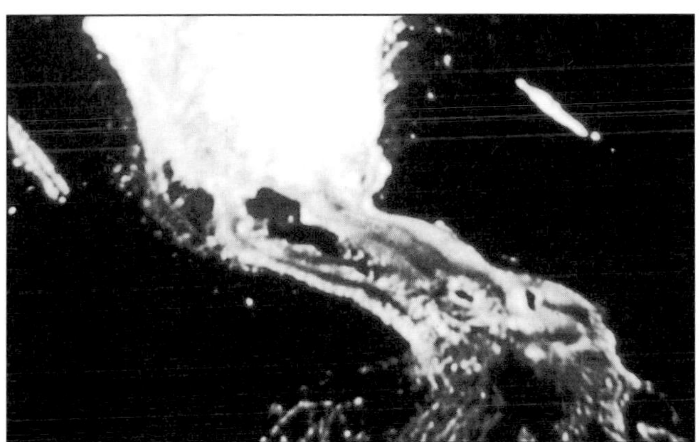

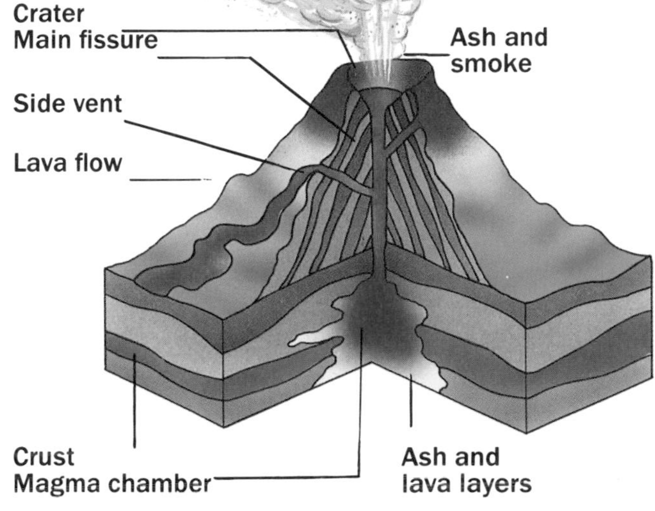

THE HOTTEST PLANET

Mercury is the planet nearest the Sun. During the day, the temperature on Mercury reaches 660°F, which is more than six times hotter than the highest temperature recorded on Earth.

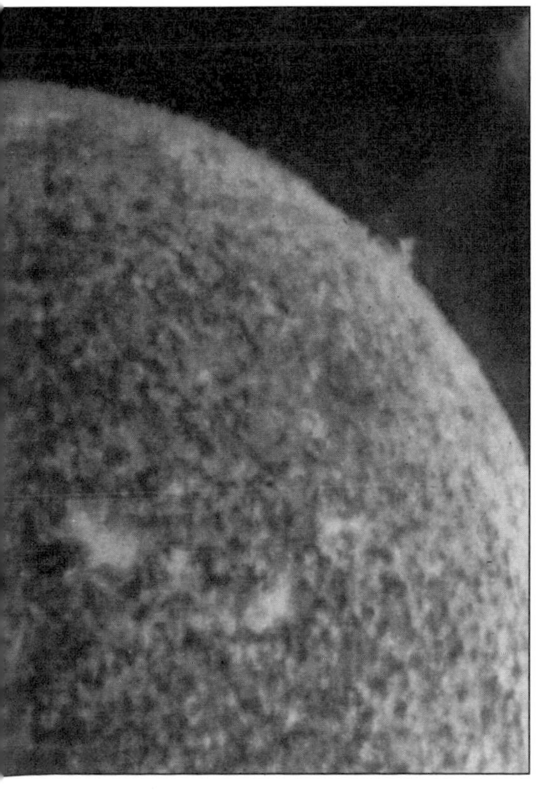

◁ Giant flames, called prominences, stream out from the Sun. The largest are nearly 40 times the size of the Earth.

△ The surface of Mercury is like that of the Moon: rocky, airless and waterless, with many meteorite craters.

Heat energy can move, and it can travel in three different ways: by radiation, convection or conduction. It travels through empty space as radiation, or heat rays. In gases and liquids, hot currents called convection currents carry the heat. And heat travels through solids, such as metals, by conduction.

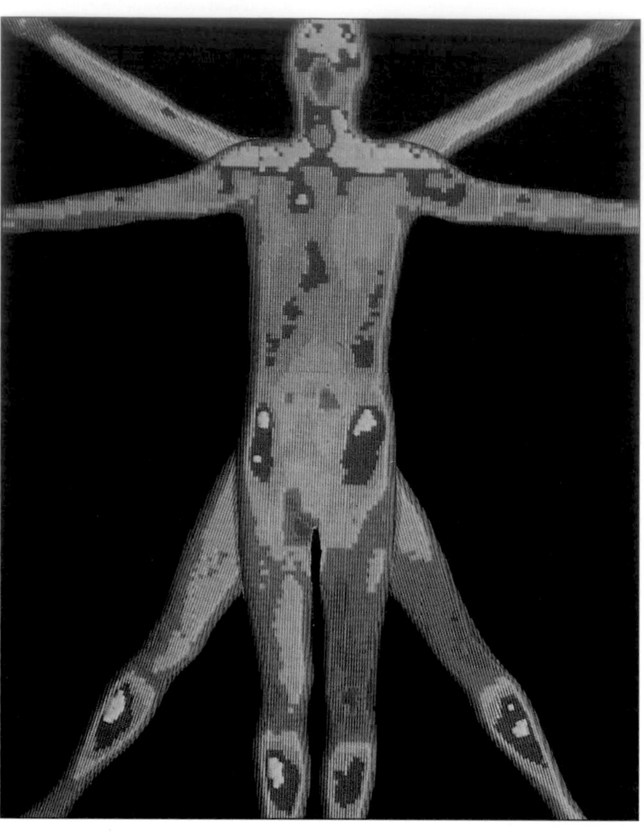

△ Doctors use special photographs taken using heat radiation to detect diseased tissues, which are usually warmer than healthy ones.

HEAT RAYS

Heat rays are also called infrared radiation, because they are similar to light. Like light rays, they are electromagnetic waves that travel through space at great speed. Infrared radiation has a slightly longer wavelength than red light. Both light and infrared radiation travel at the same speed: nearly 186,000 miles per second. More infrared radiation is given out than absorbed by anything that is hotter than its surroundings. Cold objects absorb more infrared rays that fall on them than they emit. Dark colored objects absorb and emit heat better than light colored ones.

FLOWING HEAT

When a gas, such as air, is heated by a candle, the heated air expands. The hot air becomes less dense than the cooler air around it, and so it rises. As the warm air rises, cooler air moves in to take its place. Soon a steady current of air is set up: warm air rises, carrying heat with it; when this air has cooled, it falls and is warmed again. These are convection currents. On a larger scale, convection currents take place in the atmosphere, causing winds. Air is heated by the Sun in a hot region, such as the tropics. The heated air rises and air flows in from colder regions to take its place. Convection currents carry heat in liquids as well as in gases. Peas in gently boiling water in a saucepan are carried to the surface by convection currents.

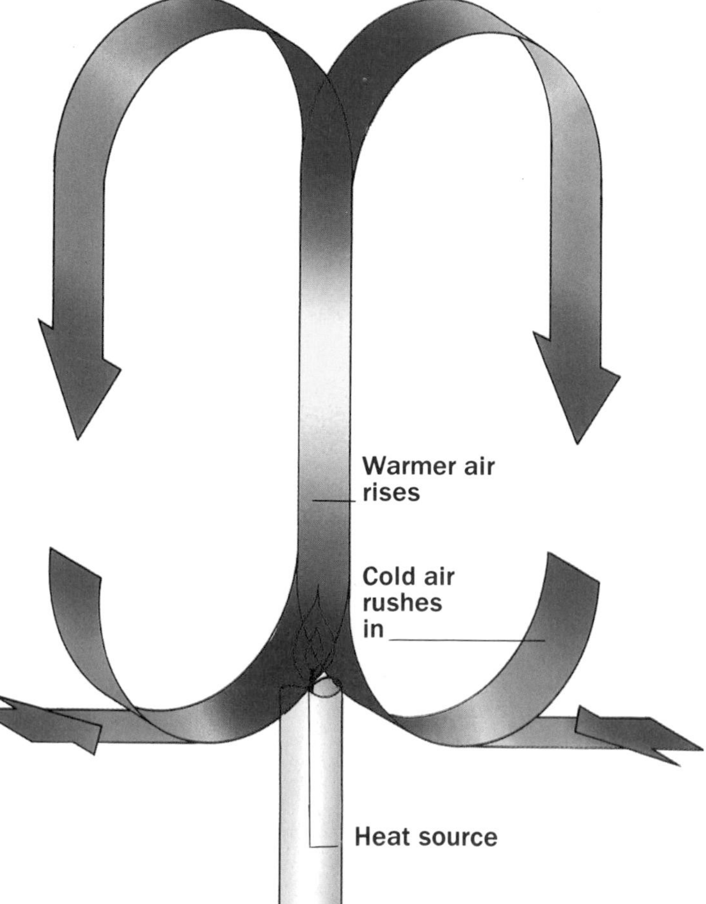

CONDUCTION

When one end of a metal bar is held in a candle flame, metal atoms near the flame get extra heat energy from it. They start to vibrate more rapidly, bumping into neighboring atoms and transferring energy to them. They in turn jostle their neighbors, and pass energy to them. This process, called conduction, carries heat energy along the bar. When you pick up a metal object, it often feels colder than it really is. This is because the heat of your fingers is conducted away rapidly by the metal. A poor conductor, such as a piece of cloth, does not feel cold.

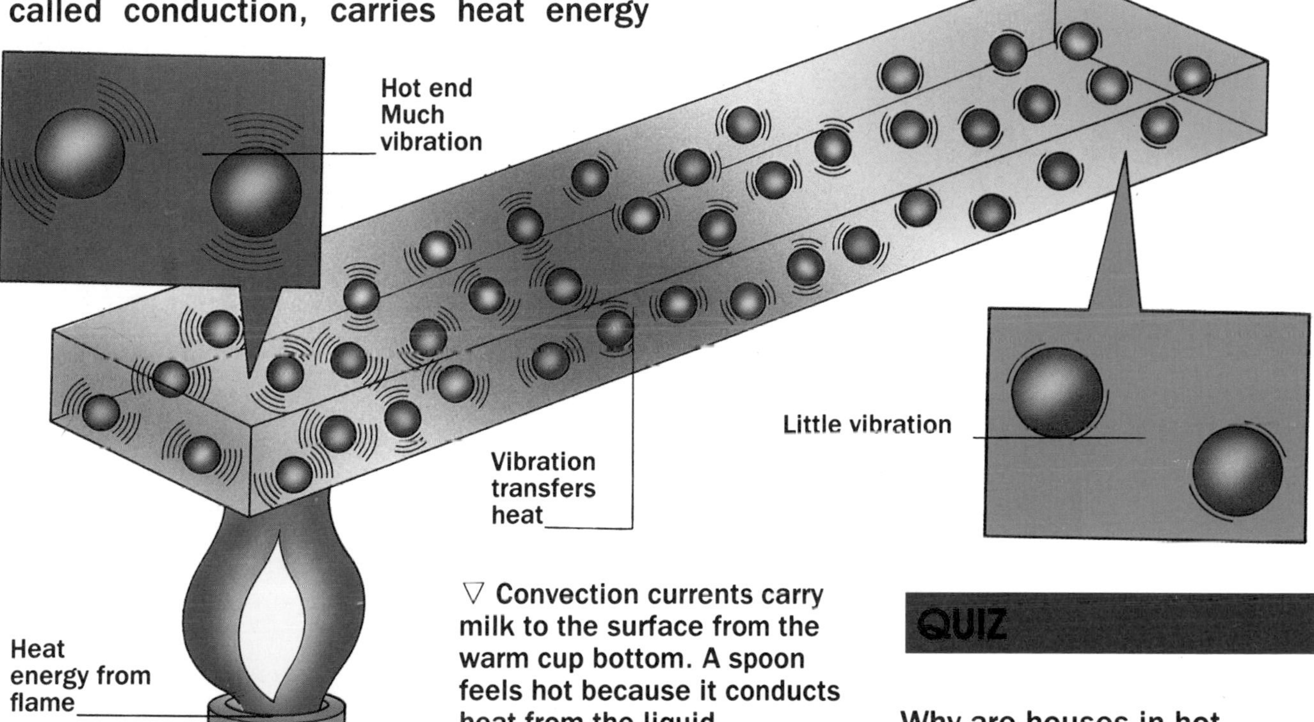

▽ Convection currents carry milk to the surface from the warm cup bottom. A spoon feels hot because it conducts heat from the liquid.

QUIZ

Why are houses in hot climates often painted white, and why is the Space Shuttle also white? Because light colors reflect most of the Sun's heat rays, while dark colors absorb them.

MELTING AND BOILING

When a solid is heated, its atoms or molecules vibrate more rapidly. If the heating continues, some molecules start to move more freely, and the solid begins to melt. Eventually, it becomes a liquid. If the liquid is heated further, the molecules obtain enough energy to leap through the surface, and the liquid boils.

HIDDEN HEAT

While a liquid is boiling, its temperature stays the same even though it is being heated. The heat being supplied, rather than increasing the temperature of the liquid, is used to give molecules enough energy to escape from the surface and become a gas or vapor. The energy needed to turn a boiling liquid into a gas or vapor is called the latent, or hidden, heat because it does not cause a temperature rise.

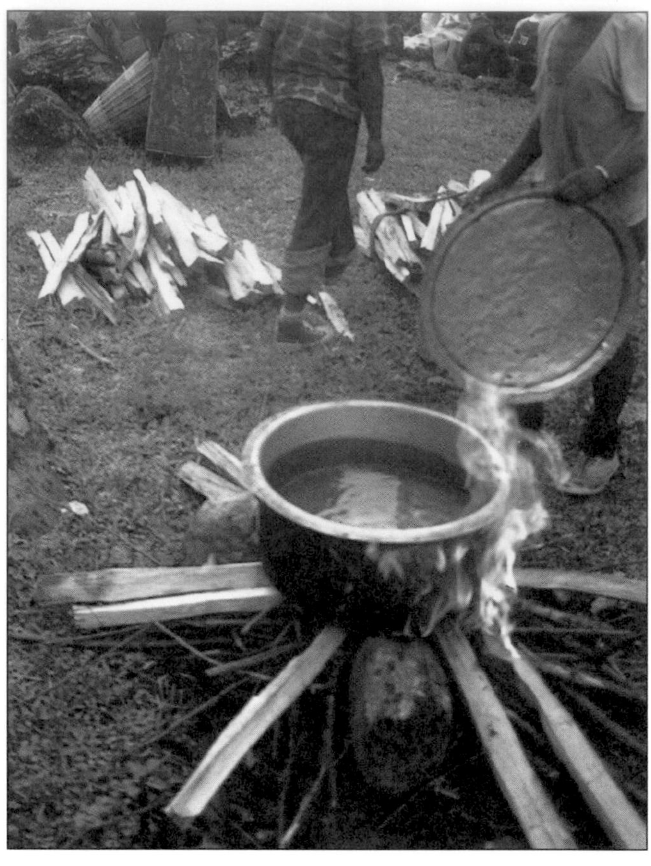

△ In high mountain regions, the low air pressure allows water to boil at a temperature below its normal boiling point.

▽ A painrelief spray works by vaporizing rapidly. This extracts heat from the injured muscle and kills pain.

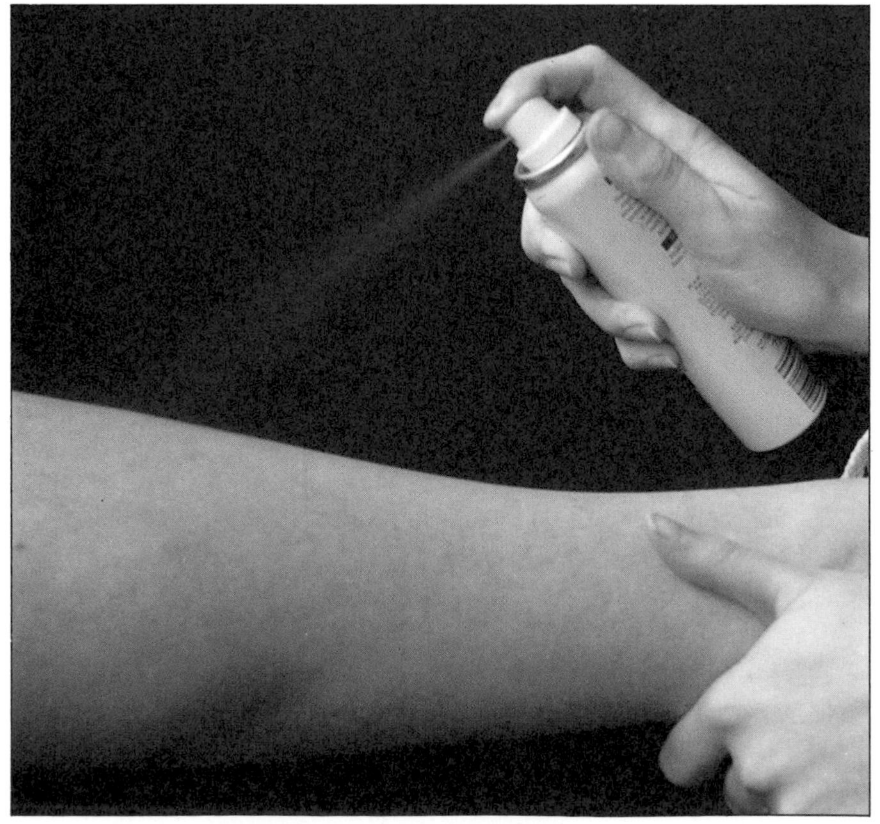

ICE TRICKS

Squeeze two ice cubes together. When you release the pressure, the cubes will have joined. This happens because the ice on the sides of the cubes that join melts when you apply pressure, and then it refreezes when the pressure is released. Next, hang a heavy weight over a cube of ice using metal wire or a thin piece of string. The wire will cut its way through the ice, which will refreeze when the wire has passed through.

MELTING AND BOILING POINTS

The melting point is the temperature at which a solid melts; the boiling point is the temperature at which a liquid boils. A pure substance at normal pressure always melts and boils at the same temperatures. But if the substance is impure, or the pressure is changed, the melting and boiling points change. Salt water boils at a higher temperature than pure water. Water boils at a lower temperature if the pressure is reduced.

△ Icicles form when dripping water freezes. The drips freeze along the icicle, which is why icicles get their pointed shape. As the temperature rises, the ice melts and the water starts to drip again.

◁ Dry ice is frozen carbon dioxide, which is a gas at room temperature. When it is warmed, it turns back into a gas without turning into a liquid first.

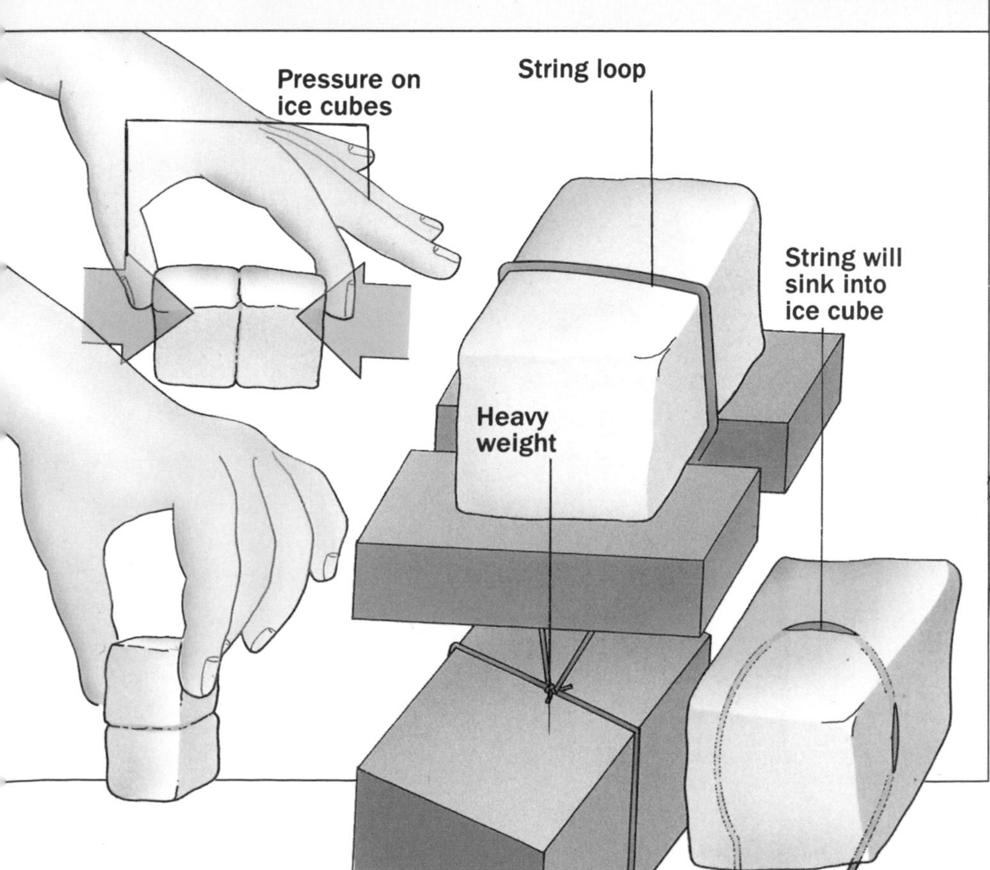

QUIZ

Why do cooks boil vegetables in salty water? The main reason is to improve the taste. But it also helps the food to cook more quickly. Why? Because salty water boils at a higher temperature than pure water.

Some materials conduct heat more easily than others. Gases and liquids are poor conductors. Metals are good conductors, but some are better than others. Copper conducts heat three times better than iron or steel, 1,000 times better than glass and 10,000 times better than air. Poor conductors are called insulators.

KEEPING WARM

Woolen clothes keep us warm because they trap a layer of air. The air is an insulator, so heat cannot easily escape through it. For the same reason, polar explorers wear several layers of clothing, rather than a single thick garment, because more air is trapped in this way. Glass fiber, a poor conductor of heat itself, traps air and is used to insulate house attics. A thermos uses a double-walled glass bottle to keep hot liquids hot (or cold liquids cold). The space between the walls is a vacuum, so that no heat can be conducted across. The walls are silvered to prevent radiation – the mirrorlike surfaces reflect radiant heat. The bottle is insulated from its container.

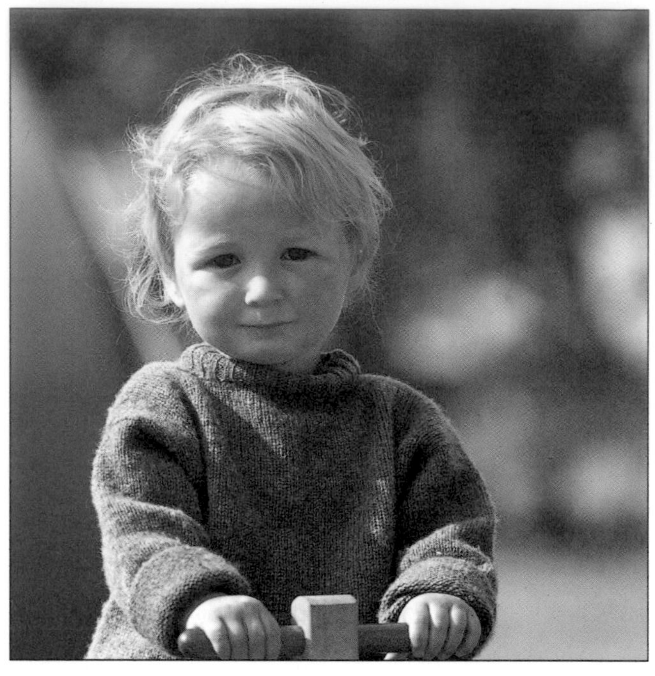

△ A sheep's wool traps air and keeps the animal warm, just as clothing made out of wool keeps its human wearer warm.

▽ Glass fiber is a good attic insulator because it traps a layer of air. It is also put into walls to prevent heat loss.

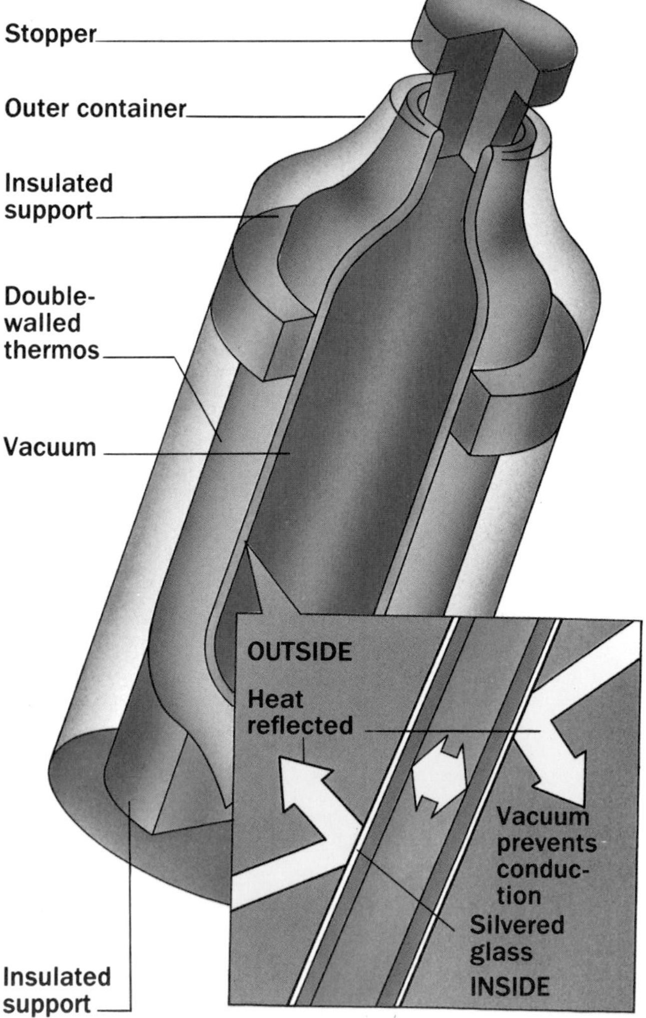

COOLERS

Insulators can help to keep things cold. Houses built with well-insulated walls are cool in summer, as well as warm in winter, because heat cannot pass through the walls. In a car's cooling system, water is circulated around the hot engine to carry away unwanted heat. The water flows through thin pipes in a radiator. Cool air drawn in by a fan flows over these pipes, cooling the water.

In a refrigerator, a liquid called the refrigerant evaporates to form a gas in the pipes around the freezer. The heat needed for evaporation is absorbed from the inside of the freezer. A compressor then changes the gas back into a liquid. This process produces heat, which is released into the air by a radiator at the back of the refrigerator.

THE REFRIGERATOR

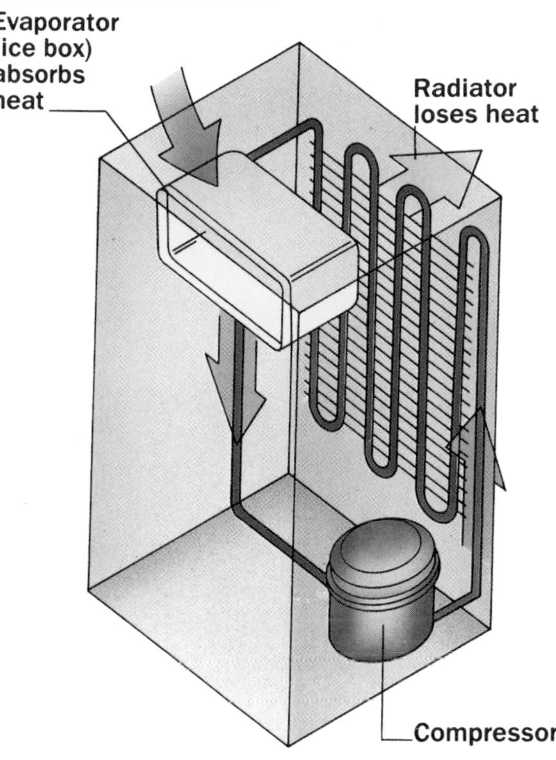

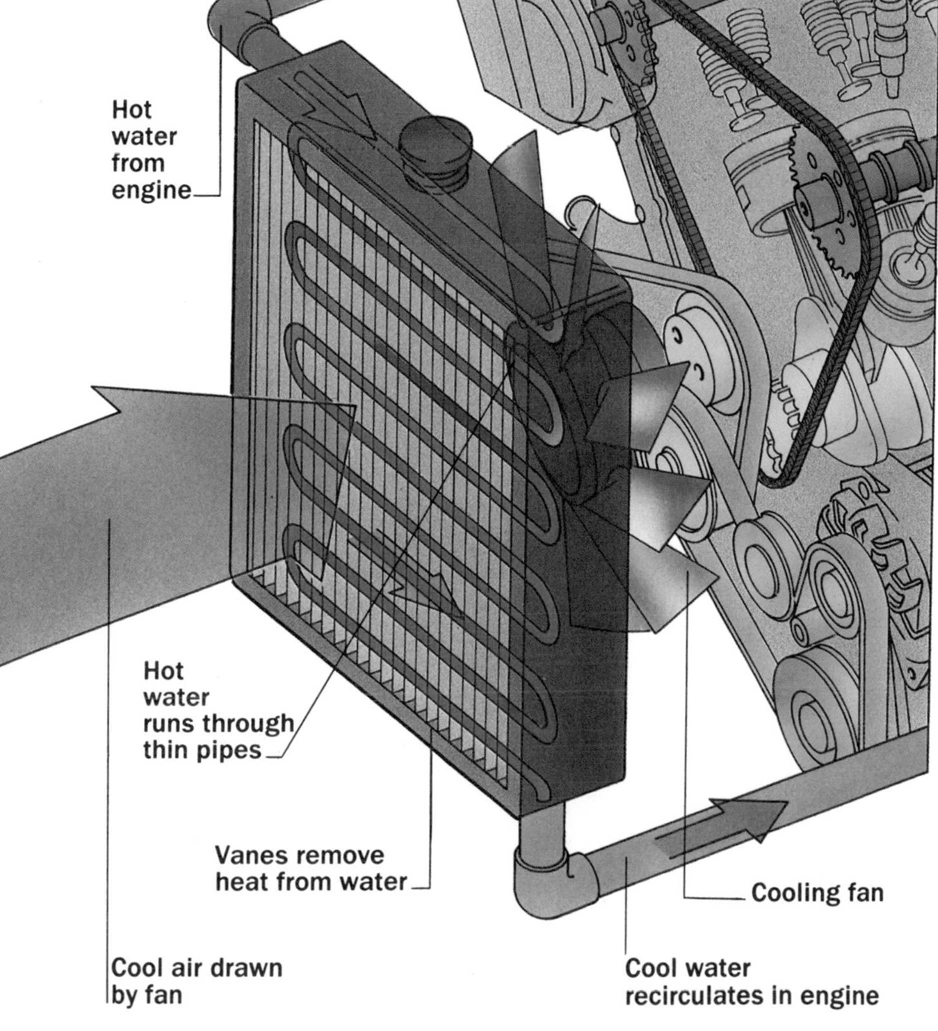

◁ **Car cooling system**

PROJECT

Take objects made of different materials and place them in sunlight to warm up. Then touch each one. They are all at the same temperature, yet some feel hotter. Why? Some objects absorb heat while others reflect it.

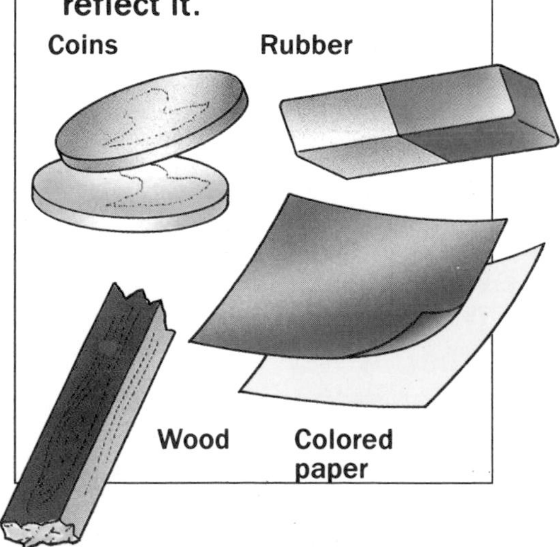

EXPANSION

Almost all materials expand (get bigger) when heated. This is because the atoms or molecules that make up the material move more vigorously as temperature increases. They, therefore, take up more room, and the material expands. When a hot object cools down, it contracts (gets smaller) and returns to its original size.

△ A large suspension bridge may be up to three feet longer in summer than in winter. Gaps are left in the road for expansion.

EVERYDAY EXPANSION

There are many everyday examples of expansion and contraction. On a hot day, overhead telephone wires or power lines hang slackly. On a cold winter day, the wires contract and stretch tightly between the poles. Railroads are built with angled gaps between lengths of rail, so that the rails do not buckle when they expand in summer. The supersonic airliner Concorde heats up during flight because of friction with the air; it grows up to 10 inches longer.

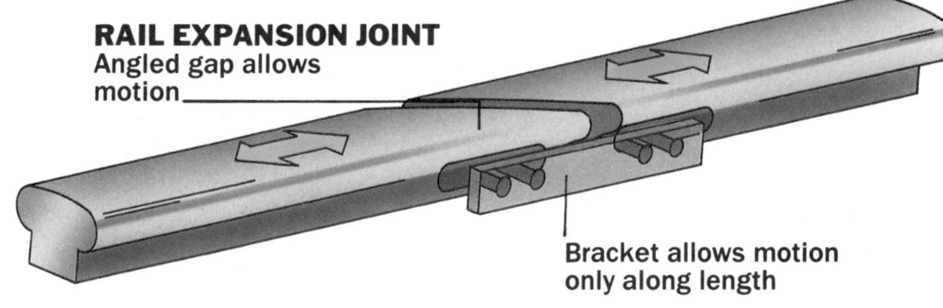

FROZEN WATER

Water behaves very strangely when it is cooled to near its freezing temperature. Above 39°F it contracts when cooled. But when cooled below this temperature, water expands, so that between 32°F and 39°F water is less dense than warmer water and floats on top of it. In winter, the colder water is in a layer on top, which is why the surface of a pond freezes first. This is extremely important for fish and other water life. The ice protects the water below it from freezing air, and the warmest water is on the bottom, where the fish stay during winter.

▽ Fish can survive winter in a frozen pond because the warmest water is at the bottom. And ducks can walk on the ice at the surface.

THE THERMOSTAT

Thermostats are switches that turn on at a certain temperature, and turn off at another, higher, temperature. They are used to control electric cookers and heaters. The heart of a thermostat is a bimetallic strip, which is made from two strips of different metals sandwiched together. When the bimetallic strip heats up, it bends because one metal expands more than the other. If the strip is part of an electrical circuit, the circuit is broken as the strip bends and this switches off the current. When the temperature falls, the bimetallic strip bends back and reconnects the current.

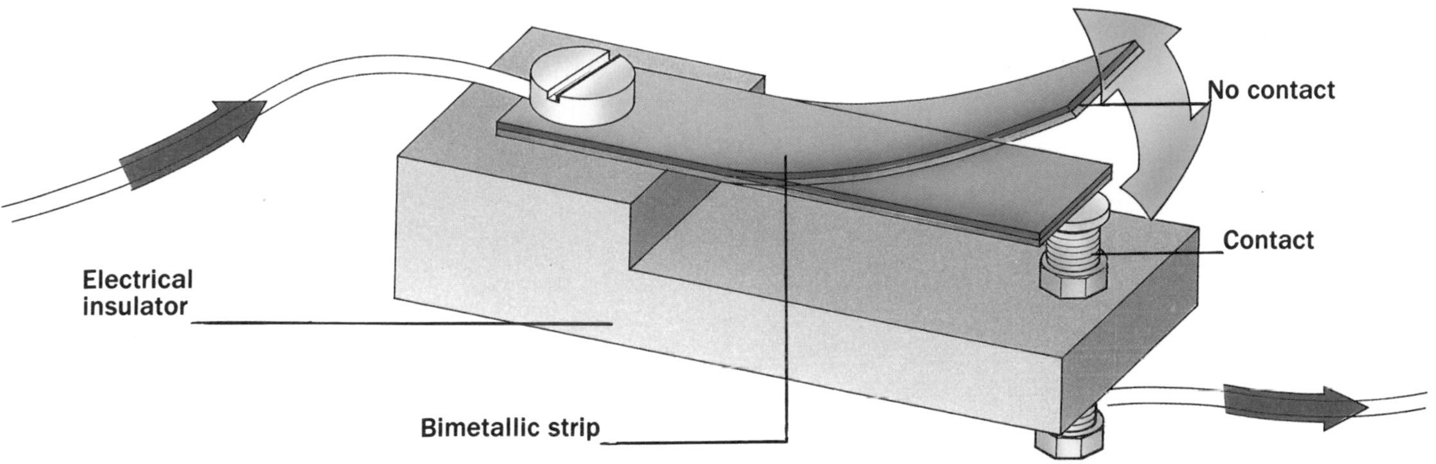

SLINKY SNAKE PROJECT

This project shows how metals expand. First, put a strip of transparent sticky tape on a piece of aluminum foil. Next, cut a snake from the foil, with the tape running along the snake's body. Coil the snake by wrapping it around a pencil. Put the coiled snake under a table lamp, where the heat of the lamp will warm it. The snake will uncoil as the foil expands.

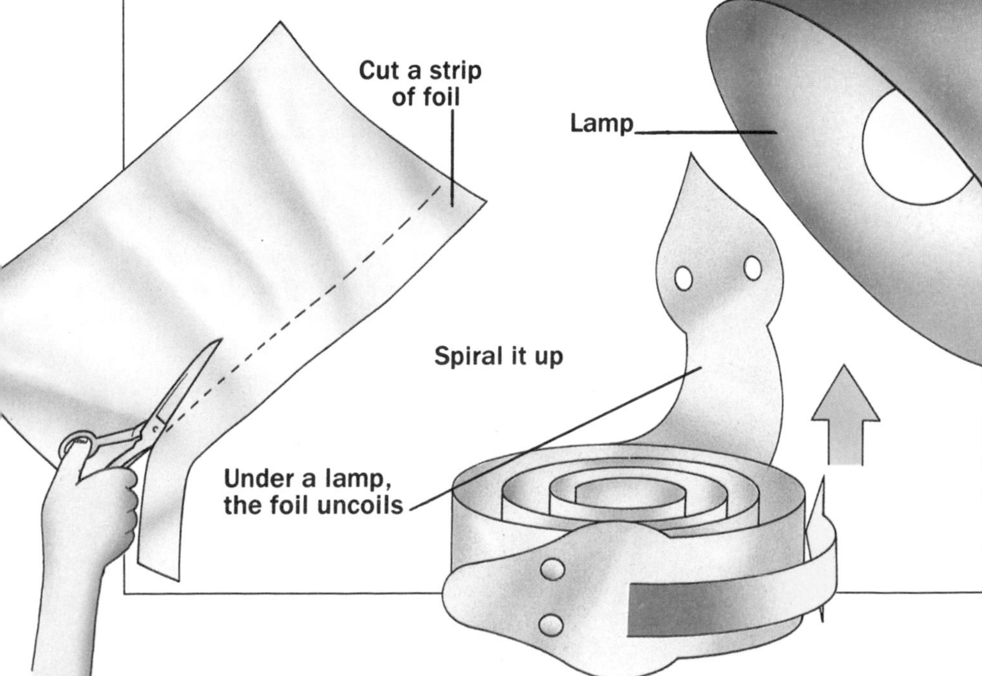

QUIZ

If you float an ice cube in a glass full to the brim with water, what will happen as the ice melts? Will the water spill out of the glass? No, because the ice occupies more volume than the water it turns into when it melts.

Burning is a chemical reaction or change – a change that produces a new substance and is hard to reverse. Many chemical changes need heat or another form of energy to get started, and many also produce heat. In striking a match, for example, friction against the box produces enough heat to light it.

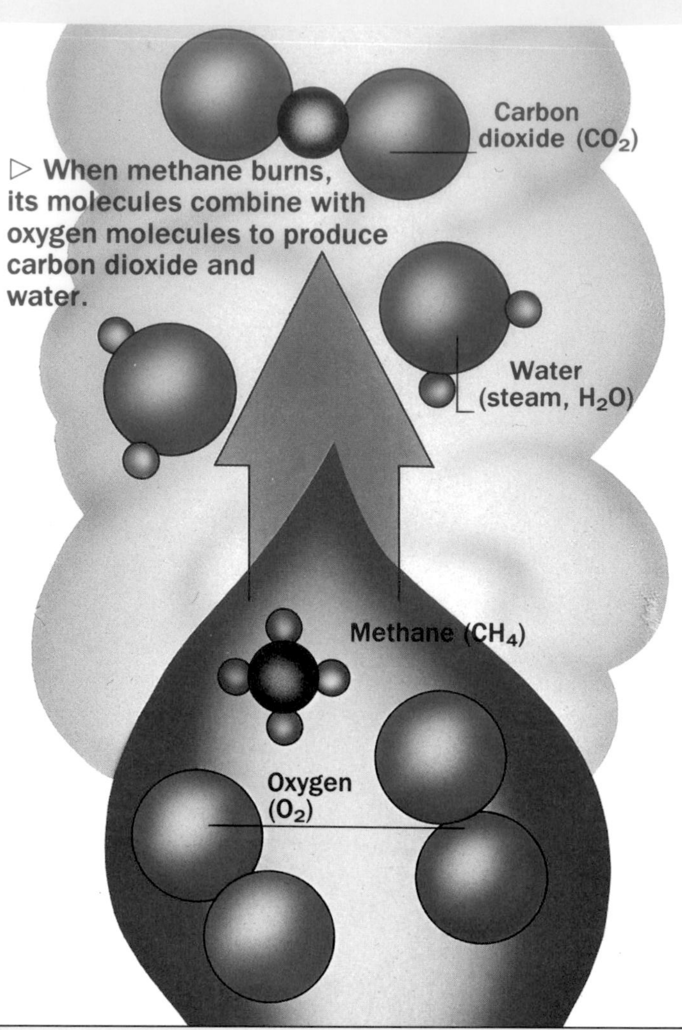

▷ When methane burns, its molecules combine with oxygen molecules to produce carbon dioxide and water.

OXYGEN AND BURNING

The chemical reaction in burning is between the substance being burned – the fuel – and oxygen in the air. It releases energy because the molecules of the fuel are full of energy. The burning process breaks these energy-packed molecules into different low-energy molecules. For instance, when coal burns, carbon in the coal combines with oxygen in the air to form carbon dioxide. Natural gas is mostly methane; it burns to produce carbon dioxide and water.

EXPERIMENTS

You can estimate the amount of oxygen in air. Ask an adult to supervise this experiment. Put a candle on a tinfoil "boat" floating in a bowl of water and light the candle (a short candle will balance more easily). Lower a large jar over the candle and the tinfoil. At first, the water does not enter the jar; the air in the jar keeps it out. As the oxygen is used up by the burning candle, the water rises in the jar. When all the oxygen is gone and the candle goes out, estimate the fraction of air left in the jar.

FUELS

Most of the fuels we use are fossil fuels: coal, oil, and natural gas. They are called fossil fuels because they were formed long ago from the remains of plants and animals. Coal was formed from giant plants that grew on Earth about 300 million years ago. Oil and gas were formed from the remains of algae and other small plants that lived in the sea millions of years ago. All of these fuels contain carbon and so, when they burn, they produce carbon dioxide. Over the last 100 years, the amount of carbon dioxide made from burning fuels has increased. Scientists think that this will cause the atmosphere to warm up like the air in a greenhouse.

◁ Smoke from a power station contains chemicals that cause the atmosphere to warm up.

Heat affects things in different ways. Write a message with lemon juice. To read it, put it in a moderately hot oven (with adult supervision) for ten minutes.

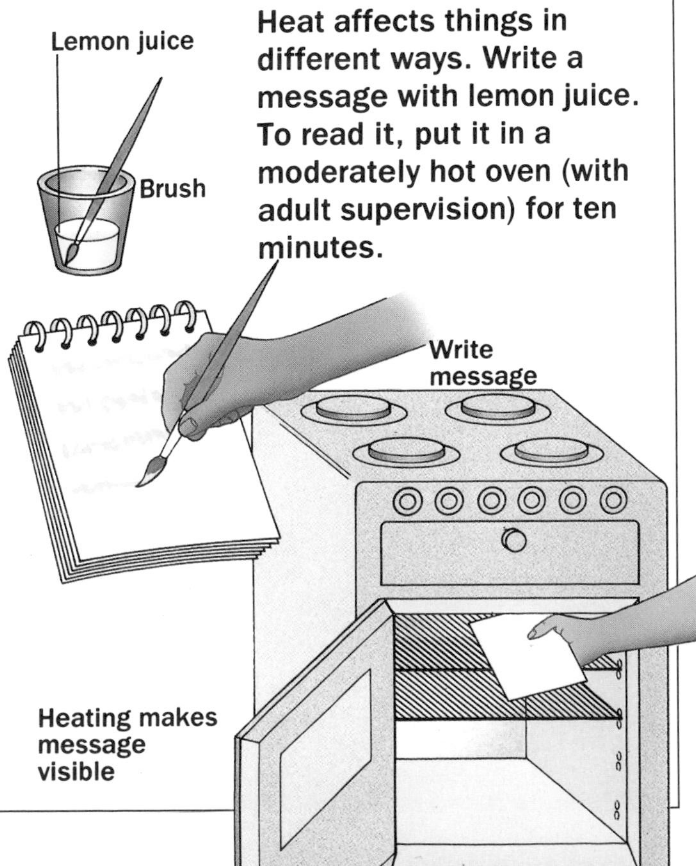

FIRE FIGHTING

A fire needs three things to start and keep going: heat, fuel, and oxygen. If any of these is missing, the fire goes out. If the doors and windows of a burning building are closed, the fire might be starved of oxygen and go out. Water sprayed onto a fire puts it out by removing heat or cooling the burning material. If somebody's clothes are on fire, wrapping them in a blanket cuts off oxygen and puts out the flames.

△ A fire fighter uses foam to blanket a burning aircraft, so cutting off oxygen and putting out the fire.

FAST AND SLOW BURNING

Gunpowder is a mixture of carbon, sulfur and a chemical called saltpeter, which contains oxygen. When gunpowder explodes, the carbon and sulfur burn, using the oxygen in the saltpeter. A different process, respiration, takes place in living things. It is a form of slow burning that releases energy from food.

EXPLOSIVES

There are two kinds of explosives, called low and high. A low explosive, such as gunpowder, burns relatively slowly and produces a weak explosion. A high explosive burns extremely quickly and produces a very powerful blast. Dynamite, made from nitroglycerine, is the best-known high explosive. Another high explosive is TNT (trinitrotoluene), which is easier to make and handle.

FIREWORKS

Fireworks are made from gunpowder and other substances that produce special effects such as colored flames and sparks. Green colors are given by substances containing barium, blue colors by copper compounds, and red colors by strontium salts. Sparks are formed by burning finely powdered steel, iron and aluminum. All these substances are packed into a cardboard tube or cone, with a paper lighting fuse at the top. In a Roman candle, for instance, the tube contains small packets called stars, which give out lots of colored sparks when they burn. The stars are separated by layers of gunpowder. The candle burns down until a star is reached. As it starts to burn, the gunpowder explodes, throwing the star high into the air.

△ The first safe high explosive, dynamite, was invented by the chemist Alfred Nobel. Here it is being used to demolish a tower block.

▷ The Chinese first made fireworks around 2,000 years ago, soon after they invented gunpowder. But fireworks then were not as spectacular as these.

ENERGY FOR LIFE

All living things need energy. They get it from energy-rich foods called carbohydrates, which are substances that contain hydrogen and carbon (such as sugars). A plant makes these foods for itself by absorbing carbon dioxide from the air and converting it by photosynthesis. Animals either eat plants to obtain carbohydrate foods, or eat other animals. Animals can also use fats and even proteins for energy. But an animal has to convert them into carbohydrates before using them. The energy held in foods is released by respiration, which is similar to burning. Respiration involves a complicated series of chemical changes, but the overall result is that oxygen combines with food substances to produce carbon dioxide, water and energy.

▽ Doctors test athletes to see how they react to vigorous exercise. Their fitness depends partly on how well they take in oxygen when they breathe.

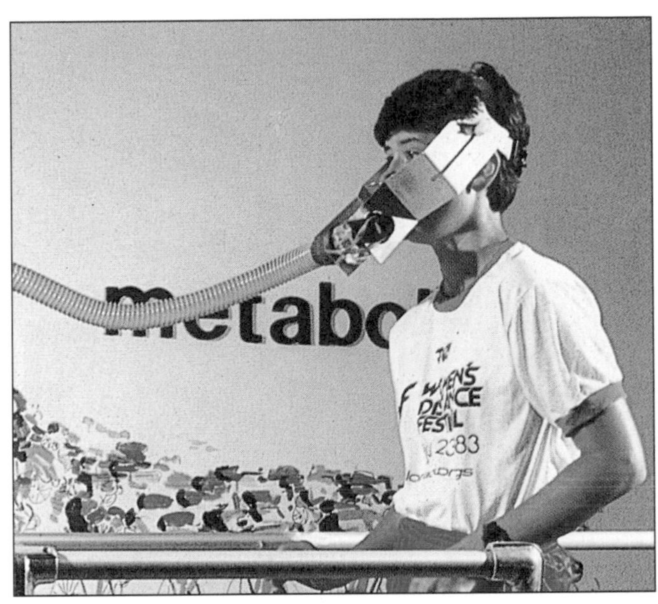

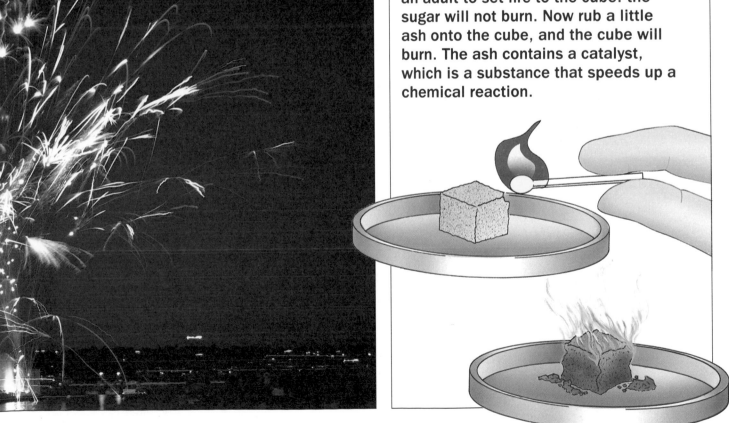

FLAMING SUGAR CUBE

Put a sugar cube on an ashtray. Ask an adult to set fire to the cube: the sugar will not burn. Now rub a little ash onto the cube, and the cube will burn. The ash contains a catalyst, which is a substance that speeds up a chemical reaction.

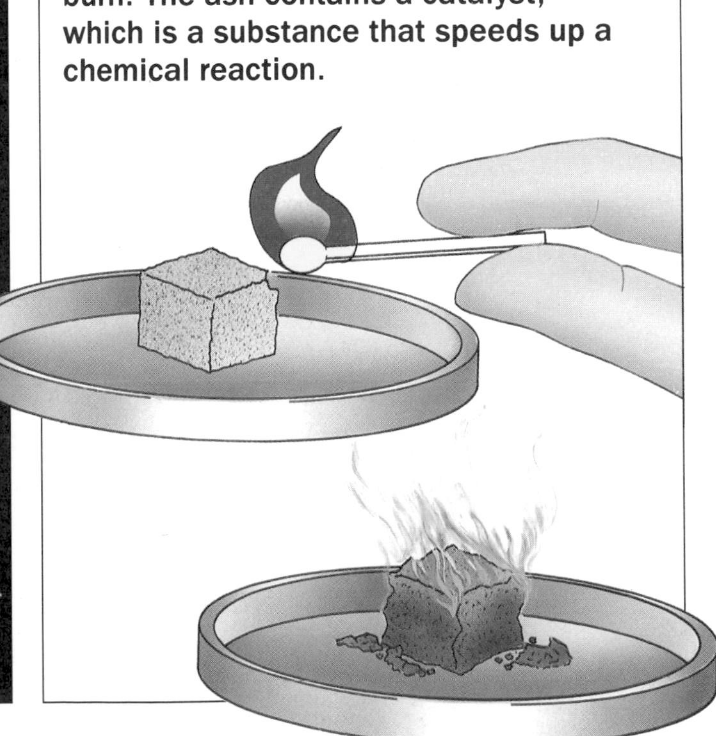

There are two main kinds of engines: external combustion engines in which the fuel is burned outside the engine, and internal combustion engines in which the fuel is burned inside it. A steam engine is an external combustion engine; a gasoline or diesel engine is an internal combustion engine.

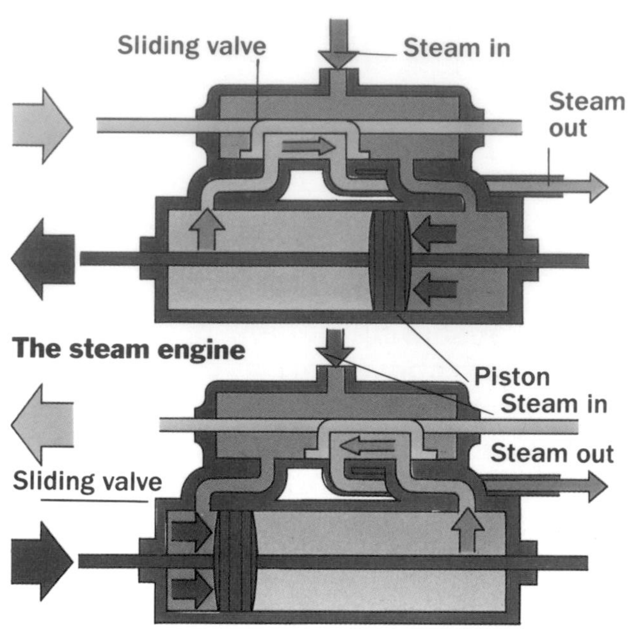

The steam engine

STEAM ENGINE

The first steam engines were huge machines. In 1712, the British engineer Thomas Newcomen built a vertical engine that was 33 feet tall. Then in 1782 the Scotsman James Watt invented the double-acting steam engine. Steam was fed into one end of a cylinder, where a tight-fitting piston was pushed along by the steam pressure. The piston was connected by a rod to a wheel, and sideways movement of the piston caused the wheel to turn. When the piston reached the end of the cylinder, a sliding valve let steam in front of the piston and forced it back again.

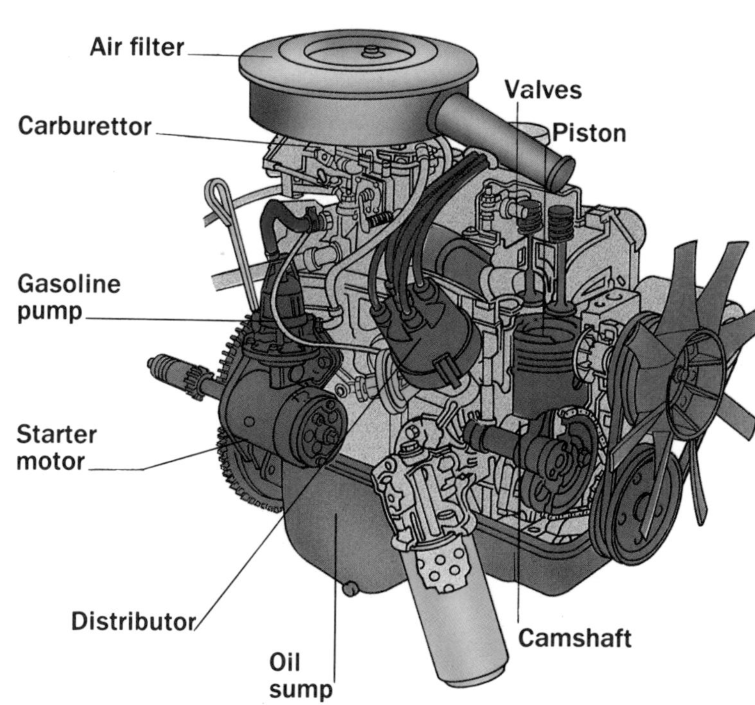

GASOLINE ENGINE

The usual car engine is called a four-stroke engine. This is because it works in four movements, called strokes, of the pistons. During the first stroke, the piston moves down. At the top of the cylinder, a valve opens to let in a mixture of gasoline and air. On the second stroke, the piston moves up to compress the fuel-air mixture. When the mixture is fully compressed, a spark plug ignites the mixture with a small electric spark. The mixture burns, and the expanding gases drive the piston downward. This is the third stroke. The piston then moves up again, forcing the burned mixture out of the cylinder through the exhaust valve. A diesel engine works in a similar way, but has no spark plug; compression of the fuel is enough to ignite it.

The four-stroke gasoline engine

TURBINES

A turbine consists of a wheel with blades – like a small windmill – mounted on a shaft. The wheel is made to turn by a stream of water, steam or hot gas flowing over the blades. In steam turbines, high-pressure steam flows over the blades. Often a series of steam turbines is used in power stations. In a gas turbine, also called a jet engine, air is drawn into the front of the turbine and compressed by fans connected to the turbine shaft. The compressed air passes into a combustion chamber where a fuel, such as kerosene, is burned. The hot gases produced expand and flow through the drive fans before passing out of the engine as a high-speed exhaust. The drive fans make the compressor fans turn. If the turbine is being used to work machinery, the turbine shaft is connected to the machinery. In gas turbine driven ships, the shaft is connected to the propeller. Jet engines in airplanes are also a sort of gas turbine, but it is the hot exhaust that makes the airplane move.

▽ Power stations use huge steam turbines. The shaft turns so fast that the tips of the blades move faster than sound.

△ The fans at the front of an airliner engine draw in air. They are turned by a drive fan at the back of the engine.

TO CREATE POWER

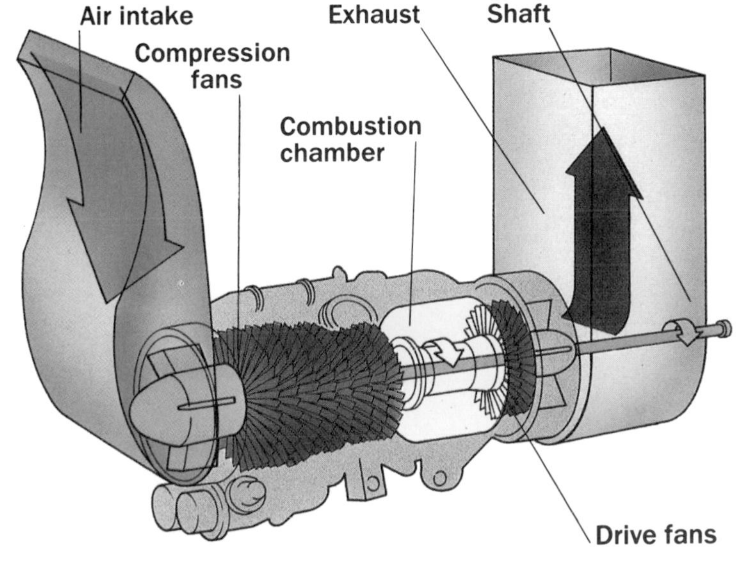

▷ A gas turbine engine can create large amounts of power, but it also creates large amounts of hot exhaust.

Heat has many uses in industry. For example, it is used for extracting metals from their ores. Iron is produced by heating iron ore in a blast furnace with coke. The ore is usually hematite, which contains iron and oxygen. Coke is mainly carbon, made by roasting coal. The resulting pig iron is used to make steel.

△ Molten pig iron can be poured into molds to make ingots. It can also be cast into more complicated shapes.

SHAPING UP

Hot materials are easy to bend and form into various shapes. This is why a blacksmith heats a horseshoe to red heat before hammering it into shape. This method of shaping a metal is called forging. Some car engine parts are made by forging. Casting is another way of shaping metals. Molten metal is poured into a mold and left to cool. Wheels for railroad cars are made by casting. Molten glass or plastic can also be molded, or blown into hollow shapes. Other plastic shapes are made by extrusion, which involves squeezing them through a specially shaped hole.

▽ Large pieces of hot metal can be forged into shape by using very powerful hydraulic hammers or presses.

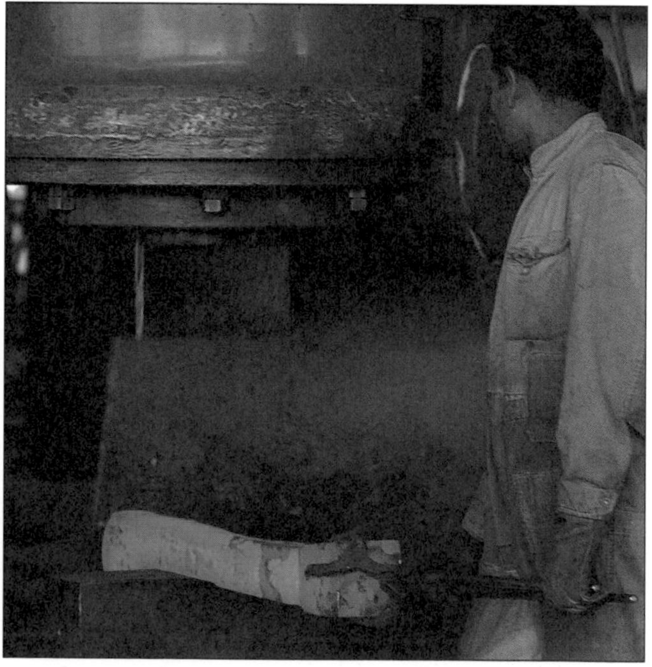

◁ A glass worker blows air into the center of a molten glass ball, expanding the glass to form a bottle.

AT AN OIL REFINERY

Many useful substances can be made from crude oil, or petroleum. The first step is to heat it, causing it to boil off gases. The gases pass into a tall distillation column. As the gases pass up the column and cool, they change into liquids that collect on the trays set across the column. Different liquids – called fractions – collect on different trays and are drawn off through pipes. The lightest fractions with the lowest boiling points are drawn off at the top of the column. Butane and propane are collected as gases before cooling. Lower down, gasoline, kerosene and fuel oils are produced. Heavy black bitumen, or tar, is left at the bottom.

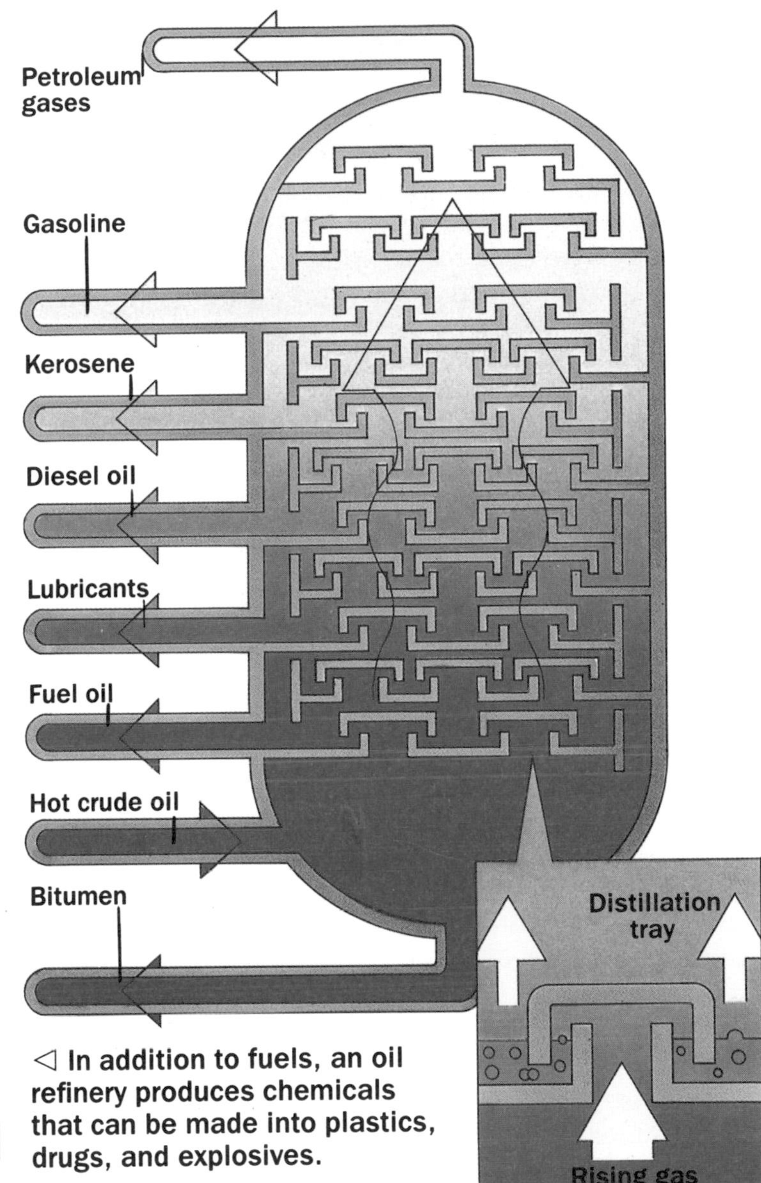

◁ In addition to fuels, an oil refinery produces chemicals that can be made into plastics, drugs, and explosives.

PROJECT

Fill a glass halfway with warm water and put a mark on the side to show the level. Stirring the water, mix in as much salt as will dissolve. Does the water level rise? Where does the salt go? Next pour some of the salt solution onto a saucer, and put it in sunlight. After a while, the water will evaporate, leaving behind small salt crystals.

Dissolve some salt into warm water

Pour mixture into a saucer

Once evaporated in sunlight, salt deposits can be seen

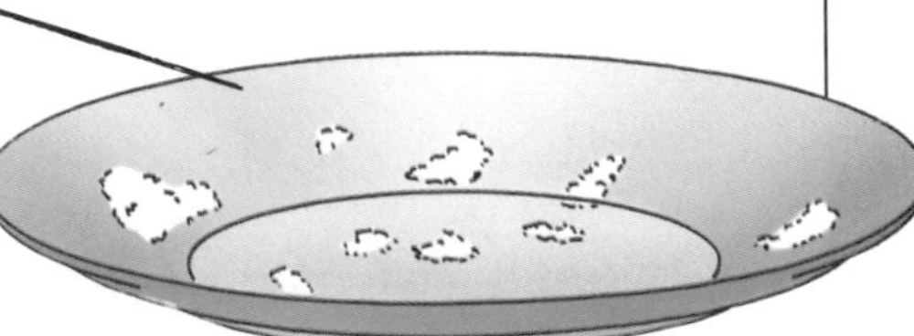

COLORS OF THE RAINBOW

Sunlight appears colorless but really it is made up of different colors. Sometimes you can see these colors – on the surfaces of bubbles or if there is oil on water. You may also see the colors across the sky in the form of a rainbow. In each case "white" light is being separated into different colors called the spectrum.

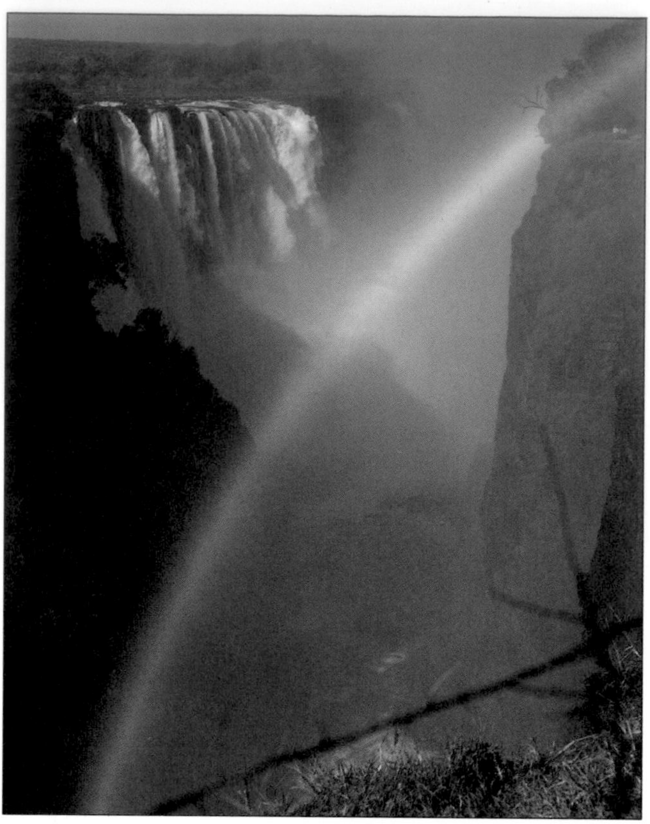

△ It is impossible to reach the end of a rainbow – you can only see it shining in the sky at a distance.

HOW A RAINBOW IS MADE

When the Sun comes out during a shower you may see a rainbow. The sunlight shines on the droplets of rain and gets separated into the colors of the spectrum. From a distance the light appears as a colored arc across the sky. People divide the rainbow into seven bands of color – red, orange, yellow, green, blue, indigo and violet. The colors always appear in the same order, with red on the outside and violet on the inside of the arc. The diagram shows how light which enters each raindrop is reflected, bent and separated into all the colors of the spectrum, which together form a rainbow in the sky.

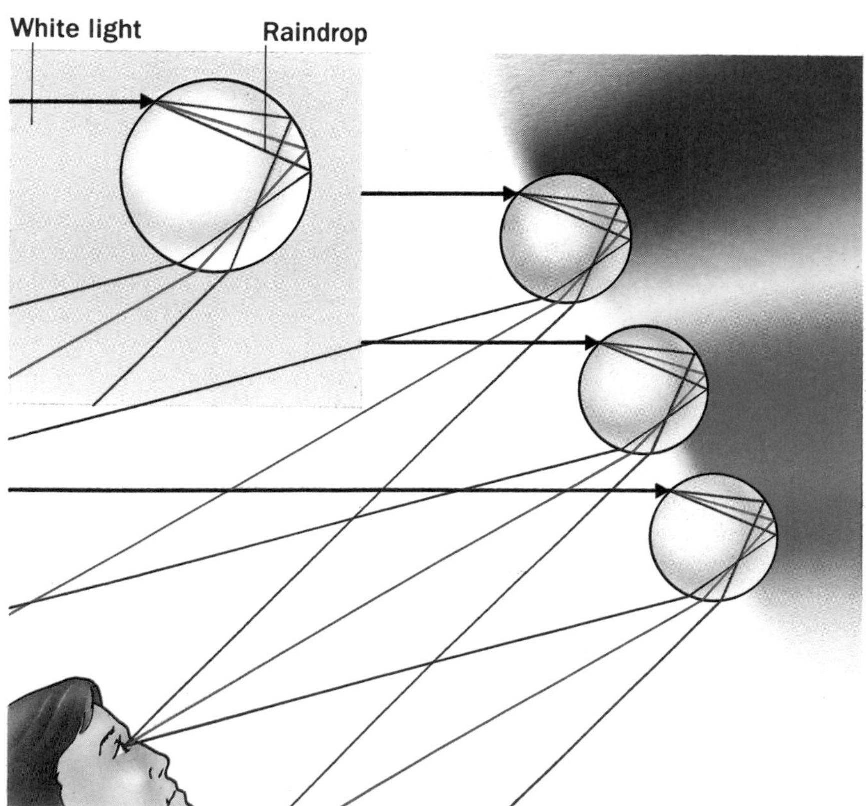

MAKE A RAINBOW

You can see the colors of the spectrum by making your own rainbow. On a sunny day fill a pan of water and rest a mirror at an angle inside it. Stand the pan in front of a window so that sunlight falls onto the mirror. Then hold a piece of white cardboard in front of the mirror and move it around until you see a rainbow appear on it. You may have to move the mirror to get this right. The mirror and the water act as a "prism" – they separate white light into the colors of the spectrum.

THE NORTHERN LIGHTS

Sometimes dazzling displays of colored lights appear in the sky at night in parts of the world which are far from the equator. These lights are caused by huge explosions on the surface of the Sun known as "flares." During a flare, millions of tiny particles are sent out from the Sun. They travel very fast and some eventually reach the Earth's atmosphere. The Earth's magnetism bends the paths of the particles so they only reach the Earth's atmosphere near the poles. As they travel through the air they bump into other particles. These collisions produce light. In the North they can be seen best in parts of Canada, but they can also be seen in northern Scotland and Scandinavia. They are called the Northern Lights or "Aurora borealis." Similar lights can be seen in the South where they are called "Aurora australis."

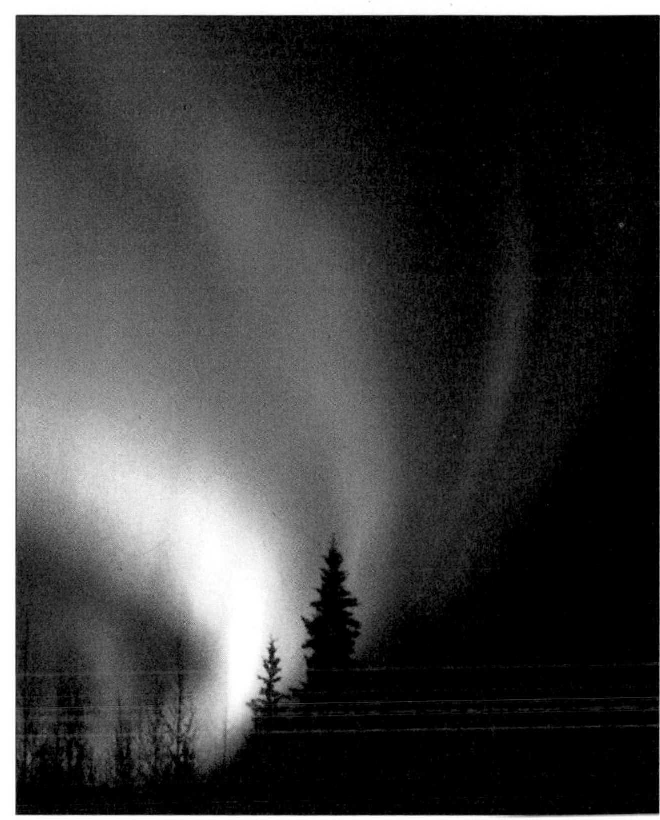

△ The Northern Lights make an impressive display of color which looks like a constantly moving curtain in the sky.

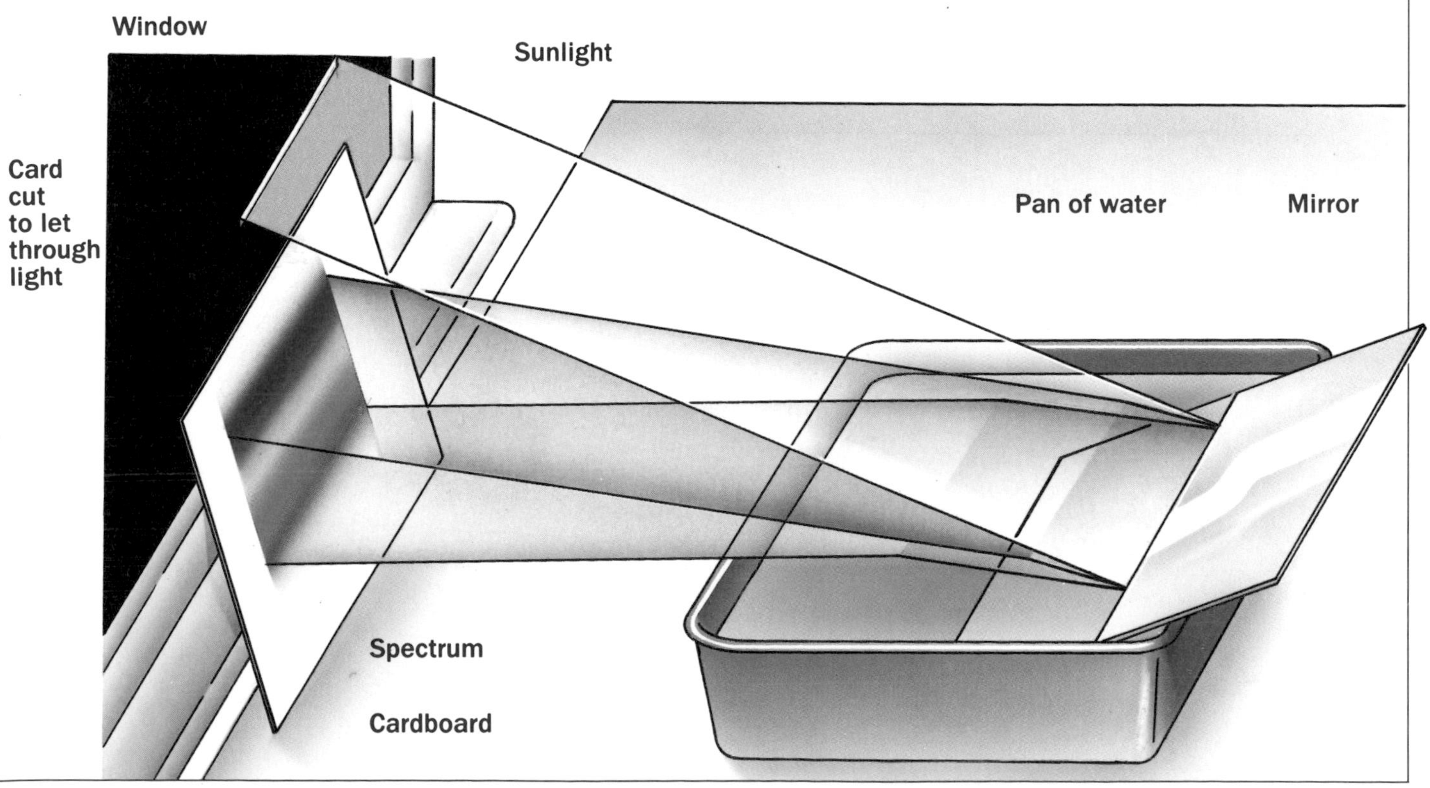

Window

Sunlight

Card cut to let through light

Pan of water

Mirror

Spectrum

Cardboard

IN THE SHADE

Light always travels in straight lines called rays. Some substances allow light to travel through them. These are called transparent substances. But opaque substances do not let light through them. When light falls onto an opaque substance like metal or wood, a shadow may be cast behind the object.

ECLIPSES

The Earth and the Moon are constantly traveling around the Sun. Sometimes the Moon passes between the Sun and the Earth. When this happens the Moon blocks light because it is opaque and a shadow is cast on the Earth. If you are on the part of the Earth in total shadow, the Sun will appear to be completely hidden by the Moon. This is called a "total eclipse of the Sun." Other parts of the Earth will be in partial shadow. From these areas only part of the Sun will be hidden by the Moon. This is called a partial eclipse of the Sun.

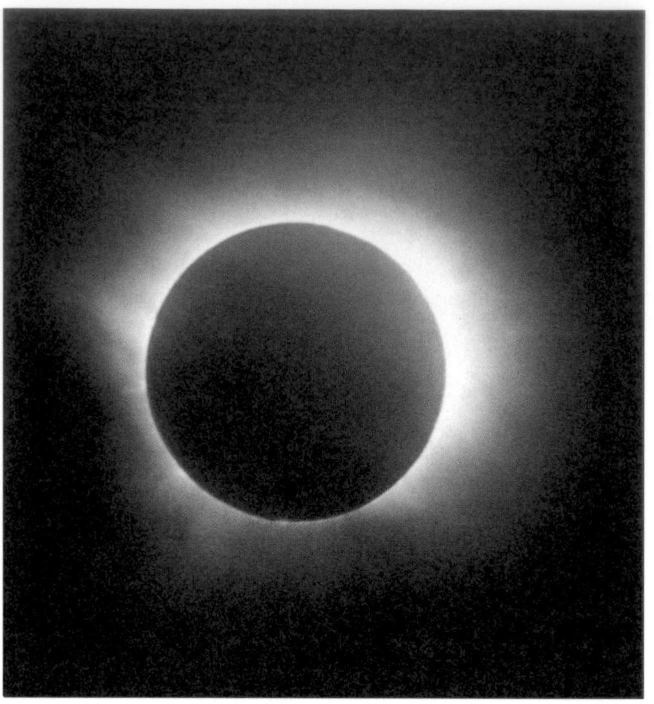

△ In a total eclipse of the Sun only the Sun's outer atmosphere shines around the Moon.

▽ Shadows are strongest in bright light. These trees cast several shadows as they block light from the Sun.

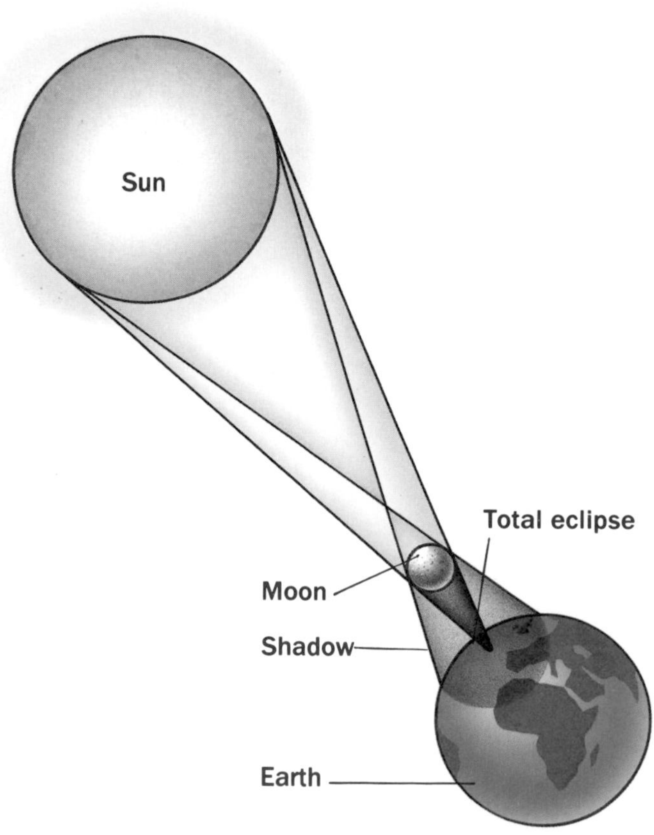

WITHOUT SHADOWS

To take a good photograph it is important to have just the right lighting. The person being photographed (the subject) needs to be well lit by floodlights. But this light could cast a shadow on the screen behind. To get rid of this shadow the photographer uses "backlights" placed on each side of, and slightly behind, the subject. The backlights light the screen to get rid of the shadows. This lighting should produce a perfect photograph without unwanted shadows.

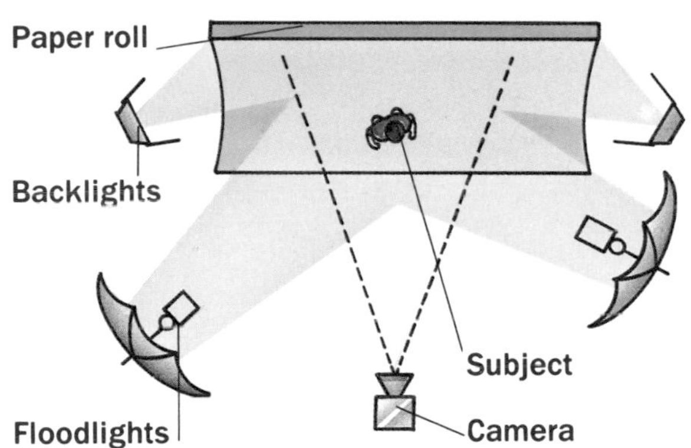

△ The lights being used to take this photograph provide just the right illumination with no shadows to spoil the results.

MAKE A SHADOW CLOCK

During the day the Sun appears to move across the sky. It casts different shadows at different times. You can use the Sun to tell the time with this shadow clock. Place the clock on a sheet of white paper so it faces the Sun. Mark where the shadow falls and write the time beside the mark. Do this several times until your clock is complete.

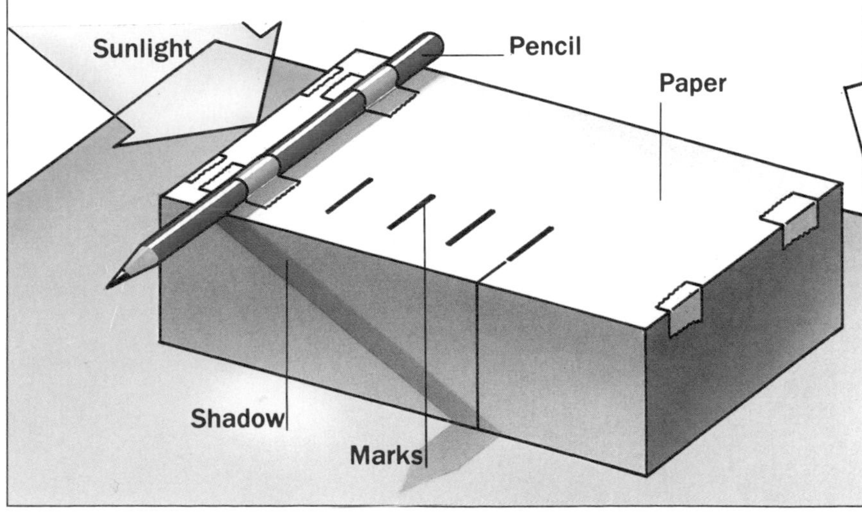

QUIZ

These pictures show the same person in the same place on the same day. Can you explain why the shadows are different lengths and point in different directions?

REFLECTION

When light from the Sun or from an electric light bulb reaches an object some of it bounces off again. This is called reflection. It is this reflected light that you see when you look at something. Mirrors are good reflectors so are surfaces like this white sheet of paper.

△ On a sunny day in calm water a reflection can look almost as real as the scene itself – but it is really just an illusion.

REFLECTION

The diagram shows how you might see a reflection of a friend in water. Sunlight falls on the friend. Some of this light is reflected straight into your eyes. This allows you to see your friend. But some of the light is reflected onto the water between you. Because water reflects some of the light, some of it bounces back up to your eyes. Light normally travels in straight lines so it seems to you that this reflection is coming from below the water. Flat, shiny surfaces like glass, water and polished metals reflect light very well. You may see a reflection of yourself when you look into them.

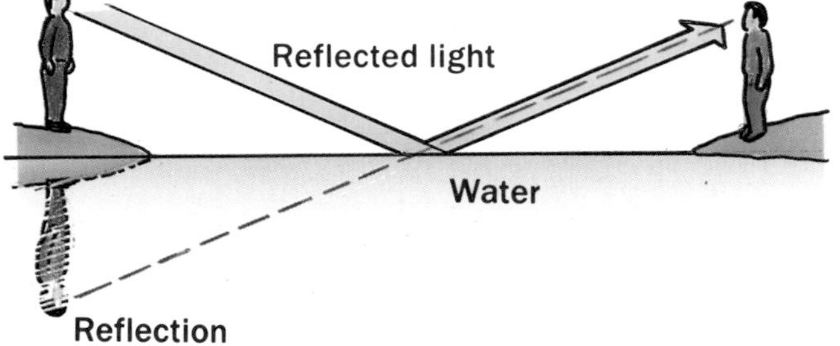

MAKE YOUR OWN PERISCOPE

Periscopes can help you see over walls and around corners. You can make one yourself by following the instructions in the diagrams. Start by cutting the cardboard so that the mirrors are a little wider than the periscope case. Make sure you cut the holes and slots to fit the mirrors too. Carefully slot the mirrors in position as shown. Do you know how the reflecting mirrors allow you to see around corners?

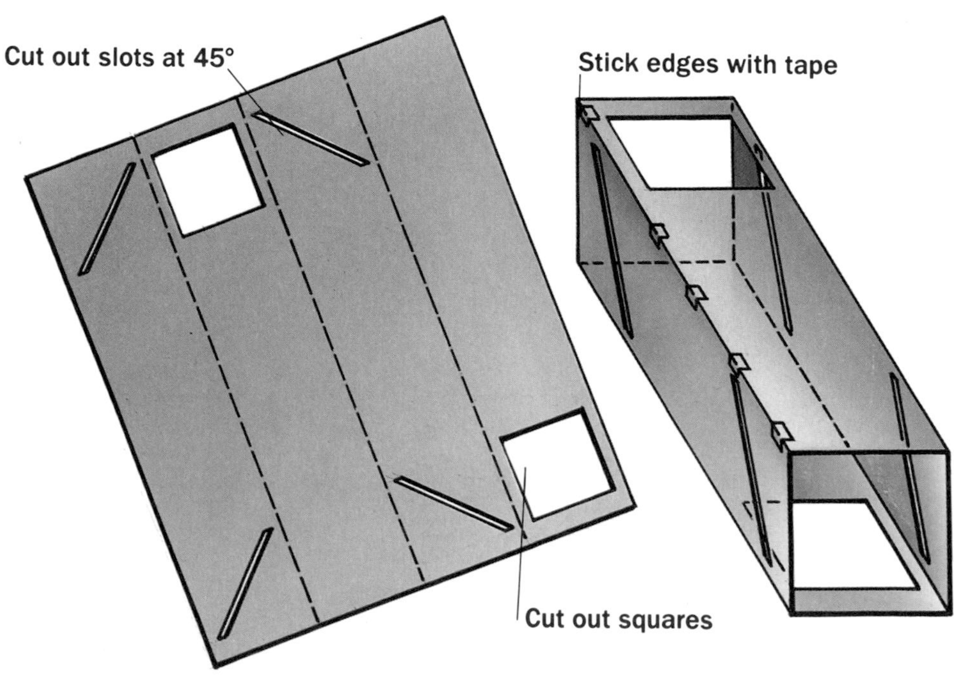

CONVEX AND CONCAVE

Not all mirrors are flat – some kinds are curved. A mirror that curves inward is called a concave mirror. A mirror that curves outward is known as a convex mirror. The reflections from curved mirrors look different to those from flat mirrors. You can see this by looking at yourself in a spoon. The front of the spoon is like a concave mirror and in it you will appear upside down. But if you bring the spoon very close to you, you will see a large image of your eye the right way up. The back of the spoon is like a convex mirror – in it your reflection will be upright but small.

△ Have you ever been in "the hall of mirrors" at an amusement park? These mirrors make people look very strange – like the people in the photograph. They use mirrors which curve in and out. Some parts of the mirrors are convex and some are concave. Your reflection is stretched in some places and squeezed together in others.

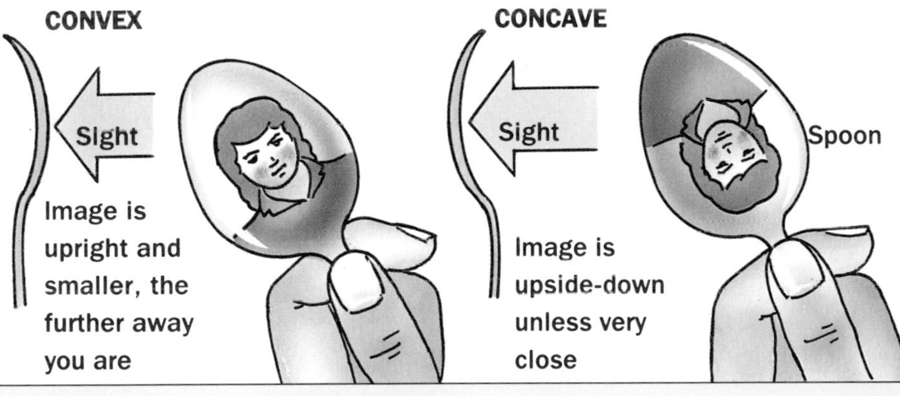

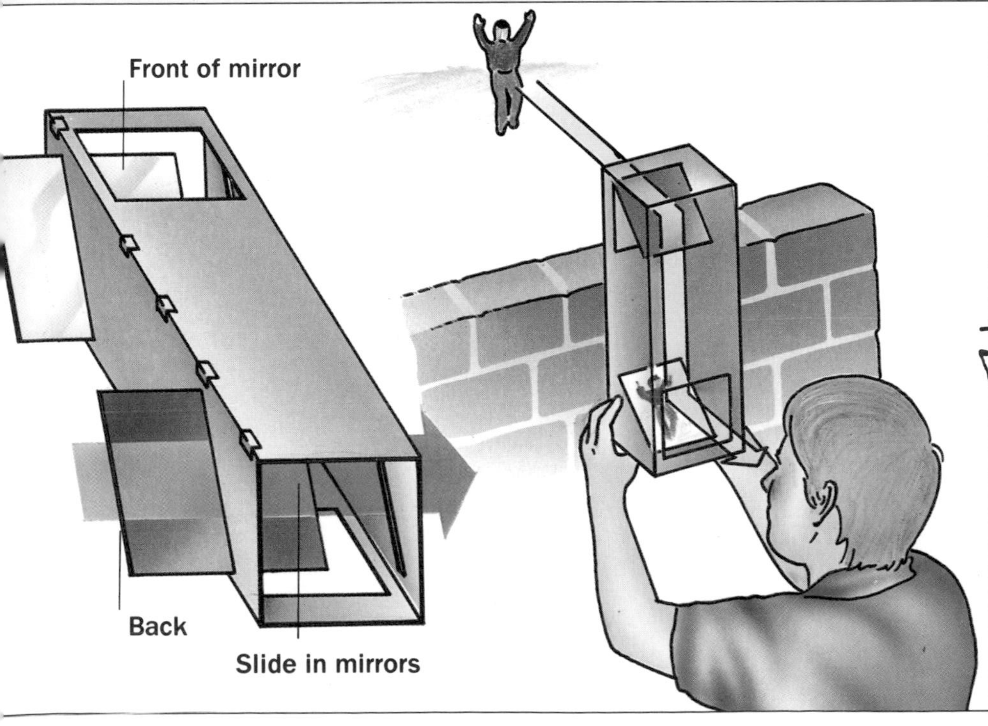

QUIZ

Even flat mirrors can be misleading. Can you read the sentence below? It has been written in mirror writing. Try reading it in a mirror – you will find it much easier.

How well can you read backwards without using a mirror?

CHANGING DIRECTION

Although light travels in straight lines you have seen how it can be reflected and made to change direction. Light travels at different speeds through different substances. When light passes from one substance to another, it may also change direction. This process, refraction, makes light appear to bend.

△ The straw in the photograph appear to be bent. Light from the straw is being refracted as it passes from the water to the air.

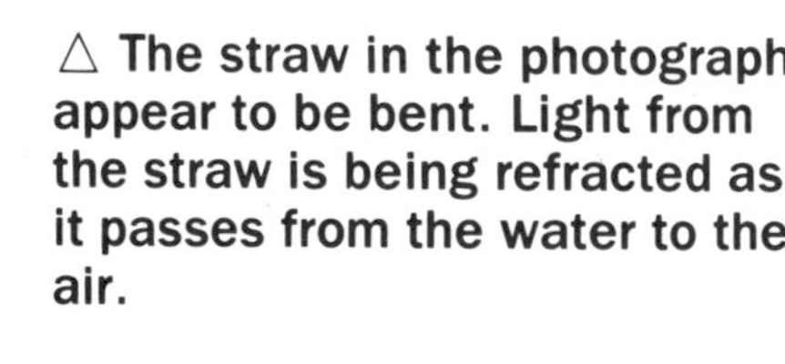

▷ Reflectors are able to collect light from one direction and reflect it back in the same direction.

REAPPEARING COIN

You can see the effects of how light appears to bend for yourself. Try this experiment using a bowl, a coin, and some water. Put the coin in the bottom of the bowl and move backward until the coin just disappears from sight. Stand still while a friend pours water into the bowl. You should find that the coin comes into view again. This happens because the water causes the light from the coin to change direction so that it travels to your eyes.

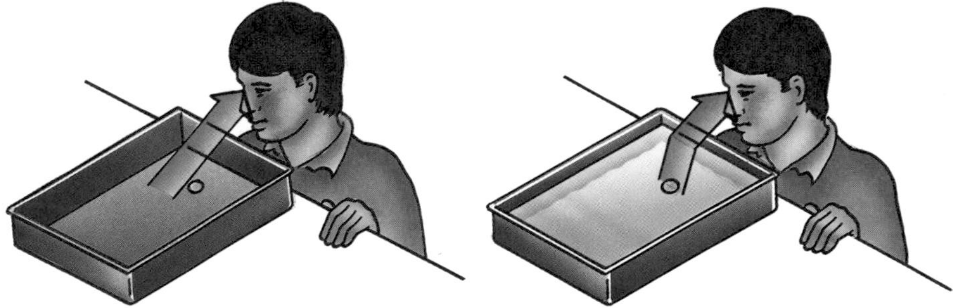

Line of sight will not reveal coin

MIRAGE

People in the desert sometimes think they see water. But this is really just an illusion known as a mirage. You may have seen mirages yourself on the road on a hot day. Mirages are caused by refraction of light as it passes through air of different temperatures. On a hot day the air near the ground is much hotter than air higher up. As the light passes from the cooler air to the hotter air it gets refracted and appears to come from a point nearer the viewer. This makes objects appear closer than they are.

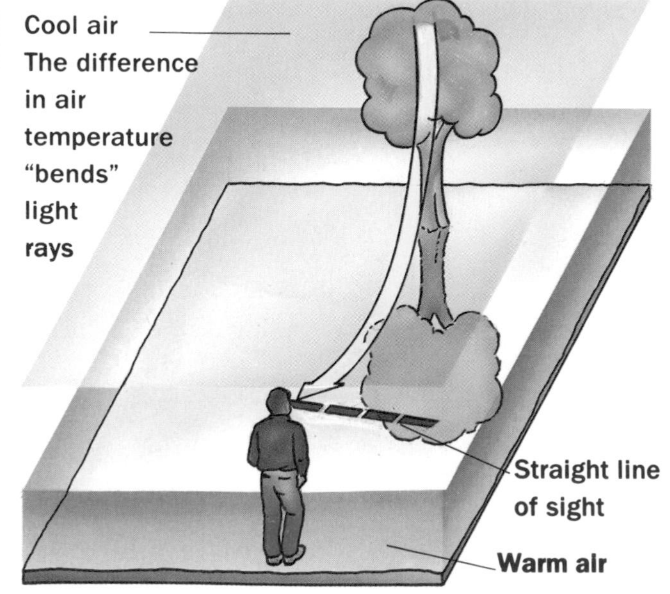

FIBER OPTICS

Optical fibers are used to channel light from place to place. They are solid glass rods which are as thin as hair. They are flexible and can be bent and twisted like wire. Light travels along the fiber by bouncing from side to side along the length of the rod. There is a cladding which surrounds bundles of the rods to protect them from damage and to prevent light coming into the cable.

△ Optical fibers are already being used by telephone companies. They can carry more information than electric cables and are likely to be used more in the future. The optical fibers carry information as light signals. These signals travel at the speed of light in the material.

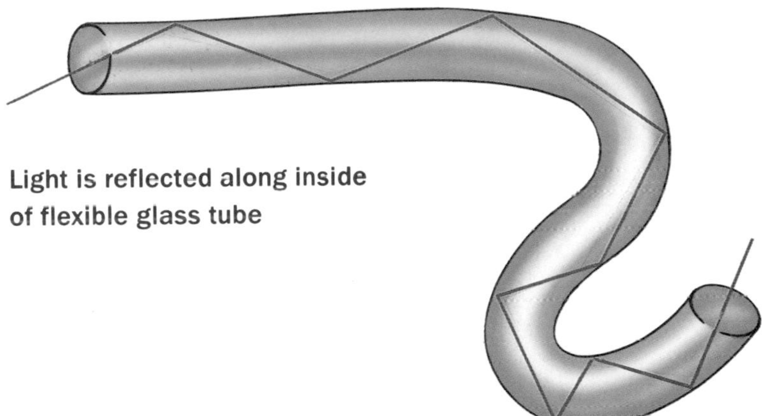

Light is reflected along inside of flexible glass tube

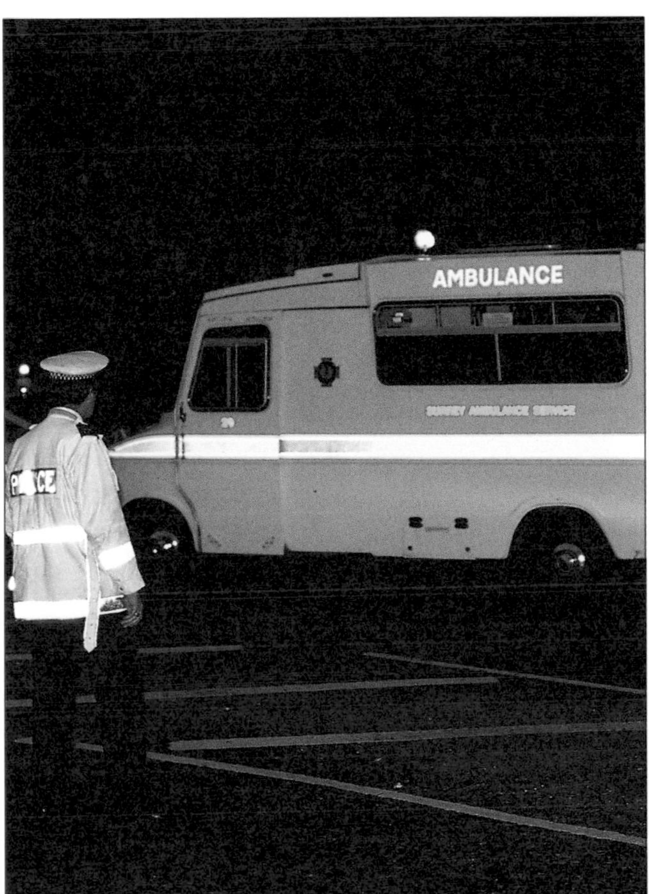

REFLECTORS

If you have a bicycle it will probably have “reflectors” fitted to it. These help other road users to see your bicycle at night. Underneath the smooth outer surface of a reflector there is a layer of plastic shaped with many angles. The angles ensure that any light falling on the reflector is reflected back to source. Reflectors worn by the police work in the same way to ensure motorists can see them.

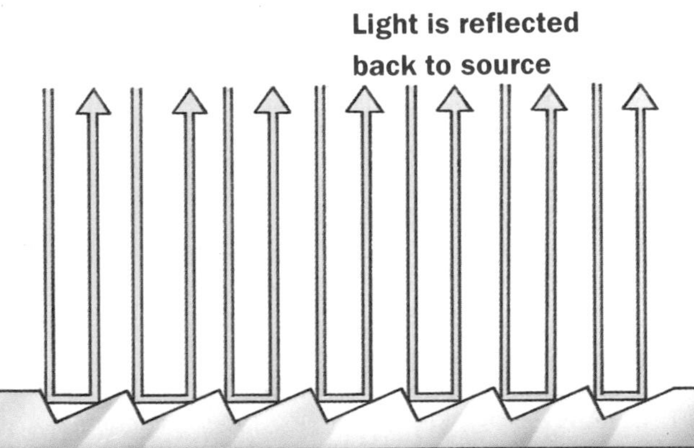

Light is reflected back to source

LENSES

Lenses are specially shaped pieces of transparent material like glass or plastic. They are curved on one or both sides, and can be used to refract ("bend") light. They may make objects appear larger or smaller. They are used in instruments which help us to see things we cannot see with our eyes alone.

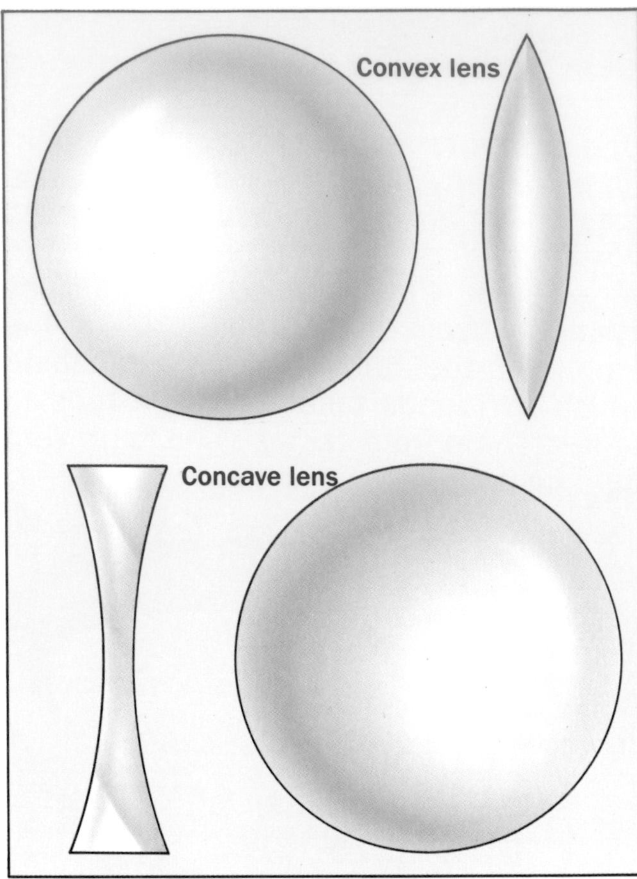

△ The drawing shows lenses as they appear from the front and the side. Convex lenses are thicker in the middle than at the edges. But concave lenses are thicker at the edges.

TYPES OF LENSES

Lenses that curve outward are called convex lenses. Lenses that curve inward are called concave lenses. The diagram below shows what happens to light as it passes through each type of lens. Light passing through the convex lens is bent inward – it converges. Light passing through the concave lens is bent outward – it diverges. Convex lenses can magnify small objects, but things appear smaller when they are seen through a concave lens.

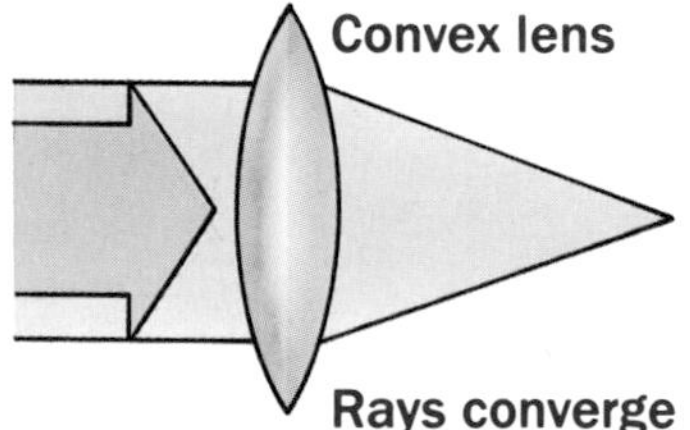

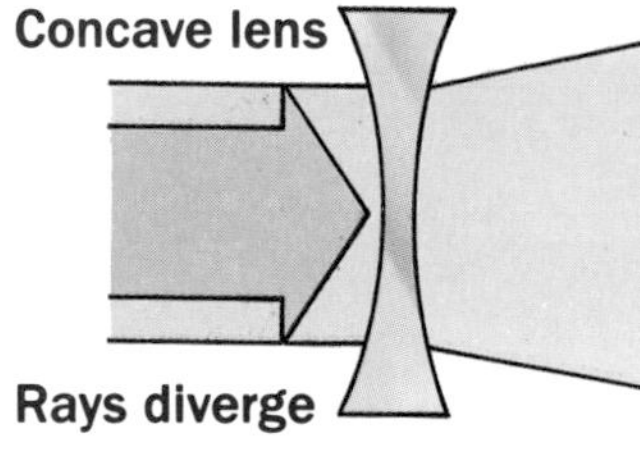

THE LIGHT MICROSCOPE

A microscope is an instrument that is used to make small objects – especially tiny living things or cells – appear larger so they can be studied. A very thin slice of the specimen to be viewed is placed on a glass slide and lit up by a light attached below. The light passes through the specimen on the glass slide and then through a number of lenses. The lenses magnify the image of the object by refracting the light so that it diverges. Microscopes can magnify things so that they appear hundreds of times larger than their real size. They are often used by doctors and scientists working in laboratories.

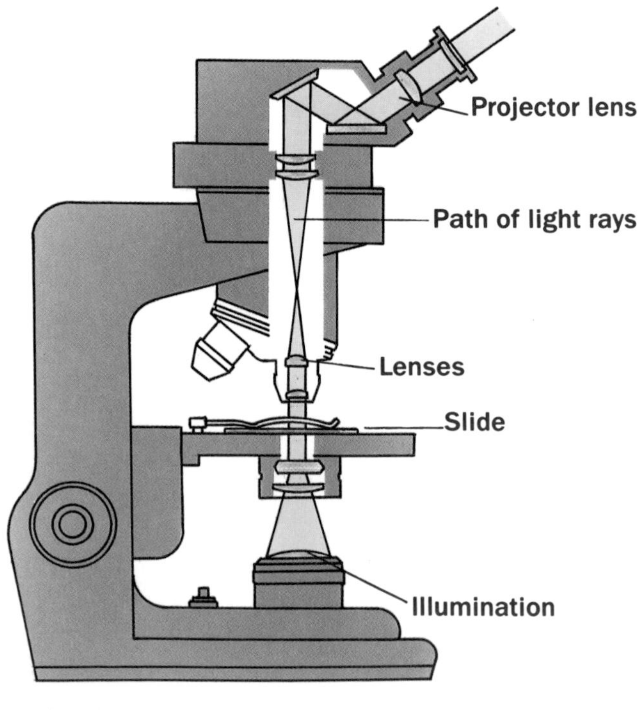

TELESCOPES

Astronomers use telescopes to study the night sky. Telescopes allow distant objects – such as planets or groups of stars – to be seen more clearly. Telescopes gather light so they make images clearer. There are two main types of telescope. The top diagram shows a refracting telescope. This uses a lens to collect and focus light from the sky and a smaller lens to magnify the image. The reflecting telescope below uses two mirrors to reflect light through a small lens. This lens then magnifies the image.

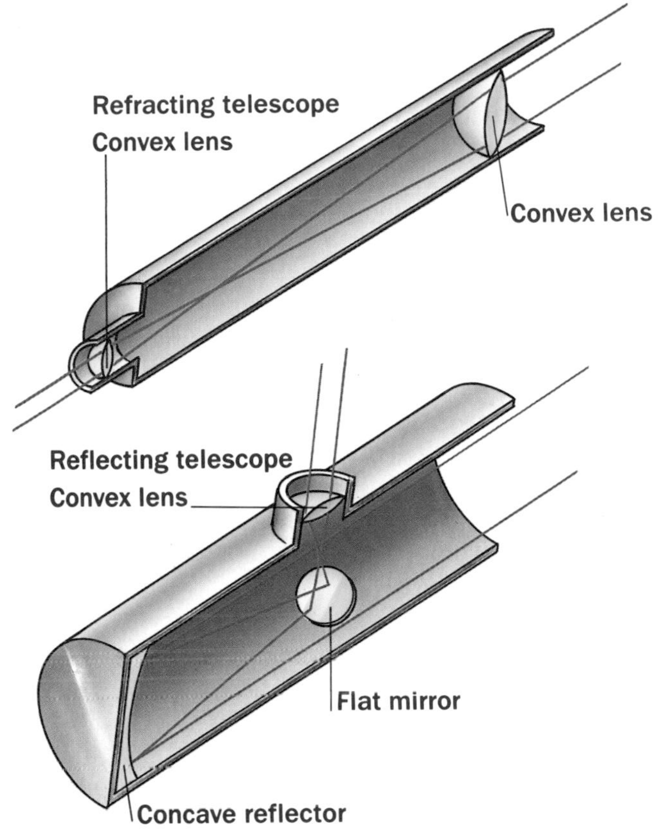

◁ This telescope is designed for observing the night sky. A system of lenses collects light so that the stars can be more clearly seen.

MAKE YOUR OWN TELESCOPE

Stand a shaving mirror by a window so that it points towards the Moon. Then hold a flat mirror so that you can see a reflection of the shaving mirror in it. Look at the reflection in the flat mirror through a magnifying glass, – the Moon will look brighter. **WARNING: Always look at the night sky. Viewing the Sun through a telescope is dangerous.**

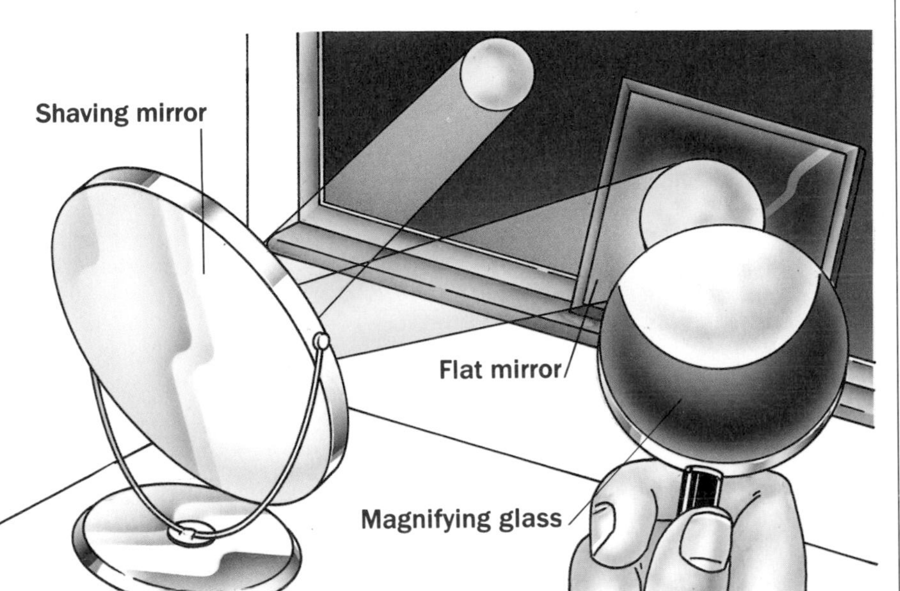

Most objects do not produce light of their own. Instead they *reflect* light which falls on them. The color an object appears depends on the color of light it reflects. There are only three primary colors of light – red, blue and green. All other colors are made by mixing these primary colors together.

△ You can see plants of many different colors in the photograph. Each one is reflecting a different combination of colored light into your eyes.

REFLECTING COLOR

Ordinary white sunlight or electric light is made up of many colors. The diagrams below show how the colors reflected by an object give it its color. Something which appears white reflects all the colors in white light. However, an object which appears red reflects only red light – the other colors of the spectrum will be absorbed by the object. Something which appears black does not reflect any light at all – all the colors of the spectrum are completely absorbed.

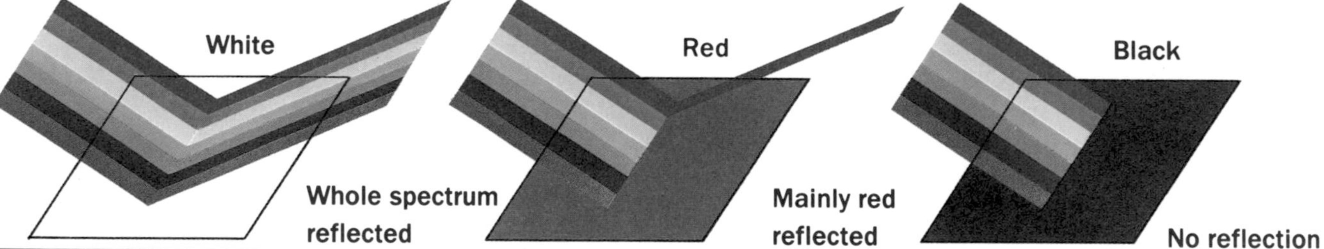

MIXING COLORS WITH LIGHT

Different combinations of colored light mix to make different colors. You can try mixing light yourself. Put colored transparent paper – one red, one green and one blue – over the ends of three flashlights. Shine them onto white paper. Divide a circle into seven equal segments and color them with the colors of the spectrum. Spin the circle. What do you see?

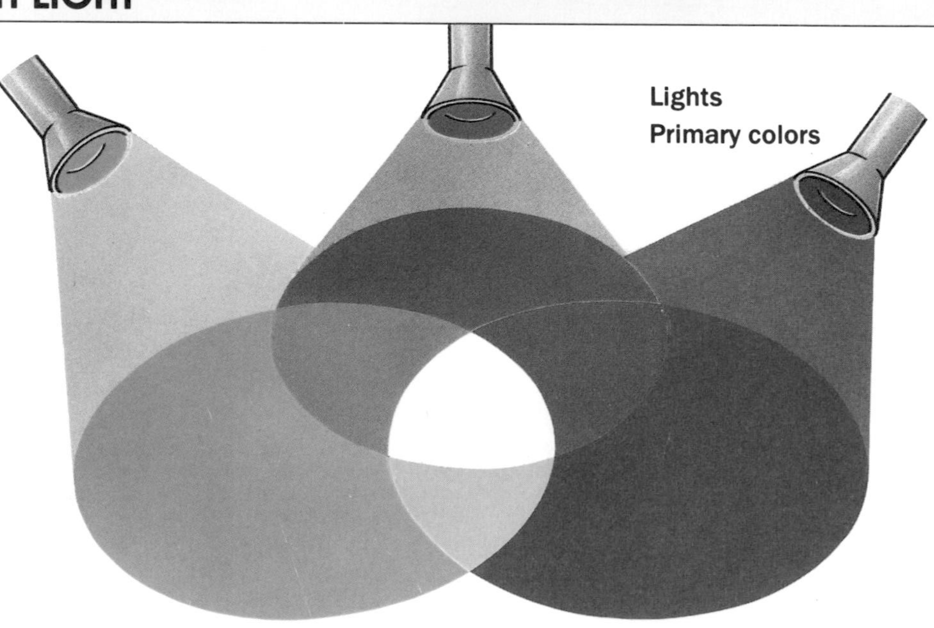

COLOR TELEVISION

A television receives signals from transmitters and turns them into pictures. The inside of the television screen is coated with many dots of special chemicals called phosphors. These dots are arranged in groups of three, so that each tiny part of the screen can produce all the three primary colors of light–red, blue and green. As the signal comes into the television it is translated into a pattern of colored dots on the screen. If you look closely at a television picture you will see that it is made up of lots of tiny colored dots. As the pattern of red, blue and green changes, so the picture and the colors it appears change too. To your eye the dots merge to form a single picture with many varieties of color and contrast.

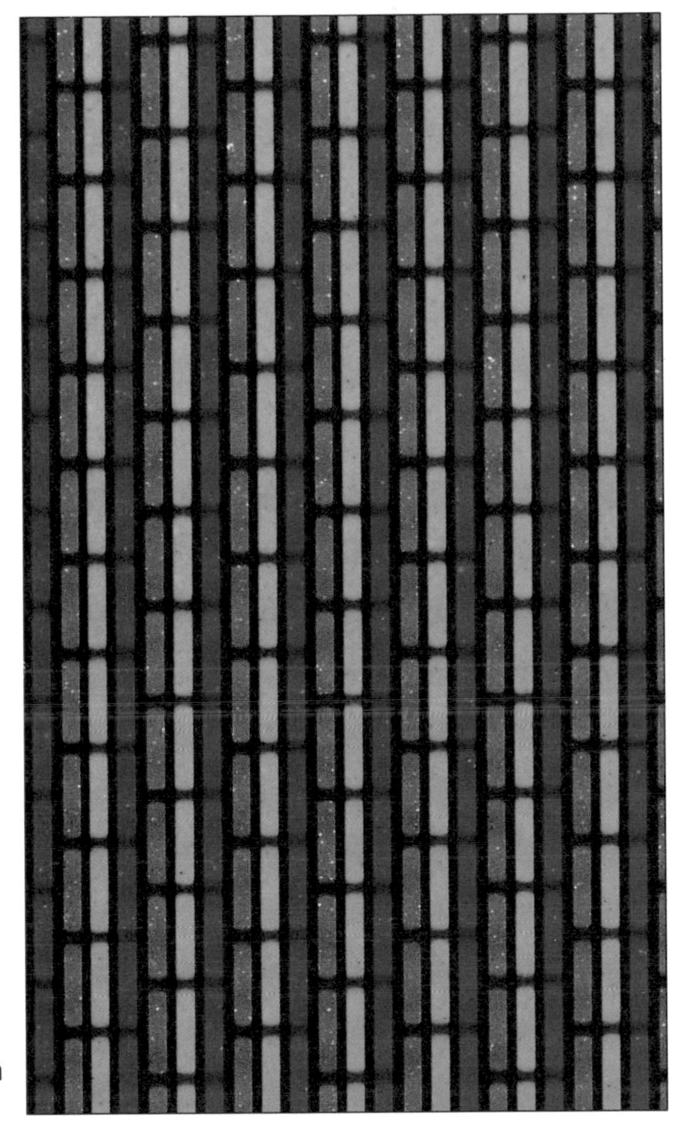

▷ The picture shows part of a color television screen magnified. You can see that the picture is made up of lots of tiny red, blue and green dots. These dots combine to make all the colors you see on the screen.

Colors of the rainbow

Spin

Put pencil through circle

NEWTON'S WHEEL
When spinning all the colors appear white

QUIZ

Some people find it difficult to see colors. What number can you see in the dots below? If you cannot see a number you probably do not have normal color vision.

Answer: 4

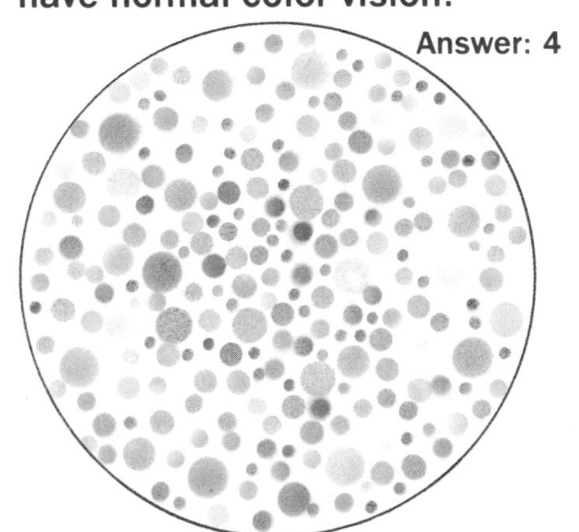

ARTIFICIAL LIGHT

The Sun provides most of the light we need during the daytime but we need other sources of light after sunset. The simplest way to make light is with fire, for example in the form of a candle. But the most popular and convenient source of artificial light today is electric light.

△ Electric light enables us to carry on with our lives even after the Sun has set. Once darkness falls, most cities are illuminated by millions of electric lights.

HOW A LIGHT BULB WORKS

When a light is switched on, electricity flows through the filament, a thin coil of tungsten wire. Because the wire is so thin it gets very hot – as hot as 4,800°F. When electricity passes through it, the filament glows white and gives out light. There is no air in the bulb so that the filament does not burn out. It may be filled with another gas or with nothing at all – a "vacuum."

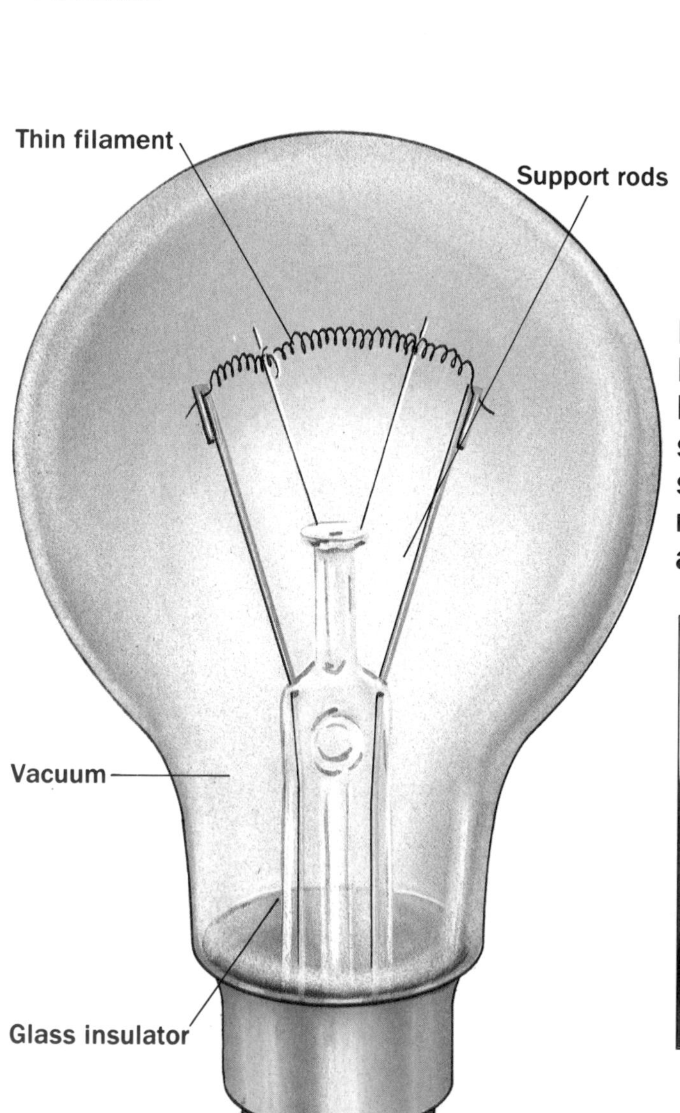

MEASURING LIGHT LEVELS

Many people need to measure light. Photographers and movie makers need to know how bright the light is in their studios. Light levels are important for some sports like baseball and tennis. To measure light levels accurately you need a light meter.

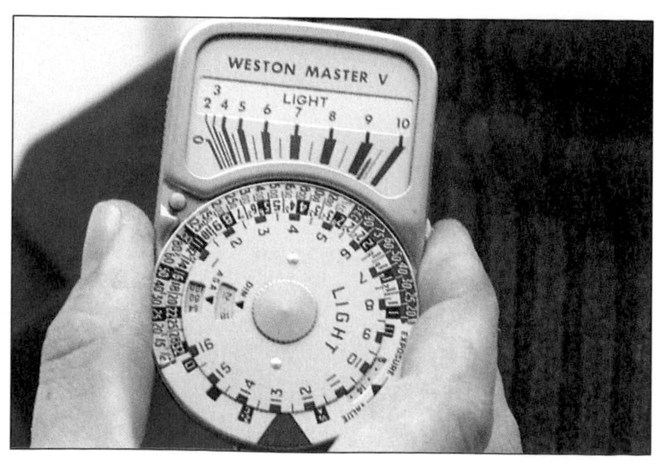

DIFFERENT ARTIFICIAL LIGHTS

Electric light bulbs may be convenient ways of lighting our homes but they are not suitable for all forms of lighting. Neon lights, used for street signs, and strip lights, used indoors, are both types of electric light. But they do not have a filament – instead they are filled with a gas which produces light when an electric current passes through it. To produce the figures on a digital watch or calculator a liquid crystal display is used. The display contains a special chemical called liquid crystal. When electric current is applied to parts of it, those parts turn black to make the figures. This technique is also used in computer graphics and pocket TVs.

▷ The hands and figures on this watch face are coated with a special chemical which is "luminous" – it glows in the dark. The light is produced by the chemical and lasts for a long time.

COLORED LIGHT AND COLOR

Theater sets use artificial colored light to change the colors on stage. You can try this yourself. Draw the colors of the spectrum on a piece of white cardboard. Cover a flashlight with red cellophane so it produces red light. In a dark room look at the cardboard with the red light. Some of the colors will appear shades of red (those which reflect red light) and some will appear black. Try the same experiment with blue cellophane.

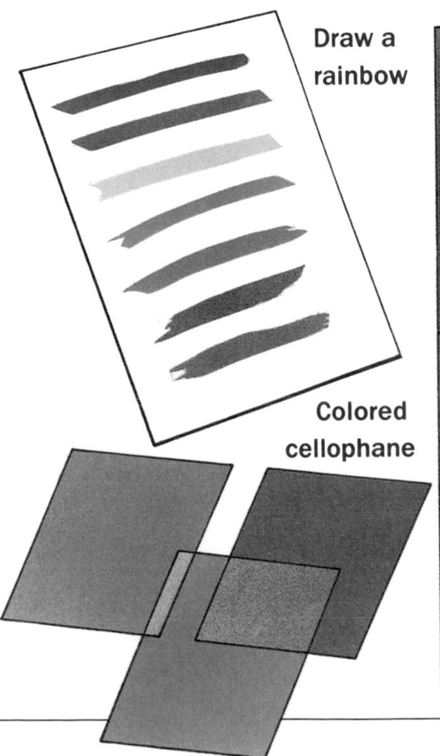

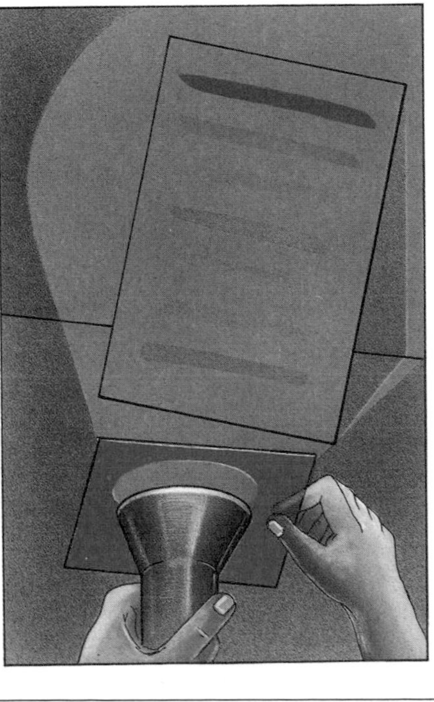

LIGHT FOR LIFE

Green plants need carbon dioxide, water and sunlight to make new substances. To use the chemicals they get from the plants they eat, animals need oxygen from the air, and they give out carbon dioxide. Plants and animals depend on each other to keep the balance of different gases in the air.

△ The sunflowers in the photograph all face the same direction. Plants always grow toward the light since they need light in order to make the chemicals with which they make stems, leaves and roots. Without light, plants grow thin and spindly and eventually die.

PHOTOSYNTHESIS

Plants take in carbon dioxide from the air and water from the soil, and make chemicals such as cellulose, starch and sugar from them. The plants then use these chemicals to make stems, leaves and roots. To do all this a plant needs energy in the form of sunlight and a special substance called chlorophyll, which is found in the leaves. This process is called photosynthesis.

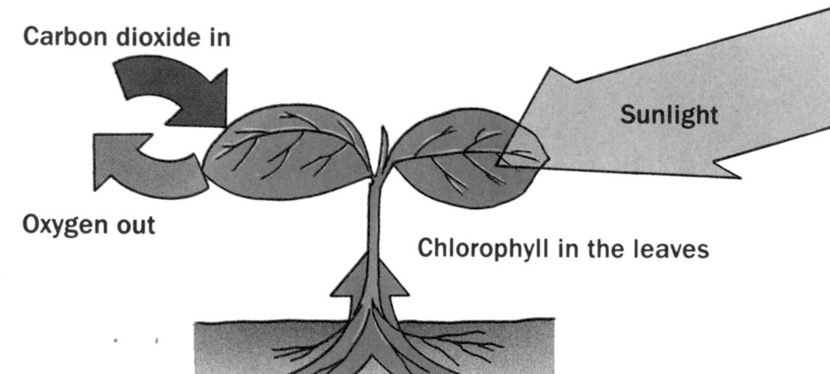

Water and minerals are taken through the roots

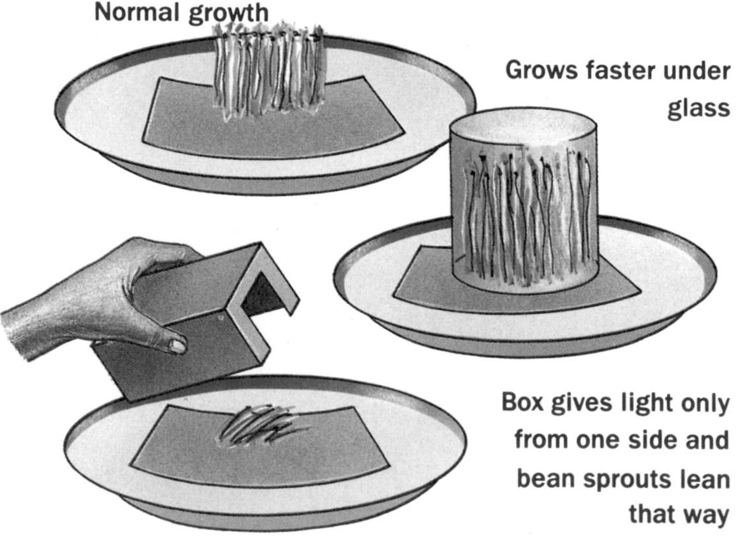

MORE ABOUT LIGHT AND PLANTS

You can find out more about plants by doing these investigations with bean sprouts. Bean sprouts grow quickly and easily so you will get results in a few days. Take three saucers and place some damp blotting paper in each one. Sprinkle some bean seeds on top of each blotting paper. Place an upturned glass over one set of seeds and a box with a hole cut in one side over another. Leave the third set to grow normally. What differences do you expect to see between the sets of seeds when they grow?

CAMOUFLAGE

Many animals have different colors and patterns on their skins or coats which make them difficult to see. They are "camouflaged." Camouflage helps to protect an animal from predators. Polar bears, for example, have white coats which camouflage them in snow. Camouflage may also help the predator. Tigers' stripes help them to hide in long grass when they are hunting prey. Some animals have bright colors that warn off other animals. Some butterflies have patterns like eyes on their wings. These frighten away birds which might otherwise eat them. Other animals use color to attract a mate. The male stickleback fish has bright blue eyes and a red chest which helps him attract a female in the mating season.

△ This glow-worm can produce its own light which it flashes to attract a mate. Different types of glow-worms produce different patterns of light.

▽ Can you see the lizard? Its mottled brown skin merges well with the stone background. The lizard is difficult to see until it moves.

INVISIBLE RAYS

Light is a type of radiation. But the light we see is only a small part of the radiation which comes from the Sun. A lot of the Sun's radiation is in the form of infrared and ultraviolet rays, two types of radiation which we cannot see. They are part of the "invisible spectrum."

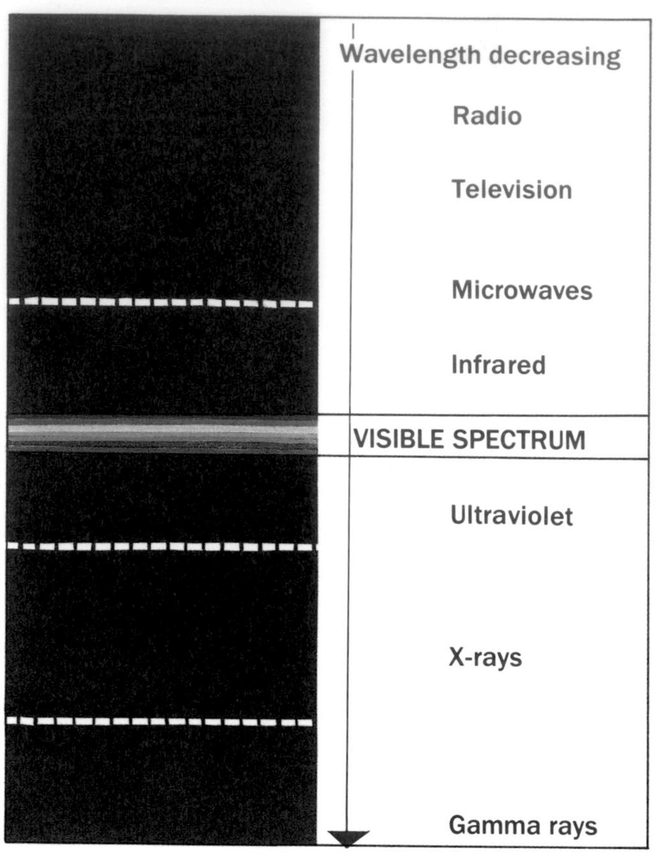

△ The diagram shows the main types of radiation. They all have different wavelengths. Radio waves have the longest and gamma rays have the shortest.

THE INVISIBLE SPECTRUM

Although we cannot see infrared or ultraviolet rays we can feel their effects. Ultraviolet light causes skin color to darken and can be harmful. We feel infrared as heat. There are also other types of radiation which we cannot see.

All this radiation travels at the same speed – the speed of light, which is about 186,000 miles per second (almost 300,000 kilometers per second). The radiation travels as "waves" rather like ripples in a pond. The only difference between the different types of radiation is the lengths of their waves (wavelengths) and their effects.

PROTECTION FROM INFRARED RADIATION

Set up two glasses of water as shown in the diagram. Put them both out in the sun. Take the temperature of the water in each glass every half hour for about two hours. Which one heats up more quickly and which one gets hotter? Then put the glasses in a cool place out of the sun. Which one cools down faster? What effect does metal foil have on infrared radiation?

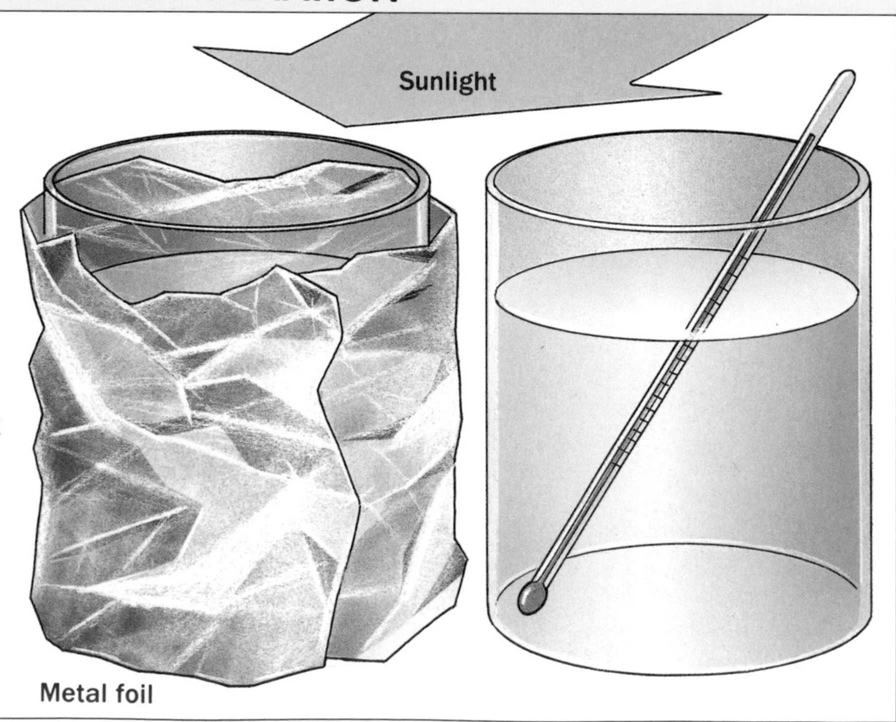

Which one is warmer?
Which one heats up faster?

WHEAT GRAIN

It is possible to collect and use energy from the Sun to provide heat and hot water for homes. This can be done with solar panels. Installed on the roof of buildings, facing the Sun, they are black to absorb the Sun's radiation. Below the surface there is a fluid, usually water, that heats up when the panels get hot, and is then used for washing, or in radiators for heating homes. Another form of solar power is solar cells. They use the Sun's light, not its heat, to make electricity. They are made up of two silicon layers, each of which contains an electric charge. When light hits the cell, the charges begin to move between the two layers, producing a small electric current. The advantage of solar power is that it can be used in remote places, it is free, and unlike fossil fuels, will not run out. The Sun is also the source of other kinds of energy, such as wind, wave and water power.

△ Solar panels provide energy for homes without damaging the environment or wasting limited resources.

▽ You cannot see or feel ultraviolet light but you may see and feel its effects if you sunbathe for too long.

ULTRAVIOLET RADIATION

The color of your skin depends on the amount of a pigment called melanin it contains. Melanin helps to protect your skin from the harmful effects of ultraviolet light. In sunshine your skin will produce more melanin to protect you. But if your skin is fair and you lie in sunshine it is likely to burn. A lot of exposure to ultraviolet light may also cause skin cancer. It is best not to lie in hot sunshine but if you do you should use suntan lotion which will give your skin extra protection. The diagram shows how the lotion works. When it is spread over the surface of the skin it forms a protective barrier. It reflects some of the ultraviolet light away before it reaches you. Different strengths of lotion reflect different amounts of ultraviolet and protect you to different extents.

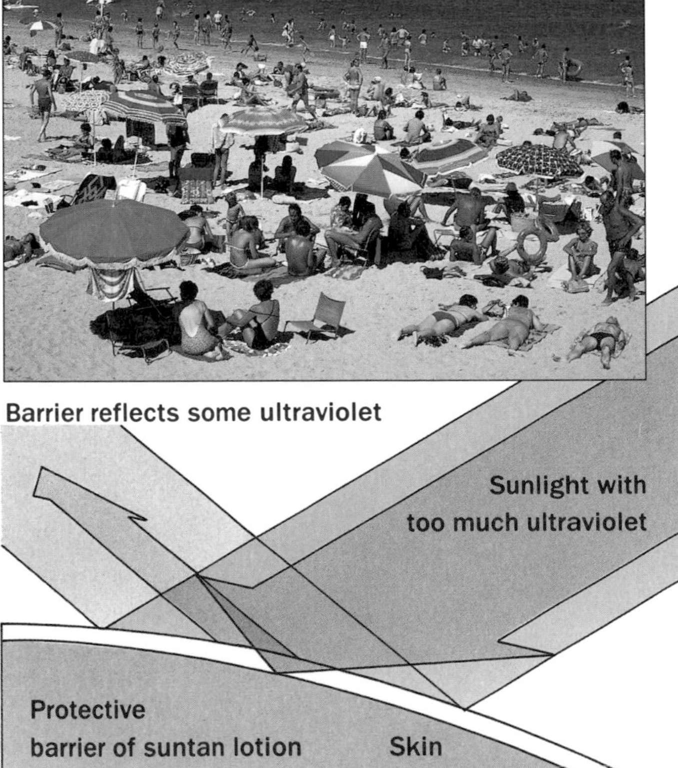

Lasers are machines which produce a special kind of light. Laser light can be focused onto a very small spot and cause intense heat. Lasers can "cut" (burn) through steel! Laser light has many uses – in industry, in surgery, to make holograms and compact disks and for taking accurate measurements.

WHAT MAKES A LASER?

Ordinary light is made up of many colors. But laser light contains light of just one wavelength. Whereas in ordinary light the waves travel in different directions, in a laser the light waves travel in the same direction and in step with each other. The diagram shows how a laser works. Inside the laser is a tube filled with a chemical. Energy is supplied to this chemical which makes it produce light. Some of this light bounces backward and forward between the two mirrors. But some shines through the hole and emerges as a beam of laser light.

△ Sometimes laser light is used for entertainment. This spectacular laser show is produced by beams of laser light. Laser light can travel long distances without fading.

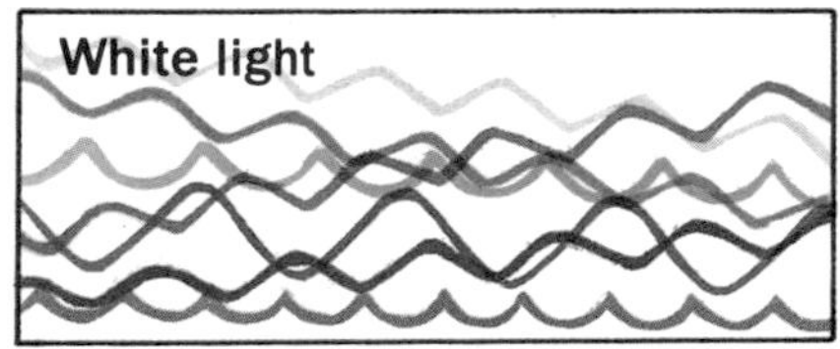

Many wavelengths out of step

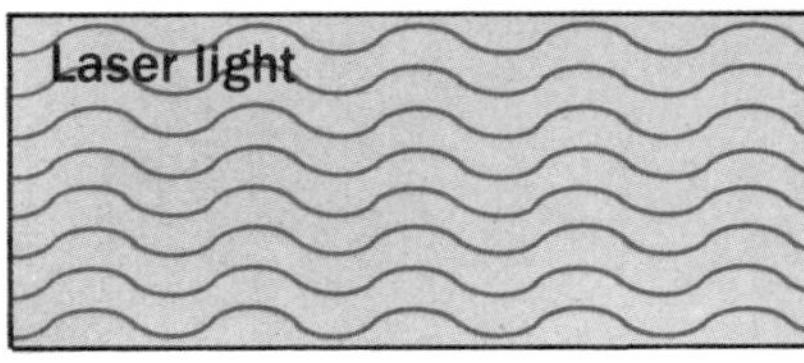

Single wavelengths in step

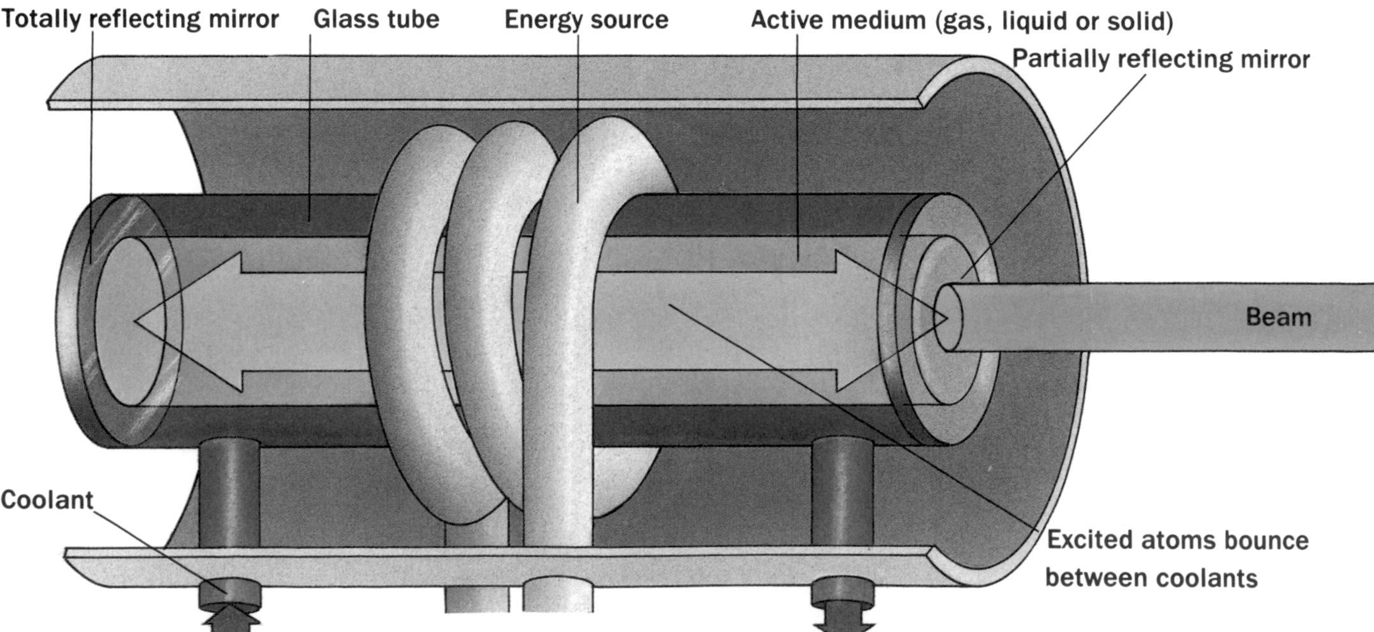

LASER SURGERY

Precision lasers are used by surgeons. Laser beams make excellent "knives." They are sterile and seal up small blood vessels as they cut, reducing bleeding. Their most common use is in eye surgery. If the retina becomes separated from the back of the eye, a laser beam can weld it back into place without the need to cut open the eye. Lasers are also used to remove stomach ulcers. The laser is directed into the body through a tube which the patient swallows. Outside the body lasers are used to treat skin growths and remove tatoos. Dentists may also use lasers instead of a drill to remove decay from teeth.

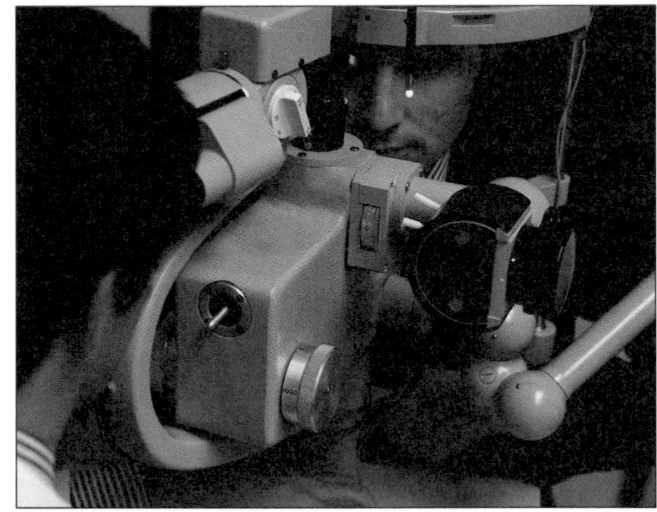

△ A laser can be directed into the eye in order to repair the retina.

▽ A hologram can appear as a 3-D image and can be very realistic.

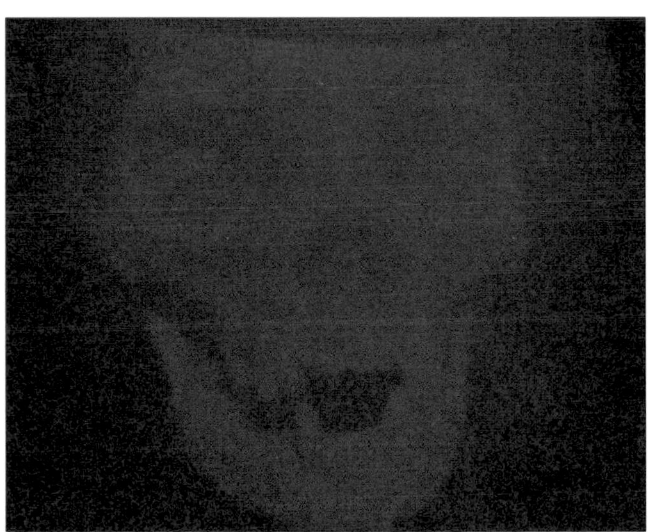

HOLOGRAMS

A hologram is a type of photograph which is made with a laser. Unlike ordinary photographs holograms are three dimensional. They look solid and real and even appear different from different angles – just like a real object. The reason holograms look so real is that they are accurate recordings of the light reflected from an object. Many uses are being found for holograms. They are very difficult to forge and so are being used on credit cards.

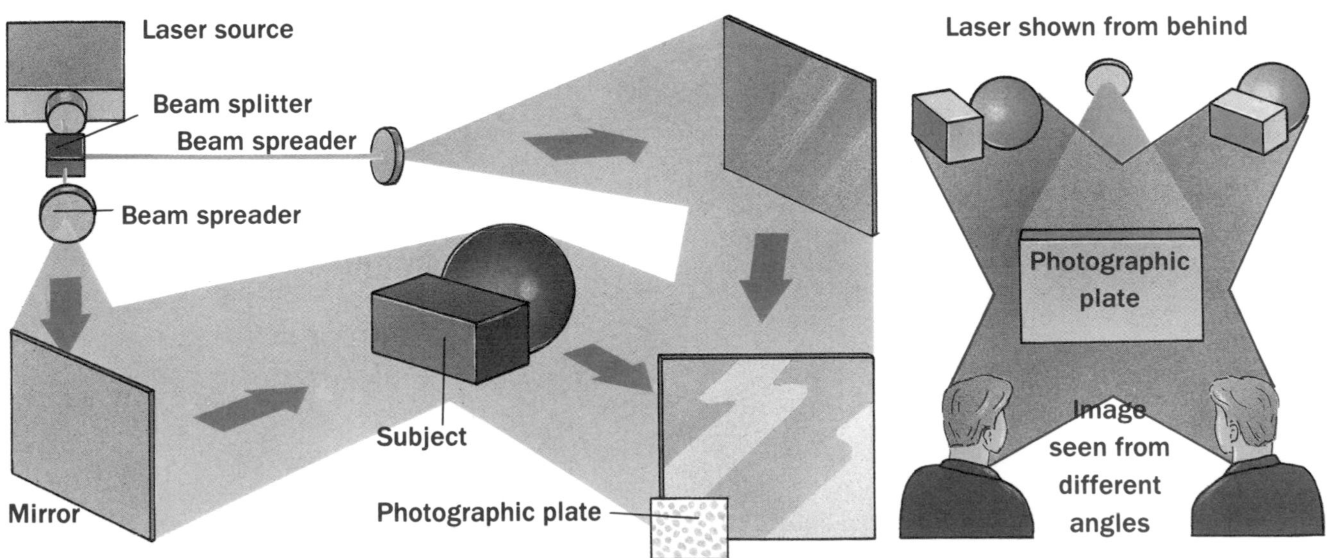

Things have to move to make sounds. Banging and scraping noises occur when things strike each other or rub together. A strong wind whistles through trees and howls around buildings. Moving parts inside machines make sounds. The sounds themselves move too, rushing through the air at high speed.

SHAKING WITH SOUND

Really loud noises can make things shake. Also, shaking causes sounds. Clapping your hands together disturbs the air around your hands so that this air shakes, or vibrates. The vibrations spread out through the air and reach your ears, and you hear the sound.

Most things that vibrate give out sounds. Striking a bell, for example, makes the whole bell vibrate. The vibration causes the air around the bell to vibrate too, and the sound of the bell spreads out in all directions. The sound dies away as the vibration comes to a stop. Musical instruments are vibrating when they produce musical notes.

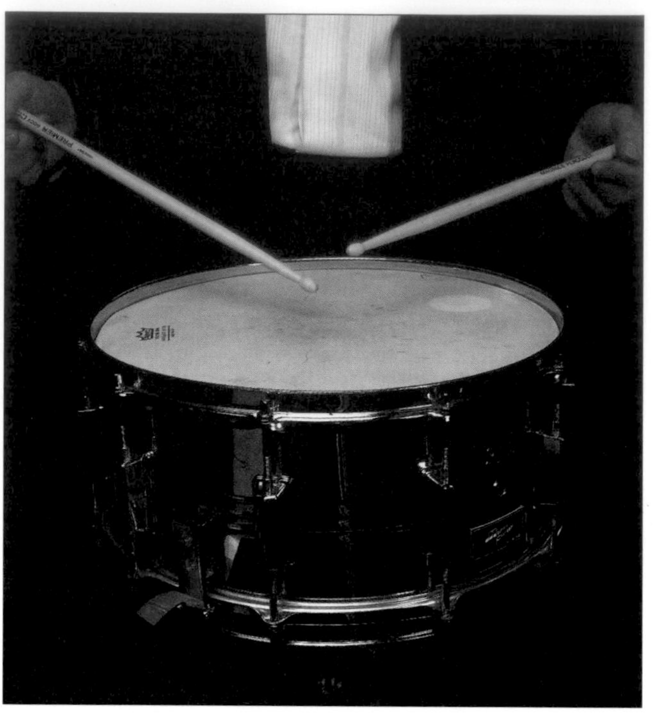

△ A drummer makes the skin on a drum vibrate when he strikes it with a stick. The skin vibrates and gives out sound.

THE SPEED OF SOUND

When you listen to people talking, you hear their voices as soon as they move their lips. The sound seems to travel instantly from their mouths to your ears. In fact, the sound takes a short time to reach you – about one hundredth of a second from a person across a room. This time is so short that you do not notice it.

The speed of sound in air is about 1,000 feet per second. This is about a million times slower than the speed of light. You can therefore see things happen some distance away before you hear them – like a flash of lightning and the thunder it makes. Count the seconds between the flash and the thunder. Divide by five, and this is the distance of the flash in miles.

△ The sound of thunder takes some time to travel through the air and reach you after a flash of lightning.

SPEAKING AND SINGING

Lightly touch your "voice box" while you are talking. You will be able to feel your throat vibrating. This is because you have two bands called vocal cords inside your throat. When you speak, the vocal cords vibrate and make the air in your throat and mouth vibrate, and out comes the sound of your voice.

You have to breathe out and push air through your vocal cords to make a sound. Open your mouth and make a sound without moving your mouth: this is the sound of your vocal cords. When you speak, you use muscles in your throat to control the cords, and you move your mouth and lips to vary the sound. You get different notes in singing by changing the spacing between your vocal cords.

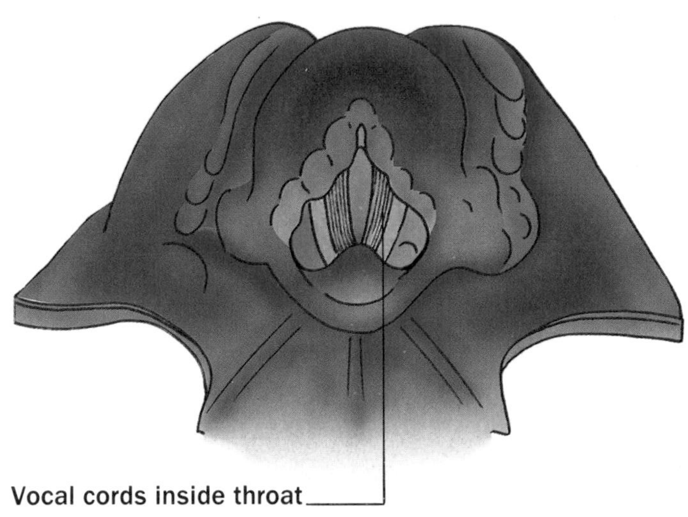

▷ We make sounds as soon as we are born. But it takes a while to learn how to make sounds that others can understand.

BALLOON NOISES

Blow up a balloon and stretch the neck sideways between your fingers. It makes a sound because escaping air causes the neck to vibrate. Pull hard to close the gap and a higher note is produced. Then loosen the neck to open the gap, and the note that comes out is lower. Your vocal cords make sounds in a similar way to the air vibrating in the neck of the balloon.

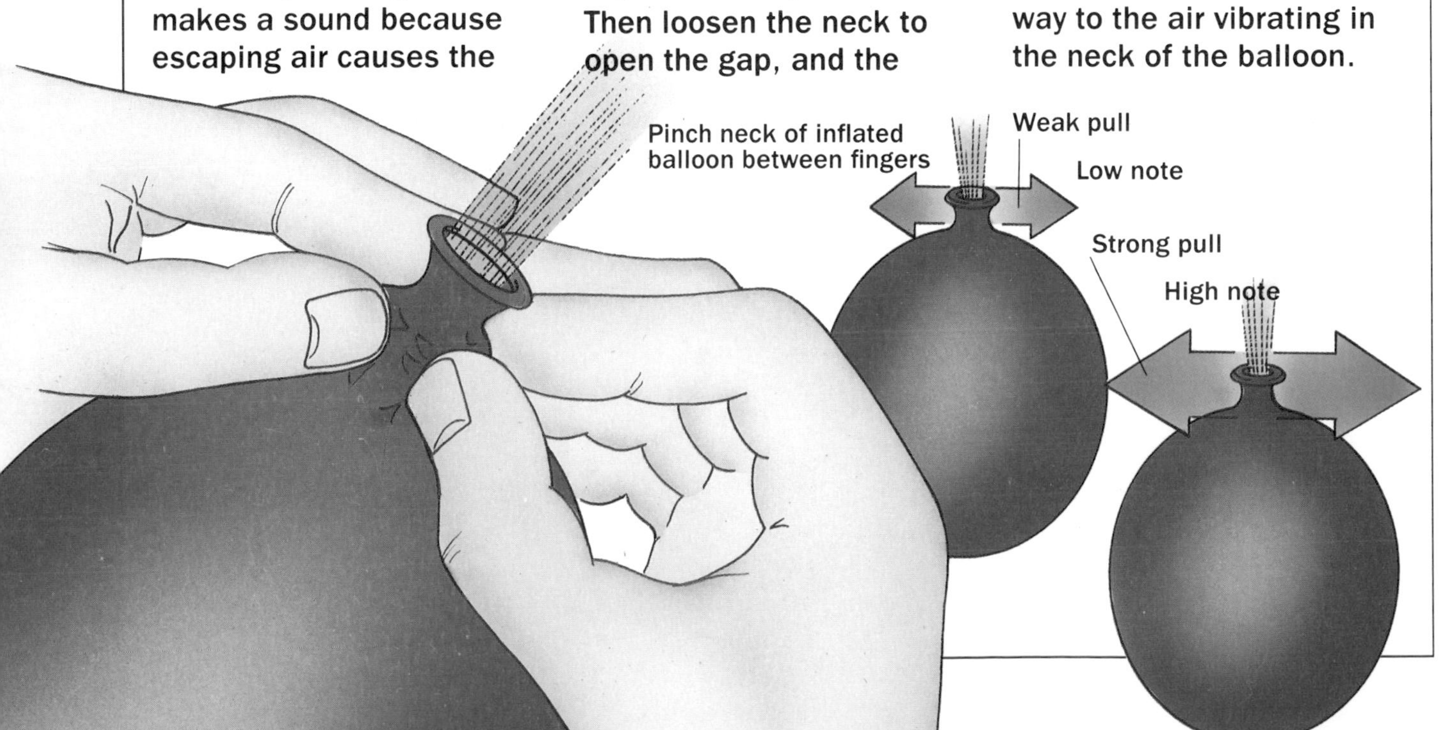

WAVES IN THE AIR

Sound travels through the air in waves. These are not like water waves, in which the water level goes alternately high and low. A sound wave consists of alternate regions of high-pressure air and low-pressure air moving through the air. A vibrating surface pushes the air to produce the pressure changes.

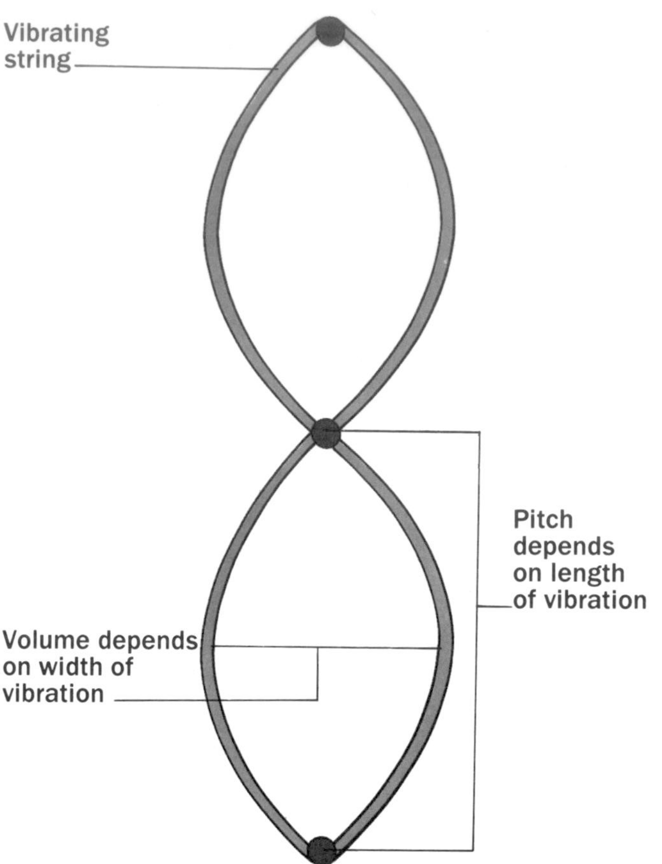

LOUD AND SOFT

When you shout to make a loud sound, you have to use a lot of effort. Being quiet and making little sound involves using little effort. The loudness or softness of a sound is called its volume. A loud sound has a high volume, and a soft sound has a low volume.

An object, such as the string on a guitar, must vibrate strongly to make a loud sound, which is why it takes more effort to vibrate it. The size of the pressure changes in the sound, or the amplitude of the sound, is greater than with a soft sound. The amplitude depends on the distance that the sound-making object moves as it vibrates.

▽ The strings inside a piano have different lengths. Short strings give high or treble notes, whereas long strings give low or bass notes.

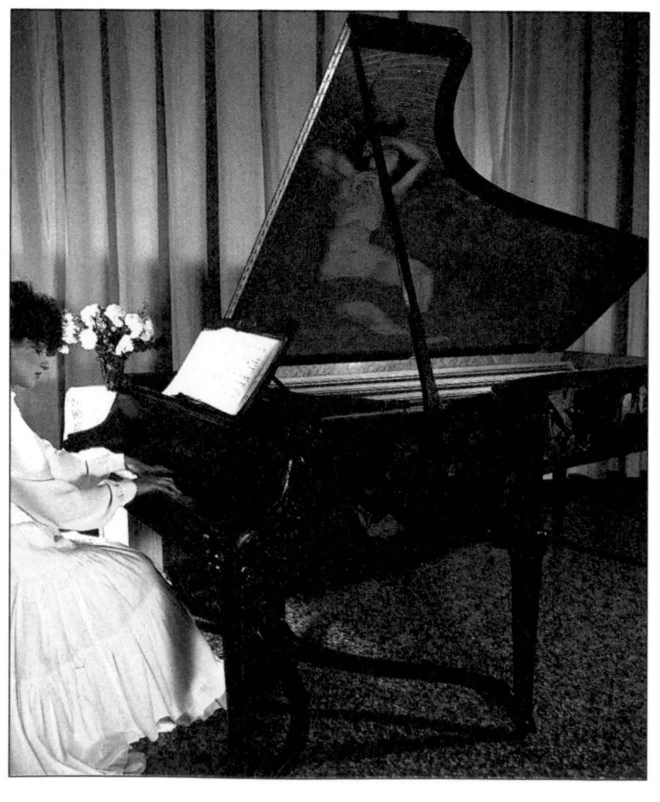

HIGH AND LOW

Human voices and most musical instruments do not only sound loud or soft. They also produce high or low notes. These notes differ in pitch. Women and young children have high voices, whereas most men have low voices.

The pitch of a sound depends on how often the pressure of the air changes. This in turn depends on how often the object producing the sound vibrates. A string that vibrates quickly gives a high note, whereas slow vibration gives a low note. The rate of vibration is called the frequency of the sound. The wavelength of the sound, which is the distance between the pressure peaks, also varies with pitch. A high sound has a shorter wavelength than a low sound.

NOTES FROM A RULER

Hold a ruler over the edge of a table and twang it to make it vibrate. Hear how using more effort makes the ruler vibrate more widely, and gives a louder sound. Move the ruler to lengthen or shorten the vibrating part. The vibration gets faster and the pitch rises as the vibrating part gets shorter.

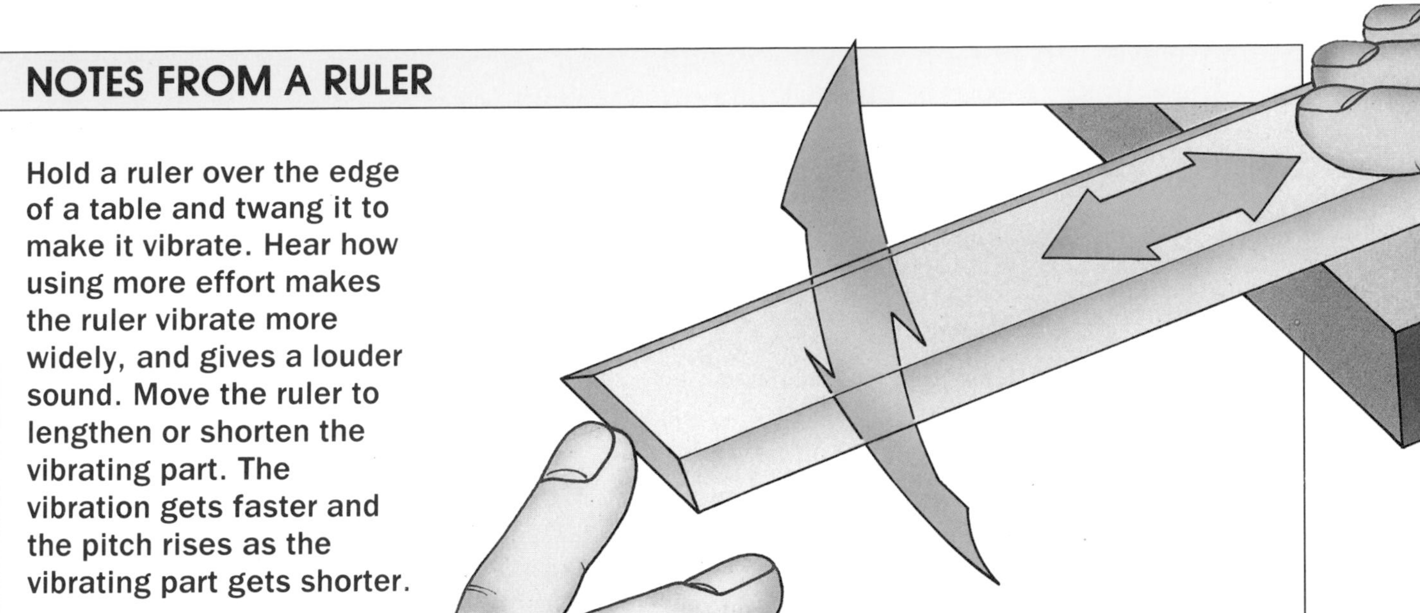

MEASURING SOUND

Loud sounds, like the roar of traffic or aircraft, can be a nuisance. They can also be dangerous. Very loud sounds can damage hearing and cause deafness. A special meter measures the loudness of sounds in units called decibels. The softest sound that a person with normal hearing can detect has a level of about 1 decibel. Sounds of 120 decibels or more can be painful.

People who work with noisy machines may have to protect their ears, because listening to loud sounds can harm their hearing. Listening to tape players with earphones can also cause damage if the volume control is set too high.

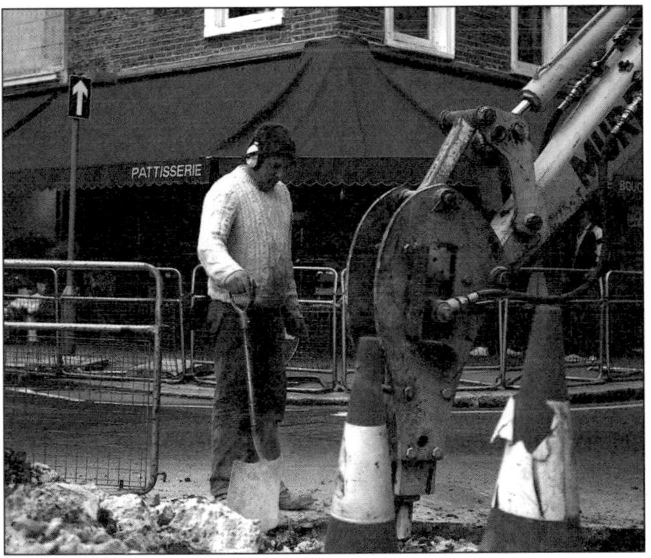

△ This workman is wearing ear muffs to protect his hearing from the loud noise of the machine.

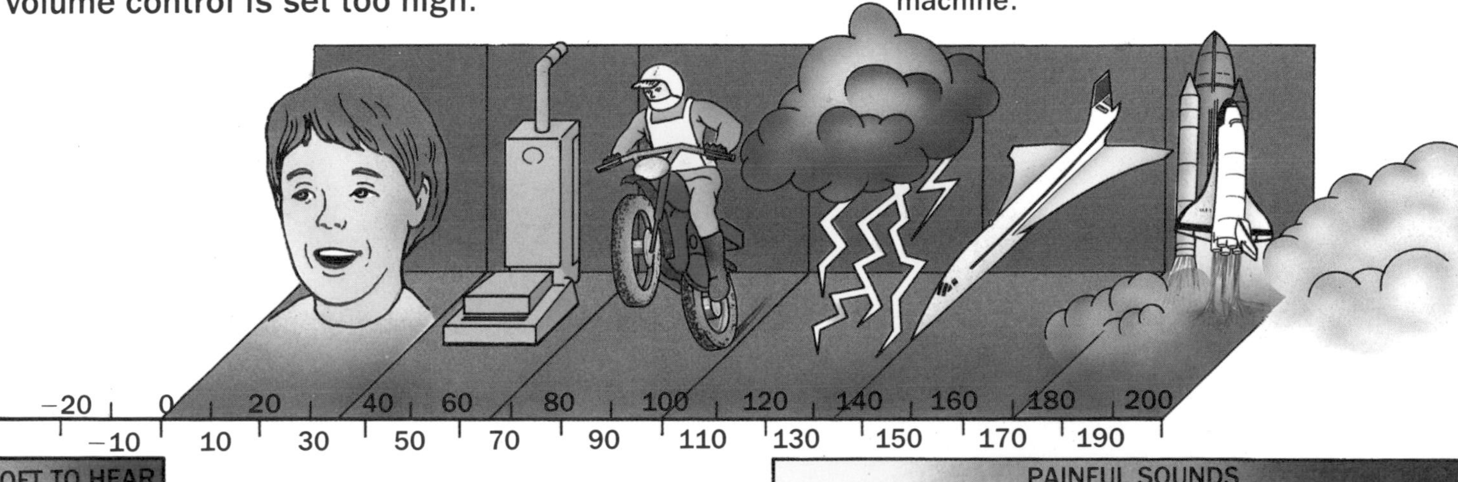

SOUNDS ON THE MOVE

Sound waves do not only travel through air. They pass through other kinds of materials. Water and hard materials can transmit sound. Sounds can penetrate walls and windows, and enter a building from outside. But some materials soak up sound, and it is possible to make a room soundproof.

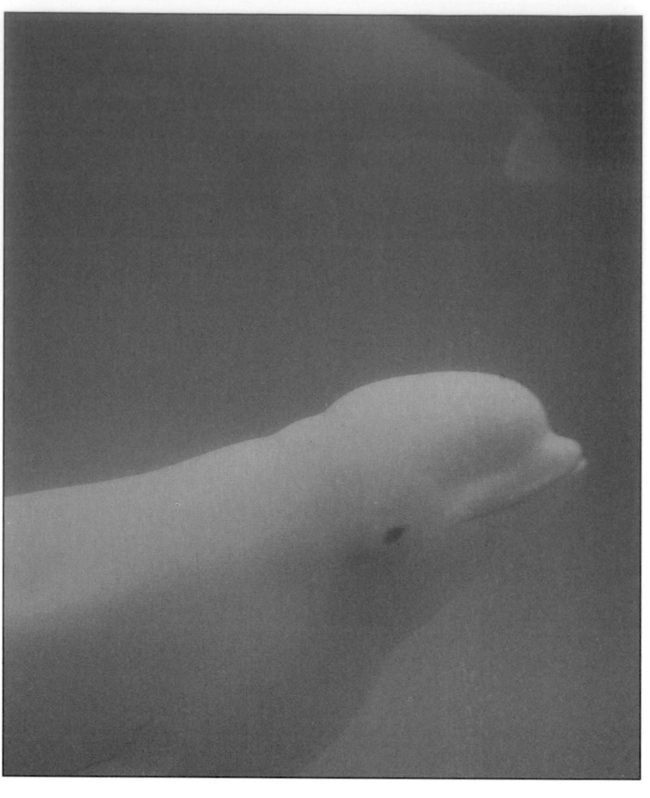

△ Sounds travel long distances through water. Dolphins are able to communicate with each other in the sea by using sound when they are far apart.

PIERCING SOUNDS

All things are made of many tiny particles called molecules. When sound waves pass through a material, they make the molecules vibrate. As the molecules move together, there is a region of high pressure. They then move apart, and a region of low pressure follows.

The molecules are close together in hard materials like steel and in liquids like water. Sound travels more quickly through these materials than through air, and it travels farther too. This is why sounds come through glass windows and brick or stone walls to enter buildings.

SONIC BOOM

Supersonic aircraft such as the Concorde can fly faster than the speed of sound. However, these aircraft may make a loud bang called a sonic boom as they pass overhead at supersonic speed.

Air moves out of the way as an aircraft passes, causing pressure changes that form sound waves traveling at the speed of sound. When the aircraft moves at the speed of sound or faster, a very sudden increase in air pressure occurs. This strong pressure then moves out and is heard as a boom when it reaches the ground. The boom may cause damage, so supersonic aircraft usually fly slower than the speed of sound over land.

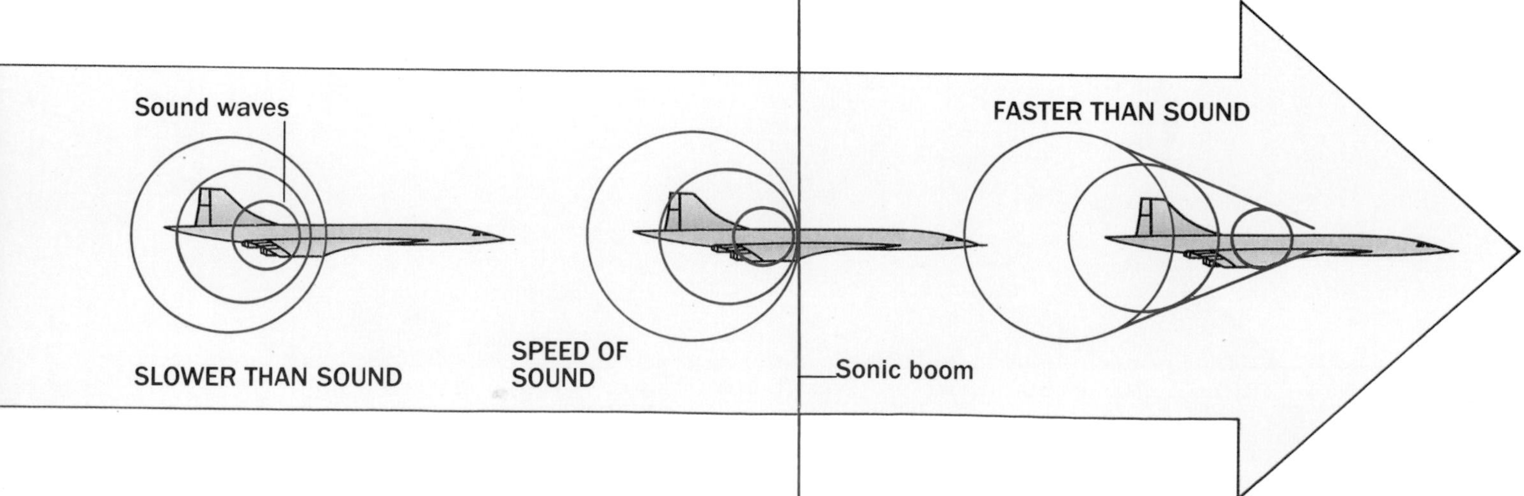

STOPPING SOUND

Soft materials soak up sound because their molecules do not easily cause each other to vibrate when sound waves strike them. Recording studios have walls that contain soft materials to prevent outside noises from getting in.

Windows containing two panes of glass – called double glazing – cut down sounds. This is because sound does not travel through the air gap between the panes as easily as it does through glass. Mufflers on cars cut out the sound of the engine. They contain materials that soak up sound, or a series of plates called baffles, that block the sound.

SILENT WORLD

The astronauts who went to the moon could not talk to each other in the usual way – they had to use radios. This is because the moon has no air. There are no molecules to transmit sound from one place to another, and so everything that happens on the moon happens in total silence. The only way to make sound travel directly from one astronaut to another would be for them to touch helmets. Sound waves could then travel through the material of the helmets.

No sound travels

Sound travels

▽ This room is lined with materials that soak up sounds, and it is totally silent inside. It is used for testing the noise levels produced by the engines of new cars.

▷ There is no sound in space because space is totally empty. Astronauts outside a spacecraft use radio to talk to the crew of the spacecraft.

QUIZ

Tap your teeth very gently with a pencil. Why are the sounds so loud? The sound waves travel through your head to your ears without going through the air.

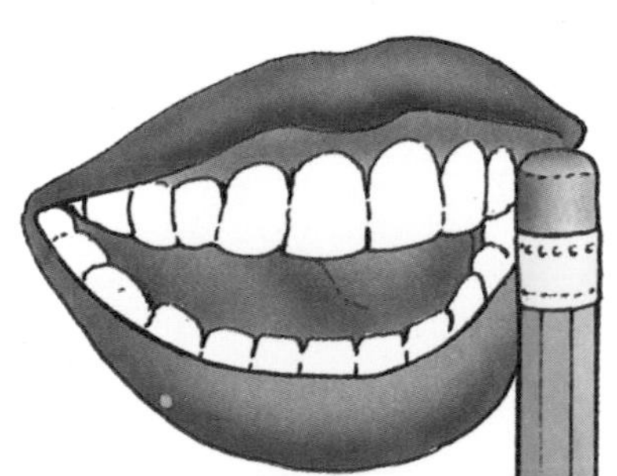

BOUNCING SOUNDS

Sound waves moving through air may strike a surface, like the wall of a room. The waves bounce off a hard surface and move back into the air. Soft surfaces like curtains soak up many of the sound waves and the sound does not return. The way in which sounds bounce before they reach us can change their quality.

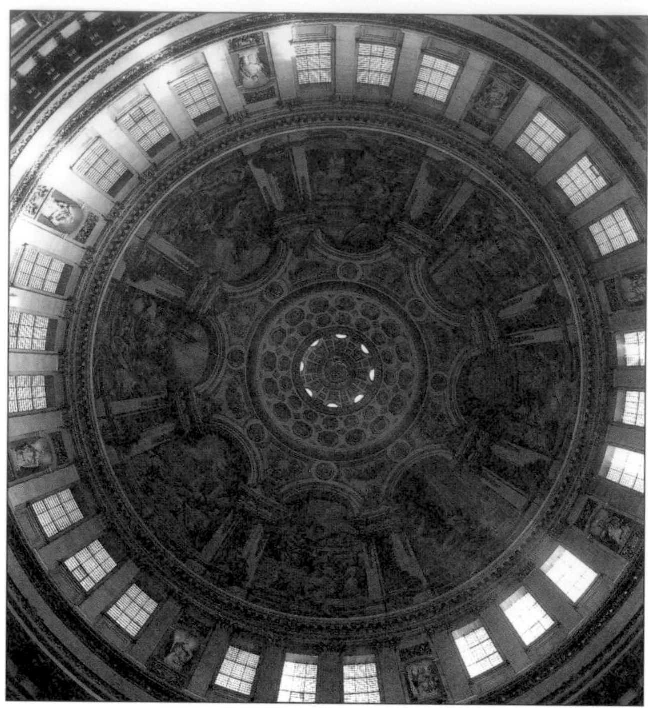

△ Sound bounces around the Whispering Gallery at St. Paul's Cathedral, London.

ECHOES

If you stand in front of a high wall or cliff and shout, the sound of your voice may come back to you slightly later. This is an echo. The sound waves travel from your mouth to the wall or cliff, bounce off it and return to your ears. You may hear lots of echoes in large places like gymnasiums and under wide domes. The sound waves bounce around several times. The echoes lengthen the original sound so that it takes time to die away.

GOOD LISTENING

When you listen to music in a concert hall, you hear sounds bouncing from the walls and ceiling, as well as the sounds coming from the stage. All these sounds mix together to give the music a good quality of sound. The shape of the hall and the materials on its walls and ceiling greatly affect the quality of the sound. Builders of halls have to study acoustics, which is the science of sound.

▽ The interior of a concert hall is designed to produce a good sound for the audience.

CAPTIVE SOUNDS

If you are ill, the doctor may want to listen to the sounds inside your body, such as the beating of your heart. The sounds are very soft, but the doctor can hear them with a stethoscope. This instrument has a long tube with a small, flat funnel at one end and earpieces at the other.

The doctor puts the funnel on your body. The sounds enter the funnel, which feeds them into the tube. They travel up the tube, bouncing from one side to the other. The stethoscope captures the sounds coming from the body and sends them directly to the doctor's ears. The sounds do not spread out as they would in the open air, and this makes them loud enough to hear.

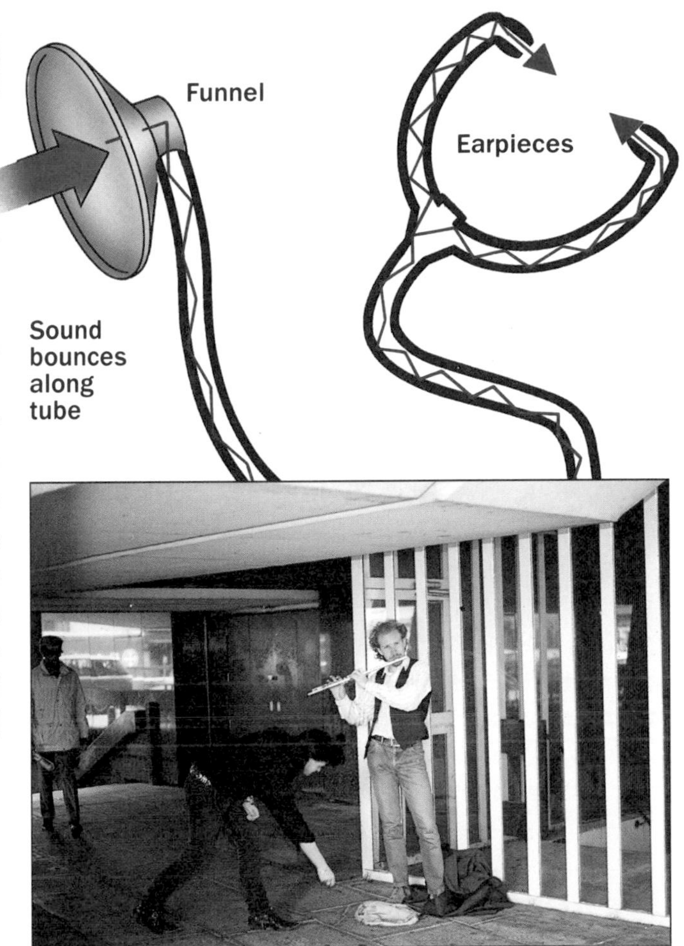

▷ Music played inside subway stations can bounce along the sides of passageways. This makes the sound louder than it would be outside.

TICKING TUBE

Two people take a long cardboard tube each and point it toward a wall. Each tube should be at the same angle to the wall. One person places a ticking watch at the end of one tube. The other person listens at the end of the other tube, and should be able to hear the watch ticking. Without the tubes, the watch cannot be heard.

The sound waves from the watch travel along one tube, then bounce off the wall and enter the second tube to reach the ear of the listener.

TOO HIGH TO HEAR

Strange as it may seem, there are lots of sounds that we cannot hear. This is not because our hearing is imperfect in any way. The sounds are too high in pitch for our ears to detect, although some animals can hear them. This kind of sound is called ultrasonic sound or ultrasound. It can be used for many purposes.

SOUND NAVIGATION

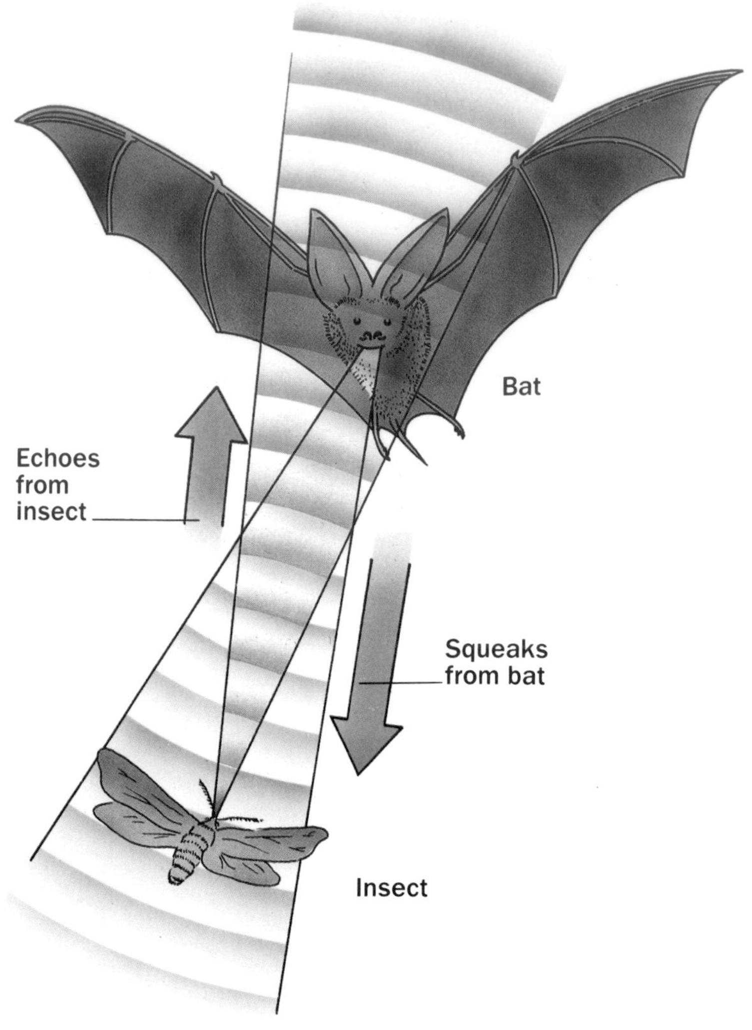

Several animals use sound, rather than sight, to find their way and to get their food. Bats sleep by day and feed by night. They fly around in total darkness, avoiding obstacles and eating insects. A bat emits squeaks of high-pitched sound, too high for people to hear. The sound waves bounce off obstacles and insects and return to the bat's large and sensitive ears. The bat is able to determine the distance and direction of obstacles and insects from the echoes it hears. This is called echo location, and high sounds work better than low sounds. Other animals, such as some whales and dolphins in the sea, also use echo location to find food and to navigate.

▽ A sonar screen displays a picture of the water beneath the ship. Shoals of fish can be detected by sonar.

SONAR

Ships use beams of ultrasound to measure the depth of water, to chart the seabed and to find shoals of fish. The system is called sonar, which stands for Sound Navigation and Ranging. A transmitter under the ship's hull sends out regular pulses of sound. These bounce off the seabed or shoals of fish and return to the ship. A detector picks up these echoes, and turns them into a picture on a television screen.

The time it takes for the echoes to return depends on the depth of the seabed or fish. Sonar measures this time and shows how deep things are. It can even show the outlines of objects such as submarines or wrecks on the seabed.

FIRST PICTURE

One of the most important uses of sound is the ultrasound scanner. This instrument is able to show a picture of an unborn baby inside its mother. Doctors can use the scanner to check that all is well with the baby before it is born.

The scanner works in the same way as sonar. A transmitter sends a beam of ultrasound into the mother's body. A detector then picks up echoes that come back from the baby. The beam scans the baby and builds up its picture on a screen. It seems that ultrasound scans are harmless to both mother and baby.

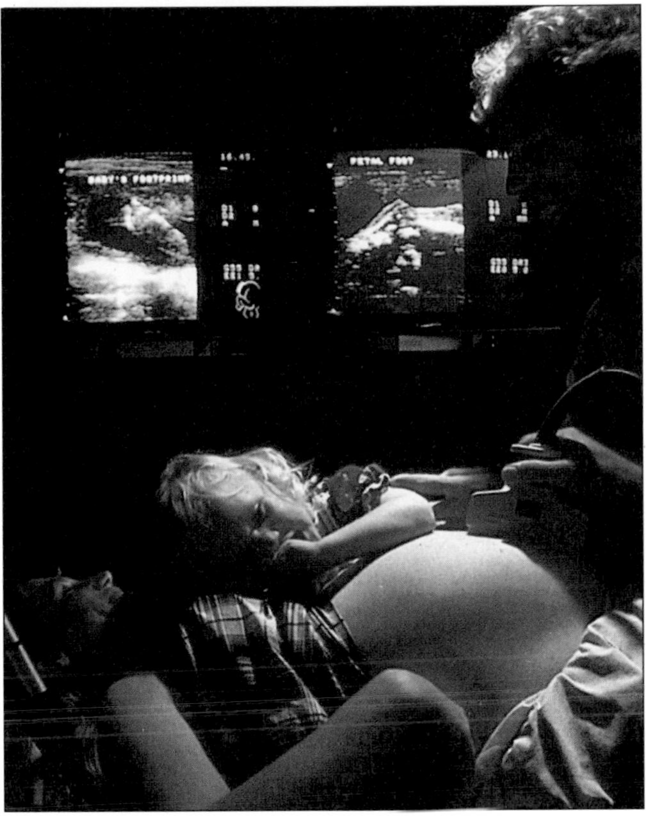

▷ The pictures of an unborn baby made with an ultrasound scanner show parts inside the baby's body as well as the whole baby.

SOUND AT WORK

Industry also makes good use of ultrasound. Detectors can check metal parts for internal faults such as cracks. A beam of ultrasound bounces off any faults in the metal and can reveal that the part may be about to break.

Ultrasound waves vibrate very fast – over 20,000 vibrations per second. Powerful beams of ultrasound can make materials vibrate so much that they heat up. Ultrasonic welding machines are used to weld plastic parts together.

▽ Ultrasonic detectors can test the metal of an aircraft to check for any cracks.

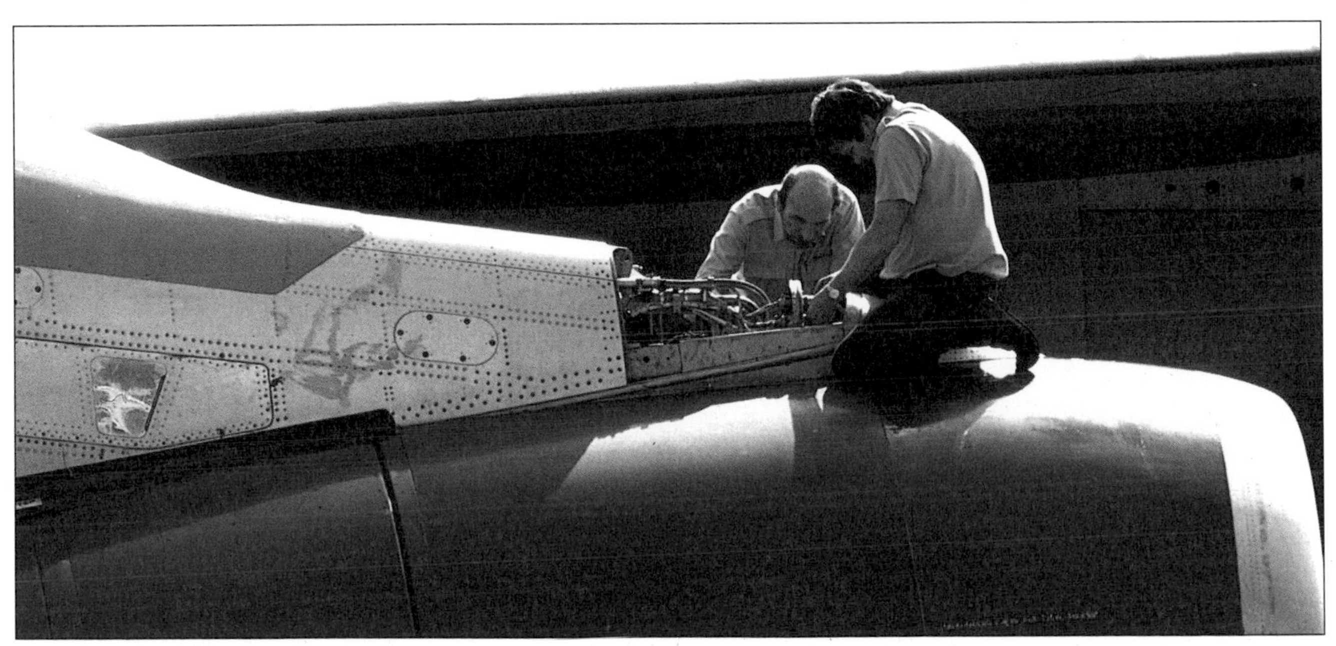

Our voices and musical instruments are not very loud. Speakers who have to address a large crowd need to shout. Singers and musicians cannot sing or play loudly enough to entertain the huge audiences that want to hear them. These people, therefore, often use sound systems to boost their voices and music.

△ Bands that perform at big concerts and festivals have powerful sound systems which make their music very loud.

SOUND SYSTEMS

A sound system uses the power of electricity to make sounds louder. It works by first turning the sound waves into an electrical signal. The strength of this signal is then increased, or amplified, and the stronger signal is then turned back into sound waves. The sound waves are now much louder.

A microphone turns sound into an electrical signal, and an amplifier strengthens the signal. A loudspeaker turns the signal back into sound.

ELECTRIC EARS

Singers and performers sing and play into microphones, which are like electric "ears." Inside each microphone is a diaphragm that vibrates as the sound waves strike it. The diaphragm is linked to a detector. This turns the vibration into an electrical signal that varies in strength at the same rate as the vibration of the sound waves.

There are several different kinds of detectors. One kind contains a small coil of wire suspended inside a magnet. As the sound enters the microphone, the coil moves back and forth in the magnet's field. This causes the coil to generate an electrical signal. A cable carries the signal to the sound system.

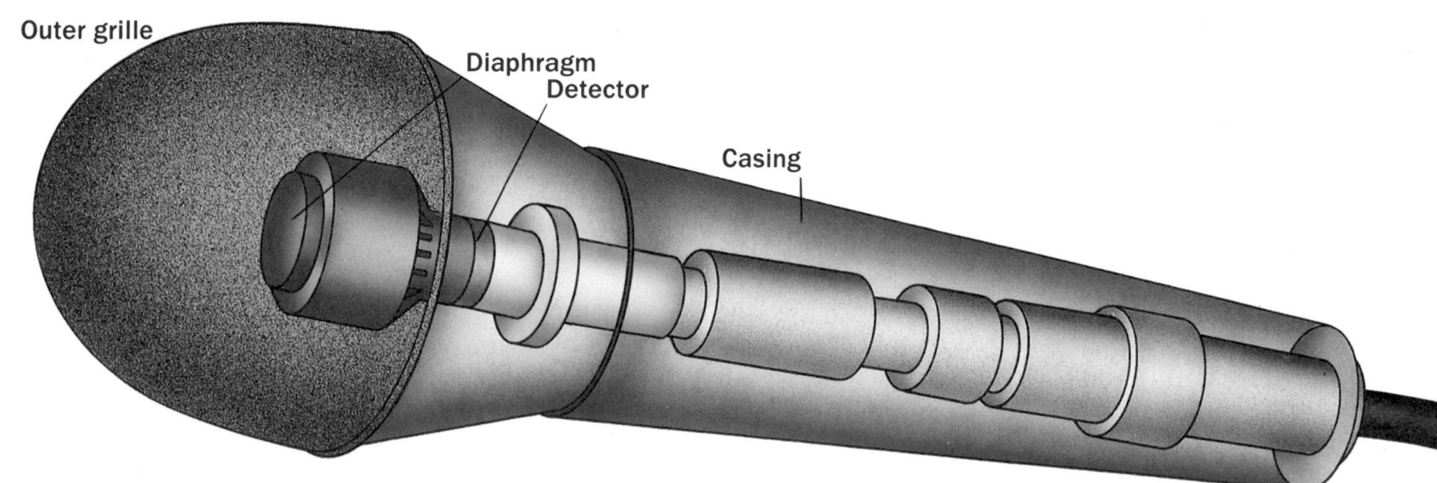

STRENGTHENING THE SIGNALS

Microphones are often connected to a mixer in a sound system. This combines the electrical signals from microphones. An engineer uses the mixer to set the final volume levels of all the sounds.

The signals from the mixer go to the amplifier, or a microphone may connect directly to the amplifier. The signals from the mixer or microphone are quite weak and go to transistors or electric valves in the amplifier. These use the weak signals to control a stronger current in the amplifier. They make the current vary at the same rate as the signals, which is the rate of vibration in the original sound. The current is turned into strong signals.

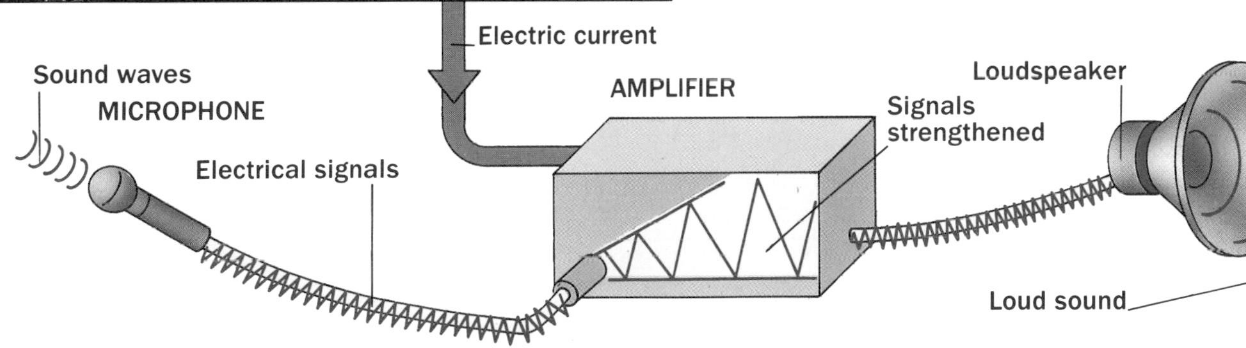

SOUND PRODUCERS

Strong signals from the amplifier go to two sets of loudspeakers placed, if it is a rock concert, on each side of the stage. The loudspeakers turn the signals back into sounds. A simple system may have just one loudspeaker.

A loudspeaker contains a moving coil and magnet like those in a moving-coil microphone, but much larger. The varying signal goes to the coil, making it vibrate. The coil is connected to a cone, which also vibrates. This vibration has the same rate as the original sound, but is much stronger. Out comes the sound at high volume. A set of loudspeakers has loudspeakers with cones of different sizes for high, mid-range, and low sounds.

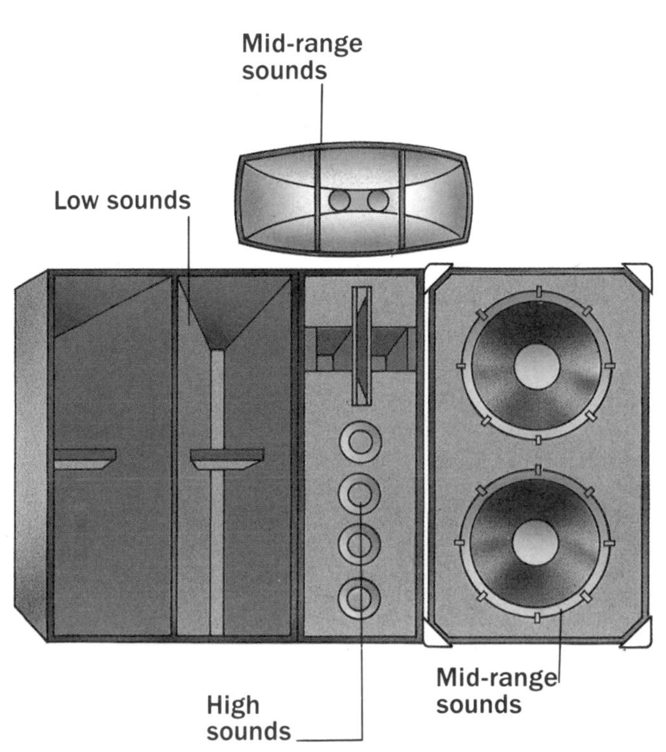

Many of the musical instruments that people play are electric instruments. These include the electric guitar and synthesizer. An electric instrument itself makes little or no actual sound when it is played. Instead, it produces an electric signal, which goes to an amplifier and loudspeaker to give the sound.

WIRING THE GUITAR

The electric guitar and the bass guitar, which is a kind of electric guitar, both have strings and are played like an acoustic (nonelectric) guitar. Beneath the strings, which are made of metal, are one or more pickups. The pickup produces an electric signal that varies at the same rate as the strings vibrate. It contains a coil of wire wound around a magnet or set of magnets. The vibrating string makes the magnetic field vary, which generates a varying electric signal in the coil. The signal goes along a wire to an amplifier and loudspeaker, and out comes the sound. Controls can change the volume and tone of the sound.

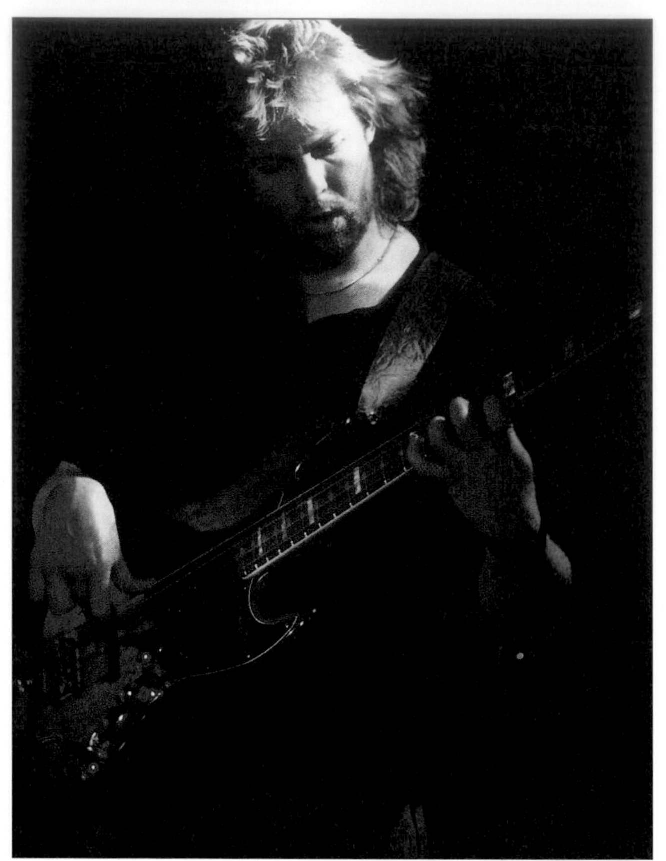

△ The electric guitar was invented to make the guitar louder. However, the instrument now has a sound all of its own.

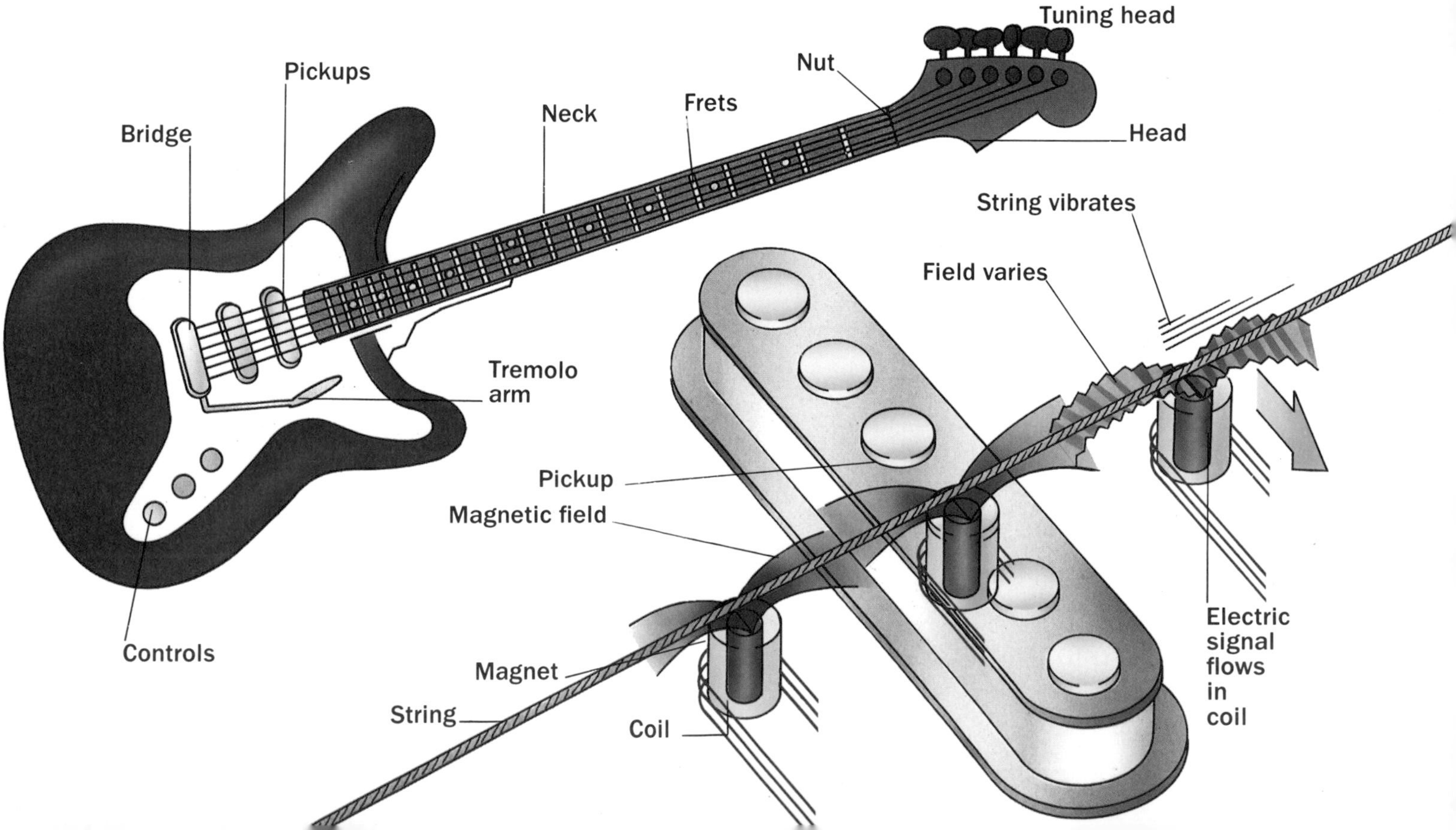

Tuning head
Pickups
Nut
Bridge
Neck
Frets
Head
String vibrates
Field varies
Tremolo arm
Pickup
Magnetic field
Controls
Magnet
String
Coil
Electric signal flows in coil

MUSIC MACHINES

Most synthesizers have keyboards and are played in a similar way to the piano or organ. Other synthesizers can be played like a guitar, wind instrument or drum. All contain electronic parts that generate an electric signal when the synthesizer is played. The signal goes to an amplifier and loudspeaker to produce a sound.

A synthesizer can produce many different sounds. These may be the sounds of musical instruments or totally new sounds. The controls on the synthesizer can change the kind of signal that is generated by the electronic components to get different sounds. A sound sampler is a similar kind of machine that can store any sound in the form of an electric signal and then use it.

▽ Although this synthesizer looks like an organ, it can sound like other kinds of instrument – or even an orchestra.

COMPUTER CONTROL

The kind of music made by synthesizers is sometimes called electronic music. A small computer can be included, connected to a synthesizer and sampler. The computer can store notes played on the synthesizer in the form of electric signals. It can then send the signals back to the synthesizer to produce the music. The computer is able to correct any mistakes that were made in the playing. A home computer and synthesizer can be connected to a stereo system to make electronic music.

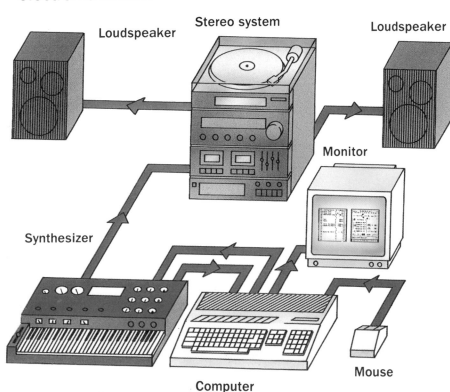

Loudspeaker
Stereo system
Loudspeaker
Monitor
Synthesizer
Mouse
Computer

QUIZ

How many musicians make the music that you hear in movies, on television, and radio? Often it is only one person using a computer and synthesizer to produce all the different sounds.

DISTANT SOUNDS

Sounds come into our homes from distant places when we listen to the radio. We can speak to people almost anywhere on the telephone. Electricity, radio waves or light rays carry the sounds. These travel so fast that the sounds reach us almost instantly, and we can talk with people as if they were next to us.

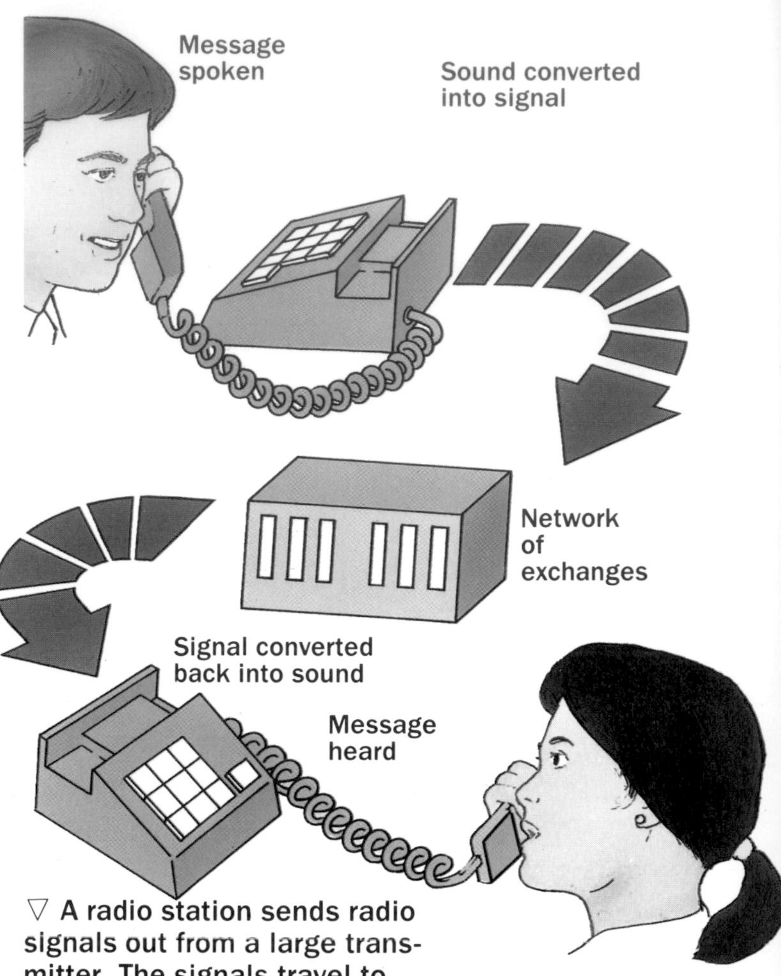

TALKING TO ALL

When someone calls you on the telephone, a microphone in their mouthpiece converts the sound of their voice into an electrical signal. This travels to the earpiece of your telephone, which contains a small loudspeaker to change the signal back into sound. The sound may travel along wires as a coded electrical signal, or it may be changed into a radio signal that moves through the air, or a light signal traveling along glass fibers. The signal is directed through telephone exchanges that connect the two telephones together.

▽ A radio station sends radio signals out from a large transmitter. The signals travel to receivers throughout a country.

TUNING IN

A radio receives sound in the form of signals from a radio station. Microphones at the station turn the voices or music into an electrical signal. This signal is then changed into radio waves that vary at the same rate as the vibration of the sound waves. There are two ways to vary the radio waves: AM (amplitude modulation) and FM (frequency modulation), meaning that either the amplitude or the frequency (and wavelength) of the radio waves varies. The radio receiver changes the radio signal into an electrical signal, which a loudspeaker changes into sound.

AM (amplitude modulation)

Amplitude

FM (frequency modulation)

Wavelength

Sound wave

SOUNDS ON THE MOVE

Radio enables people to contact each other when they are on the move. Vehicles such as taxis and police cars have receivers and transmitters so that drivers can talk to their headquarters. There are also radios called walkie-talkies that people can carry. CB (Citizens' Band) radio is used by drivers to talk to each other over short distances.

Many people have cellular telephones that they can use wherever they are. These work by radio, which links the telephone to satellites that are part of the telephone network.

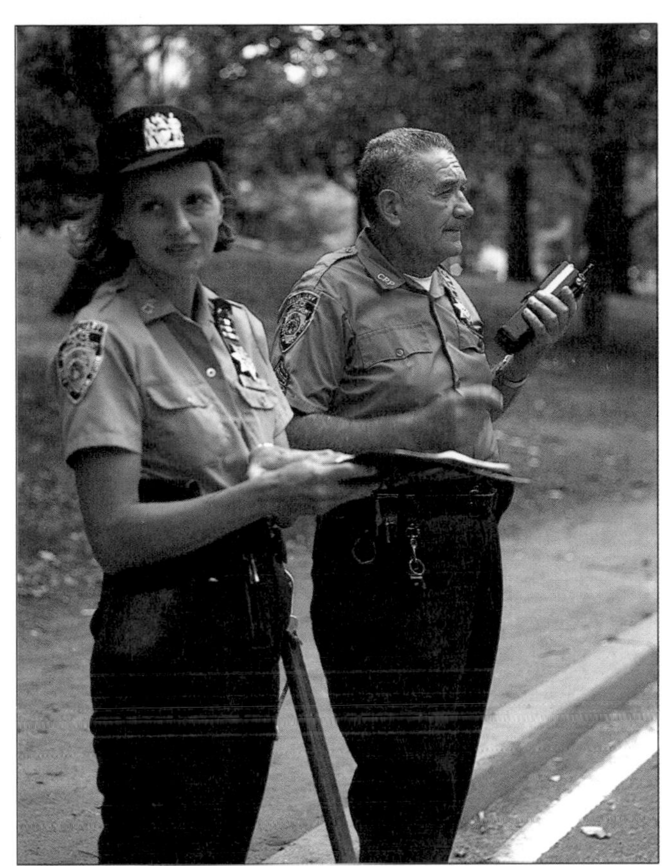

▷ A police officer uses a portable radio to talk to other officers or to his headquarters. He can quickly call for assistance and send or receive vital information.

SPARKING SOUNDS

Connect a metal part of a steel file near the handle to a battery with a wire. You can do this with sticky tape. Connect another wire to the other terminal of the battery, and scrape the loose end of this wire along the file. See how small sparks fly. Place a radio nearby, turn it on and notice how noises come from the radio as the sparks occur. This is because the sparks send out short bursts of radio waves that the set picks up and turns into sounds. You may need to turn up the volume of the radio to hear them.

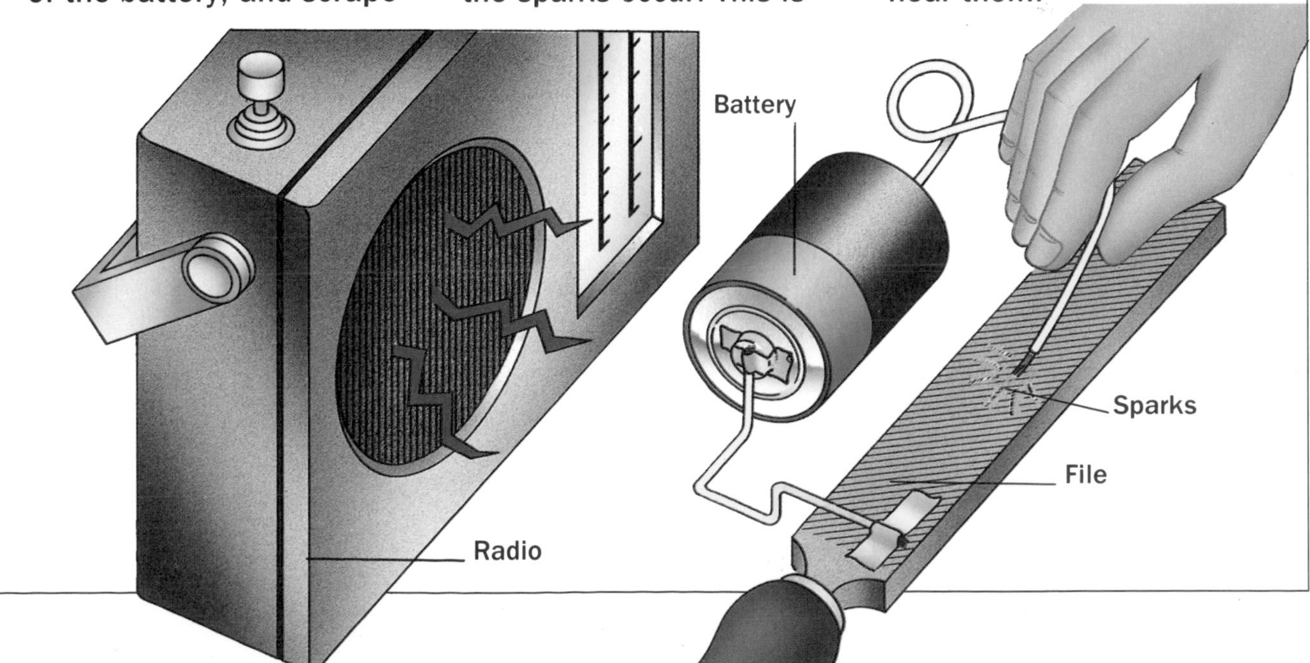

encyclopedia of science

ELECTRICITY AND MAGNETISM

CONTENTS

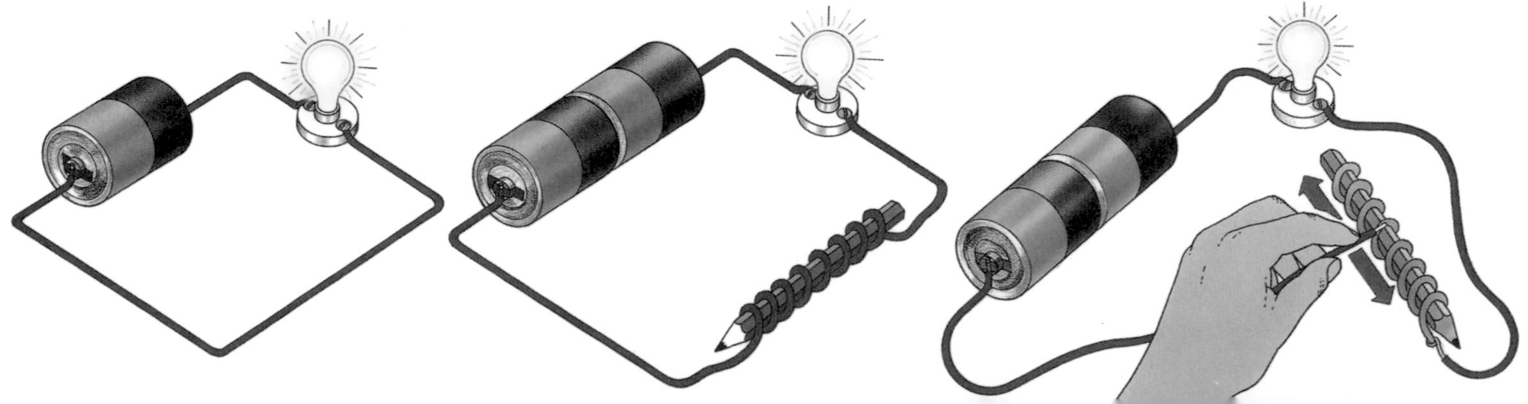

INTRODUCTION

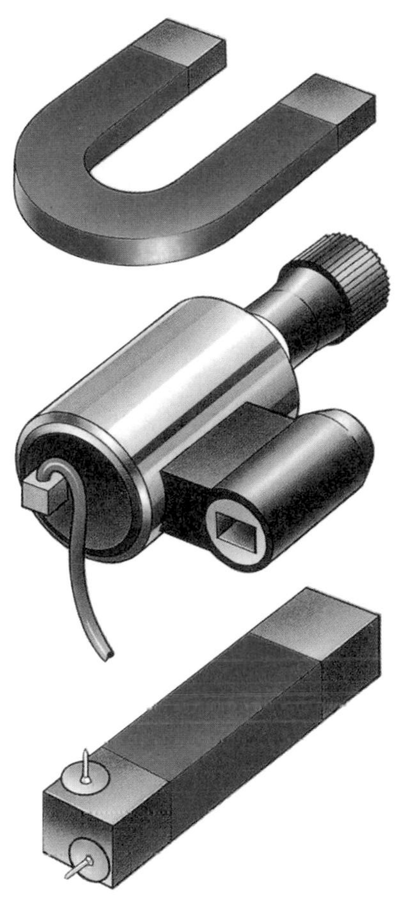

It is very difficult to imagine life without electricity. But electrical appliances have only become widespread during the last 70 years. And in many parts of the world electricity is still nonexistent or unreliable. In these parts, people have to rely on fire for heat, and light, and animals for transport.

Electricity occurs naturally – when lightning strikes there is a huge electric charge. In our bodies, electrical currents carry messages along nerves. But electricity can also be generated by large power stations, to supply homes and industries. Today we have developed sophisticated electrical equipment, such as a computer that will store X-rays, a compact disk that can record images, even a videophone.

Electrical energy can be turned into mechanical energy by using magnetism. The electromagnet is the basis of many items of electrical equipment. Magnets have many uses, from keeping a refrigerator door shut, to storing millions of numbers in a computer.

All things are made up of tiny particles. Some of these particles are electrically charged. This charge may be negative or positive. Electric current is a flow of negatively charged particles from one place to another. Sometimes you can see a flow of charge in the form of a spark. Lightning is a huge spark of electricity.

△ Lightning is extremely powerful. One flash can be seen from far away and can destroy trees, damage buildings and even kill people. The sound of thunder always follows the lightning flash.

HOW DOES LIGHTNING STRIKE?

Lightning occurs when there is a gigantic flow of negative charge — or electricity. A flash of lightning is caused by huge amounts of electric charge leaping from one cloud to another. The diagram shows how the charge moves and produces sparks. Electric charge builds up inside a cloud when small drops of water and ice hit against each other. The bottom of the cloud becomes negatively charged compared with the ground below. This negative charge leaps from the cloud to the highest point on the ground, such as a tree. The huge flow of charge heats the air and produces the noise of thunder.

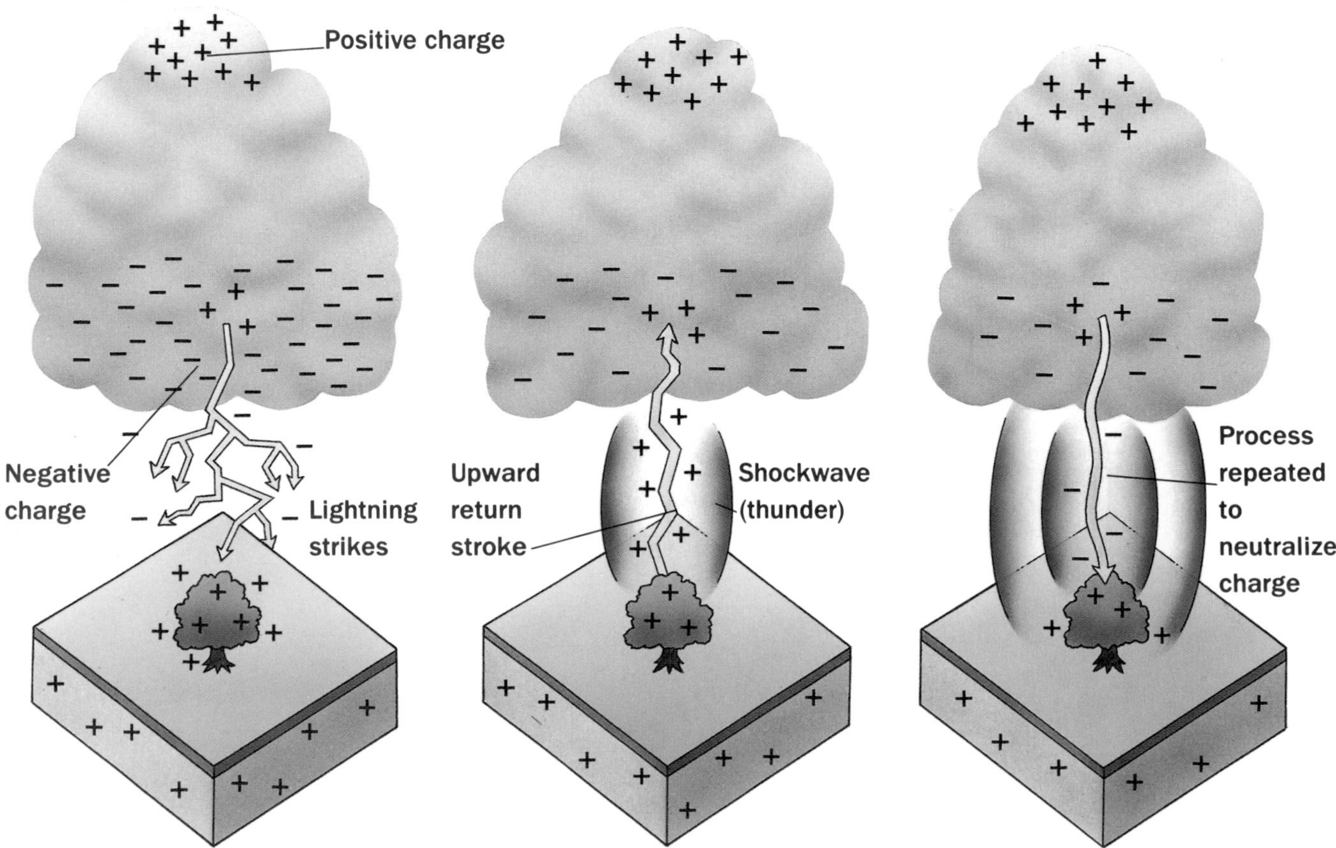

CHARGED CHIMNEYS

Industrial smokestacks often allow dirt and harmful chemicals into the atmosphere. This pollution can harm living things, including people, who need air to survive. Electric charges can be used to help cut down the amount of pollution which gets into the air. A layer of charged particles can be put on the inside of the smokestack. These charged particles pull particles of dirt (which are also charged) toward them and hold them inside. Like charges always repel each other – unlike charges attract each other.

△ The inside of this smokestack is charged to prevent too much dust and soot from getting into the air. If the smokestack is given a positive charge, then any dirt or soot with a negative charge will be attracted.

LOOKING AT CHARGE

Electric charge which moves is called an electric current. But there can also be a build-up of charge which doesn't move and this is called static electricity. You can cause static electricity to build up by rubbing materials together. Charge a blown up balloon by rubbing it on your sweater. The charged balloon will pull certain things towards it. It can "bend" a thin stream of water.

Balloon charged with static electricity can pick up small pieces of paper

Water "bends" towards charged balloon until it touches the balloon

QUIZ

This boy is taking off his sweater. But why is his hair standing on end? And what are these sparks around his head? Try to explain what is happening. Does the same happen to you when you take off your sweater?

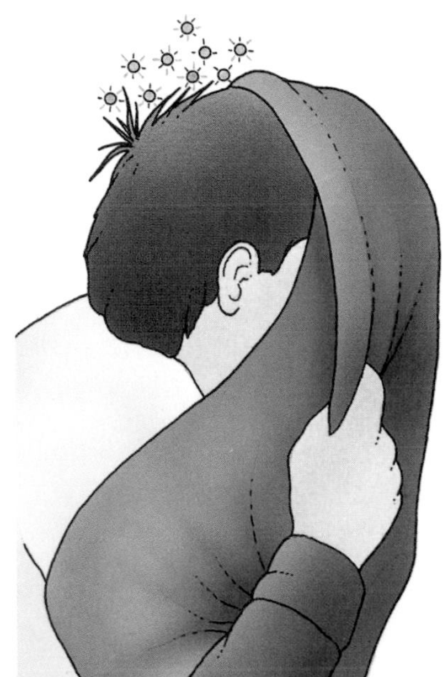

ELECTRICITY FROM CHEMICALS

Static electricity is not very useful for powering machines. Instead we use current electricity in homes and industries. An electric current is a *controlled* flow of electric charge. Batteries are convenient sources of current electricity that is produced from chemicals inside the battery.

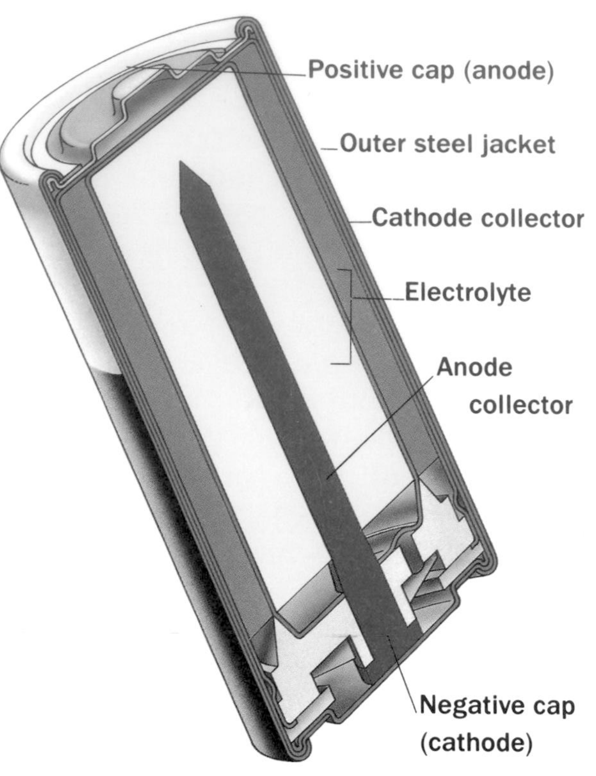

Negative charge flows from the negative end round the appliance and back to the positive end.

HOW IT WORKS

A battery can be used to make an electric current when one is needed. Inside a battery there are two metal parts which are each covered by a special chemical. When the battery is connected to an appliance the chemicals inside the battery react with each other to produce charged particles. The negative charges collect at one end of the battery while the positive charges collect at the other. A stream of negative charge then flows round the appliance and back to the battery. As long as this current continues to flow, the appliance will work.

USING BATTERIES

Flashlights, personal stereos and many other portable appliances need their own supply of current electricity. They get this supply from batteries. Batteries come in many different shapes and sizes depending on what they are needed for. Very small batteries are needed inside hearing aids and pocket calculators. Some batteries last for a long time before going "dead." The type of battery depends on the type of metals and chemicals inside it. The most common batteries use zinc and carbon but others use lithium, magnesium or lead. New types of battery are being developed.

▷ The photo shows some of the batteries now available. Batteries come in many different sizes – small enough to power a hearing aid, large enough to power a car.

RECHARGEABLE BATTERIES

When chemicals in a battery have been used up the battery is "dead" and no longer provides current electricity. Many batteries have to be thrown away at this stage. But others can be "recharged." This means that the chemical reaction which has taken place is reversed so the battery can be used again. Rechargeable batteries may last for a very long time and be recharged time and time again. Car batteries are rechargeable and it is possible to get small rechargeable flash-light batteries too. Some vehicles, such as wheelchairs, are completely powered by rechargeable batteries. Rechargeable batteries are less wasteful than others.

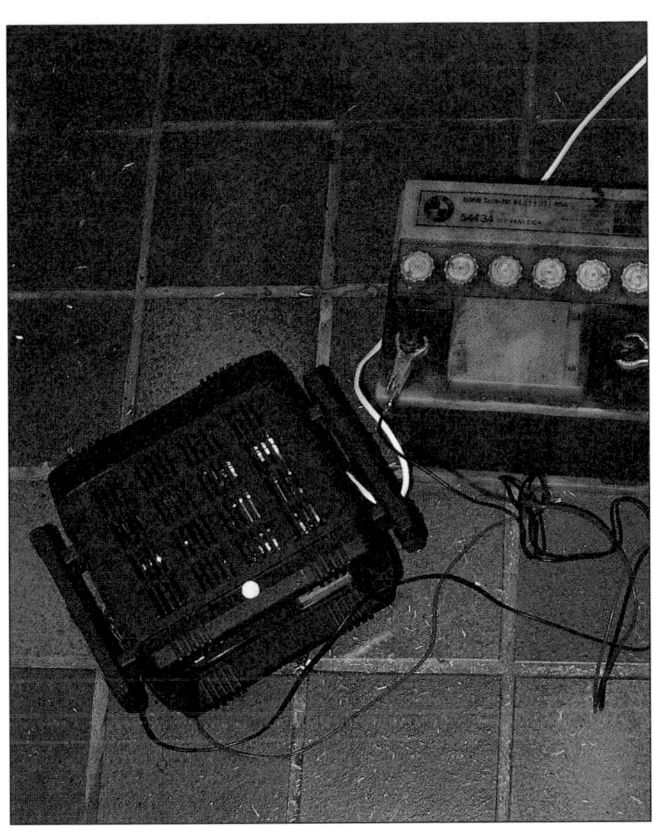

▷ Some car batteries are rechargeable. They can be plugged into the mains and recharged overnight.

MAKE SOME BATTERIES

Stick two pieces of metal that are different into a lemon. Make sure they do not touch each other. Connect a piece of wire to each piece of metal. Touch the wires onto your tongue (but not to each other). You will feel a tingle as a current is produced. Make a pile of copper and nickel coins. Arrange them alternately with pieces of blotting paper soaked in salt water between each one. Make sure the coins do not touch each other. Use your battery to light a flashlight bulb. You can attach the wires with tape.

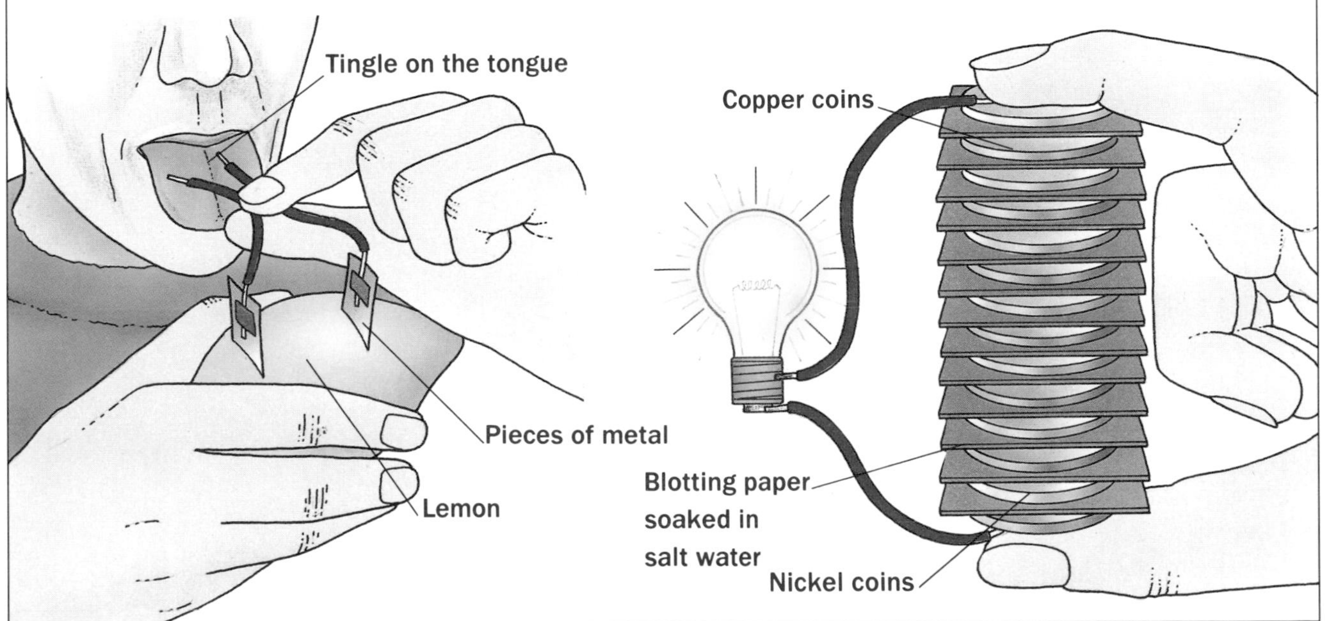

The path an electric current takes as it flows is called a "circuit." In a simple flashlight the circuit is made by the two wires, the battery and the bulb. Electric current flows from the battery to the bulb along one wire. As long as there are no breaks in the circuit, the current will flow and the bulb will stay lit.

TYPES OF CURRENT

The electric current that flows from a battery always travels in the same direction. This type of current is called direct current (DC). But most of the electricity you use comes from the supply lines from the power station. This current is constantly changing direction — backwards and forwards. It changes direction as often as 50-60 times per second. It is called alternating current (AC). AC is used for the mains supply because it can be transmitted more cheaply that DC. For most purposes AC is more efficient.

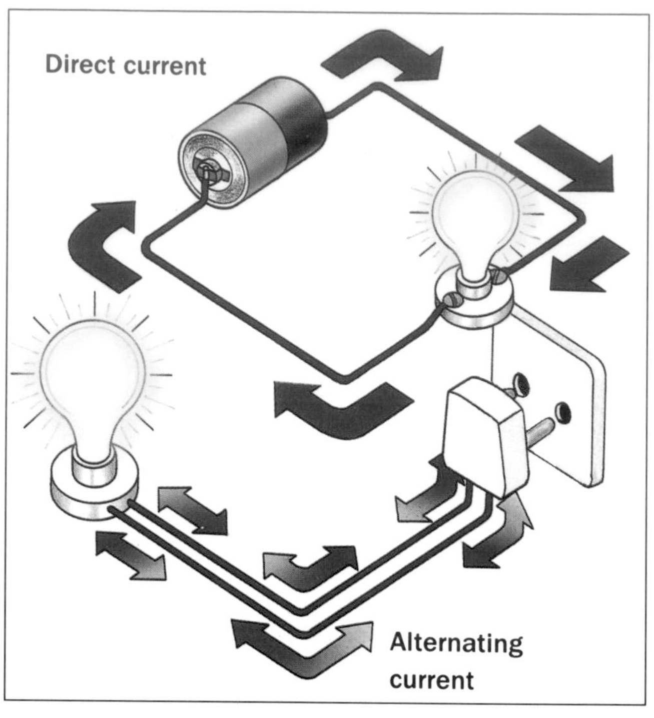

△ The bulb in your flashlight is powered by direct current from a battery. But the lights in your home receive alternating current from the mains. You cannot tell by looking at a bulb if it is powered by AC or DC.

MAKING A CIRCUIT

The diagrams show you how to make your own simple circuit. You will need to use insulated wire which has had the plastic removed at each end – ask an adult to help you prepare the wire. The paper clip forms a switch. When the switch is "on" the bulb should light. If it does not light, check that there are no breaks in the circuit. To turn the bulb off, move the paper clip to the "off" position as shown in the diagram. Moving the paper clip breaks the circuit.

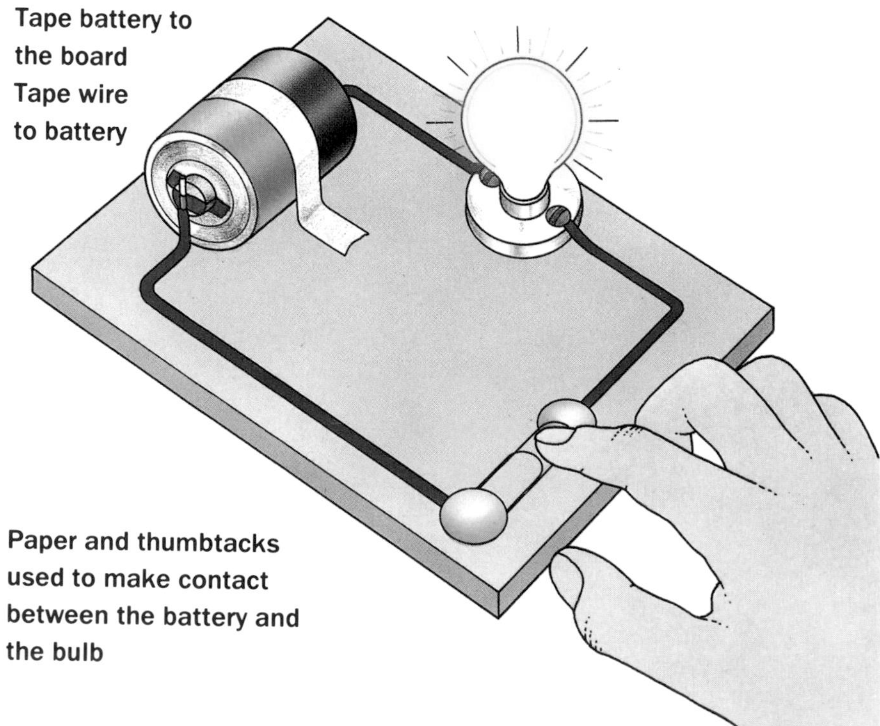

SWITCHES

A switch is simply a way of breaking a circuit. All electric appliances are fitted with a switch so that they can be turned off when they are not in use. When a switch is turned "on" the circuit is complete and the current flows. But when a switch is put in the "off" position, a gap is made in the circuit. However the gap made by the switch needs to be quite large. The diagram below shows what can happen if the gap between two wires is too small – a spark of electricity may jump between them.

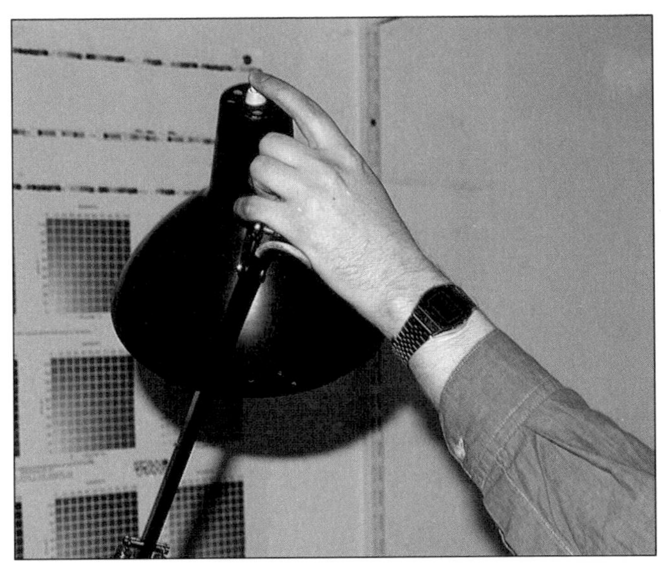

△ Look around you and notice just how many things are operated by pressing a switch. In the "off" position a gap is made in the circuit. Electricity does not flow easily through the air in this gap, so the current stops. If the gap is very small, the electric current may jump between the two ends. This is what happens when there is a bad connection.

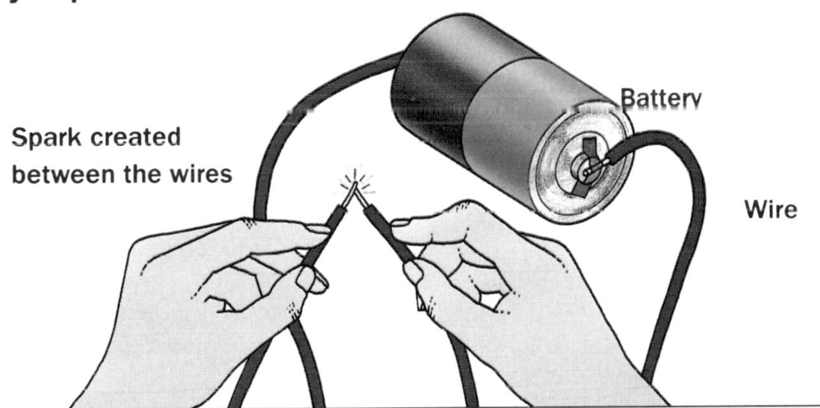

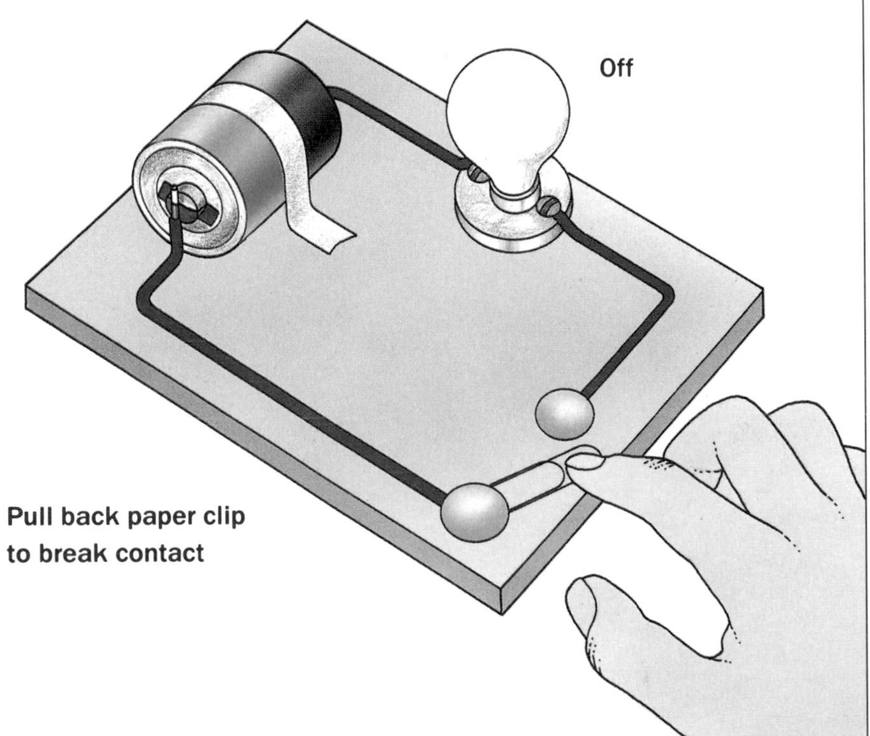

QUIZ

These trailing wires do not work properly. Why not? They are also dangerous. Can you suggest how they might give someone a shock or even start a fire? If you see a loose wire like this you should tell an adult so it can be fixed.

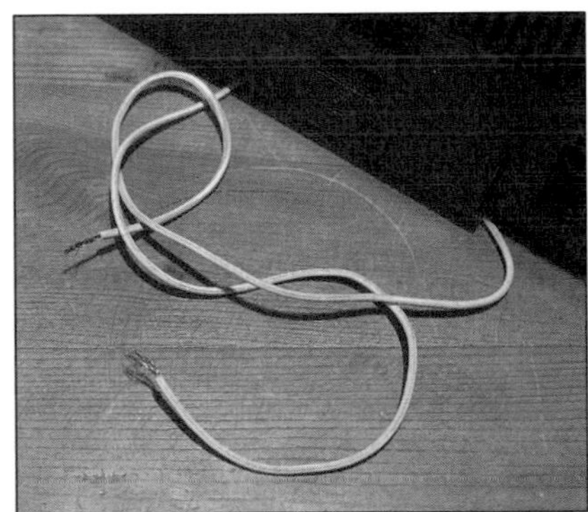

CONDUCTORS AND INSULATORS

Electricity flows through some materials very easily. These materials are called conductors. Metals are good conductors of electricity. But electricity cannot flow through other substances, such as wood and plastic. These materials are insulators. Conductors and insulators are used for different purposes.

GOOD CONDUCTORS

All metals conduct electricity. The best metal conductor is silver which is used in circuits in computers. But silver is expensive. The best low cost metal conductor is copper. The power lines supply electricity along copper wires. Water is a weak conductor of electricity – but you should not touch electric appliances with wet hands or you may get a dangerous shock. The best conductors of all are known as "super conductors" and can conduct electricity at very low temperatures. These materials are only now being fully developed but may have a great effect on life in the future.

△ Cables are often covered with materials that do not carry an electric current easily.

▽ This tiny microchip circuit is made from aluminum which is a good conductor of electric current.

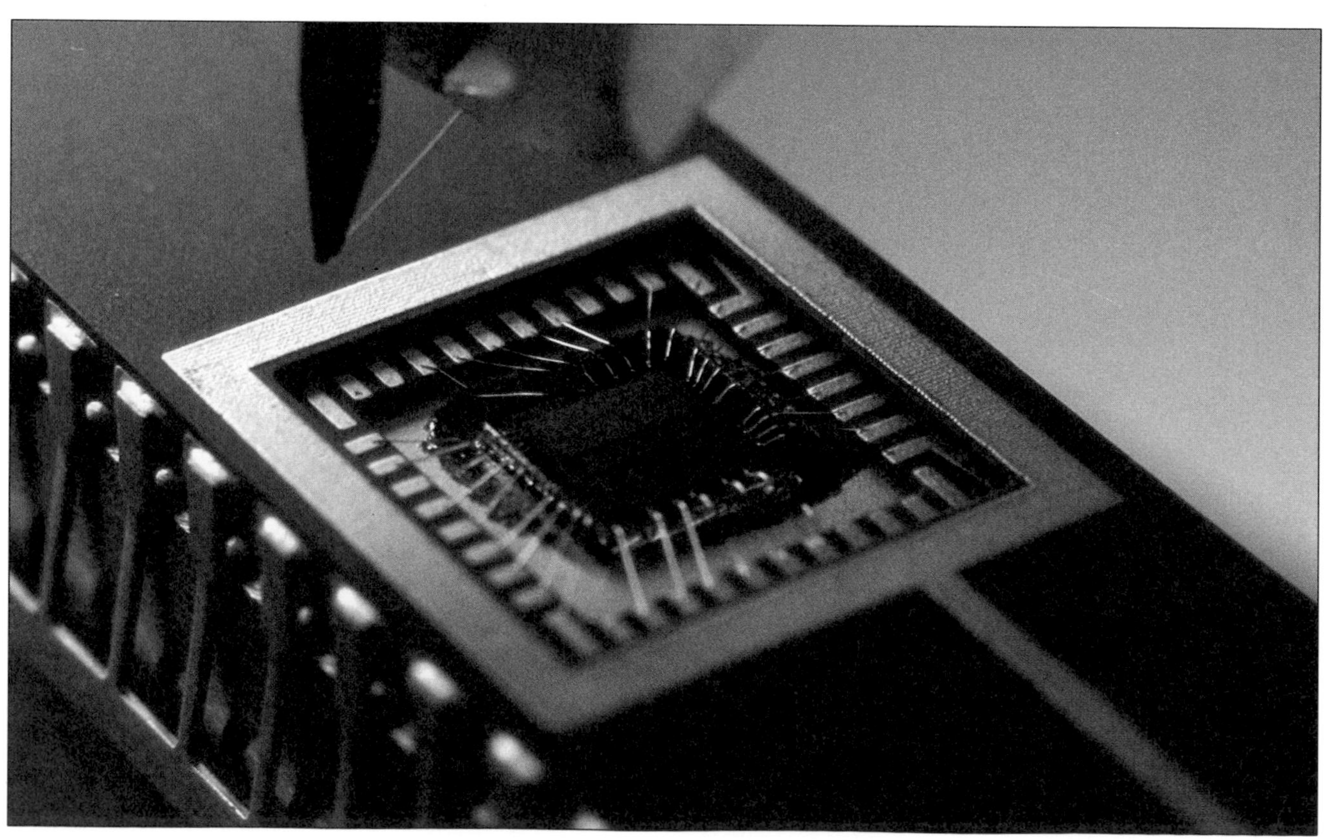

INSULATORS

Insulators are used to prevent electricity flowing where it is not wanted. You have seen how air acts as an insulator in a switch. The wires in household appliances are insulated from you and from each other by a plastic coating. Plugs and sockets are usually made of plastic or rubber so that you can touch them safely. Materials called ceramics also make good insulators. Ceramics are not flexible like plastic but can withstand very high temperatures. They are used in car engines and to coat electric oven rings so that you can cook without getting a shock through the saucepan if you should touch it.

△ Plastic is used to insulate wires as it is flexible and does not need to withstand high temperatures. Any break in the insulation could be dangerous and should be repaired.

EXPERIMENTS

Find out which materials are conductors and which are insulators by doing the experiment below. Check that the bulb lights when you touch the two ends of the wires together. Then fix them well apart on the plate. Use a variety of objects and materials to fill the gap between the wires. You can test wood and different types of metals by placing them in the circuit. Those which light the bulb are conductors. Those which do not are insulators. Try dipping the wires in water to see if water is a good conductor.

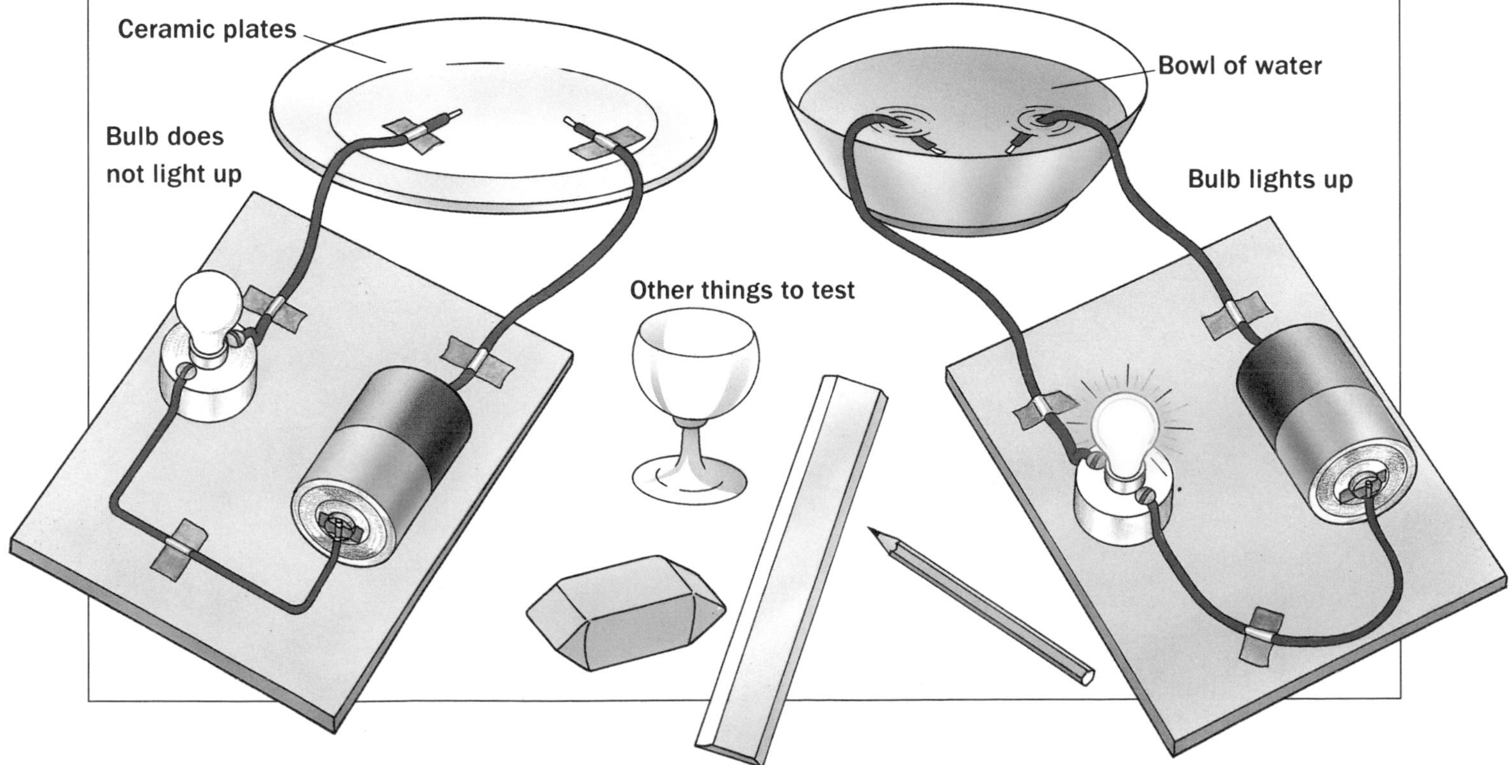

Copper is a good conductor – it hardly resists the flow of electricity through it at all. But thin copper wire allows less current through it than thick wire. And the longer the wire, the more it resists the flow of electricity. Coils of wire or other pieces of poor conductors can be put into circuits to reduce the current.

RESISTANCE

A thick wire can carry more electric current than a thin wire – rather like a wide road can carry more cars than a narrow one. So a thin wire in a circuit resists the current and reduces it. A long wire has a similar effect, reducing the current flowing through it. The diagram compares *resistance* in a circuit to a blockage in a bicycle pump. To get air through a blocked pump you have to pump harder. One way to keep a bulb shining brightly in a "blocked" circuit is to use an extra battery.

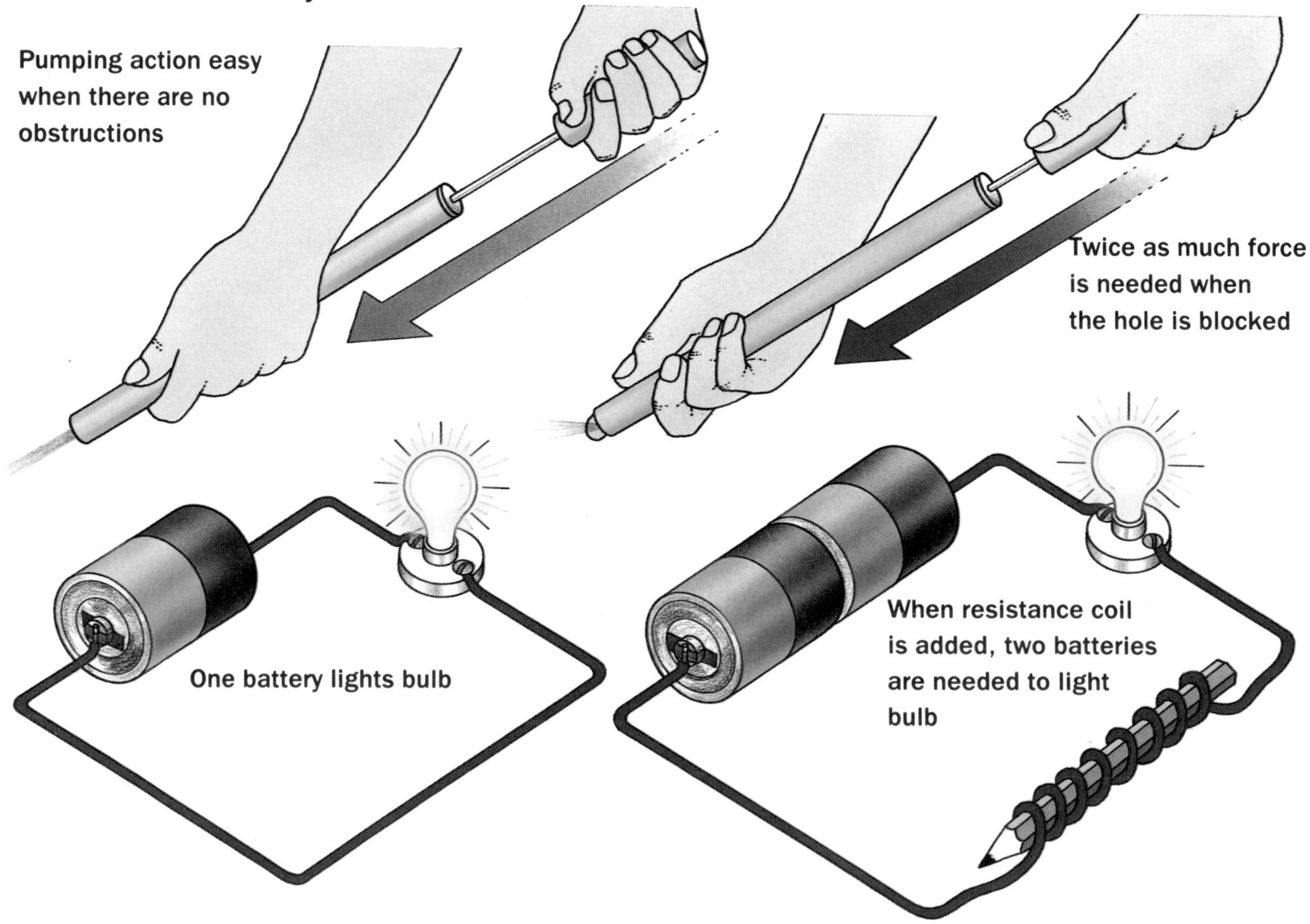

△ This shows some typical resistors used in circuits.

Pumping action easy when there are no obstructions

Twice as much force is needed when the hole is blocked

One battery lights bulb

When resistance coil is added, two batteries are needed to light bulb

USING RESISTANCE

Every time you turn up the volume on the television you alter the amount of current flowing in its circuit. The volume control is linked to a resistor made of a coil of wire. When the volume is turned up, less of this coil is included in the circuit so more current flows around it. The control for a toy car works in a similar way. When the lever is pushed in, less coil is included in the circuit, there is less resistance, and the car moves faster.

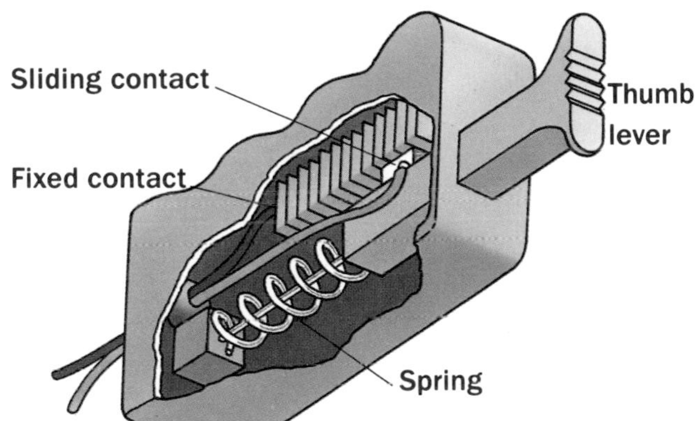

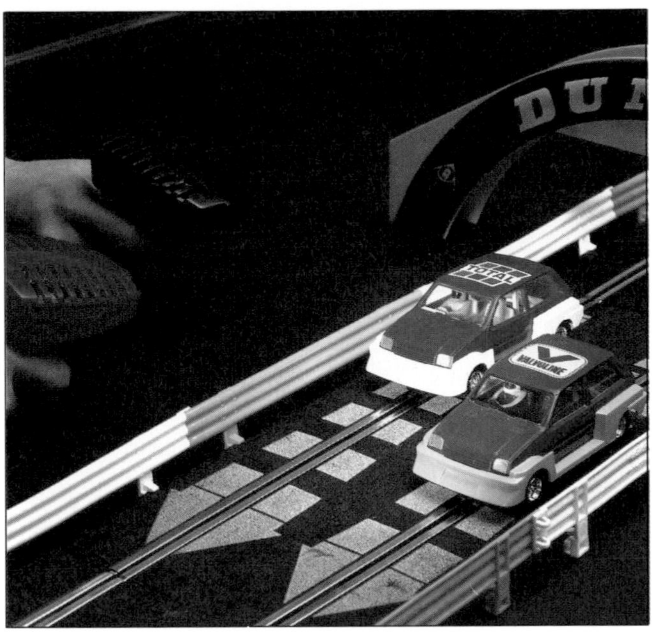

△ These children make their cars go faster or slower by changing the amount of current flowing through them.

MAKE A DIMMER SWITCH

You can make this dimmer switch. Use two batteries in your circuit and arrange them just as they are in the diagram – you may need to tape them together. Connect the wires as shown. As you move the free end of wire up and down the coil, you will find the bulb gets dimmer and brighter. When more of the coil is included in the circuit the resistance is greater, the current is reduced and the bulb glows less brightly. The amount of resistance depends on the size of the coiled wire.

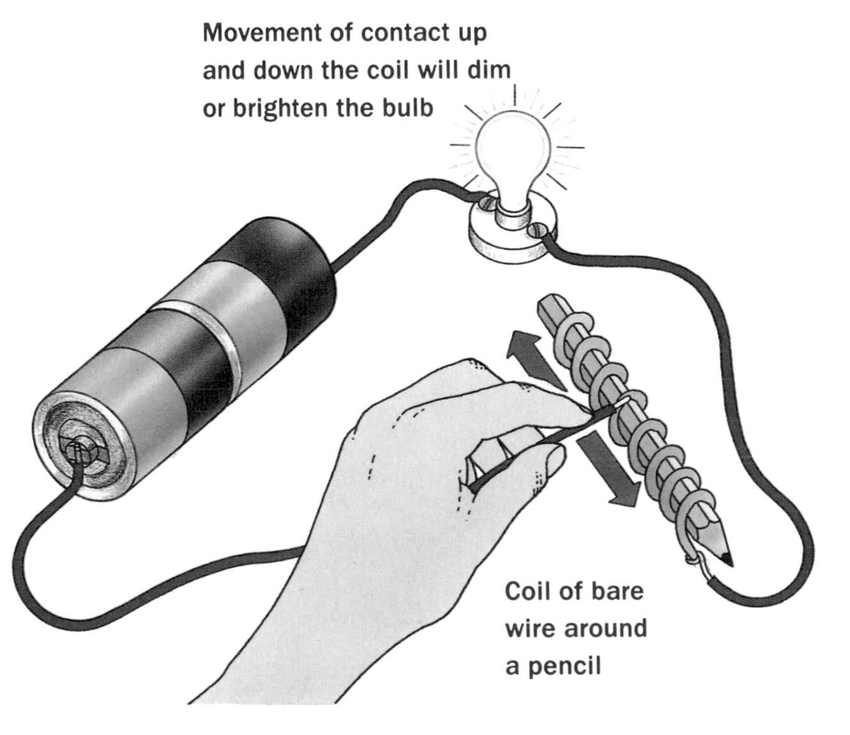

HEAT AND LIGHT FROM ELECTRICITY

Heat and light can be produced by electricity. When an electric current flows through a coil of thin wire the wire gets hot and may also glow. Electric stoves, heaters and light bulbs all contain coils of different types of wire which give off heat and light as they resist the flow of the current.

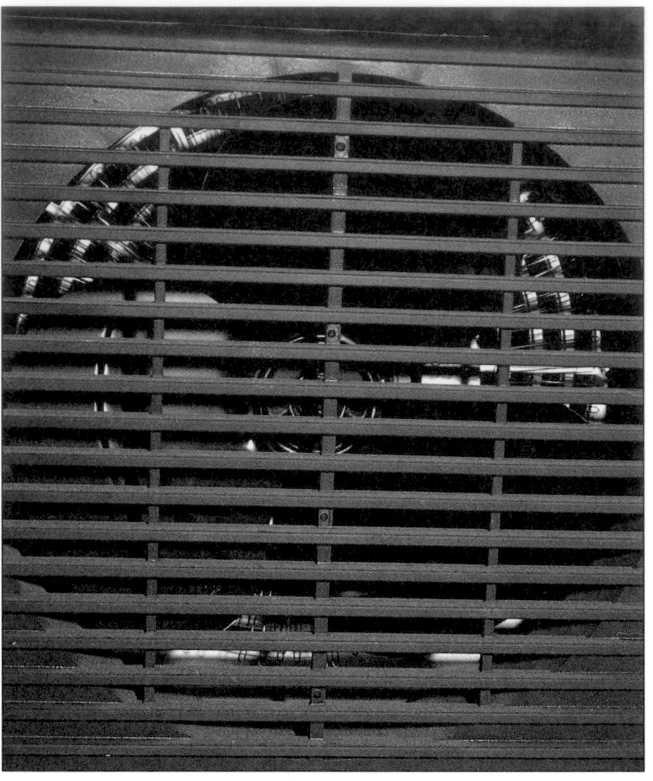

△ Inside this electric heater is a thin wire coiled tightly around an insulator. When the heater is switched on the wire gets red hot and the heat is blown into the room.

INSIDE A WIRE

The diagram shows what happens when a current flows through a thin wire. A wire is made of billions of tiny particles called atoms. Atoms are made up of a nucleus that contains positively charged particles and electrons which each have a negative charge. When the electrons move in an ordered way, a current is produced. In a very thin wire the electrons bump into atoms more frequently than in a thicker wire. It is these collisions which produce heat when a current flows through a small space. Many electric heaters have a thin wire which glows when an electric current passes through it.

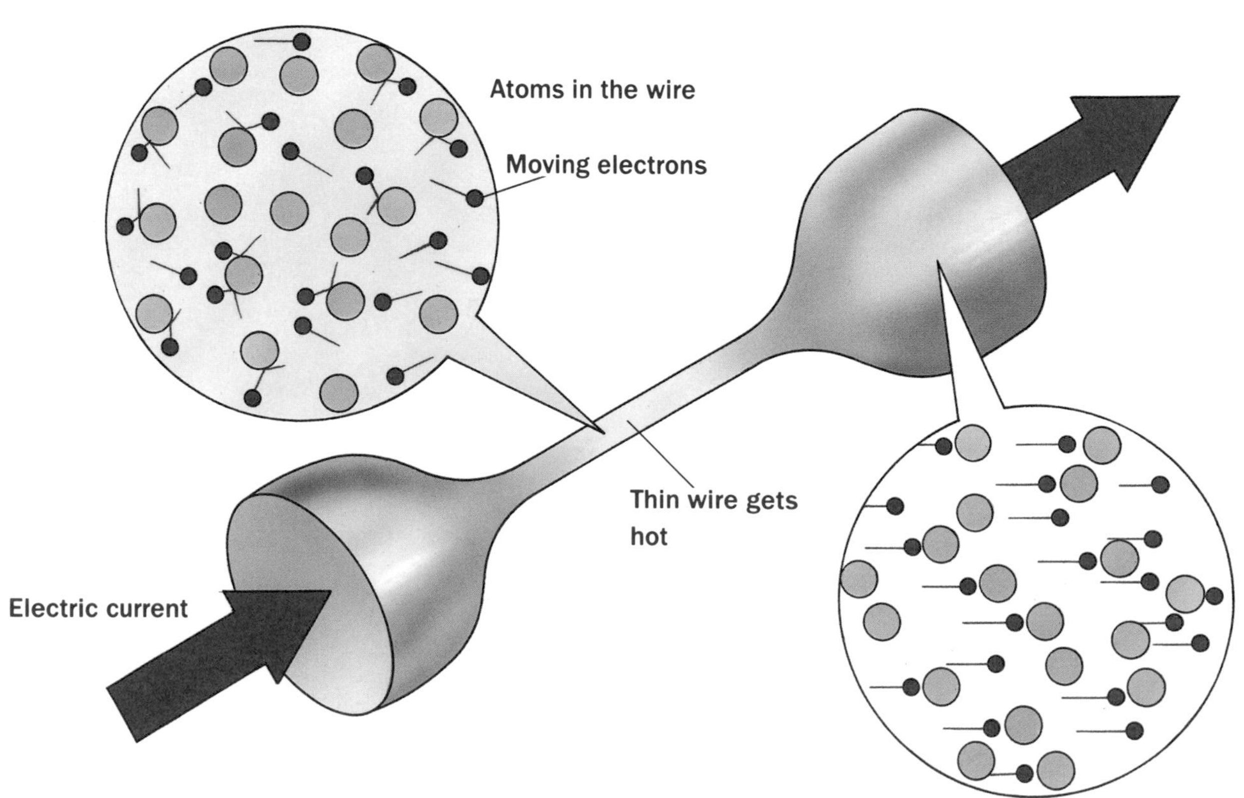

LIGHTING UP

One of the most important uses of electricity is to provide artificial light. The simplest way to provide electric light is with a light bulb. When a light bulb is connected into a circuit it glows brightly. The part of the bulb which glows is called the filament. The filament is a coil of very thin wire made up of the tungsten metal. When electricity flows through the filament the wire gets very hot – as hot as 4,800°F. It glows white and gives out light. The filament is supported to prevent it falling inside the bulb. The hot filament would burn in air because air contains oxygen. So the bulb is filled with another gas such as argon. Some bulbs glow more brightly than others. The brightness of the bulb depends on the amount of current flowing through the filament. Light bulbs are very fragile.

△ Close-up of a light bulb filament. The coil glows when a current flows through it.

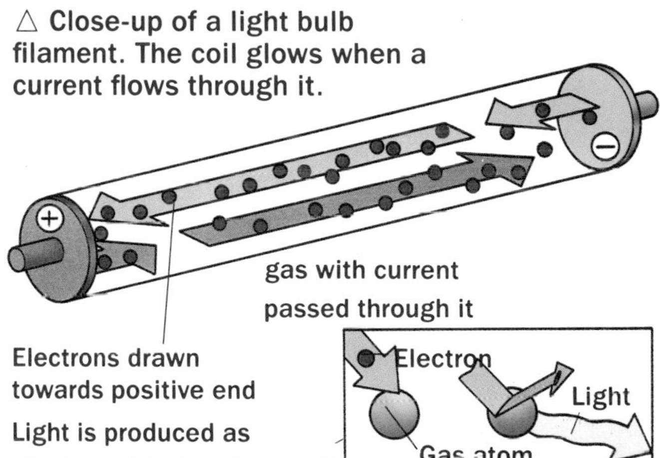

NEON LIGHT

Not all electric lights use a filament. The neon light in the photograph is produced when an electric current is passed through a tube of the neon gas. The current provides energy as light. Different gases can be used to produce different colors of light. Neon makes red light, sodium makes yellow light and mercury makes blue light. Colored lights are not much use indoors. Fluorescent strip lights are used in offices to produce a whitish light. A fluorescent light works as an electric current is passed along the tube. This causes the atoms to move more quickly. As they stop moving, they give out white colored light.

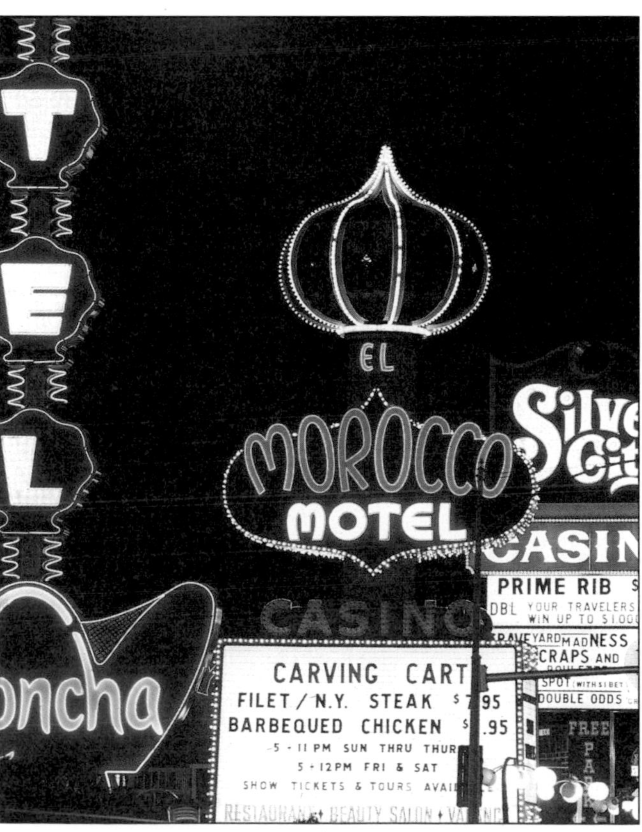

▷ Neon lights make very bright street signs and are a familiar sight in busy cities. Each color is achieved by using a different gas in the light.

ELECTROLYSIS

In a battery chemicals react with each other to produce an electric current. But an electric current can also be used to cause chemical reactions. Electric currents can be used to split chemicals into the substances they are made of. This process is called "electrolysis." Electrolysis can be used to purify metals.

WHAT IS IT?

Electrolysis is a way of using electric currents to separate the chemical substances in a liquid. Some liquids are made up of positively charged particles and negatively charged ones. For example, when salt (sodium chloride) is dissolved in water it separates into positive sodium particles and negative chlorine ones. If a battery is connected to a cathode and an anode which are dipped into the liquid, the negative particles collect at the positive end (anode) of the battery while the positive ones collect at the negative end (cathode) of the battery.

△ Charged particles in a liquid move when an electric current flows through it. The gas appears at the anode while the metal coats the cathode.

EXTRACTING METALS

Aluminum is a very important metal that is used in cookware and electricity cables. But it is not found in its pure form. Instead it is found in a rock called bauxite which is a mixture of aluminum, oxygen and other materials. Electrolysis is used to get the pure metal. Molten alumina (aluminum and oxygen) is poured into a container. The oxygen particles are negatively charged and the aluminum ones carry a positive charge. When an electric current is passed through the liquid, aluminum collects at the cathode where it can be removed.

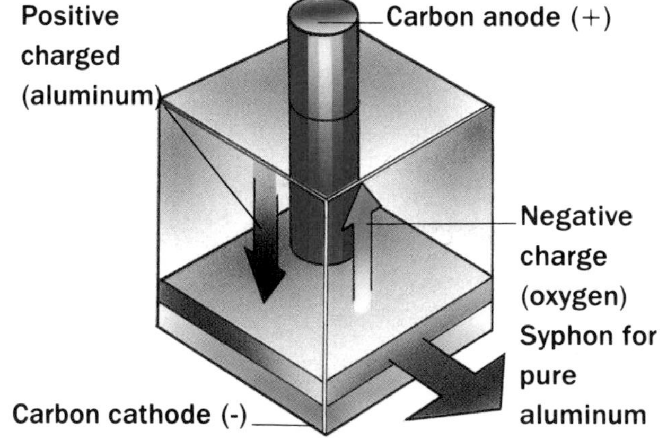

▷ Soft drink cans are often made from aluminum which has been obtained through electrolysis.

ELECTROPLATING

"Silver" jewelry or cutlery is not always solid silver it may be "silver plated." This is done by electrolysis. The diagram below shows how a piece of metal may be coated with a thin layer of another metal. It is attached to the negative terminal of an electricity supply and dipped into a liquid containing positive silver particles. When the current flows, the silver collects on the metal and coats it. This can be done with many metals. Iron nails are often coated with zinc to protect them from rusting.

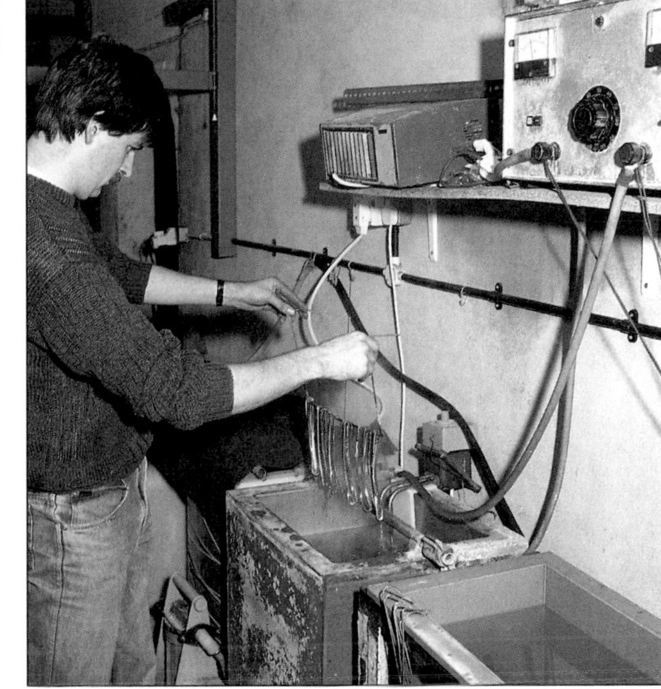

△ Silver plating through electrolysis.

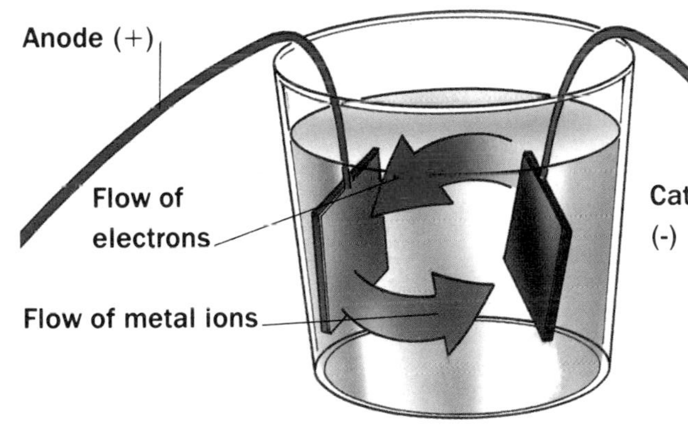

COPPER PLATING

You can copper plate an iron nail or disc. Attach a copper coin to the positive terminal of a battery. Connect a nail or iron disc to the negative terminal. Dip the coin and the disc into a beaker of copper sulphate solution. Positively charged particles of copper in the liquid will move towards the iron disc and coat it with a layer of pink copper. The bubbles around the coin are of oxygen gas.

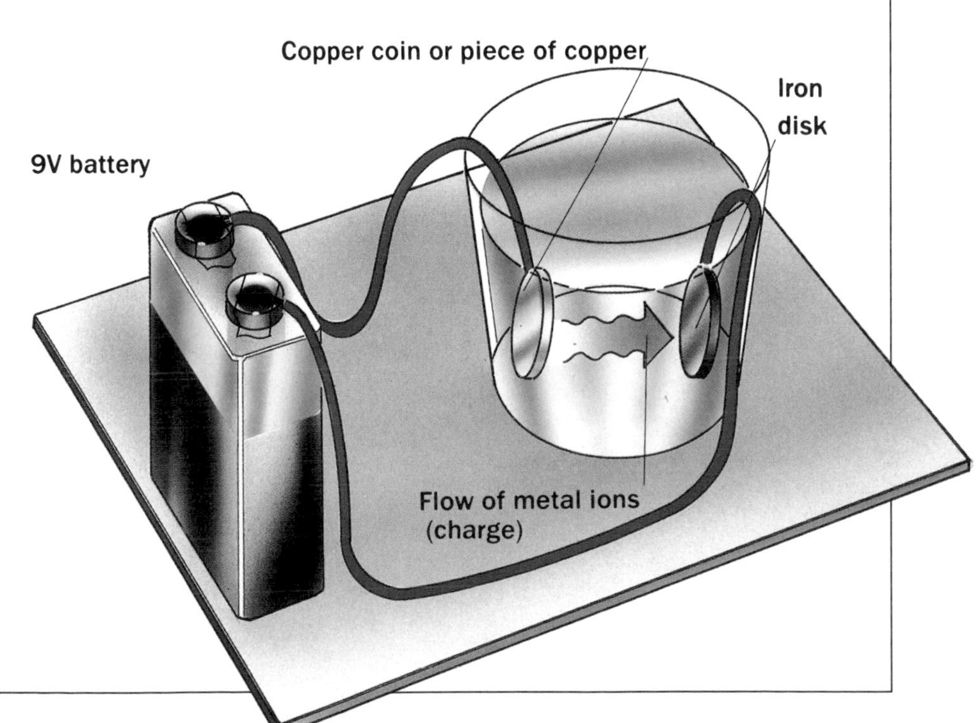

ELECTRIC MOTORS

The force exerted by a magnet can push or pull the charged particles making up an electric current to one side. When the current is flowing through a wire, the magnet makes the whole wire move. This idea is used in electric motors. An electric motor uses electricity and magnetism to produce movement.

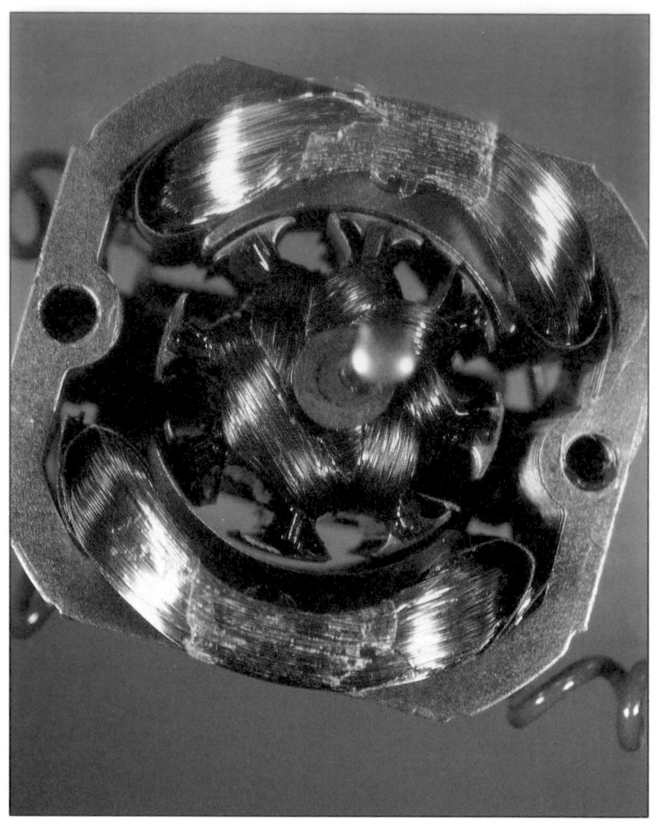

△ When the motor is switched on, the coil spins round. This movement can be used to turn parts in a machine.

HOW THEY WORK

The diagram shows how an electric motor works. In an electric motor there is an electric current in a coil of wire. A magnet is placed around the coil and this makes the coil move. In the drawing the battery is connected to a coil of wire which is in the shape of a square. The current flows up one side of the coil and pushes the other side up. This movement is repeated again and again so that the coil spins round and round between the magnets. Whatever is attached to the rotating coil - such as a food whisk - will turn with it.

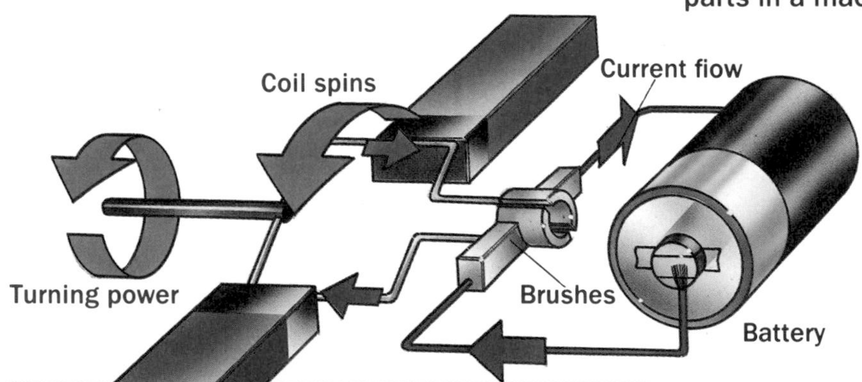

▽ Many bicycles use a dynamo to power their lamps. As you pedal and turn the wheel, this movement is used to turn a magnet within a coil of wire to produce an electric current.

USING A DYNAMO

A dynamo is the opposite of an electric motor, almost like an electric motor in reverse. In a motor an electric current is used to produce a turning movement. In a dynamo, a turning movement is used to produce an electric current. So a dynamo generates electric current. A dynamo does this by turning a magnet within a coil of wire. Dynamos can be of many sizes depending on what they are to be used for.

MOTORS IN ACTION

The electric motor uses electricity to produce movement. There are many ways of using motors. In the home electric motors do all kinds of useful work: they churn water and clothes around in washing machines; and they turn the wheels in electric toy cars. Electric motors are also used outside the home: they can be found in underground trains, golf carts and escalators. You can probably think of many more examples. But all electric motors produce circular movement, ideal for turning wheels. Scientists are aiming to produce reliable electric cars to reduce pollution.

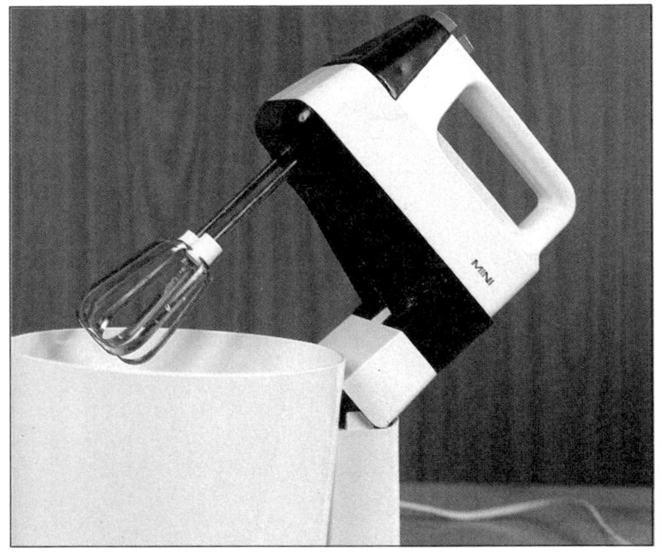

△ The moving parts in kitchen appliances are driven by electric motors.

EXPERIMENT TO SHOW AN ELECTRIC MOTOR IN ACTION

You can see the effect that a magnet has on an electric current by setting up this apparatus. You will need two small magnets, wire, tape, modelling clay and a battery all connected together as shown in the diagram. When you turn the switch you should see the coil twitch – it is being pulled by the magnets. The coil will not spin like a motor. This is because the current will keep flowing in the same direction rather than keep changing as it does in a motor.

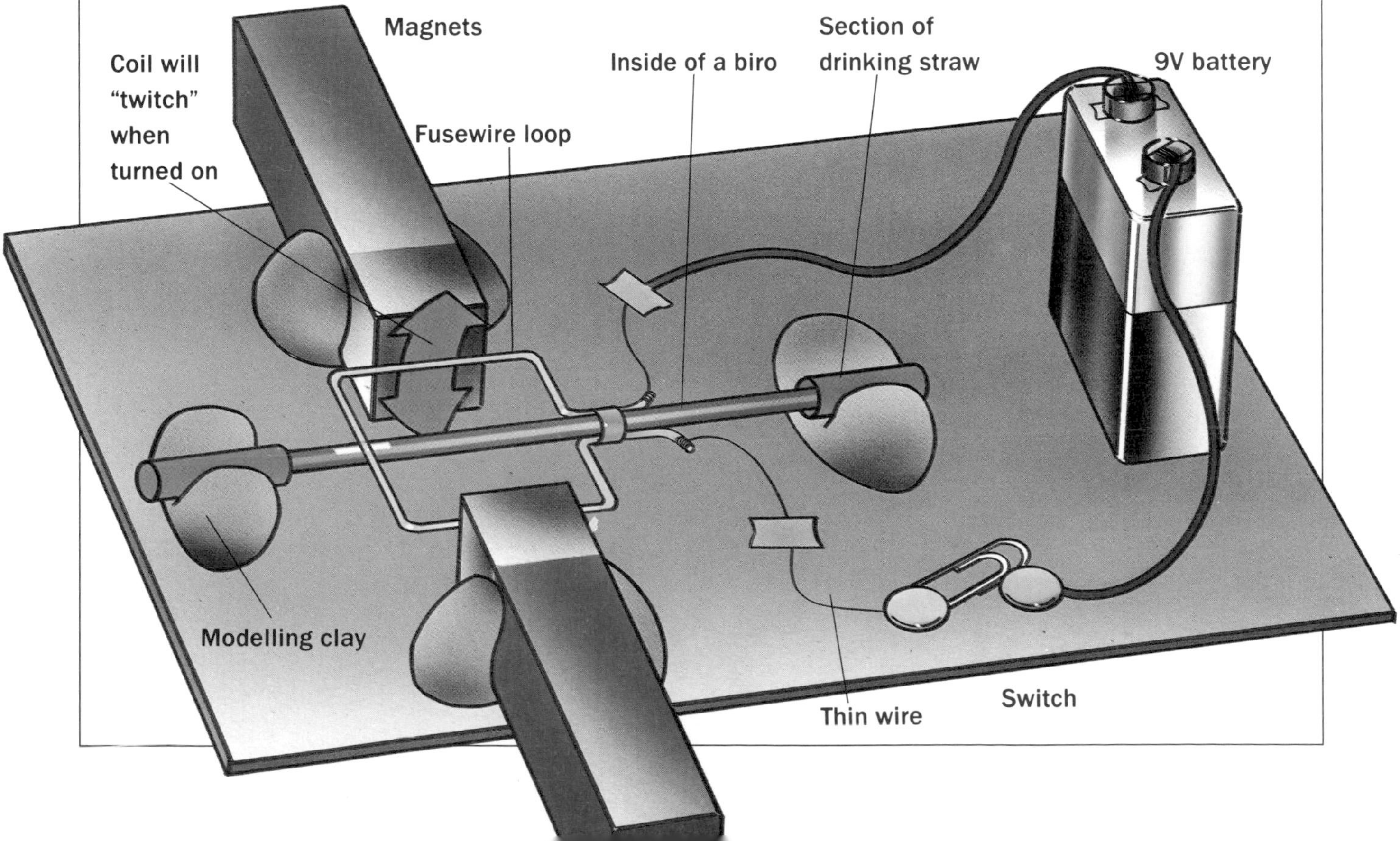

Magnets

Coil will "twitch" when turned on

Fusewire loop

Inside of a biro

Section of drinking straw

9V battery

Modelling clay

Thin wire

Switch

You have seen how an electric current can produce movement in an electric motor and how it is also possible to produce an electric current from movement. At a power station electricity is produced – or "generated" — by turning magnets at great speed inside coils of wire.

MAKING ELECTRICITY

The diagram below shows how the turning movement of a windmill can be converted into an electric current to light a bulb. The "generator" or dynamo is like a motor in reverse. As the windmill turns it makes a coil of wire rotate between two magnets. An electric current is generated which is being used to light a bulb. A dynamo like this can be used to power bicycle lights. In this case, the coil is rotated by the wheels as they turn. The electricity supplied to your home is generated in a power station in a similar way. However, in a power station it is the magnets which rotate inside a coil of wire. Moving the magnets in this way can generate huge amounts of current.

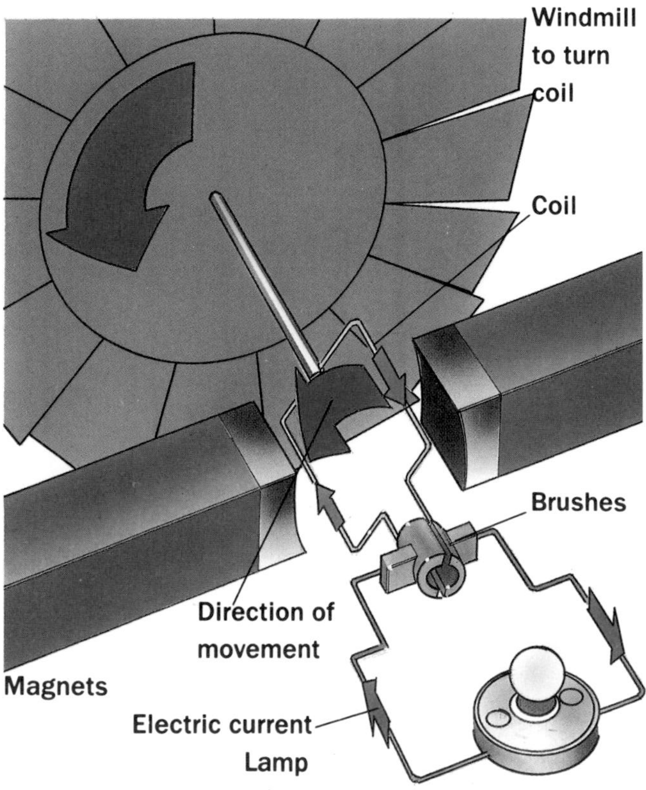

POWER STATIONS

Power stations produce electricity on a large scale for homes and industries. Huge "turbines" turn magnets inside coils of wire to generate a current. A turbine is like a series of big wheels or fans. It may be spun around by steam or water. Steam to drive the turbine may be produced by using coal or oil to boil water. Or the energy may come from nuclear reactions. Once the electricity has been generated it must be carried across the country to where it is needed. These diagrams show how the turbine is designed to spin around.

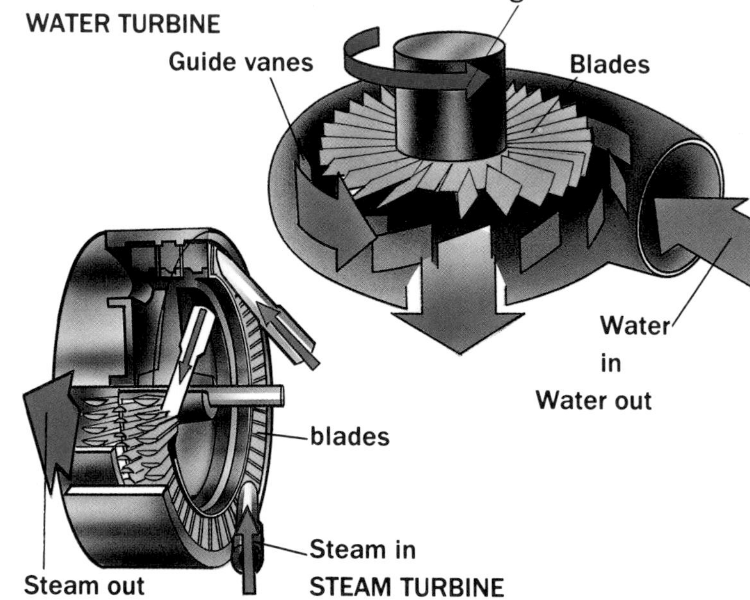

▽ Energy from a dam of water or tidal barrier can be used to turn a turbine to generate electricity.

ELECTRICITY SUPPLY

Electric current is carried from power stations in thick cables. Some of these are buried beneath the ground and some are carried high above the ground with metal structures called pylons for support. A system of pylons and cables connects all the power stations in the country into one huge network called the grid. The diagram shows how electricity might reach your own town from the network. The electric power carried by these cables is very great. So, before the current can safely be used in your home, this power has to be reduced or "transformed" at a substation. The grid network allows power to be switched from one area to another as demand for it changes. If a power station fails, a local electric current from another power station is sent along the cables in the grid. This maintains the power supply in the area. In this way power cuts can often be avoided.

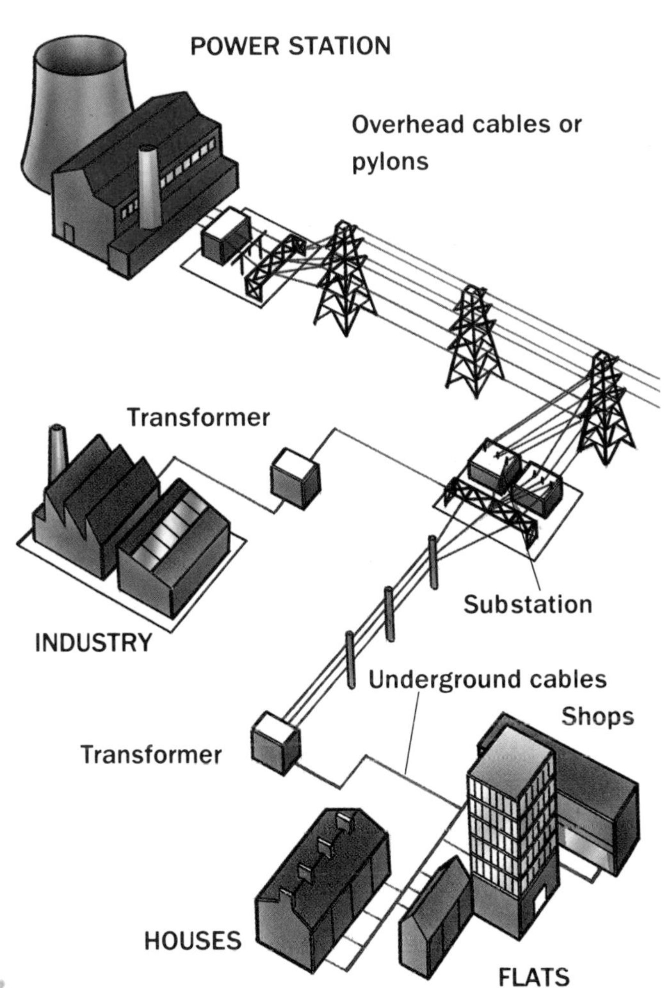

PROJECT – MOTOR TO GENERATOR

Do this experiment to see for yourself how motors and generators are related. You will need to find two small electric motors from a toy car, for example. Connect one motor to a battery – it should turn. Switch the first motor off while you join it to a second motor. This should be connected to a bulb. When you turn the switch on, the first motor will make the second motor act like a dynamo. The current generated by the dynamo lights the bulb.

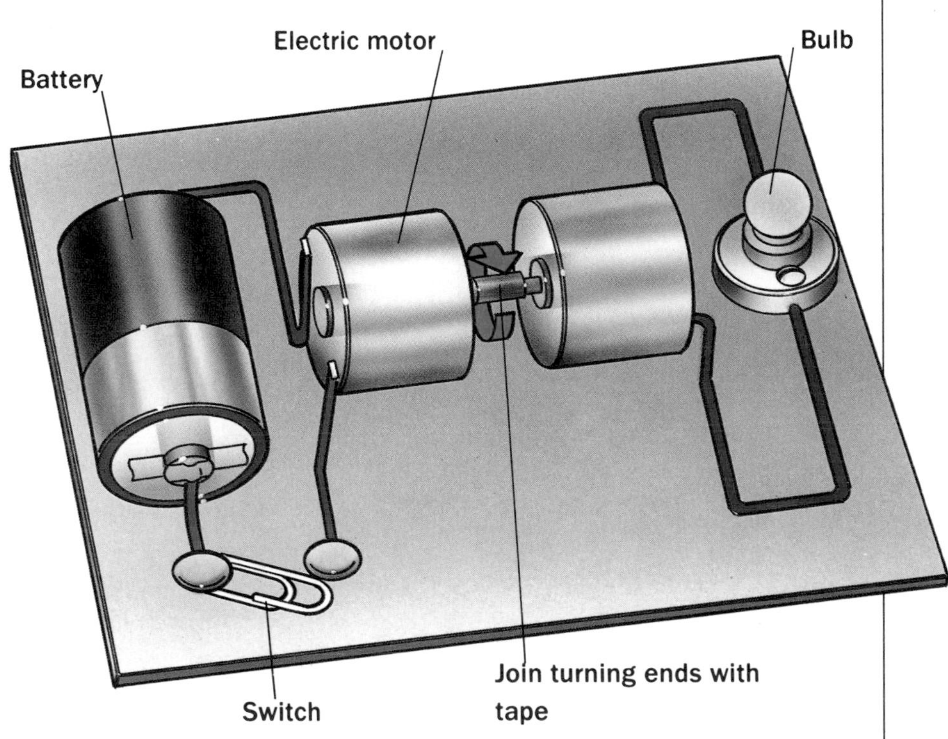

ELECTRICITY IN THE HOME

You use electricity in the home for many purposes — to power lights, televisions, stoves, videos and much more. Electricity is supplied to two kinds of circuits in the home — the lighting circuit and the sockets. Electrical appliances are connected to the power supply by putting a plug into a socket.

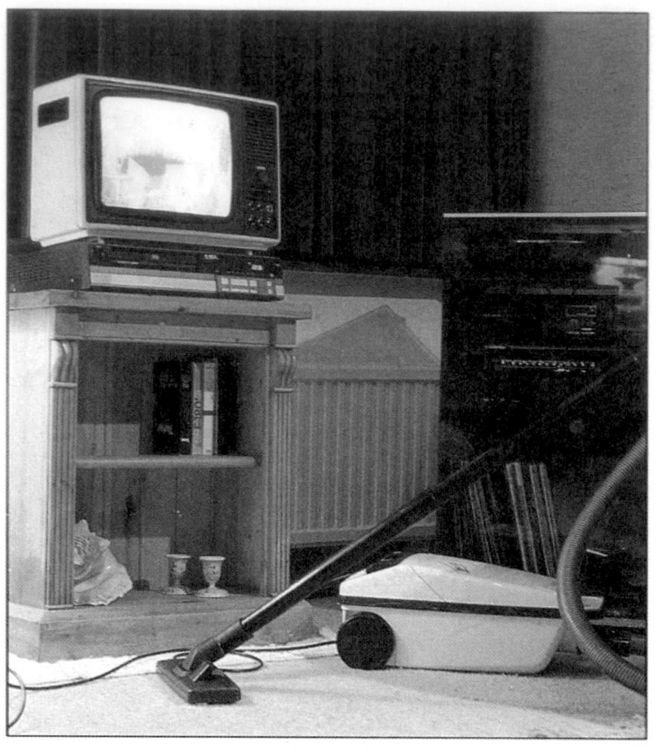

△ Life without electricity would be very different. All of the appliances in the photograph need a supply of electricity to power them.

APPLIANCES

An appliance is a machine that you use to do some sort of work for you. You probably use many electrical appliances in your home. Appliances may use electric power to produce light or heat; to drive a motor or to produce sound. Different appliances use different amounts of current. Those producing heat, such as a stove, use much more than those producing light or sound, like the television. Each appliance has a circuit that can be connected into the power supply.

HOUSE WIRING

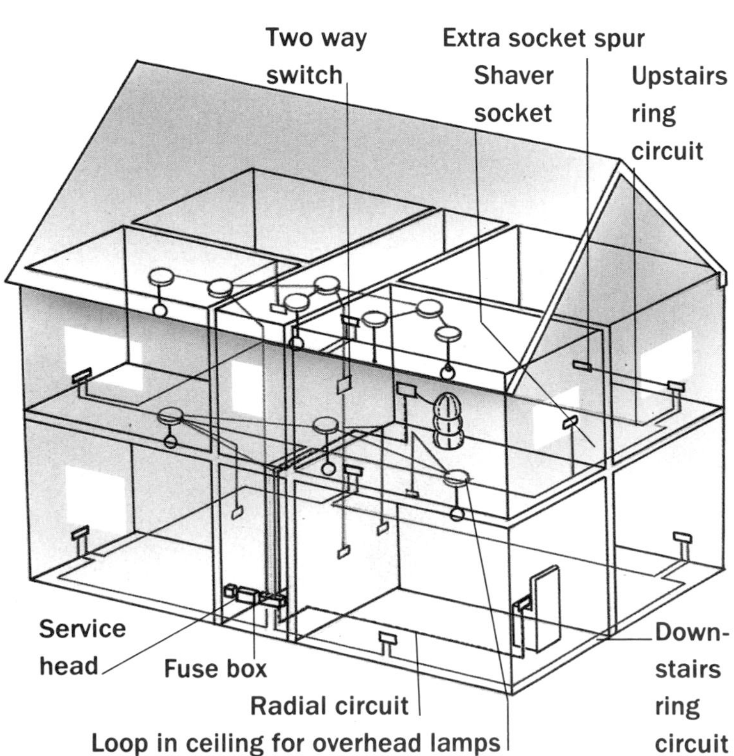

The diagram shows how electrical wiring is usually arranged in a house. Electricity enters the house through a wire, flows through the fuse box and separates into two types of circuits. One type of circuit powers the main lights. Other circuits supply electricity to the sockets. This runs around the house, usually between the walls or under the floorboards. At a number of places in each room the circuit opens into a socket. Appliances can be connected to the circuit at these sockets. The current flows into the appliance through one wire and then back to the "neutral" wire. The amount of electric current which enters a house is measured by a meter. This is a small motor connected to a counting device. A dial on the meter shows how much electric current has been used. In many countries, it is cheaper to use electricity during the night when there is less demand for power.

PLUGS AND FUSES

A plug carries wires leading from an appliance and connects them to the wires in the main circuit. Inside a plug there is a live wire (coated in black insulation) and a neutral one (which is white). The live wire carries the current to the appliance. The current returns to the power supply through the neutral wire. In some countries plugs also have a ground wire. The ground wire does not usually carry a current — it is there as a safety device. If there is a fault in the appliance and it becomes "live," or is connected to the power supply, the ground wire provides a route for the current to flow safely to the ground.

Most circuits carry a fuse or a circuit breaker. A fuse is a thin piece of wire included in the circuit. If too much currrent flows round the circuit the fuse melts and breaks the circuit before damage is done. A circuit breaker works in a similar manner, but no metal melts and the breaker can be reset after the problem has been corrected. The diagram shows how a fuse completes a circuit and how a blown fuse breaks it.

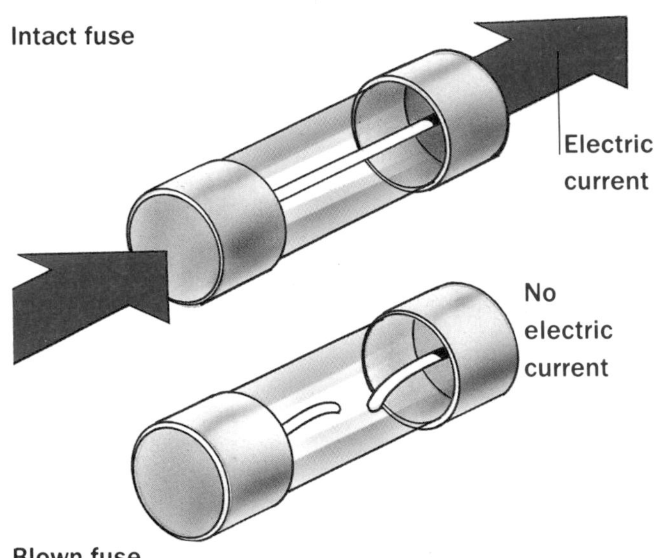

QUIZ

Electricity is a very versatile source of power: it can cause light, movement and sound and it can be used to make things hot or cold. Look at the different appliances drawn opposite. They are all everyday items and they use electric current to produce different effects. Can you say what they are? Can you think of other machines that use electric motors to produce circular motion? How many different ways is electricity used in a washing machine?

MAGNETS

More than 2,000 years ago, the Greeks found a type of black stone with strange powers. Iron nails and pins clung to the stone. If a piece of the stone was hung from a string, it always pointed in the same direction. These black stones from Magnesia (a place in modern day Turkey) were called magnets.

▲ Magnetite is also called lodestone, or "leading stone." In the ancient world, lodestones were used like compasses to guide travelers.

WHAT IS A MAGNET?

Some substances, such as magnetite, are natural magnets. A magnet can attract, or pull closer, small pieces of iron. The power of attracting pieces of iron in this way is called magnetism. Some magnets are called permanent magnets. They keep their magnetism, unless they are dropped, knocked, or get too hot. Some materials can be made to act like magnets when an electric current is passed through them. They are called electromagnets. They are not permanent magnets, because their magnetism can be turned on and off with an electric current.

DIFFERENT KINDS OF MAGNETS

Most magnets are made from iron or steel, a metal made by adding carbon and other substances to iron. Magnets can also be made from more expensive metals, such as nickel and cobalt. Strong magnets are made by mixing aluminum, nickel, cobalt, iron, and samarium.

Some magnets are long and narrow. They are called bar magnets. Other magnets are curved like horseshoes, and are called horseshoe magnets. Magnets can also be made in shapes like rings, or thin cylinders like pencils. These magnets are made from materials called ferrites, which contain iron. Electromagnets are often shaped like thick flat plates or cylinders.

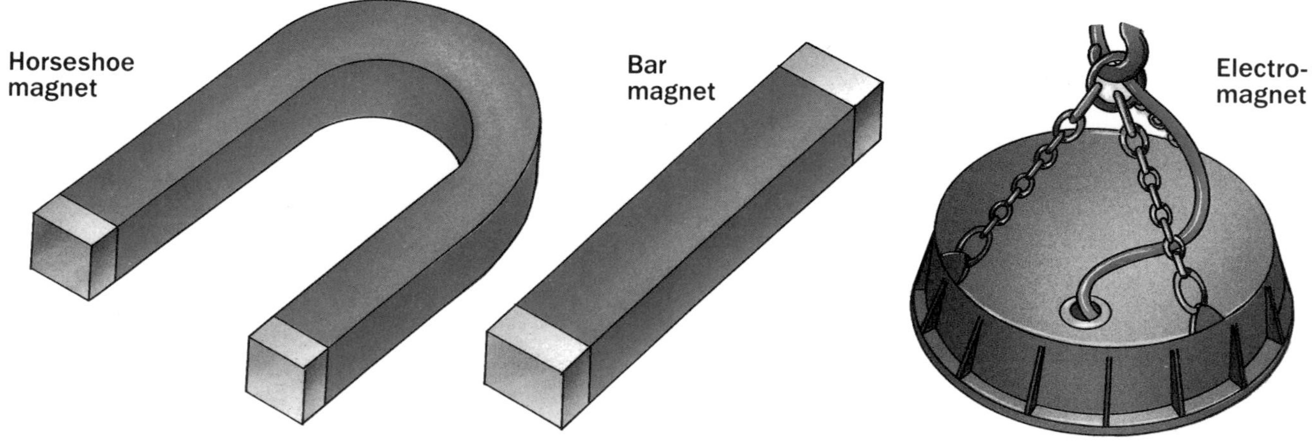

WHAT CAN A MAGNET ATTRACT?

If you play with a magnet, you will notice that not all things are attracted to it. Materials that are attracted to a magnet are called magnetic materials. Other materials are called non-magnetic.

See which of these things are attracted to a magnet: a pin, a paper clip, a plastic fork, a piece of paper, aluminum foil, different types of coins, a pencil, and a drinking glass.

You will find that objects made of iron, or containing iron, are attracted to a magnet. Most other metals, such as the aluminum in kitchen foil or the copper in coins, are not attracted.

Glass is not attracted to a magnet

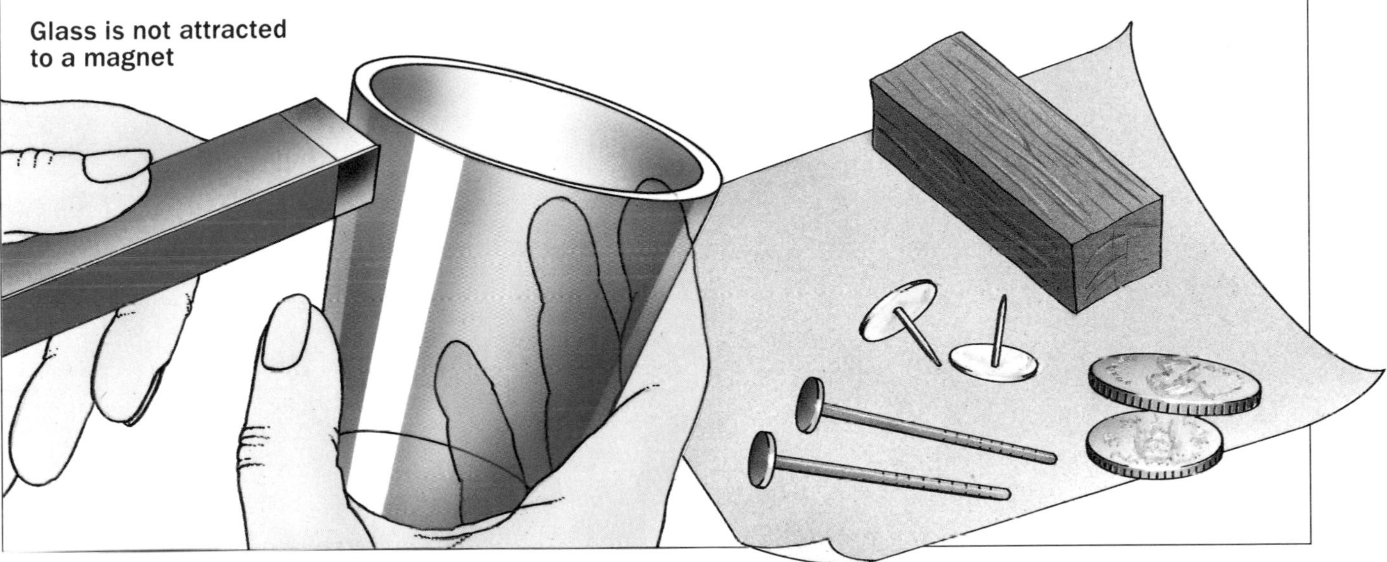

Quiz

Magnets are very useful around the home. They are sometimes used to keep doors closed. When you close a refrigerator door, what makes it close tight? A strip of magnet around the door opening holds the steel door shut. Magnets are also used to keep chess pieces on the board. Do any of the gadgets listed below use magnets? – telephone, cassette recorder, vacuum cleaner, refrigerator, washing machine, radio, television set, and home computer. Can you find other magnets in your home?

Magnetic door catch

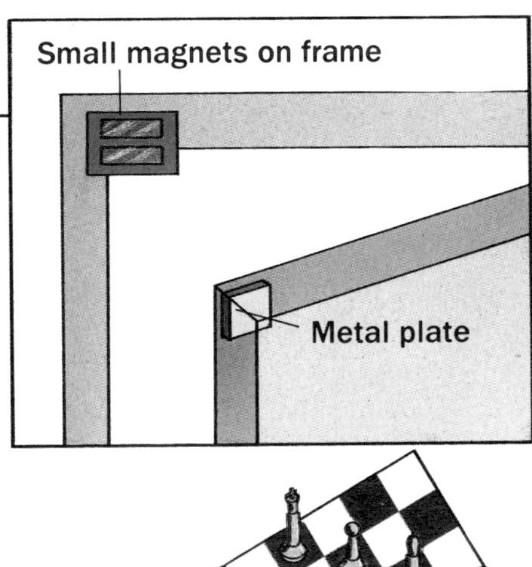

Magnetic board games

MAGNETS AT WORK

Magnets are used in many household gadgets. Electric motors use magnets and motors are used in many appliances, such as vacuum cleaners. A cassette recorder uses tiny magnets on the tape to store sounds. In a television set, magnets are used to move the electron beam which makes the picture.

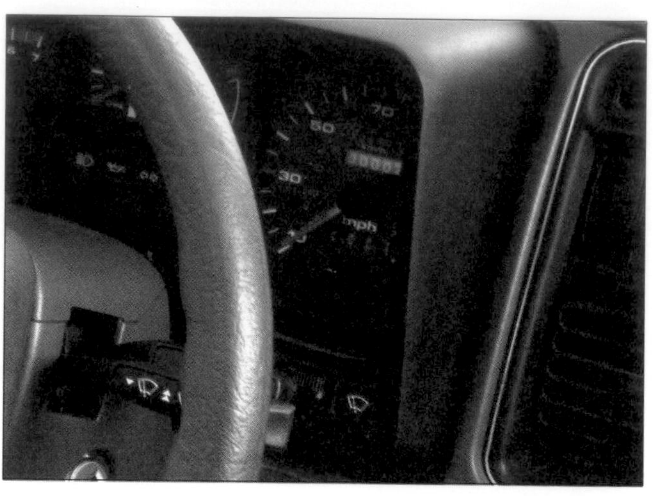

▲ The speedometer is an instrument which shows how fast a car is moving. It works with a magnet that spins around as the car moves.

MEASURING SPEED

A speedometer is driven by a cable that is connected to the wheels of the car or truck. The cable rotates, or turns around, very rapidly as the vehicle moves along. Inside the speedometer, the cable is attached to a small magnet. The magnet is turned around by the rotating cable. The magnet is inside a flat metal cup which is connected to the pointer on the speedometer dial. As the magnet turns around, it attracts the metal cup, causing the cup to turn. This turns the speedometer pointer, and shows the speed on a dial – the faster the magnet spins, the more the pointer moves.

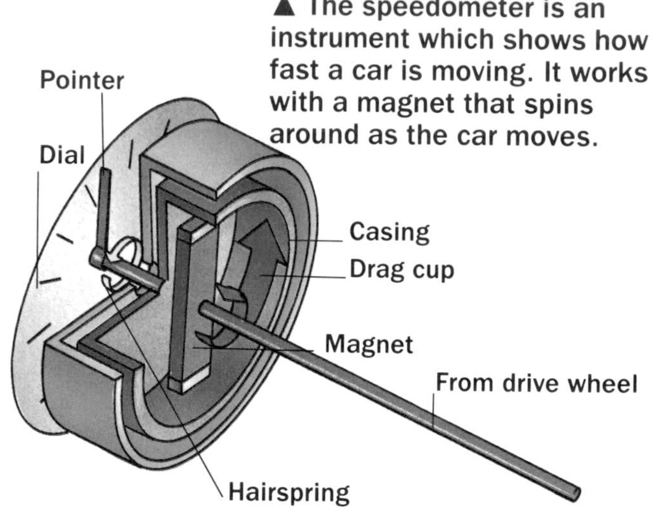

NO BURGLARS, PLEASE!

A magnet can be used in a burglar alarm that will sound when a window is opened by an intruder. In many burglar alarms a magnet is fitted onto the window pane. A special switch is then fitted to the frame of the window. When the window is closed, the magnet is near the switch. The magnet attracts a metal bar inside the switch, keeping the bar pressed against an electrical contact, or wire, connected to an electric bell. This stops the bell from ringing. If the window is opened, the magnet moves away from the switch and cannot attract the metal bar. A small spring pulls the bar away from the electrical contact. This breaks the electrical circuit and causes the bell to ring, sounding the alarm.

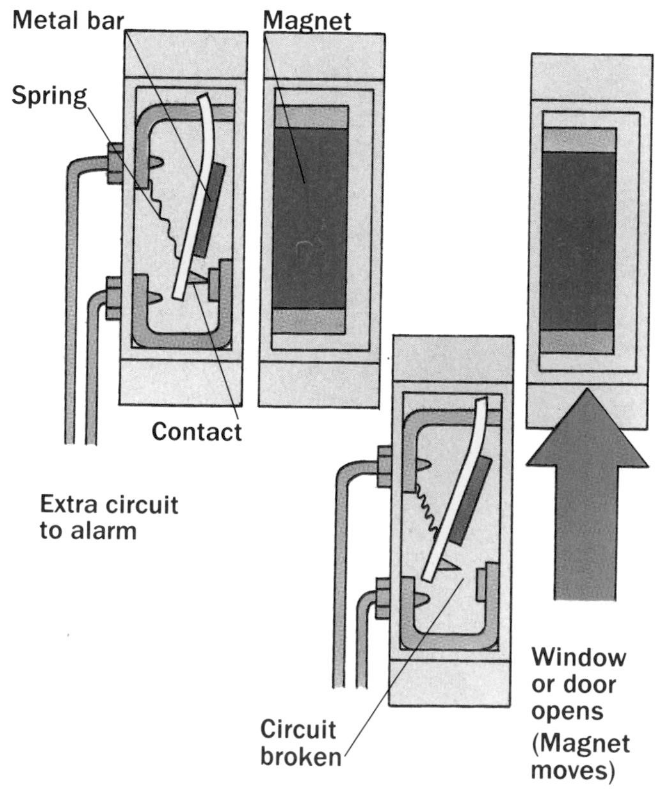

COIN TESTER

When a coin is put into a vending machine, an electric current passes through the coin. Only the correct coins conduct the right amount of electricity and are accepted by the machine. Other coins are rejected. The coin then rolls by a magnet which attracts it, slowing it down.

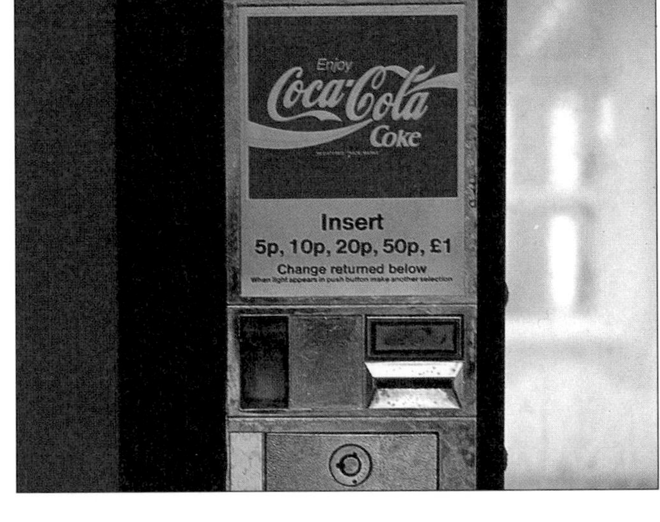

▲ Machines that sell tickets, drinks or candy check the coins put in. They use electrical and magnetic tests to make sure the coins are the correct ones.

Electric current test – and rejects coin

Reject slot

Magnetic test: slows coin down

MAKE A BURGLAR ALARM

You can make a model burglar alarm using simple equipment. You will need a strong magnet, a small flashlight bulb in a holder, a battery, thumb tacks, some thick cardboard, wire, and string, all connected together as shown in the diagram. You can use tape to make the connections, but metal must touch metal. The magnet is tied to the door, so that it is pulled away when the door is opened. The bent cardboard strip will topple over, completing the electrical circuit. The bulb will light up warning you that there is an intruder.

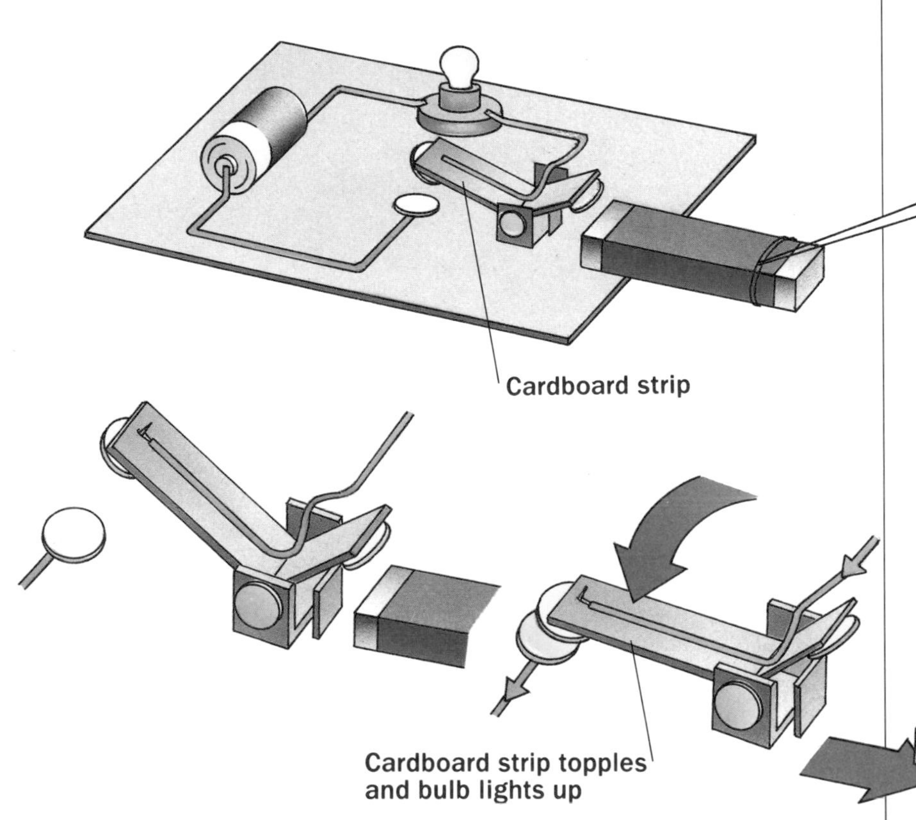

MAGNETIC STRENGTH

Not all magnets are the same strength. You can see this if you experiment with different magnets. One magnet might be able to pick up many paperclips or pins. Another might be able to pick up only a few. The magnets used in industry, or by scientists in their experiments, often need to be very strong.

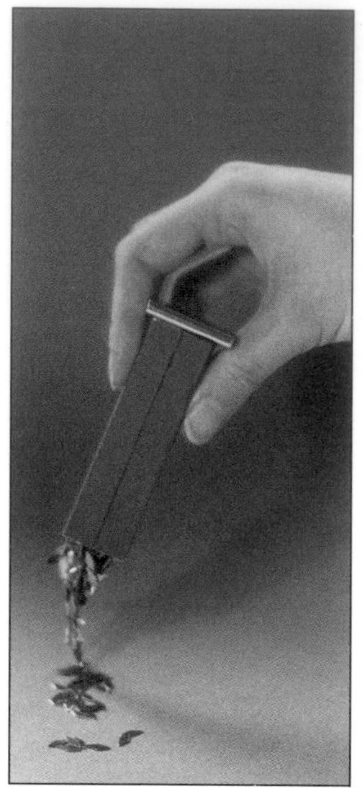

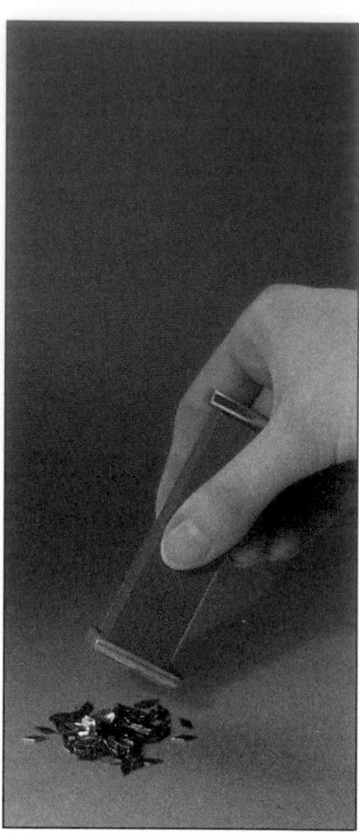

▲ Magnets should be joined with keepers when not being used. This helps to conserve their strength.

LOCKING MAGNETS

Magnets need to be treated carefully or they will lose their magnetic power. When you finish experimenting with a magnet, place a small piece of metal over the ends. The metal piece is called a keeper. If you have two magnets, place them side by side, and then put the keeper over the ends. Using keepers like this is called "locking" the magnets. Locking a magnet prevents it from losing its magnetism.

Unlocked magnets

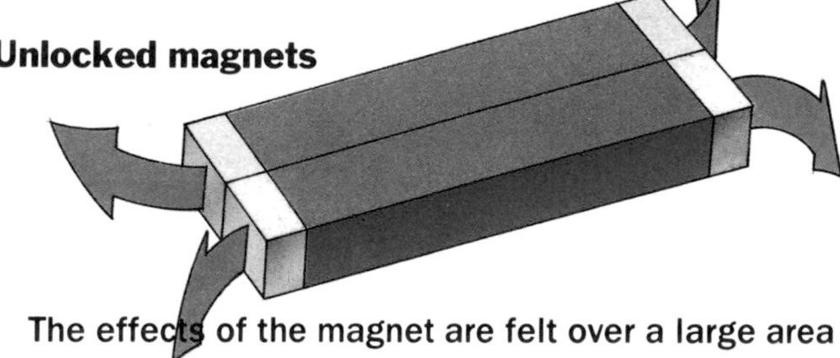

The effects of the magnet are felt over a large area

Locked magnets

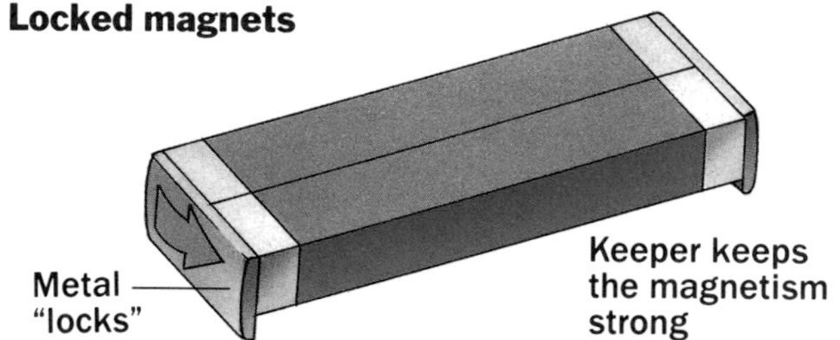

INDUSTRIAL MAGNETS

The magnets used in industry need to stay very strong. Most permanent magnets are made from steel or mixtures of iron with other metals. One common alloy, or mixture of metals, is called alnico. This name shows that the alloy is made from aluminum, nickel, and cobalt, as well as iron and sometimes copper and titanium. Alnico alloys can be made into very strong magnets – 30 times stronger than permanent magnets made from other materials. These magnets are used in electrical instruments and appliances. Samarium-cobalt magnets have become important in small, powerful motors.

▲ The photograph shows the use of industrial magnets to separate different kinds of metal.

INDUCED MAGNETISM

When a paperclip, or any small piece of iron or steel, is attracted to a magnet, the clip itself becomes a magnet. You can see this by arranging paperclips on a magnet. Each paperclip becomes a magnet and attracts other clips. This type of magnetism is called "induced" magnetism.

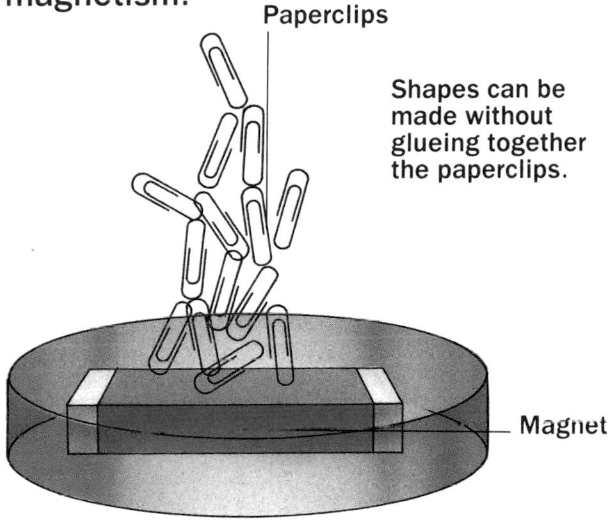

▼ This toy is made from a magnet and metal pieces which become induced magnets and cling to each other.

CAN YOU BLOCK A MAGNET'S POWER ?

Can a magnet attract a thumb tack through water? You can find out with a magnet, a glass bowl of water and a tack.

Place a nail on one side of a sheet of paper and move a magnet on the other side. Does the nail move or is the magnet blocked?

Repeat the experiment with a wooden, glass and plastic sheet. You could also try it with a magnetic metal sheet.

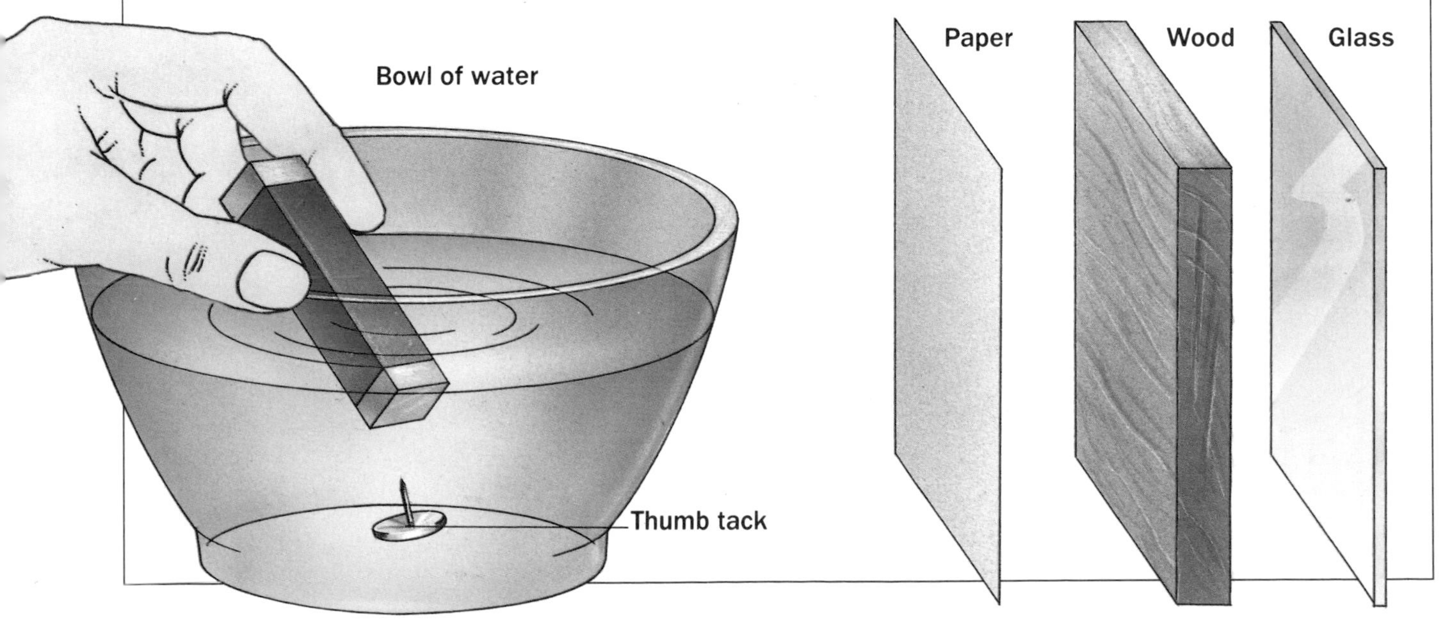

POLES APART

The power of a magnet is strongest at two points, called the poles. The poles are usually near the ends of the magnet. They are called the north pole and the south pole. If a magnet is hung on a thread so that it can swing freely, the north pole points to the north. The south pole points south.

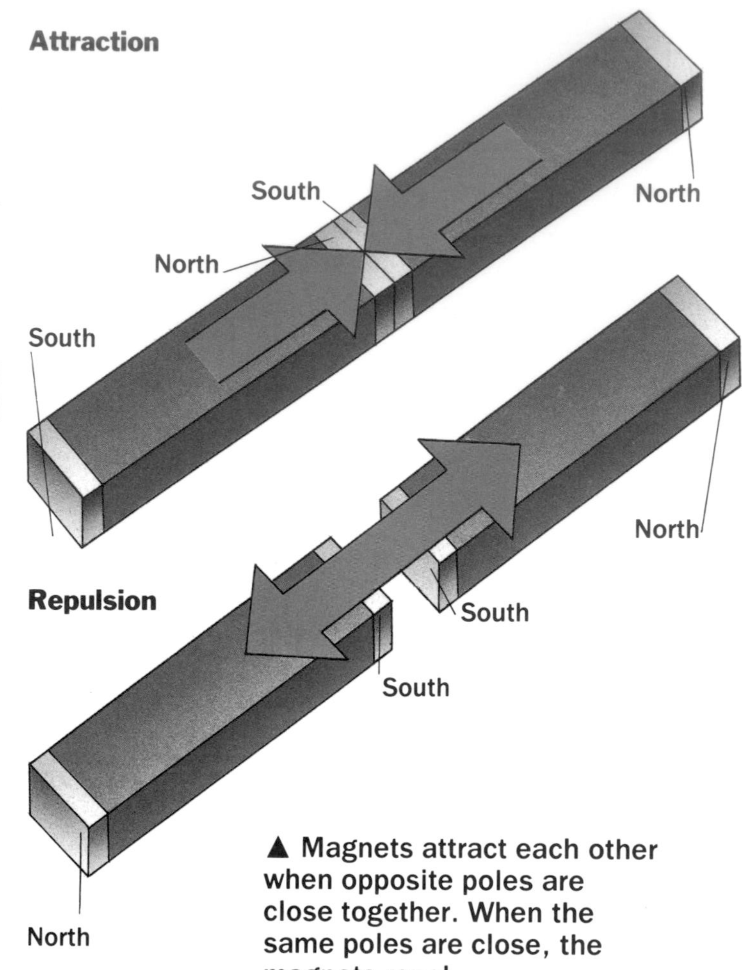

▲ Magnets attract each other when opposite poles are close together. When the same poles are close, the magnets repel.

ATTRACTION AND REPULSION

If you have two magnets, you will notice that they do not always attract each other. Magnets only attract each other if a north pole is near a south pole. If two of the same poles are placed close together, the magnets push apart, or repel each other. Scientists have made up a rule to describe this. They say: Like poles repel, unlike poles attract. If the magnets are very powerful, it may be impossible to make like poles touch. This principle of attraction and repulsion is used in many machines.

THE MAGLEV TRAIN

The word "maglev" stands for "magnetic levitation," or floating in the air using magnets. The maglev train is a train without wheels. It floats above the track using magnets. Maglev trains are fast, quiet and cause no pollution as they run. But they do need special track which is costly to build. The train shown here has electromagnets underneath. When the magnets are turned on, they are attracted to the iron or steel suspension rail. This lifts the train off the track. In some systems, the suspension rail is made up of permanent magnets that attract the electromagnets. The train is driven along the track by a linear motor. This type of motor has an electromagnet as poles that move along the train. As the poles move, they are attracted to the iron or steel reaction rail and the train is dragged along.

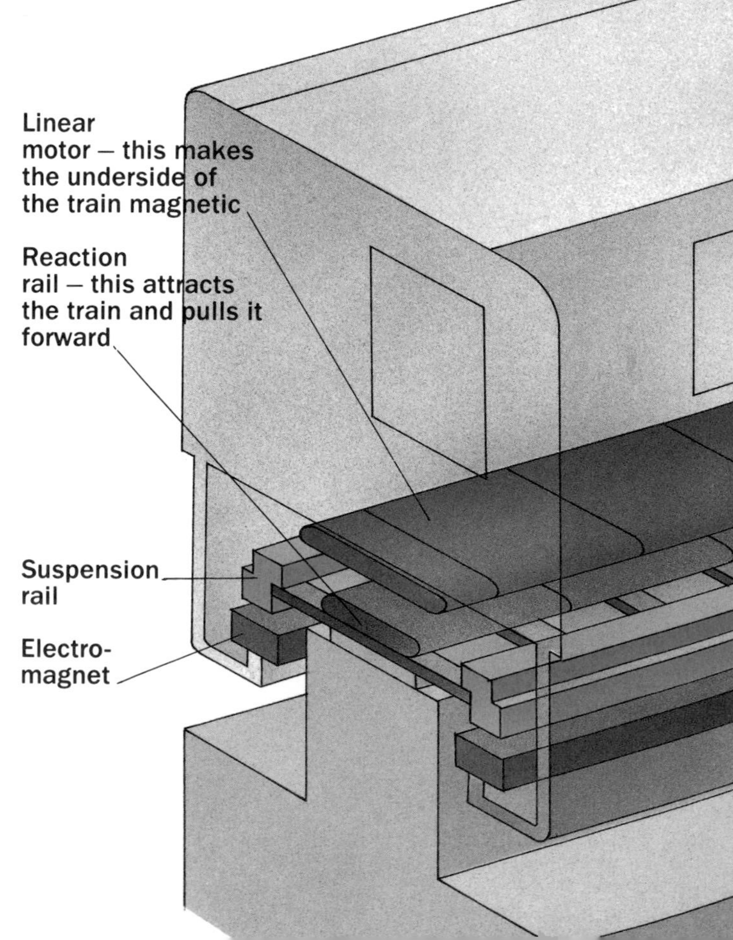

DO-IT-YOURSELF MAGLEV

If you have two strong magnets, you can show your friends how maglev works. Place one magnet on top of the other, with the two north poles together. Put a pencil between the magnets. Now tape the sides of the magnets together with pieces of adhesive tape. Remove the pencil, leaving a space between the magnets. Place the magnets on a table so that one magnet floats above the other one. Press down on the top magnet, to feel the "spring" of the magnetic force of the magnets.

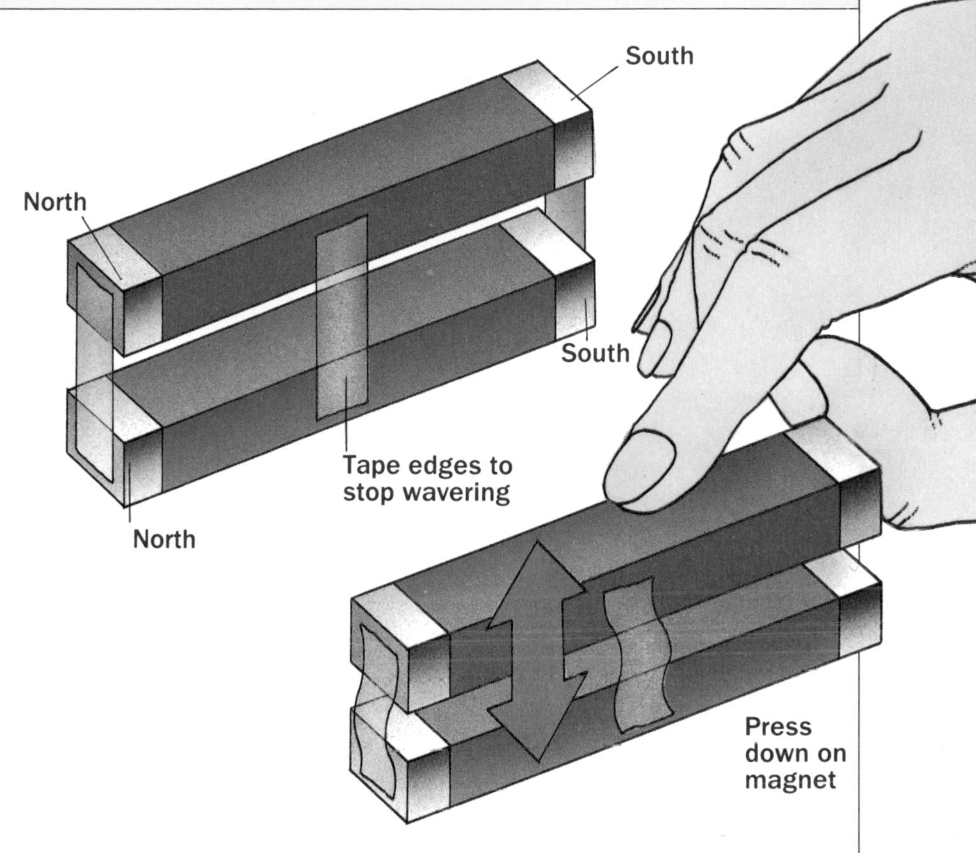

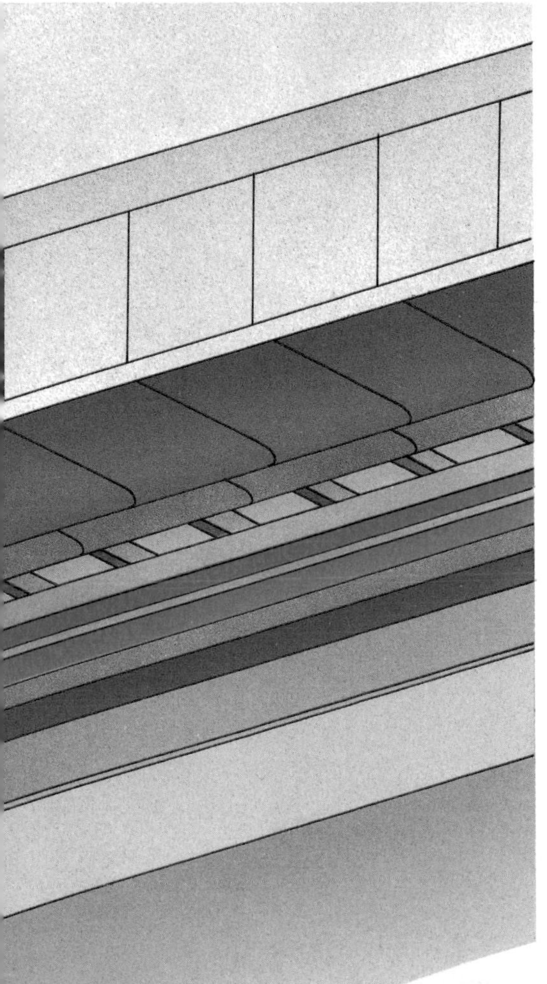

▲ Maglev trains are fast and the track is expensive to build. They are used only for short journeys in Japan.

MAGNETIC FIELDS

If you hold a pin near a magnet, you can feel the magnet attracting the pin. Scientists describe this by saying there is a magnetic field around the magnet. A magnetic field is the space around a magnet where you can feel the force of the magnet on the pin. The magnetic field is strongest close to the magnet.

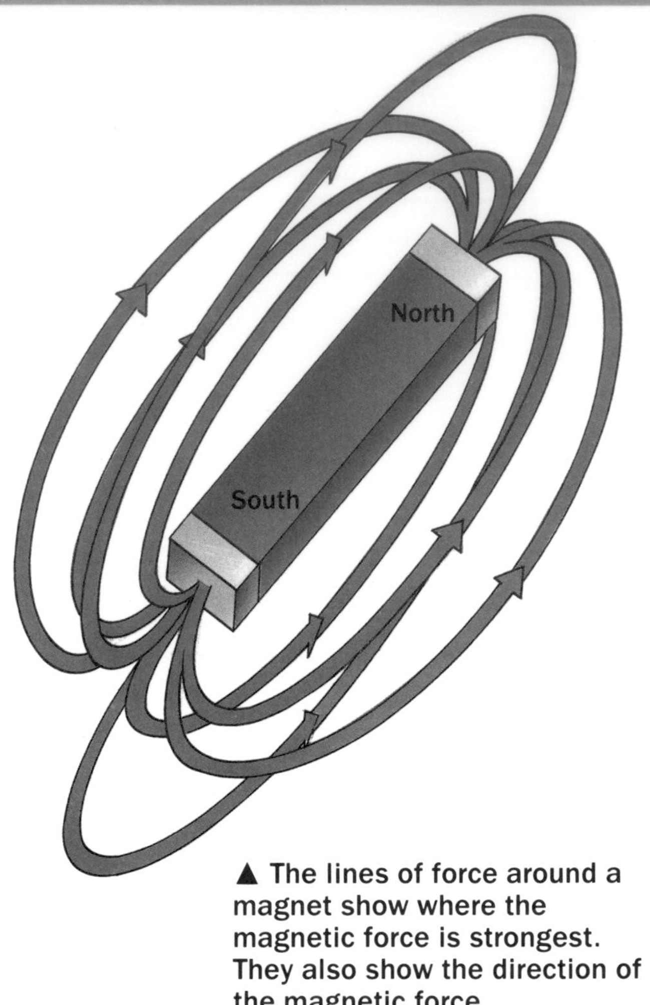

▲ The lines of force around a magnet show where the magnetic force is strongest. They also show the direction of the magnetic force.

LINES OF FORCE

A pattern of imaginary lines can be used to describe a magnetic field. These lines are called lines of force. They provide a kind of picture of the magnetic field around a magnet. Lines of force show the direction of the magnetic force near a magnet. They are drawn so that they always run from the north pole of a magnet to the south pole. They are closest together near the poles where the magnetic force is strong. Away from the poles, where the magnetic force is weaker, the lines are further apart so as to show this.

SEE LINES OF FORCE FOR YOURSELF

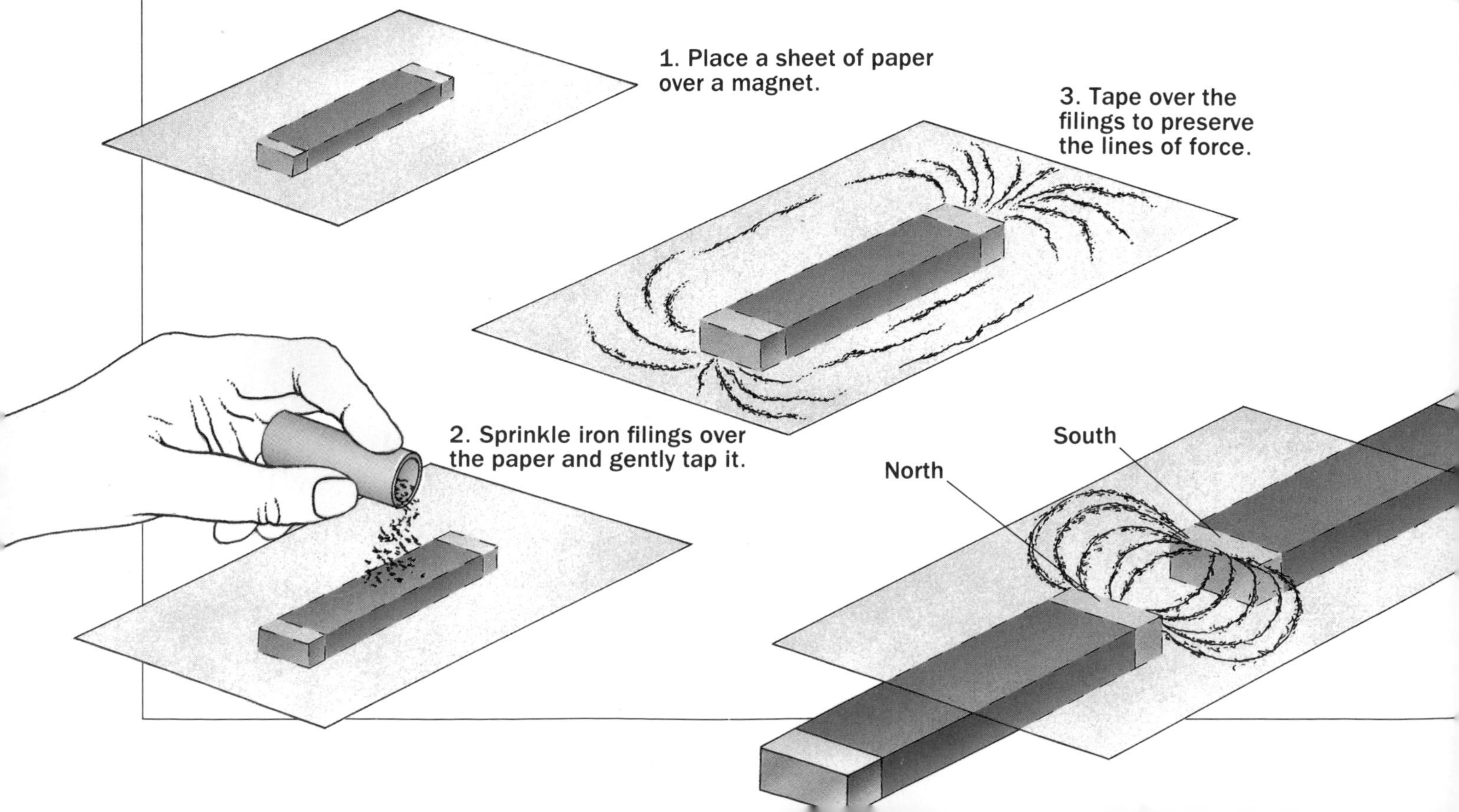

1. Place a sheet of paper over a magnet.

2. Sprinkle iron filings over the paper and gently tap it.

3. Tape over the filings to preserve the lines of force.

North

South

MAGNETIC ANIMALS

Some animals have a built-in magnet that acts like a "compass" and helps them to find their way. Birds use the Earth's magnetic field to navigate when they migrate. If a magnet is fixed to a pigeon's back, the bird becomes confused and cannot find its way on cloudy days. Many whales, dolphins, and porpoises follow the Earth's magnetic field when they migrate across the oceans. Some snails have magnets on their tongues which they use to find their way home. These snails always point north when they are resting. Compass termites from Australia always build their nests pointing to the north. Perhaps they use the Earth's magnetism to line up their mounds. Even humans have a built-in compass. There is magnetic material just behind your nose! Scientists know this because blindfolded people taken many miles from home can find their way back more accurately than people without a blindfold.

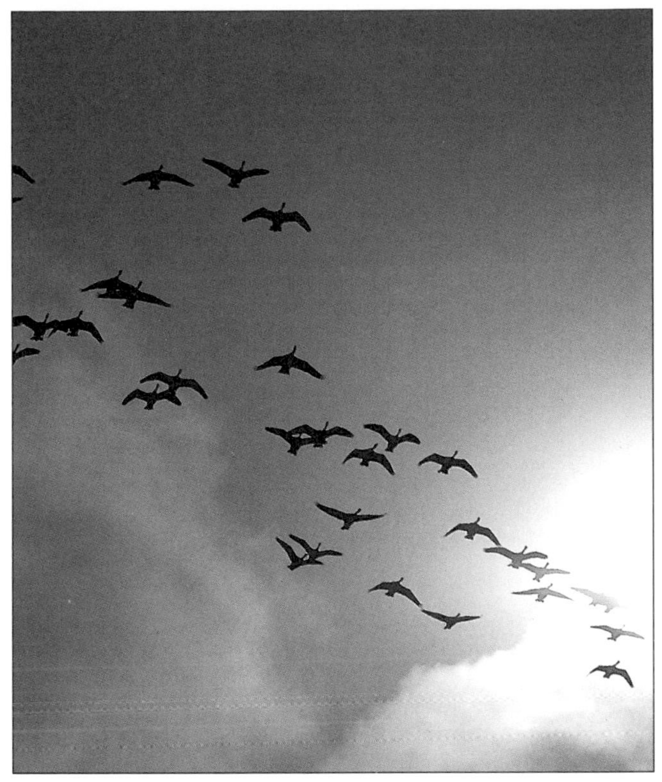

▲ Migrating birds have built-in compasses that they use for navigation. Changes in the magnetic field of the Sun can make them lose their sense of direction.

You can reveal the positions of lines of force around a magnet by using iron filings. These are small pieces of iron, about the size of salt grains. Place a sheet of paper over a magnet and sprinkle the filings onto the paper. Tap the paper gently, and the filings will arrange themselves in lines in the magnetic field. Repeat the experiment with two magnets under the paper. First of all put two north poles close together, and then place a north pole near a south pole.

WHAT HAPPENS HERE?

What pattern of filings would you expect to occur around a horseshoe magnet? Remember that the magnetic field is strongest near the poles. Repeat the experiment on the left with iron filings, a sheet of paper and two horseshoe magnets. When the magnets attract each other, you will feel how the magnetic force pulls them together and see the pattern of filings. When the magnets repel each other, you will be able to see how the pattern of filings changes and feel how the magnets push each other apart.

COMPASSES

The best-known use of a magnet is to help travelers find their way. The Chinese were using magnets in this way in the 11th century. They used a magnetic needle stuck through a straw floating in a bowl of water. The needle turned to point north and south. Similar compasses were introduced to Europe around 1200.

ALWAYS NORTH

The Earth behaves like a giant magnet with a magnetic field surrounding it. The magnetic field of the Earth is produced by the molten metal which is found deep below the Earth's surface, at the core or center of the Earth. As the Earth spins, electric currents are created in the molten metal. These currents produce the Earth's magnetic field. The field produced is like the field of a bar magnet with one pole in northern Canada. This is called the north magnetic pole. The south magnetic pole is in the Antarctic. A compass needle points to the north and south magnetic poles.

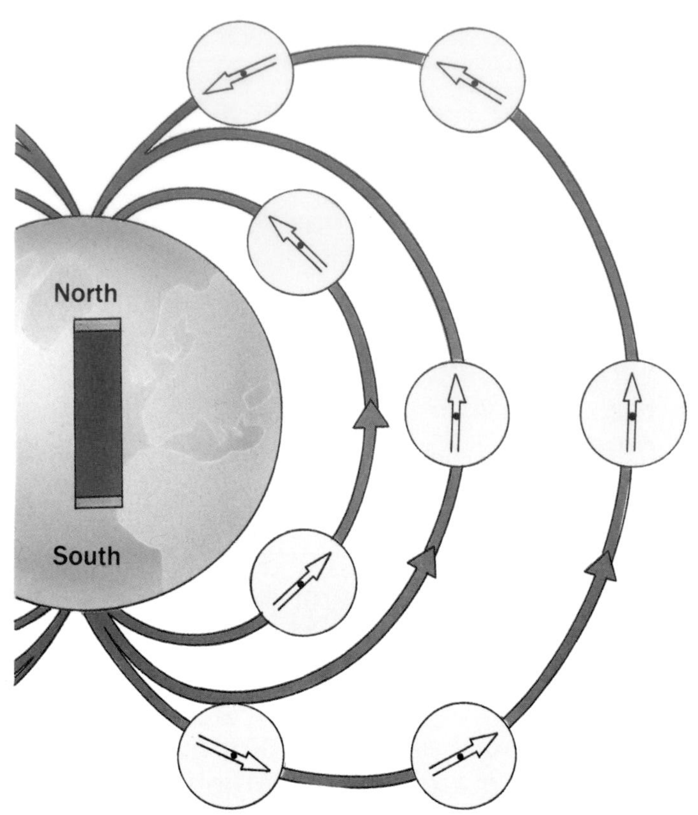

▲ Compasses point in the direction of the magnetic field surrounding the Earth, towards the magnetic poles.

REAL NORTH?

The north magnetic pole is about 1,000 miles (1,600 km) away from the true North Pole. The south magnetic pole is about 1,500 miles (2,400 km) from the about 2,400 km (1,500 miles) from the true South Pole. It is as if the imaginary bar magnet inside the Earth is slightly tilted to one side. The angle between the direction a compass points and true north is called the magnetic declination or variation. Navigators using compasses have to remember this when they work out the direction of true north. Scientists studying old rocks have found that the Earth's magnetic poles move about two inches each year. They have also found that the strength of the Earth's magnetism changes slowly.

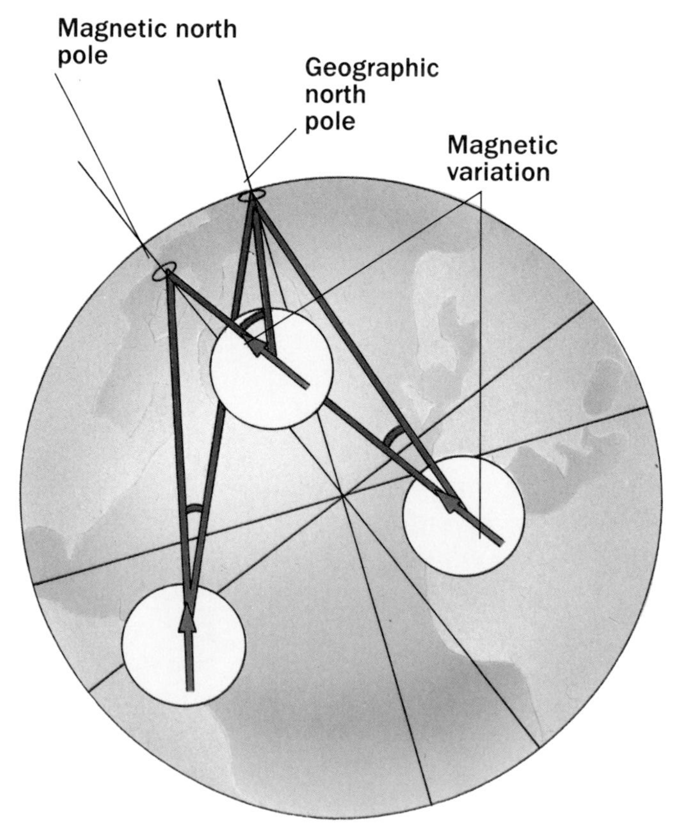

THE MODERN COMPASS

A modern compass, such as those used by hikers, has a thin needle balanced on a fine point so that it can turn easily. Below the needle is a card marked with the points of the compass: north, east, south and west. A ship's compass has a card, also marked with the points of the compass, instead of a needle. On the underside of the card are strips of magnetized metal. The card floats in a bowl of liquid. The bowl is mounted so that it remains steady in rough weather. This means that the compass gives accurate readings in stormy seas.

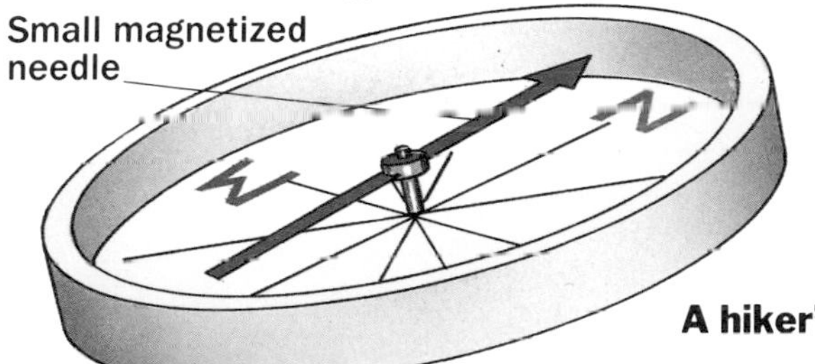

A hiker's compass

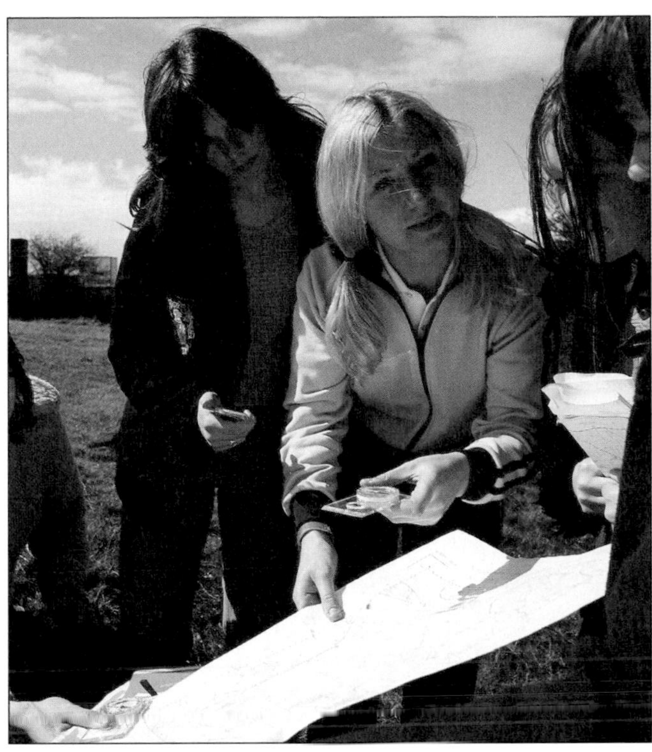

▲ In the sport of orienteering, runners must find their way in rough country using a compass.

MAKE YOUR OWN COMPASS

Make a compass from a bar magnet and some thread. Tie one end of the thread around the magnet. Make sure the magnet is balanced when it is hung from the thread. If you have a thin magnetized needle, you can make a water compass. Cut an inch or two from a drinking straw. Push the needle through the center of the straw, at right-angles to it. Plug the ends of the straw with clay. Put the straw and needle in a bowl of water. The magnet will turn to point north-south.

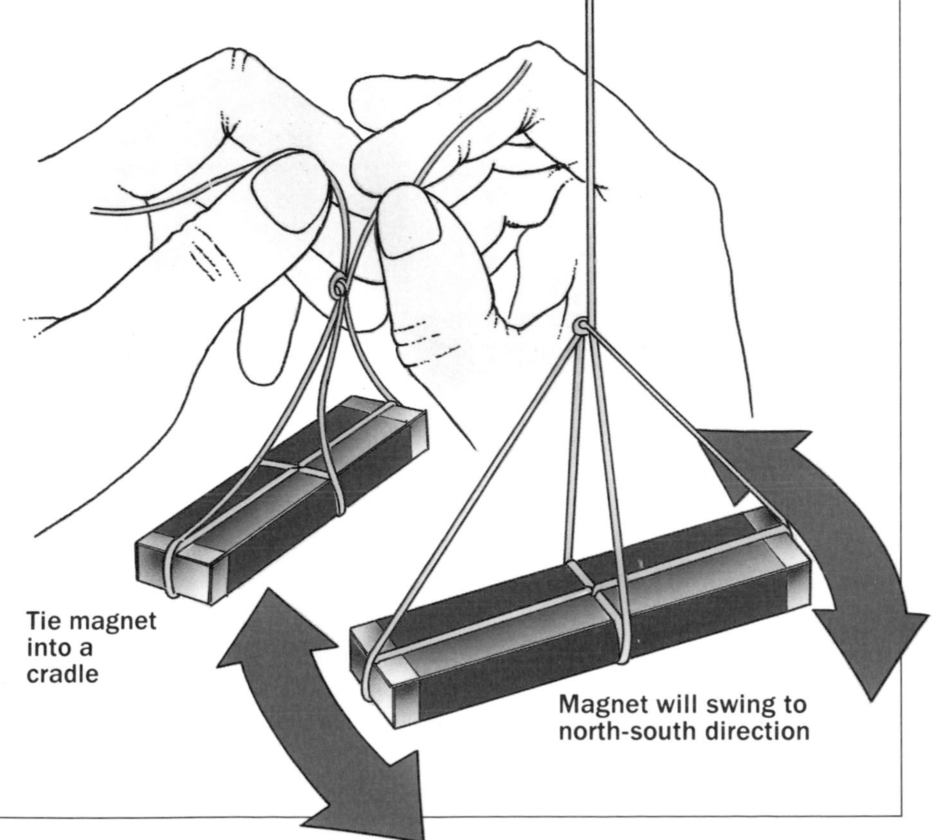

ELECTRIC CURRENTS AND MAGNETS

There is a close connection between electric currents and magnetism. Electric currents produce magnetic effects. Magnetism produced in this way is called electromagnetism. Many electrical machines and household appliances such as electric bells and loudspeakers work because of electromagnetism.

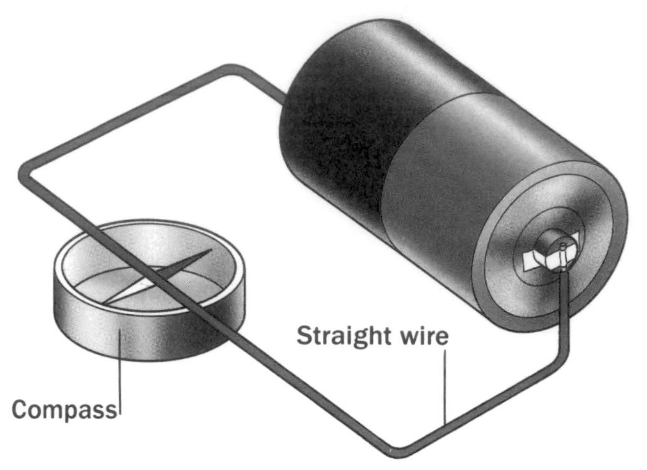

▲ A compass needle swings to point away from the wire when an electric current flows through the wire.

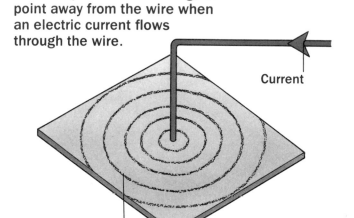

CURRENT AND FIELD

You can easily see the effects of the magnetism produced by an electric current. Connect a wire across the terminals of a battery. Bring the wire near a small compass needle. The needle will swing to point at right angles to the wire. The current in the wire is producing a magnetic field that is affecting the compass needle. The lines of force drawn around the wire are circular. They form rings around the wire. The magnetic field can be detected if a wire is passed through a card and iron filings are scattered on the card. When a strong current flows through the wire, the filings form rings around the wire.

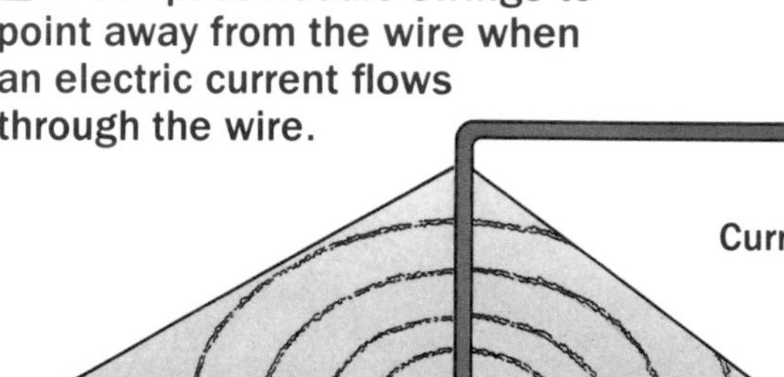

THE MAGNETIC COIL

If the wire carrying an electric current is wound into a coil, the magnetic effect is greater. This can be done by winding a wire around a pencil, and then removing the pencil. A coil of wire made like this is called a solenoid. When an electric current flows through a solenoid, the magnetic field of a solenoid is just like the field of a bar magnet. The lines of force run from one end of the coil and travel to the other end. The more turns of wire in the coil, the stronger the magnetism produced. Also, the greater the electric current flowing, the greater the magnetic effect. So powerful batteries produce the best effects. When the battery is disconnected from the coil, the magnetism stops.

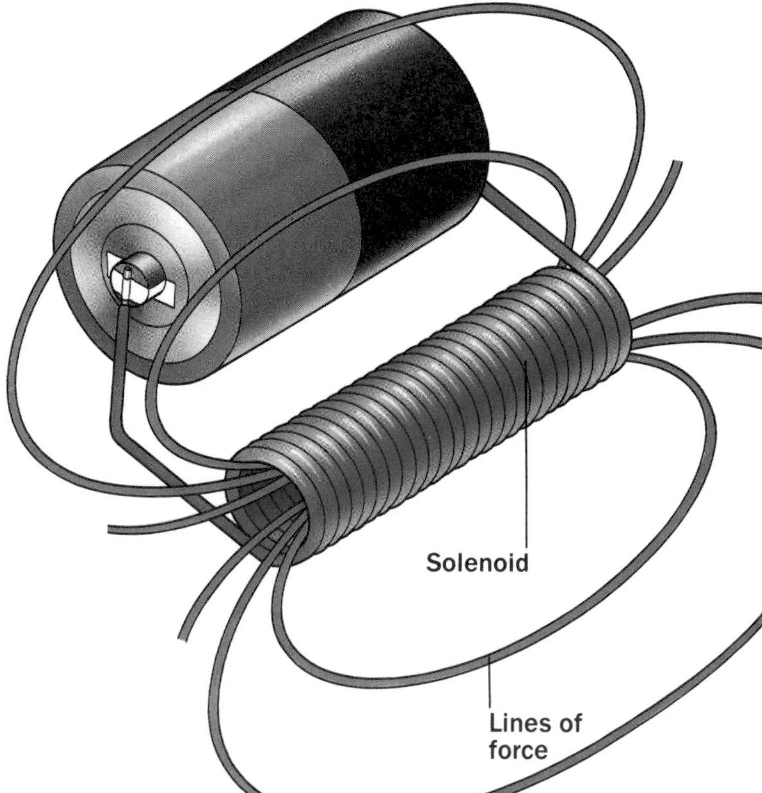

THE POLES OF A COIL

Connect a coil to a battery and place a compass needle near each end of the coil. You will see that one end of the coil attracts the north pole of the nearby compass needle. At the other end of the coil, the south pole will be attracted. This is because the coil is acting like a bar magnet, with a south pole at one end and a north pole at the other. What will happen if you reverse the connections to the battery? Are the poles reversed?

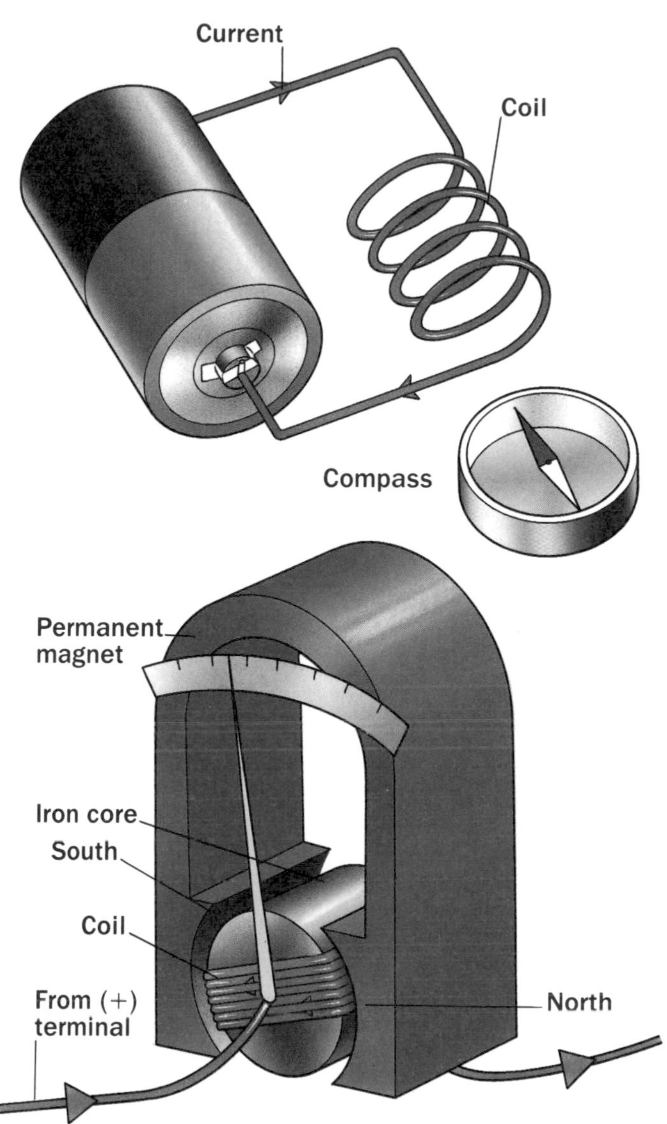

MEASURING CURRENT

The size of an electric current is measured with an instrument called a galvanometer. This consists of a small coil of wire between the poles of a permanent magnet. The coil is wrapped around an iron core which can rotate, or turn. When an electric current flows through the coil, the coil becomes magnetic. This causes the coil to turn between the poles of the magnet.

MAKE YOUR OWN CURRENT INDICATOR

A simple current indicator can be made with a compass and a coil of wire, as shown in the diagram. Turn the coil and compass until the compass needle lies parallel to the coil. When the ends of the coil are connected to a flashlight battery, the needle will swing toward the coil. What would happen if you used a larger battery? Would it make the needle swing further than a small battery?

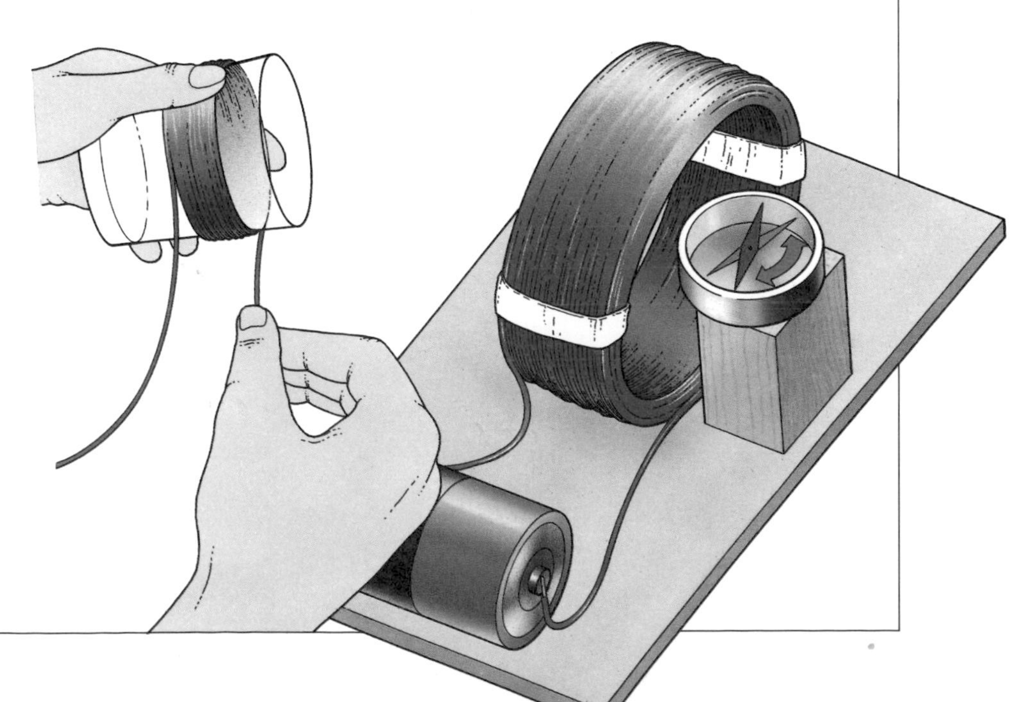

ELECTROMAGNETS

When an iron bar is placed inside a solenoid, the magnetic effect of the coil increases. The lines of force produced by the current-carrying coil flow through the iron, making it into a strong magnet. A magnet made in this way is called an electromagnet. They are useful because they can be turned off and on.

MAKE AN ELECTROMAGNET

An electromagnet can be made by wrapping plastic-covered wire around a steel nail. If you connect the ends of the wire to a battery, the nail will become a magnet and will attract pins and paperclips. If you switch off the current, by disconnecting the battery, you will probably find that the nail still acts as a magnet. This is because steel keeps its magnetism. If, instead of steel, you use soft iron, you will find that the magnetism disappears when the current is turned off. Soft iron does not keep its magnetism like steel. So most electromagnets use soft iron. You can make soft iron by heating a nail until it is red and letting it cool slowly. If you increase the number of turns of wire around the nail, you will find the electromagnet becomes stronger. It will pick up more pins or paperclips. Also, if you connect two batteries so that a greater current flows through the coil, the magnet becomes stronger.

MODEL RAILWAY SIGNALS

A coil of wire carrying an electric current has another surprising property. An iron or steel nail is attracted into the coil. This effect can be used to make a model railway signal.

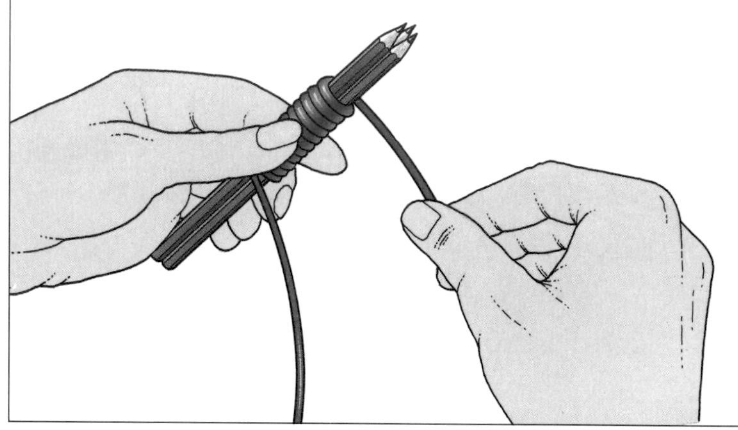

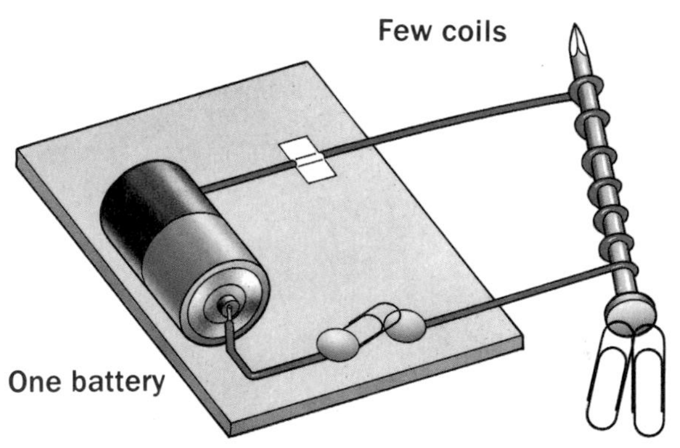

A simple electromagnet

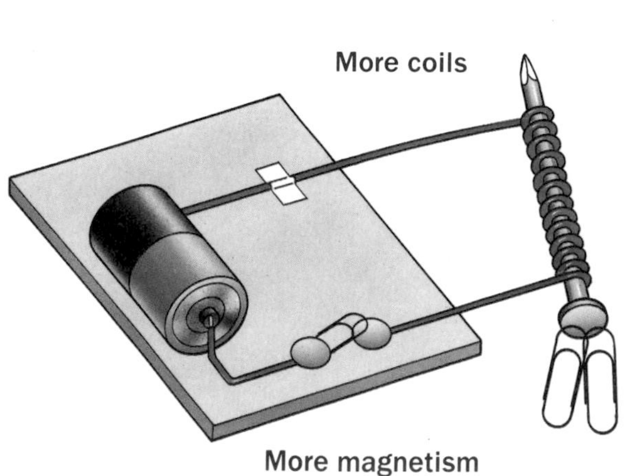

More magnetism

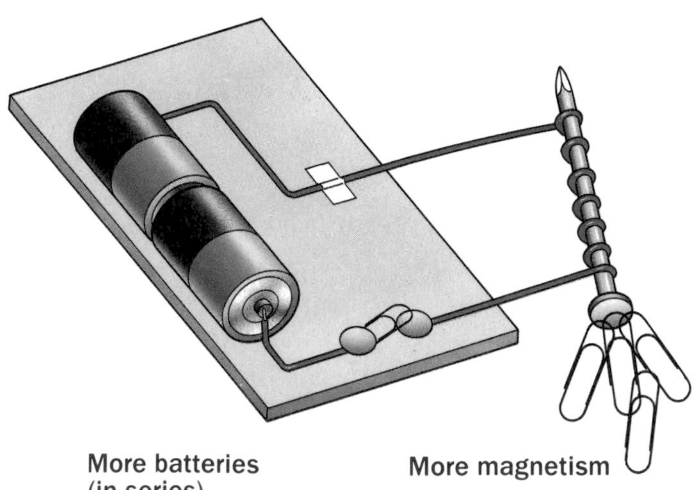

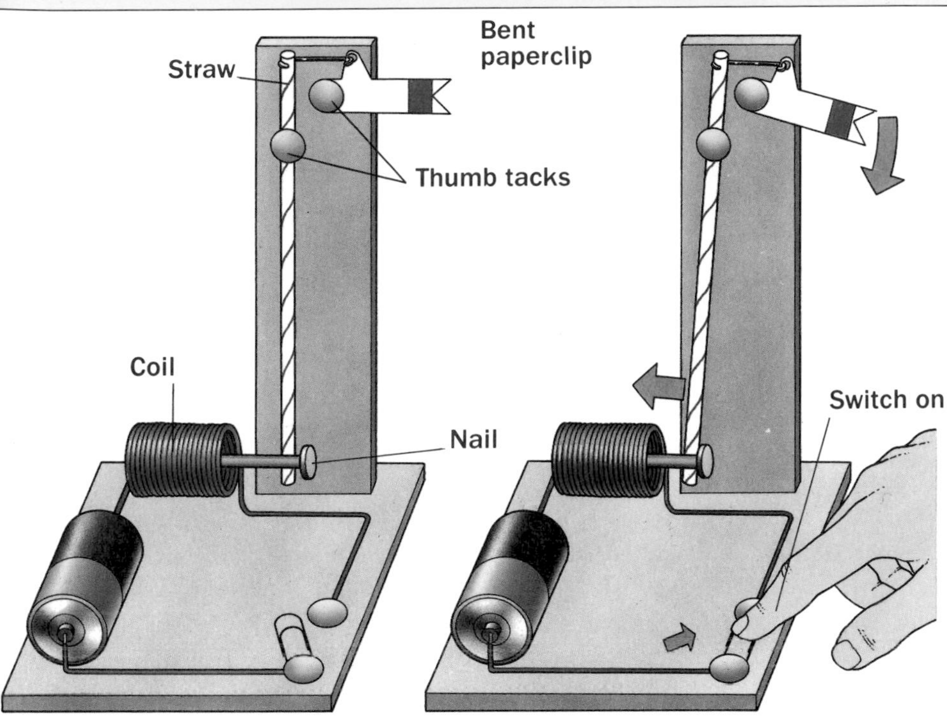

Push a metal nail through one end of a drinking straw. Then glue or nail two pieces of wood together to make an upside down T shape. With tacks, attach the straw and nail to the upright piece of wood so that the straw hangs loosely.

Fix a cardboard signal arm to the top of the straw, using cotton and tacks as shown. Wind some wire around a pencil to make a coil. Position the coil near the hanging nail, so that the nail is attracted into the coil when the current is turned on. This moves the signal arm.

DING DONG BELLS

An electric doorbell uses an electromagnet. In the type of bell shown, a current flows through the coil when the doorbell button is pressed. This magnetizes the soft iron core. The metal chimes are attracted and move towards the core. As each chime hits the core, it produces a musical note. The chimes are different lengths and so produce two different notes, making a "ding dong" sound. The movement of the chimes breaks the electrical circuit and the iron core loses its magnetism. The chimes swing back to their original position. The process repeats as long as the doorbell button is being pressed.

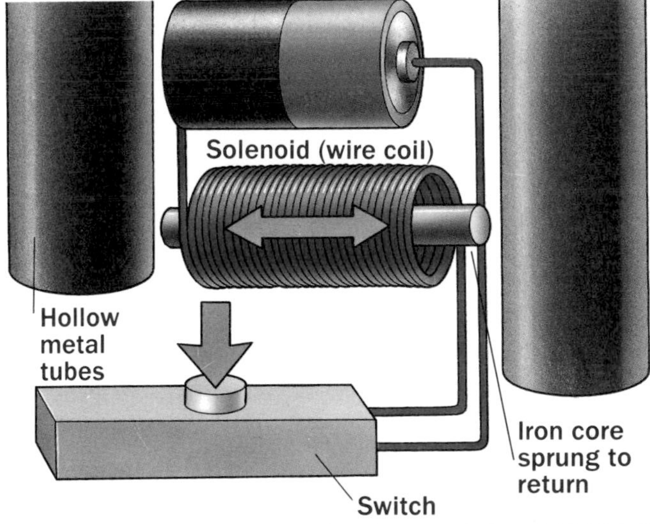

► All doorbells use an electromagnet to make a hammer hit against the bell or chime. The movement of the hammer is used to break the electric circuit and keep the bell ringing.

ELECTROMAGNETS AT WORK

Electromagnets are used in many different ways. They are found in electric motors, video machines, computers, loudspeakers, and telephones. In a television set, they are used to control the beams which form the picture. In hospitals, they are used to remove metal splinters from wounds.

THE SCRAPYARD CRANE

An electromagnet's strength and ability to be turned on and off makes it ideal for moving heavy loads of metal in a scrapyard. A powerful electromagnet, hanging from the arm of a crane, is often used. The electromagnet consists of a large coil of wire inside a steel casing. A non-magnetic plate underneath the coil makes sure the magnetic lines of force spread beneath the magnet. The electromagnet is strong enough to lift a scrapped car. When the crane has carried the scrap to the correct spot, the driver turns the electric current in the coil off. The scrap immediately drops to the ground.

▲ In a scrapyard, electromagnets are used to move metal scrap and also to separate iron and steel from other scrap.

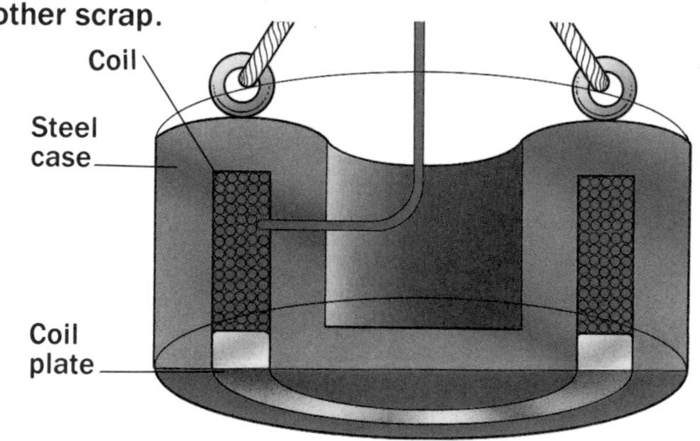

THE CAR HORN

A car horn is similar to an electric bell. When the horn button is pressed, an electric current flows through the coil of an electromagnet. The energized electromagnet attracts an iron bar. As the bar moves toward the coil, it pushes the contacts apart. This breaks the electric circuit and the current stops flowing. A spring pulls the bar back to its original position. The contact points close together, and the current starts to flow again. The process repeats. In this way, the bar is made to vibrate rapidly back and forth. The bar is attached to a thin metal sheet, or diaphragm. The diaphragm also vibrates making a loud sound. The sound travels down a horn that concentrates the sound forward.

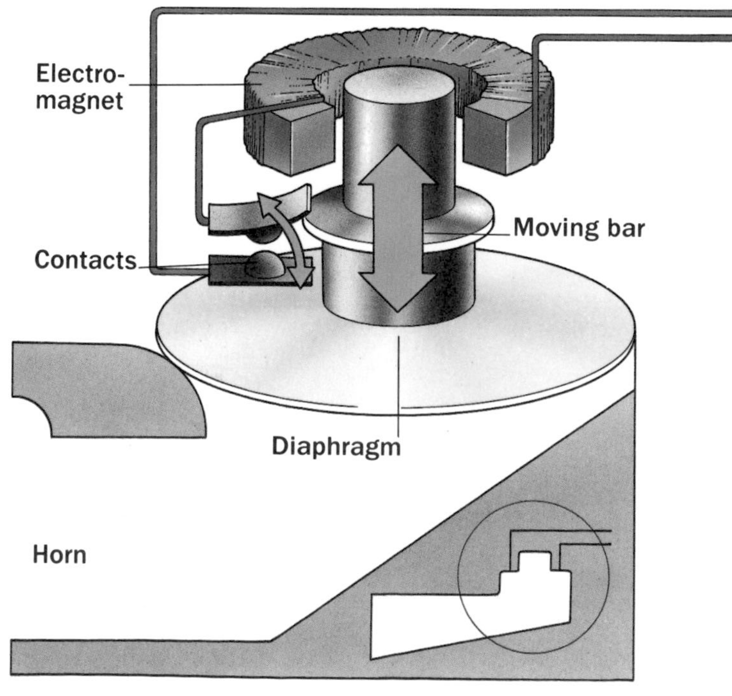

MAKE AN ELECTROMAGNETIC CRANE

To do this you will need a long steel nail, plastic covered wire, a flashlight battery, two square cardboard boxes, a cardboard tube, a sewing spool, a pencil, a paper clip, two paper fasteners, scissors, strong glue, and some thick cardboard.

First, cut one of the boxes in half to form the base. Make a hole in the top of the base and insert the cardboard tube. Make a hole in the bottom of the other box. Insert the top of the tube through the hole and glue the tube to the top box as shown.

Cut a piece of thick cardboard to form the arm of the crane. Attach the arm to the cotton reel as shown. Insert the cotton reel inside the top box, with the arm lying in slots cut in the front and the pencil through two holes in the sides.

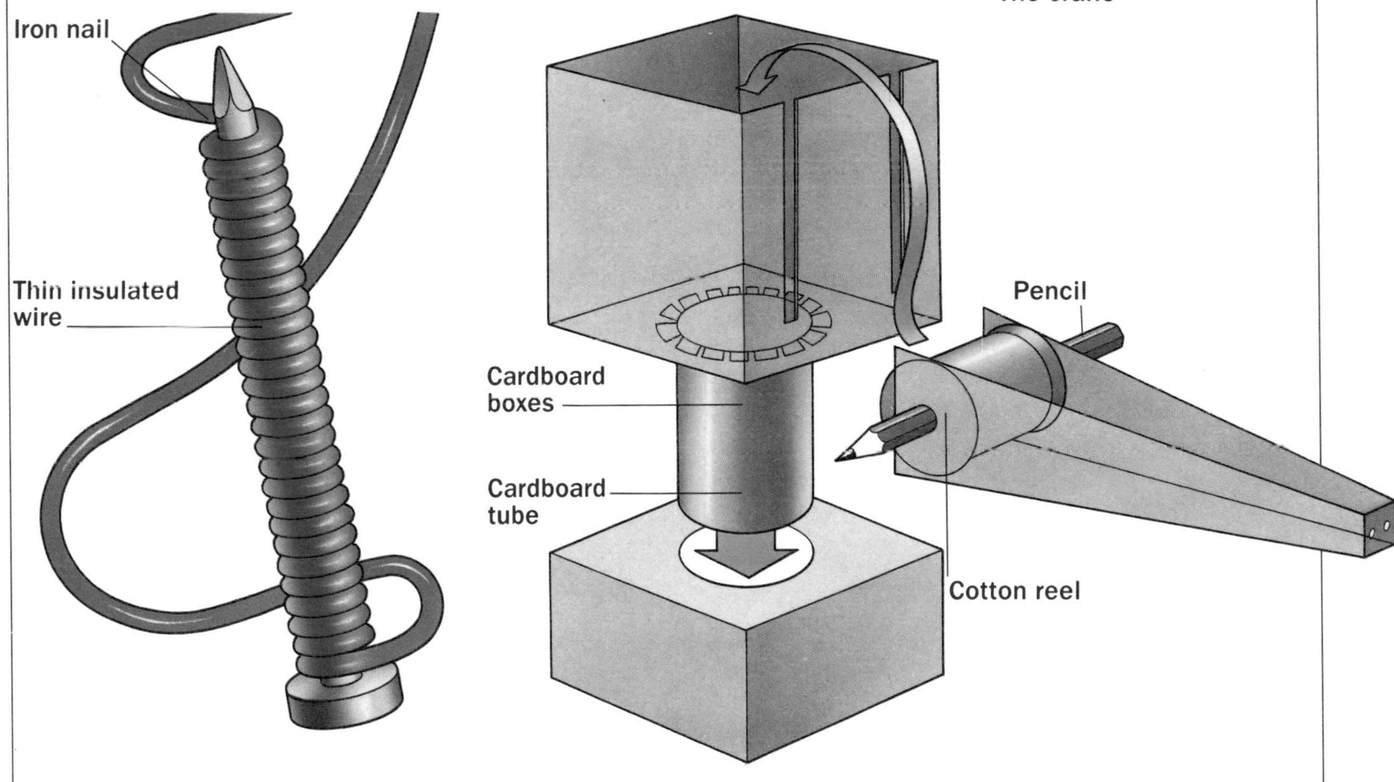

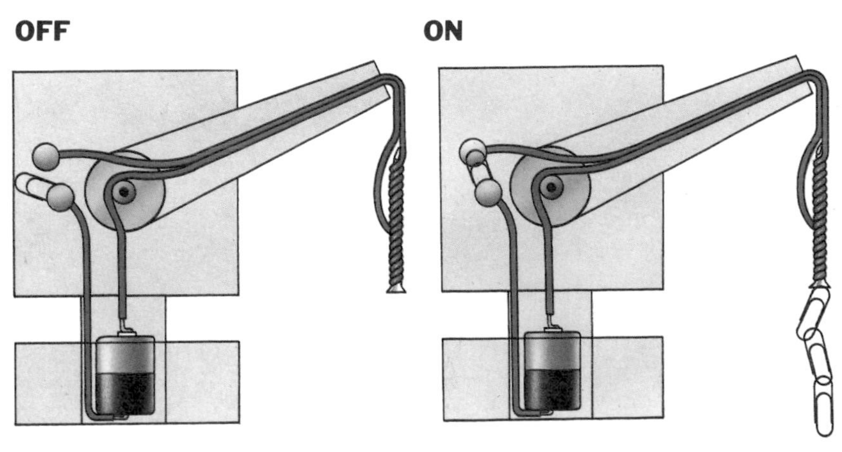

Make a switch on the side of the crane using paper fasteners and a paper clip. Then make an electromagnet by winding about 30 turns of plastic-covered wire around the nail. Connect the battery to the electromagnet and switch as shown.

MAGNETS AND SOUND

Tape recorders use magnets to record sounds. A microphone converts the sounds we wish to record into an electrical signal. This signal is stored as a pattern of magnetism on a plastic tape. The tape player reproduces the electrical signal from the pattern. The loudspeaker turns the signal back into sound.

▲ A sound system is often made up of separate units. The record or cassette deck plays the record or tape, producing an electrical signal. The signal is increased in size, or amplified, by the amplifier unit.

MICROPHONES

Inside a microphone, there is a thin plate of metal or cardboard called a cone. The cone moves back and forth as sound waves hit it. In the moving coil microphone, a small coil of wire is fixed to the cone. This coil is near a magnet. The coil moves when the cone is moved by sound waves. When a wire moves in a magnetic field, an electric current flows in the wire. For this reason, an electric current is produced in the microphone's moving coil and passed to the amplifier, which magnifies the current. The current gets stronger or weaker as the sounds vary. A loudspeaker works in the opposite way to a microphone. The current from the amplifier is passed through a coil near an electromagnet, causing the coil to move. The coil is fixed to a cone which also moves causing the air to vibrate.

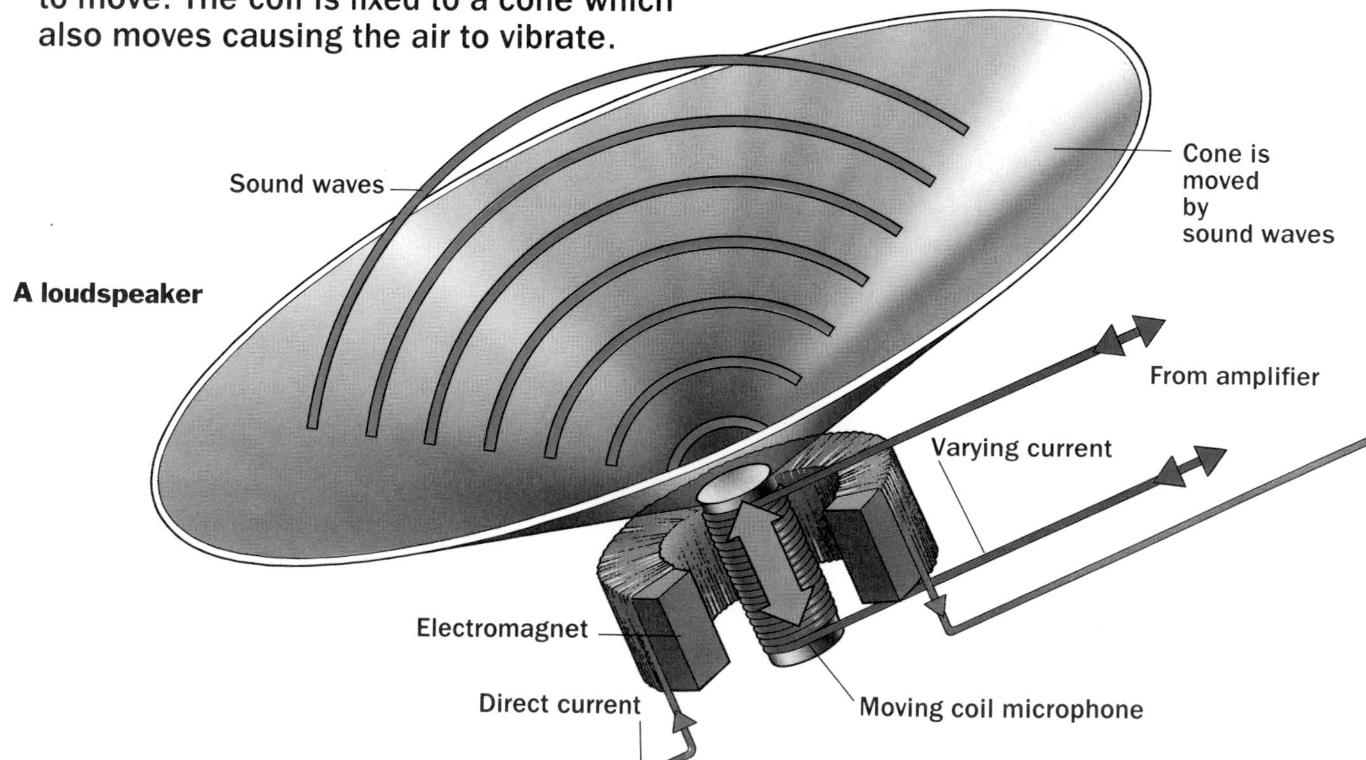

A loudspeaker

THE TAPE RECORDER

In a tape recorder, electrical signals from the amplifier are sent to the record/replay head. This contains coils of wire wrapped around cores, or rings, of metal which have a small gap cut in them. As the signals pass through the coils, a varying magnetic field is produced at the gap. The tape moves past the record head. This tape is made of a thin ribbon of plastic, covered with particles of magnetic material. As the tape moves past the head, the particles are magnetized into a pattern that represents the original sound. To play back the recording, the recorded tape is moved past the head. As it moves, the magnetic pattern on the tape produces a weak electric current in the head. This current is passed to the amplifier and loudspeaker.

▲ A tape recorder has an erase head as well as the record/play head. When recording, it is used to remove any previous recordings from the tape.

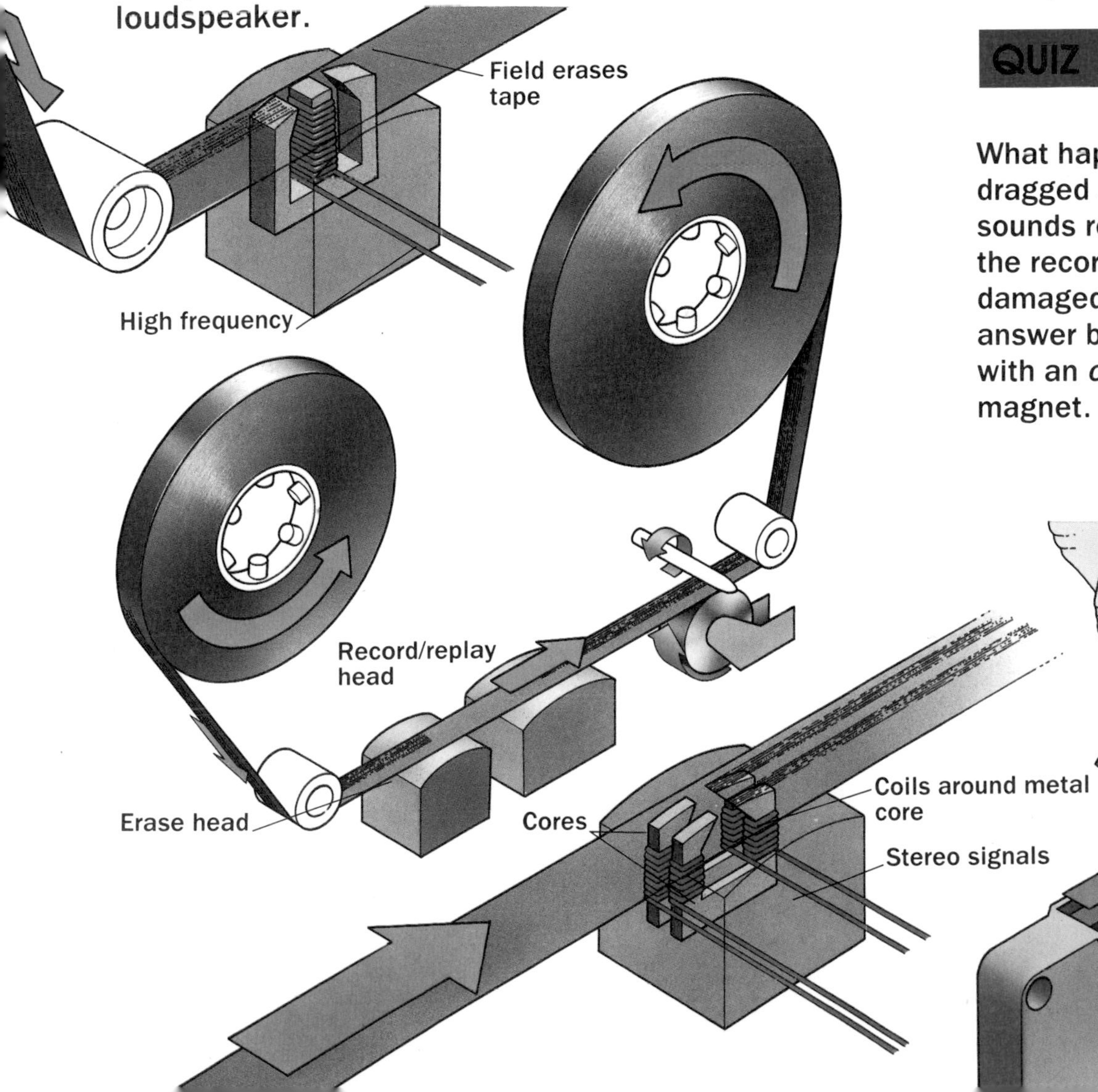

QUIZ

What happens if a magnet is dragged across a tape with sounds recorded on it? Will the recording on the tape be damaged? You can find the answer by experimenting with an *old* tape and a magnet.

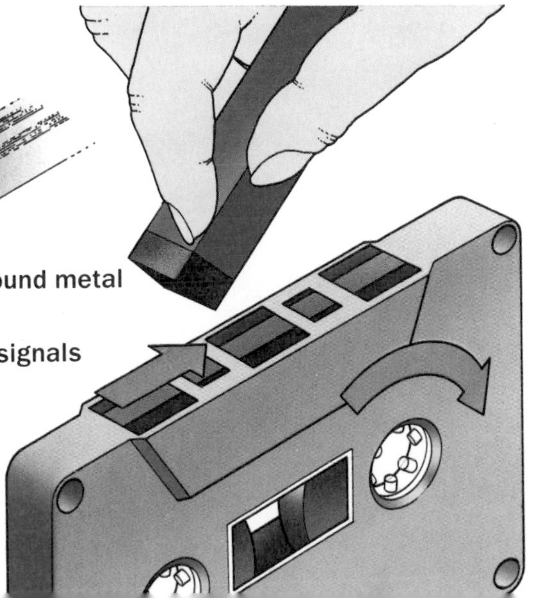

THE GENERATOR

Almost all our electricity supply is produced by generators containing magnets. In a generator, coils of wire rotate in a magnetic field to produce an electric current. Electric motors also contain magnets. But in a motor, a current passed through coils in a magnetic field causes the coils to rotate.

FARADAY'S EXPERIMENT

In 1831, an English scientist called Michael Faraday discovered how to use magnets to produce an electric current. He connected a coil of wire to a galvanometer, an instrument used to detect electric currents. When a bar magnet was pushed into the coil, the galvanometer needle moved slightly. Faraday realized that an electric current was produced as the magnet moved.

▲ The electric current flows in one direction as the magnet is moved into the coil. When the magnet is pulled out, the current moves in the other direction. When the magnet is still, no current is produced.

ELECTRIC CURRENT

Faraday put his discovery to good use by inventing the dynamo or generator, a device for producing currents of electricity. This consisted of a coil of wire which was turned, or rotated, between the poles of a permanent magnet. The ends of the coil were connected to two half-circles of metal. Pieces of carbon, called brushes, pressed against the metal half-circles. As the coil turned, an electric current, called direct current, was produced.

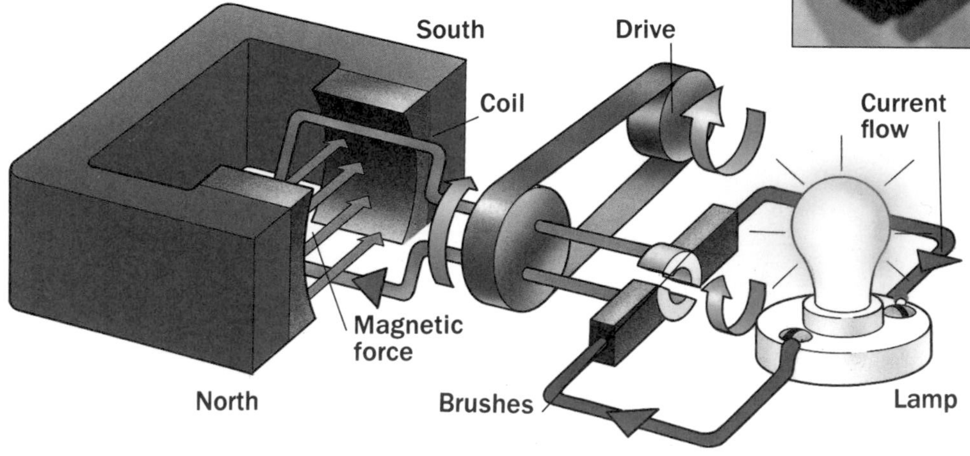

▲ A bicycle generator consists of a cylindrical permanent magnet which is turned by the bicycle wheel. The rotating magnet causes an electric current to flow in the coil of wire inside the generator. A wire carries the electric current to the bicycle lamp and the lamp lights up.

GENERATORS IN USE

In an electric power station, huge generators are used to make electricity. These are often turned using steam power. Steam produced by boiling water is led through a pipe to a machine called a turbine. In hydroelectric power stations, water from a high dam is fed to the turbine. Inside the turbine, there are vanes like the vanes (blades) of a windmill. As the steam or water flows through the vanes, the turbine turns around. This turns an electromagnet inside a coil of wire. The effect is exactly the same as in a small generator, and electricity is produced in the coil.

▲ Some submarines have a generator powered by a nuclear reactor. A nuclear reactor has the advantage of being able to function under water for a long time without having to refuel.

◀ All power stations except hydroelectric ones use a fuel to produce steam which is then used to generate electricity. The fuel can be oil, gas, coal or nuclear fuel.

MOTORS

An electric motor is like a dynamo in reverse. It uses an electric current to provide a circular movement. Inside an electric motor there is a coil of wire. When an electric current is passed through the coil which is in a magnetic field, this coil turns around.

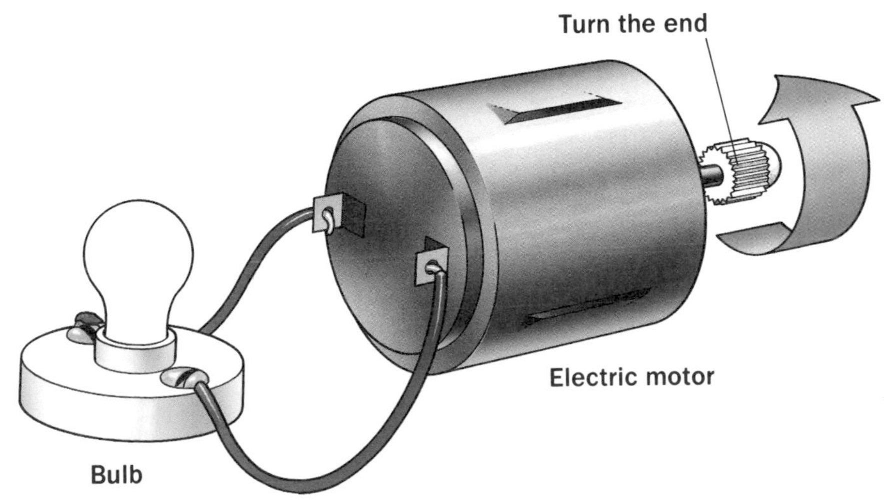

encyclopedia of science

MOTION

CONTENTS

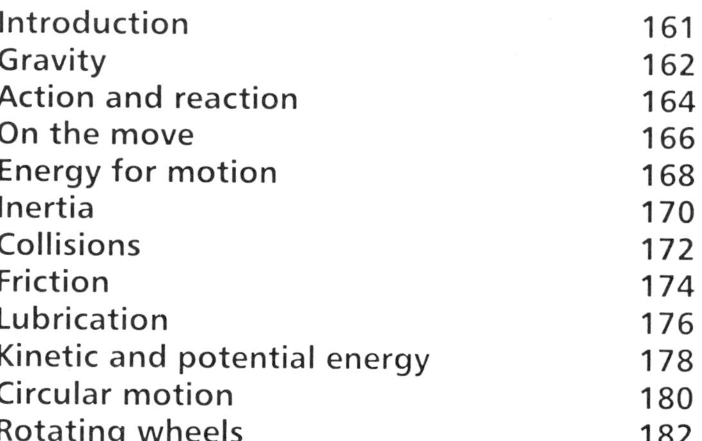

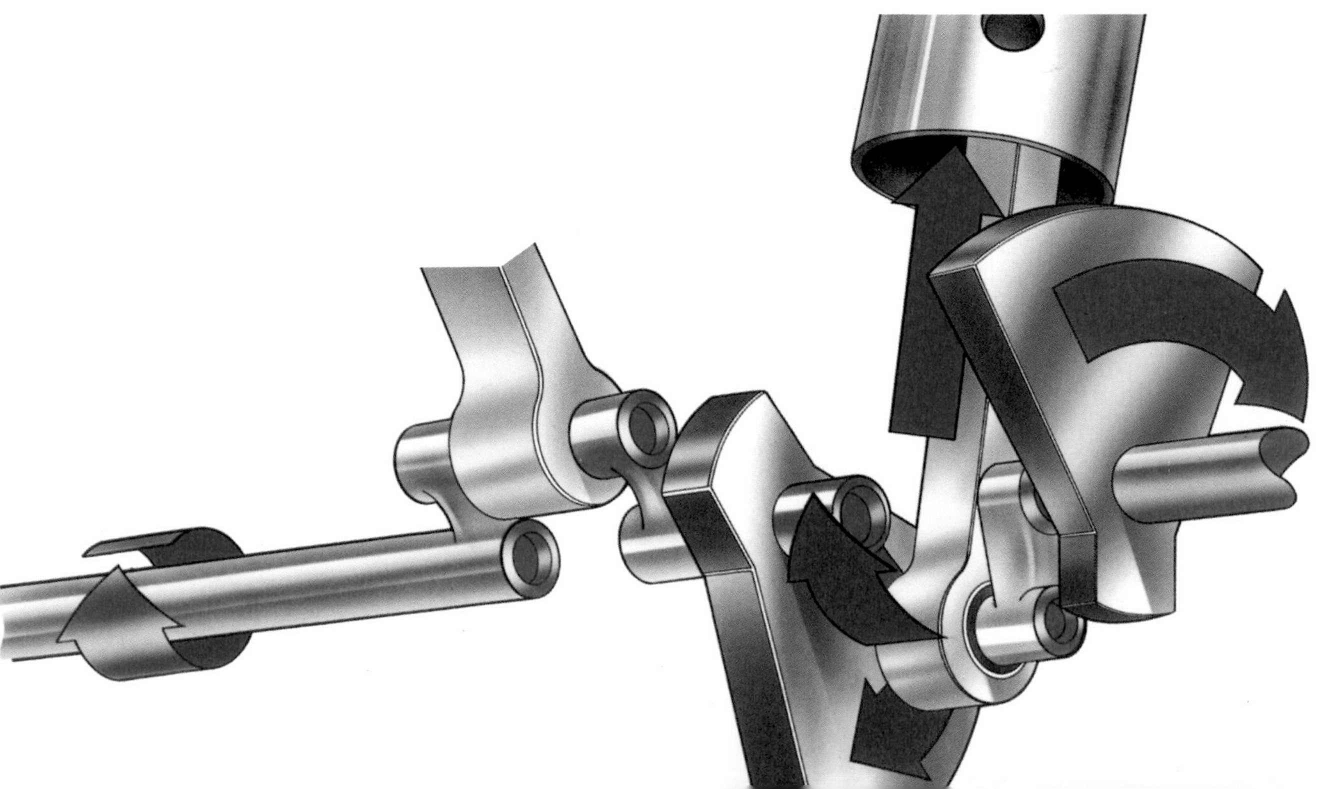

INTRODUCTION

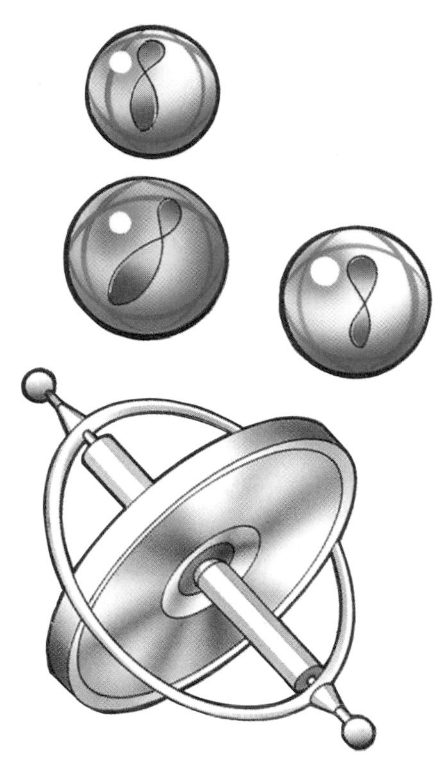

Nearly everything we do involves movement, from walking down the street to throwing a ball or lifting a heavy box. Human movements like these are made using our muscles, which contract and relax to move our bones. In the very earliest times, nearly all work had to be done using the muscle power of human beings or animals such as horses and oxen.

But if we want to travel faster than a horse can gallop, or lift something that is very heavy, we have to use machines. Even simple machines, such as levers and pulleys enabled ancient engineers to build pyramids and construct huge stone buildings. Today, we have cars, trains and planes to carry us at high speeds. Construction engineers use tower cranes to build skyscrapers. All of these, from muscles to machines, involve movement.

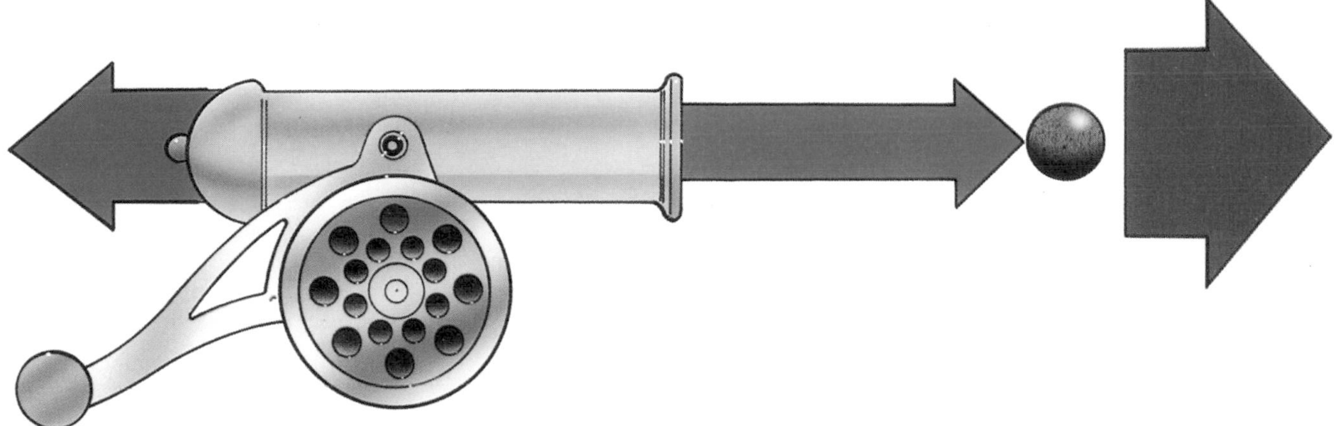

GRAVITY

All of us experience the force of gravity. It is a force that acts between an object and the Earth, and it makes things fall by pulling them down. Gravity also keeps everything resting on the ground or on the floor. Gravity still acts on everything, even though the ground or floor prevents movement. It gives everything weight.

FALLING

When you use your muscles to throw a ball up in the air, the force of gravity pulls down the whole time. It first acts in the opposite direction to the upward movement of the ball so that the ball's speed lessens. When the ball stops for a moment at the top of its climb, gravity still pulls on it and it begins to fall back down to Earth. The size of the force of gravity that pulls an object down is the same as its weight. The weight depends on its mass – the amount of matter in it. Gravity makes the speed of falling objects increase at the same rate, whatever their weight.

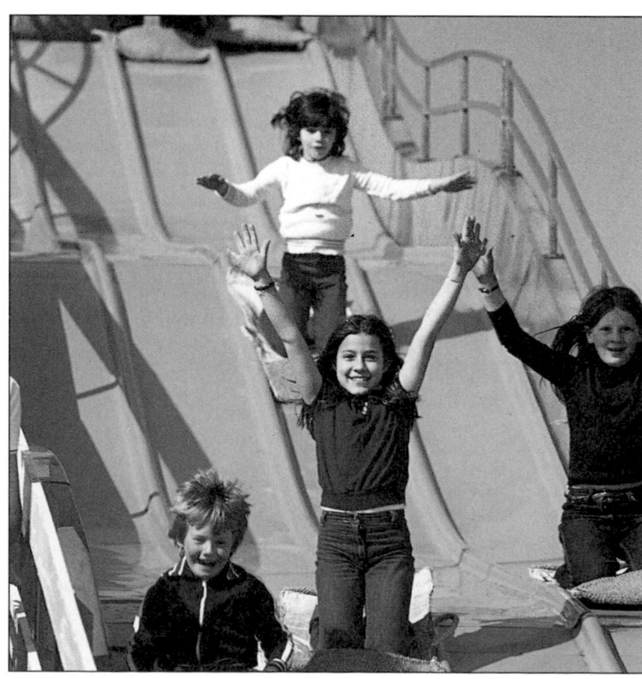

△ Gravity makes things fall. The steeper the slide, the more effect gravity has, and the faster you slide down.

FLYING

Birds, aircraft and balloons are all able to overcome the force of gravity. They can float or fly. This is because they all produce a force called lift that pushes them upward. The lift is stronger than the force of gravity pulling them down. As a result, they move upward and rise.

The wings on birds and aircraft produce lift as they move through the air. The wings must move fast, which is why aircraft have to rush along a runway to take off. Birds use muscles to flap their wings to get enough lift and fly. Balloons get their lift from the hot air or gas they contain.

Once in flight, lift may lessen. When it becomes equal to gravity, the bird, aircraft or balloon stays at the same height. If lift lessens further, gravity will be greater and the object will descend.

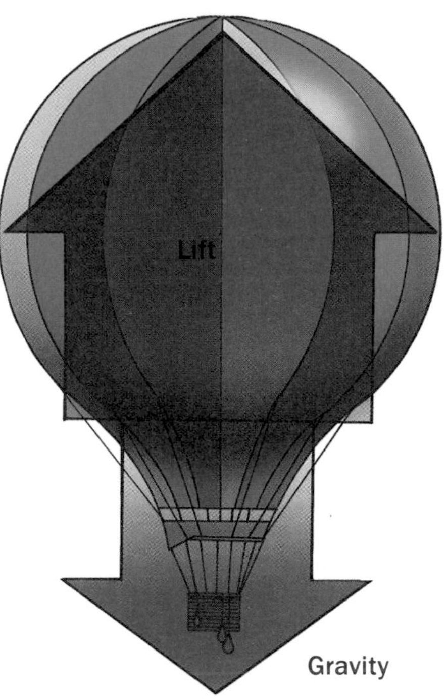

◁ Hot air balloons have burners that heat the air in the balloon. The hot air is lighter than the cool air around the balloon, and produces lift.

FAST OR SLOW?

Drop two boxes, one of which is empty and one full. Guess which will hit the ground first. They always fall together whatever their weight.

Roll two balls made of plasticine down a slope. Let them go at the same time. Both balls move together because gravity pulls them down.

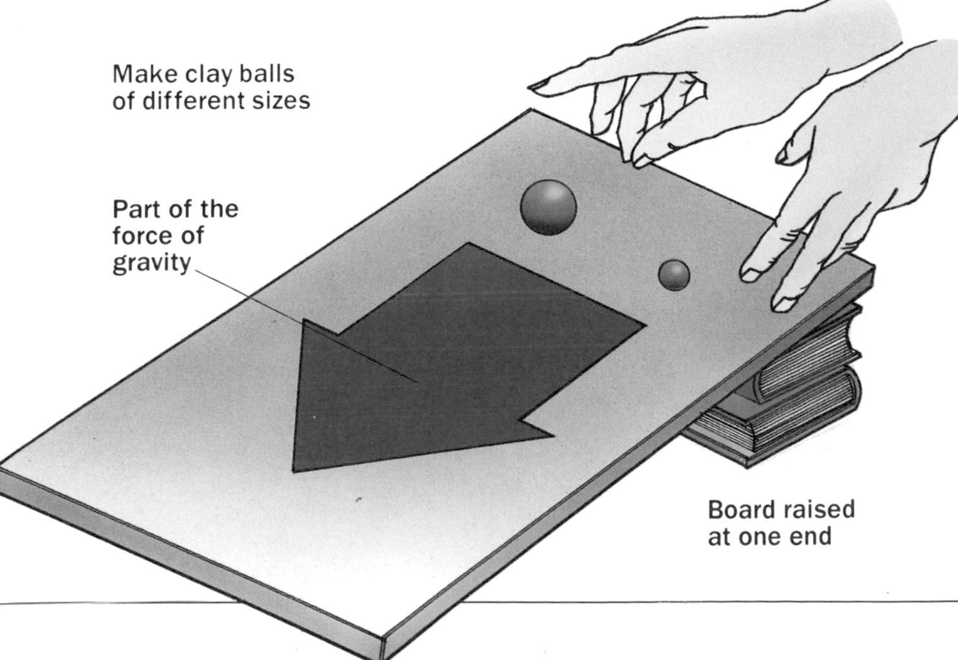

QUIZ

How much would you weigh on the Moon? In fact, you would have only a sixth of your weight on Earth. This is because the Moon is smaller than the Earth. Its force of gravity is only a sixth of the Earth's gravity.

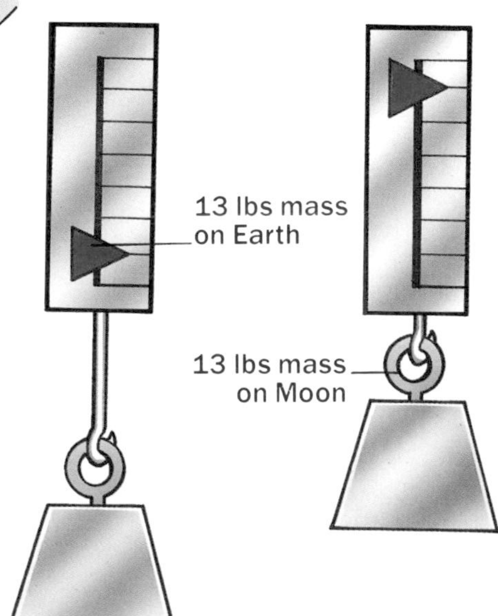

Forces always act between two objects; one object must push or pull on another. Forces also come in pairs that act on both objects in opposite directions. The jet engines on an aircraft produce a powerful force that pushes air backward. A force in the opposite direction pushes the engines – and the aircraft – forward.

▽ Action and reaction cause a cannon to recoil when it fires. As the cannonball shoots from the barrel, the cannon recoils or jerks backward. Two forces act: the action moves the cannonball, the reaction moves the cannon.

PAIRS OF FORCES

When you walk, muscles act in pairs to move your legs. As you step forward, your feet push backward on the ground. You can discover this for yourself if you step on some ice: your feet slip back and you may lose balance and fall over. But normally, your feet grip the ground. As you push against it, the ground exerts an equal force on your feet.

The force with which you move your feet is the action. The equal and opposite force with which the ground pushes back is the reaction.

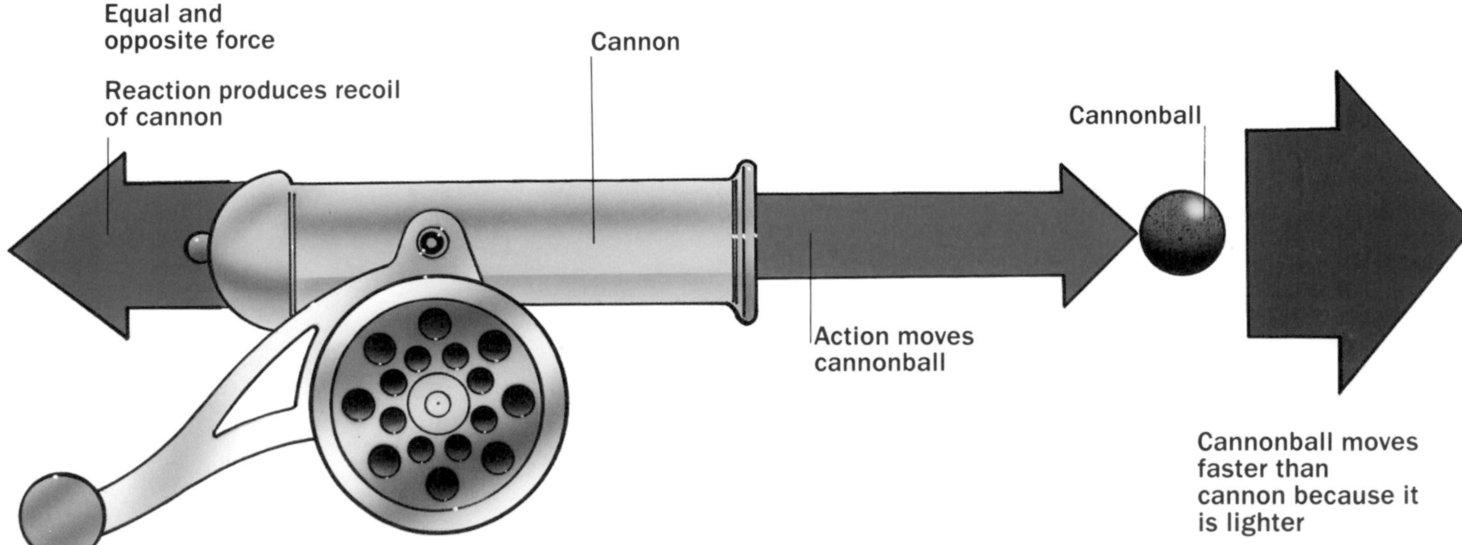

FEELING THE FORCES

It is difficult to get an idea of action and reaction because you may not feel both of these forces when you move. When you walk, for example, you are not really aware of the ground pushing on you. But you can feel how action and reaction operate if you are able to move easily. Put on some roller skates and throw a large ball forward. As you throw the ball, you will move backward on the skates.

△ The action of the skater produces a reaction from the ice, which moves the skater forward.

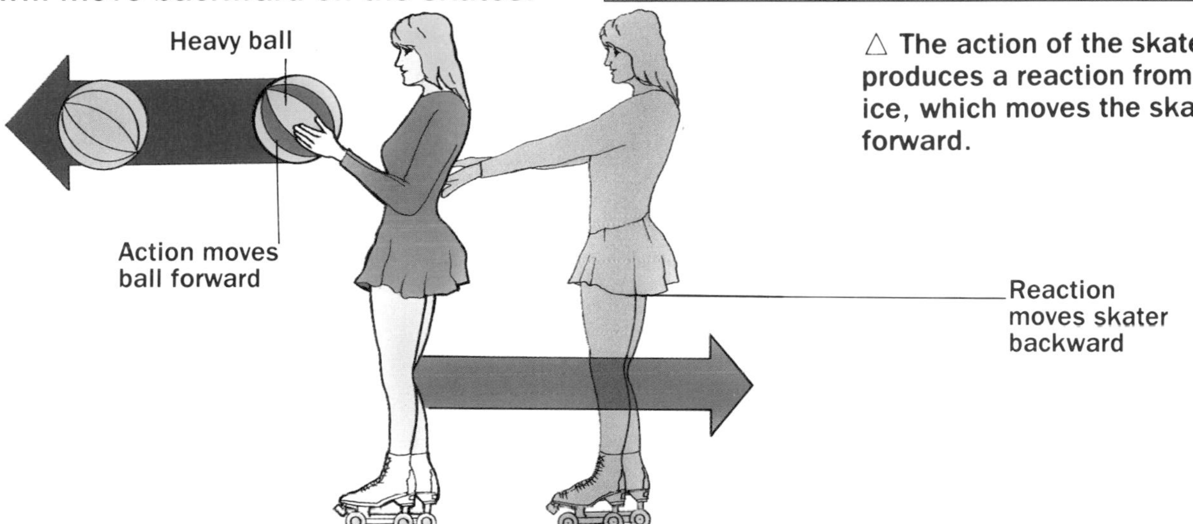

SEEING THE REACTION

Blow up two balloons and tie the necks. Fix a short straw to each one with sticky tape. Thread the balloons on a long piece of string. Untie the neck of the first balloon, and it will shoot along the string at high speed. The reaction to the force of the escaping air drives the balloon forward. The second balloon moves back as air escapes from the first.

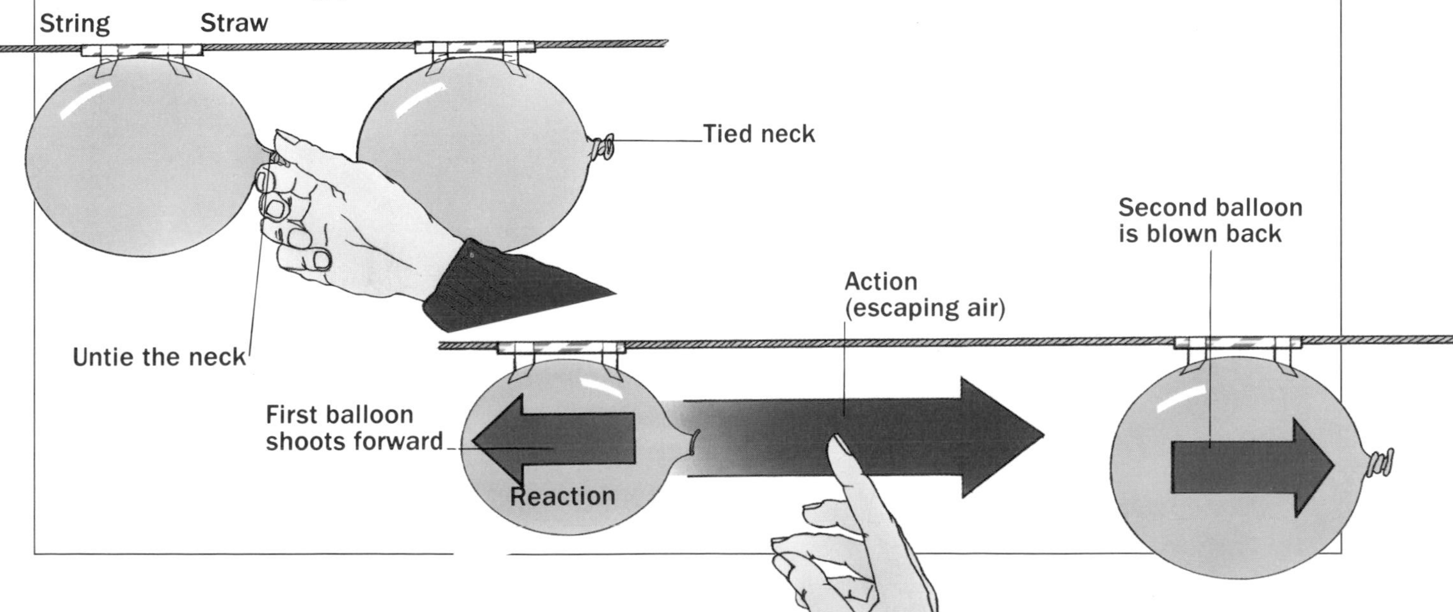

Things seldom move in straight lines. They generally change direction as they move, turning to right or left, or rising or falling. They may also move faster or slower. This is because forces acting on them are constantly changing. A ball moves in a straight line unless acted upon by another force like the wind.

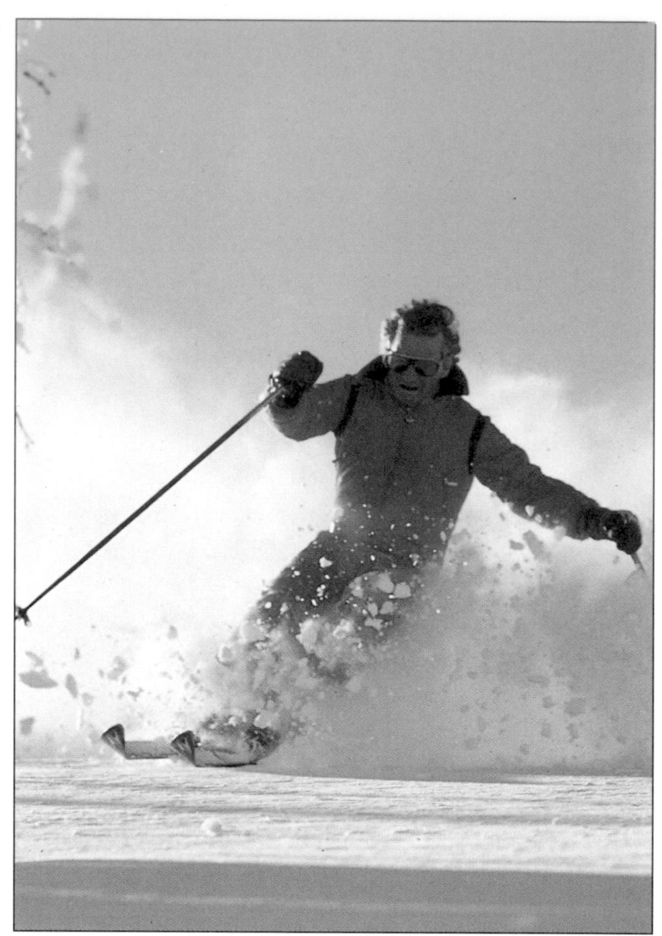

△ A person on skis moves with great speed across the snow, using balance to change direction.

SLIDING AND SKATING

Moving at a steady speed in one direction does not require any force at all. Balls rolling over a flat surface move in this way. But most movement needs some force to continue; you need to pedal a bicycle, for example, to keep it moving.

Once something is moving, it will continue to move without force. People sliding on ice move in this way. They get up speed by running, and then slide over the ice without any further action. There's little force to stop sliders or to make them change direction. They move easily in a straight line at the same speed.

Sliding and skating on ice is great fun. You move effortlessly because the skate blades have a very smooth surface.

CHANGING DIRECTION

Once on the move, an object will change direction only if a force pushes or pulls it to one side. When the side force stops, the object continues moving in a straight line, but in a new direction.

Kicking a football to score a field goal can be very difficult. You can use enough force to reach the goal and aim straight for it, but the ball still misses the net. Other forces cause it to change direction. Gravity makes it fall while a wind can turn it.

Steering a vehicle causes a side force to act on it. Turning the rudder of a boat makes water push on the stern so that the boat heads on a new course. The front wheels of a bicycle or car steer in the same way.

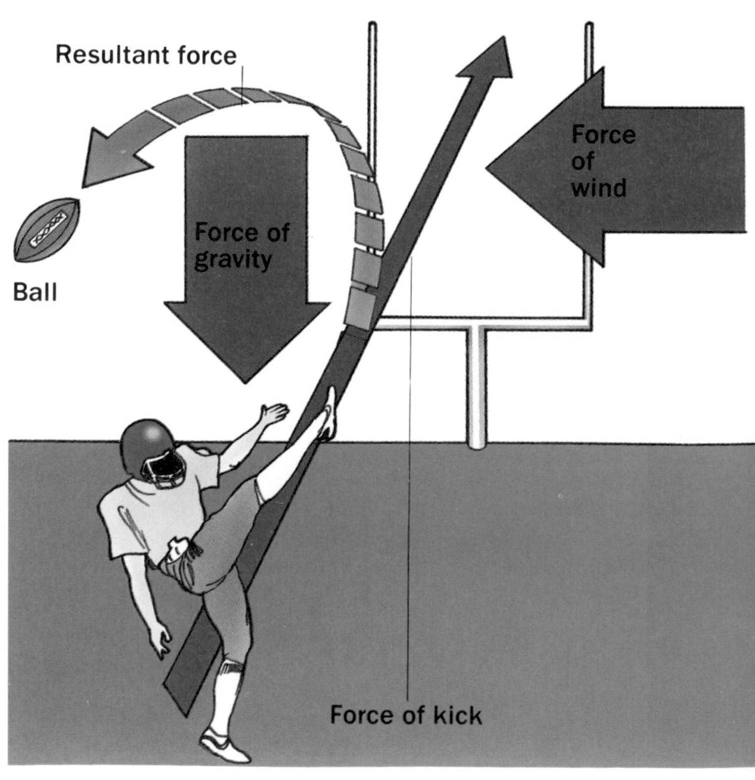

FASTER AND FASTER

Riding a bicycle downhill is exciting. You do not need to pedal, yet you go faster and faster. The force of gravity pulls you down the slope, acting all the time to make you speed up.

This increase in speed is called acceleration. The force of gravity makes a falling object increase its speed by 33 feet a second for every second that it continues to fall.

The greater the force that acts on a moving object, the greater its acceleration. A powerful car has a big engine that produces a lot of force. It can therefore increase speed quickly and move ahead of other less powerful cars.

SLOWER AND SLOWER

After riding a bicycle down into a valley, you will be faced with getting up the other side. You now have to overcome the force of gravity, which pulls you back down the hill. Unless you start pedalling again, the bicycle loses speed and you go slower and slower. If you cannot pedal hard enough to overcome gravity, the opposing force will bring you to a stop.

A force acting in the opposite direction to the direction of movement causes speed to decrease. The loss of speed is called deceleration. It is sometimes necessary for a car to decelerate or stop rapidly. Powerful brakes produce a very strong force that slows the car quickly.

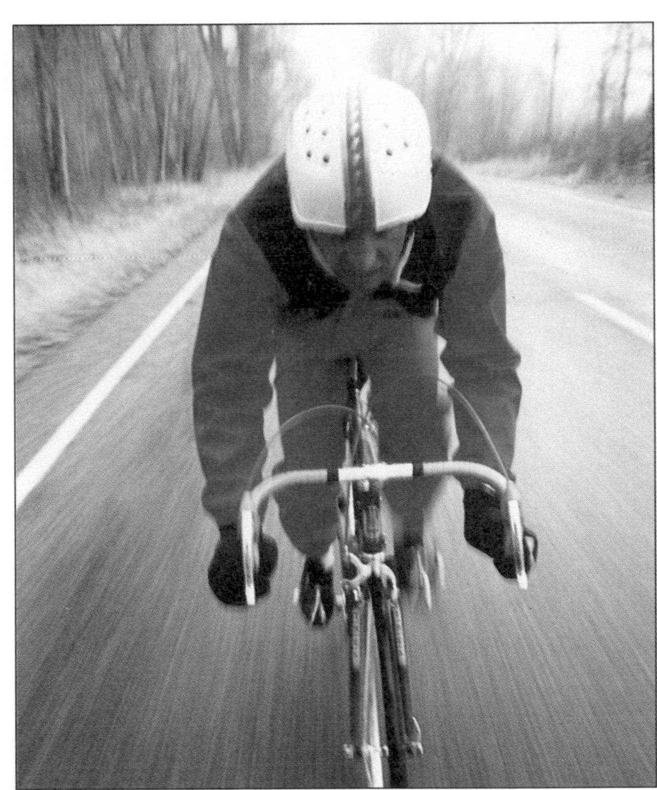

△ A bicyclist struggles to get up a hill. A lot of force is needed to overcome gravity and keep going.

◁ This ball was photographed several times as it dropped. It traveled farther between photographs because gravity made it accelerate.

ENERGY FOR MOTION

Anything that is moving has kinetic energy. The bigger an object is and the faster it moves, the more energy it has. The kinetic energy of an object comes from the force producing movement, like muscles or motors. These sources have a supply of energy that they turn into kinetic energy.

△ A racing car develops a huge amount of kinetic energy. It contains a very powerful engine that burns gasoline.

BURNING FOR POWER

Cars, motorcycles, lorries, diesel trains and aircraft have internal combustion engines, which burn a fuel like gasoline, diesel fuel or kerasone. Burning produces heat, a form of energy, which the engine turns into kinetic energy. This kinetic energy then causes movement. Energy to move muscles comes from the "burning" of the food we eat.

▽ A diesel train has an internal combustion engine which turns fuel into kinetic energy.

ELECTRIC TRANSPORT

Electric trains have motors that use electricity to make things move. They do this by using the electric current to produce powerful magnetic fields that turn a shaft. Electric trains get their electricity from a cable or live rail. Diesel-electric trains have a diesel engine that drives an electric generator.

MOVEMENT OLD AND NEW

At first people used their own muscles or the muscles of animals like oxen to drive machines and vehicles. Muscles turn the energy in food into movement. An early machine to make movement was the waterwheel. This uses the energy of moving water to drive a shaft. Windmills work in the same way, but use the energy of moving air in the wind.

We still use these sources of movement today. Hydroelectric power stations contain turbines that work in the same basic way as waterwheels, and

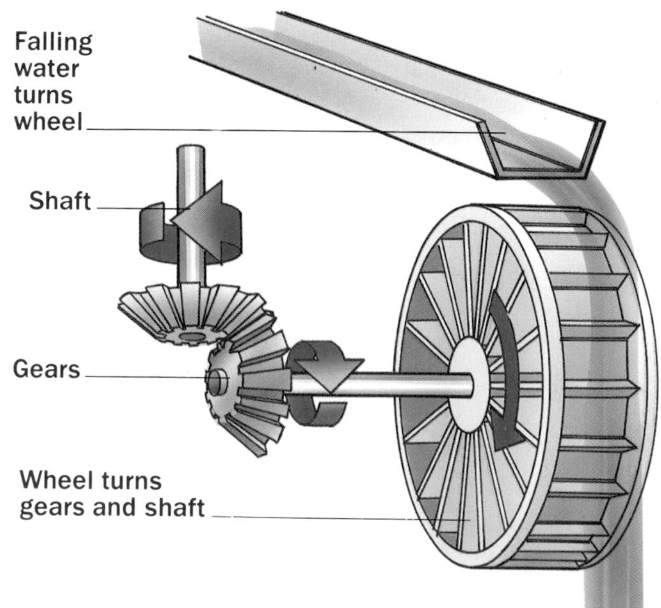

Waterwheel

wind generators are modern kinds of windmills. Both drive electric generators to produce electricity. These machines do not consume fuel to make electricity.

Wave generators turn the movement of waves in the sea into electricity. Solar cells turn the light of the Sun into electricity, which can then power an electric motor and produce movement.

▷ Windmills can be adapted so their sails drive generators to produce electricity.

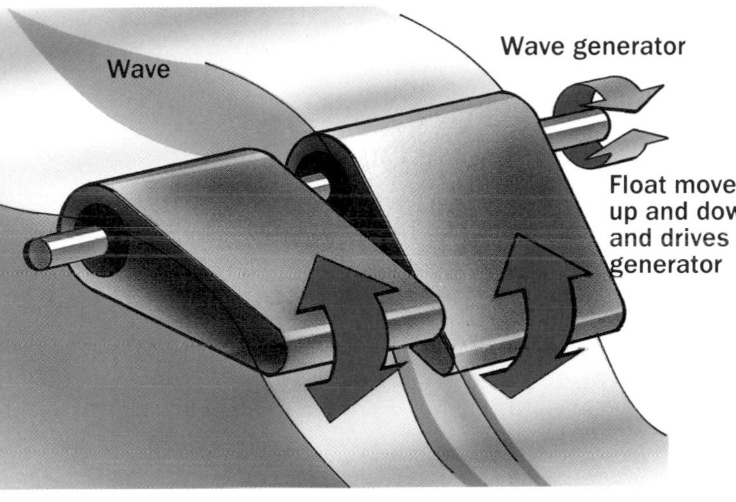

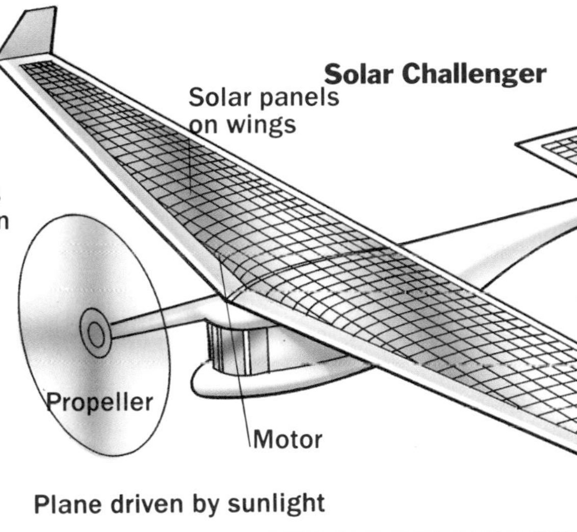

Plane driven by sunlight

MAKE A SAND WHEEL

A sand wheel works in the same way as a waterwheel, but is easier to use. The wheel is made of a cylinder of cardboard with flaps. Sand from the funnel hits the flaps and turns the wheel. The shaft turns a cam, which is a device that converts rotary movement into movement that goes to and fro. The cam has teeth that strike one end of a lever, making the lever move up and down. The other end goes up and down regularly like a hammer.

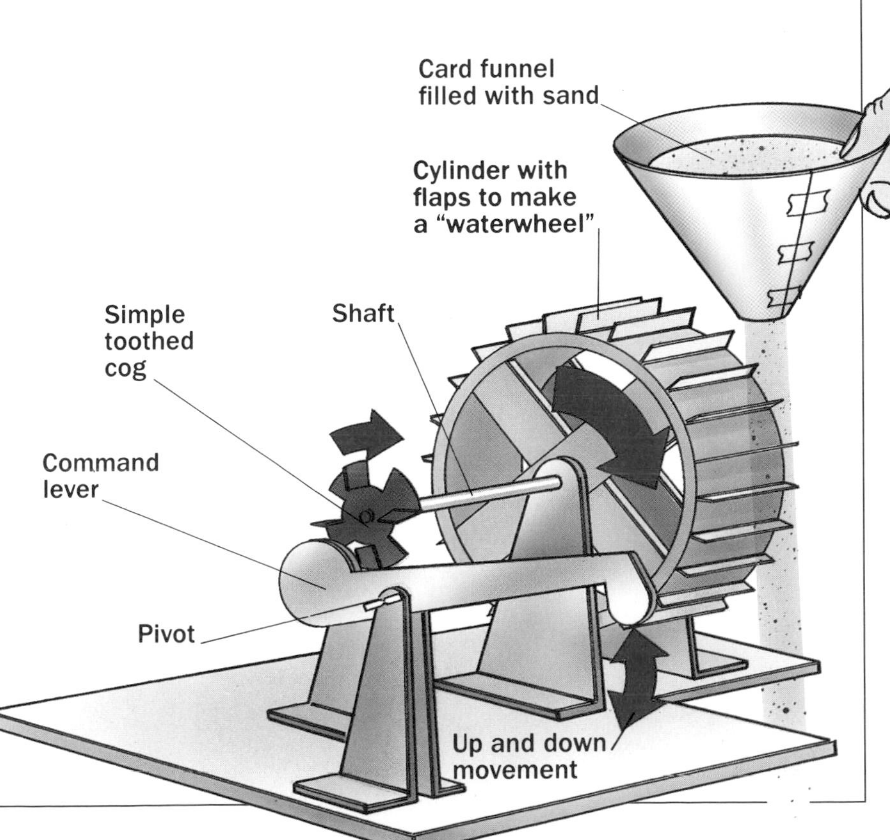

INERTIA

It is easy to push a bicycle, but hard to push a car. We say that something has inertia if an effort is needed to get it moving. In fact, everything has inertia. A light object has a small amount of inertia, and a heavy object has a lot of inertia. The force required to stop something moving also depends on its inertia.

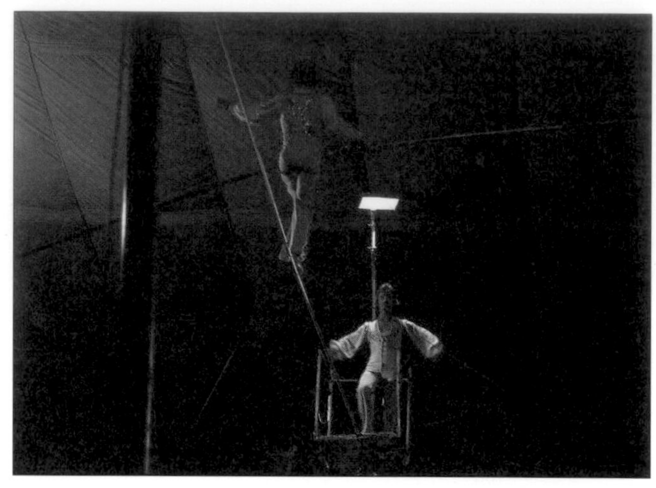

△ This tightrope walker is using a pole to balance. The inertia of the pole is small, and it can be moved quickly to help the walker balance.

INERTIA IN ACTION

Getting a heavy car moving at a certain speed takes more energy and therefore more force than getting a light bicycle to move at the same speed.

Bicycles and cars have gears to help the engine or rider increase speed easily and therefore overcome the effects of inertia. Using a low gear when you start moving sends a lot of force to the wheels. The bicycle or car picks up speed quickly. Once something is moving, inertia resists any change in speed. Less force is needed and a higher gear can be used. Brakes exert a lot of force because inertia must again be overcome to slow and stop. Passengers have inertia too, and will jerk forward if they are free to move and the car stops suddenly. This is why you wear seat belts to prevent you from being pushed forward and injured when a car stops suddenly.

▽ A shot putter can throw the shot only a short distance because it is heavy and has high inertia.

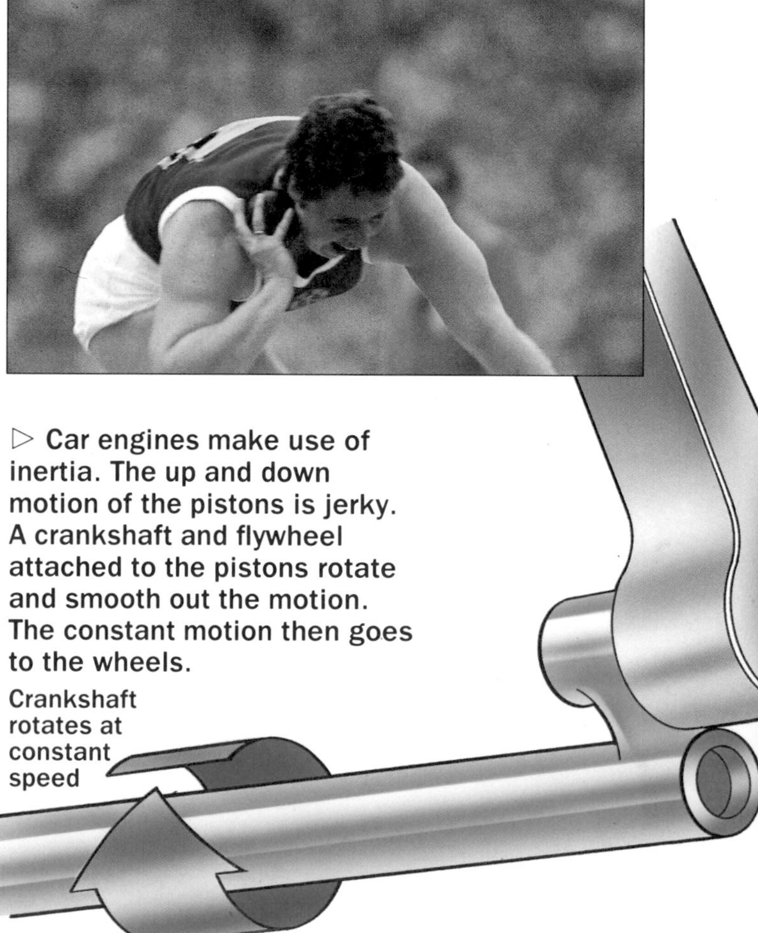

▷ Car engines make use of inertia. The up and down motion of the pistons is jerky. A crankshaft and flywheel attached to the pistons rotate and smooth out the motion. The constant motion then goes to the wheels.

USING INERTIA

It is possible to make use of inertia when we need to keep something moving at the same speed. This happens in the turntable of a record player, which must turn at a constant speed. The turntable is heavy, and its high inertia prevents it from changing speed if the force of the motor driving the turntable alters slightly.

A flywheel is a heavy disk that is used in the same way in car engines. Some toys contain a flywheel connected to the wheels which keep them moving.

TOY TRUCK

Attach a string to a toy truck and fix a weight to the other end of the string. Place the truck on a table with the string over the edge. Let go: the weight pulls the truck quickly to the edge. Try again, but this time load the truck with some weights. Now the truck moves more slowly because the extra weight gives the truck more inertia.

Heavy webs on crankshaft have high inertia helping to maintain constant speed

Piston moves up and down

Crank changes movement of piston into circular motion

QUIZ

Place a piece of cardboard on a table and put a large coin on top. Can you move the cardboard without disturbing the coin? Flick the cardboard with your finger as hard as you can. It should fly out from under the coin! This is because the inertia of the coin makes it stay still.

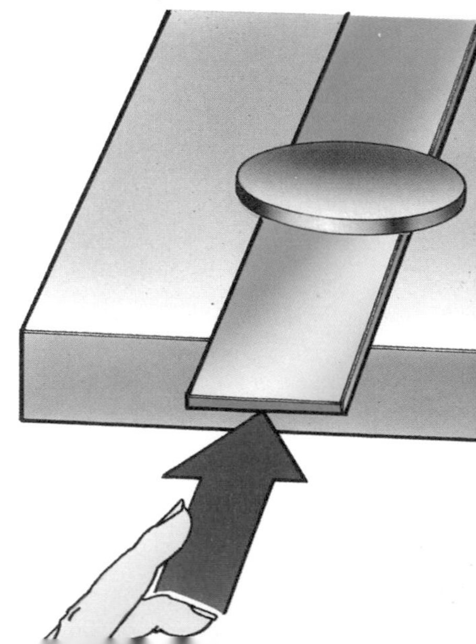

A moving object may collide, perhaps with another object on the move or with an obstacle. As it comes to a stop, the moving object loses its kinetic energy. This energy has to go somewhere; energy often goes to the other object which may start moving or change the energy it receives into heat.

TRANSFERRING MOTION

A moving object often collides with another that is free to move, like the balls in a game of pool or billiards. As one ball strikes another, it sets the other ball rolling. The first ball transfers kinetic energy to the second ball, which starts to move. It may transfer all its energy, so that the first ball comes to a stop. The second ball then moves off at the same speed as the first ball. If the first ball transfers only part of its energy, both balls continue to move at a slower speed.

△ Games like pool use collisions. The players use wooden poles to make one ball collide with another.

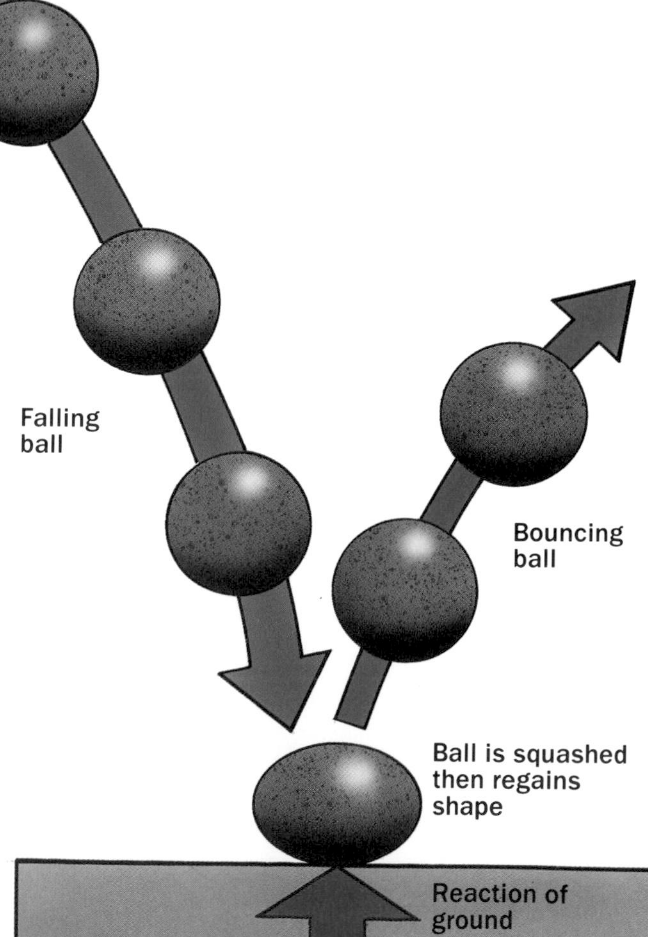

BOUNCING

A collision often results in a bounce. In this case, one or both of the objects is elastic, like a rubber ball. An elastic object changes shape when a force acts on it, but regains its shape when the force stops. The ball changes shape as it strikes the ground. Then it regains its shape, which causes it to push against the ground and bounce so that it also regains its kinetic energy.

△ Children can bounce on an inflatable because inflated objects are elastic.

ABSORBING MOTION

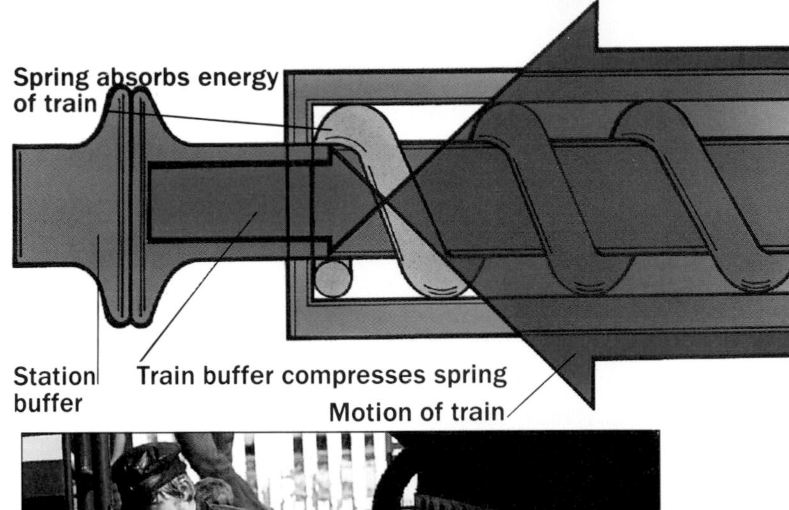

Not all collisions result in movement. Soft surfaces can absorb motion so that anything striking the surface stops. The objects in the collision absorb the kinetic energy of the moving object. The energy changes into sound (the noise of the collision) and into heat.

Springs are very good at absorbing energy. Sprung bumpers on a railway train can bring the train to a halt without damaging anything if a collision occurs at slow speed. Shock absorbers work in much the same way. In the human body, disks of cartilage between the bones of the spine act as shock absorbers when you land after a jump.

▷ A train has bumpers to absorb movements between the carriages or trucks, which is important when the train stops.

COLLIDING COINS

Take some coins of different sizes. Tape two rulers to a table top so that they form a narrow channel. The coins should be able to slide easily along the channel.

Place a marker on one ruler a short distance along the channel. Put a coin by the marker, and flick another coin up the channel to strike the first coin. Note how far the coins move. Try different coins, and try to flick with the same force each time. See how lighter coins move farther. See also how flicking a heavier coin makes the other coin move farther.

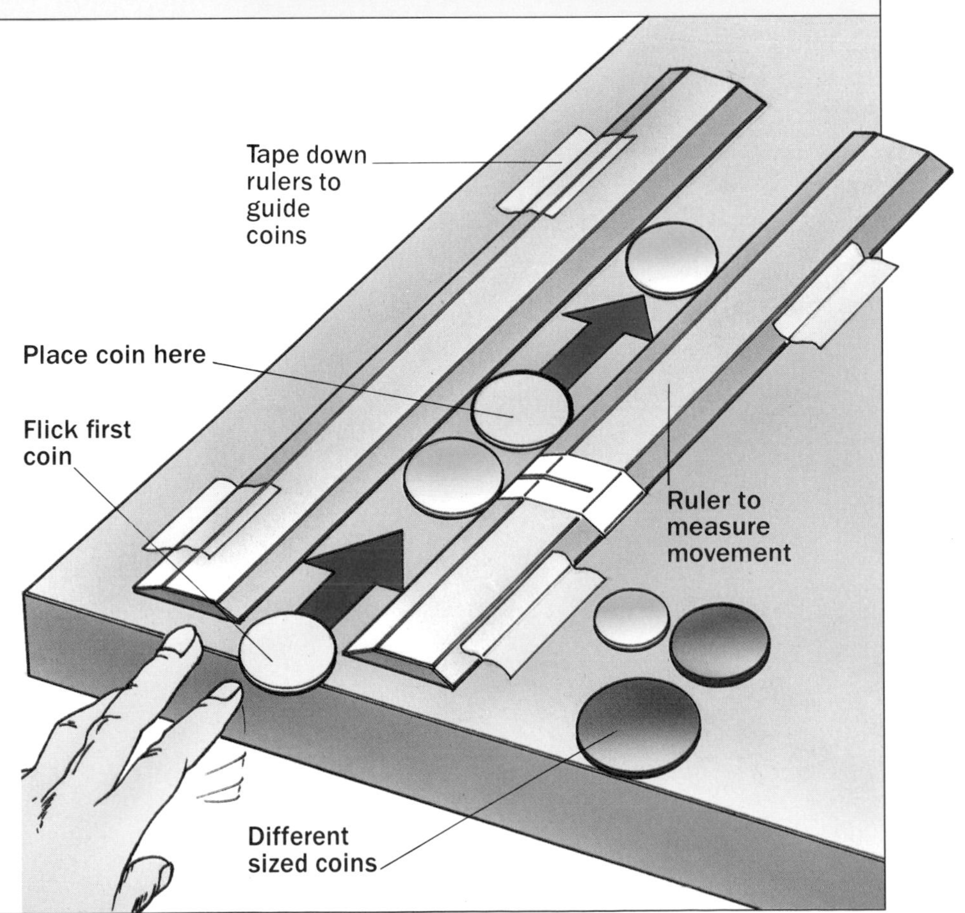

All movements come to a stop unless force is used to keep things moving. The reason is that things rub against other surfaces, or even only against air or water, as they move. This contact produces friction, which slows and stops motion. In the human body, layers of cartilage reduce friction between bones.

△ A bird lands on some water, extending its feet to cause friction with the water and quickly bring it to a stop.

FORCE AGAINST MOTION

As an object moves through air or water, it pushes the air or water aside. The air or water moves, taking some kinetic energy from the object, which moves slower. Sliding against another surface, especially if it presses hard, also takes energy and slows the object. In this case, the energy turns into sound and heat.

Friction is a force which always acts in the opposite direction to the movement. The size of the force varies, and falls to zero when the object stops.

BRAKES

Friction is used to make brakes work. It provides an extremely strong force able to stop a fast moving car in several seconds. Bicycles have brake shoes that press against the rim of each wheel. Cars have disk brakes, in which pads press against a disk at the center of the wheel. Levers and pedals operate the brakes.

The pressure of the shoes on the rim or pads on the disk produces friction. Greater pressure gives a stronger force of friction and slows the bicycle or car more quickly.

Bicycle brake

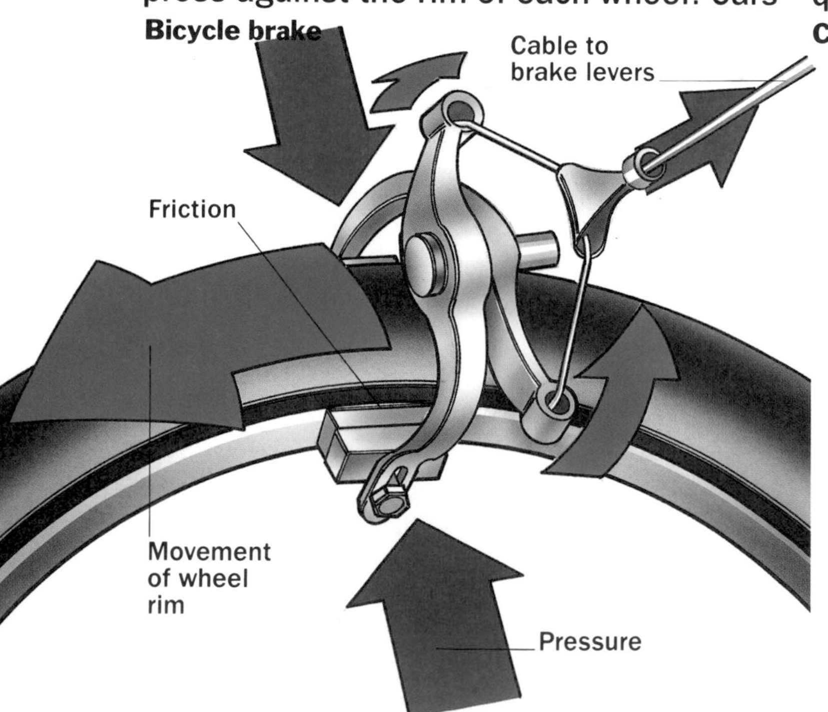

Car disk brake

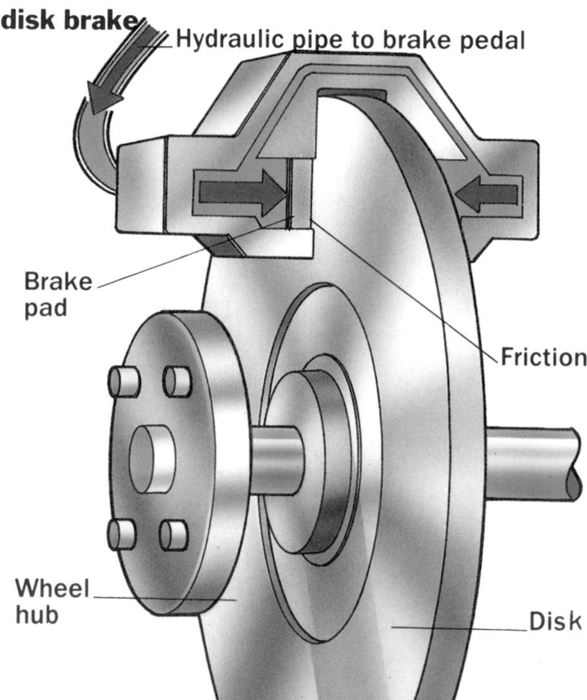

PARACHUTE

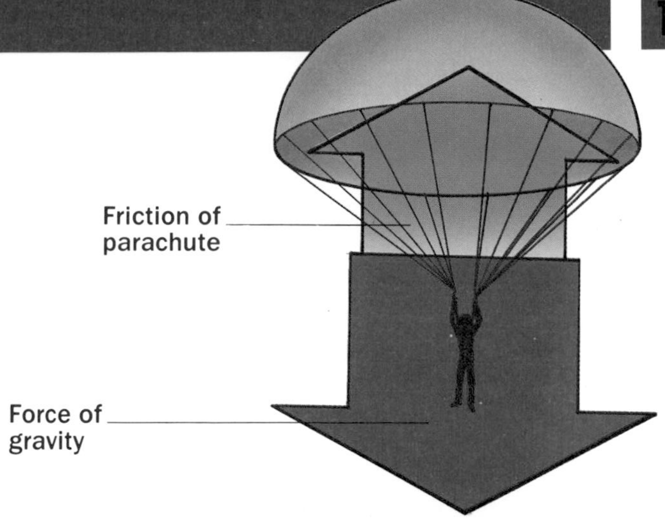

Parachutes make use of friction to lower people safely from the skies. People can use parachutes to escape from aircraft in emergencies, or if they make parachute jumps for sport.

When the parachute opens, it billows out and the large canopy pushes against the air. A strong force of friction develops between the parachute and the air. It acts upward to oppose the force of gravity pulling the parachutist down. The fall slows to a low speed at which the parachutist can safely land on the ground.

▷ Some parachutists like to fall freely through the air before opening their parachutes.

DEMONSTRATE FRICTION

Fix a rubber band to a piece of cardboard. Place it on a table, and put a beaker of water on top. Pull the rubber band. It stretches before the cardboard moves. The amount of stretch shows the force of friction between the cardboard and the table.

Put different amounts of water in the beaker

Rubber band

Card

QUIZ

Why can you warm your hands by rubbing them together? Friction between the skin on your hands turns movement into heat. Press your hands very firmly together as you rub them. They get hotter because more friction develops and produces more heat.

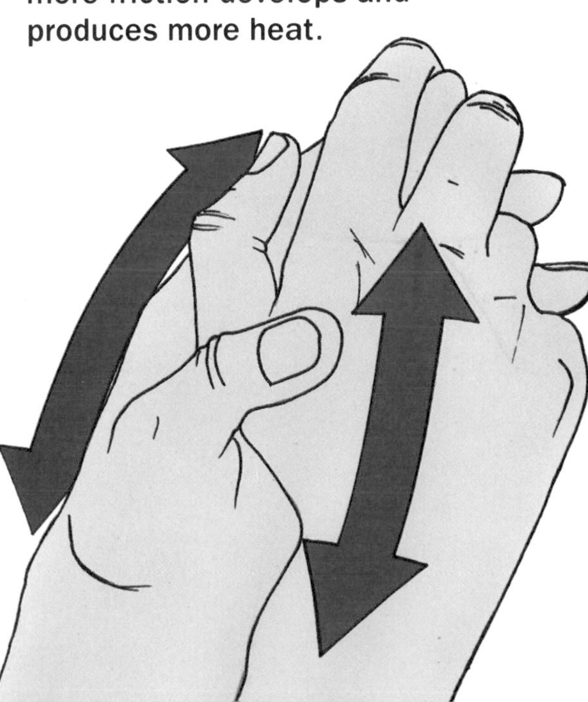

Friction is vital as a means of starting and stopping movement. But it is also a nuisance. Friction causes machines to waste some of the energy driving them by turning the energy to heat and noise. It lowers performance, and raises fuel consumption. We need ways of reducing friction to improve machines.

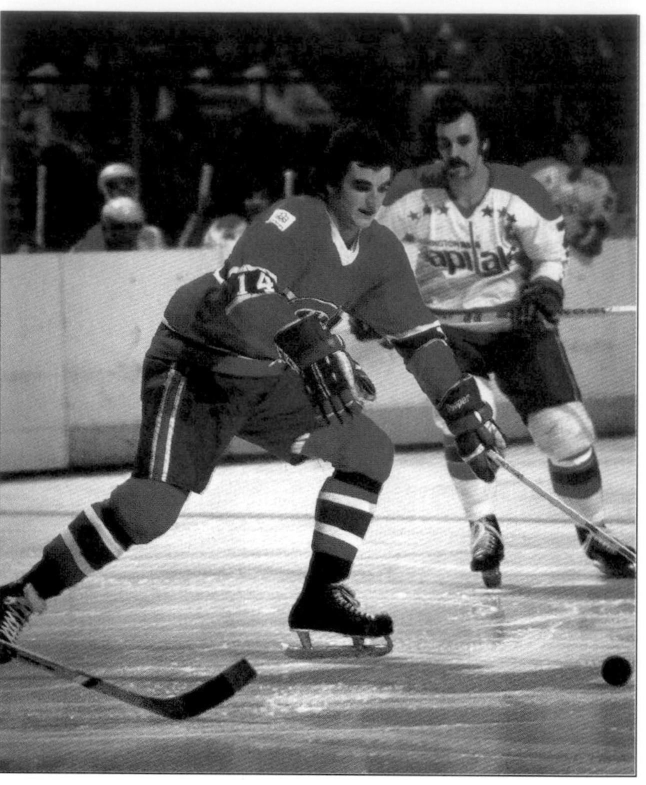

△ Skaters are freed from friction as they speed on ice. The surfaces of the ice and their skates are very smooth.

SLIPPERY SURFACES

You walk over the ground because your feet grip firmly. Friction between your feet and the ground stops them slipping and provides a good grip. Car tires are designed to grip the road strongly.

When a road gets wet, friction gets less. This happens because a film of water covers the road, and there is less contact with it. The tread on tires squeezes out the water film to maintain friction. A covering of ice greatly reduces friction, making the road very slippery and dangerous.

LUBRICATION

We can reduce friction in machines by lubrication. Oil is put into the machine, where it coats surfaces that rub and makes them slippery. All surfaces have tiny projections that catch against each other as they rub. Without lubrication, this would cause great friction, slowing and overheating the machine. The oil film separates the two surfaces so that their small rough spots do not catch.

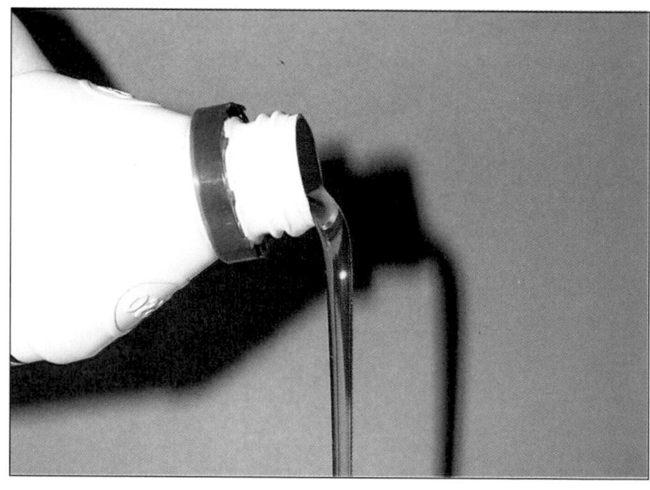

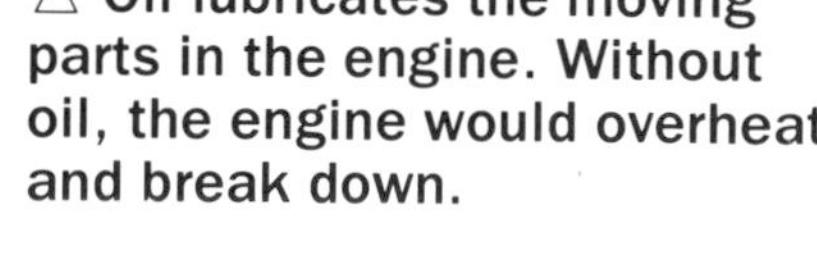

△ Oil lubricates the moving parts in the engine. Without oil, the engine would overheat and break down.

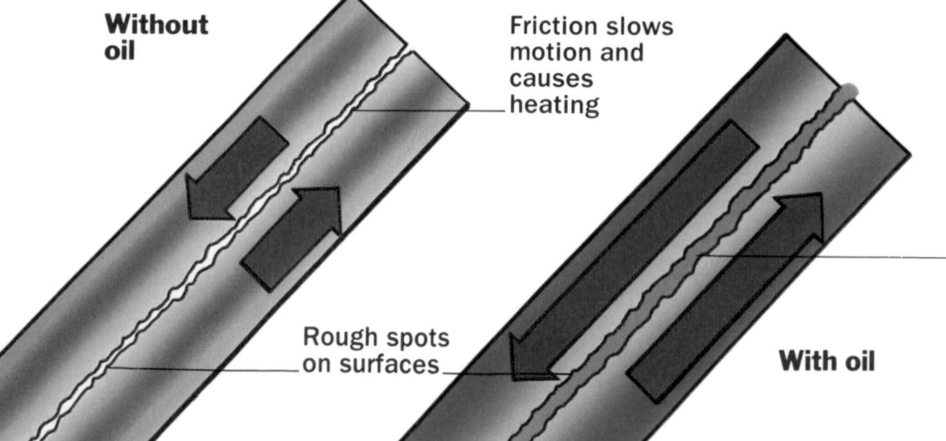
Without oil
Friction slows motion and causes heating
Rough spots on surfaces
With oil
Oil film separates surfaces. Less friction produces faster motion and less heat.

BEARINGS

Lubrication is not the only way to reduce friction in machines. Rolling is another way. Placing small steel balls or cylinders between two moving surfaces allows one surface to roll over the other just as a vehicle rolls over the ground on wheels. The balls or cylinders do not rub against the surfaces as they roll, so very little friction occurs.

A ball bearing contains a set of balls between two rings. The inner ring can rotate easily while the outer ring does not move. The bearing can be used to support a rotating shaft, which is fixed to the inner ring of the bearing.

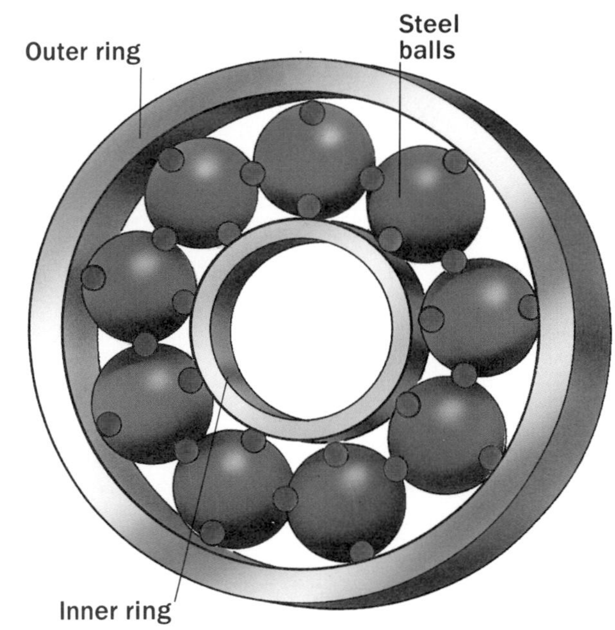

STREAMLINING

A third way of reducing friction is very important in transport, especially in aircraft. Streamlining gives the transport a shape that moves more easily through air or water. It has a pointed nose or bow and smooth sides, which do not push strongly against the air or water.

Reducing friction by streamlining an aircraft or car can give it a higher speed. Streamlining can also save fuel if speed is not increased.

▽ Many birds are streamlined so that they can swim at speed, catch prey and dive through the air or water.

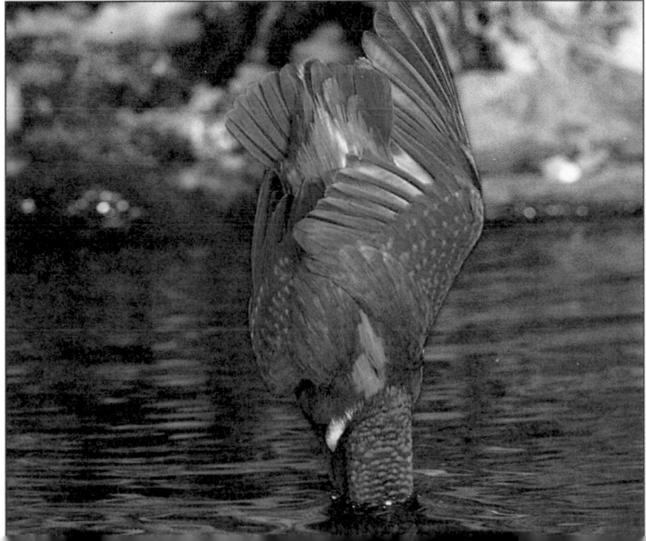

TEST FOR FRICTION

Take two pieces of wood and put one on the other. Lay a hand on the top piece and try to move it. Friction is probably too strong. Now try placing safe liquids like soap between the two pieces and see how good they are for lubrication by reducing friction.

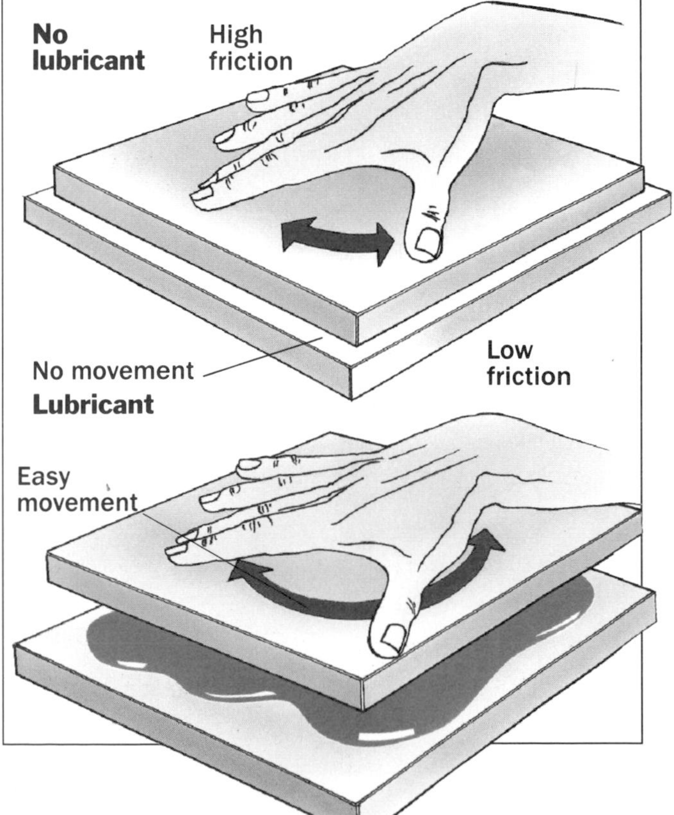

Things have energy when they are stationary as well as kinetic energy when they move. This stationary form of energy is called potential energy. It is "stored energy" that can be turned into kinetic energy to cause motion. When movement stops, kinetic energy may turn back into potential energy.

△ A trapeze artist swings to and fro to gain speed before soaring up into the air to grasp another trapeze.

THE PENDULUM

Kinetic energy constantly changes to potential energy and back again in a pendulum. At the bottom of each swing, the weight moves fastest and has the greatest kinetic energy. Then as it rises, the pendulum begins to slow until it stops. The kinetic energy of the pendulum changes to potential energy, which depends on the height of the weight. As the weight stops, it has no kinetic energy, only potential energy. When it moves down again, its potential energy changes back into kinetic energy.

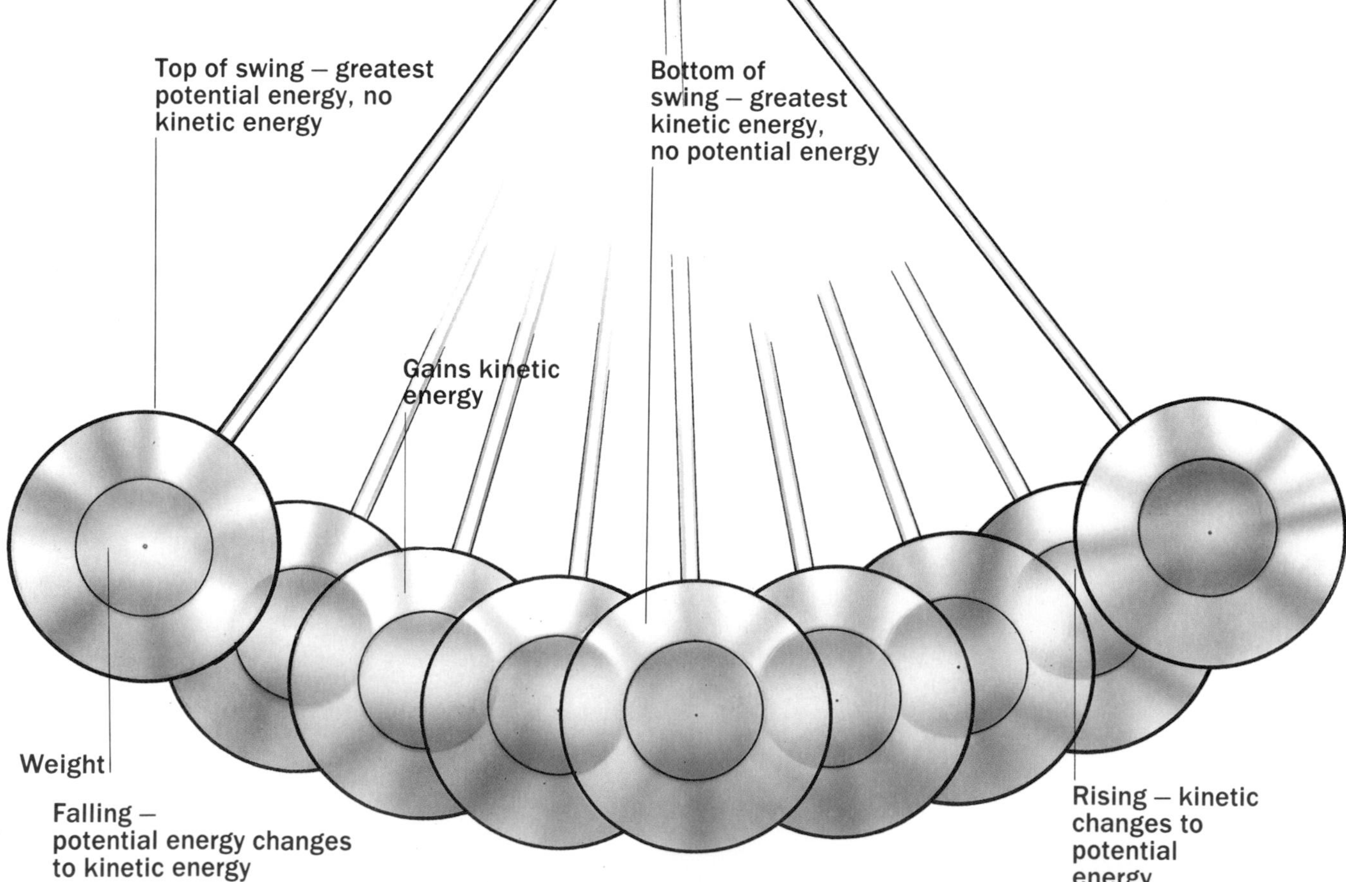

STRINGS AND SPRINGS

Another form of potential energy depends on the length of an elastic string or spring. Changing the length takes energy, which the string or spring "stores" as potential energy.

A bow makes use of this potential energy. Pulling back the string stores potential energy in the string and bow as it stretches. When the string is released, its potential energy changes to kinetic energy as it fires the arrow.

Stretching or compressing a spring also stores potential energy. The spring moves back to its former length when it is released, changing its potential energy into kinetic energy. The spring in a toy or watch works in this way. Winding it up stretches a spring, which then drives the wheels of the toy or hands of the watch as it slowly regains its shape.

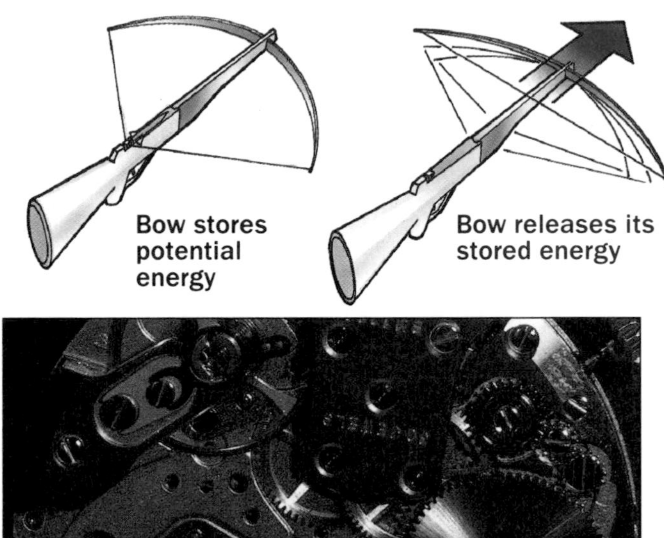

▽ A roller coaster gives a thrilling ride as it swoops up and down. It is powered solely by the force of gravity.

△ This clock mechanism contains a set of wheels driven by a mainspring to turn the hands.

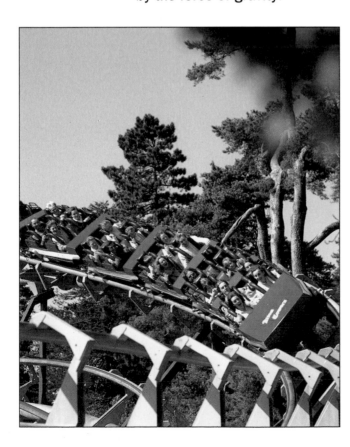

FAIRGROUND RIDES

Many of the most exciting rides in fairgrounds or theme parks make use of potential and kinetic energy. You enter a car that is first hauled up to the top of a steep incline. Then the car plunges down a steep slope to begin a thrilling ride that takes you up and down more slopes and perhaps even around a circular loop.

The car speeds through all these ups and downs without a motor to drive it along the track. This is because the top of the incline is higher than any other part of the ride. The car gets a great store of potential energy, which then changes into kinetic energy as gravity pulls the car and it moves. This store of potential energy is enough to send the car through the complete ride, even up and around any loops in it.

Movement often happens in a circle or part of a circle. To turn a corner, you have to move around a section of a circle, for example. Circular motion is different from movement in a straight line. An object moves in a straight line without any force, but force is needed to keep something moving in a circle.

CENTRIFUGAL FORCE

As you zoom around on a fairground ride, you are pushed down in your seat. A strong force pushes you away from the center of the circle in which you are moving. This is called centrifugal force, but it does not really exist! What is happening is that the car is pushing against you as you move around in a circle.

Throwing the hammer, which is in fact a weight on a cord, shows the forces in circular motion. The thrower moves the hammer in a circle, and the weight flies out. In fact, the weight is trying to move in a straight line, but the cord pulls it into a circle. The thrower has to pull on the cord with a force called centripetal force to stop the weight flying away. When the thrower lets go, the weight carries on moving in a straight line.

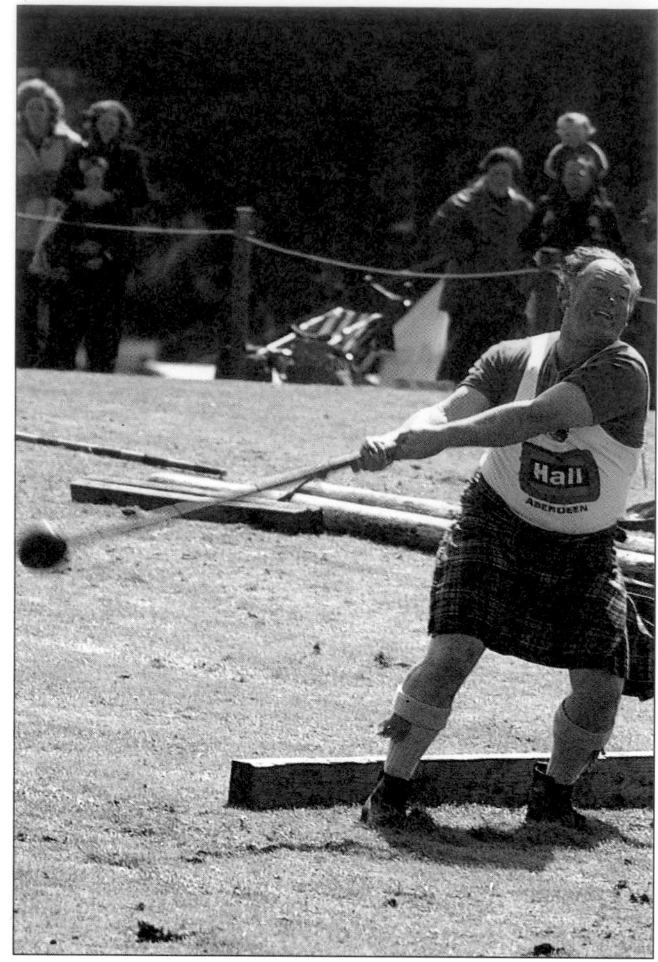

△ A hammer thrower has to pull very hard and rotate as fast as possible before letting go of the hammer.

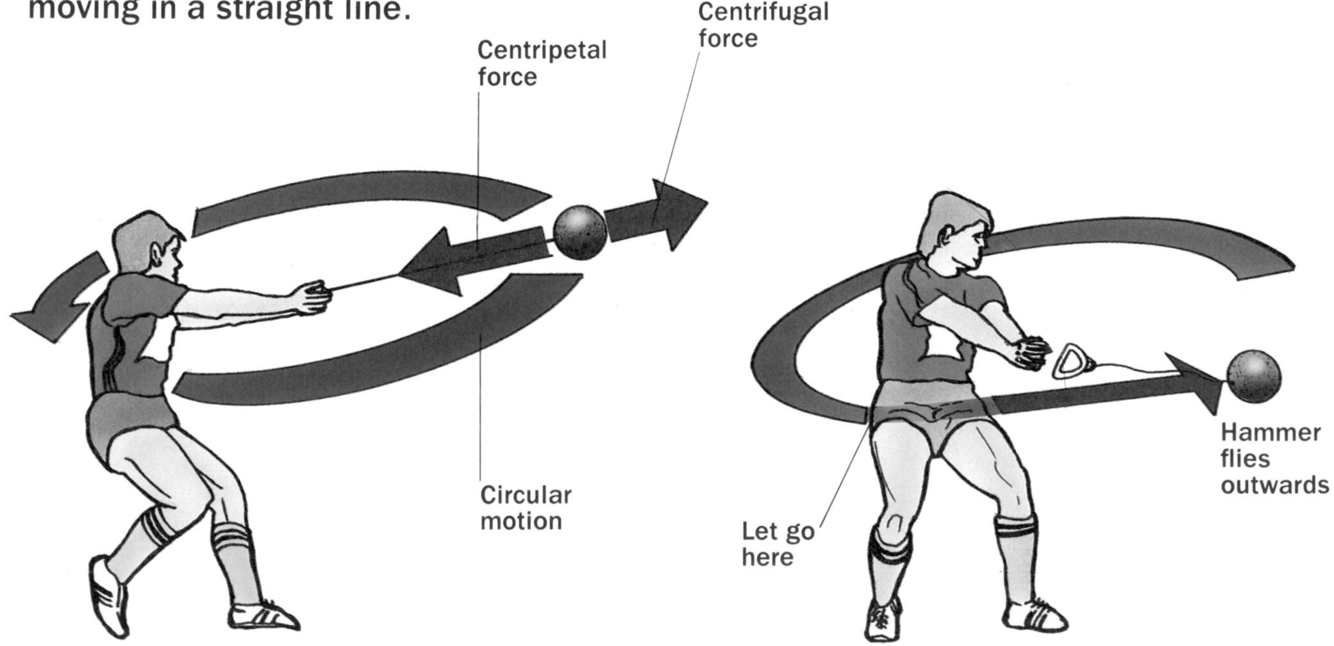

SPEED WITHOUT EFFORT

Try spinning on a revolving chair. If you tuck your legs in, you suddenly speed up. Now stick your legs out. You slow down. This effect happens because of the energy in circular motion. An object has more energy of movement when it is moving faster. Also, a wide object that is rotating has more energy than a narrow object of the same mass. When you pull your legs in, you suddenly become narrower. However, your total amount of energy does not change. Therefore, you move faster to keep the same amount of energy. Sticking your legs out makes you suddenly wider. To keep the same energy, you slow down.

△ A top can twirl on a point on the surface and spin faster and faster as you apply more force.

UPSIDE-DOWN WATER

Put some water in a bucket, grasp the handle firmly, pick it up and whirl it quickly around. At the right speed, the water will stay in the bucket, even if the bucket tilts upside-down. But get the speed wrong and the water will slosh out, so take care. The water keeps trying to move straight on. You stop it by pulling the bucket in a circle. The water cannot flow toward the top of the bucket and stays inside.

Swing the bucket around

The water stays as if a force pushes it into the bucket.

QUIZ

Bicyclists and motorcyclists lean over when they turn a corner at speed. Why do they not fall over? Leaning over causes the centripetal force that pulls the bicycle or motorcycle into a circle. It enables the rider to make a sharper turn. Without leaning, the rider would fall outward.

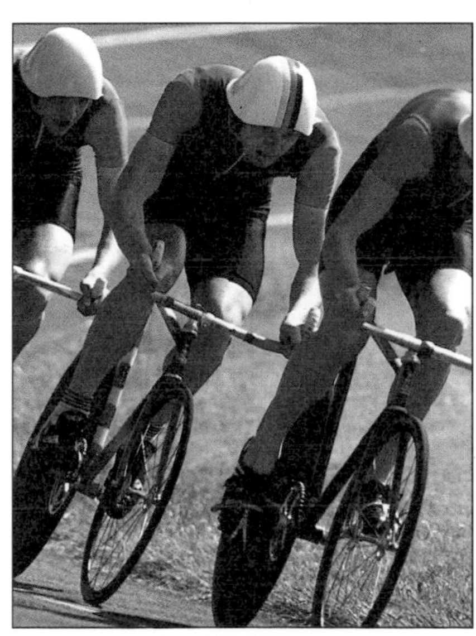

Wheels rotate to move bicycles, trains and cars. We also use other wheels to produce motion. These are toothed wheels or gear wheels, which can change the speed at which the pedals power a bicycle or the engine drives a car. Gyroscopes are also rotating wheels and they move in an unusual way.

THE WHEEL AND AXLE

A wheel has an axle, a central shaft that turns to make the wheel rotate. The rim of the wheel moves faster than the axle. This enables you to speed along the road on a bicycle. The pedals pull the chain, which turns the axle of the back wheel. The rim of the wheel moves faster than the chain, so that the bicycle moves faster than your feet turn the pedals.

The chain passes over toothed wheels on the pedals and the back wheel. These two wheels are different sizes. If the hub wheel has half the number of teeth as the pedal wheel, it makes a full turn when the pedal wheel makes a half turn. Many bicycles have a set of hub wheels of different sizes that give different speeds. These are called gears.

△ The pedals turn the front wheel in a penny-farthing, an early form of bicycle.

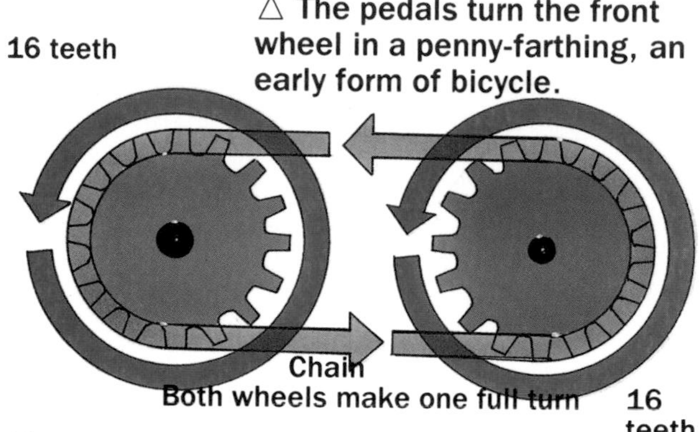

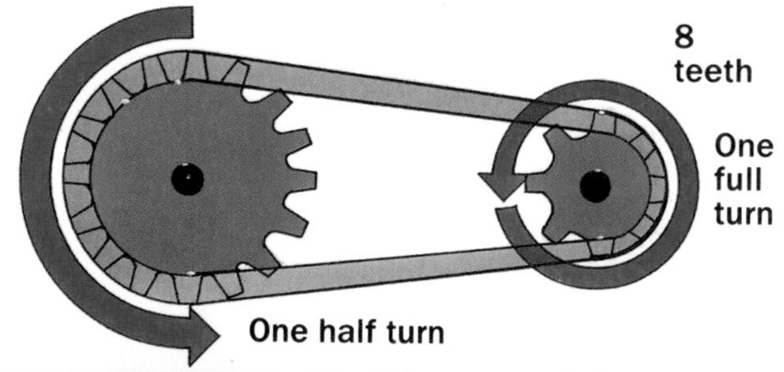

BALANCING ON A BICYCLE

If you roll a coin along the ground, it will stay upright and move some way before toppling over. You are able to ride a bicycle because the rotating wheels, like the rolling coin, do not easily topple over. If you begin to tilt to one side while riding a bicycle, you move the handlebars slightly to swivel the wheel in the direction of the tilt. A strong force then moves the wheel back upright, and you keep your balance on the bicycle. This balancing movement is called precession.

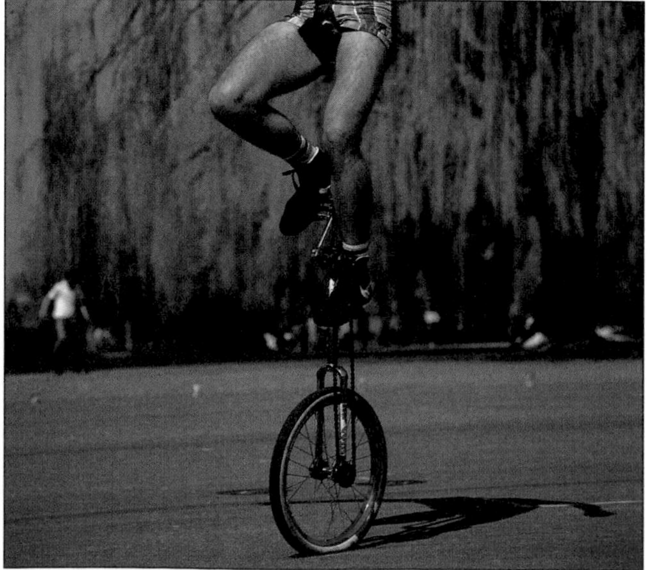

▷ Some riders can balance so well, that they can ride a unicycle.

GYROSCOPES

The gyroscope is capable of amazing feats of balance. A toy gyroscope can be made to stand on its pivot without falling over. The wheel in the gyroscope must spin very quickly to make it stand on its end. The gyroscope then begins to tilt and starts moving in a circle. After a while, the wheel slows and falls over. If it could be kept rotating, the gyroscope would continue to balance.

Precession occurs in the gyroscope. As it begins to tilt, the force of gravity pulls it down vertically. Another force acts to move the wheel in a horizontal direction, causing the whole gyroscope to move in a circle around the pivot. Gyroscopes can be used in very accurate compasses.

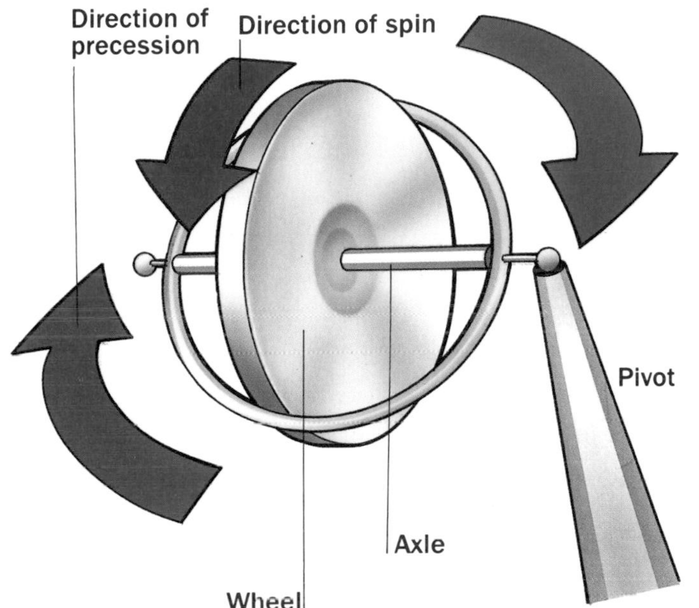

▽ Gyroscopes like this one make attractive toys but they can also be used in accurate instruments like a compass.

DEMONSTRATE PRECESSION

Remove the front wheel of a bicycle from its forks. Hold it upright by the axle and tilt the wheel slightly. Now ask someone to start the wheel spinning in the same direction as it would spin if you were riding the bicycle. Swivel the axle slightly. The wheel will move in an odd way and then right itself. This movement is called precession. It acts at right angles to the direction of the swivel. The movement keeps a bicycle upright when you pedal.

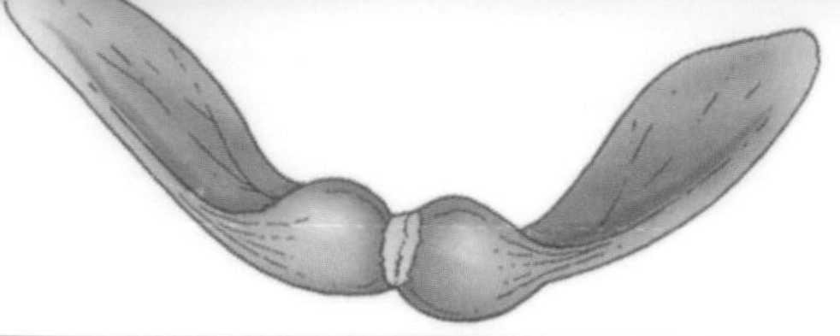

encyclopedia of science

PLANTS

CONTENTS

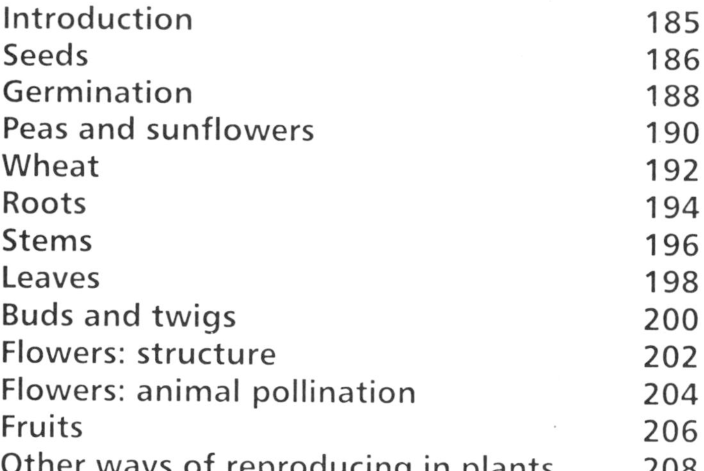

INTRODUCTION

Plants grow all around us and we often pay little attention to them. But without plants, our lives and the lives of all other animals would be impossible. Plants produce the oxygen we breathe. They also trap the energy in sunlight, which is the original source of energy in all of our food.

People have studied plants since the start of history depending on them for food, and also for fuel, clothing, building materials and medicines. The scientific study of plants is known as botany. The earliest botanists spent much of their time discovering and naming the different types of species of plant. Apart from this they looked for plants that would help to cure diseases.

Today, botanists use the latest scientific techniques to study how plants work. The knowledge that botanists gain is used in many ways to benefit us. These benefits include the breeding of better varieties of crops, and the use of chemicals in plants as medicines.

SEEDS

Plants cannot move around like animals. This is because they need a supply of water and mineral salts from the soil. They get these through their roots. Seeds form on parent plants after flowering. Each seed contains a young plant called an embryo. Seeds allow plants to spread to new places and to survive dry seasons.

STRUCTURE

A tough coat, the testa, surrounds the seed and protects the embryo. There is a small hole in the testa called the micropyle. Inside the seed are leaflike structures called cotyledons. Flowering plants are divided into two groups, depending on how many cotyledons they have. Lilies, grasses and palms are known as the monocotyledons and have one per seed. Herbs, shrubs and broadleaf trees, the dicotyledons, have two.

The embryo has a root known as the radicle and a tiny shoot called the plumule. Most seeds contain a food store for the embryo. Seeds form inside fruits. Fruits give the seed extra protection and help to disperse the seeds.

△ Nuts are very hard fruits.

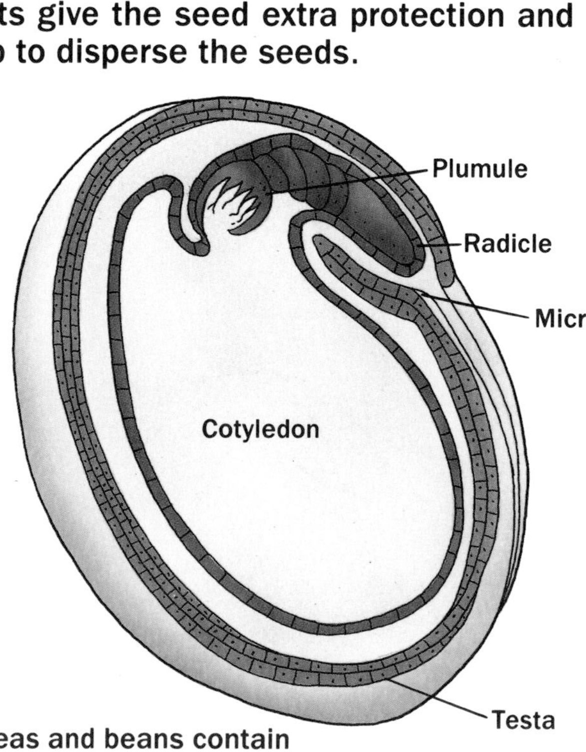

△ Peas and beans contain food in large cotyledons. These seeds are valuable food for humans.

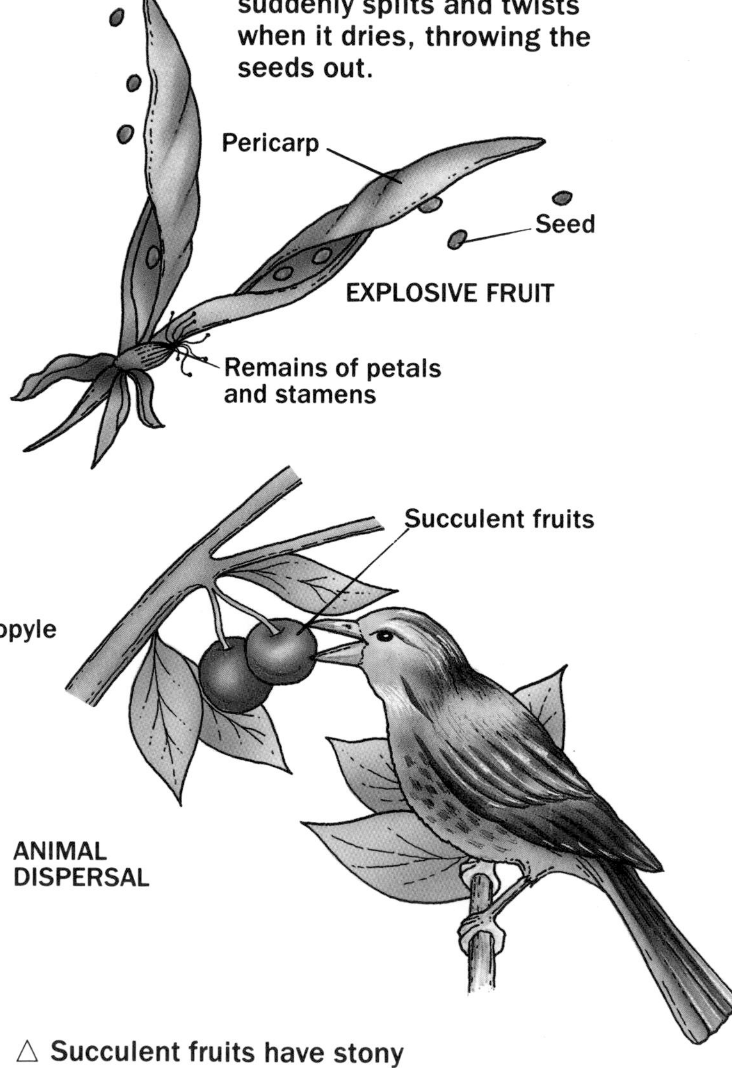

▽ Lupin pods are explosive fruits. The pericarp (shell) suddenly splits and twists when it dries, throwing the seeds out.

△ Succulent fruits have stony seeds. These pass through animals that eat them and are deposited with feces.

DISPERSAL

It is important that young plants start life a good distance from their parents, so that they can get plenty of light and nutrients. The way in which seeds are carried away from the parent plant is called dispersal. Seed dispersal usually involves natural forces, because plants cannot move themselves.

Fruits are important in the dispersal of seeds. In botany, the name "fruit" includes many structures besides the familiar fruits that we enjoy eating. Fruits develop from a part of the flower called the ovary. This surrounds the seed. The wall of the ovary (the pericarp) forms the outside of the fruit.

Fruits that open to release or throw out seeds are known as dehiscent fruits. Forces develop in the pericarp as it dries and cause it to split. Some dehiscent fruits produce very small seeds, which are easily blown away. Fruits that do not open are known as indehiscent fruits. These rely only on either wind, animals or water for dispersal.

△▷ Each part of a dandelion "clock" breaks off to be carried by the wind. In the lime, a leaflike wing breaks off with the fruit and works just like the sycamore fruit.

Dried bract on stalk

Lime fruit

Ovary

WIND DISPERSAL

Sycamore

Ovary

Wing extensions of ovary

▷ Sycamore fruits have wings that make them spin and fall slowly. This allows them to be blown quite long distances by the wind.

DID YOU KNOW?

Seeds of the coconut palm are dispersed by the sea. The large woody coconuts are covered by a fibrous husk and can float for a long time. Ocean currents sometimes carry them for great distances.

Hooked fruits on cat's tail

ANIMAL DISPERSAL

◁ Many fruits have hooks or spines. These catch in the fur of animals, and in this way the seed is carried away.

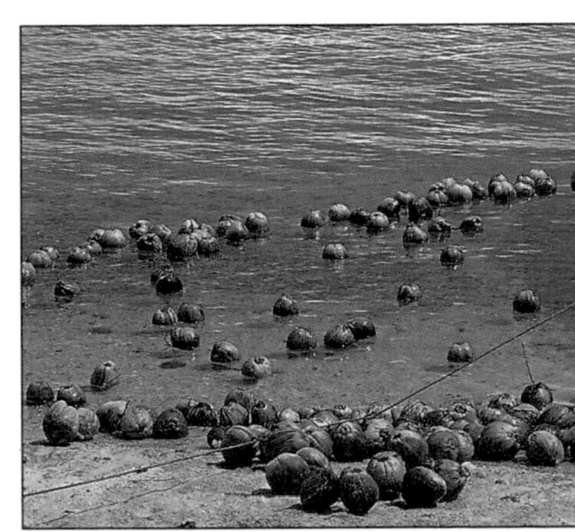

GERMINATION

If a seed is dispersed to a suitable place, the embryo inside eventually starts to grow. The first stage of growth is called germination. Before it can germinate, the seed absorbs water from the soil. It also needs oxygen and the right temperature. The embryo grows into a seedling using food stored in the seed.

DORMANCY

Many ripe seeds will not germinate at first, even if they are placed in good conditions. These are called dormant seeds. Seeds become dormant so as not to grow at times when conditions would normally be too poor for the seedlings to survive. Dormant seeds start to grow only after they receive a signal. In some seeds, the signal is a period of cold followed by warmer temperatures. This tells the seed that winter has passed.

△ Most seeds dry out as they ripen, for example, the seeds in these poppy pods.

ABSORBING WATER

Put equal layers of dried peas or beans into two jars. Cover the seeds in one of the jars with a layer of water.

Do not add any water to the control jar. This one is set up to show what the seeds were like at the start.

After one day, the seed layer in the first jar is deeper. The seeds have absorbed water and swollen.

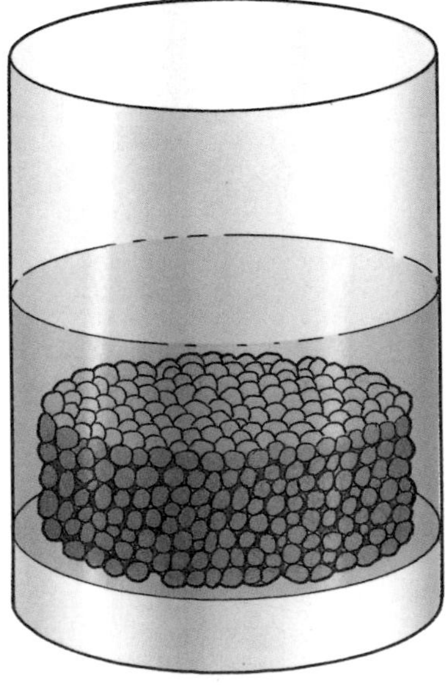

Start of experiment

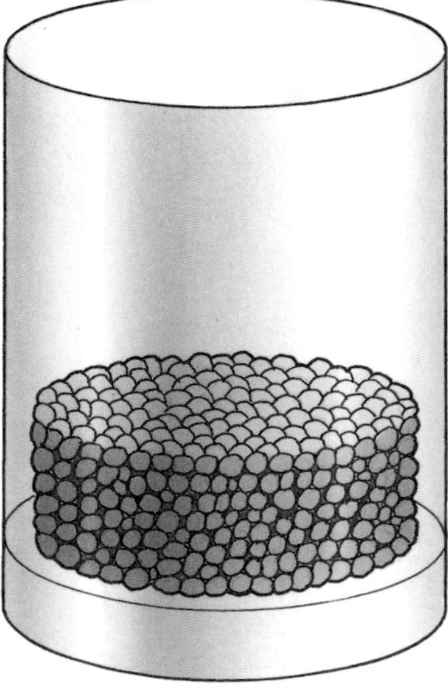

Control

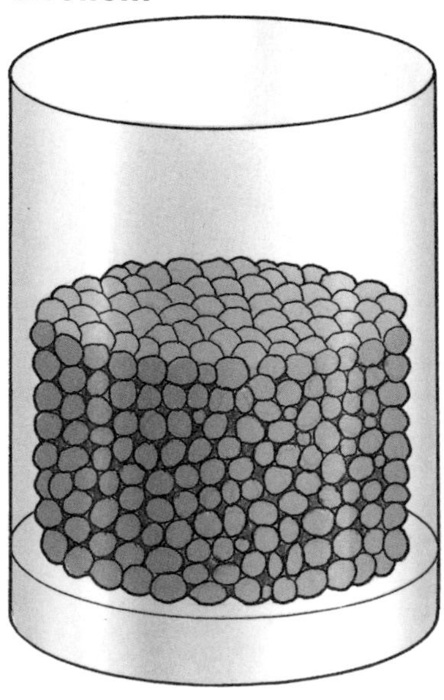

After one day

RAPID GROWTH

Once a seed germinates, rapid changes start to happen. First, the radicle swells and pushes its way through the testa. It then grows down into the soil and absorbs water and minerals for the seedling. Food stored in the seed is turned into forms that can be used by the seedling as it grows. The plumule grows upward to form the shoot. When the shoot reaches the light, it turns green and starts to make its own food using sunlight. Making food using energy from light is known as photosynthesis.

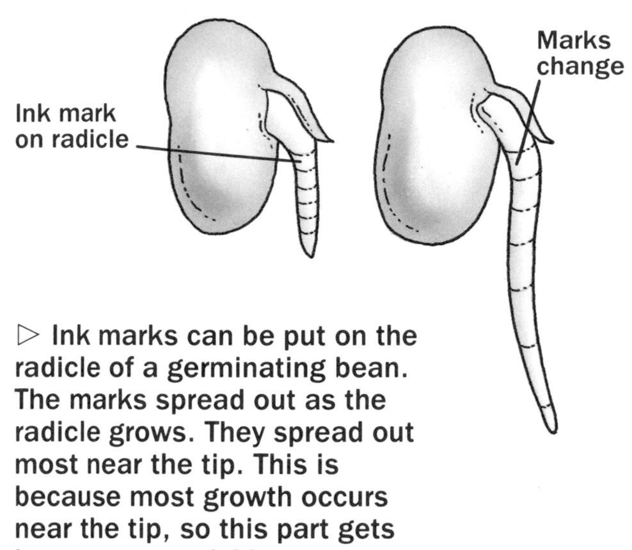

▷ Ink marks can be put on the radicle of a germinating bean. The marks spread out as the radicle grows. They spread out most near the tip. This is because most growth occurs near the tip, so this part gets longer more quickly.

WATER IN GERMINATION

Set up four jars as shown in the pictures. Use peas sold for use as seed. Cover each jar with plastic wrap. See which peas germinate. Peas will germinate if they are kept moist. But when covered with water, they get too little oxygen.

DID YOU KNOW?

Many dormant seeds can remain alive for more than 10 years. In nature, a "seed bank," composed of dormant seeds, often builds up in the soil. If all of the parent plants are killed – for example, by a fire – there is a good chance they will be replaced from the seed bank. Scientists store rare or important seeds in refrigerators. Cold can slow down the rate at which dormant seeds die.

PEAS

The way in which seeds germinate depends on the number of cotyledons and what their function is.

The garden pea is a dicotyledon. In pea seeds, the main function of the cotyledons is to store food. After the radicle has pushed its way out of the seed, the shoot begins to grow. For a short time, growth happens only in the part of the shoot between the cotyledons and the plumule. This part is called the epicotyl. The plumule is a delicate region at the tip of the shoot. Later it will be the main area where shoot growth occurs. The shoot is bent over as it is pushed through the soil. This protects the plumule from damage. Once it has emerged from the soil, the shoot straightens and the first leaves form. The cotyledons remain inside the seed and never emerge above ground. When their food store has been used, they shrivel up.

This type of germination, where the cotyledons never function as true leaves, is called hypogeal germination. The broad bean, acorn and hazelnut also have hypogeal germination.

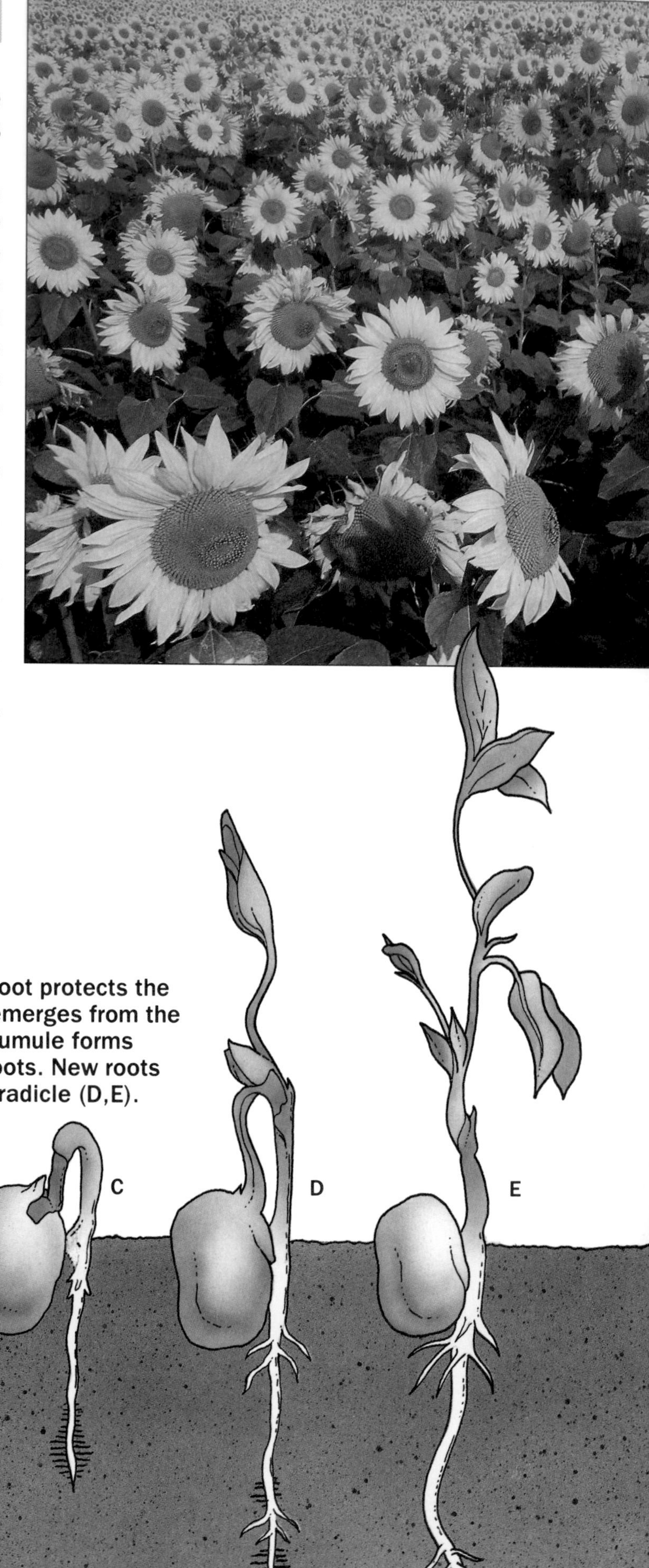

▽ Germination starts with the appearance of the radicle (A). As it grows, it produces fine root hairs which help it to absorb water and salts (B).

▷ The bent shoot protects the plumule as it emerges from the soil (C). The plumule forms leaves and shoots. New roots grow from the radicle (D,E).

SUNFLOWERS

The sunflower is a dicotyledon, like the garden pea. Each sunflower "seed" is actually an indehiscent fruit that contains one seed.

Germination starts in the sunflower in the same way as in the pea. The radicle bursts out of the seed coat and fruit, then grows downward. Next, however, the length of stem between the radicle and the cotyledons starts to elongate. This part of the stem is called the hypocotyl. By lengthening, it pulls the cotyledons up into the air. Again, the stem is bent to protect the plumule from damage. When the cotyledons are free, the stem straightens. The cotyledons turn green and are the first leaves. They produce food by photosynthesis, and this helps the plumule to form the main shoot and larger leaves. This type of germination is called epigeal germination.

△ These sunflowers grew from seeds that all germinated at about the same time.

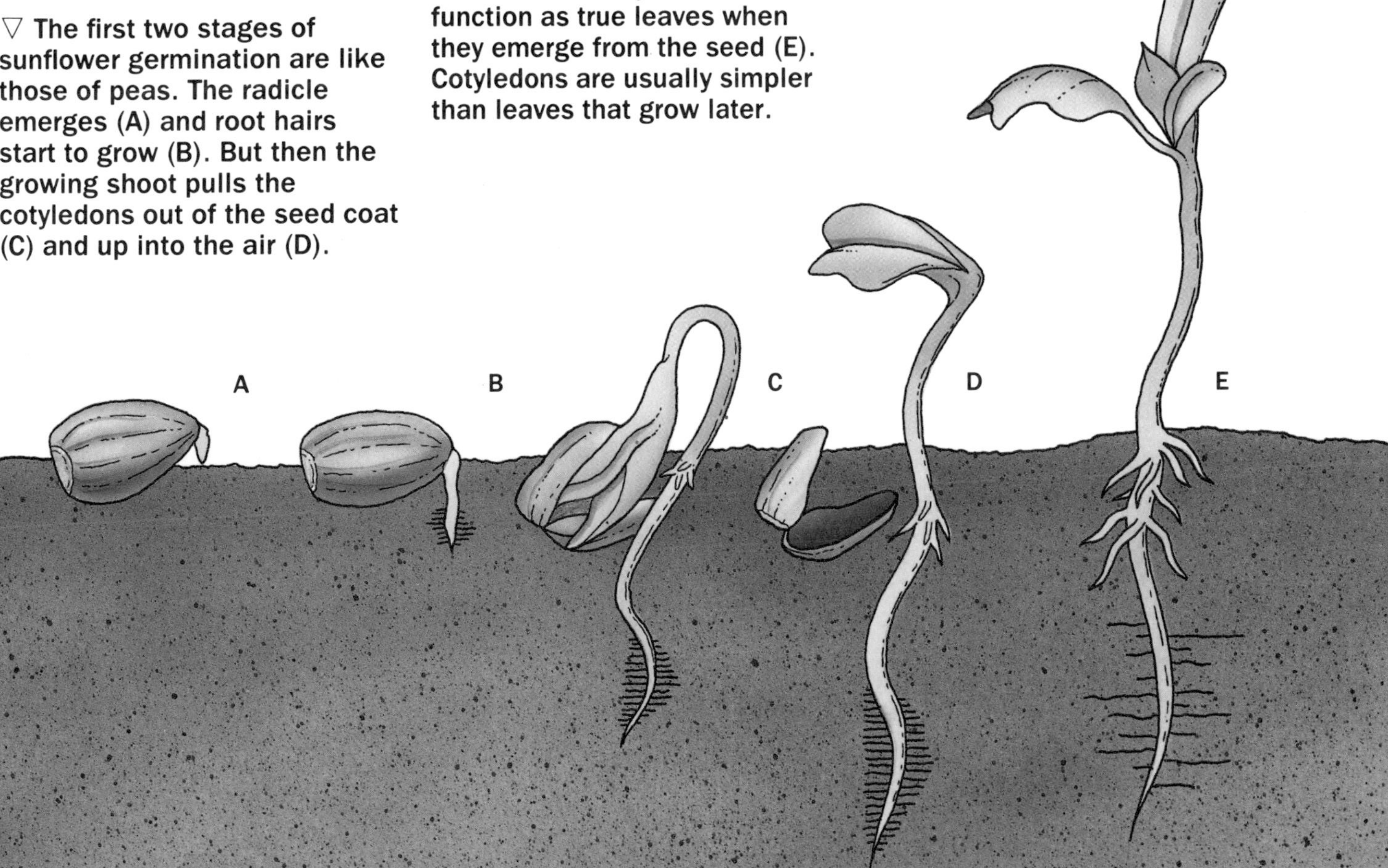

▽ The first two stages of sunflower germination are like those of peas. The radicle emerges (A) and root hairs start to grow (B). But then the growing shoot pulls the cotyledons out of the seed coat (C) and up into the air (D).

▷ Sunflower cotyledons function as true leaves when they emerge from the seed (E). Cotyledons are usually simpler than leaves that grow later.

WHEAT GRAIN

Wheat is one of the most important grain crops in the world. Its most common use is to produce flour for baking. Wheat grain provides a good combination of proteins and carbohydrates. It is easy to grow and the grains can be harvested cheaply using machines. Wheat grain can also be stored for a long time.

The wheat grain is a fruit with a single seed inside. Wheat is a monocotyledon. The food store fills the part of the seed outside the embryo. The cotyledon stays below ground during germination. It absorbs food from the store and passes it to the growing parts of the seedling. In wheat, the plumule grows straight up through the soil. The plumule is protected from damage by a tough cap called the coleoptile.

Soon, the first true leaves break through the coleoptile as the shoot grows. The cotyledon withers away as the food in the seed is used up. New roots do not grow from the radicle. Instead, they come singly from the base of the shoot.

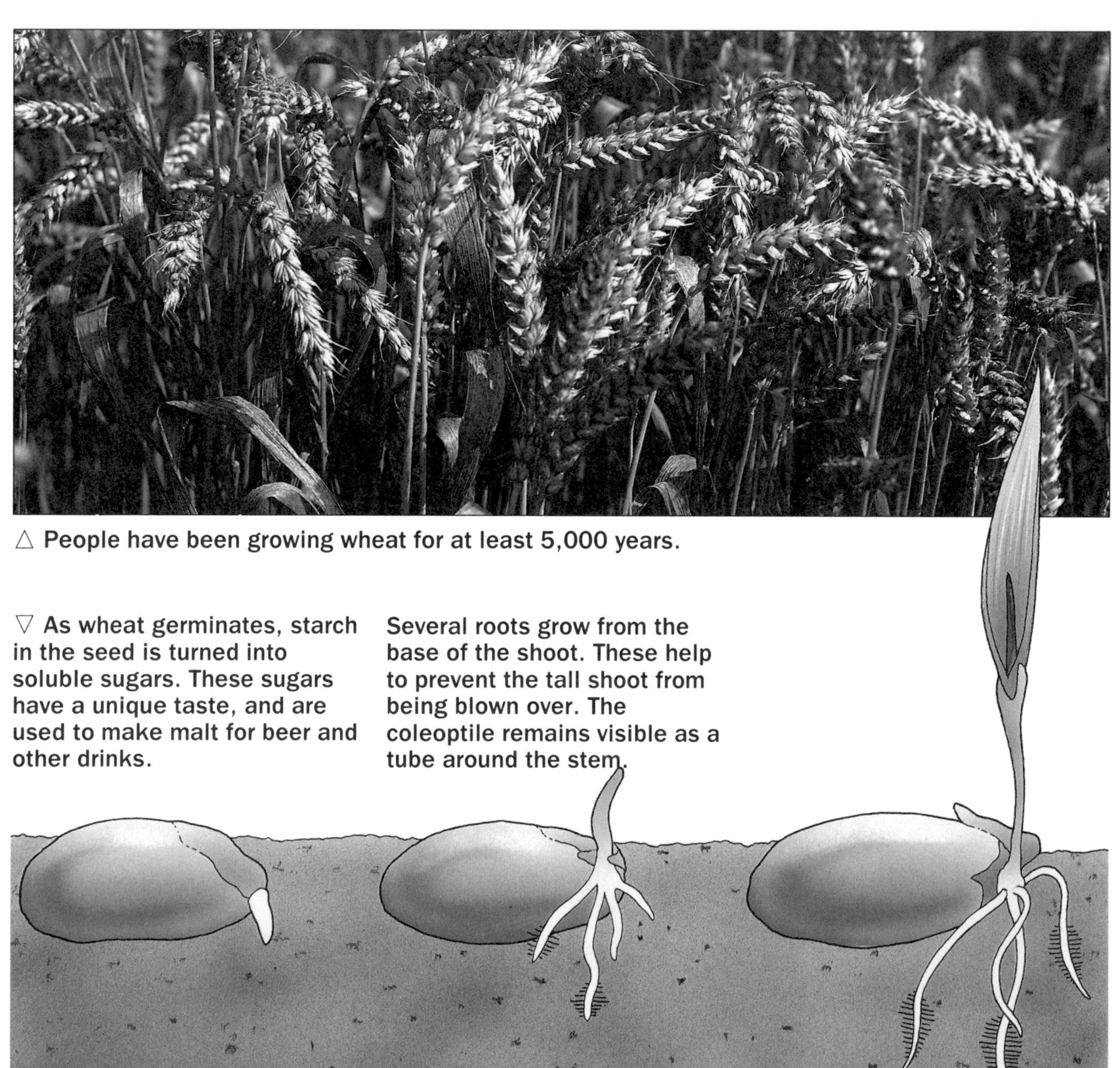

△ People have been growing wheat for at least 5,000 years.

▽ As wheat germinates, starch in the seed is turned into soluble sugars. These sugars have a unique taste, and are used to make malt for beer and other drinks.

Several roots grow from the base of the shoot. These help to prevent the tall shoot from being blown over. The coleoptile remains visible as a tube around the stem.

AFFECTING GROWTH

Seedlings behave in ways that increase their chances of finding sunlight, water and minerals.

This determines the response of shoots and roots to gravity. Shoots grow upward, away from gravity. Roots grow downward, toward gravity.

Sunlight affects the growth of shoots. Place cress seeds in good light and the seedlings will grow with stout but short stems. If they are placed in deep shade or darkness, the seedlings become tall and spindly. They grow tall in order to try to reach light.

Light has the opposite effect on radicles. It makes them grow long and spindly, and they produce no lateral roots. They are using all their energy trying to find the soil, where it is dark. The soil contains the mineral salts and water that the plant needs.

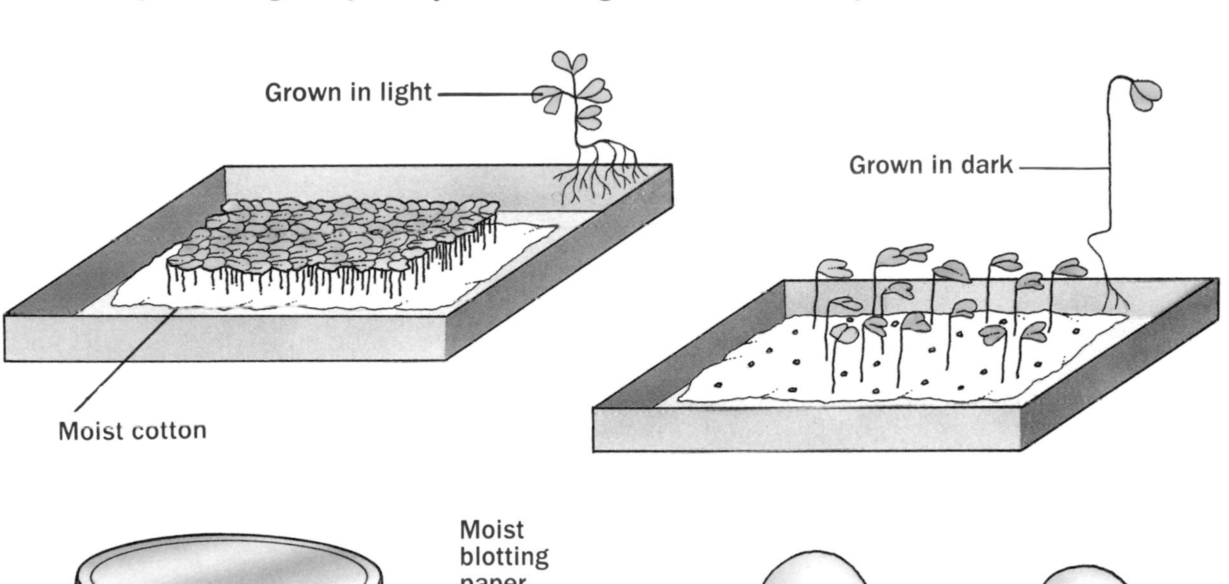

◁△ To test the effect of light on radicles, put beans in a jar, as in the picture. Cover half the jar with black paper and see what happens.

ROOTS

Roots have a number of different jobs. They anchor the plant, preventing the shoot from being toppled by the wind and the force of gravity. They absorb water from the soil, together with dissolved minerals. These substances are carried to the leafy shoots. Some plants have roots that store food for later use.

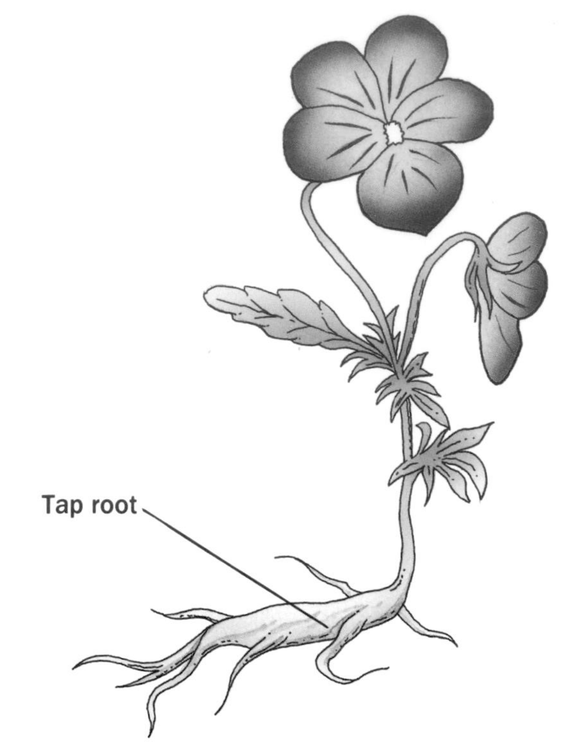

ROOT SYSTEMS

There is a good chance to examine roots when a tree is blown over in a storm. Large amounts of soil are often pulled up with the roots, although some roots break off in the ground. The tangle of roots on a plant is called the root system. The root system usually reaches out as far as the shoots or branches do. Sometimes, a thick main root can be seen. Smaller lateral roots grow out from the main root. This type of root system is called a tap root system. Tap roots often become swollen with stored food, as in the carrot, beet and parsnip. In other plants the roots are all of similar size. This is called a fibrous root system.

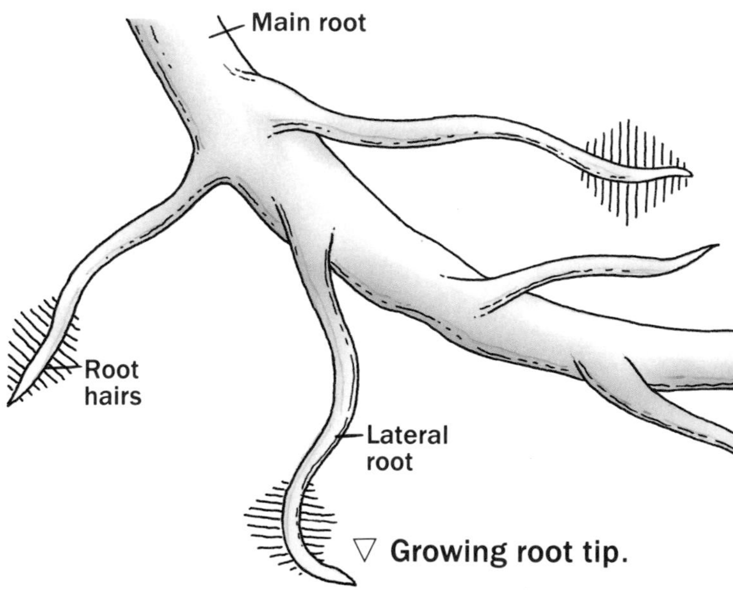

STRUCTURE

Like all living organisms, plants are made up of tiny building blocks called cells. Different types of cells are grouped together to form tissues. Roots grow longer because cells in the tip of the root divide into two and enlarge.

Long thin cells called root hairs absorb water and minerals from the soil. The water and minerals then pass through the cortex and enter the xylem tissue. The xylem forms a star-shaped core which runs up and joins to xylem in the stem and leaves. Special tubular cells in the xylem carry the water up to the leaves. Food made in the leaves passes down to the growing root through the phloem tissue. The root cap protects the root tip as it pushes through the soil.

▽ Growing root tip.

◁ Tap root systems are found mainly in dicotyledons. Food stored in the root allows the plant to survive harsh periods, such as winter. Tap roots often grow to great depths in search of water.

▷ Most monocotyledons and many dicotyledons have fibrous root systems. The main roots grow from the base of the stem – in this case a bulb. These roots have smaller lateral roots than tap root systems do.

Fibrous root

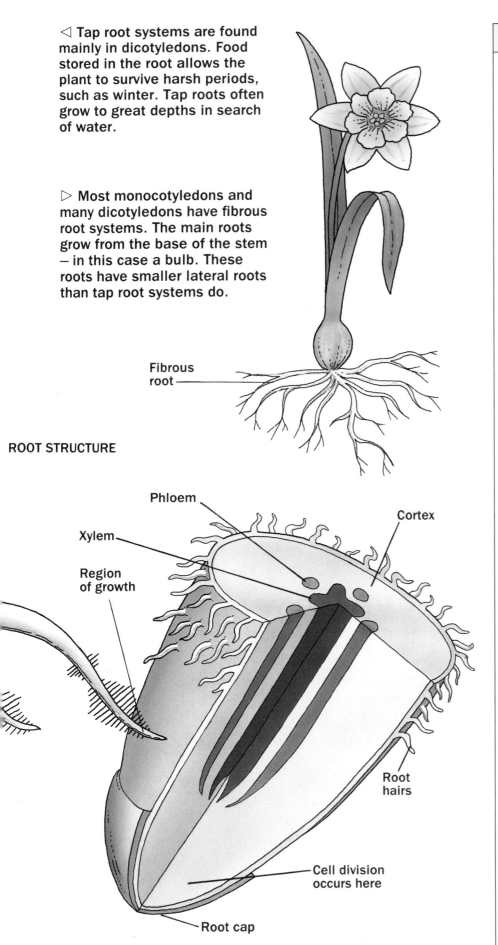

ROOT STRUCTURE

Phloem
Xylem
Region of growth
Cortex
Root hairs
Cell division occurs here
Root cap

EXPERIMENT

The importance of gravity in root growth is shown by this experiment. Cut a pad of blotting paper to fit tightly in the bottom of a jar. Fix three bean seeds to the pad using pins (do not stick them through the bean). Soak the paper and let the seeds germinate with the jar upright. Now set the jar on its side. The young roots bend and grow downward in response to gravity.

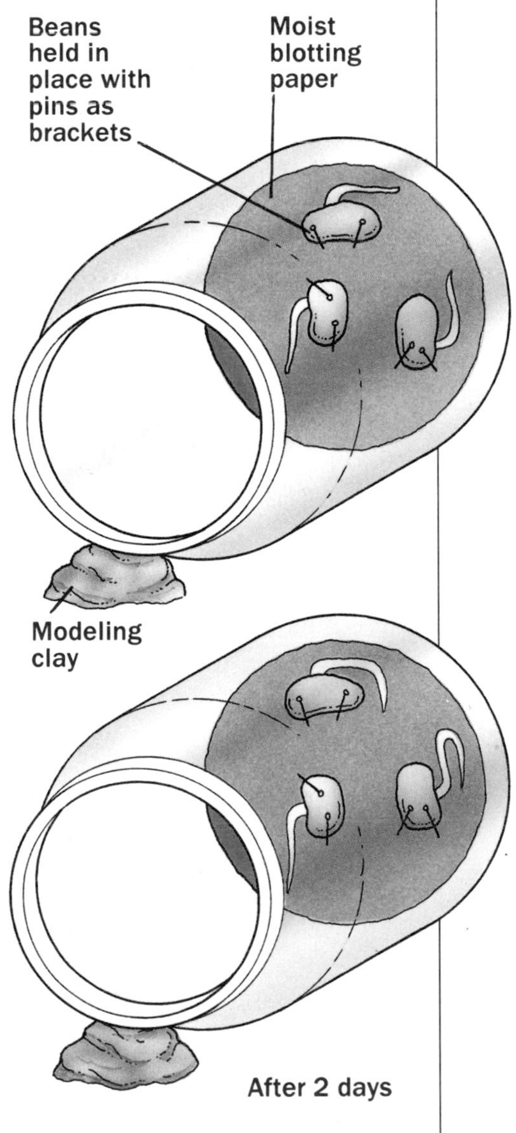

STEMS

Stems form part of the shoot. Their main job is to support the leaves, buds and flowers. The way in which the leaves and flowers are exposed to sun and insects is very important. Plants often have green stems, which make food in the same way as leaves do. Stems also allow water and nutrients to be moved inside the plant.

△ Flowers are held up by the strength of stems.

CHARACTERISTICS

Each stem is made up of a number of similar units joined end to end. A stem unit consists of a straight piece of stem, known as an internode. Internodes join together at swollen areas called nodes. Leaves and buds are attached at the nodes. If a bud starts to grow, it can form a side branch or a flowering stem.

Usually there is an obvious main stem. If the main stem dies, a side stem can grow to take its place. The stems of plants that do not have leaves – like cacti – are the main place where food is formed. The "bulb" of the buttercup is a special food-storing stem. Such stems are called corms.

INSIDE STEMS

Two different types of growth occur in stems. Non-woody shoots grow by the division of cells in the stem tip. This occurs in all young stems. Later, woody tissues grow in dicotyledons.

The outer layer of non-woody stems is called the epidermis. It is covered by a waxy layer to prevent drying out. The xylem and phloem tissues are strands running up the stem. The phloem is on the outside and the xylem on the inside. Each strand runs to an individual leaf.

The height to which plants can grow depends on how strong the stem is. There is a substance called lignin that can form in xylem and some other tissues. It increases the strength of stems and makes them woody.

▽ Typical structure of a plant.

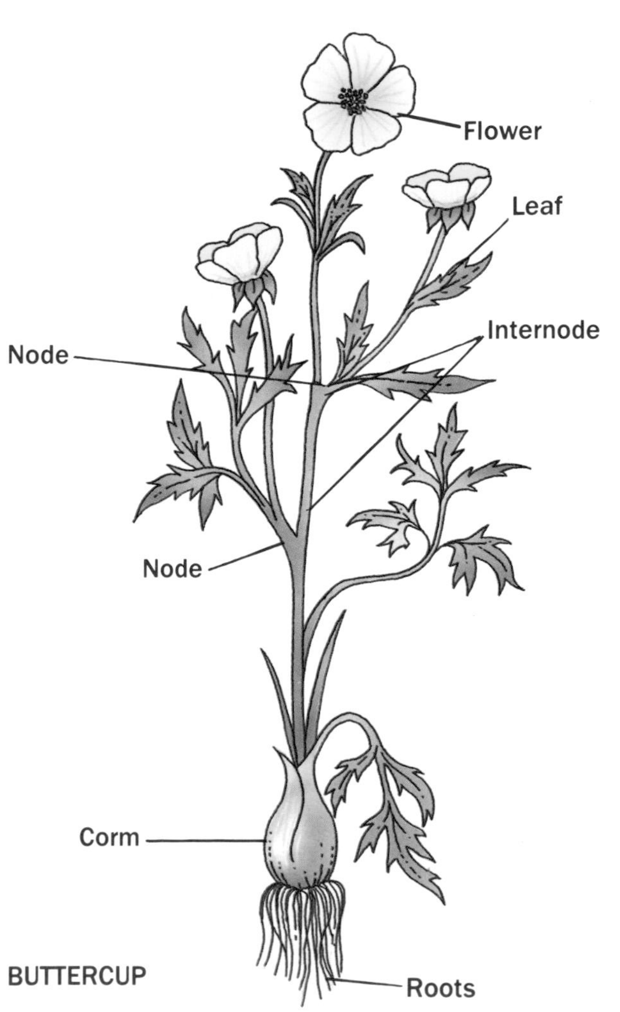

TOWARD THE LIGHT

Stems grow toward light. Place a potted plant on its side under bright light. After a few days the stem starts to bend upward. This is not caused by gravity. The stem also bends sideways if lit from the side. It bends because cells on the dark side grow faster than those on the light side.

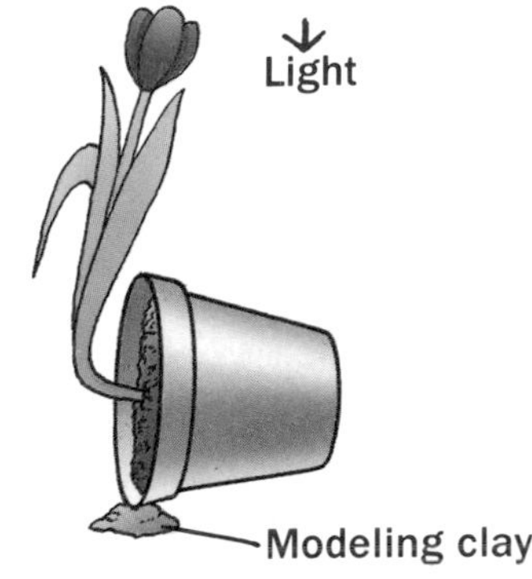

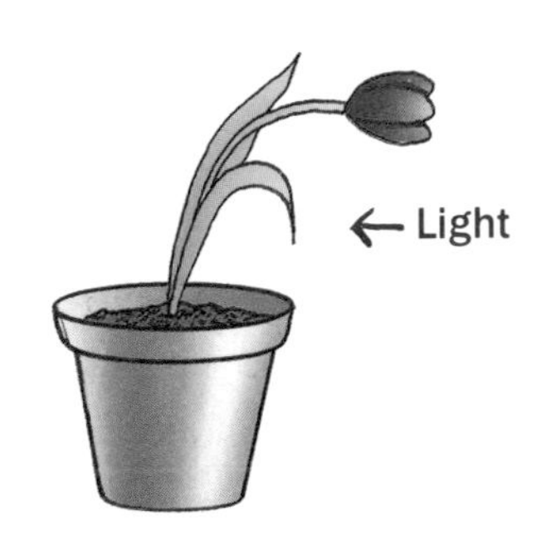

DID YOU KNOW?

It is possible to tell the age of a tree by counting the number of rings in its trunk. These are known as growth rings. A new ring forms each year of the tree's life. The oldest living tree in the world is a bristlecone pine in California. It is more than 4,600 years old!

▽ This stem has formed cambium and is just about to start making woody growth.

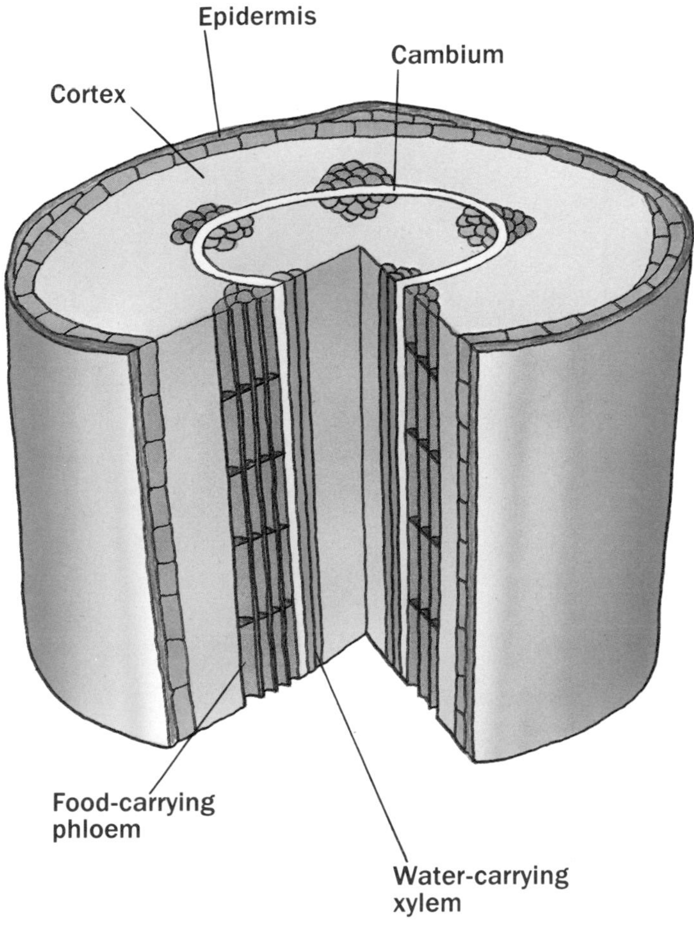

PLANT STEM

WOODY STEMS

Woody growth makes stems stronger and thicker, and allows strong boughs and branches to form. A ring of cells called the cambium runs up the stem. It passes between the xylem and phloem tissues, going through each of the strands. The cells in the cambium start to divide and form new xylem cells on the inside and new phloem on the outside. The xylem cells become soaked with lignin and form strong wood. Weaker cells form rays that radiate through the stem. Bark forms on the outside and makes the swelling stem waterproof.

▽ Wood forms in rings.

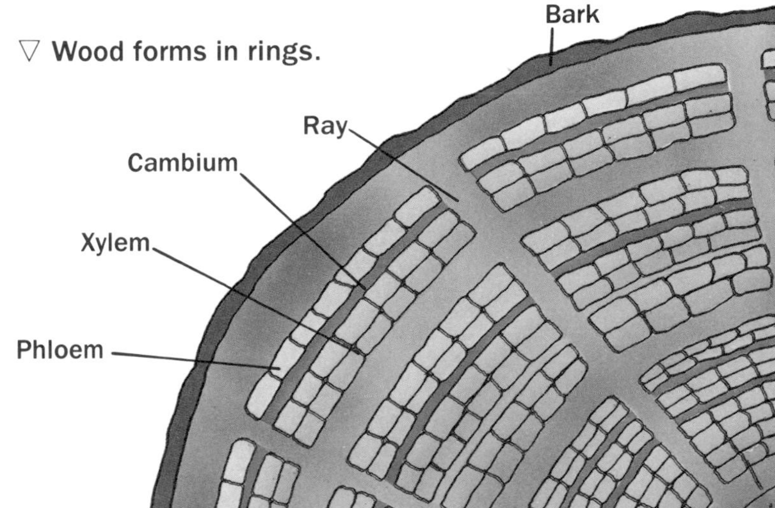

Leaves come in a huge number of shapes and sizes, but they all have one function in common. They produce food for the plant by photosynthesis. The leaf changes the energy in sunlight, using a green pigment called chlorophyll. This energy is used to make sugar from carbon dioxide (CO_2) and water (H_2O).

STRUCTURE

Leaves are usually flat to trap as much sunlight as possible. They are also thin. If leaves were thick, some of the cells would not get enough light or CO_2 for photosynthesis, but would still need to use up food.

The leaf is kept firm by the midrib and veins. The midrib and veins have xylem to bring water from the stem. They also have phloem to take sugar that has been made in the leaf to the stem.

Photosynthesis happens inside the leaf cells. Palisade cells contain lots of chlorophyll and absorb most of the light. The spongy mesophyll layer has air spaces. CO_2 enters the leaf through holes on the underside called stomata.

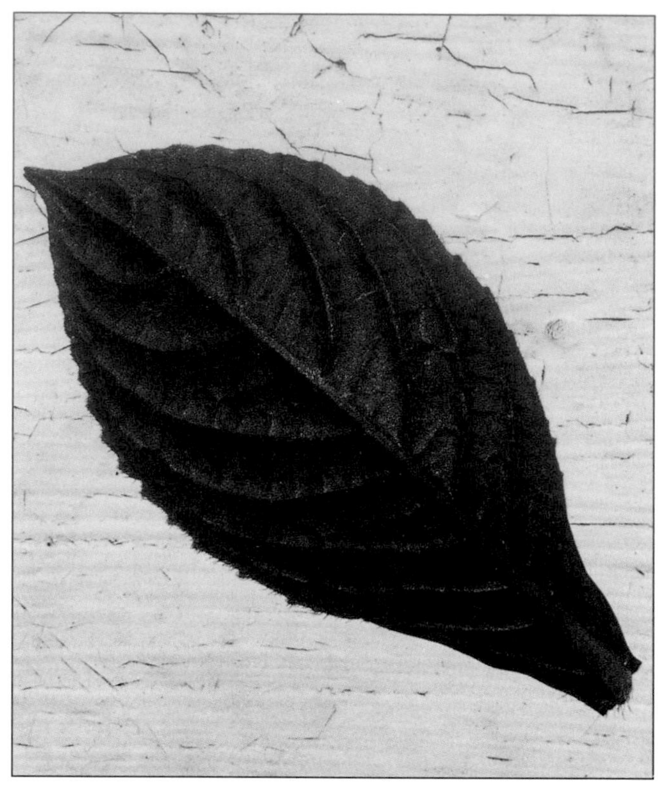

△ Veins carry sugar and water around inside the leaf. In dicotyledons the veins usually form a branching network. The veins in monocotyledons are arranged in parallel lines.

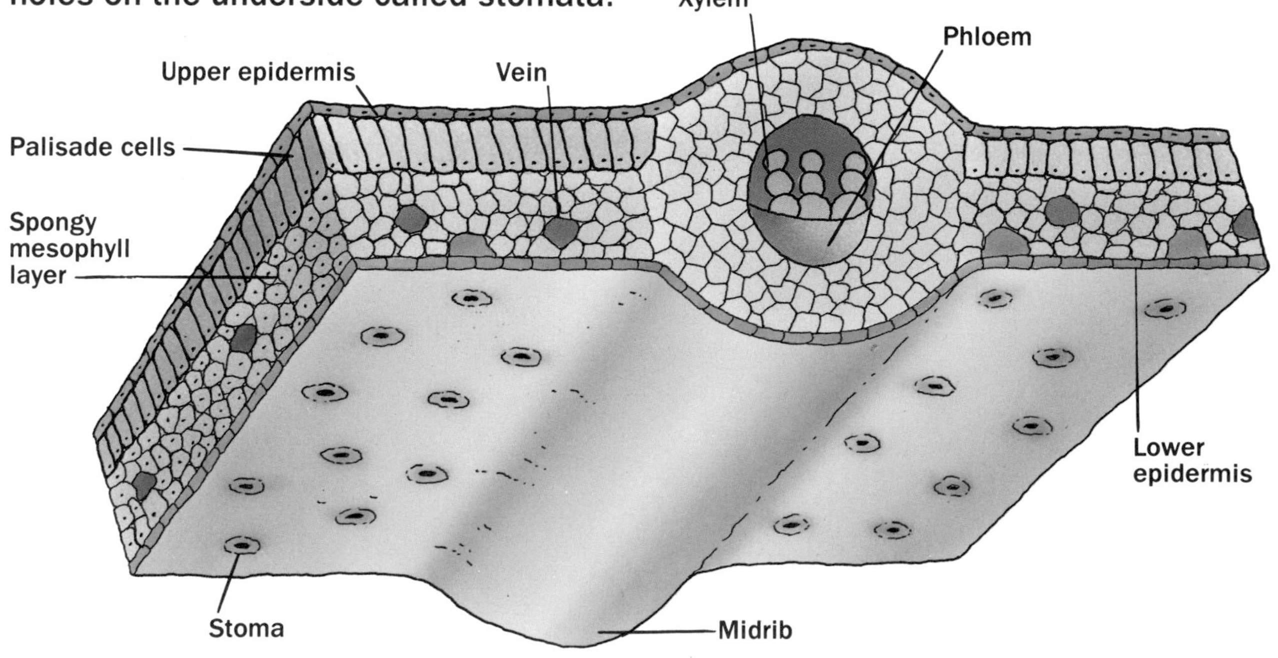

△ The epidermis is covered in a waxy layer called the cuticle. This helps to prevent the leaf from losing water and wilting. But the cuticle also keeps CO_2 out, so there are stomata to let CO_2 enter the leaf. They are usually on the shaded side to keep water loss small.

BREATHING

Stomata are special pores that control the movement of gases in and out of leaves. Each stoma can be opened or closed. The stomata open during the day to let CO_2 into the leaf for photosynthesis. In bright sunshine, lots of water evaporates from the mesophyll cells and passes out through the stomata. If the soil is dry, the plant could wilt and die. To prevent this, the stomata close in very dry weather. They also close at night.

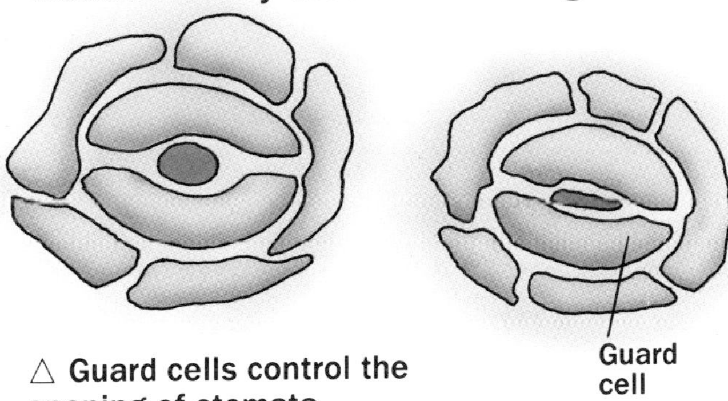

△ Guard cells control the opening of stomata.

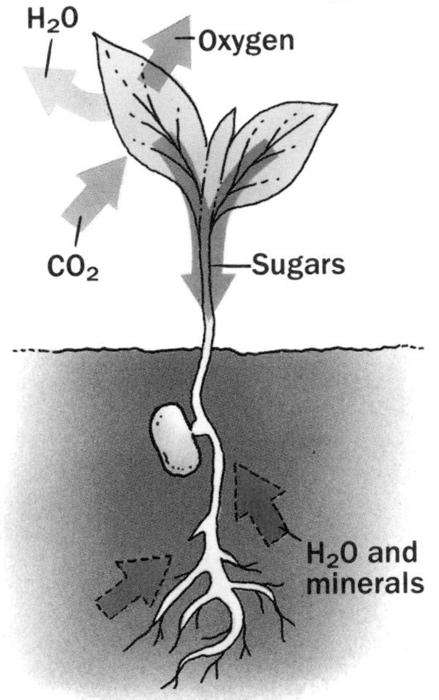

△ In photosynthesis, CO_2 and H_2O are combined to form sugars using energy from sunlight. Oxygen is given out as a waste product. There was no oxygen in the atmosphere before plants appeared on Earth and produced it.

LEAF ARRANGEMENTS

Leaves usually fit around the stem in a way that catches the most sunlight. They position themselves so that one leaf is in the shade of others as little as possible. Stand under a beech tree and notice how the leaves seem to fit together and blot out the sky.

▽ Three different arrangements of leaves.

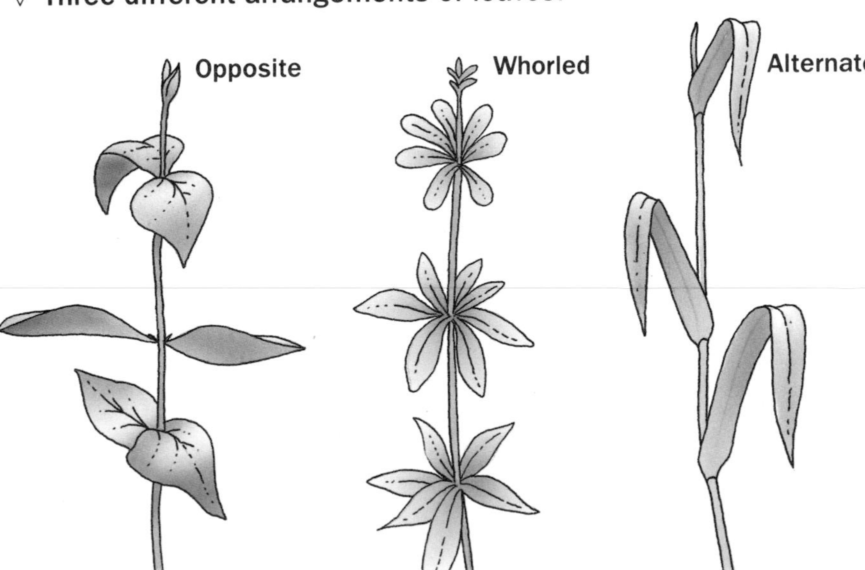

DID YOU KNOW?

The enormous leaves of the giant water lily from the Amazon can support the weight of a child. The raised rim of each leaf acts like the sides of a boat. Thick veins keep the leaf from folding up as it floats on the water.

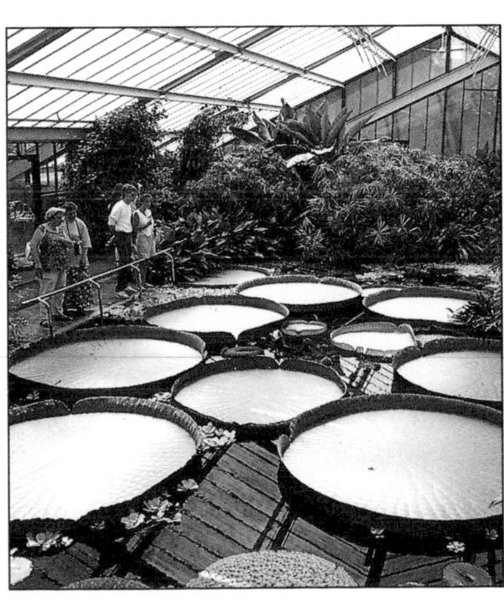

Most countries have both good and poor seasons for plant growth. Plants often grow when conditions are good, but form buds to pass through the poor season. Buds are miniature shoots with a stem and tightly packed leaves or flowers. They can rapidly expand into leafy shoots when good conditions return.

△ Buds contain next year's shoots and flowers.

STRUCTURE

Deciduous plants form buds and lose their leaves as the winter approaches. Good examples are the broadleaf trees like oak, beech and horse chestnut. Many other plants form winter buds even though they are not fully deciduous. The buds are a safeguard against very severe frosts, which may kill all the green shoots.

Buds are formed during the summer. This happens when the tree senses that the days are becoming shorter. Usually a large bud forms at the end of each shoot or twig. Smaller buds form in the leaf axils – the angles between each leaf and the stem. Each bud is surrounded by small, tough leaves called bud scales.

During the winter the buds stay dormant. This dormancy is broken by a signal that spring has arrived. In trees, the signal is often a rise in temperature after a period of cold.

▽ The large winter buds of horse chestnut are often called "sticky buds." The horse chestnut is one of the earliest trees to come into leaf in the spring. The buds start to swell as the stem inside lengthens (A). As the bud scales bend back, fluffy leaves can be seen inside (B). These are folded up in the bud, but now start to expand (C). The stem starts to grow from the bud, pushing the leaves upward (D).

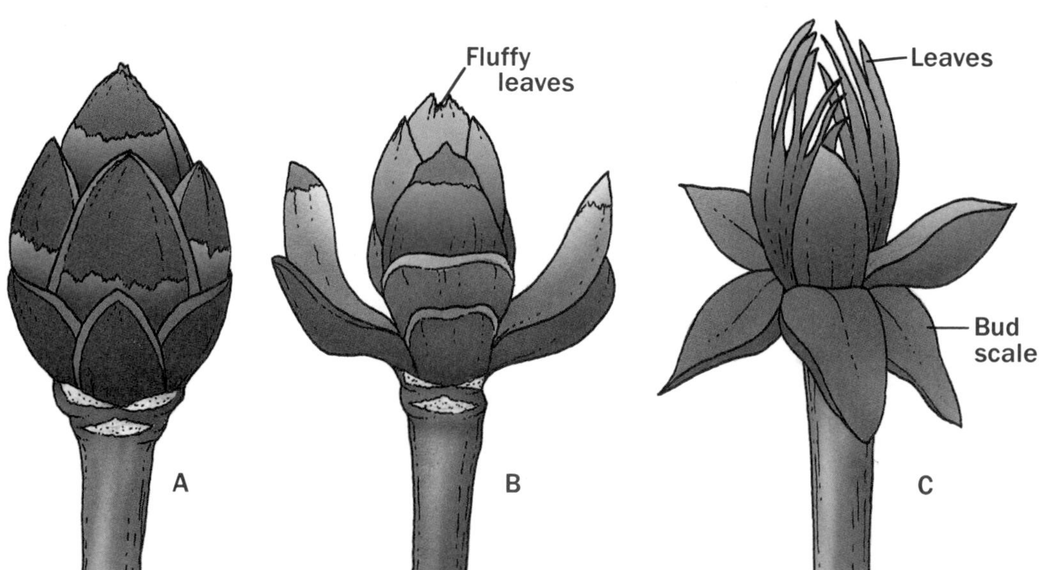

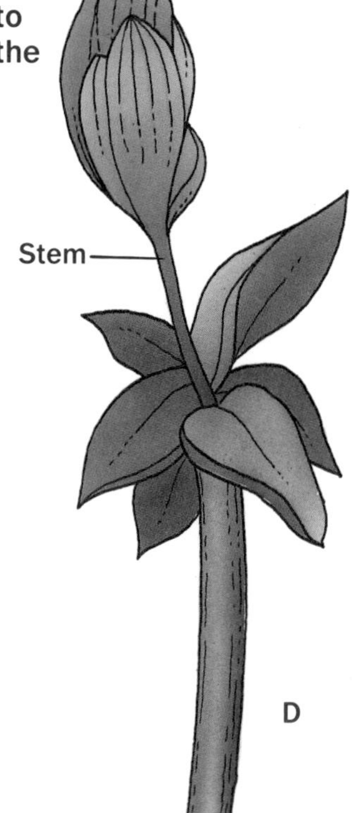

LEAF FALL

All trees shed their leaves. Deciduous trees lose all their leaves at once in the autumn. Evergreens drop leaves in ones and twos all through the year. A few deciduous trees lose their leaves in very hot conditions. Getting rid of the leaves helps to stop the tree from drying up when the soil is frozen or very dry.

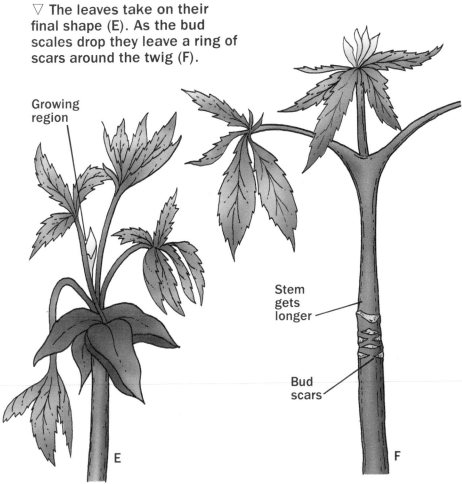

△ Deciduous forests change color in autumn.

Deciduous trees prepare for leaf fall in late summer. They sense the shortening days or lower temperatures. Useful substances are withdrawn from the leaves. This is what causes them to change from green to red or yellow. A layer of cork forms at the bottom of the leaf stalk. The leaf falls off when the weak cells in the cork layer break.

▽ Scars left by leaves do not form rings.

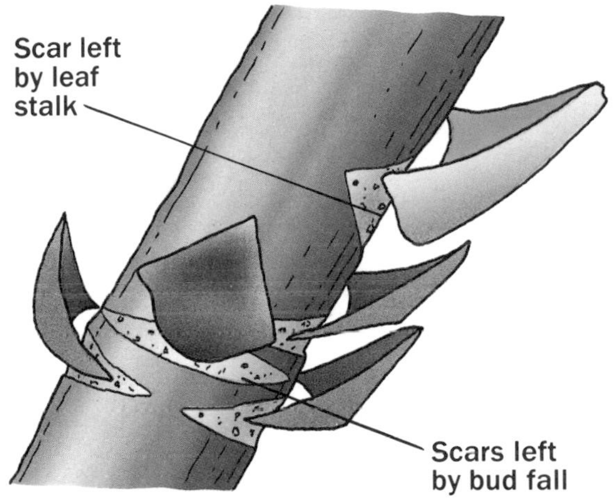

▽ The leaves take on their final shape (E). As the bud scales drop they leave a ring of scars around the twig (F).

DID YOU KNOW?

Dragon trees, like this one on Tenerife, are some of the few monocotyledons to form wood. Some species of dragon tree produce a red resin which is known as "dragon's blood."

Flowers are the special parts of plants that make seeds for reproduction. They also carry the structures that are necessary for pollination. Reproduction that involves pollination and seeds is one form of sexual reproduction. Plants and their flowers are often both male and female at the same time.

△ Brightly colored flowers attract insects. The insects feed on sugar produced by the nectaries and on pollen.

STRUCTURE

The parts of a flower are arranged in rings (known as whorls) around the stem or stalk. Sepals protect the flower in the bud. They are usually green. The petals are usually larger and often colored.

The male parts of a flower are called the stamens. Stamens are made up of anthers on top of stalks called filaments. Pollen forms inside the anthers. The female parts are called the carpels. The top of the carpel (the stigma) traps pollen. Below this is the style, and inside is an ovule. The ovule will later form the seed. All the parts of a flower join to a receptacle, which is an enlarged part of the stem.

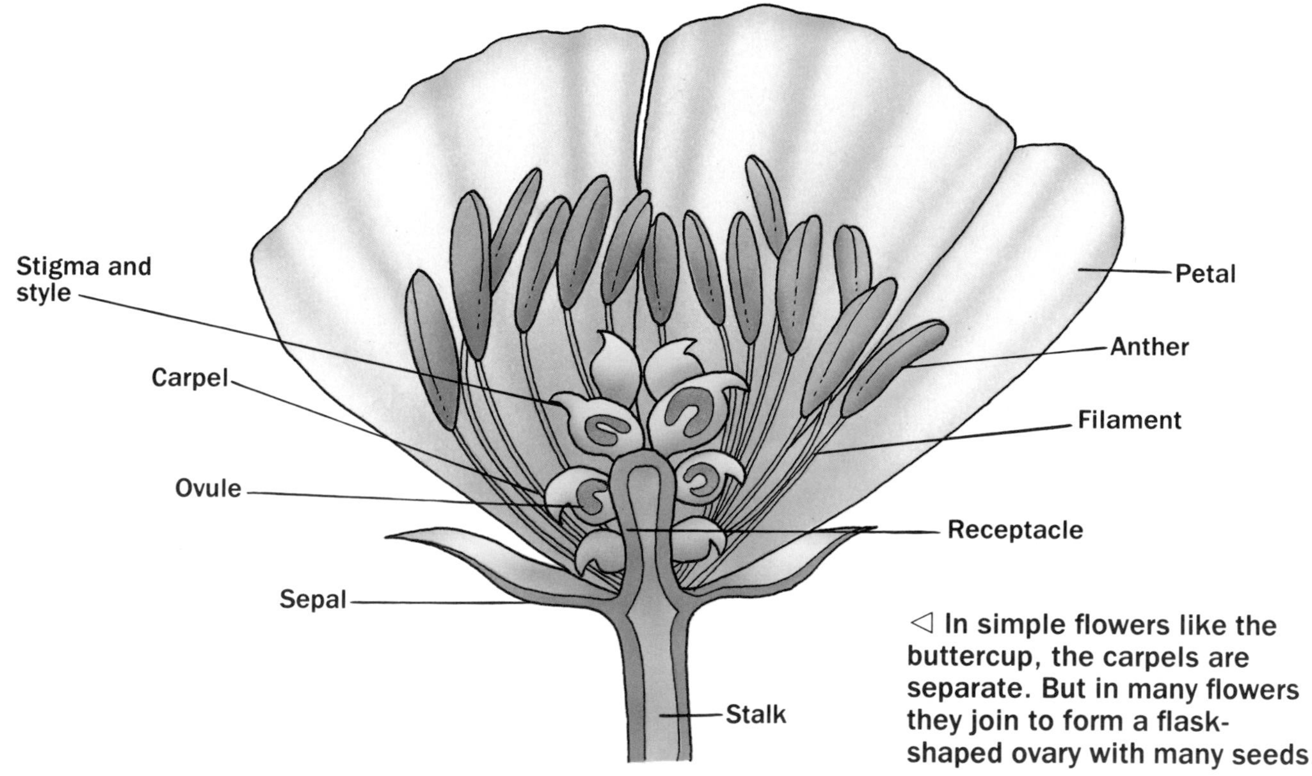

◁ In simple flowers like the buttercup, the carpels are separate. But in many flowers they join to form a flask-shaped ovary with many seeds.

POLLINATION

Pollination is the name given to the transfer of pollen from anthers to stigmas. This transfer is necessary for seeds to form. Movement of the pollen may be brought about by insects or sometimes by other animals. Pollen is also often carried in the wind and sometimes by moving water. Many flowers are specially structured to undergo pollination by only one of these methods.

Insect-pollinated flowers are usually easy to see and brightly colored. The male and female parts are often hidden inside. Wind-pollinated flowers have small green petals and no nectaries or scent. The anthers hang out to shed pollen. The stigmas are feathery to catch pollen that is blowing past.

Pollination between flowers on separate plants is known as cross-pollination. It allows characteristics of the parents to be mixed in new ways. This lets the species adapt if living conditions change. Pollination between flowers on the same plant, or even within the same flower, is known as self-pollination. It does not allow mixing of characteristics.

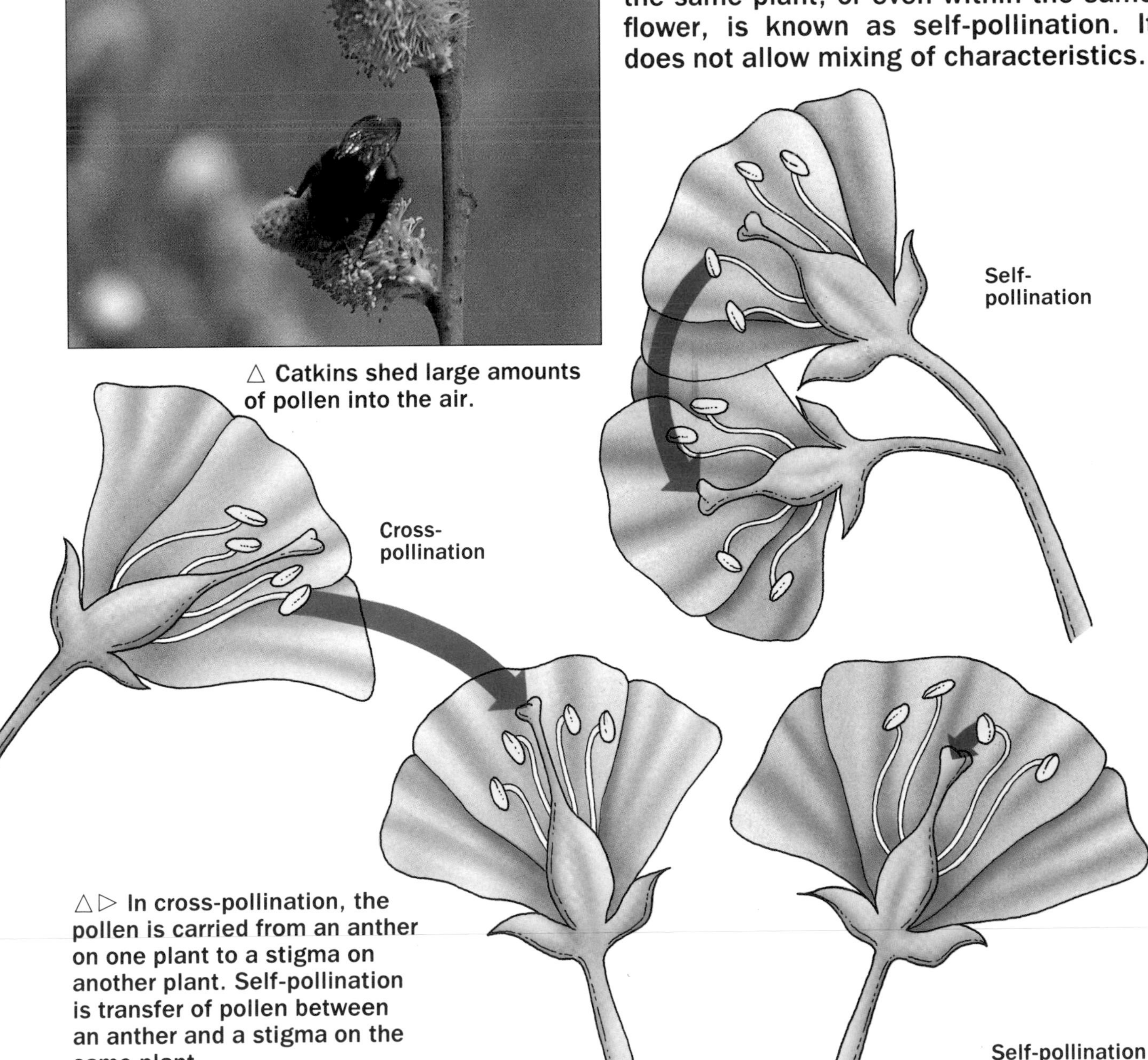

△ Catkins shed large amounts of pollen into the air.

△▷ In cross-pollination, the pollen is carried from an anther on one plant to a stigma on another plant. Self-pollination is transfer of pollen between an anther and a stigma on the same plant.

ANIMAL POLLINATION

Plants such as buttercups have simple flowers that are open and regular in shape. They can be pollinated by almost any small creature that crawls onto them. But because of their simple shape, self-pollination often occurs.

Many flowers have a design that increases the chances of cross-pollination by insects. In one sort of design, the petals are joined together to form a tube. The nectaries are at the bottom of the tube. Insects have to crawl into the tube to feed from the nectaries. They are then more likely to brush against the anthers and stigmas.

The petals of insect-pollinated flowers are often different sizes. Special petals provide a place for insects to land. Colored lines – called honey guides – help insects to find the flower tube. Only insects of the right size and shape can enter these flowers and cause pollination. This helps to make pollination more likely, because pollen will not be wasted on insects that can go to lots of different species of flower.

Many flowers are pollinated by bees and butterflies. Pollen easily sticks to their hairy bodies. These insects have long tongues to reach the nectar.

△ Hummingbirds need lots of sugary nectar. They visit and pollinate large, brightly colored flowers.

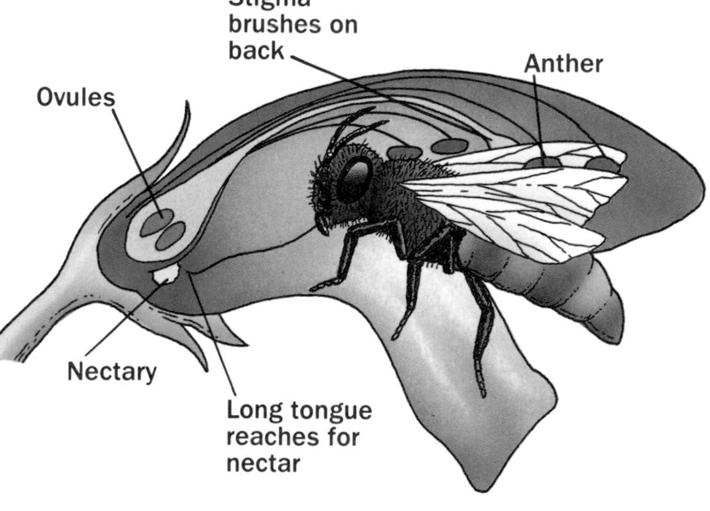

△ The white deadnettle is pollinated by bees with long tongues. As the bee pushes into the flower the stigma and anthers brush on its back.

◁ The lower petals of lupin and gorse flowers are pushed down by the weight of a bee when it lands. The stigma and anthers brush the bee's underside.

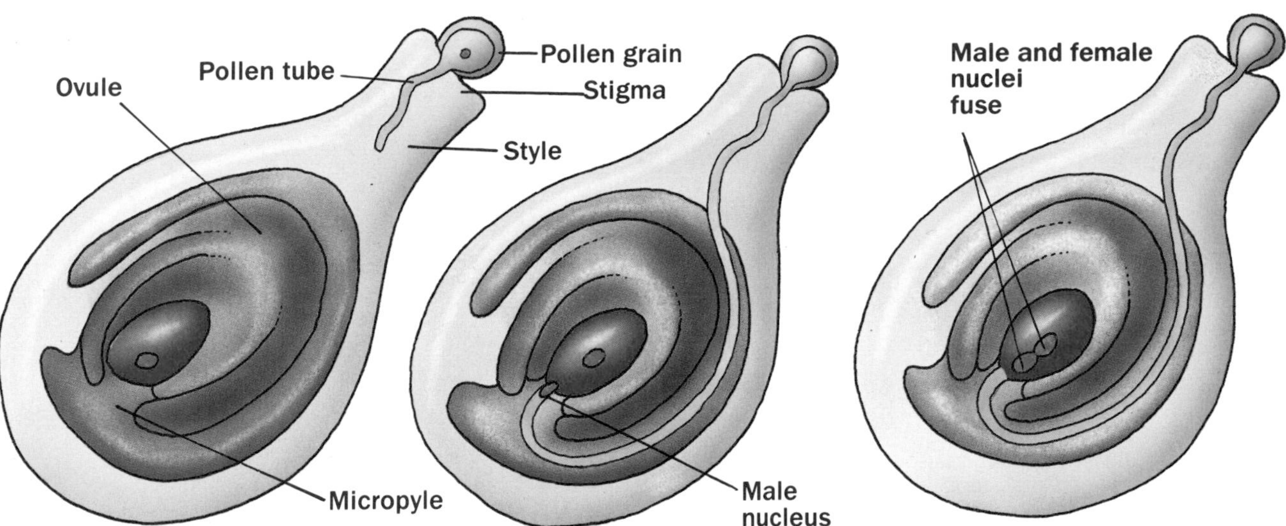

△ When a pollen grain lands on a stigma, a pollen tube starts to grow.

△ A pollen tube grows down through the style, through the micropyle, and into the ovule.

△ The male nucleus passes down the pollen tube and fuses with the nucleus in the ovule.

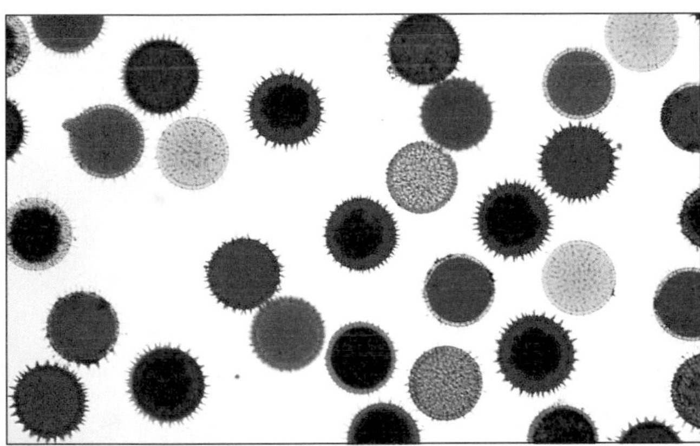

△ Patterned coats of pollen grains

DID YOU KNOW?

Honey possums feed entirely on pollen and nectar using a brush-tipped tongue. They dart from flower to flower. Like insects, they help to pollinate the flowers.

▽ A honey possum in Australia

FERTILIZATION

Seeds are formed by sexual reproduction. In sexual reproduction, special cells called gametes are produced by male and female plants or animals. These cells fuse (join together) in a process called fertilization. In flowers, this happens after pollination. The male gamete is the pollen grain and the female gamete is an egg cell inside the ovule.

During pollination, grains of pollen become stuck to the stigma. If the pollen and stigma are of the same species, the pollen grain sends out a pollen tube. The pollen tube grows down through the style into the swollen part of the carpel, which contains the ovule. Only one tube reaches the ovule, and the rest die. The successful pollen tube enters the ovule through the micropyle.

When fertilization happens, the end of the pollen tube breaks. A tiny particle called a nucleus moves from the tube into the ovule. This fuses with the female nucleus of the egg cell.

The fertilized ovule now grows into a seed inside the ovary. If the flower contains several ovules inside an ovary, a separate pollen grain fertilizes the egg cell in each of the ovules.

FRUIT FORMATION

The final event in the life cycle of a flowering plant is the formation of seeds and fruits.

After fertilization, the petals, sepals, stamens, styles and stigmas start to shrivel up. The fertilized egg cell divides many times to form the tissues of the embryo. Other cells in the ovule divide to form a food store known as endosperm. The outer layers of the ovule form the testa. The micropyle remains as a hole in the coat of the ripe seed. It sometimes lets water enter the seed at germination.

Fruits develop from the ovary. The number of seeds in the fruit depends on the number of carpels that joined to form the ovary. Fruits called multiple fruits are formed from several ovaries.

△ Fruits form if the ovule is fertilized.

▽ Sometimes parts of the flower besides the ovary help to form the fruit. The apple flower has a receptacle that encloses the ovary. The outer flesh of the apple is formed from the receptacle. The true fruit wall can be seen as a line.

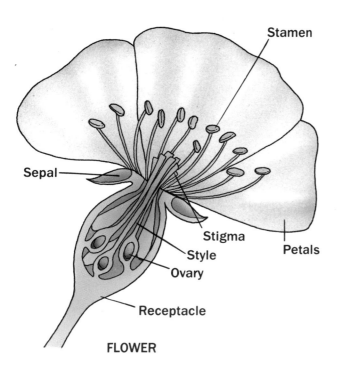

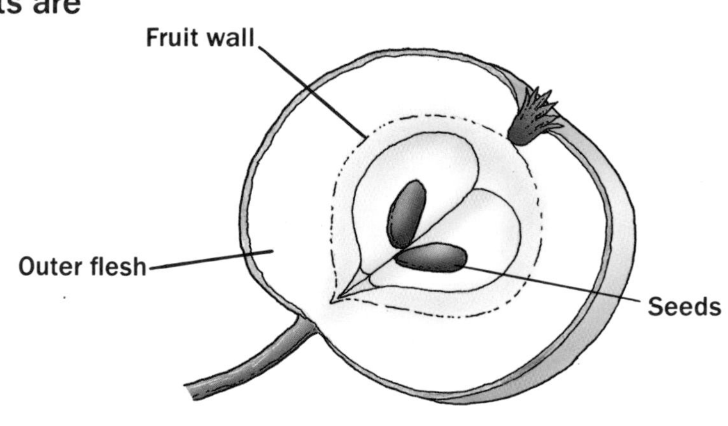

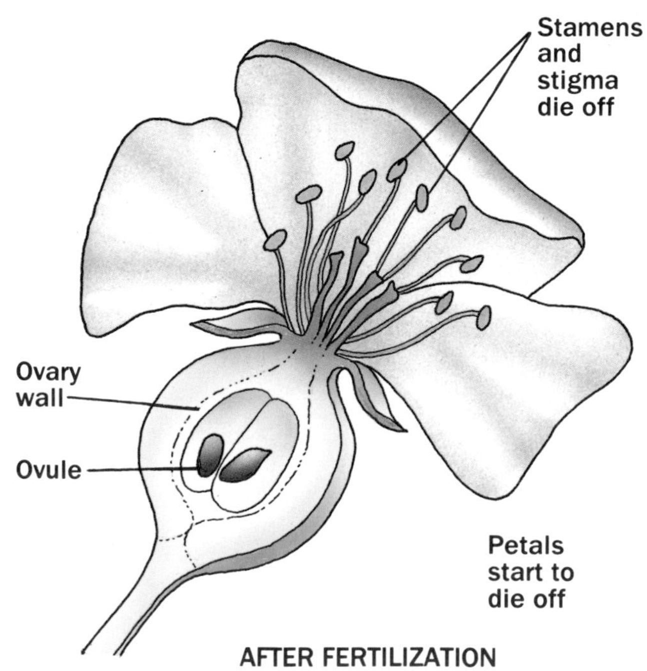

DIFFERENT FRUITS

See how many different kinds of fruits you can find. Remember that vegetables like peas in their pods are actually fruits.

Examine each fruit carefully and try and understand how it has formed. Get an adult to help cut the fruit open so that you can see the number and arrangement of the seeds. Can you see if there is more than one ovary? Is the fruit dehiscent or is it indehiscent?

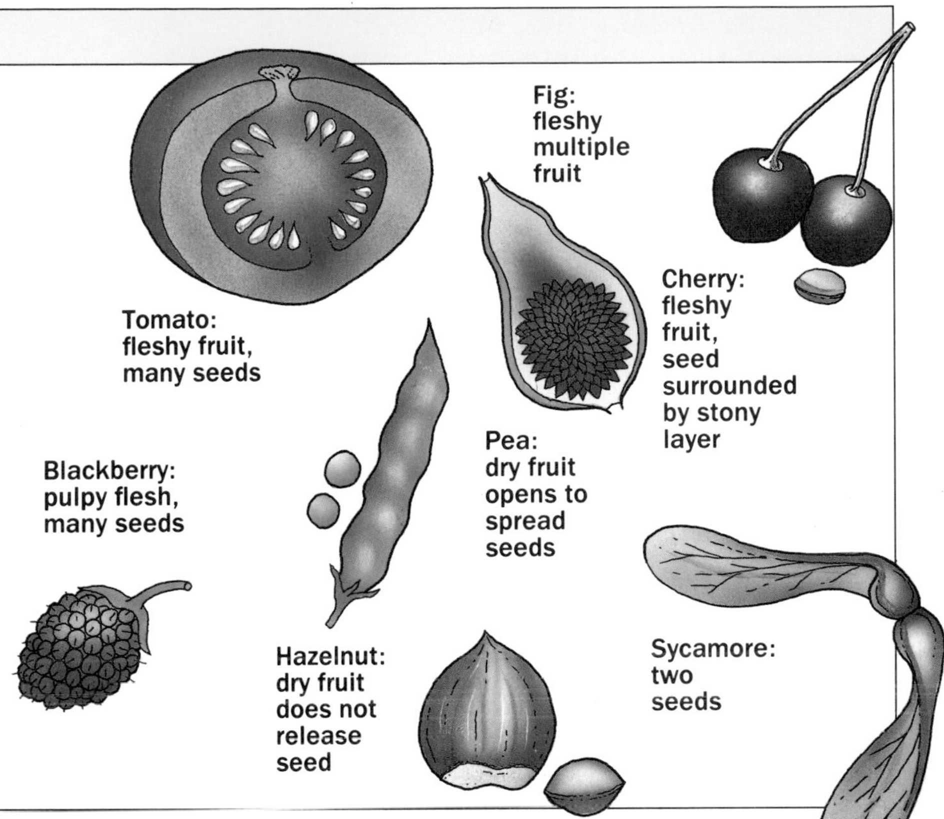

▽ The stigmas in rose-bay willow herb are raised above the anthers. This lessens the chance of self-pollination occurring. The ovary is formed from fused carpels. Willow herb fruits are dehiscent. They split open when they are ripe. The seeds have strands that act like parachutes for wind dispersal.

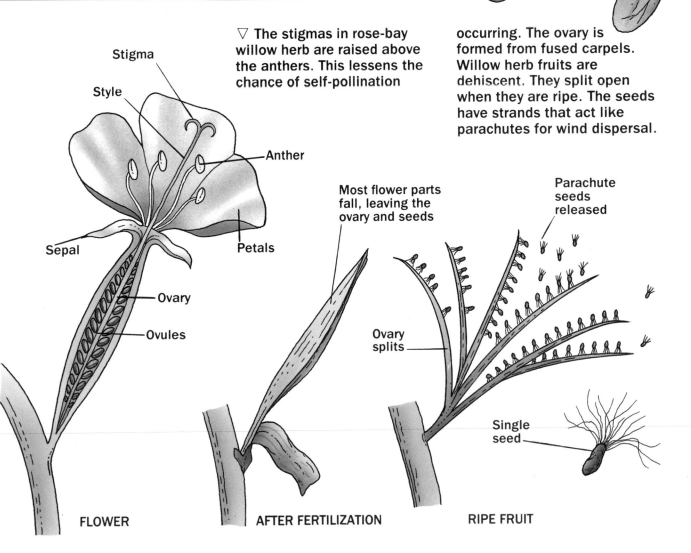

Stigma
Style
Anther
Sepal
Petals
Ovary
Ovules
Most flower parts fall, leaving the ovary and seeds
Parachute seeds released
Ovary splits
Single seed
FLOWER
AFTER FERTILIZATION
RIPE FRUIT

Seeds are usually the only method of reproduction in annual plants – ones that complete their life cycle in a year and die. Many perennial species – those that live for several years – also reproduce vegetatively. Offshoots grow from the parent plant, then become separate and start to live on their own.

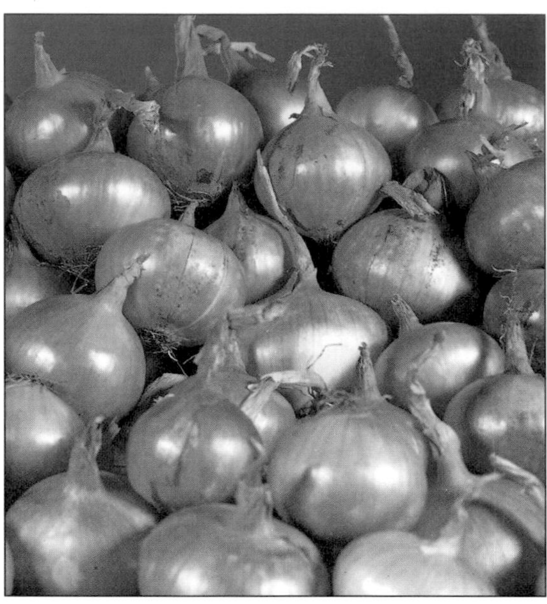

△ Onions are typical bulbs.

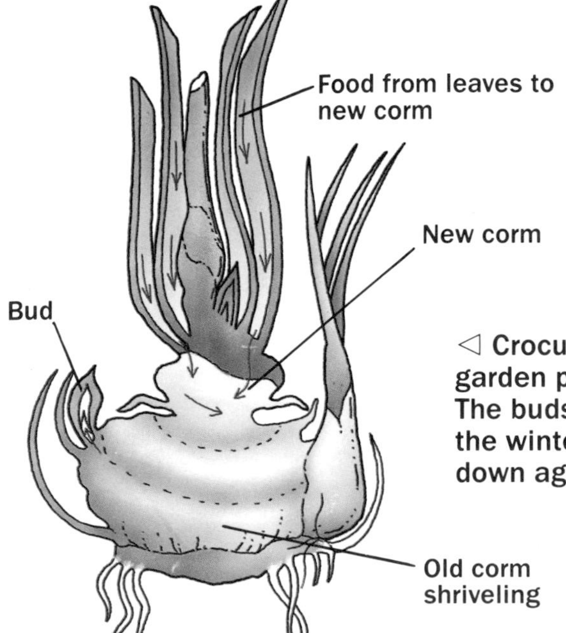

◁ Crocuses are common garden plants that have corms. The buds start to grow early in the winter and the leaves die down again by early summer.

BULBS AND CORMS

Perennial plants often store food made during good weather for later use. The food is stored in the parts, or organs, that can produce new plants. Producing new plants without using seeds is known as vegetative propagation.

A corm is simply a short piece of stem that is swollen with food. It survives the winter, or (in some species) hot, dry periods, underground. Buds are formed on the corm before the leaves die down. Later, the main bud forms new leaves using the food in the corm. These leaves produce a new corm on top of the old one. Other buds may also grow into shoots that form corms. So one corm can produce several new corms. Each new corm grows special roots called contractile roots. When fully grown, these roots shrink and pull the corm deeper into the soil.

Bulbs are mostly made of small fleshy leaves that store food. These leaves are called bulb scales. At the bottom of the bulb there is a piece of stem. Roots grow down from this. Each year the main bud grows to form new leaves and flowers. Food produced by the leaves helps to make new scales inside the bulb as the outer ones die. New bulbs can form if other buds, called lateral buds, grow.

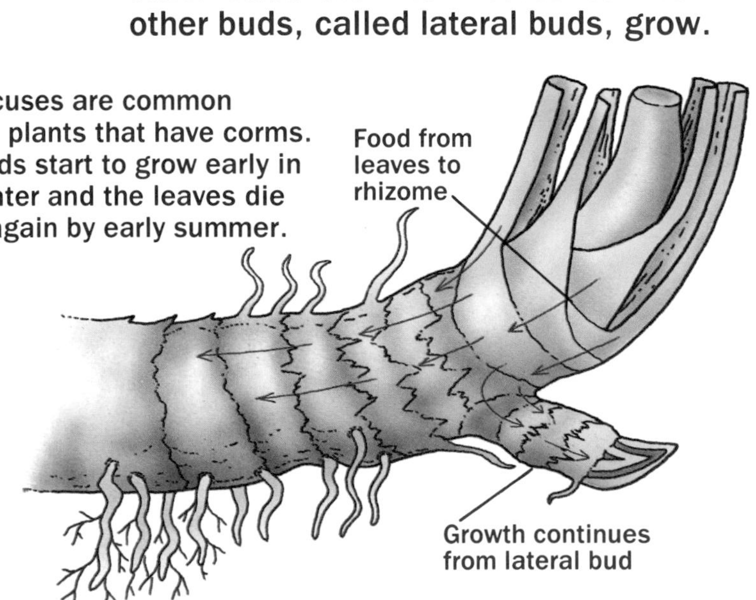

▷ Many iris species have rhizomes, although some have bulbs. The tip of the iris rhizome turns up to form the leaves and flowering shoot.

▽ Strawberries propagate by runners growing from the stem.

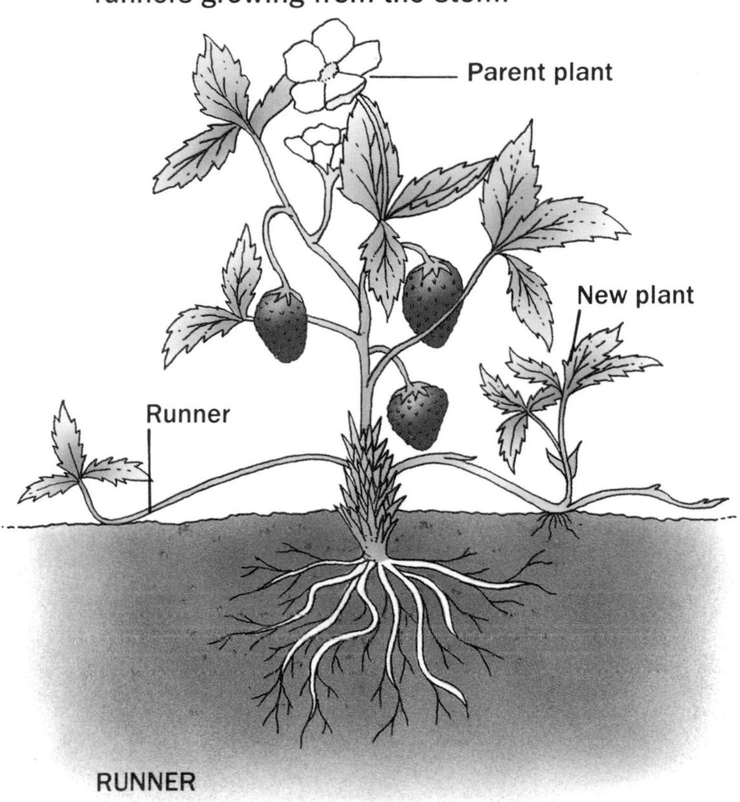

RUNNERS, RHIZOMES AND TUBERS

Runners, rhizomes and tubers are also organs for vegetative propagation.

Runners are horizontal stems that grow from buds on an adult plant. New plants develop on the runner from buds at the nodes. Roots grow down into the soil to anchor the new plant.

Rhizomes are similar to runners, but they grow underground. In irises, food is stored in the rhizome. Leaves and flowers form when the end of the rhizome grows upward. New rhizomes start to grow from lateral buds.

Potatoes are examples of special rhizomes called tubers. Ordinary rhizomes grow out from the potato plant. The ends swell and store food. The "eyes" of potatoes are compressed stems with buds. These turn into next year's plants.

▽ Bulbs are produced by spring flowering plants like snowdrops, daffodils and bluebells.

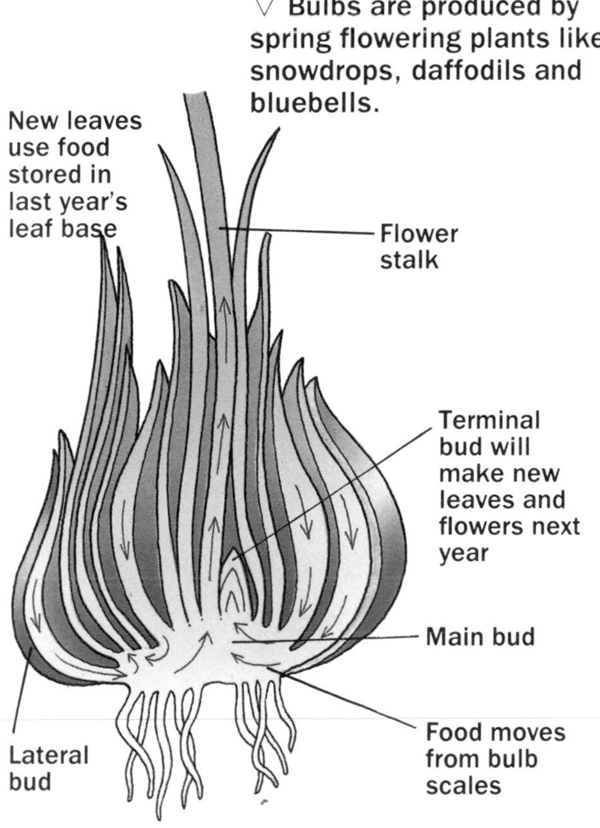

POTATO PROJECT

It is easy to grow potatoes. Fill a large pot with earth. Plant a single tuber four inches deep. Remember to water the pot sometimes. Examine the new tubers when the plant is flowering.

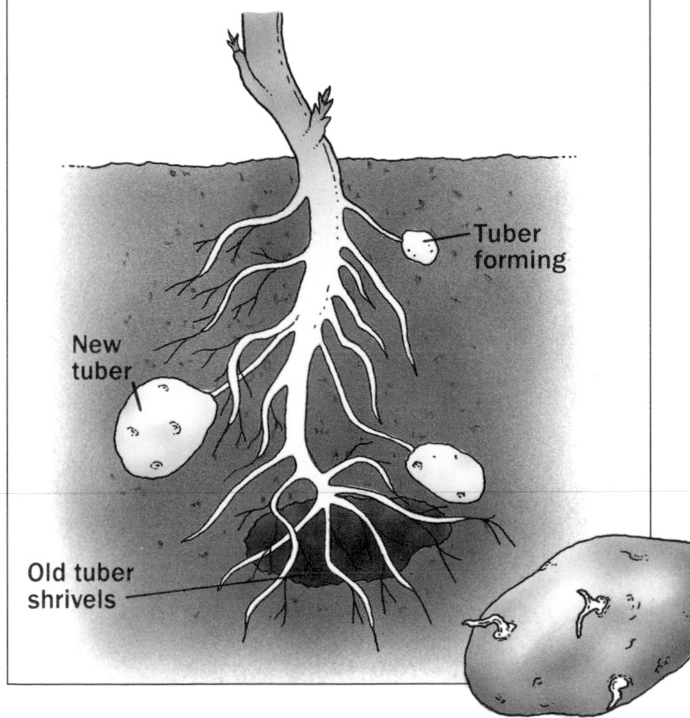

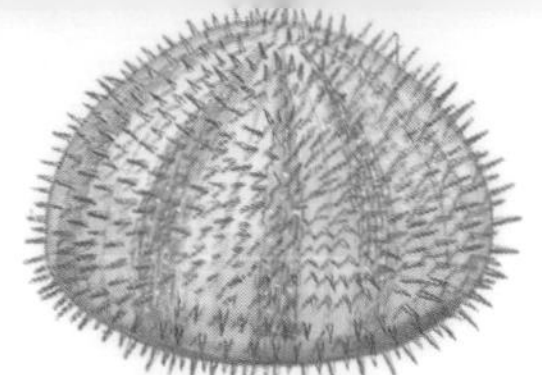

encyclopedia of science

INVERTEBRATES

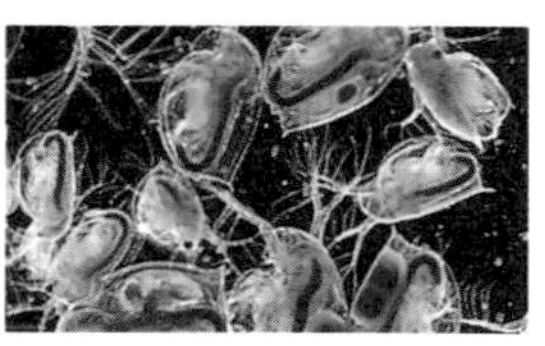

CONTENTS

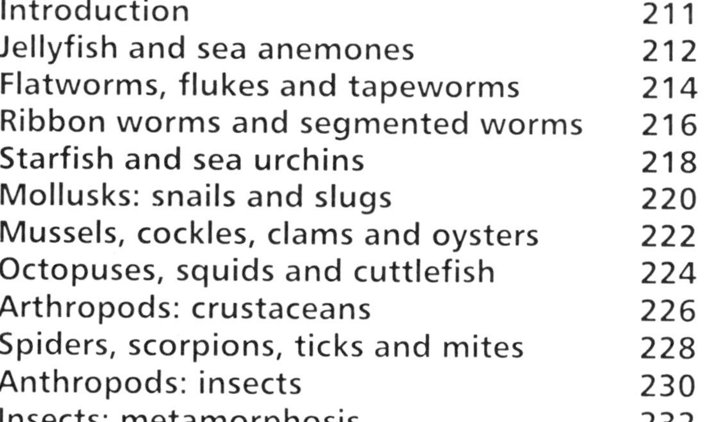

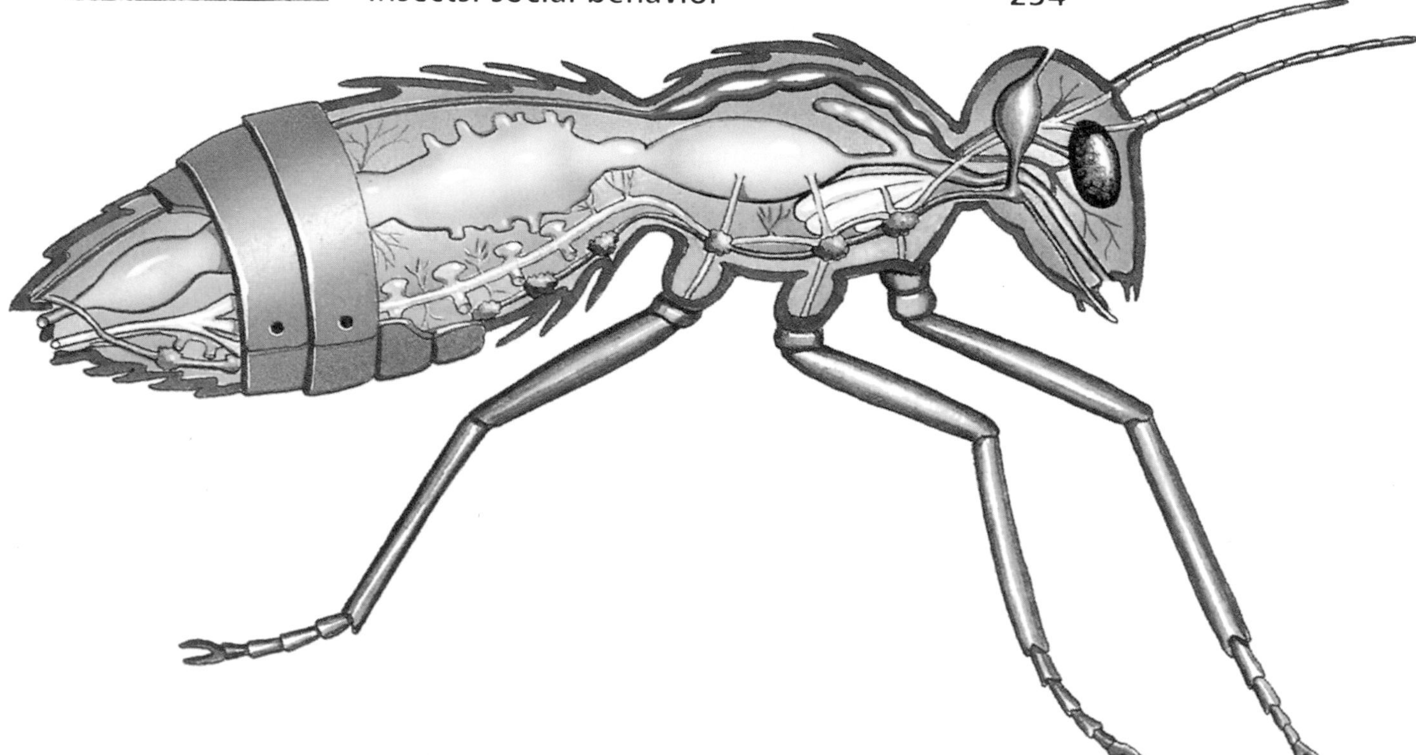

INTRODUCTION

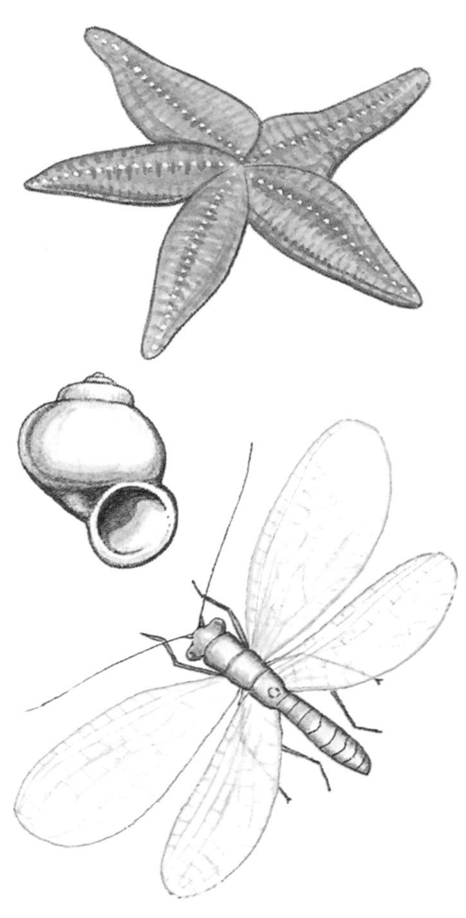

The animal kingdom can be divided into two main groups: animals with backbones (vertebrates) and animals without backbones (invertebrates). This chapter is about invertebrates.

When we think of animals, we usually think of animals that are vertebrates. Vertebrates include mammals (such as dogs, lions and people), birds, reptiles, amphibians and fish. But the great majority of animals in the world are invertebrates.

There are not only great numbers of invertebrates, but there are very many different types. For example, there are nearly a million known species of insect, and about 8,000 new species are discovered every year. There are only about 4,000 species of mammal.

This section describes the most important groups of invertebrates. It tells you about some of their main features and ways of life, and what distinguishes one group from another.

Jellyfish, sea anemones, corals and hydras all belong to a group of animals called the coelenterates. Coelenterates are very simple animals. They all live in water, and nearly always in seawater. They have a strange life cycle in which they live in two quite different forms: polyps and medusas.

△ Coral is formed by some species of polyp. The polyps build limestone skeletons. When they die, new polyps add more limestone.

JELLYFISH

Jellyfish, like other coelenterates, are made up of two layers of cells: the outer layer is for protection, and the inner layer is the lining of the stomach. Between these layers is a jellylike material, called mesoglea. This usually makes up most of the animal. Jellyfish vary in size from a few millimeters to three feet across.

Jellyfish are carnivores – that is, they eat animals. They have tentacles around their mouth. The tentacles catch prey and draw it into the mouth. They have special cells called nematocysts. Some nematocysts sting and paralyze prey; others are very sticky and catch hold of the jellyfish's prey.

▽ Medusas produce an egg that develops into a larva called a planula. This attaches to a rock and grows into a polyp. The polyp grows new medusas, which break off.

▽ This jellyfish is at the medusa stage of its life cycle. It spent the first part of its life as a polyp, which looked very different.

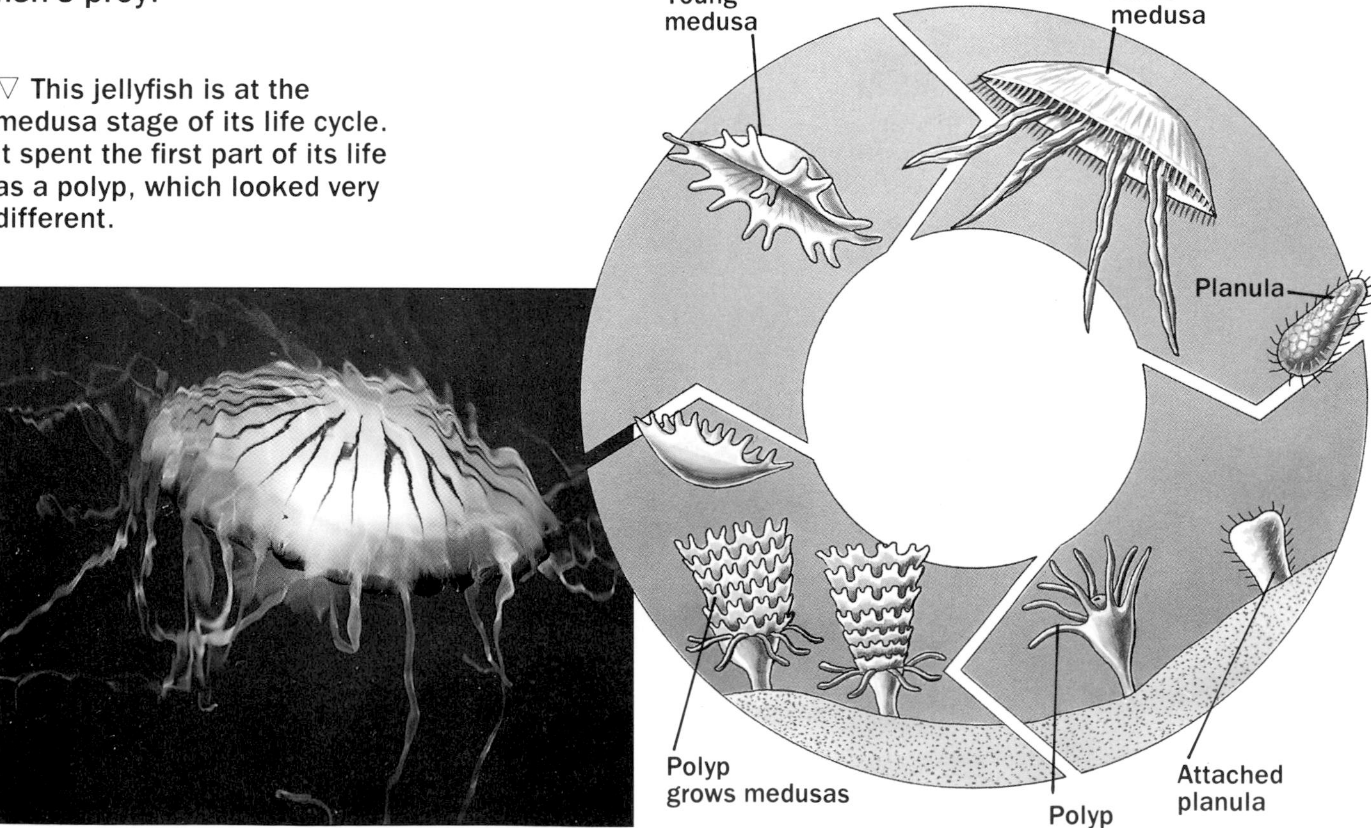

SEA ANEMONES

Sea anemones are brightly colored and look like flowers growing in the sea. They vary in size from a few millimeters to about three feet across. Anemones live attached to rocks, although they can move around slowly.

Sea anemones are a type of polyp. They do not have a medusa stage in their life cycle. They produce tiny new anemones, called budding, which break off from the parent. Sometimes sea anemones split down the middle, called fission, and the two halves separate.

Like jellyfish, sea anemones have tentacles covered in nematocysts. When prey comes too close, it is paralyzed. Sticky nematocysts hold the prey. The prey is then drawn down into the gut.

HYDRAS

Hydras are unusual coelenterates because they live in fresh water. Hydras are polyps. Like sea anemones, they do not have a medusa stage.

Hydras look rather like thin sea anemones with long tentacles. They are rarely more than ⅓ inch long. Hydras live attached to rocks and plants. They catch tiny plants and animals with their tentacles, which have nematocysts.

Hydras attach themselves by what is known as a basal disc at the bottom of their bodies. They can move slowly by walking on this disc. But if a hydra needs to move more quickly, it bends over and its tentacles take hold of a hard surface. The basal disc then lets go, and the hydra turns a cartwheel!

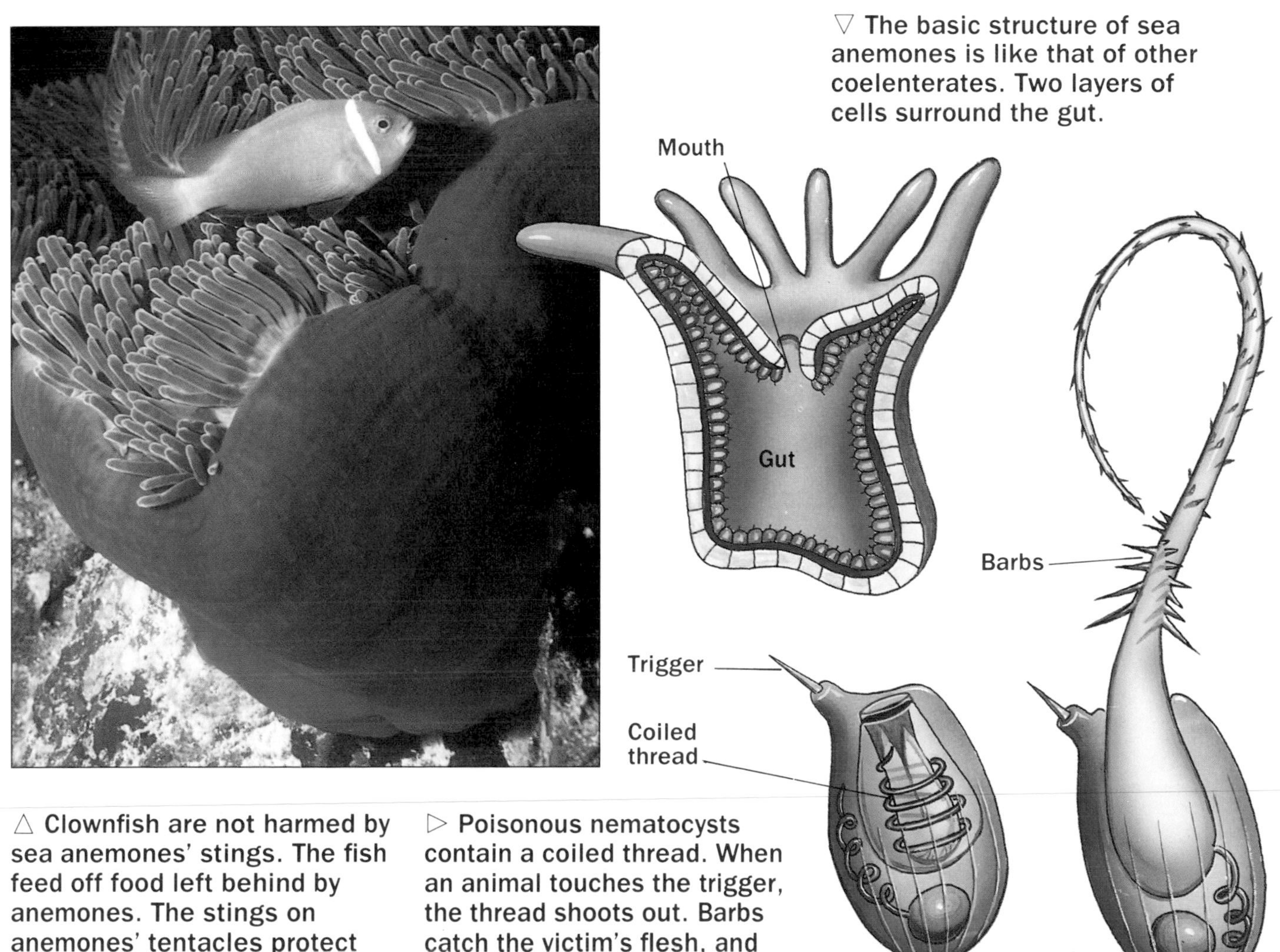

▽ The basic structure of sea anemones is like that of other coelenterates. Two layers of cells surround the gut.

△ Clownfish are not harmed by sea anemones' stings. The fish feed off food left behind by anemones. The stings on anemones' tentacles protect the fish from attack.

▷ Poisonous nematocysts contain a coiled thread. When an animal touches the trigger, the thread shoots out. Barbs catch the victim's flesh, and the thread injects poison.

FLATWORMS, FLUKES AND TAPEWORMS

There are four main types of worm: flatworms, ribbon worms, roundworms and segmented worms. Worms have soft bodies which are usually long and thin. They have no legs. The main senses they use are touch and the ability to detect chemicals that are around them. Many have simple eyes or light-sensitive spots.

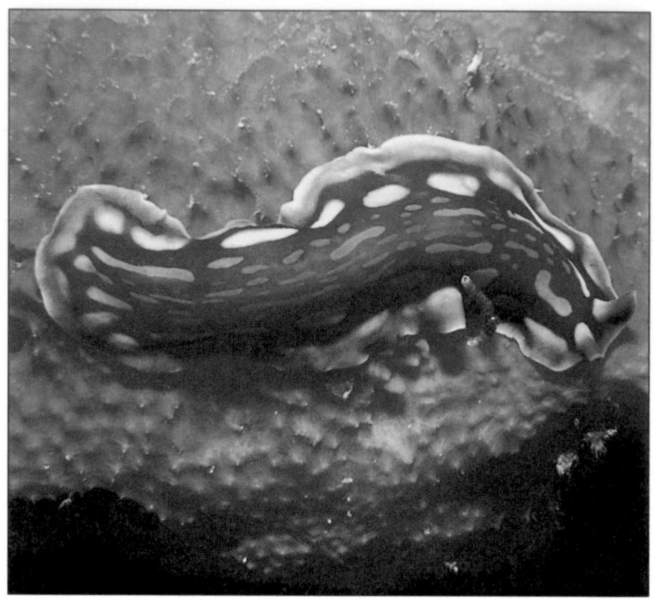

△ Most turbellarians, such as this one, live in water, but a few live on land. Turbellarians are the only group of flatworms that are not parasites.

FLATWORMS

Flatworms are also known as platyhelminths. As the name flatworm suggests, most of them have flat bodies, which are often leaf-shaped. Their bodies have a simple structure with three layers. There is an outer layer that forms the skin of the animal. The inner layer forms the intestine. And there is a middle layer of muscles and other organs between the inner and outer layers.

Many types of flatworm are parasites. Parasites live on or in an animal or plant, which is known as the host. Parasites get their food by feeding off the host.

Other flatworms live in water. These are called turbellarians. They are usually found in the mud or living among the tiny plants at the bottom of the water.

FLUKES

Flukes are parasitic flatworms. They are leaf-shaped and have suckers and hooks to attach themselves to their host. Some flukes cause little damage, but others can kill their host.

Several types of flukes infect mammals. The adult flukes can live in the human intestine and bladder, where they mate. Eggs pass out of the body with feces. The eggs hatch into larvae called miracidia, which live in water. The larva burrow into snails, where they produce hundreds of another form of larva, called cercariae. The cercariae leave the snail and again live in water. They can then burrow through the skin of a host.

Human host
Cercariae
Female fluke
Male fluke
Water snail
Egg
Miracidium

△ The blood fluke causes the disease bilharzia (also called schistosomiasis) in humans, particularly in Africa.

TAPEWORMS

Tapeworms are another group of parasitic flatworms. The adult lives in the intestine of its host (for example, a human) and absorbs digested food. The body of a tapeworm has three parts: a head, a neck and a body. The head has hooks and suckers, which hold on to the intestine wall of the host. The body grows many segments. Each forms sacks of eggs. The end segments drop off and leave the host with feces. They then release the eggs. The eggs enter a second host (for example, a pig), usually in drinking water, and hatch into larvae. The larvae burrow from the host's intestine into its flesh. If a human eats the flesh (and it has not been properly cooked), a larva can form into a new adult.

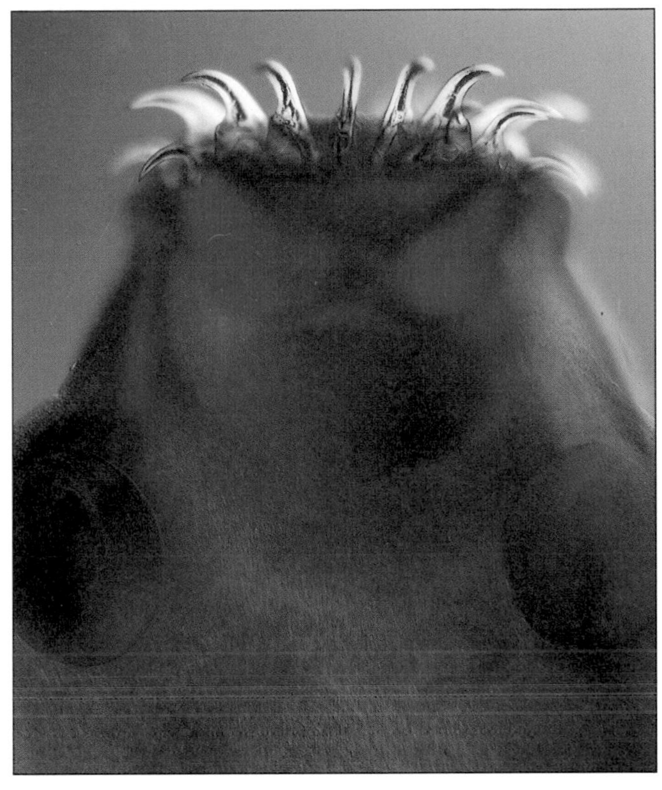

△ Tapeworms have no eyes on their heads, and their other senses are poor. When living in an intestine, they do not have to look for food or watch out for danger.

▽ The pork tapeworm has humans and pigs as hosts.

DID YOU KNOW?

Most flatworms are less than two inches long. Some tapeworms are this length, and have just four segments. But tapeworms can be over 100 feet long. They grow to almost the length of the intestine they are living in. New segments are added from the neck, so the oldest segments are farthest from the head.

Ribbon worms, roundworms and segmented worms are more complex in their structure than flatworms. They have better developed nerve and blood systems. Roundworms and segmented worms have a fluid-filled cavity around the intestine. This gives them four instead of three layers in their structure.

RIBBON WORMS

Ribbon worms are also called nemertines. They are usually quite small (two inches long or less), although the bootlace worm can grow to several feet in length. Most of them live in the sea, but a few live in fresh water or on land. They feed on small animals such as mollusks or other worms.

Ribbon worms have an unusual way of catching food. A tube shoots out through a special pore in the head. The tube is made to shoot out when the worm fills it with fluid. In some ribbon worms, the tube wraps around the prey. In others the tube has spikes and stabs the victim. A few have tubes that can sting.

△ This ribbon worm is one of the few that live on land.

ROUNDWORMS

Roundworms are also called nematodes. They have narrow, round bodies that get thinner at the ends. Some are very small, but the largest can be three feet long.

Many roundworms live in the soil or in water. These feed off the dead remains of plants and animals. Other roundworms live as parasites on plants and animals, and some can cause serious diseases.

Many species of roundworm infect people. The ascaris roundworm breeds in the human intestine and produces eggs. The eggs leave the intestine with feces. They can then get into the food of cattle and pigs. The eggs hatch into larvae in the animal's intestine. The larvae burrow out of the intestine and into muscle. This may then be eaten by a human host.

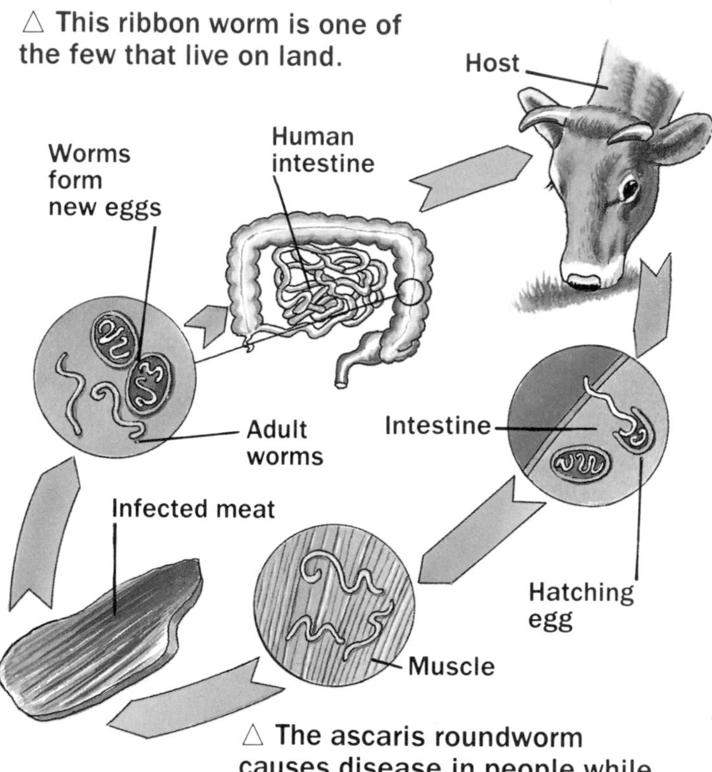

△ The ascaris roundworm causes disease in people while it is living in the human intestine.

△ Tentacles on a polychaete.

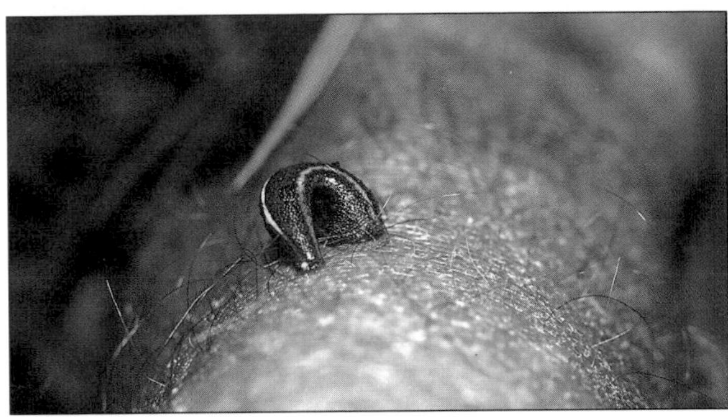

◁ Leeches do not feed often. But when they do, they can drink more than their own body weight in blood.

SEGMENTED WORMS

Segmented worms are often called annelids. The segments make them look as if they are made of a series of rings.

One group of segmented worms lives in or near the sea. This group is called the polychaetes (pronounced *poli-keets*). They have long tentacles around their mouth. They use these to gather particles of food from the water.

A second group is called the oligochaetes. This group includes the earthworms. Earthworms move through the soil eating dead plant material. They are important to farmers and gardeners because they break up the soil. This lets water and air into the ground.

The third group is the leeches. These are parasites that suck blood from animals. Their bodies are quite flat, and they have suckers to hold on to their host. Most leeches live in water.

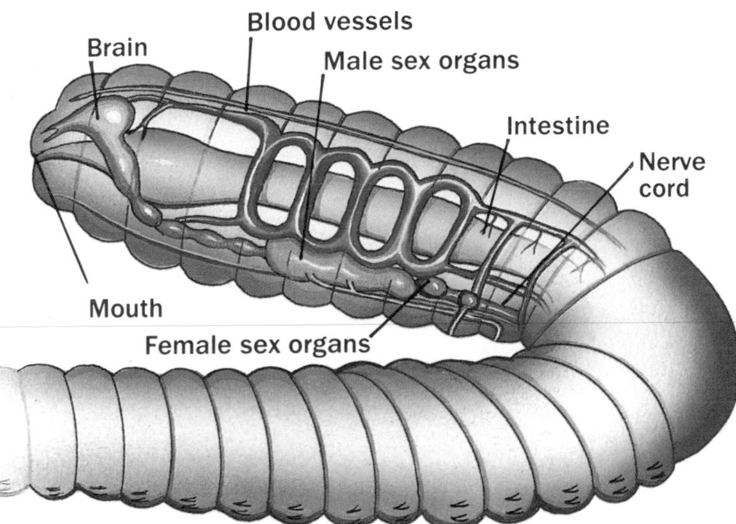

EXPERIMENT

You can watch earthworms move through the soil. Get an adult to help make a narrow tank with glass sides. The tank can be held together with strong tape. Only the large sides have to be made of glass. Make sure that air can get in. Fill the tank with loose, damp soil. Find two or three worms and put them in the tank. Then watch. Remember to put the worms back where you found them after a few days.

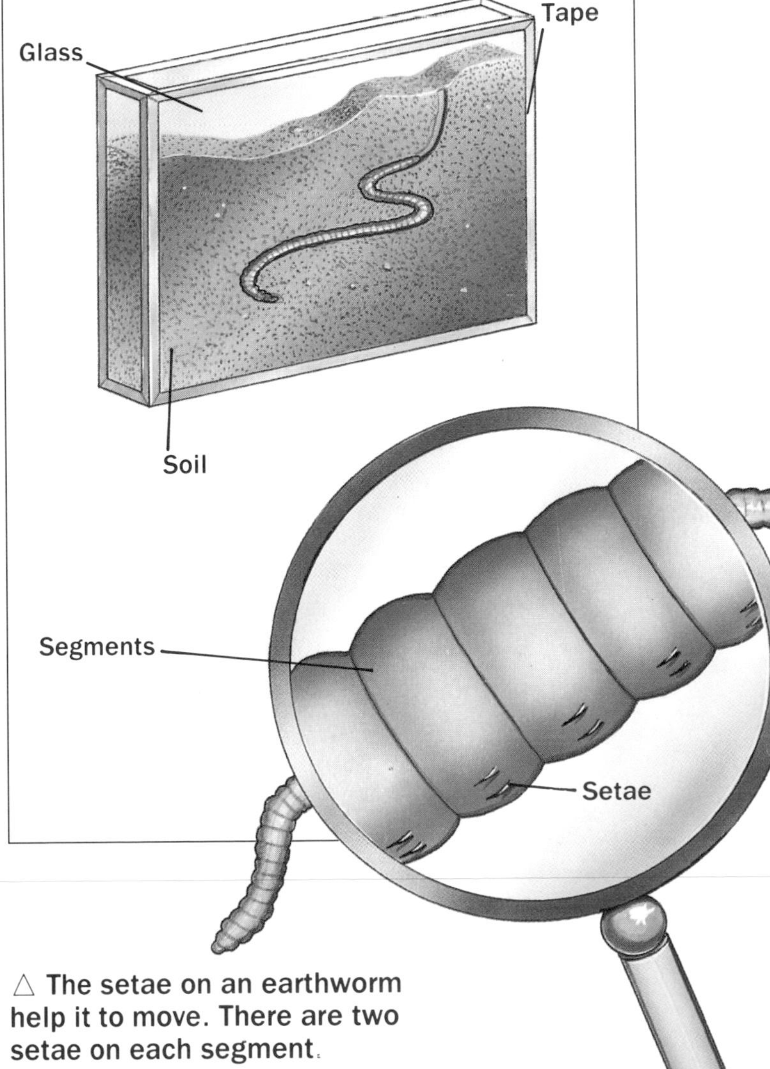

△ The setae on an earthworm help it to move. There are two setae on each segment.

Starfish and sea urchins belong to a group called the echinoderms (pronounced *ekino-derms*), which means spiny-skinned. They are unusual because they are symmetrical in several different directions. They all live in the sea, sometimes in shallow water and sometimes in very deep oceans.

STARFISH

Starfish have five arms. But starfish move by walking on dozens of very small feet. These feet are tubes. Each tube foot moves when water is pumped in and out of it. A system of canals carries water to the feet. There are pumps on the canals. These control how the water moves. Starfish suck water in from the sea through a filter.

Starfish feed mainly on shellfish, such as mussels and scallops. A starfish first pulls the shell of its prey open just a crack. Then the starfish turns its stomach inside out through its mouth and pushes the stomach into the shell. The stomach then digests the victim.

If a starfish is caught by one arm, it escapes by letting the arm drop off. A new arm grows in its place.

△ Brittle stars are relatives of starfish. But their arms are much longer than those of starfish. They move by walking with their arms instead of by using tube feet.

△ Each tube foot has a sucker at the end. This allows a starfish to hold on to hard surfaces, such as rocks or the shells of its prey.

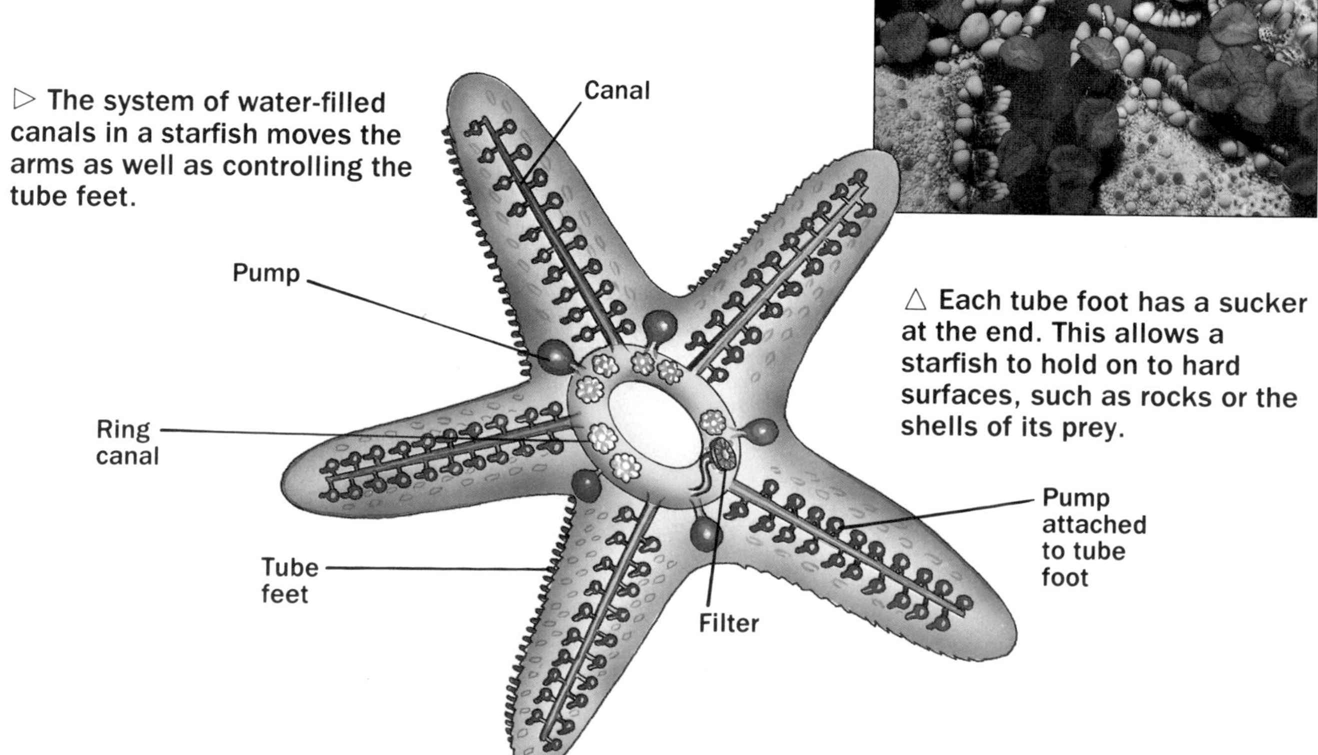

▷ The system of water-filled canals in a starfish moves the arms as well as controlling the tube feet.

SEA URCHINS

Sea urchins live on rocky shores and in shallow water. They measure from one third to twenty inches across. Their bodies are surrounded by hard plates that make a shell. The shell is covered in spines. Sea urchins have a mouth with teeth. They feed on tiny plants and animals. Some also have pincers on stalks. These can catch particles of food and pass them down to the mouth. Like starfish, sea urchins have tube feet.

SEA CUCUMBERS

Sea cucumbers are echinoderms with soft bodies. They are symmetrical in the same way as the other echinoderms, but this is quite difficult to see. They usually live buried in sand, which they burrow into using their tube feet. Sea cucumbers use tube feet near the mouth for gathering food. Some species leave these feet sticking out of the sand to collect particles of food from the water. Other species eat dead material that has sunk to the bottom of the sea.

▽ The tentacles on this sea cucumber are long tube feet, which it uses to catch food.

▽ Sea urchins breathe with small gills near to the mouth.

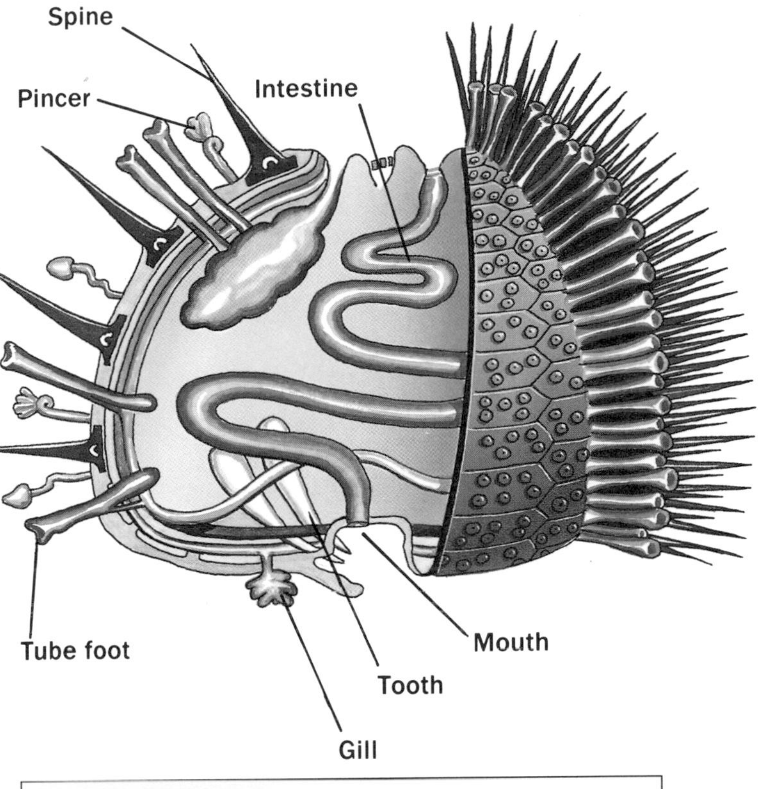

COLLECTING

You can collect the skeletons of starfish and sea urchins. The skeletons are the spiny skins or shells. They can be found on the seashore, especially in places where there are rocks (remember that rocks can be dangerous). The spines often fall off dead sea urchins, but be careful of living ones – the spines sometimes sting.

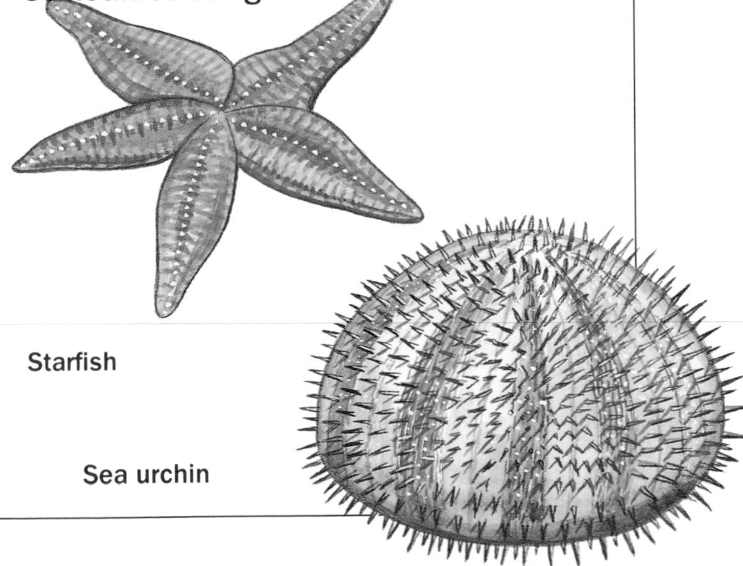

Mollusks are a large group of animals, with over 100,000 species. The word mollusk means soft-bodied, although many mollusks have a shell. There are three main groups of mollusks: gastropods, bivalves and cephalopods. The groups look quite different from each other, but have many things in common.

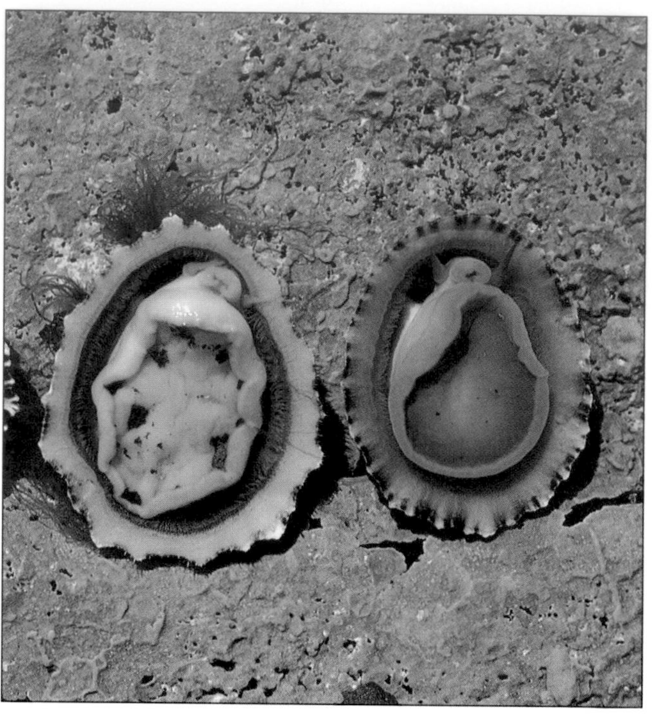

△ Limpets are a type of gastropod. They have powerful suckers underneath their bodies. They cling tightly to rocks on the seashore.

SNAILS

Gastropods are a group of mollusks that includes snails, slugs, limpets and periwinkles. Gastropod means stomach-foot. Many live on land, although some live in water. Gastropods either have one shell or no shell at all. Snails can pull their bodies inside their shells.

All gastropods have basically the same internal structure as a snail. Snails feed on plant material. Inside their mouths is a radula, which is like a tongue covered with teeth. They use this to scrape off particles of food. The food passes into the crop, where it is stored and digestion starts. The food then goes through a complex digestive system. Waste material from digestion passes out of the anus and the excretory pore. Snails breathe using a lung.

▽ Snails have two pairs of tentacles on their heads. These are snails' main sense organs. One pair has simple eyes, which can detect areas of light and dark.

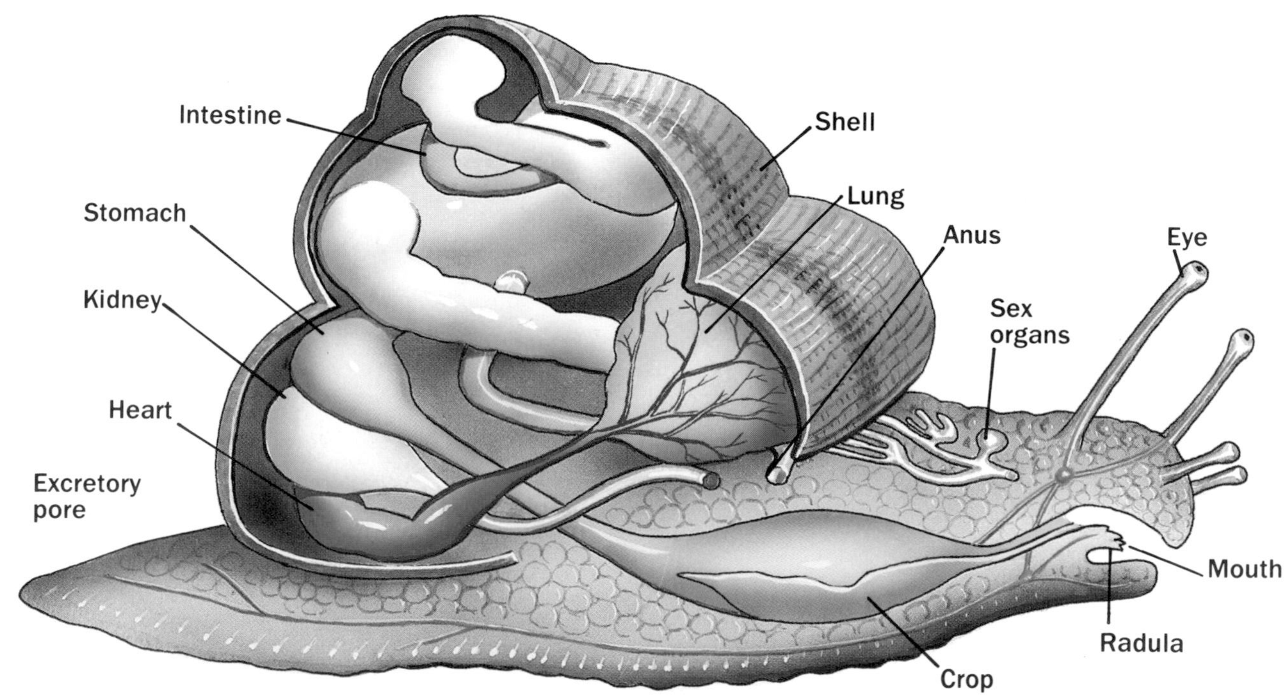

MOVING

When slugs and snails move, muscles expand and contract along the bottom of the animal. This moves first one section along, then another. Gastropods secrete mucus to make movement easier. This mucus is slippery under parts of the foot that are moving. But it becomes solid under contracted parts so that the snail can grip to the ground. You can often see shiny trails of dried mucus that slugs or snails have left behind.

MATING

Snails and slugs are hermaphrodites. This means that all snails are both male and female at the same time. When two snails mate, the first thing they do is fire "love darts" into each other's bodies. These contain chemicals that stimulate mating. Sperm is then passed from each snail to the other. The eggs inside both bodies are fertilized. Once the eggs have been laid, they hatch into tiny snails.

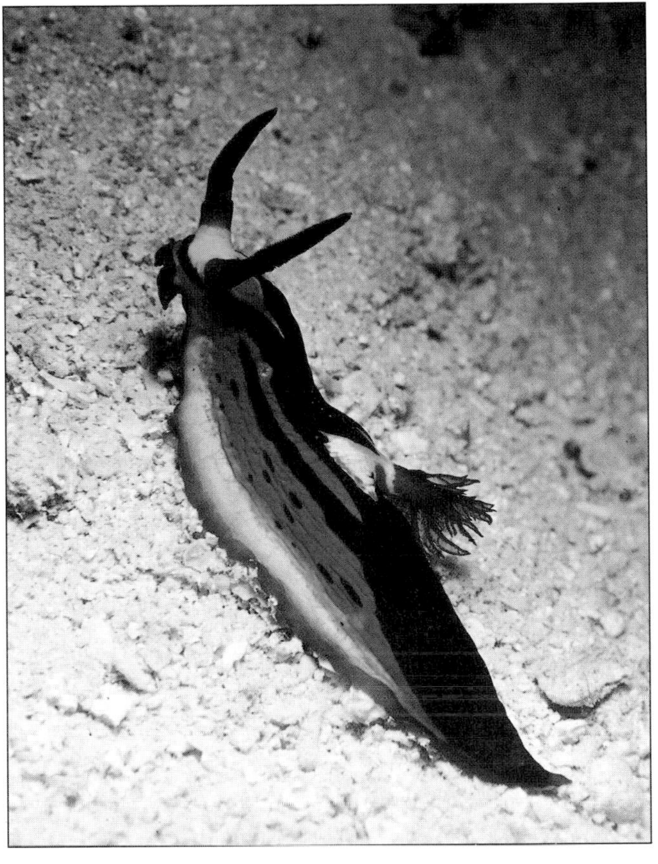

△ Sea slugs are a group of gastropods that live in the salt water of seas and oceans. They have no shells and are often brightly colored.

▷ Some species of snail die after they have mated and then laid their eggs.

▽ Although slugs and snails move very slowly, some species of slug can climb as much as 30 feet up trees.

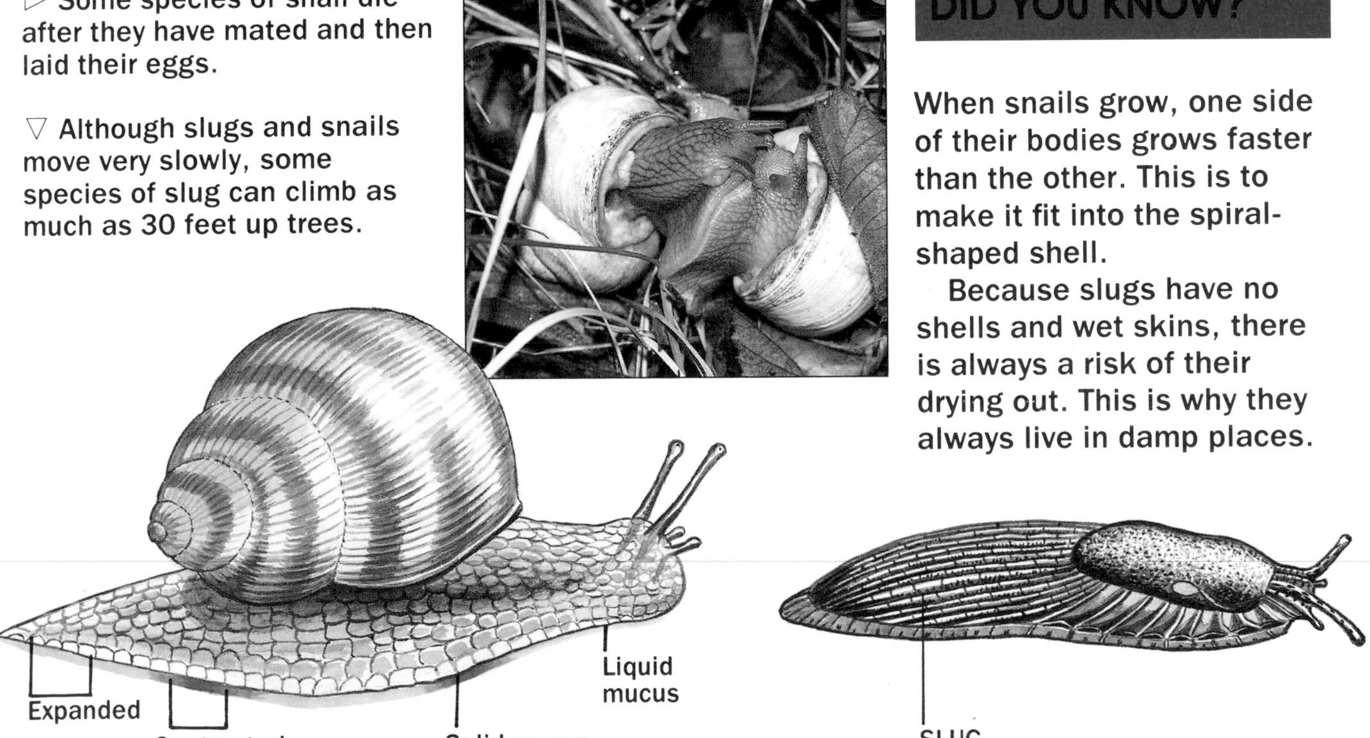

DID YOU KNOW?

When snails grow, one side of their bodies grows faster than the other. This is to make it fit into the spiral-shaped shell.

Because slugs have no shells and wet skins, there is always a risk of their drying out. This is why they always live in damp places.

Bivalves are mollusks that have two separate shells (bivalve means two-shelled). These shells hinge together. Examples are mussels, cockles, clams and oysters. Most bivalves live in the sea, but a few live in fresh water. Like some other types of mollusk, many bivalves are eaten by people.

FILTER FEEDERS

Bivalves get their food by filter-feeding. They have special gills that are covered in tiny hairs called cilia. The cilia move in a way that draws water into the shell through a tube known as a siphon. Particles of food in the water are trapped by sticky mucus, which is produced by the gills. Movements of the cilia pass the particles down to the mouth. The water leaves through another siphon.

Some bivalves can move using a foot, and scallops can swim. But many never move. Oysters cement themselves onto rocks, and mussels attach themselves with strong threads. At one time, people made clothes from these threads.

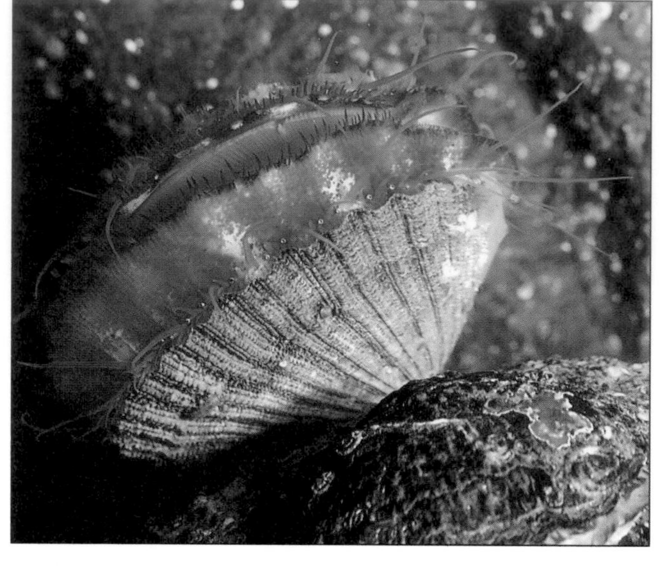

△ Scallops swim by opening their shells then clapping them shut to send out a jet of water.

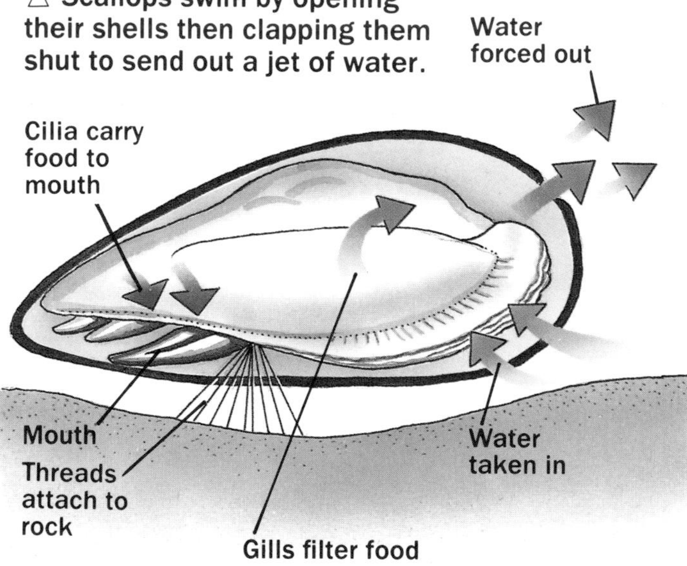

△ The mussel is a typical example of a bivalve. It feeds by filtering water, although it has less well-developed siphons than other bivalves.

▽ Clams burrow into sand for safety. The foot pushes down into the sand (A). Blood pumps into the end of the foot, which expands to make an anchor (B). Muscles shorten the foot to pull the clam down (C). The foot is pushed down to repeat the process (D). Water pumped through the siphons and the gap between the shells loosens the sand.

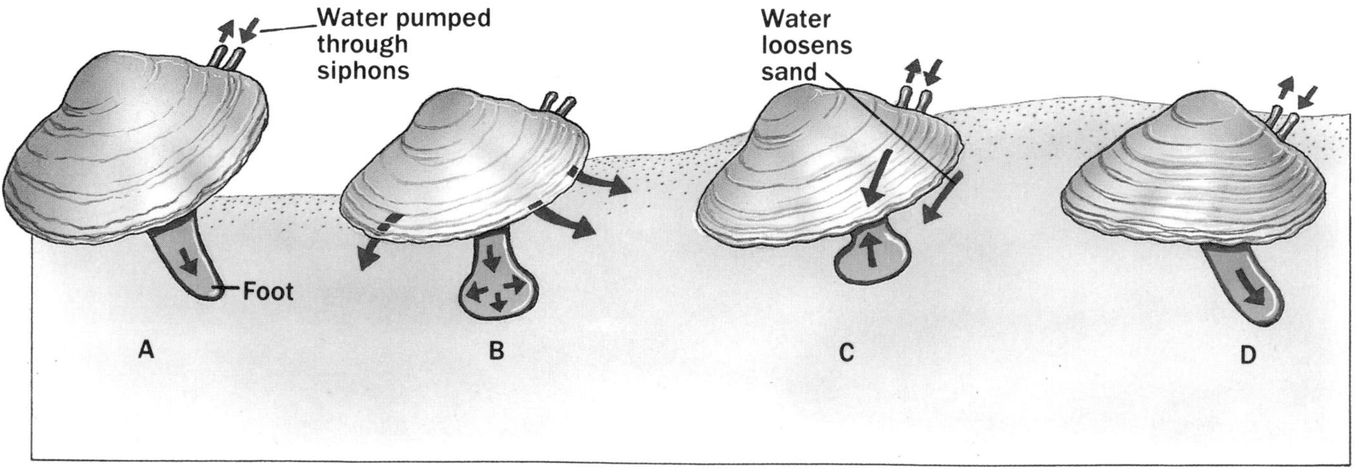

FOOD TEST

Discover what slugs and snails like eating. Find two or three gastropods. Put them into a box with a lid to stop them from escaping. An old shoe box is good. Put the box in the shade, somewhere that is not too hot, cold or dry. Now put various kinds of plant food into the box. (If you use food from the kitchen, make sure that it was going to be thrown away.) Cut the food so that it is all about the same size (get an adult to help with this). You will then be able to tell how much has been eaten.

What food do the animals like eating? Which food do they eat the most? Try the experiment first with one sort of gastropod, then with another.

Do not keep the animals for more than two or three days. Remember to put them back just where you found them.

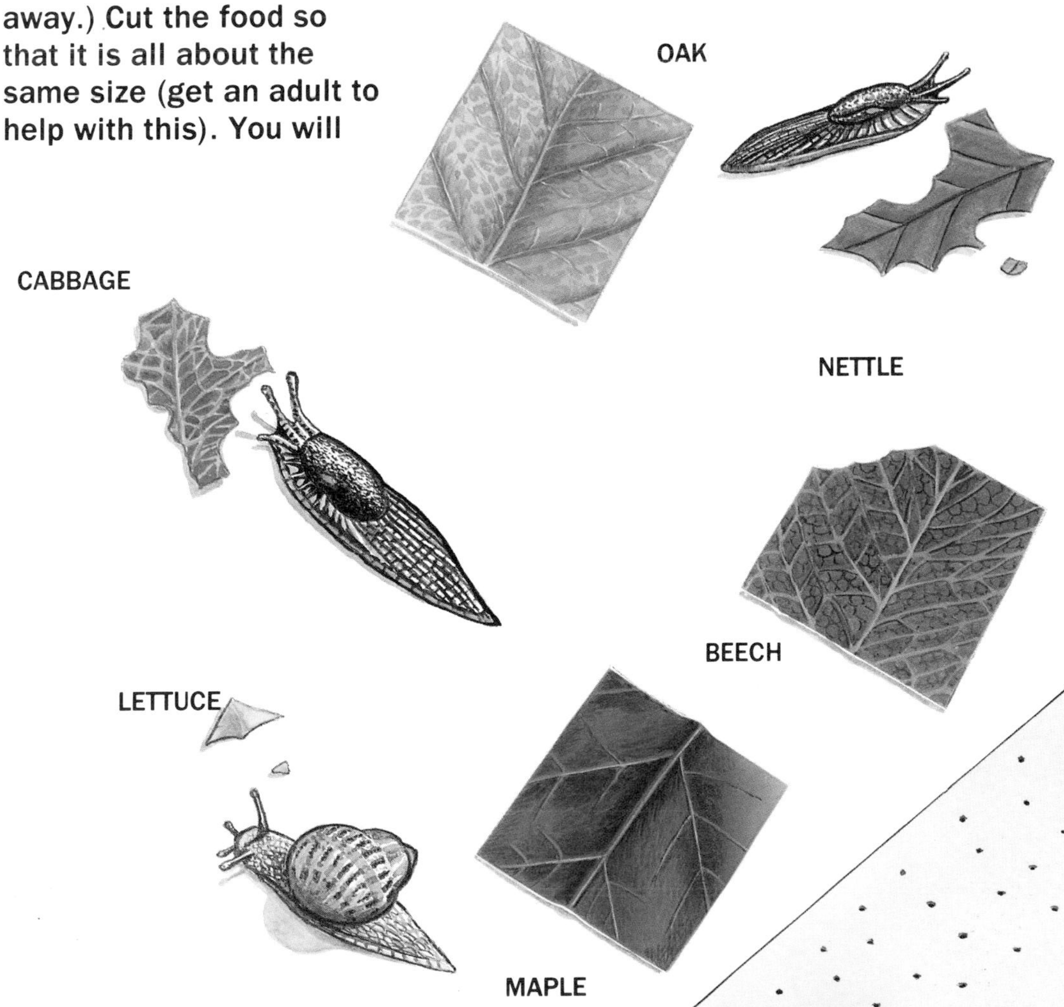

OAK

CABBAGE

NETTLE

BEECH

LETTUCE

MAPLE

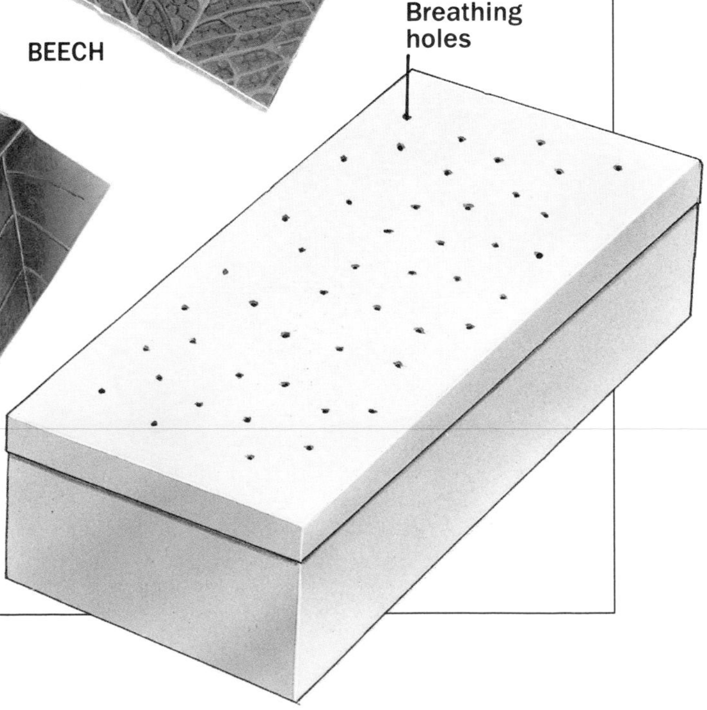

Breathing holes

▷ Make sure that there are holes in the lid of your box so that the animals are able to breathe.

Cephalopods are the largest of the mollusks. Cephalopod means head-foot. There are three main groups: octopuses, squids and cuttlefish. None of these has any visible shell. They all have large heads with big eyes that give them good eyesight. They have several arms attached to the head.

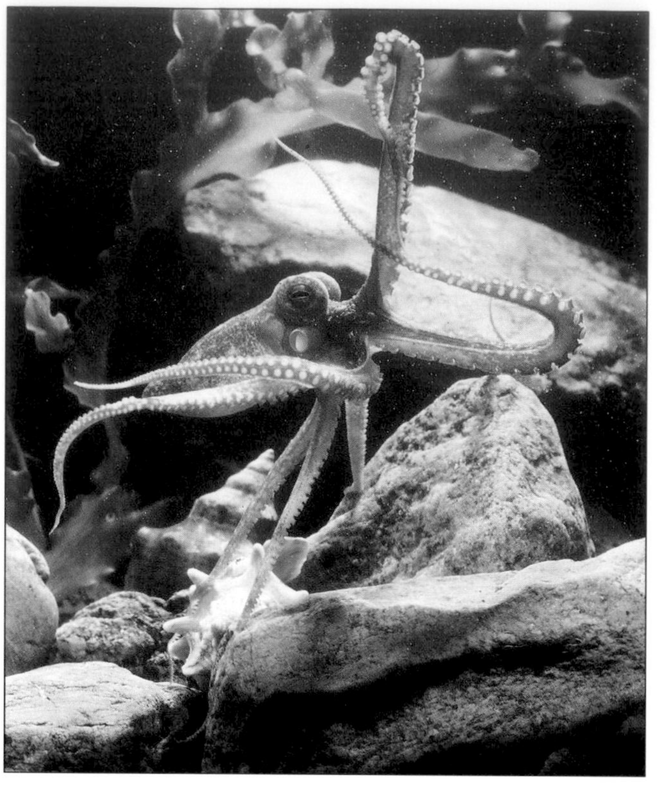

△ Octopuses live in rocky areas near the shore where there are plenty of places to hide from danger and wait for prey.

JET-PROPELLED ANIMALS

Cephalopods move by jet propulsion. They squirt water out of the mantle cavity through the siphon. Squids and cuttlefish move mostly in this way, but octopuses usually walk using their arms.

Octopuses have eight arms. They use them to catch their prey, as well as for walking. The arms have suckers which can grip very strongly. Squids and cuttlefish have two long tentacles for catching prey as well as having arms.

Although cephalopods do not have visible shells, squids and cuttlefish do have a special sort of shell inside their bodies. These shells help to support the body and keep the animal afloat. In cuttlefish this is called the cuttlebone, and in squids it is called the pen.

When cephalopods are attacked, many of them release a jet of dark-colored ink to confuse the attacker. They can also change their color to camouflage themselves in different places.

▽ The cuttlefish has internal organs typical of cephalopods. The beak is used to attack prey. Octopus beaks can inject poison that is deadly to the small animals they attack.

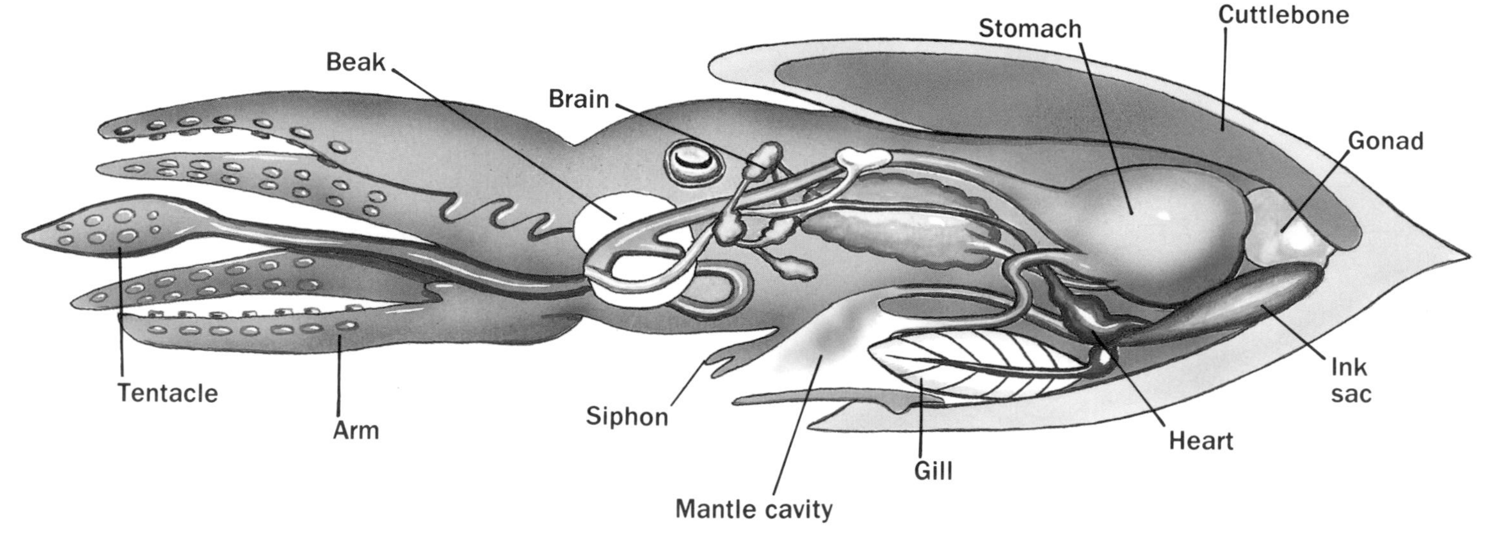

COLLECTING AND IDENTIFYING SHELLS

If you go to the sea, you will find many shells of dead mollusks on the shore. You can also find mollusk shells on land or by fresh water. Can you tell what kind off mollusk the shell comes from? With bivalves – like clams – you will usually only find one of the two shells. See how many of the ones shown here you can find.

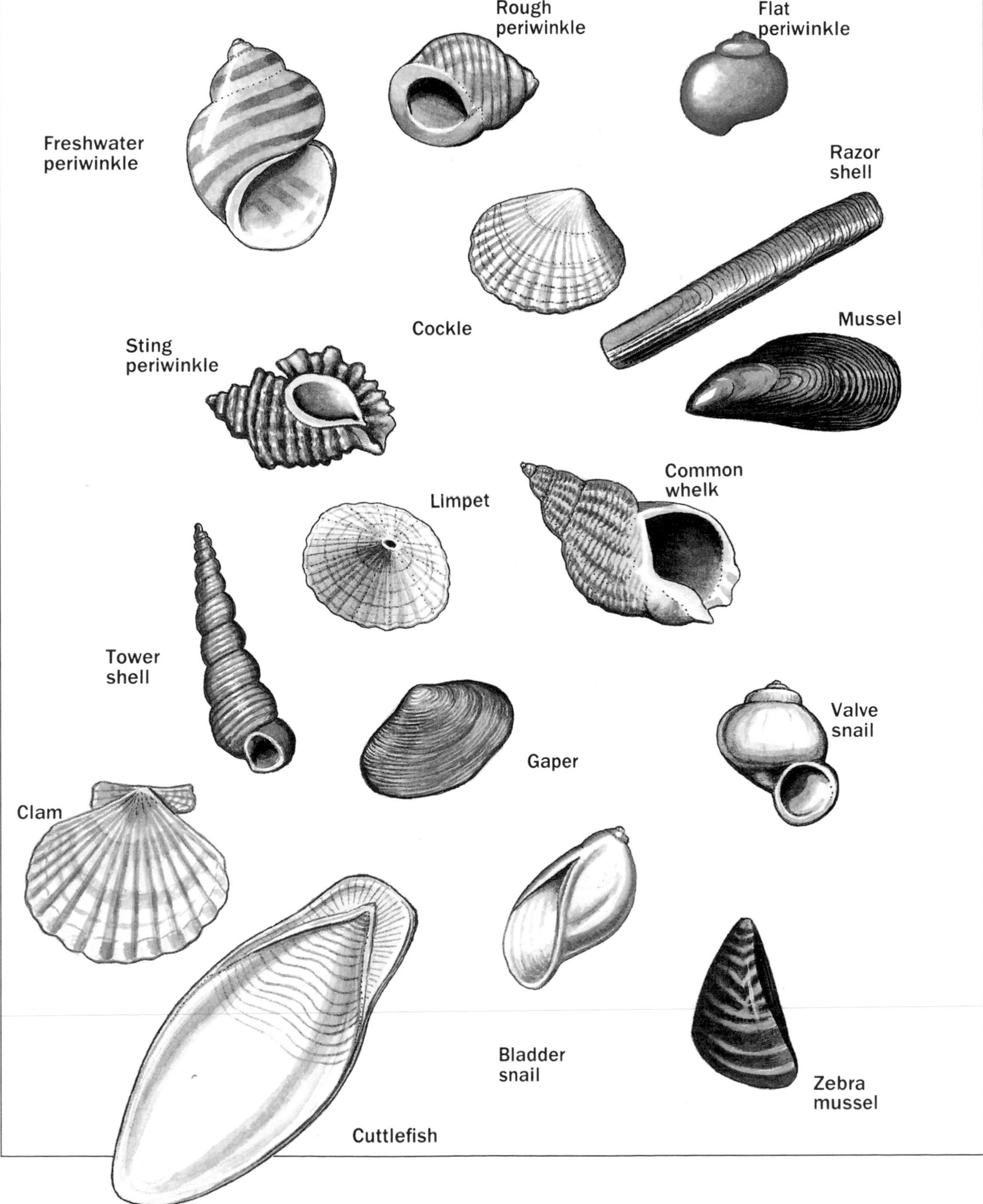

Arthropods are the most common type of animal on earth. There are well over one million species, and four out of every five animals alive is an arthropod. They live in water and on land, and many can fly. Arthropod means joint-legged. Types of arthropod include crustaceans, arachnids and insects.

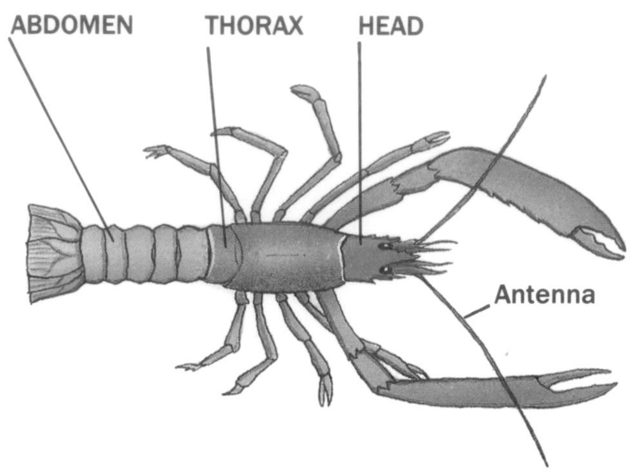

5 legs each side

TEN LEGS

Crustaceans live in the sea. Large crustaceans, such as lobsters and crabs, usually have ten legs. But other species have more or fewer. One pair of legs often has claws attached. Crustaceans also have pleopods. These look slightly like legs, but have a different structure and different uses.

The whole body is covered with a hard skeleton. Muscles are attached to the inside of the skeleton. The body is usually divided into three main sections: the head, thorax and abdomen. The head has eyes called compound eyes. These are made up of many tiny eyes all clustered together. The head also has two pairs of antennae. The thorax contains most of the internal organs, such as the stomach and the sexual organs. The abdomen contains much of the intestine.

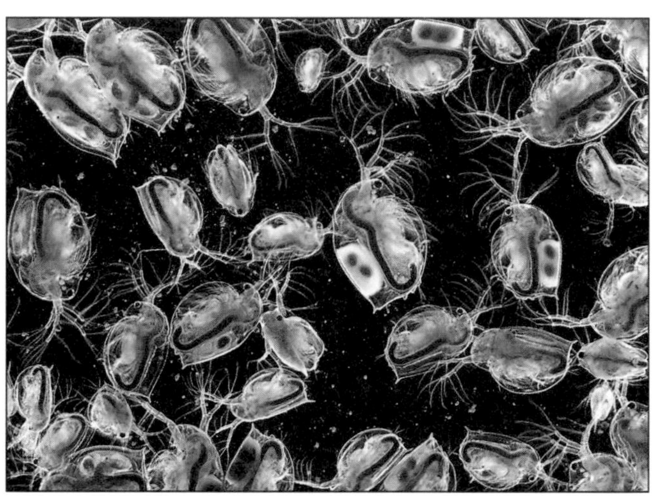

△ Water fleas are small crustaceans.

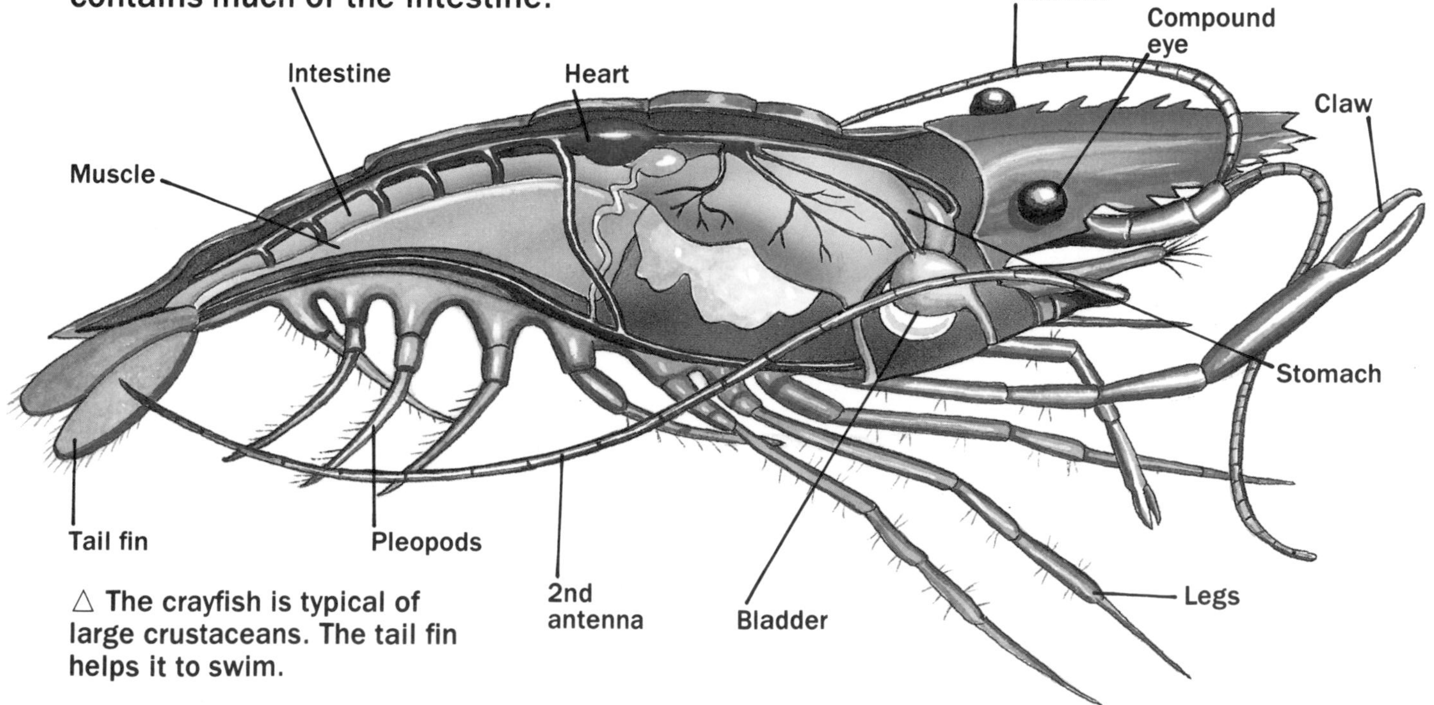

△ The crayfish is typical of large crustaceans. The tail fin helps it to swim.

BARNACLES

Barnacles do not look like typical crustaceans. They live attached to hard surfaces, such as rocks or the hulls of ships. Barnacles attach themselves by a stalk called a peduncle. This is very short in some species and quite long in others. The peduncle has a cement gland that glues the barnacle down.

Barnacles have a shell-like plate called a carina. The plate opens to let out special netlike feet called cirri. These catch scraps of food floating in the water.

Barnacles mate by extending a long tube (penis) to neighboring barnacles. Sperm passes along the tube.

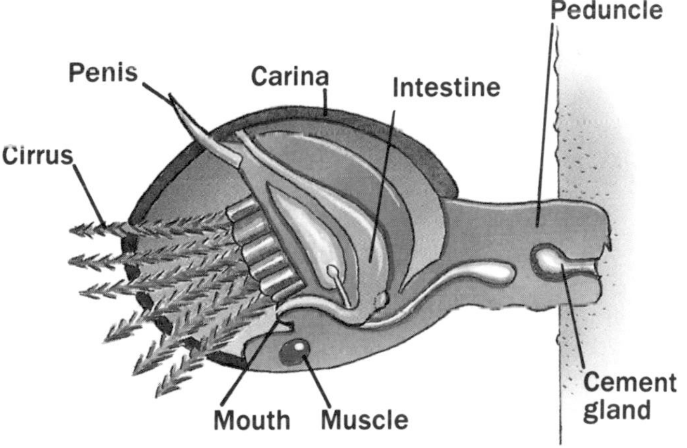

DID YOU KNOW?

Unlike most crustaceans, woodlice are unusual because they live on land. However, woodlice can dry out easily, so they do various things to keep moist. They live in damp places, such as dead wood, rotting leaves and under stones. They usually come out only at night to avoid the hot sun. They also roll themselves into balls. This saves water and is also a defense against enemies.

▽ Fiddler crabs are so called because their claws remind you of a violin and a bow.

The arachnids are a large group of arthropods that live on land. They include spiders, scorpions, and ticks and mites. Like all arthropods, arachnids have a hard external skeleton. The body is divided into two parts: a head and thorax that are joined together (the cephalothorax), and an abdomen.

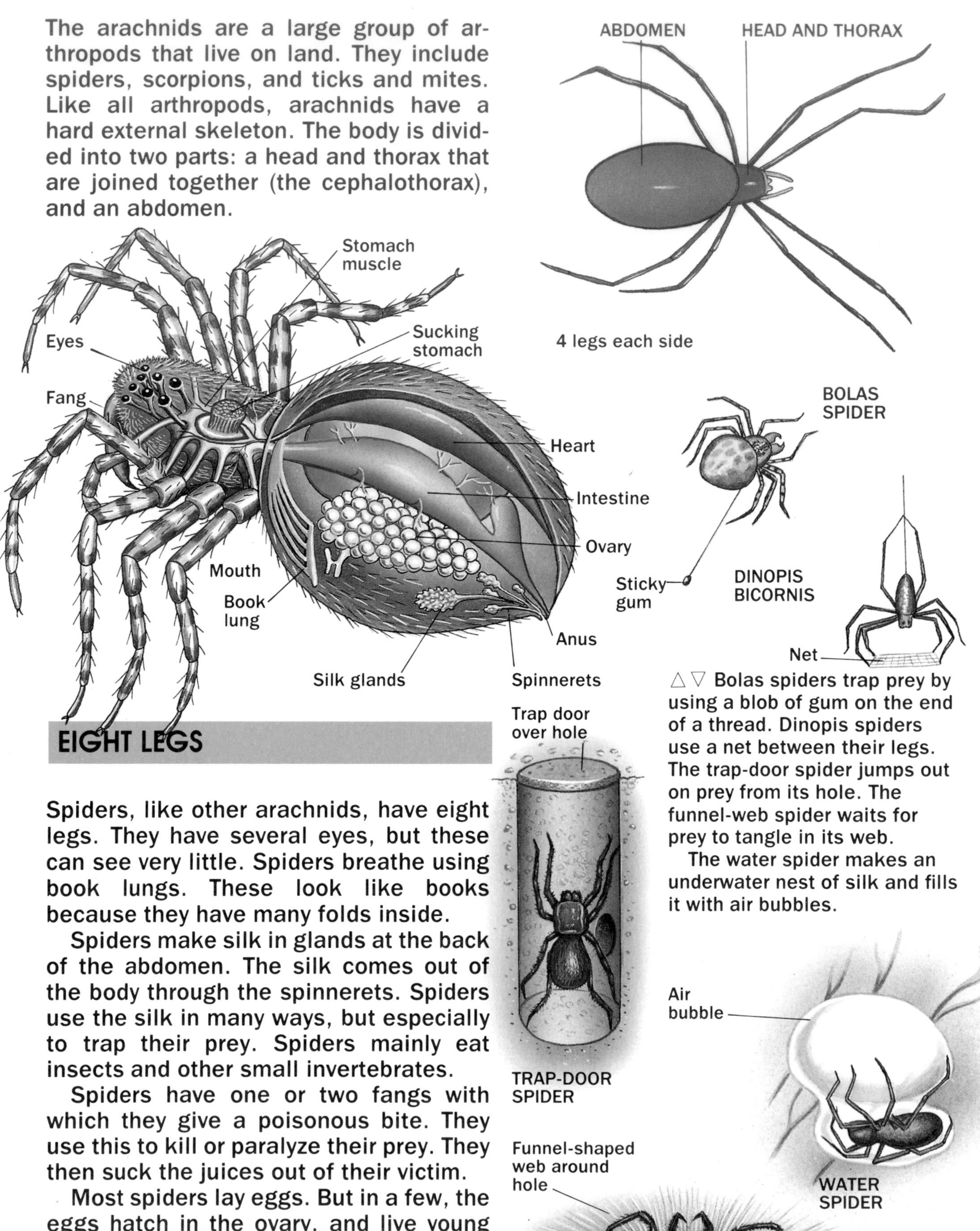

△▽ Bolas spiders trap prey by using a blob of gum on the end of a thread. Dinopis spiders use a net between their legs. The trap-door spider jumps out on prey from its hole. The funnel-web spider waits for prey to tangle in its web.

The water spider makes an underwater nest of silk and fills it with air bubbles.

EIGHT LEGS

Spiders, like other arachnids, have eight legs. They have several eyes, but these can see very little. Spiders breathe using book lungs. These look like books because they have many folds inside.

Spiders make silk in glands at the back of the abdomen. The silk comes out of the body through the spinnerets. Spiders use the silk in many ways, but especially to trap their prey. Spiders mainly eat insects and other small invertebrates.

Spiders have one or two fangs with which they give a poisonous bite. They use this to kill or paralyze their prey. They then suck the juices out of their victim.

Most spiders lay eggs. But in a few, the eggs hatch in the ovary, and live young are born. As in all arthropods, the skeleton cannot grow, so spiders molt and form new ones as they get bigger.

SCORPIONS

Scorpions hunt by night for insects and spiders. They catch their prey with two powerful pincers, which they use to tear their victims apart. Scorpions have a sting in the end of their tails. If their prey puts up a fight, they curl the tail forward to sting it.

Most species of scorpion are not really dangerous to people. They will very rarely attack somebody deliberately. Many scorpions can give a nasty sting, however, and a few can be deadly.

Scorpions give birth to live young. The tiny scorpions then ride around on the mother's back. One mother can often carry as many as 30 of her babies.

△ There were scorpions very like this one living on Earth 450 million years ago.

TICKS AND MITES

Ticks and mites are very similar, but mites are larger. They look as if they only have one body segment. Most of them are parasites.

Ticks and mites have a mouth that has a beak with teeth. They use this to grab on to host animals, such as cats, dogs, fish, insects or people. They then suck blood or other fluids from the victim. Some species also feed off plants.

Ticks and mites can carry diseases, such as Rocky Mountain spotted fever. Some can get into the skin of humans and cause an irritating rash.

△ Mites are less than 0.04 in long.

DID YOU KNOW?

A spider starts its web by letting the wind blow a thread from one support to another (1). It then spins a second thread between the supports by crawling along the first thread (2). It pulls the second thread into a V-shape, which makes a basic frame (3). It then adds arms to complete the frame (4). The web is finished by joining all the arms together with a spiral (5). Building a web usually takes a spider about an hour.

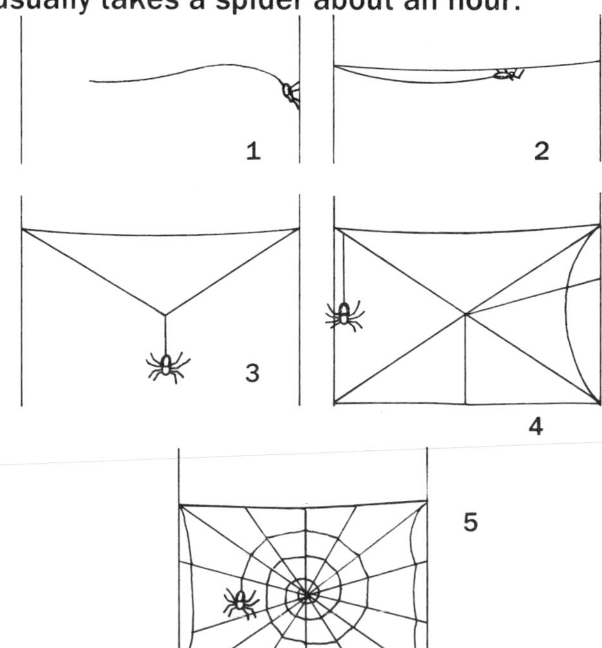

Insects are the largest group of arthropods. It is unusual to go through a day without seeing many insects. Flies, bees, ants, beetles, moths, butterflies and many other animals are all insects. They mostly live on land, and many can fly. Like other arthropods, they have a hard external skeleton.

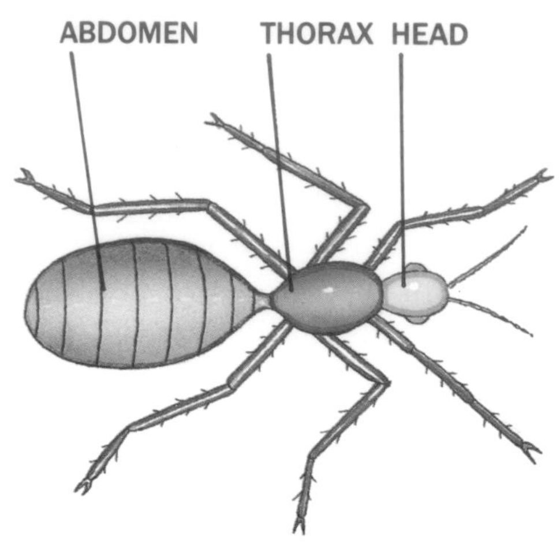

3 legs each side

SIX LEGS

Insects have three main body parts: the head, the thorax and the abdomen. They have six legs attached to the thorax, and usually have one or two pairs of wings.

The head has a pair of antennae. These act as sense organs to detect smell or movement. Insects have compound eyes, like those of crustaceans. Often they have simple eyes as well. Many insects have several other sense organs, such as special ears on their legs.

Insects breathe through holes in the sides of their bodies called spiracles. These are connected to tubes inside the body known as trachea. The trachea branch into many fine tubes. These take air to the organs of the body. Muscle movements in the abdomen make air move in and out of the spiracles.

▽ This hover fly has a typical insect body structure.

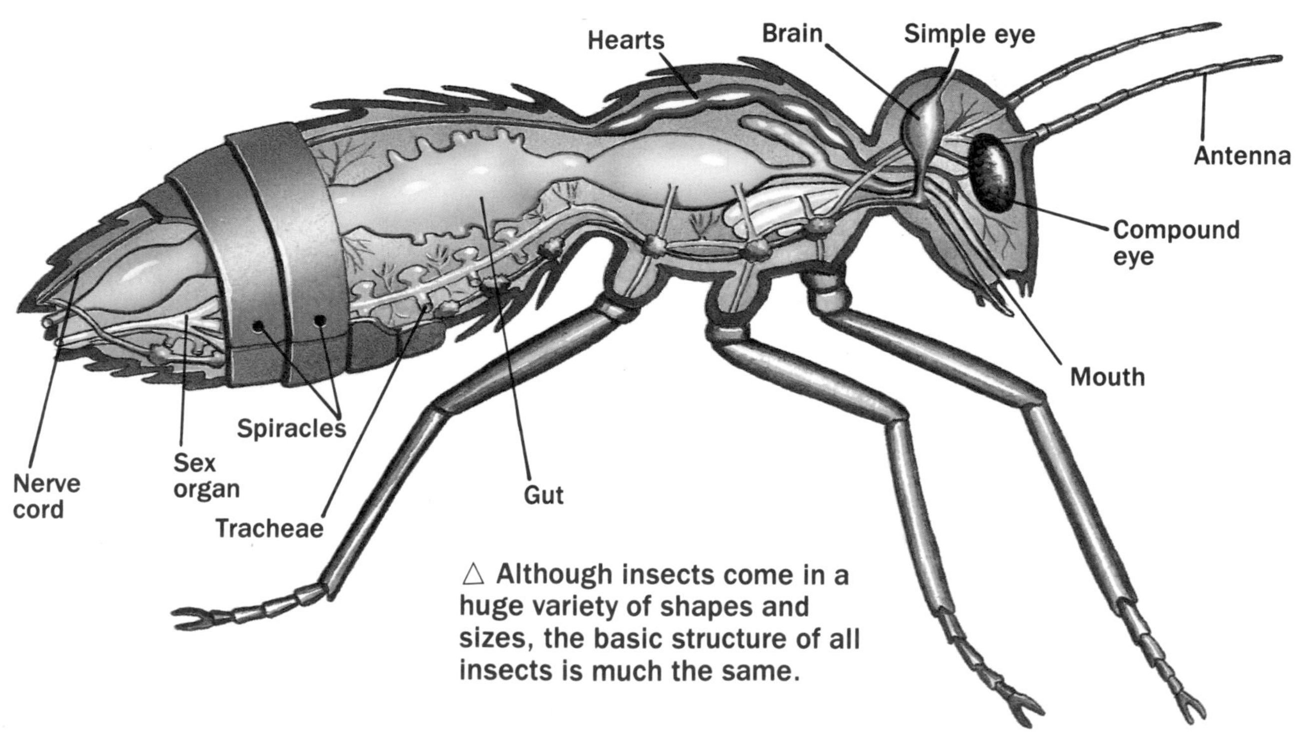

△ Although insects come in a huge variety of shapes and sizes, the basic structure of all insects is much the same.

GROWTH AND DEVELOPMENT

All insects start life as eggs. An egg laid by an adult hatches, and a new insect starts to develop. There are three ways in which insects develop into adults.

Some insects hatch as tiny versions of the adult. The external skeleton of the insect cannot grow. When the insect reaches a certain size, it molts, shedding its skeleton. A new, larger skeleton grows in its place. Each stage of growth is known as an instar.

Some insects go through what is known as incomplete metamorphosis. The egg hatches into a nymph. Some nymphs look very much like the adult, but without certain features, such as wings. Other nymphs look quite different, but change into an adult in the final stage of molting. The adult is called the imago.

Other insects go through complete metamorphosis. They hatch as larvae that look nothing like the adult. Some larvae look like worms; others have small legs. Once the larvae have grown, they transform into pupae. Pupae have protective coverings. Inside its covering an insect changes into an adult. When the change is complete, the covering opens and an adult emerges.

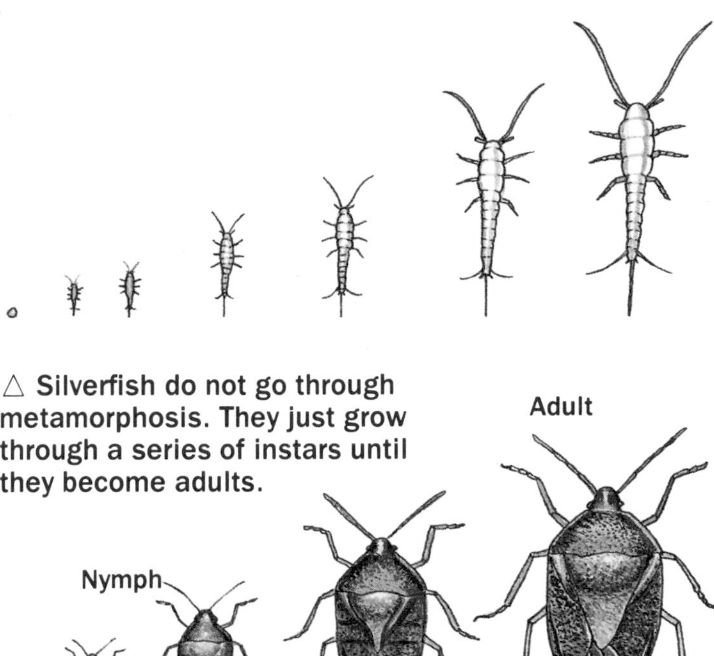

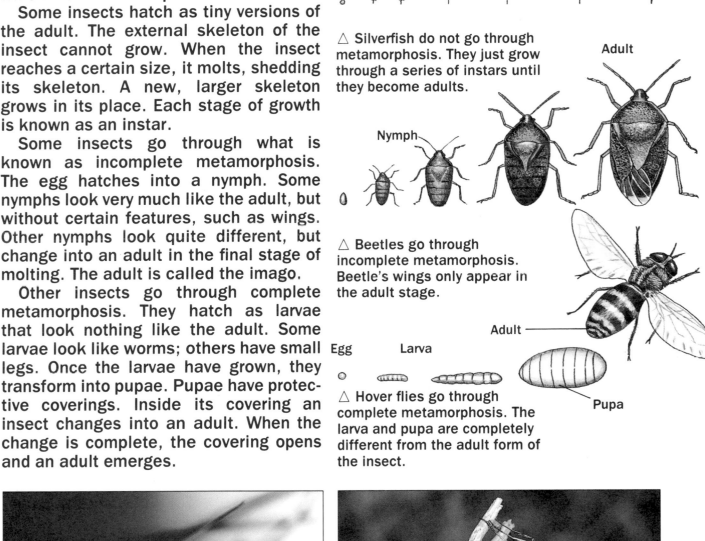

△ Silverfish do not go through metamorphosis. They just grow through a series of instars until they become adults.

△ Beetles go through incomplete metamorphosis. Beetle's wings only appear in the adult stage.

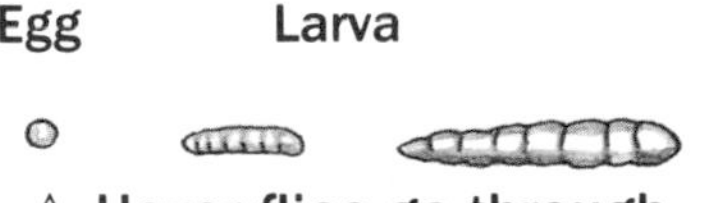

△ Hover flies go through complete metamorphosis. The larva and pupa are completely different from the adult form of the insect.

△ Emerging from an old skeleton.

△ Emerging from a pupa case.

METAMORPHOSIS

You can watch metamorphosis in a butterfly for yourself. Find a caterpillar (a butterfly larva) and put it in a large glass jar. Put some food in the jar. The food must be the same kind of leaf as you found the caterpillar on. Many caterpillars will only eat one kind of leaf. Caterpillars eat a lot, so you may have to give it many leaves. Put a twig upright in the jar. When the butterfly appears, wait for the wings to expand and harden. Then return it to the place you found the caterpillar.

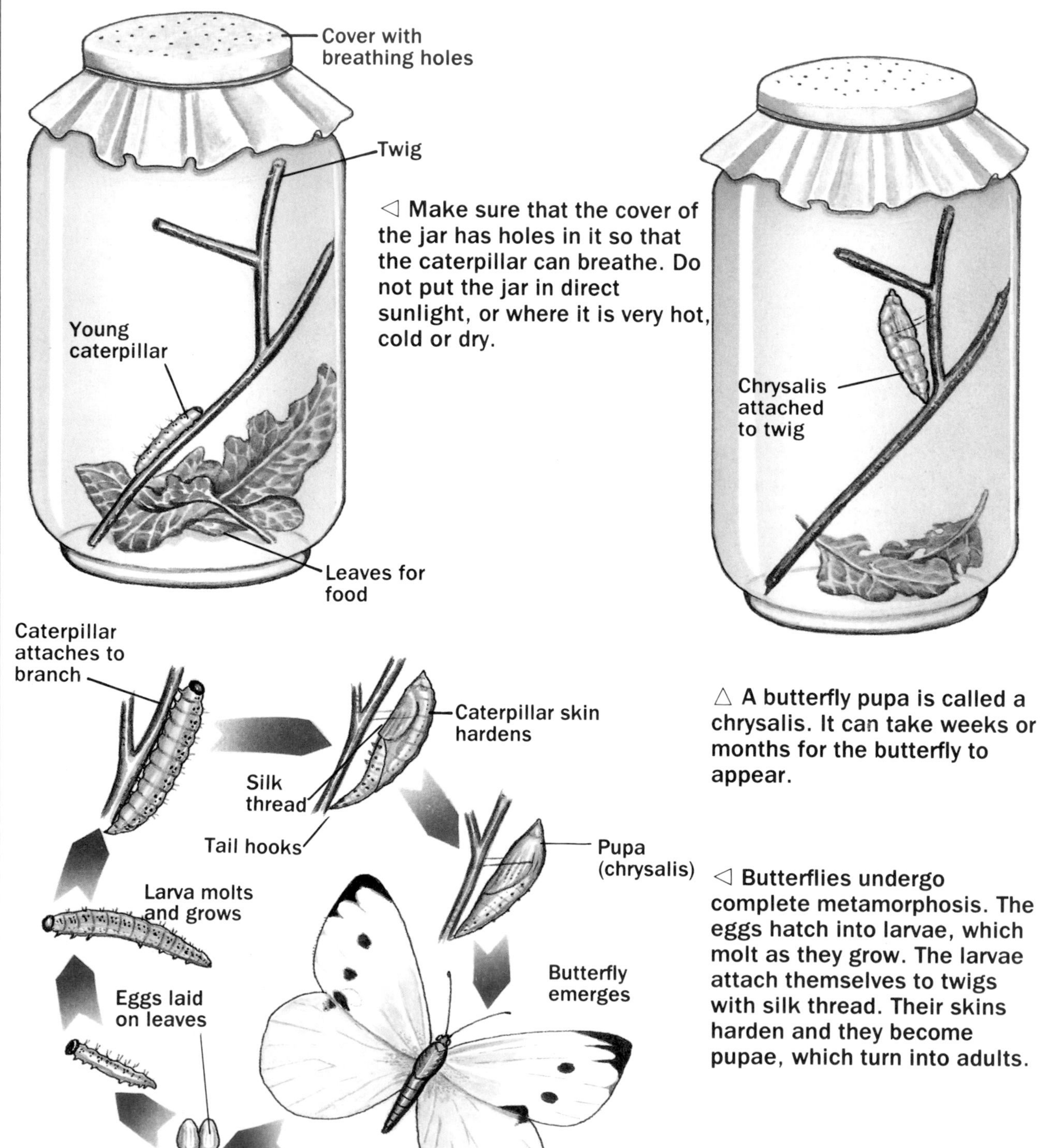

◁ Make sure that the cover of the jar has holes in it so that the caterpillar can breathe. Do not put the jar in direct sunlight, or where it is very hot, cold or dry.

△ A butterfly pupa is called a chrysalis. It can take weeks or months for the butterfly to appear.

◁ Butterflies undergo complete metamorphosis. The eggs hatch into larvae, which molt as they grow. The larvae attach themselves to twigs with silk thread. Their skins harden and they become pupae, which turn into adults.

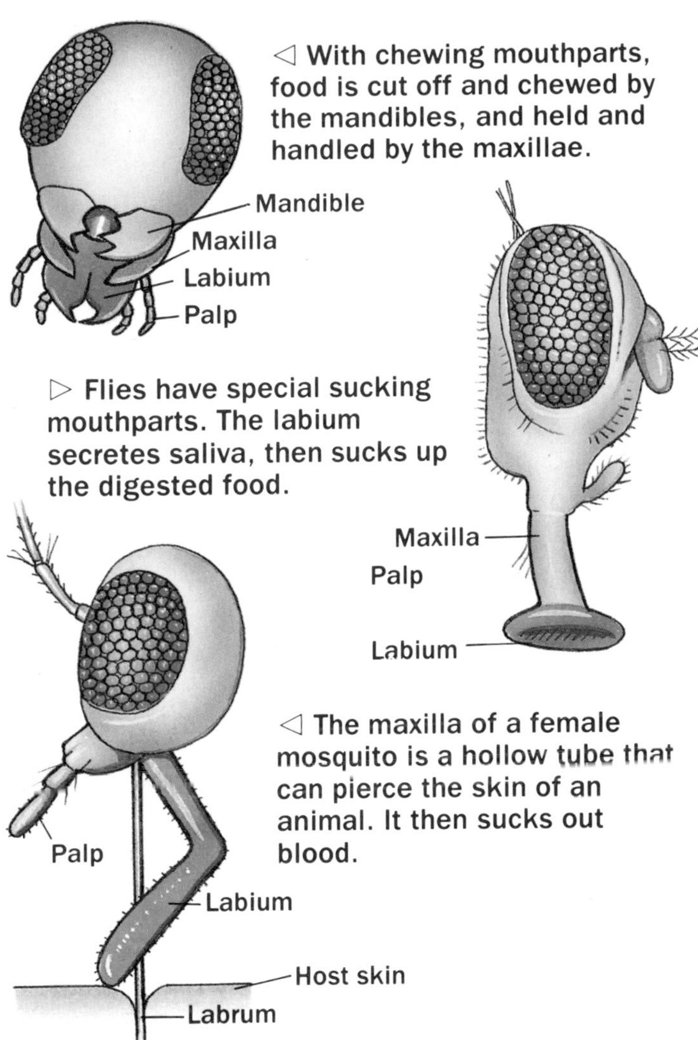

◁ With chewing mouthparts, food is cut off and chewed by the mandibles, and held and handled by the maxillae.

▷ Flies have special sucking mouthparts. The labium secretes saliva, then sucks up the digested food.

◁ The maxilla of a female mosquito is a hollow tube that can pierce the skin of an animal. It then sucks out blood.

FEEDING

Insects feed on a great variety of food and in very many ways. Each species has mouthparts that are specially designed for the way in which it feeds. There are two main types: chewing mouthparts and sucking mouthparts.

Insects with chewing mouthparts have two pairs of jaws: the mandibles and the maxillae. There are two lips: the labrum above the mouth and the labium below. The palps are used to taste food. Sucking mouthparts are a variation of chewing mouthparts, but are very much changed.

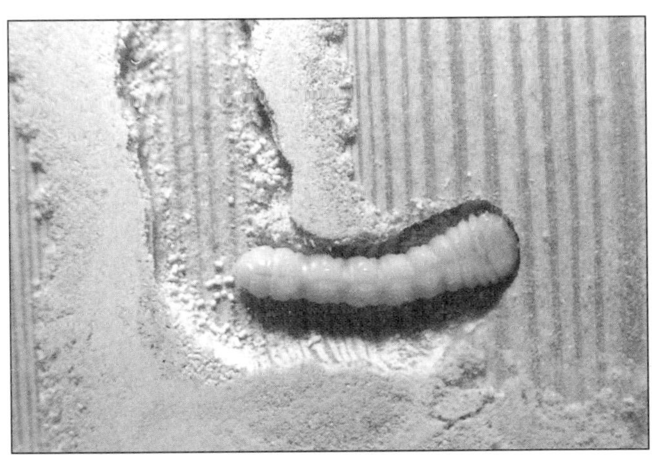

△ This larva can eat through wood.

FLYING

Many species of insect have wings. Flies have one pair of wings. They have special knoblike structures called halteres instead of rear wings. Halteres help them to balance. Beetles also have one pair of proper wings. Instead of front wings they have wing covers. Most other insects have two pairs of wings. These usually flap up and down together. Sometimes the wings on each side are joined together by special hooks along the edges.

The speed at which the wings of different insects flap varies. Some butterflies flap fewer than five times a second. Small flies flap up to 1,000 times per second. The fastest insect fliers are dragonflies, some of which can fly at 65 miles per hour.

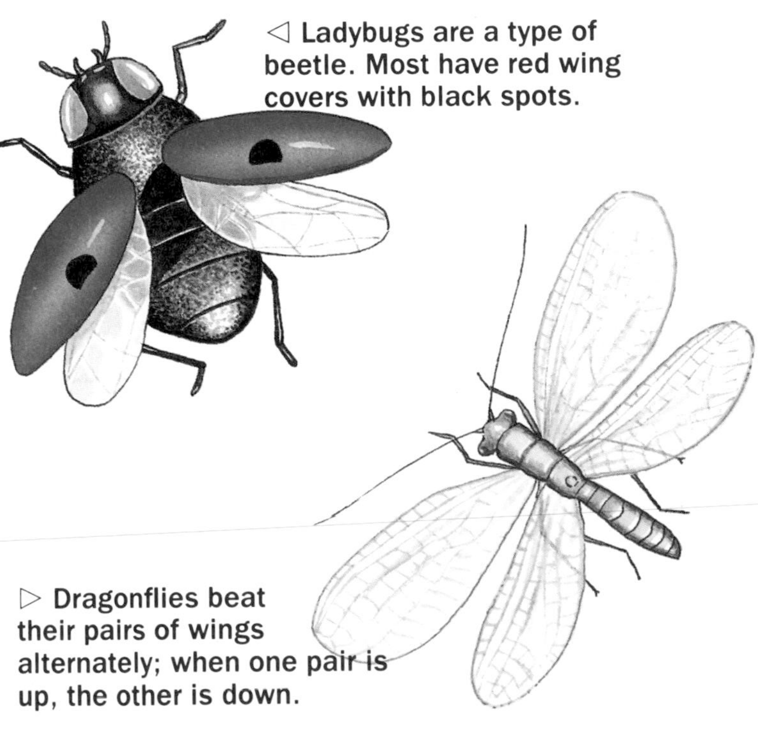

◁ Ladybugs are a type of beetle. Most have red wing covers with black spots.

▷ Dragonflies beat their pairs of wings alternately; when one pair is up, the other is down.

SOCIAL BEHAVIOR

Ants, termites, bees and some species of wasp live in large groups called colonies. Often these colonies build nests to live in. For example, African termites build nests that can be up to three times the height of a person.

The insects that live in a colony are divided into different types. Each type has a particular job. For example, some ant colonies have special "soldier ants," which have fierce jaws and protect the colony. In ant and bee colonies, it is the females who do all the work. The male's only job is to mate with the queen.

The queen is the female that lays all the eggs for the whole colony. The queen is often many times bigger than any other insect in the colony.

△ A colony of bees in its hive.

△ Soldier termites guard workers.

COMMUNICATION

Insects in colonies have to communicate with each other. This is so that the colony can run efficiently. For example, if one insect finds a supply of food, it needs to tell others so that they can help to carry it to the nest.

Insects in colonies communicate in several ways. Some do it by touch, for example, by putting their antennae together. Sound and smell are also used. The activities of a termite colony are controlled by special chemicals that are released by the queen. Bees have a dance that one bee performs to show the direction and distance of a supply of food it has found.

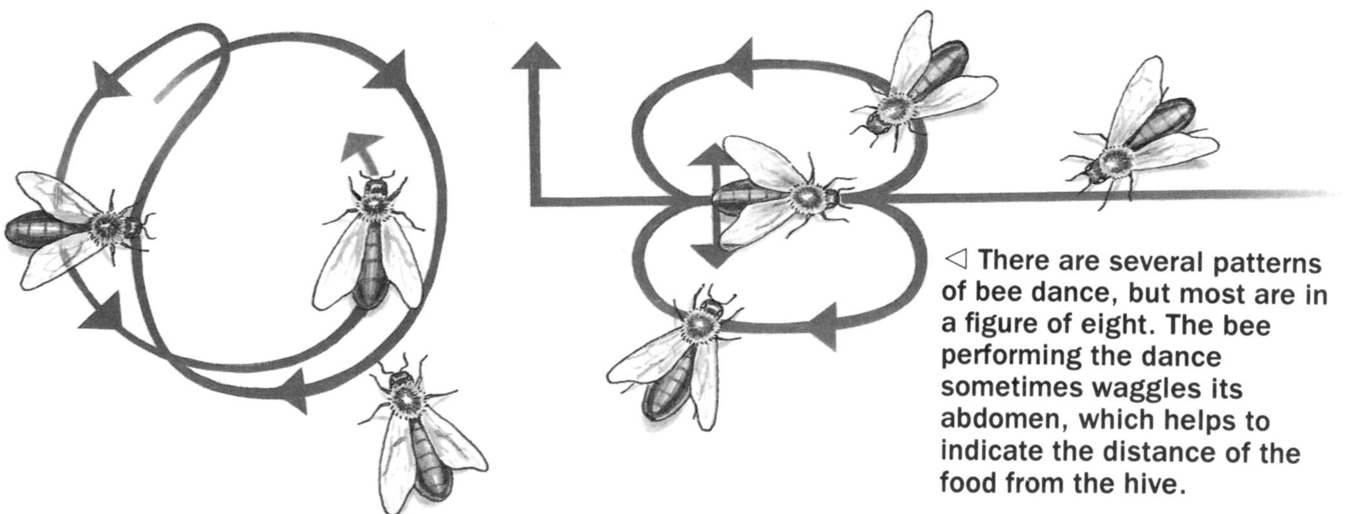

◁ There are several patterns of bee dance, but most are in a figure of eight. The bee performing the dance sometimes waggles its abdomen, which helps to indicate the distance of the food from the hive.

ANTS

When ants find a supply of food, they take as much of it as they can back to the ant nest.

If you see an ant, try to find out where its nest is. The entrance may be very small – for example, a crack between the pavement. Remember to be careful, because some types of ant can give a nasty bite.

Once you have found a nest, put some food down a few feet away from it. When one ant has found the food, it will tell others. A trail of ants will form, with some ants carrying food to the nest, and others walking back for more.

Once the ant trail has formed, try putting an obstacle like a twig across the trail. See how long it takes the ants to figure out how to cross it.

Are there any ants guarding the nest? Are any ants searching for more food?

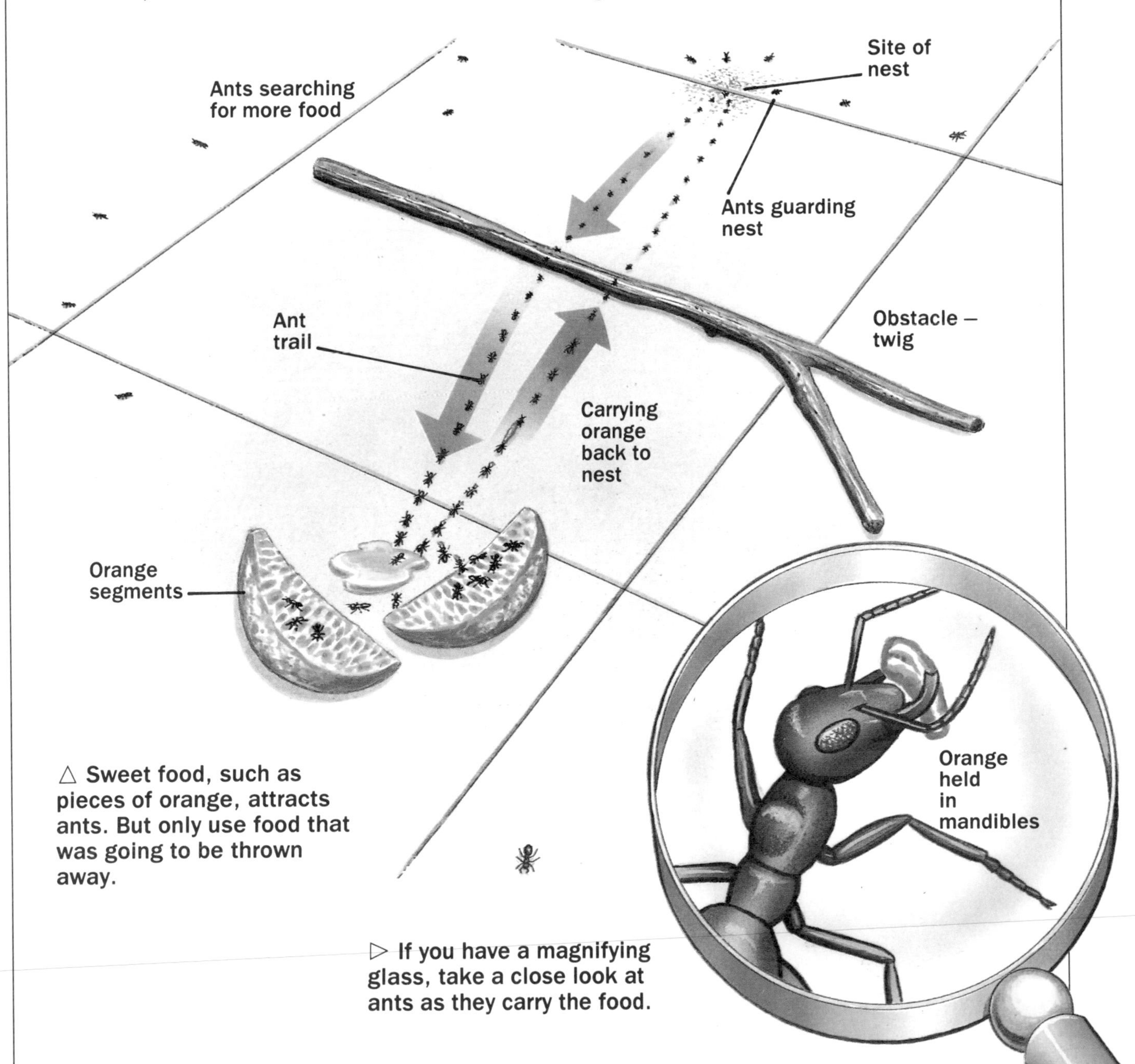

△ Sweet food, such as pieces of orange, attracts ants. But only use food that was going to be thrown away.

▷ If you have a magnifying glass, take a close look at ants as they carry the food.

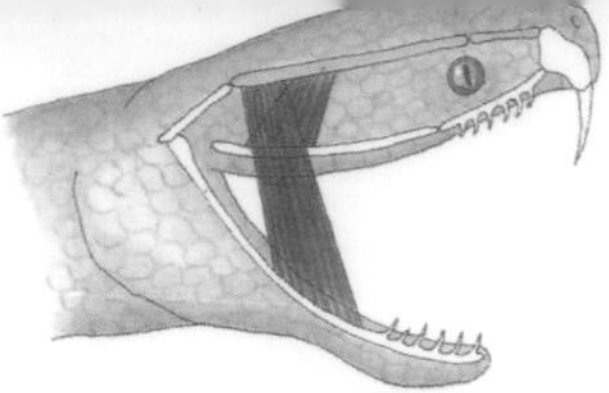

encyclopedia of science

FEEDING

CONTENTS

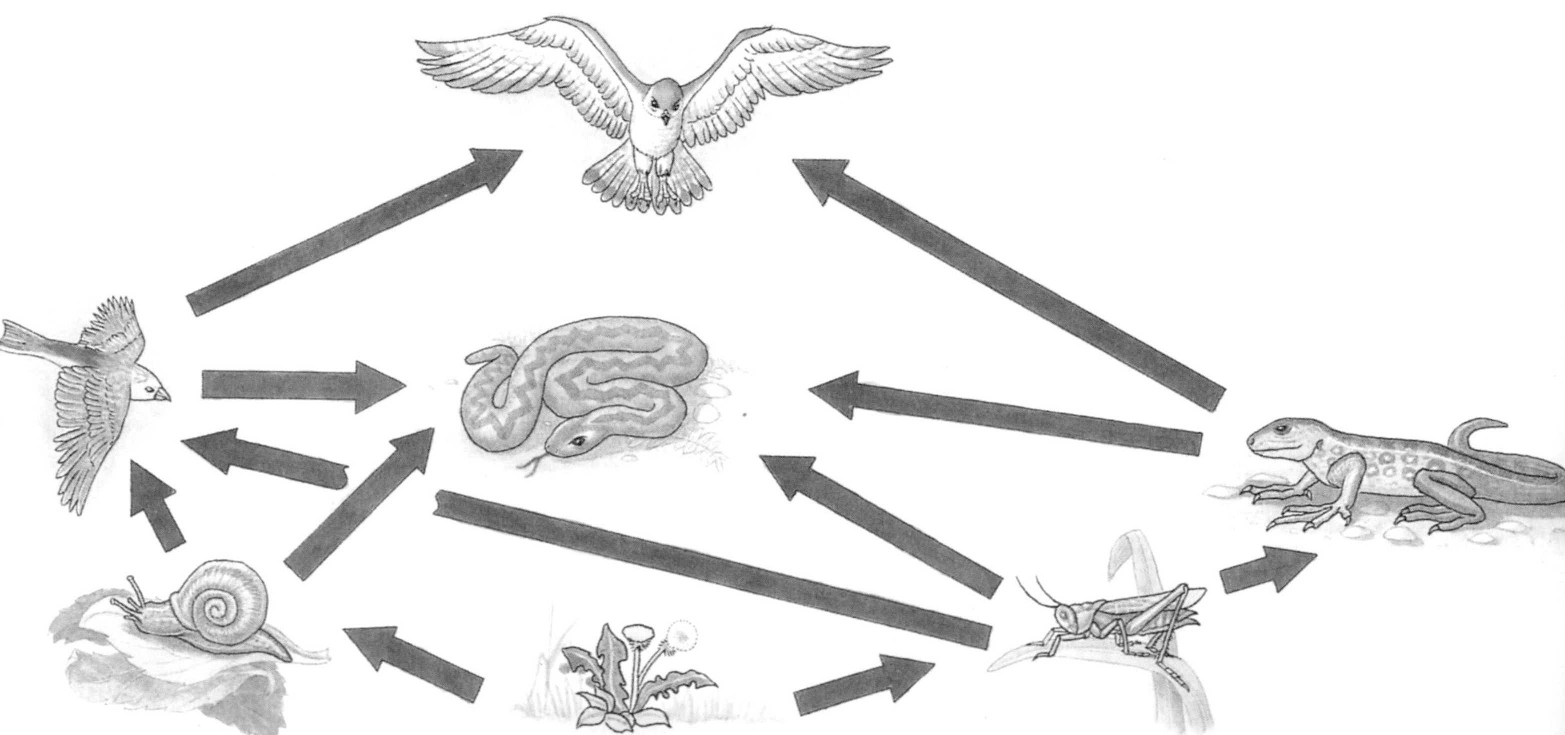

INTRODUCTION

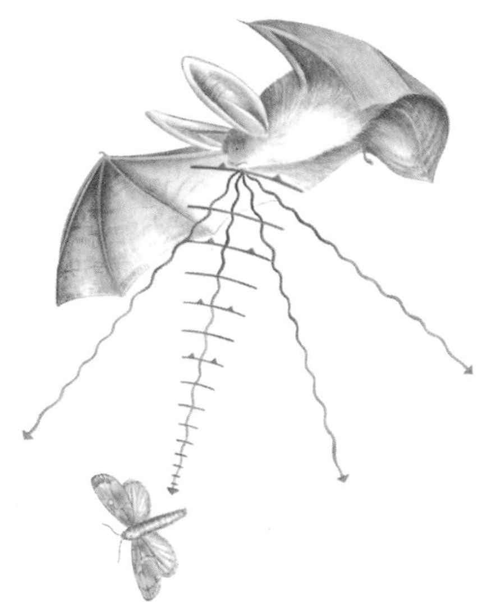

Feeding is essential to the lives of all animals. Many animals spend most of their time searching for and eating food. All animals would die if they did not eat food at some stage in their lives. There is a huge variety of methods of finding food and of types of food eaten. Many of these practises are different from the ways in which humans feed.

Many of the features of animals that you can see are connected with feeding. For example, the sharp teeth of a dog or the beak of a bird. There are many other examples, such as strong legs to run fast and catch another animal. A large number of animals have features that are designed to prevent themselves being eaten. For example, markings that make an animal difficult to see.

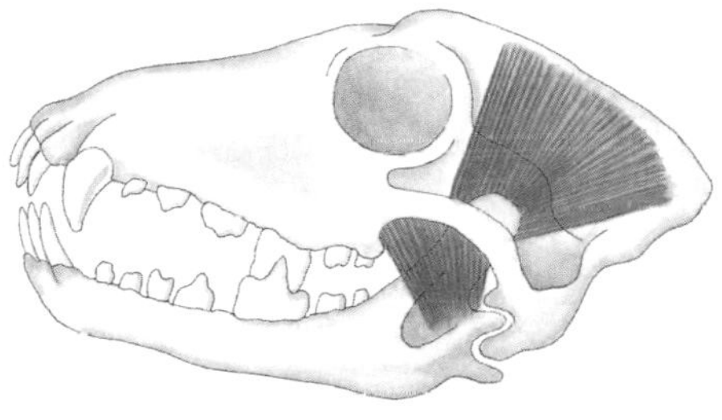

Once an animal has eaten food, it must digest it. The digestive systems of animals vary greatly. There are different problems in digesting various types of food.

DIFFERENT WAYS OF FEEDING

There are two main types of food. Inorganic food consists of simple substances, such as mineral salts and carbon dioxide. Organic food consists of complex carbon-containing substances, such as proteins, carbohydrates and fats. There are also two main methods of feeding: autotrophic and heterotrophic.

AUTOTROPHIC FEEDING

Autotrophic organisms (autotrophs) are able to make organic substances from inorganic food. Inorganic food consists of simple molecules, which contain just a few atoms. Organic food consists of large, complex molecules (which are called "organic" because they are characteristic of living organisms).

Only plants and some bacteria are autotrophic. They can make organic molecules by a process known as photosynthesis (although some bacteria use rather different processes). In photosynthesis, an organism uses the energy of sunlight to make organic materials from carbon dioxide and water.

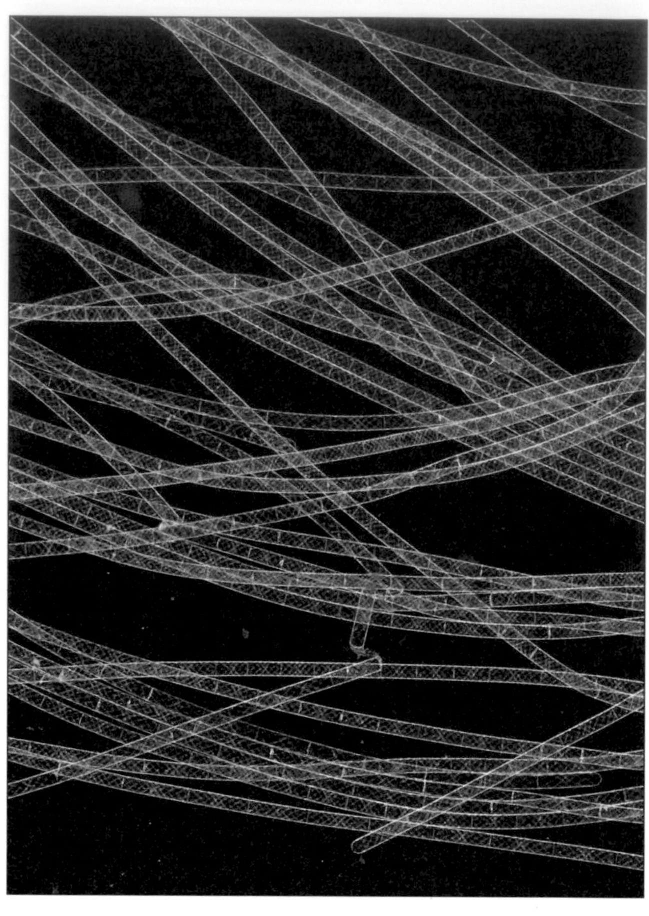

△ Spyrogyra is a tiny plant made up of strings of single cells. Like other plants, it is an autotrophic feeder.

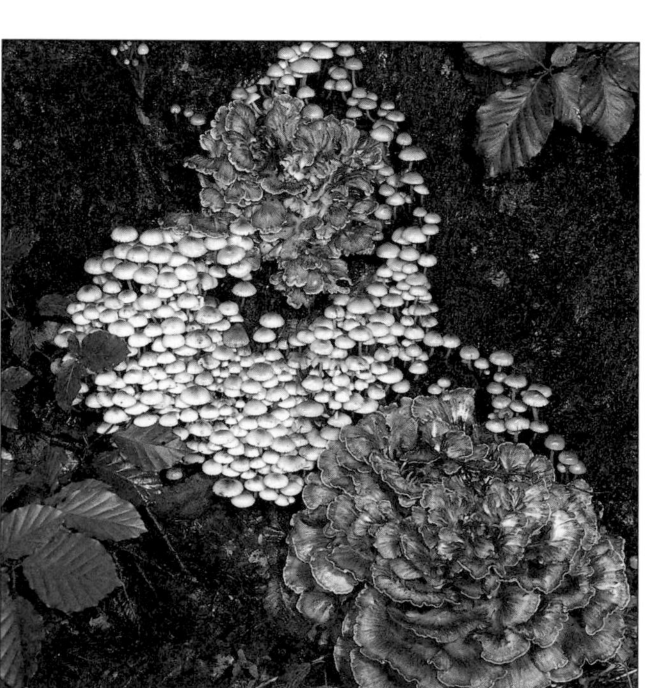

△ Fungi look like plants, but cannot photosynthesize and so are heterotrophic feeders.

HETEROTROPHIC FEEDING

Heterotrophic organisms (heterotrophs) are not able to make organic substances from inorganic food. They have to eat organic food in order to survive. The main reason is that heterotrophs get all of their energy from organic food. They cannot get energy from sunlight by photosynthesis in the way that autotrophic organisms do. Heterotrophs also get almost all of their inorganic food by feeding on other organisms – both autotrophs and other heterotrophs.

Animals are the main group of heterotrophs. There are a few others, such as fungi. All are organisms that cannot photosynthesize. This section is about feeding in animals and so talks about heterotrophic feeding.

MAJOR NUTRIENTS

There are three types of food described as major nutrients: carbohydrates, fats and proteins. These three are all organic foods. They consist of complex molecules that contain large amounts of carbon together with a variety of other chemical substances.

Carbohydrates contain only carbon, hydrogen and oxygen. There is a wide variety of carbohydrates. The main difference between them is the size of their molecules. Small carbohydrates include sugars. The sugar used in cooking is one example; glucose is another. Large carbohydrates include starch, found in great amounts in such foods as potatoes and grains. Large carbohydrate molecules may be hundreds of times longer than small ones. Animals use carbohydrates mostly for energy.

Fats, like carbohydrates, contain only carbon, hydrogen and oxygen, but arranged very differently. Biological oils are fats that are liquid at room temperature. Animals use fats as an energy store. Fats are found in large amounts in meat, milk and many seeds. They contain more energy per gram than carbohydrates do, but cannot be used so easily.

Proteins contain carbon, hydrogen, oxygen and nitrogen. Some also contain sulfur and other substances. Proteins are made up of building blocks called amino acids. There are about 20 different amino acids. They join together to make hundreds of different proteins, most containing more than 50 amino acids. The differences between proteins depend on the order in which the amino acids are joined together. Proteins have many functions, which include the formation of muscle and other tissues, and taking part in a large number of chemical reactions.

▷ Seeds are a good source of food and contain all of the major nutrients.

▽ Meat contains large amounts of protein and fat, but little carbohydrate.

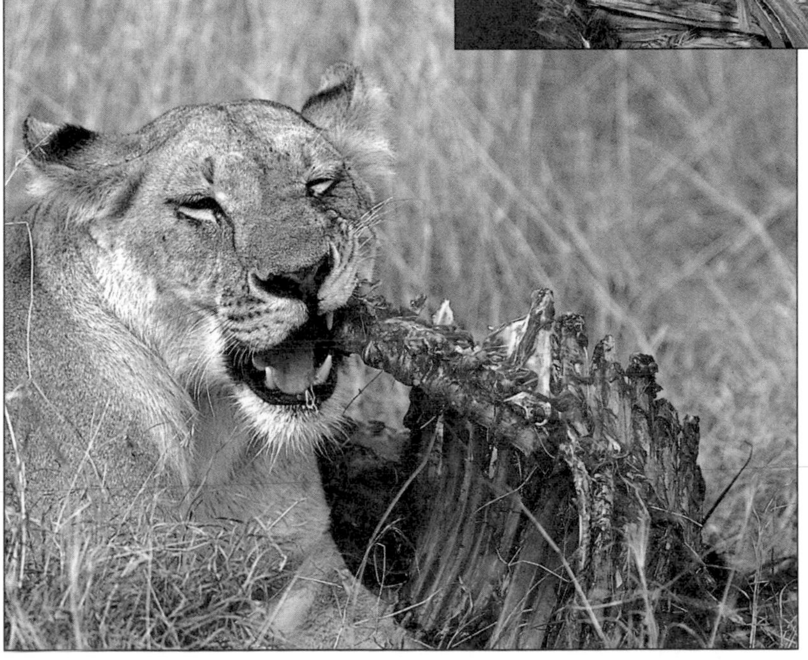

PROJECT

You can test food to see whether it contains large amounts of fat. Take a sheet of light-colored paper. Now rub a small amount of the food you have chosen on the paper (use food that is going to be thrown away). Now hold the paper up to the window or a lamp. If the food consists mostly of fat, the paper will let more light through where you rubbed it.

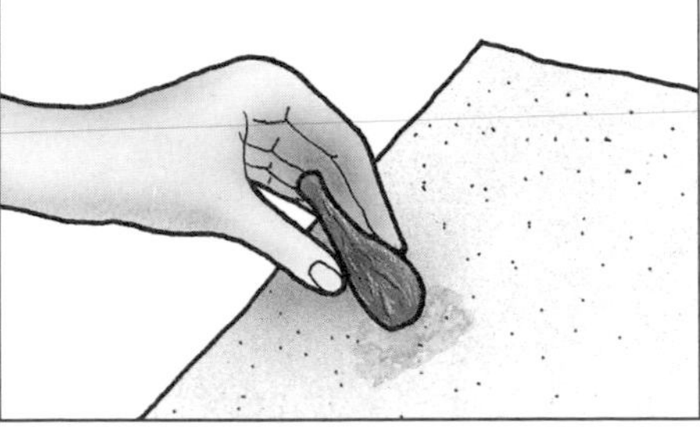

MINERALS

Minerals are inorganic food. They are described as minor nutrients, together with vitamins. The minerals that an animal needs are commonly found in nonliving material. But animals usually get all of their minerals by eating living things that contain the minerals. Animals use only small amounts of minerals, but a shortage leads to deficiency diseases.

Some of the minerals needed by mammals (such as humans) are as follows. Only some of the main functions are described.

- Calcium: used in bones and teeth
- Phosphorus: used in bones and teeth, and in producing energy from food
- Iron: part of hemoglobin, which carries oxygen and carbon dioxide in the blood
- Potassium: needed for nerves to work
- Sodium: needed for nerves to work
- Iodine: part of the body substance that controls growth
- Fluorine: needed to make teeth and bones, and to prevent tooth decay

Other minerals needed include sulfur, chlorine, magnesium, zinc, copper, manganese, chromium and cobalt.

VITAMINS

Vitamins are organic foods. Animals need them in very small amounts, but vitamins are extremely important. They are mostly involved in helping and controlling chemical reactions in the body. As with minerals, a lack of vitamins in the diet leads to deficiency diseases; for instance, a lack of vitamin C causes scurvy. Not all animals need the same vitamins; for example, humans need vitamin C, but most animals can make their own. Vitamins come from a wide variety of foods, although some foods have more of some vitamins than of others.

The vitamins are as follows. Only some of their main functions are given.

- Vitamin A: healthy skin and eyes, and resistance to disease
- Vitamin B: there are at least ten B vitamins, which are involved in many functions, but especially in the production of energy from food
- Vitamin C: repair to damaged tissues
- Vitamin D: healthy bones
- Vitamin E: affects reproduction in some animals (but not in humans)
- Vitamin K: helps with blood clotting

DID YOU KNOW?

The human body contains as much calcium as 340 sticks of chalk, as much phosphorus and sulfur as 2,500 boxes of matches, potassium as 4.5 pounds of fertilizer, sodium and chlorine as 40 teaspoonsful of salt, magnesium as in 80 indigestion tablets, iron as 6 paper clips, fluoride as 30 tubes of toothpaste, and zinc as a small battery. The rest of the minerals in the body would fill about one-tenth of a teaspoon.

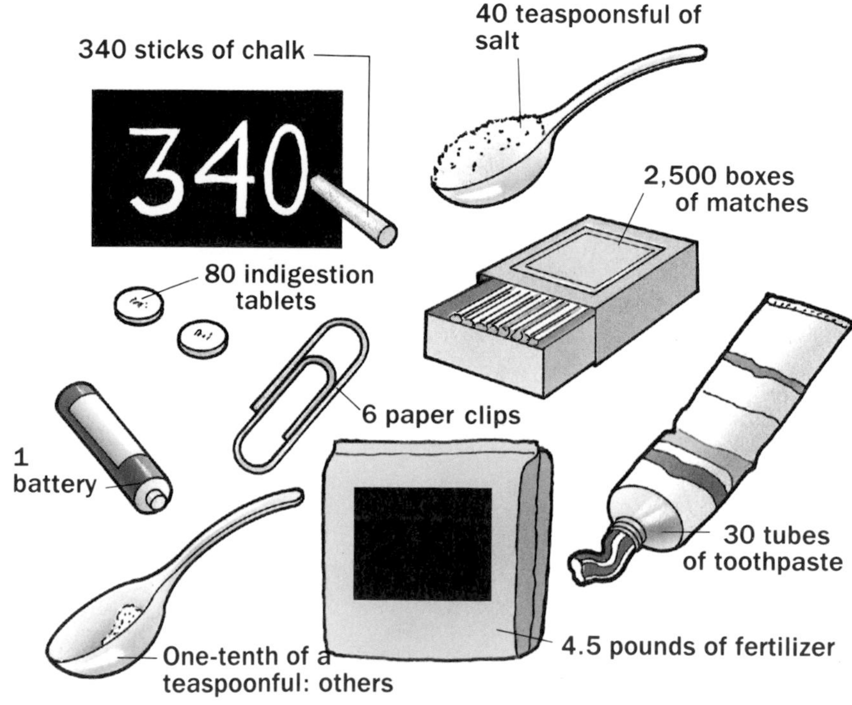

△ Many animals must drink water to survive.

WATER

A very large part of the body of every animal is water. Water has many functions. All chemical reactions in the body take place in water. Substances are carried around the body by watery fluids. Water is involved in temperature control (for example, when an animal sweats), and is important for many other reasons.

Animals obtain water in three ways. First, they can drink it directly – for example, from a pool or stream. Second, they can obtain it from the food they eat. Some animals get all of their water in this way and never drink at all. Third, animals that live in a watery environment can simply absorb water through their skins.

OTHER SUBSTANCES

In addition to the major nutrients, minor nutrients and water, there are other substances that animals take in.

Dietary fiber (also known as roughage) consists of the indigestible or poorly digestible parts of food. It is made up mostly of the cell walls of plants. Fiber gives solidity to food and increases the overall rate at which food passes through the intestine.

Different animals require different amounts of fiber. Animals that eat mostly meat get very little fiber, but need only a little. Animals that eat plants get much more, although they can usually digest plant cell walls to some degree. In animals that need fiber, a sufficient amount in the diet helps to prevent some disorders of the intestines.

▽ Elephants get large amounts of fiber when eating wood.

Many birds – especially those that eat seeds – swallow small stones. They take the stones into their gizzards to help them grind up food. Hens eat egg shells. They are able to reabsorb the minerals to make shells for new eggs. Some animals lick salt from the ground, where it is sometimes found as a natural mineral.

Animals may eat substances that are of no use to the body. Food may contain indigestible parts, such as bone. It may contain chemicals that have no nutritional value. Food that has been accidentally eaten may even contain poisons.

Animals are heterotrophic feeders – they must feed on other organisms (see page 238). Some animals eat plants (and are known as herbivores); some eat animals (carnivores); and some eat both (omnivores). The relationships between animals, the food they eat, and the animals that eat them are very complex.

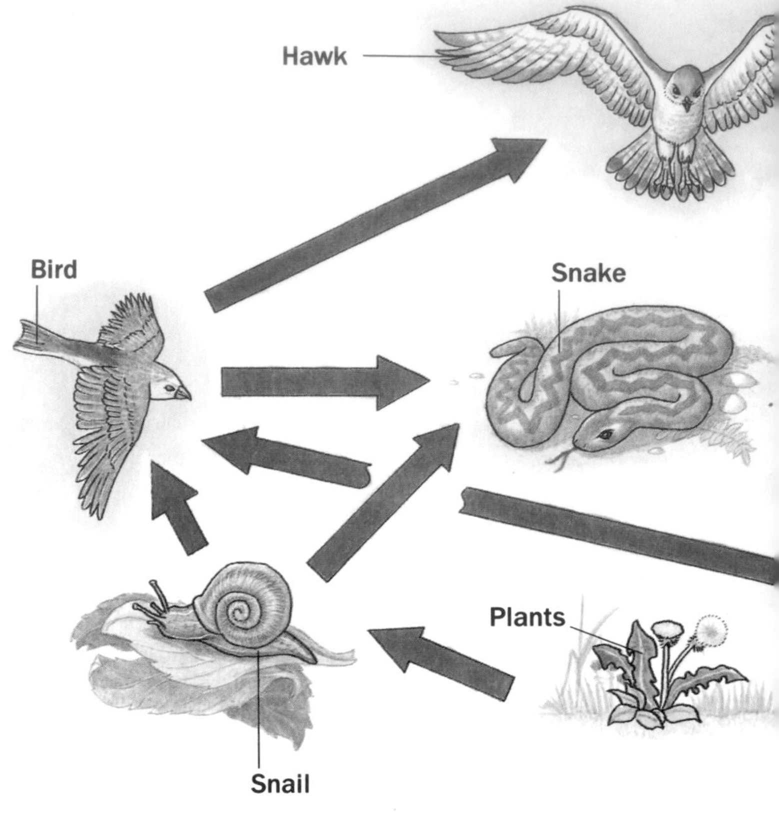

FOOD CHAINS

The simplest way to look at food relationships is by a food chain. The best way to understand food chains is to use an example.

A field has grass growing in it. Crickets live in the field and eat the grass. The crickets are eaten by lizards, which are in turn eaten by hawks.

This example of a food chain has four "links" in it. The first link, the grass, produces the nutrients needed in the chain. These nutrients include both energy and such things as minerals. The grass produces the nutrients by using energy from the sun and by absorbing minerals from the soil. The grass is therefore known as a producer.

The other links in the chain are known as consumers. They get the energy and nutrients they need from an organism lower down the chain. The first consumer in the chain must be a herbivore. Higher links are carnivores. An omnivore might be any link in the chain.

PYRAMIDS

Another way to look at food chains is as a pyramid of numbers or of biomass. Three examples of pyramids are illustrated below. A pyramid of numbers shows the number of each organism. A pyramid of biomass shows the total mass (or weight) of the organisms. At the bottom of a pyramid is a producer. Each stage up the pyramid is a link in the food chain.

The pyramid becomes smaller toward the top because at each stage the chain

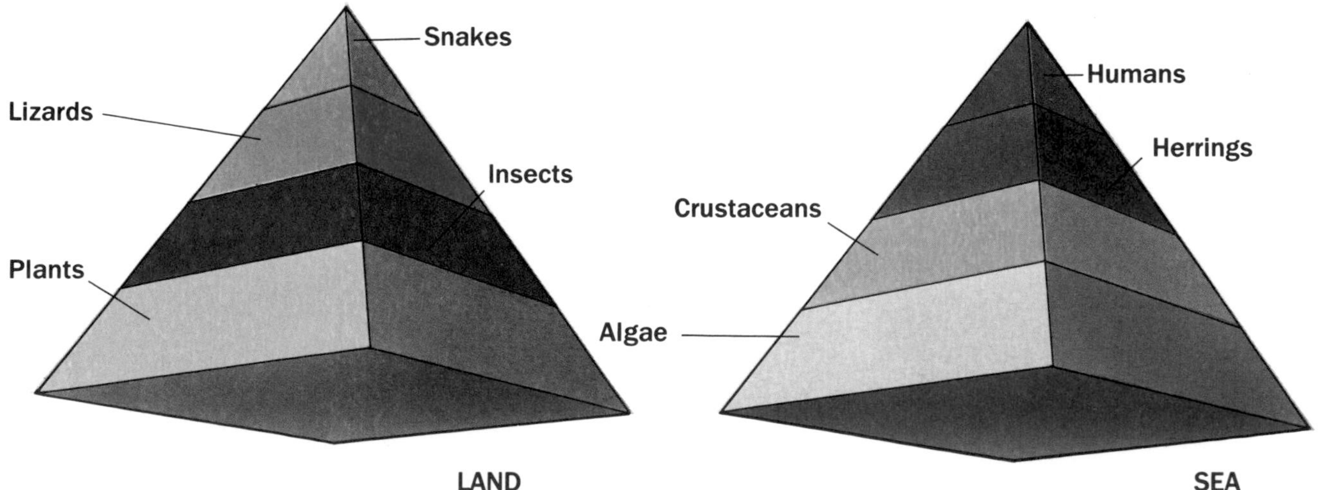

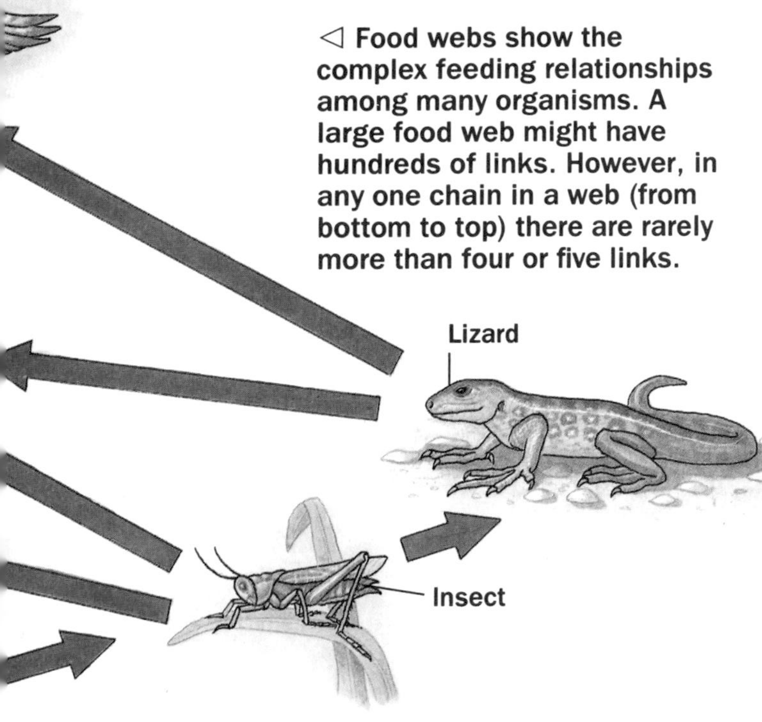

◁ Food webs show the complex feeding relationships among many organisms. A large food web might have hundreds of links. However, in any one chain in a web (from bottom to top) there are rarely more than four or five links.

loses nutrients. A large amount of the food that an animal eats is used up. In particular, food that contains energy is used up when an animal uses energy (for example, by moving). Other food is lost when an animal eats more than it needs.

Pyramids of biomass are more useful than pyramids of numbers. For example, a hundred fleas may feed on a dog. But the total weight of fleas would be much less than the weight of the dog, and they would use up far fewer nutrients.

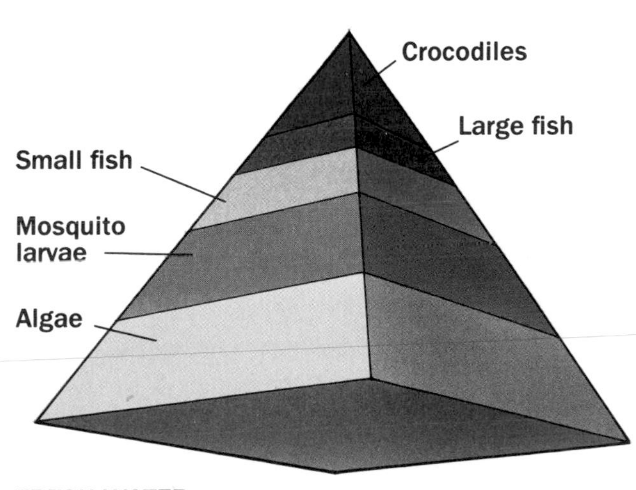

FRESH WATER

WEBS AND CYCLES

Food chains give a quite simple picture of feeding relationships. But in reality, the relationships are usually much more complex. Most animals feed on more than one other organism, and are eaten by more than one type of animal. Food webs try to show all of the relationships, or at least a large part of them. A food web is like a large number of food chains, all combined together.

The parts of a web are closely linked, and a change in one part can affect many others. If the numbers of one organism get fewer, so will the numbers of the organisms that feed on it. On the other hand, those organisms it eats may increase in numbers. For example, the Canadian lynx relies on the snowshoe hare for a large part of its diet. When the population of the hare drops, the population of the lynx drops soon afterward. When the population of the hare rises, so does that of the lynx.

Most of the nutrients in a food web are recycled. For example, when an animal dies, it decomposes; the chemicals it contains return to the soil and can be reabsorbed by plants. But energy is lost – for example, as heat from an animal's body. Energy must be replaced by producers, taking energy from the sun.

△ The Canadian lynx feeds on the snowshoe hare.

Even the smallest animal has to feed in order to get energy and nutrients. Tiny animals can feed on nothing larger than minute particles of food floating in water. But many very large animals also feed on small food particles. Some other animals do not feed on solid food at all, but only drink liquids.

MICROORGANISMS

Microorganisms are tiny, often single-celled plants and animals. They live in water or other damp environments.

Microorganisms such as paramecia are covered in cilia, which are like tiny bundles of muscular fibers on the surface of the cell. Paramecia wave their cilia to move. This action also creates currents that draw food particles into the oral groove. A particle is then taken into the cell as a food vacuole.

Amoebas surround food particles with fingerlike extensions from the cell called pseudopodia. As in paramecia, a food particle is drawn into the cell to form a food vacuole. This can happen anywhere on the surface of an amoeba.

△ A flamingo's large beak is shaped to be held upside down in the water as it feeds.

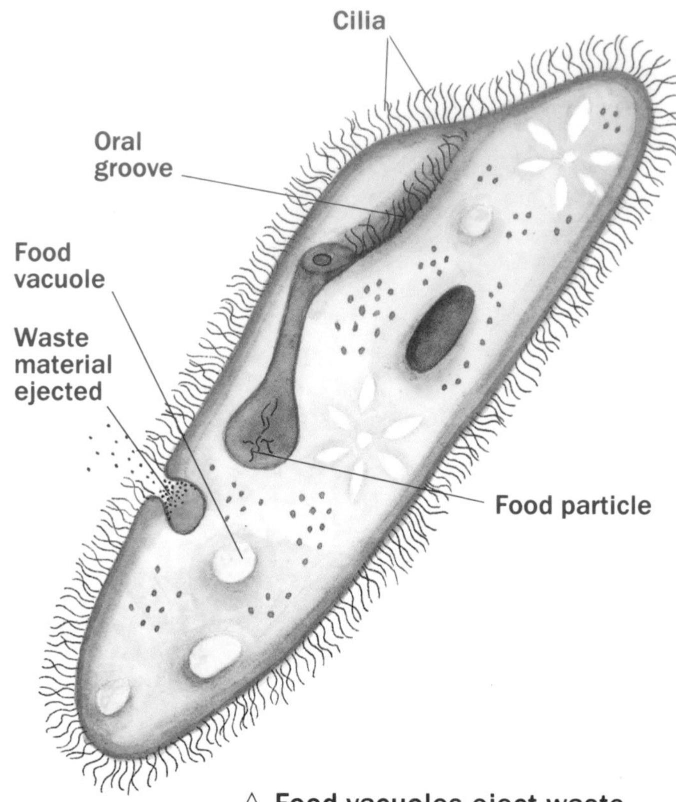

△ Food vacuoles eject waste material at the surface of a paramecium after digestion.

FILTER FEEDERS

A variety of animals use filter feeding. These animals filter small particles of food from water.

Many shellfish are filter feeders. They use cilia on their gills. (Gills are normally used to get oxygen from water.) An example of such a shellfish is the mussel. Mussels draw water past their gills by moving their cilia. The gills and cilia are covered with a sticky mucus (a substance produced by the surface of the gills). The mucus traps food particles from the water. The cilia move the mucus and food particles to the mussel's mouth.

Flamingoes are unusual filter-feeding birds. They wade in shallow lakes on their long legs, while holding their beaks upside down in the water. The opening of a flamingo's beak is surrounded by bristles. The bird moves its beak from side to side, and the bristles filter minute plants and animals from the water.

Many fish, such as herrings, use filter feeding. They have structures on their gills called gill rakers. The rakers sieve food from the water that passes over the gills. The food is usually such things as small shrimp-like animals, called plankton, and the larvae of sea animals.

Some whales filter feed – for example, blue whales. They use a large number of thin plates hanging from their upper jaws to filter tiny animals from the water.

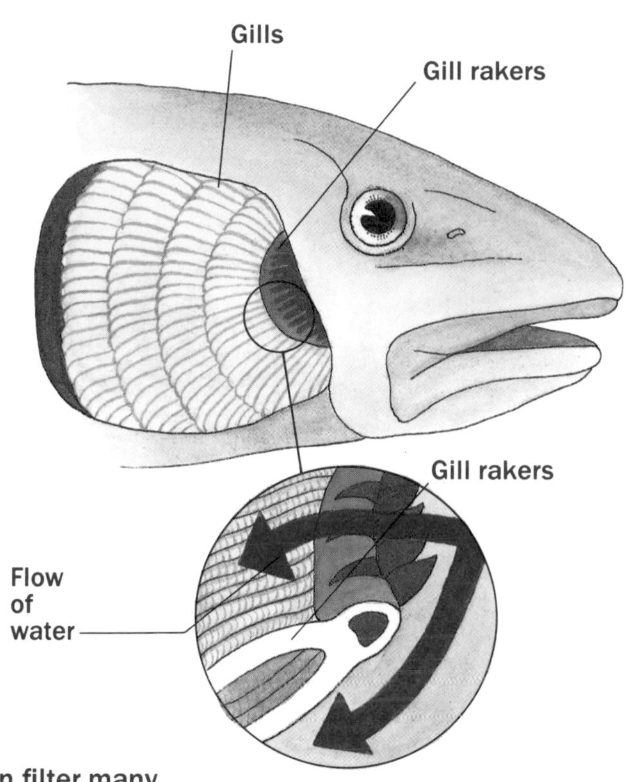

△ Gill rakers can filter many food particles from water.

DID YOU KNOW?

There is a type of spider that is colored yellow (below). The color allows it to hide in yellow flowers without being seen by bees. When a bee arrives to feed on nectar, the spider kills the bee and sucks fluid from its body.

△ Butterflies have a long proboscis, which uncurls to suck nectar from flowers.

FLUID FEEDERS

Animals that feed only on liquids are called fluid feeders. Most fluid feeders are insects. Such insects have specially designed mouthparts.

Many insects that feed on fluids are parasites – they suck blood or sap from living animals or plants (see page 254).

A number of insects feed on nectar, a sugary fluid which is made in flowers. Examples include butterflies and bees. The mouthparts of such insects usually have a long tube (called a proboscis). This tube is used to reach into flowers and suck the nectar.

Flies feed on fluid by pumping saliva onto solid food. The saliva partly digests the food and makes it liquid. The mouth then sucks up the liquid food.

A few other types of animal feed on fluids. Examples include spiders, which inject insects with digestive fluid and suck the juices out and hummingbirds, which feed on flower nectar.

Herbivores feed on plants. Different herbivores eat many different parts of plants. The main problem that herbivores have with feeding is that some plant material is difficult to digest. This is particularly a problem for mammals, because they cannot make substances that can digest cellulose.

EATING CELLULOSE

The main carbohydrate (page 239) in many parts of plants is cellulose – for example, in leaves and stems. Cellulose makes up the cell walls of plants. Herbivorous mammals have various special methods of digesting cellulose.

Most herbivorous mammals have large numbers of bacteria in their intestines which can digest cellulose. The bacteria absorb some of the digested material. But much of the material is left over for the animal to absorb.

A rabbit, for example, has such bacteria in its cecum, appendix and colon. Rabbits also help digestion by passing food through their intestines twice. They do this by eating their own feces. Rabbits extract further nutrition as the food passes through for the second time. This is called refecation.

RABBIT SKULL

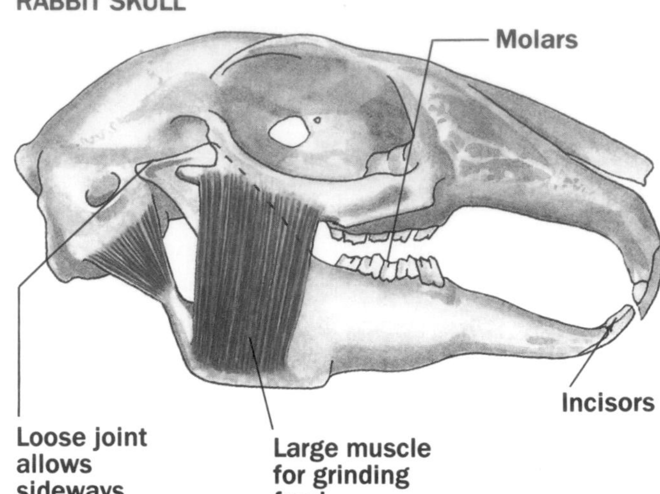

△ Rabbits eat their own feces to get extra nutrition from plant food that is hard to digest.

▷ After food has passed through a rabbit's intestine, the feces come out as green pellets, called cetrophs. Rabbits swallow these pellets, which are digested more in the stomach than in the cecum and appendix. The feces re-emerge brown.

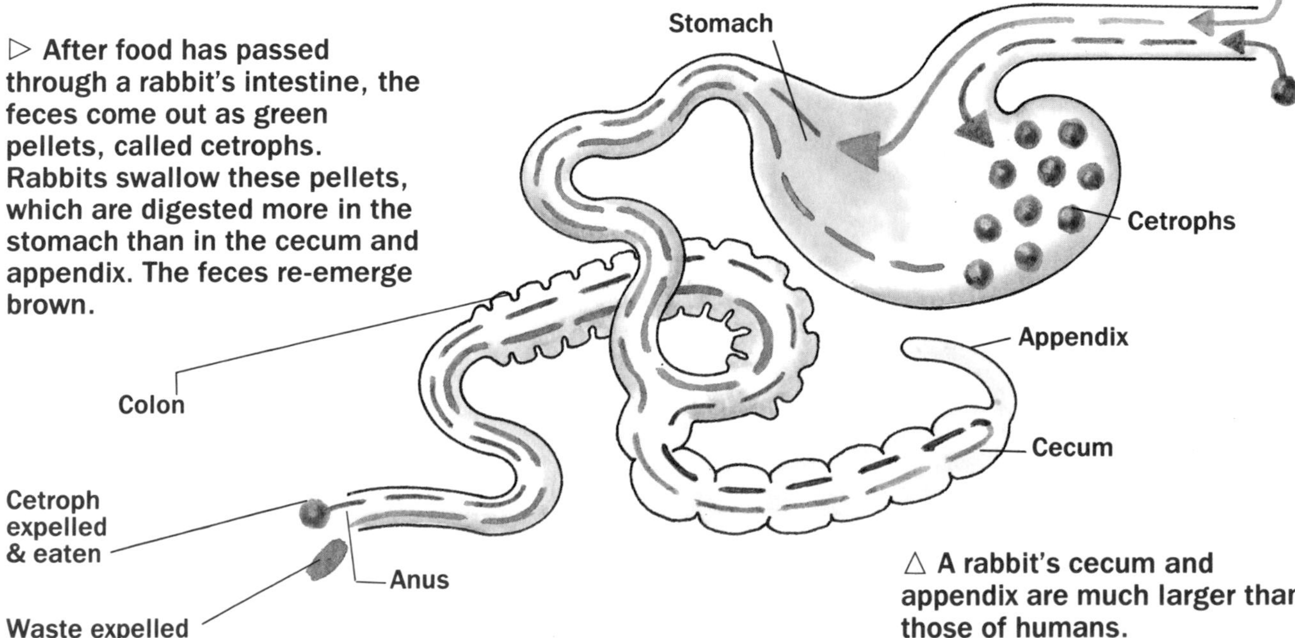

△ A rabbit's cecum and appendix are much larger than those of humans.

RUMINATION AND TEETH

Many herbivores are ruminants – including sheep, cattle, deer, antelopes, goats and kangaroos. Ruminants have several pouches in their digestive passages. Food goes first to the rumen, which contains great numbers of bacteria that can digest cellulose. After some time in the rumen, the food returns to the mouth. Here the food is chewed further (this is known as rumination, or chewing the cud). The food is swallowed again and passes through the reticulum and omasum, where more digestion by bacteria takes place. When the food reaches the abomasum, any bacteria in the food are killed by acid and digested.

The teeth and jaws of herbivorous mammals are designed for breaking up plant material. The front teeth (incisors) are shaped for tearing off food. The molar teeth are designed for grinding up food. The teeth grow for all of the animal's life (unlike the teeth of carnivores). At the same time as they grow, the teeth wear down. The tops of molar teeth wear away leaving hard, sharp ridges of enamel. These ridges are very effective for grinding up tough plant food. The jaw is designed to move easily from side to side as the teeth grind the food.

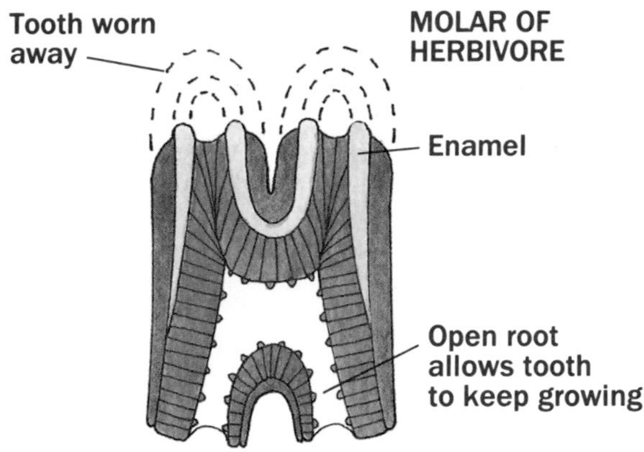

◁△ A rabbit's jaws and teeth are designed for breaking up tough plant food. The teeth wear down to leave hard ridges of enamel.

△ Cattle are ruminants. Their diet is largely grass.

Anus
Abomasum
Omasum
Food rechewed
Reticulum
Cecum
Rumen
Small intestine

▷ The abomasum is the true stomach, in which a ruminant's digestive processes take over from bacteria. Digestion and absorption of food continue along the rest of the digestive system.

Carnivores feed on animals. There are a number of characteristics that make them different from herbivores. Many of these characteristics are of the teeth, jaws and other mouthparts. The digestive systems of carnivores are shorter than those of herbivores because meat is easier to digest than plant material.

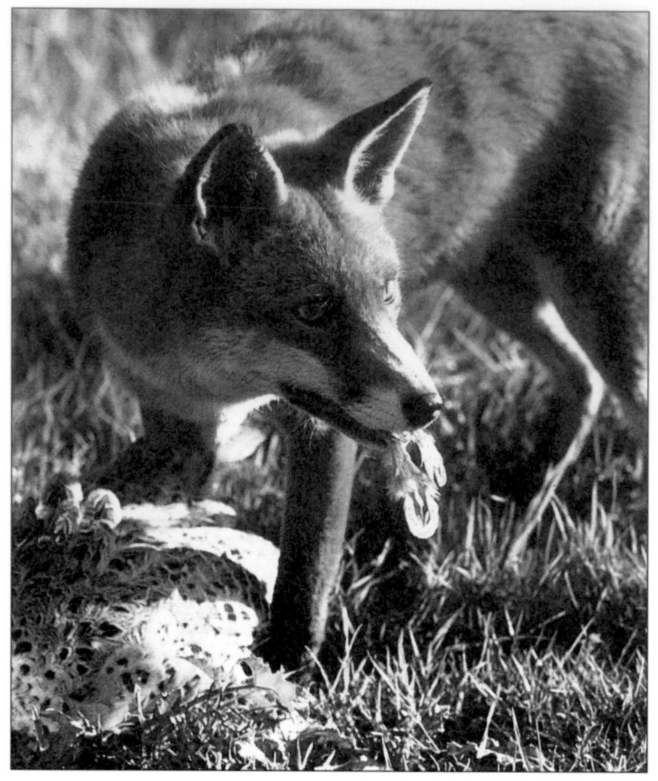

△ The fox is a carnivore that feeds on a variety of small animals.

MAMMAL CARNIVORES

The teeth of carnivores are designed for both catching and eating their prey. Dogs have teeth that are typical of carnivorous mammals. The front teeth (the incisors) are designed for gripping and tearing off pieces of meat. The canine teeth are pointed and long. They pierce the flesh of the dog's prey, stopping the prey from escaping and helping to kill it. The rest of the teeth are designed mainly for breaking up food. The large carnassial teeth move past each other like scissors, cutting through meat. The rear molars crush food into small pieces.

There is a large and powerful muscle for closing the jaws. This helps the teeth both to hold onto prey and to chew meat. The hinge of the jaw only lets the jaw move up and down, not from side to side as with herbivores. Food is therefore cut or crushed, not ground up.

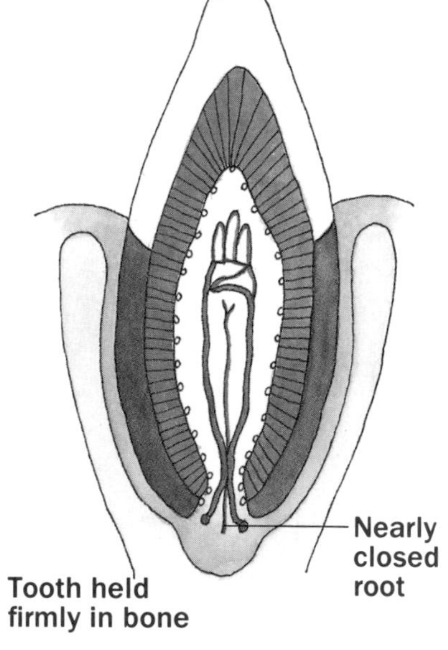

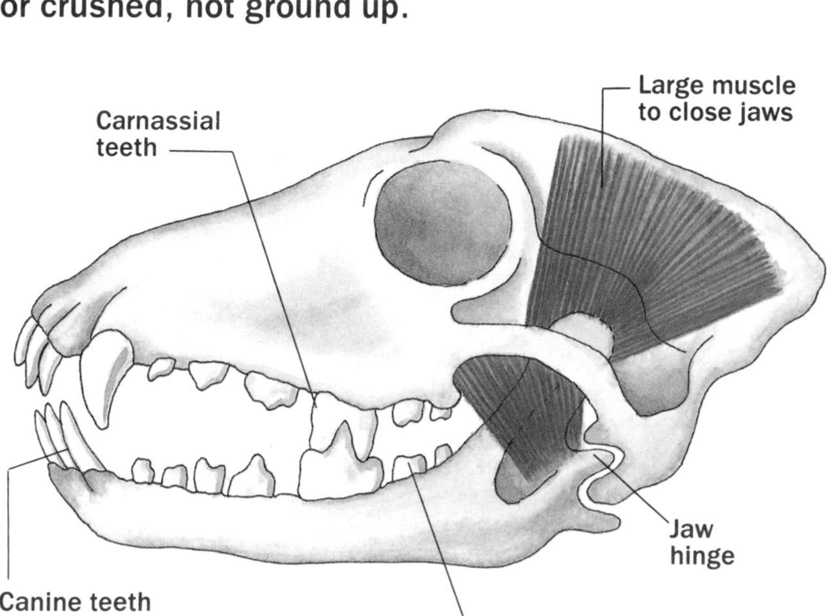

◁△ A dog's teeth are designed for gripping prey and breaking up meat. They do not grow once they have reached full size and have a root that is almost closed. The teeth do not wear down in the way that a herbivore's teeth do.

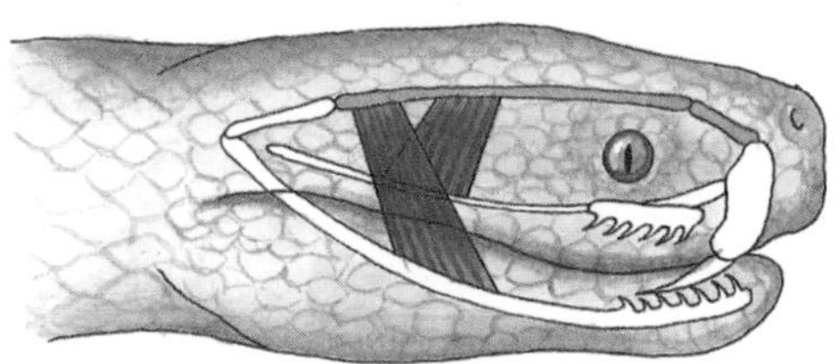

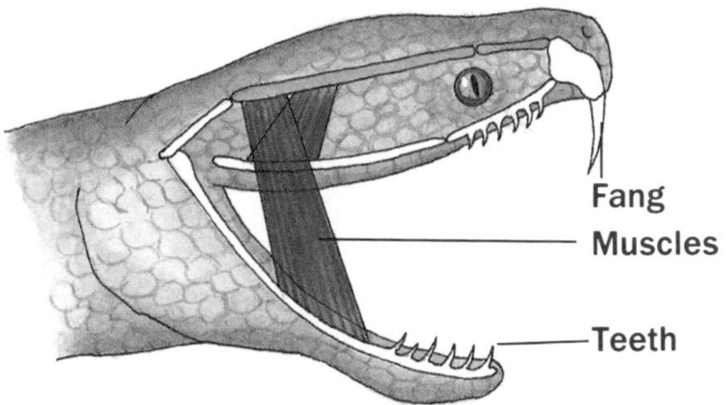

△ Many snakes have jaws that can open very widely. Many also have fangs that swing forward when the jaws open.

OTHER CARNIVORES

There are many types of carnivore in the animal kingdom. These animals have a variety of adaptations for eating meat.

Many carnivorous fish do not have teeth that can cut or crush food. They just have a large number of spike-like teeth for holding onto prey. Such fish swallow their prey whole. Other fish, like piranhas and many sharks, do have teeth that can tear through flesh.

Sharks are unusual because they have several rows of teeth. They use only the front two or so rows. The teeth in the other rows grow and move forward to replace the front rows of teeth.

Snakes do not have cutting teeth or strong jaws. As a result, they have to swallow their prey whole. To do this, snakes have long jawbones with loose hinges, which allow their mouths to open very widely. Many snakes can swallow prey that is bigger than their own heads.

Birds that have to tear up their prey before swallowing it have strong, hooked beaks. Such birds include vultures and birds of prey.

△ Sharks have rows of teeth that move forward, replacing lost or damaged teeth.

INSECTIVORES

Insectivores are carnivores that eat insects. Most frogs and toads have long, sticky tongues that they shoot out to catch insects. Chameleons have similar tongues, which they control with large muscles in their throats. A number of mammals, like anteaters, also have sticky tongues, which they use to pick up ants and termites. Bats and other small mammals use their teeth to catch insects. Many birds pick up insects with their beaks. Some insects are insectivores and have powerful mouthparts.

△ A three-horned chameleon.

DID YOU KNOW?

A few plants eat insects. One example is Venus-flytrap. When an insect lands on its special leaves, the leaves snap together to trap the insect. The plant then digests its victim.

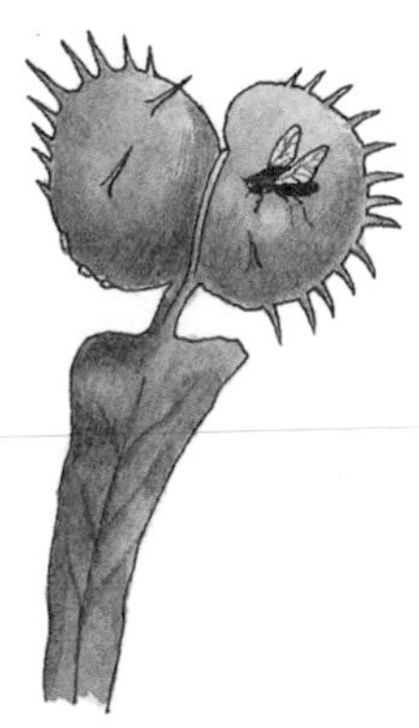

The competition between predators and prey is in some ways like a battle between armies, each with its methods of attack and defense. Predators are animals that hunt other animals (prey). Predators have many methods of catching their prey. Hunted animals have many ways of protecting themselves.

△ The horned frog looks very like a dead leaf.

▷ Skunks defend themselves by spraying foul-smelling liquid from glands near their tails.

DEFENSE

Animals have a huge variety of ways of defending themselves from predators. One obvious method is by running, flying or swimming from danger. Examples of animals whose main defense is running are antelopes and zebras. Some animals also try to confuse predators while escaping. For example, rabbits make sideways jumps while they are running away.

Hiding from predators is a method of defense. Some animals live in holes in the ground. Others spend much of their time hidden among bushes or other plants. Small animals often come out of hiding only at night when it is dark.

Another way of hiding is to use camouflage. An animal's coat, fur or feathers are camouflaged by color or patterns, which often mimic their natural surroundings. For example, a brown, speckled pattern blends in well with twigs and dry plants in a forest. Some animals do not look like animals at all. For example, stick insects look more like twigs than like insects.

Some animals look like other, dangerous animals. For example, many hover flies have yellow and black stripes like a wasp. Predators think that they will be stung if they attack. Small animals – including some butterflies – often have large spots that resemble eyes. This may fool a predator into thinking that it is attacking a much larger animal.

Many animals fight back against predators. Large animals may kick, bite, or use horns or tusks. Some smaller animals have poisonous bites or stings. Others have foul odors or poisonous skins. Poisonous animals are often brightly colored to warn predators away.

Another form of defense is to have armor plating. Animals with such protection include shellfish, snails, turtles and armadillos. Porcupines are covered in sharp quills.

△ Spots that resemble large eyes may frighten a predator.

DETECTING PREY

Before attacking, a predator has to find its prey, which it does by using senses like smell, sight and hearing.

Sight allows predators to pinpoint their prey and observe their target's movements. Animals that attack their prey from long distances have very good eyesight. For example, hawks swoop down on their prey from the air and can see small animals, like field mice, from great heights. Animals that hunt in poor light often have large eyes to let in as much light as possible.

Hearing can be used to detect any noise that the prey makes. For most animals, hearing gives a rough idea of the direction of the prey. Bats hunt at night so cannot see prey easily. They use a system called echolocation. They let out squeaks and hear the echo from the prey. Dolphins use a similar system.

Animals also use smell to find prey. They sniff out the prey's scent in the air or on the ground. Some animals, such as dogs, can follow prey for long distances by using scent on the ground.

A large number of fish can sense the tiny electrical charges created by animals. These fish use an organ called the lateral line that runs down the sides of their bodies.

△ Cuttlefish have large eyes to see prey in dark waters.

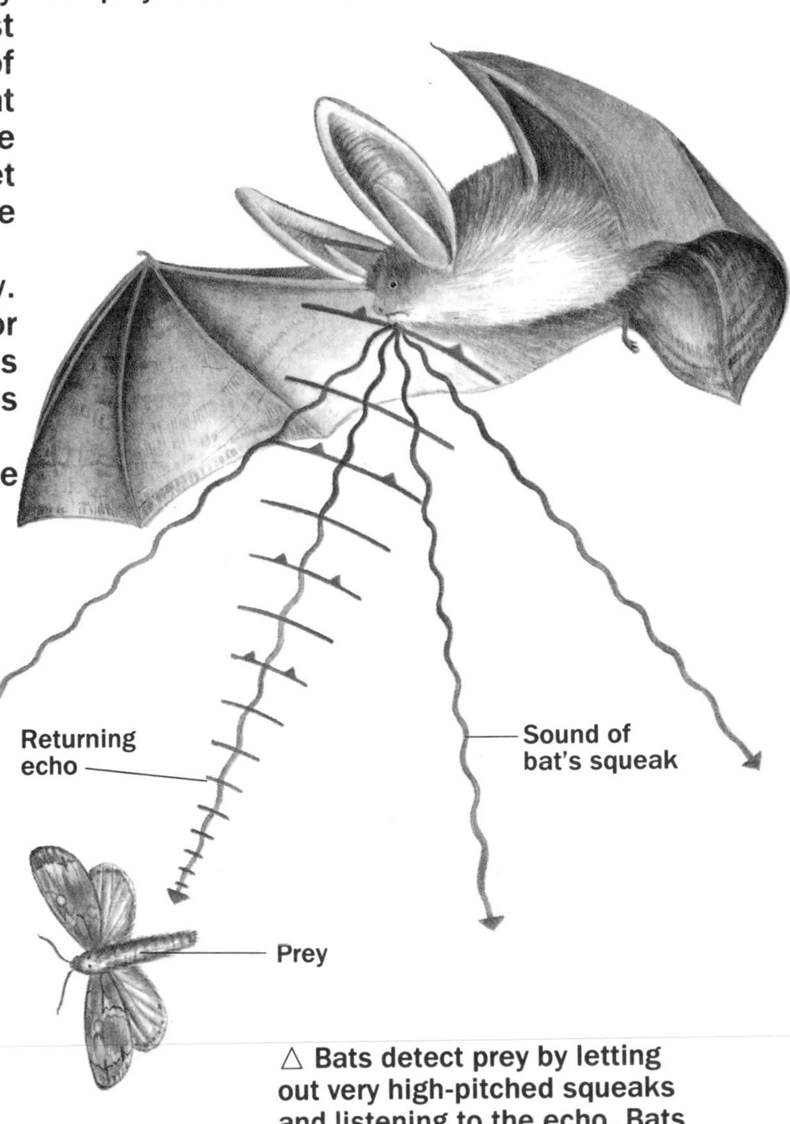

△ Bats detect prey by letting out very high-pitched squeaks and listening to the echo. Bats need large and sensitive ears to hear the tiny sound of an echo bounce off an insect.

EXPERIMENT

Find your way by using echolocation like a bat. Stand outdoors near to a large wall. Get a friend to blindfold you and turn you around a few times. Make a sharp sound, such as banging two pieces of wood together. Can you tell in which direction the wall is by listening for the echo?

CATCHING PREY

The most common way of catching prey is to chase it. Predators often stalk their prey, trying to get as close as possible before chasing. Some predators, such as wolves, can chase their prey for quite long distances. Others, such as cheetahs, move very quickly, but can run for only short distances.

Another common method of hunting is to wait in ambush for prey. For example, leopards sometimes wait in trees and jump out onto passing animals. Birds of prey swoop down from the air before their victim has time to run away.

Most spiders use webs to catch their prey. An insect flies into the web without seeing it and becomes trapped. Ant lions also set traps. An ant lion makes a conical hole in the ground and waits at the bottom.

Many predators catch hold of their prey and kill it with their teeth, beaks, other mouthparts or claws. But there are different methods. Constrictor snakes wrap their bodies around prey and crush it to death. Other snakes use poisonous bites. Spiders, octopuses, some jellyfish and a few fish also use poison. Electric eels and some other fish use electric shocks to stun or kill their prey.

△ African wild dogs hunt in packs for buffalo.

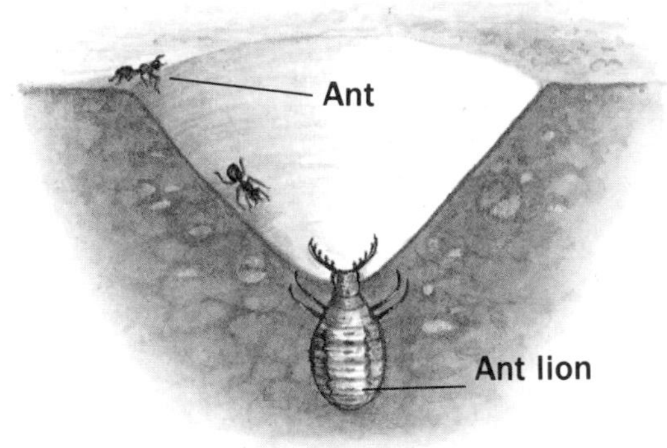

△ Ant lions wait at the bottom of their traps with only their heads showing.

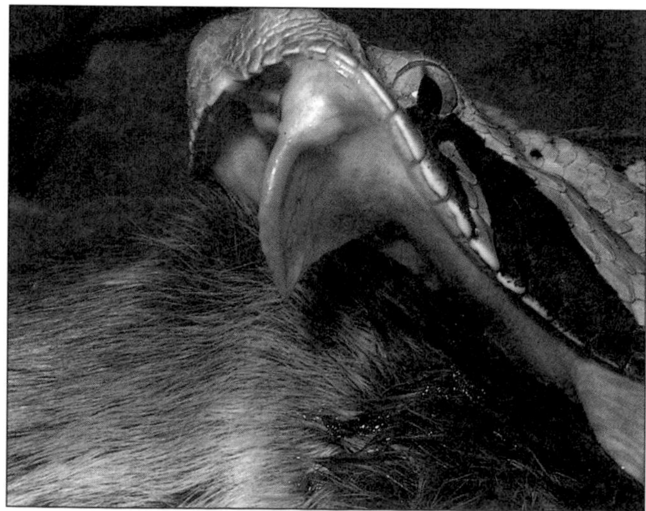

△ Poisonous snakes use their fangs to inject poison.

▽ The snapping turtle lures prey into its mouth with what looks like a small worm.

USING TOOLS

Very few animals use tools to catch or kill their prey. Humans use by far the most complex and varied tools. These tools include spears, bows and guns, among many others. Chimpanzees use thin sticks to catch termites. They lick a stick and push it into a termites' nest. Then they pull the stick out covered in termites. A few types of bird, such as Darwin's finch, use thorns to pull insects out of tree bark. Sea otters break open clams and other shellfish by smashing the shells against stones. Some birds drop snails onto the ground to break the shells. Siberian crows get water to drink in the winter by dropping stones onto frozen lakes.

PACK HUNTING

There are two main advantages to hunting in packs. First, it makes hunting more efficient. Animals that are hunted can often run very quickly and are difficult for a single predator to catch. Second, pack hunting helps animals to kill prey that is much larger than themselves. For example, a pack of African wild dogs can kill a buffalo many times the size and strength of a single dog.

Only animals that live in groups hunt in packs. Examples include wolves, jackals and lions. There are many methods used for pack hunting. One method that lions use is as follows. Some of a group of lions lie hidden on one side of a herd of, for example, zebras. Other lions start to stalk the herd from the opposite side. These lions deliberately let themselves be seen. The herd moves away from what it thinks is the danger. But the hidden lions are waiting and leap out when the herd is close.

Most animals that hunt in groups are mammals. An example of another type of animal, however, is African army ants. These ants move in huge numbers and swarm over any victim that gets in their way. The ants can move only slowly and so are little danger to large animals, which can easily run away. Their prey is mainly insects and other small animals.

▽ Sea otters open clams by knocking their shells against rocks until they break.

SPIDERS' WEBS

Find a web with a spider waiting on it. Gently touch the web with a piece of grass or a thin twig. The spider will run out to catch what it thinks is an insect.

Parasites feed off living plants and animals. A parasite's victim is called the host. Most parasites cause some harm to their host, even if the harm is not serious. A number of parasites eventually kill their hosts. Some types of animal live together and help each other. This relationship is known as symbiosis.

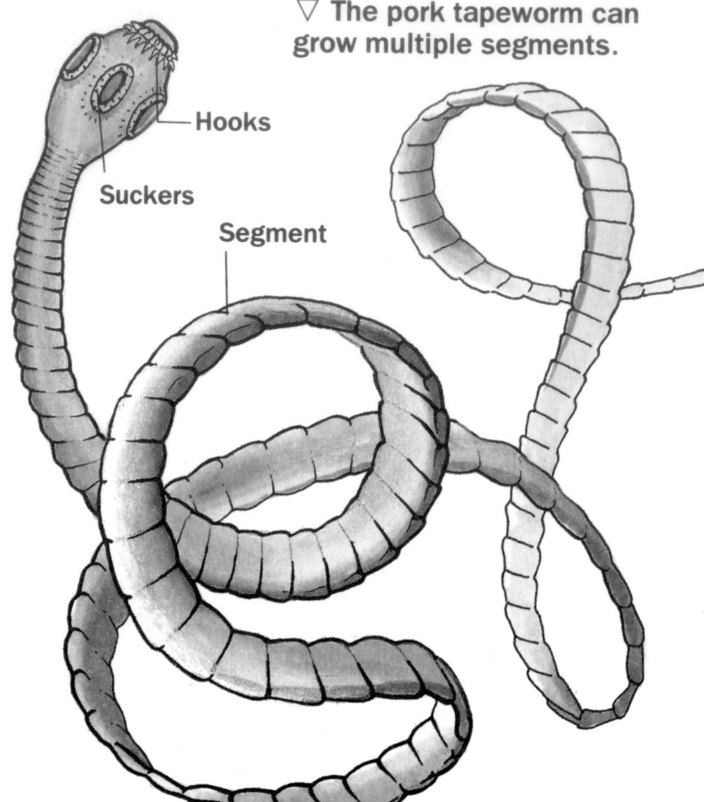

▽ The pork tapeworm can grow multiple segments.

BLOODSUCKERS

A number of insects, ticks and mites feed by sucking blood from larger animals. The insects include fleas, lice, bedbugs and mosquitoes. They all have special mouthparts for piercing skin and sucking blood. For example, the mouthparts of a female mosquito (males feed on plants) make up a long, thin tube. The labium supports the tube while the mandibles and maxillae pierce the victim's skin. The saliva duct then injects a special saliva that prevents blood from clotting (becoming solid). The mosquito sucks up blood through the labrum.

The action of sucking blood itself usually causes little harm to the host. But the saliva of bloodsucking insects can carry diseases that infect their hosts.

Leeches, a type of worm, also feed by sucking blood. They live mostly in water. Leeches attach themselves to their hosts with suckers around the mouth.

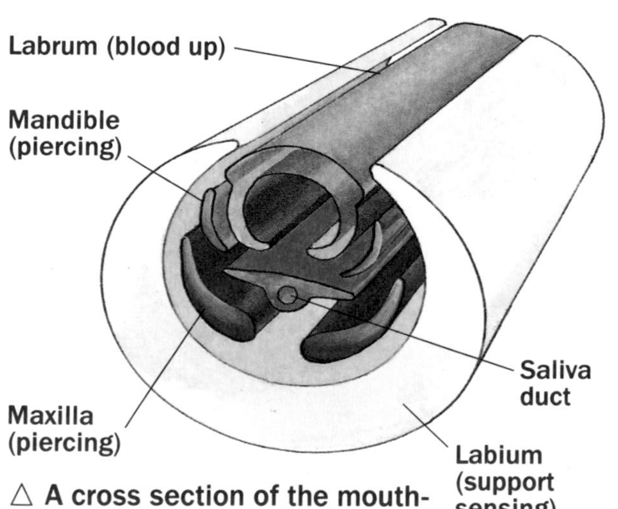

△ A cross section of the mouthparts of a female mosquito.

INTERNAL PARASITES

Some parasites live inside their hosts. Many of these parasites are worms. For example, the pork tapeworm lives in human intestines. It absorbs digested food through its skin. The head of the worm has hooks and suckers to hold on to the intestine. Some tapeworms can grow to lengths of over 33 feet. The pork tapeworm has a complex life cycle – as do many parasitic worms. Its larvae live in the flesh of pigs. Humans may be infected if they eat undercooked pork. There are many other types of tapeworm.

Flukes are another group of parasitic worms. They can infect many parts of a host's body, including the liver, lungs and intestines. Hookworms live in the intestines of animals. They are much smaller than tapeworms and suck blood from the walls of their hosts' intestines.

Some single-celled animals are parasites and cause disease. For example, plasmodia cause malaria, and some amoebas cause amoebic dysentery.

DID YOU KNOW?

Vampire bats drink the blood of birds and mammals. They have sharp teeth with which they cut the flesh of the animal before lapping up the blood. The bite causes little injury, but can spread disease. Vampire bats live in South America.

SAPSUCKERS

Some insects feed by sucking the sap (juices) from plants. These animals have mouthparts very similar to those of blood-sucking insects. Sapsucking insects include aphids (greenflies), plant hoppers, froghoppers, leaf suckers, and plant lice.

Many sapsucking insects can cause much damage to crops and so are serious pests. When such insects have been accidentally brought to new countries, some crops have been almost destroyed.

△ Ants protect aphids in return for honeydew.

SYMBIOSIS

Many animals share symbiotic relationships. A good example among fish is the cleaner wrasse. This small fish eats parasites and dead scales on large fish, such as the sweetlips. The sweetlips is a dangerous predator, but it even allows the wrasse to swim into its mouth. The large fish benefits by being cleaned, and the wrasse benefits by having a good supply of food. Cleaner wrasses wait in particular areas so that large fish know where to go to be cleaned.

A similar example, but on land, is the crocodile bird. This bird feeds on the backs of crocodiles, keeping the crocodile clean and free from parasites.

△ The mouth of a sweetlips.

There is symbiosis between aphids and ants. Aphids produce a sweet liquid called honeydew. Ants feed on this fluid. In return, the ants look after and protect the aphids.

Intestines of herbivores (see page 246) and the bacteria within also have a symbiotic exchange. The animal gains by being able to digest cellulose; the bacteria have a constant supply of food.

Sometimes symbiosis seems to benefit only one of the animals. For example, a fish called the remora holds on to sharks. The remora is carried around and protected. When the shark catches prey, the remora lets go and feeds on scraps of the shark's food in the water.

Digestion is breaking down food so that it can be absorbed and used. Breaking down food involves mostly chemical actions on the nutrients. The human digestive system is used here as an example. It is quite typical of mammals, but is in many ways different from more distantly related animals.

THE DIGESTIVE SYSTEM

Digestion starts in the mouth. Here food is broken up by chewing and mixed with saliva. The saliva makes food easier to swallow and contains an enzyme.

Enzymes are catalysts. A catalyst is a substance that makes a chemical reaction happen more quickly, but is not itself changed in the reaction. Digestive enzymes help the chemical breakdown of food. They make the chemical reactions happen hundreds or even thousands of times faster. It is mostly major nutrients (see page 238) that must be broken down into simpler chemicals. Minor nutrients (page 240) can usually be absorbed by the intestine without changing. All animals use enzymes to digest food.

The enzyme in saliva starts to digest cooked starch. It turns the starch into a sugar, which can easily dissolve. The food is then swallowed. Muscles in the esophagus move the food down to the stomach. Muscles move food all the way through the digestive system.

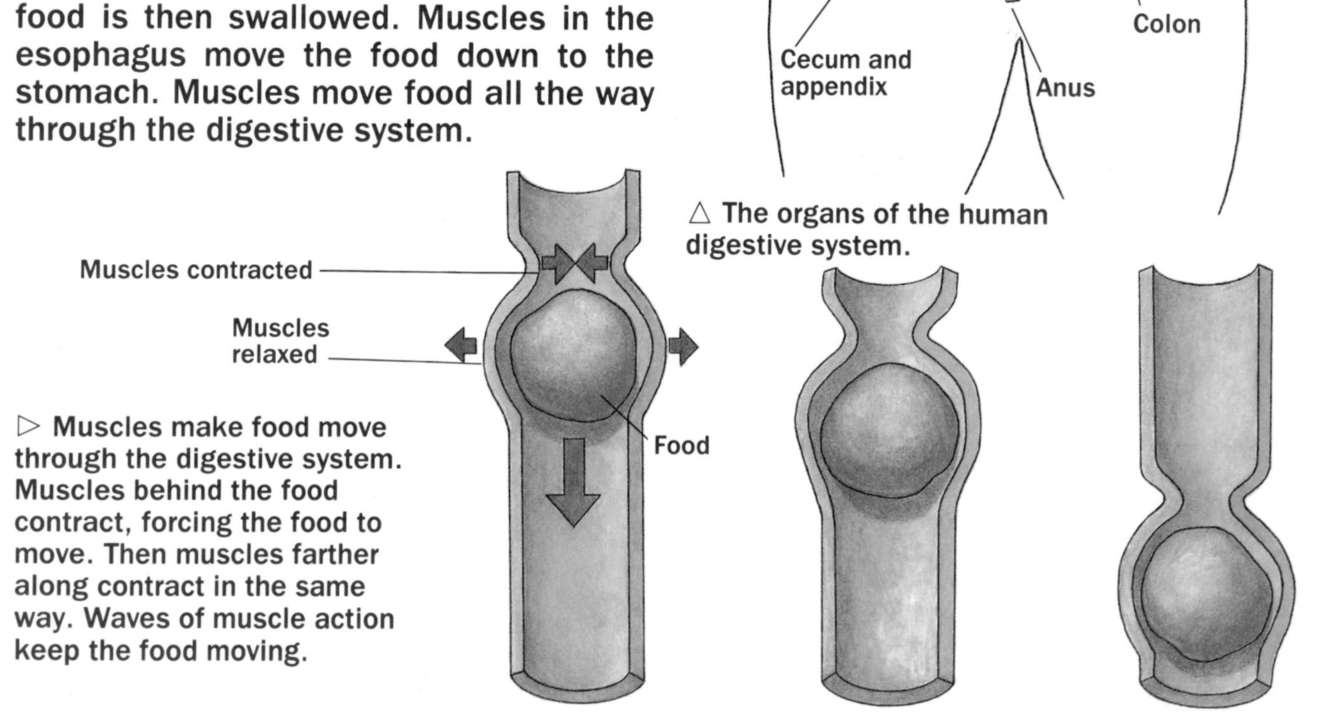

△ The organs of the human digestive system.

▷ Muscles make food move through the digestive system. Muscles behind the food contract, forcing the food to move. Then muscles farther along contract in the same way. Waves of muscle action keep the food moving.

▽ The stomach is made up of layers of muscles. The lining produces acid and enzymes.

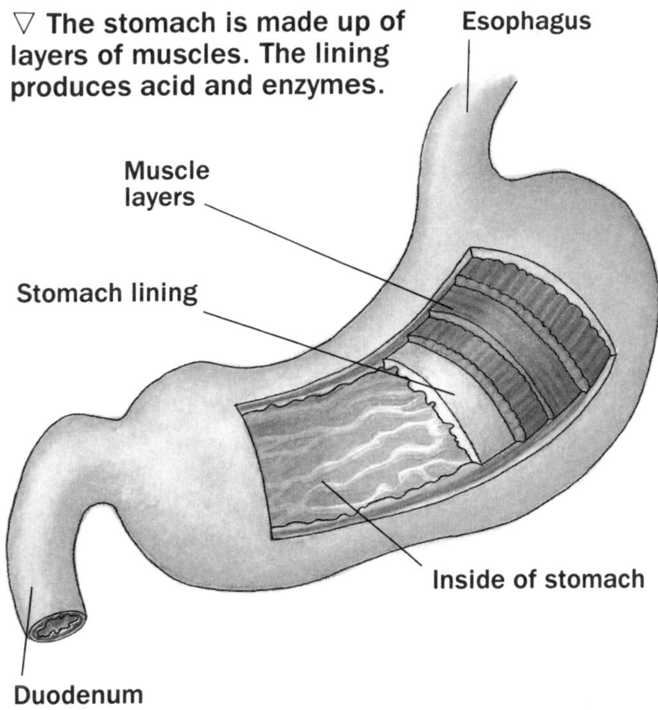

EXPERIMENT

Bile from the liver lets oils and fats mix with water more easily. Detergents have much the same effect. Fill a glass about half full of water. Add about three teaspoonsful of cooking oil (use some that is going to be thrown away). Mix the water and oil with a spoon. After a while, the oil will float to the surface. Now add a drop or two of dishwashing liquid. Mix again, and the water and oil will stay mixed.

The stomach holds food for between one and four hours. The stomach lining produces enzymes that digest proteins, and acid that helps the enzymes to work. Muscles around the stomach churn the contents. The churning mixes the contents and makes them more fluid. Muscles at the end of the stomach allow food through slowly to the small intestine.

The small intestine is where most digestion takes place. It is divided into two main parts. The first is called the duodenum. Digestive juice from the pancreas flows into the duodenum. The juice has enzymes that digest proteins, carbohydrates and fats. Bile from the liver also flows into the duodenum. Bile helps with the digestion of fats.

The second part of the small intestine is the ileum. The ileum lining produces more enzymes to finish digestion. Most absorption of food takes place in the ileum. The lining has many fingerlike villi. The villi increase the surface area of the lining, which allows more absorption to take place.

The colon, or large intestine, absorbs water to form feces, but does not digest food. Feces leave the intestine through the anus. The appendix has little or no function in humans.

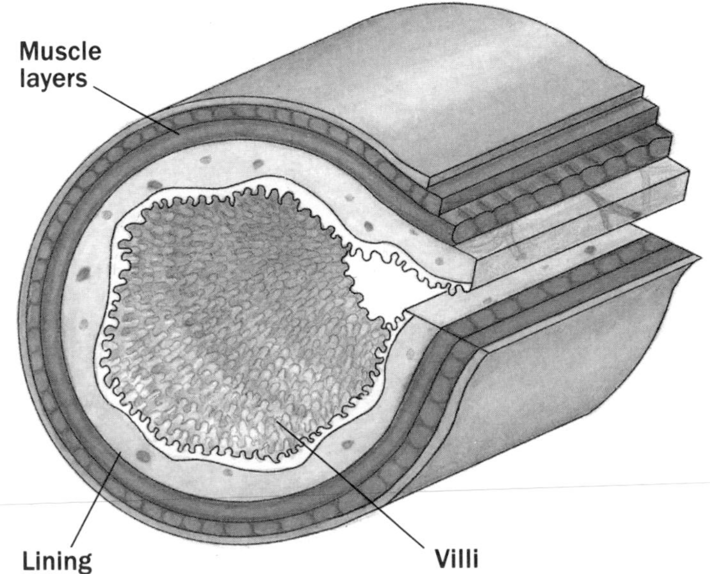

△ Like other parts of the intestine, the ileum has muscles that move food along.

DID YOU KNOW?

Food spends a different length of time in each part of the intestine. The times vary, depending on the amount and type of food. For example, carbohydrate food spends less time in the stomach than protein food.

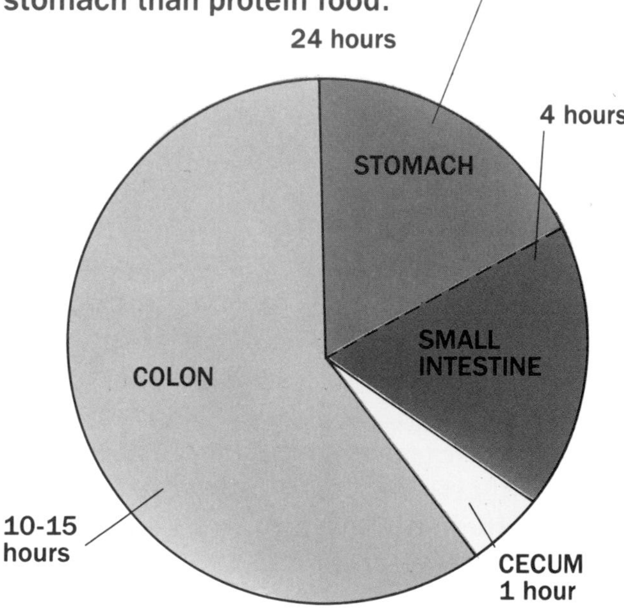

WASTE PRODUCTS

Some of the food that is taken in cannot be used or stored by the body. Also, when food substances have been used, the remaining chemicals may be harmful. Some substances taken in, such as alcohol, may be poisonous. The removal of waste products and dangerous substances is known as excretion.

Proteins are not stored. If there is more protein than necessary in a meal, the extra is converted to carbohydrate. This conversion creates a by-product called urea that must be excreted.

The body converts other materials that it does not need into substances that can be excreted, including substances similar to urea and chemical salts. Most of the conversions take place in the liver.

The main organs of excretion are the two kidneys. They act as a kind of filter for the blood. The kidneys extract urea and similar substances, water and salts. These substances leave the body with water as urine.

STORAGE

Animals often absorb more food during digestion than they need right away. Animals store extra carbohydrates and fats, and some vitamins and minerals.

Digestion converts all carbohydrates to glucose (or similar sugars). If the body does not use glucose immediately, the liver and muscles convert it to a substance called glycogen. The body can change glycogen quickly back to glucose when it is needed. Only a small amount of glycogen is stored. Any more extra glucose is converted to fat.

Fats are stored as globules of fat in special fat cells. There are fat cells in most organs of the body and especially under the skin. The body can store very large amounts of fat. The fat acts as a long-term energy store.

△ Stored fat seen with a powerful miscroscope.

PROJECT

When you cut an apple, the cut surface turns brown after a while. This is the result of an enzyme-controlled reaction. The reaction takes place with air. Enzymes are very sensitive to acidity. If the acidity is wrong, they will not work. Ask an adult for a knife and cut an apple in half. Rub the cut surface of one half with lemon juice (which is acidic). Leave the apple for half an hour. The half with lemon juice will not have turned brown. Now eat the apple!

△ Penguins give their young partly-digested food.

Crop

Gizzard

Liver

Intestine

▷ Birds have crops and gizzards; mammals do not.

VARIATIONS

Animal digestive systems vary. Amoebas (page 244) have no real digestive system. Simple animals, such as jellyfish, have a gut but with no different parts. More complex animals, such as insects, have digestive systems with several sections. Animals such as fish, reptiles and birds have systems with many or most of the parts that humans have. They may also have parts that humans do not have.

Birds, for example, have a crop in which food is stored. Birds also have a gizzard, which is a muscular bag. It contains small stones that the bird has swallowed. The gizzard churns food and the stones together to break up the food. The digestive system of some young birds is poorly developed. The adult birds feed the young with partly digested food.

Mammals – such as dogs, cats, rabbits and sheep – have digestive systems with all the parts of a human system. Sometimes parts are larger or smaller. For example, a rabbit has a much larger cecum and appendix (page 246). Another example, is the extra "stomachs" of ruminants (page 247), which are really pouches in the esophagus.

DID YOU KNOW?

The caterpillar of a cinnabar moth feeds on ragwort. Instead of excreting poison from the ragwort, it keeps the poison in its body to put off predators.

Animals need energy for everything they do. They need it for such things as movement, but also for all the chemical reactions in the body. Animals get energy from food. The amount of food they need depends on the kind of body they have and on their behavior. Some animals also need to store large amounts of food.

△ Shrews need to eat very large amounts of food.

ENERGY NEEDS

An animal that is very active uses up more energy than one that is not moving. For example, a bird uses much more energy while flying than if it is sitting on its nest. An animal that uses a lot of energy during a day needs to eat more food than one that uses little energy. For example, a human sitting down all day might need to eat food containing 10,000 joules of energy; somebody doing physical work all day might need 15,000 joules. You may have noticed that you are more hungry if you have been playing sports than if you have been watching television all day.

Mammals and birds use energy to keep their bodies warm. Other animals rely mostly on heat from their surroundings. Small mammals and birds need more energy to keep warm than large animals need. This is because a small animal has a larger surface area in relation to its volume. A large surface area means that an animal loses heat quickly. As a result, a shrew may eat more than three times its own body weight in food every day; an elephant eats only a small part of its own weight in food each day.

Some animals eat large meals for other reasons. Eating a very large meal means that an animal does not have to use energy to find more food for a long time. The disadvantage is that it may be so full that it can hardly move! Some blood-sucking animals eat very large meals. For example, leeches can suck more than their body weight of blood in one meal. This is largely because leeches only rarely find hosts.

◁ Some large snakes can swallow a whole antelope. Part of the reason is that snakes do not have teeth that can break up prey. But an enormous meal gives a snake a huge supply of energy that will last it for a long period of time.

ENERGY SUPPLIES

Animals need to store food for times when food is not available. Food for energy is stored mostly as fat inside an animal's body.

Animals need to store small amounts of fat to give themselves energy between meals. This is necessary even when there is plenty of food available because, for example, a lion might fail in its hunting for a few days. Fat may be stored for much longer. A good example of a long-term fat store is a camel's hump. Camels may not eat for many days in desert land.

Winter is a time when there is a shortage of food for many animals. It is common to build up supplies of fat during the summer. These supplies keep animals alive during the winter months.

Some animals, such as bears and dormice, hibernate which means that they sleep all through winter. When animals hibernate, the processes in their bodies (such as the heartbeat) become very slow. This not only means that they use up very little energy, but also that they do not need to look for or eat food. Animals that hibernate must build up large supplies of fat.

A few animals store food outside their bodies. For example, squirrels hide nuts and similar food. In the same way, bees store food in the form of honey.

△ Dormice and many other animals hibernate in winter.

△ A camel's hump is a large store of food energy.

PROJECT

You may eat a wider variety of food than you realize. Make notes of all the food you eat. Write down the ingredients of any mixed foods. You can get help with this by reading the labels on food packets or asking the person who made the food. At the end of a week, see how often you ate each kind of food. Find out if what you eat in a second week is very different or about the same as in the first.

encyclopedia of science

MOVEMENT IN ANIMALS

CONTENTS

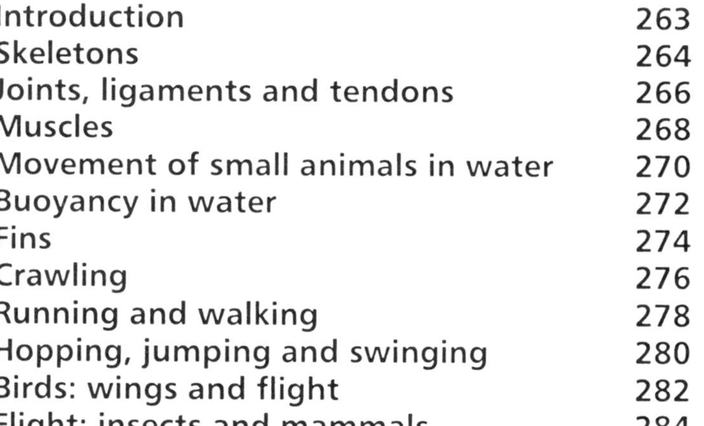

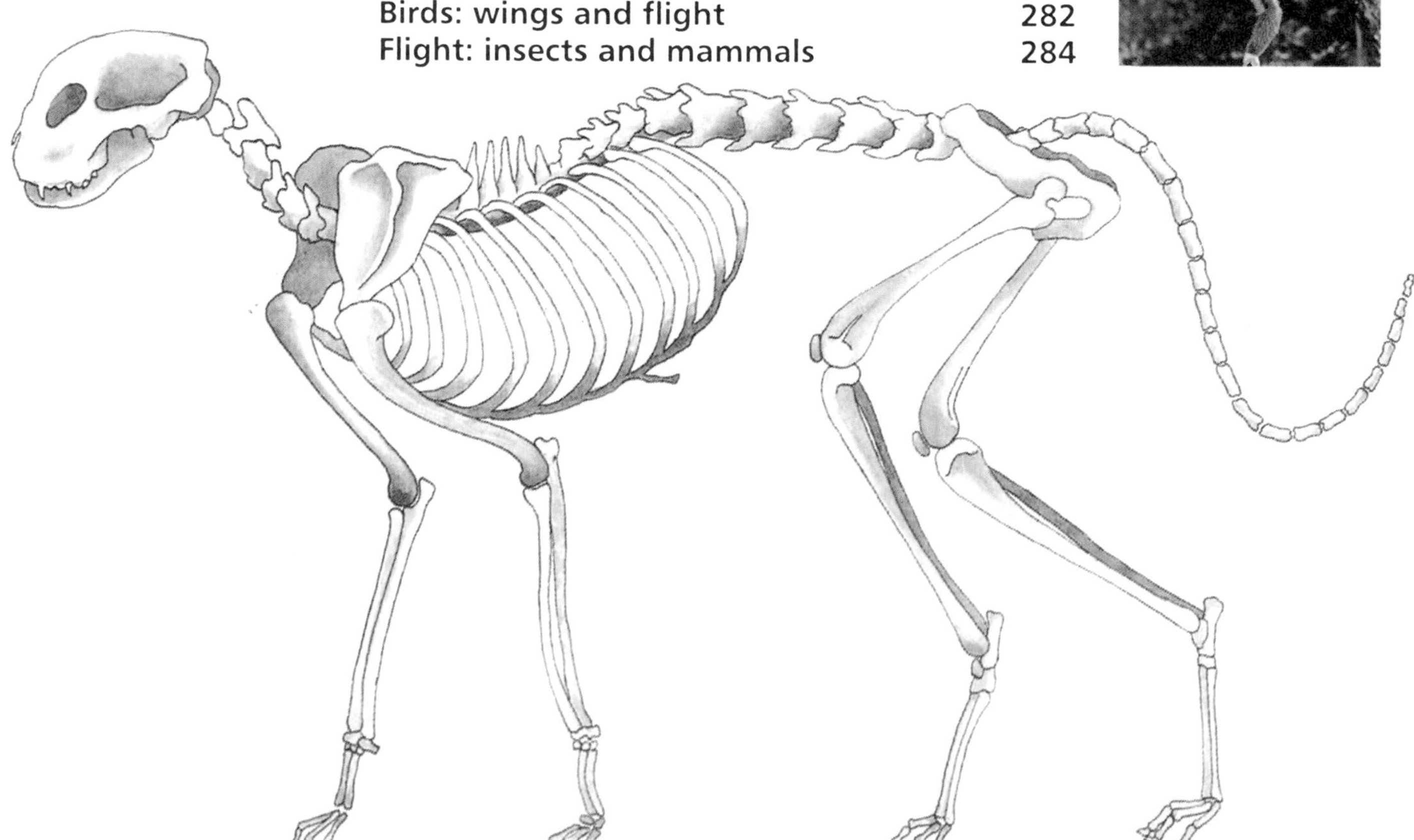

INTRODUCTION

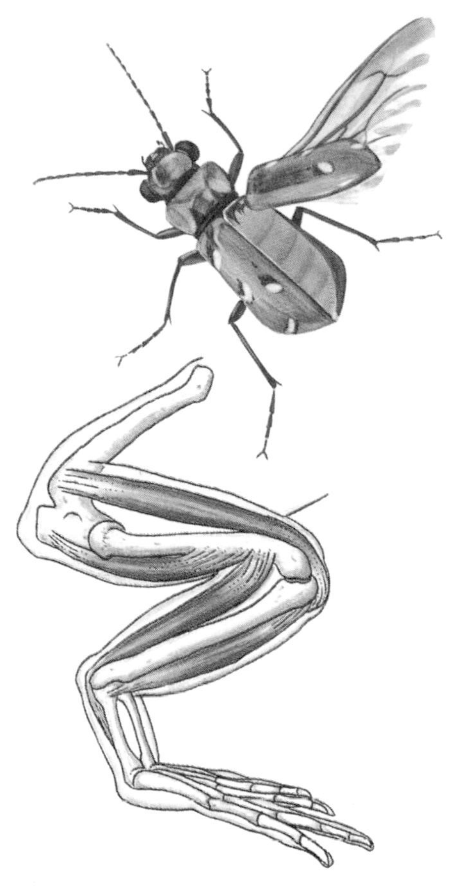

We can see movement all around us. In the living world (with few exceptions) only animals can move from one place to another using their own energy.

When you look at an animal, many of the things you first see are connected with movement. The animal may have legs, fins or wings. The animal's whole shape may help it to move. For example, a fish may be shaped to move easily through water. If you could see inside an animal, you would see many other structures to do with movement, such as muscles and bones.

There are many reasons why animals move. They search for food and water. They escape from danger and discomfort. They move to find shelter or a mate.

Animals move in nearly every environment on earth. They swim in the oceans, walk on land and fly through the air. To do this, animals have developed many, very varied ways of moving.

Skeletons have three main functions. First, they support the body of an animal and keep it rigid. Second, they are involved in movement. Third, hard skeletons can provide protection for delicate parts of an animal's body. There are three main types of skeleton: hydrostatic, external and internal.

HYDROSTATIC SKELETONS

Many soft-bodied animals, such as earthworms, have hydrostatic skeletons. A hydrostatic skeleton is like a bag filled with water: the outer layers of the animal's body surround a fluid-filled cavity. Water cannot be compressed (its volume cannot be made less by pressing). This means that if the outer layers of the animal press inward on the fluid, the fluid presses back and supports the animal's body. A hydrostatic skeleton helps with movement because muscles can push on different parts of the fluid, changing the body's shape. But a hydrostatic skeleton does not give the animal any protection.

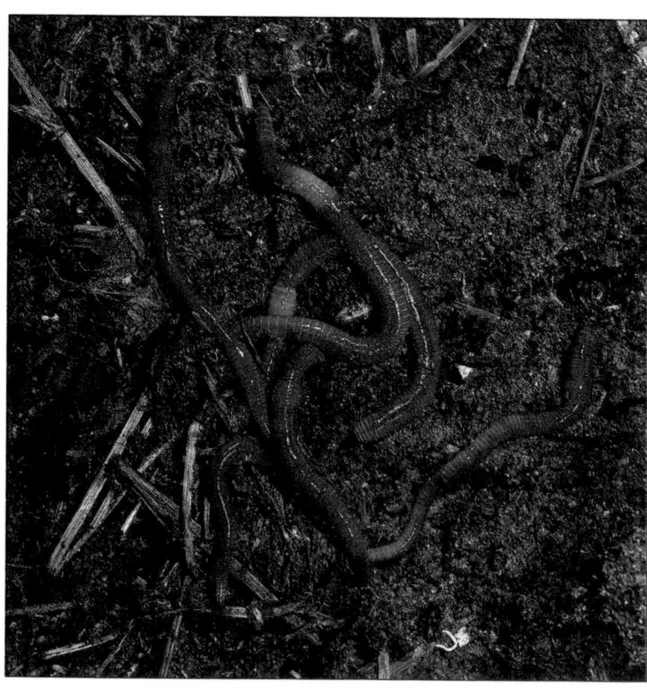

△ A hydrostatic skeleton supports an earthworm's body, and is also very flexible.

EXTERNAL SKELETONS

Many animals, such as insects, spiders and crabs, have external skeletons (known as exoskeletons). The skeleton covers the outside of the animal's body. Exoskeletons are made of a strong substance called chitin (pronounced ky-tin). They also contain proteins and calcium carbonate to make them harder. The skeleton is made up of three layers. The middle layer has spaces to make it lighter.

Exoskeletons do not bend easily and so provide support for an animal's body. Muscles for movement are attached to the inside of the skeleton. Exoskeletons give very good protection. But it is difficult for an animal to grow inside an exoskeleton because the skeleton itself cannot grow. The skeleton has to be molted and regrown from time to time as the animal gets bigger.

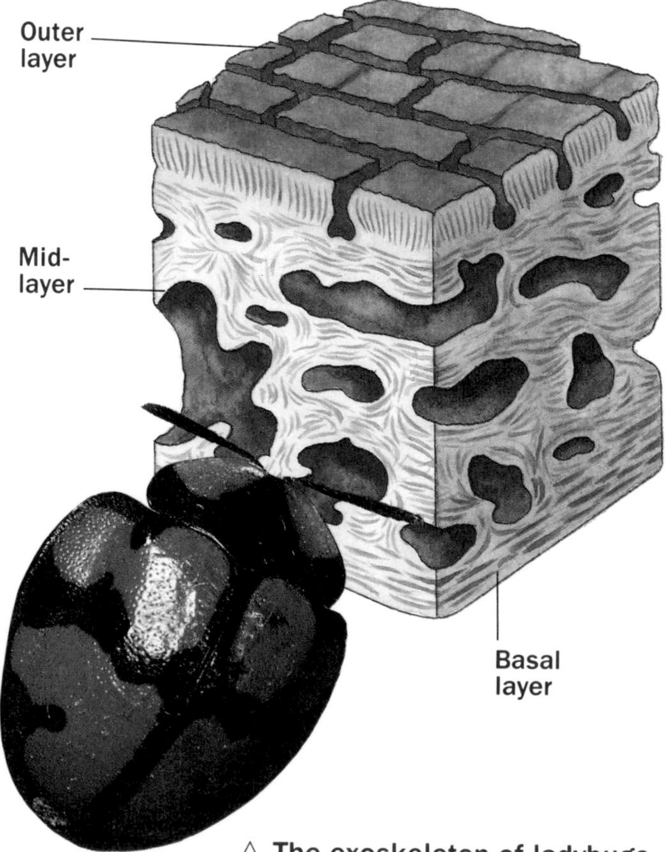

△ The exoskeleton of ladybugs and other insects is made up of three layers.

INTERNAL SKELETONS

Birds, fish, amphibians, reptiles and mammals all have internal skeletons (known as endoskeletons). Endoskeletons are inside an animal's body and are made of bone and cartilage (except for primitive fish like sharks, which have only cartilage). Bone is very hard and strong, and is made of 70 percent minerals and 30 percent proteins. Cartilage is similar to bone, but is made mostly of proteins and is softer.

Endoskeletons give support and help with movement in much the same way as exoskeletons do. But they provide protection only with special structures – such as the skull to protect the brain. Another advantage of endoskeletons is that they allow an animal to grow more easily – the bone just grows at the same rate as the rest of the animal's body.

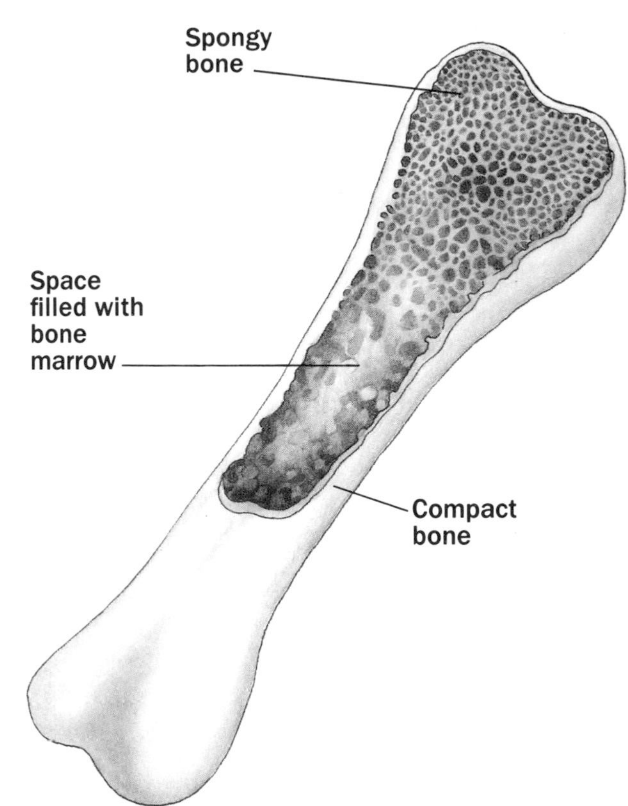

△ A typical bone has three regions. Compact bone is hard. So is spongy bone, but with air spaces. Bone marrow is soft.

▽ A mammal's skeleton (here, a cat's) has very many bones.

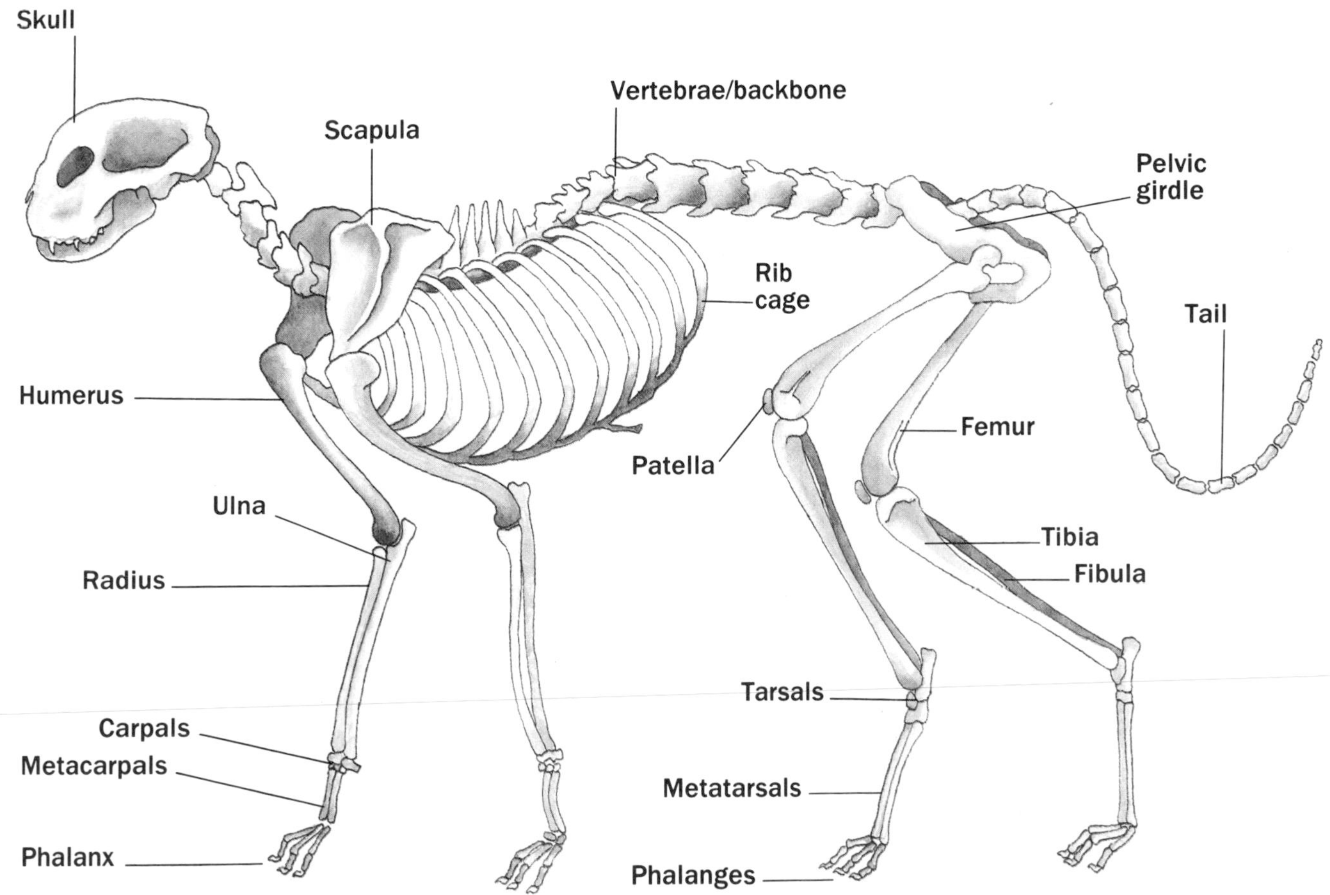

FEET

The bones in the feet of an animal reflect how it moves. A pigeon's feet help it to balance on two legs and to grip on perches. A frog has hind feet it can use in walking, but they are also shaped like flippers for swimming. A gorilla can stand on two legs, and the shape of the bones in its feet is quite like that of a bird. A horse stands on four feet, each with only one toe. Its feet are designed for running quickly, and not for balance.

▽ Many animals have the same set of bones arranged in different ways in their feet.

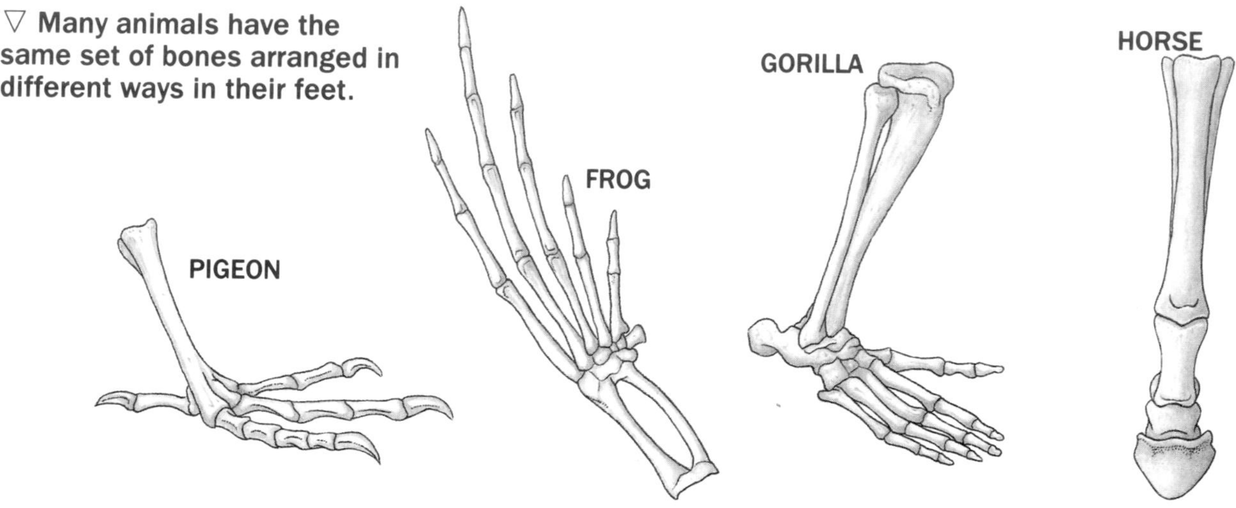

JOINTS

If an animal's skeleton did not have joints, the animal would not be able to move. A joint is where two bones meet. Some joints, known as fixed joints, cannot move (for example, in the skull). Most joints can move, however, and these can be divided into three main types.

Hinge joints are like a hinge on a door: they can bend in only one direction. An example in humans is the knee. Ball-and-socket joints allow movement in many directions. Examples are the hip and shoulder joints. The third type of joint is the pivot (or sliding, or slipping) joint. This consists of two flat ends of bone meeting. The two ends slide over each other, which allows a small amount of bending and rotating. There are examples of pivot joints in the wrists and ankles. (The joints of animals with external skeletons allow similar movements, but are made differently – see page 269.)

In joints, synovial fluid acts like oil for pads of cartilage that protect the bones from wear and tear.

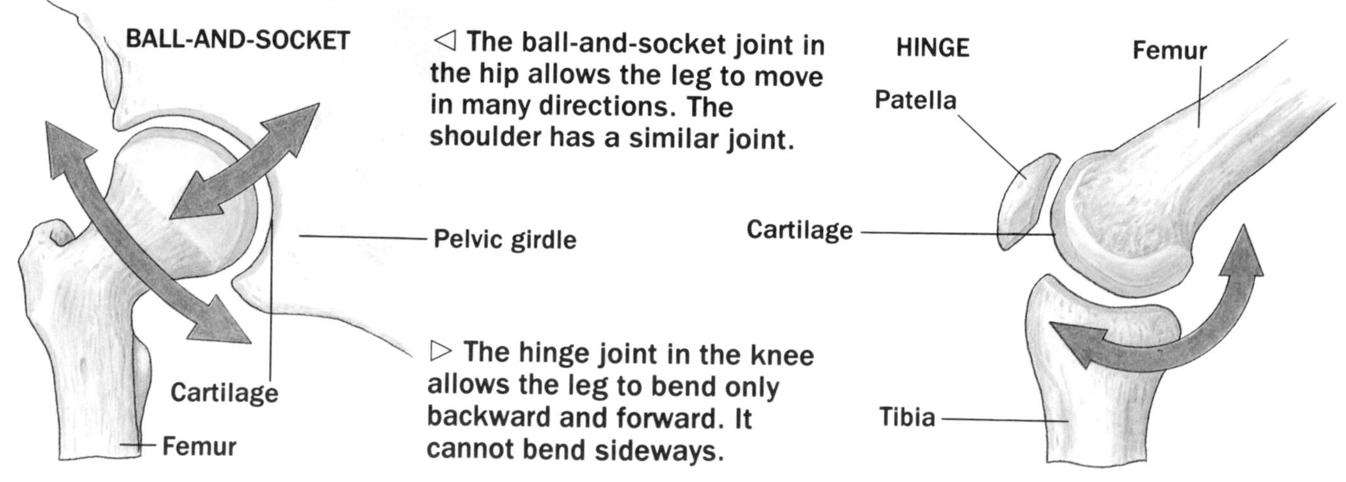

◁ The ball-and-socket joint in the hip allows the leg to move in many directions. The shoulder has a similar joint.

▷ The hinge joint in the knee allows the leg to bend only backward and forward. It cannot bend sideways.

LIGAMENTS AND TENDONS

Like cartilage, ligaments and tendons are made mostly of protein. The cartilage in a joint prevents the ends of the bones from being damaged by rubbing against each other. The ligaments hold the ends of the bones together. Ligaments are cords, bands or sheets of tissue that surround a joint. They are strong, but quite elastic to allow the joint to move. Some joints have one sheet of ligament surrounding the whole joint.

Tendons connect muscles to bones. Muscles that bring about movement must be connected to bones because they need something to pull against. The connection is usually close to a joint. Tendons are very strong, but much less elastic than ligaments. It would not help an animal to move if, when a muscle pulled, it merely stretched a tendon.

▽ The knee is a complicated joint, surrounded by many ligaments and tendons.

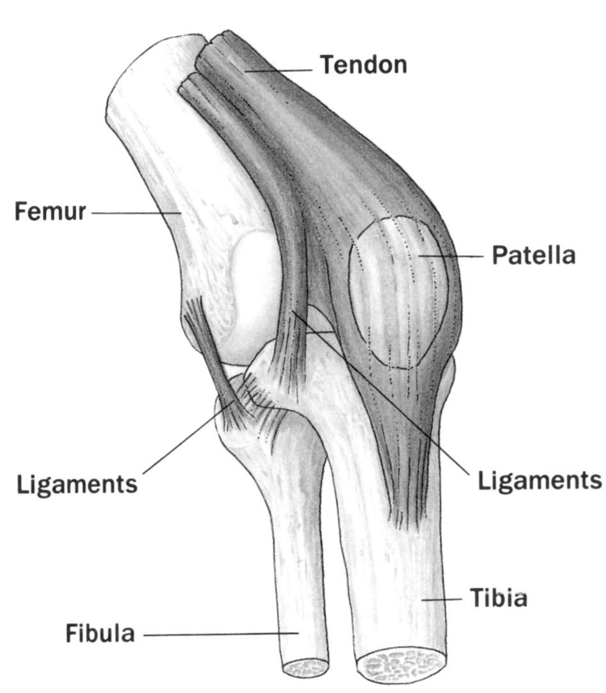

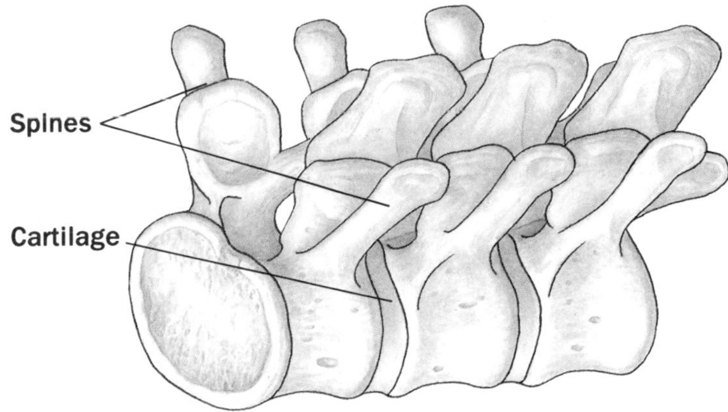

◁ The bones of the backbone are connected by pivot joints. In four-legged animals, there are spines sticking up from the backbone. These are connected by ligaments. The ligaments are like the girders of a bridge and give the backbone extra strength.

EXPERIMENT

Get an adult to help you cut three corks in half across their middles. Cut a piece of thick cardboard about 4 inches long and 1 inch wide. Glue a piece of cork in place at each end. Put the "bridge" on a flat surface, and press down in the middle. How easily does it bend? Now make the structure shown in the second diagram, using glue. Press down in the middle again. How easily does it bend this time? This structure is like the bones and ligaments in the spine of a four-legged animal.

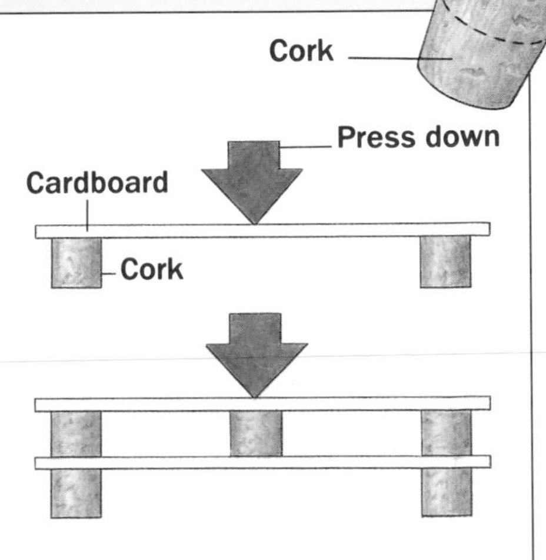

Muscles produce movement in animals. Most animals have large numbers of muscles. Muscles carry out work by contracting (getting shorter). There is more than one type of muscle – for example, in mammals, heart muscle is a special type. The muscles that produce movement are known as skeletal muscles.

STRUCTURE

Muscles are made mostly of three types of protein. These proteins together make up muscle fibrils. If you look at a fibril using a microscope, you can see light and dark bands. Each band is made largely of one type of protein. When the fibril contracts, chemical actions pull these bands of protein together so that they overlap. The fibril becomes shorter. This process uses up energy.

The fibrils are bundled together to make muscle fibers. Each fiber is in many ways like a cell, but has more than one nucleus. The fibers are bundled together to make larger bundles, which in turn make up the complete muscle. Each bundle is surrounded by a membrane (a thin sheet of connective tissue). At each end of a muscle, the membranes (particularly the outermost one) and the fibers connect to a tendon (page 267).

Muscle contractions are controlled by nerves. When a nerve message reaches a muscle fiber, the end of the nerve releases chemicals that cause the fiber to contract. Muscle fibers have what is called an "all-or-nothing response." This means that a fiber either contracts completely or does not contract at all. Differences in the distance a muscle contracts and the strength with which it contracts result from differences in the numbers of fibers contracting.

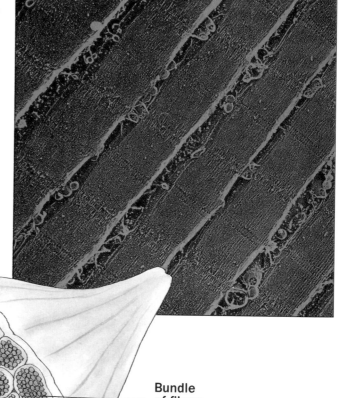

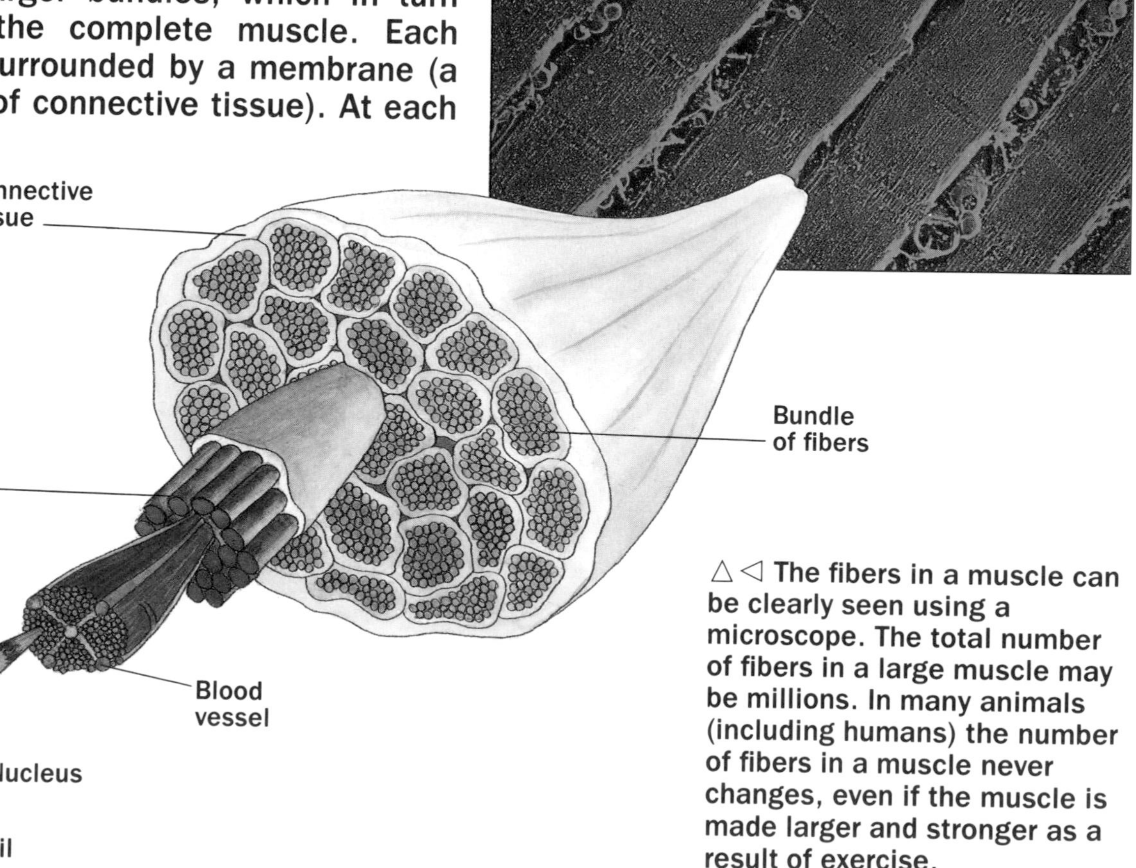

△◁ The fibers in a muscle can be clearly seen using a microscope. The total number of fibers in a large muscle may be millions. In many animals (including humans) the number of fibers in a muscle never changes, even if the muscle is made larger and stronger as a result of exercise.

HYDROSTATIC SKELETON

Circular muscle

Muscle along the body

Body cavity

△ With hydrostatic skeletons, the main muscles are arranged straight along the body and in rings around the body.

FUNCTION

The movement of skeletal muscles is controlled by the brain (except for certain "reflex actions"). Because muscles can only contract and relax, but not expand, they are usually arranged in pairs. Each one of a pair has an opposite effect. For example, the muscles at the front of the human thigh straighten the leg; the muscles at the back bend it. The bones that a muscle is attached to are like levers; a short contraction of a thigh muscle moves the foot a long way.

Muscles in animals with external skeletons work in much the same way as those in animals with internal skeletons. The muscles are still arranged in pairs with opposing effects.

In animals with hydrostatic skeletons, there is nothing solid for muscles to pull against. The muscles therefore pull against each other and against the pressure of fluid in the body.

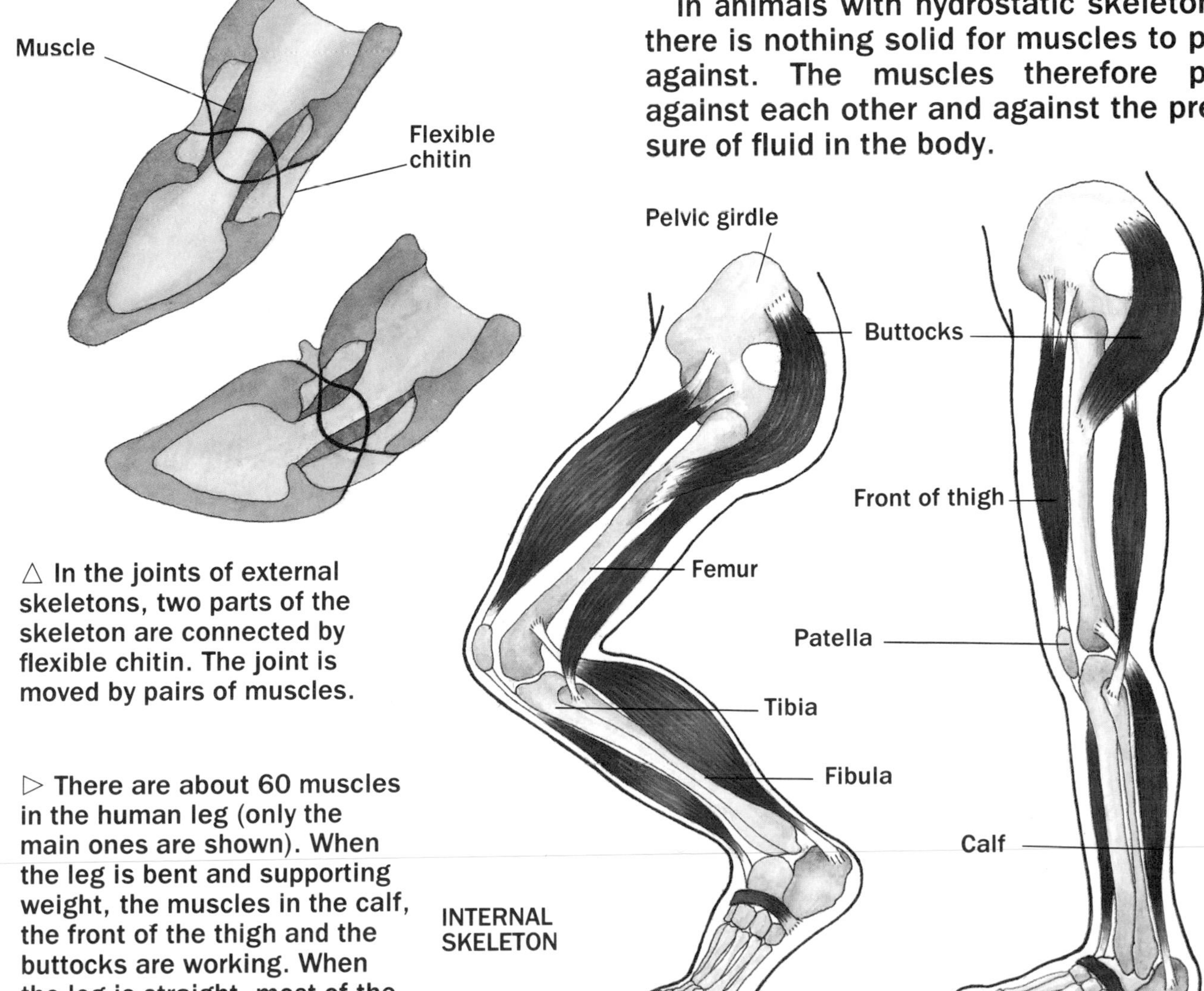

△ In the joints of external skeletons, two parts of the skeleton are connected by flexible chitin. The joint is moved by pairs of muscles.

▷ There are about 60 muscles in the human leg (only the main ones are shown). When the leg is bent and supporting weight, the muscles in the calf, the front of the thigh and the buttocks are working. When the leg is straight, most of the muscles are relaxed.

MOVEMENT OF SMALL ANIMALS IN WATER

The first life on Earth appeared in water. Many animals, including most single-celled and simple animals, still live in water. Single-celled animals do not have any sort of skeleton, or even any real muscles. There are three main methods by which they move: by amoeboid movement, with cilia or with flagella.

AMOEBOID MOVEMENT

A very simple form of movement is found in amoebas (which are tiny single-celled animals). Amoeboid movement relies on the fact that cytoplasm (the jellylike content of the cell) can flow into a tight space in the cell wall to form a projection which extends from the rest of the cell. An amoeba forms pseudopodia (which means "false feet") with its cytoplasm, and then draws the cytoplasm back and forms another pseudopodia in a different place along the cell wall.

An amoeba moves by moving its pseudopodia. Although amoeba live in water, most of their movement occurs when their pseudopodia are in contact with a solid object.

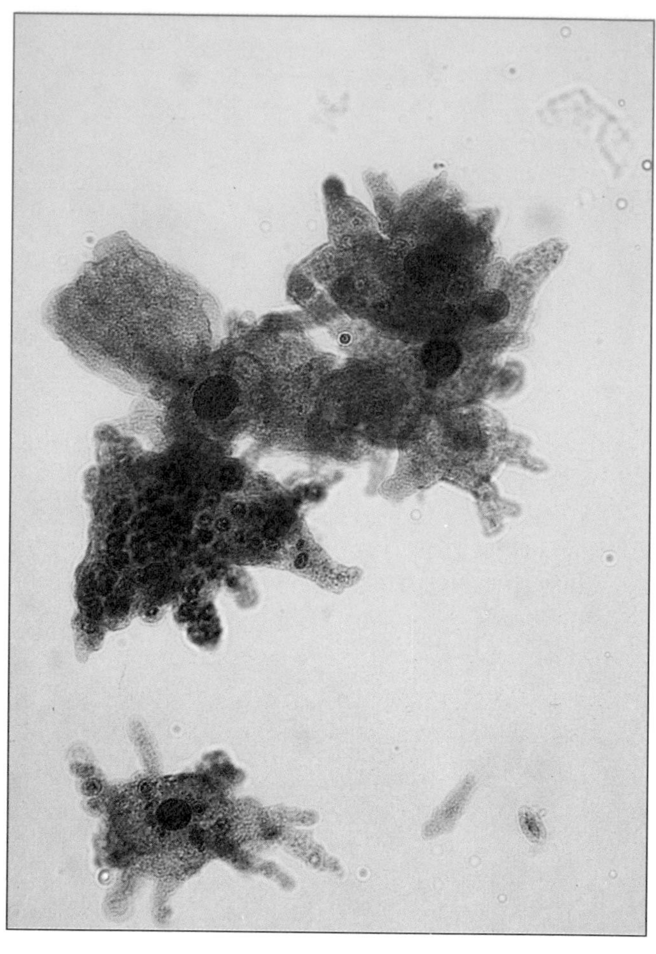

△ Through a microscope, it is possible to see several pseudopodia on all of this group of amoebas.

CILIA

Cilia are used for movement by many single-celled animals and larvae that live in water. Cilia are hairlike structures on the surface of a cell. Each contains filaments (thin strands) that contract to make it move. A basal granule controls a cilium's movement.

Cilia move an animal forward by pushing back against the water. To do this, the cilia become stiff and swing backward (the power stroke). After the power stroke, the cilia move forward again (the recovery stroke). During this stroke, the cilia are relaxed and so do not push against the water. Large numbers of cilia are arranged in patterns and work in a coordinated rhythm.

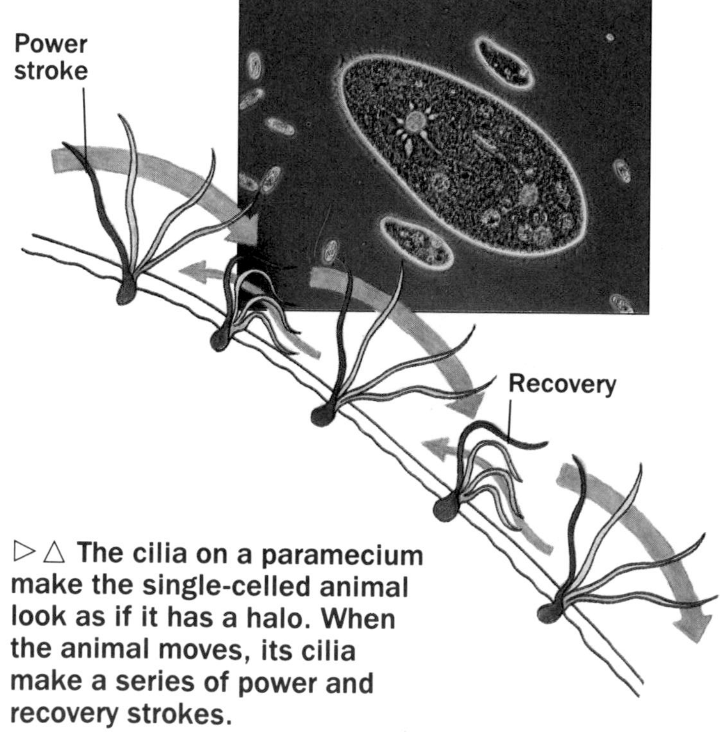

▷△ The cilia on a paramecium make the single-celled animal look as if it has a halo. When the animal moves, its cilia make a series of power and recovery strokes.

FLAGELLA

A flagellum is a long thread emerging from a cell. Flagella are like very long cilia. Their structure is similar, but most cells have only one or two flagella. Euglena is an example of an animal that uses a flagellum to move.

A flagellum can produce movement in much the same way as a cilium, by pushing backward against water like an oar. The movement of flagella is, however, often much more complex than this. A flagellum may move in waves (like an eel swimming), pushing the animal along. It may also have a corkscrewlike movement, which has an effect rather like that of a propeller.

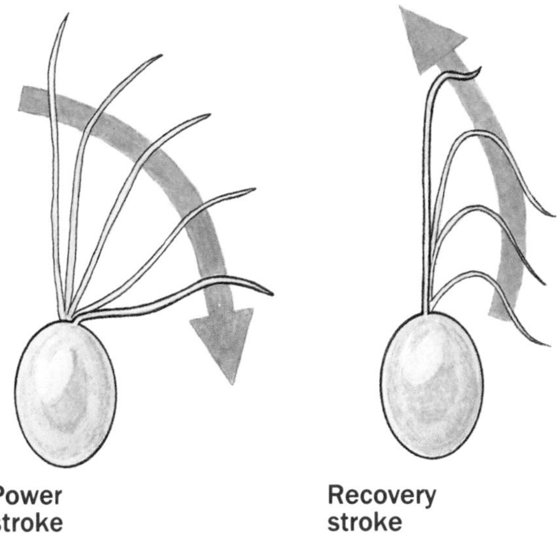

△ The basic movements of a flagellum include a power stroke and a recovery stroke, but are often more complex.

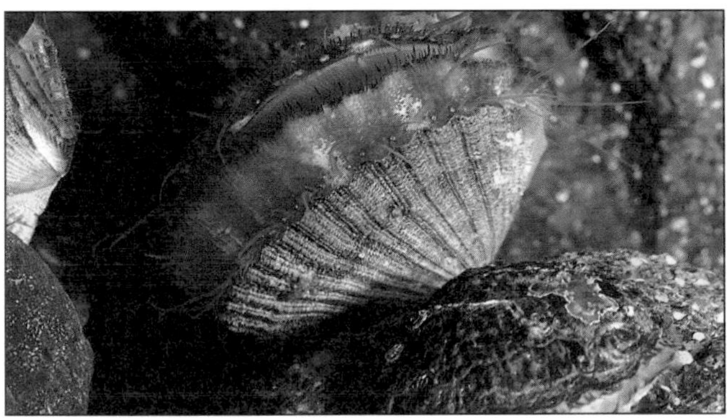

△ Scallops swim with an uneven movement.

JET PROPULSION

Some animals swim by shooting out jets of water. Squids, octopuses and cuttlefish do this by drawing water inside their bodies through a tube called a siphon. They then squirt the water out of the siphon, which pushes them along. They can point the siphon to control the direction in which they move.

Scallops, and some other two-shelled shellfish, move by clapping their shells together. When the shells open, water is drawn in. When the shells clap shut, the water shoots out again and the scallop moves along.

JELLYFISH

Jellyfish are not complex animals, although they may be quite large. They do not have skeletons, only a layer of rubbery material called mesoglea. Jellyfish are shaped like an upside down bowl or plate. They move by pulling the edges of this plate together. This movement pushes water down beneath the jellyfish, and so pushes the jellyfish upward. To move along, jellyfish swim at an angle, and so move diagonally upward. They then sink again a bit further along before pushing once more. This gives them a characteristic way of moving.

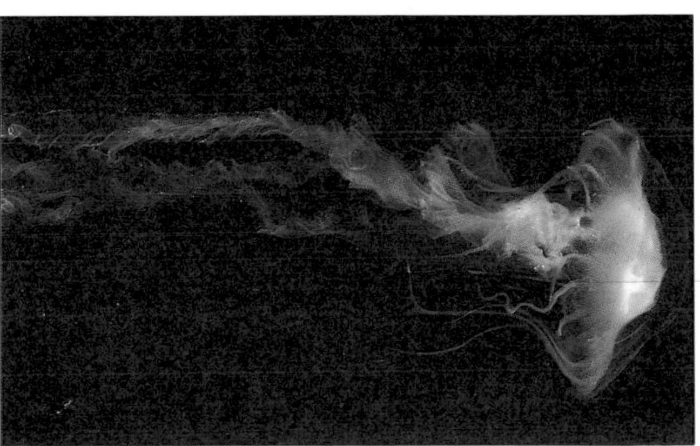

△ Jellyfish swim very slowly.

BUOYANCY

Buoyancy is the ability of a thing to float. The flesh and bone that an animal is made of are more dense than water, and so it is not buoyant. This means that, unless it has some way of floating, a fish has to keep swimming to stop it from sinking. Swimming all the time uses a lot of energy. Many fish have a swim bladder to stop them from sinking.

A swim bladder is sausage-shaped and filled with air. In some fish, the amount of air in the bladder is controlled by releasing and absorbing air from the blood. In other fish, the swim bladder opens into the throat. The amount of air in the bladder is controlled by taking in or letting out air through the fish's mouth.

Some other animals that live in water have different ways of floating. Cuttlefish, for example, have air-filled spaces in their cuttlebone.

EXPERIMENT

To see how a swim bladder helps a fish to float, you will need a glass bottle (or jar) with a screw top. With the bottle empty, screw on the top and place it in a sink full of water. Then fill the bottle one-quarter full of water and put it in the sink again. Now try with the bottle half, three-quarters and completely full. Then see if you can make the bottle float, but beneath the water's surface.

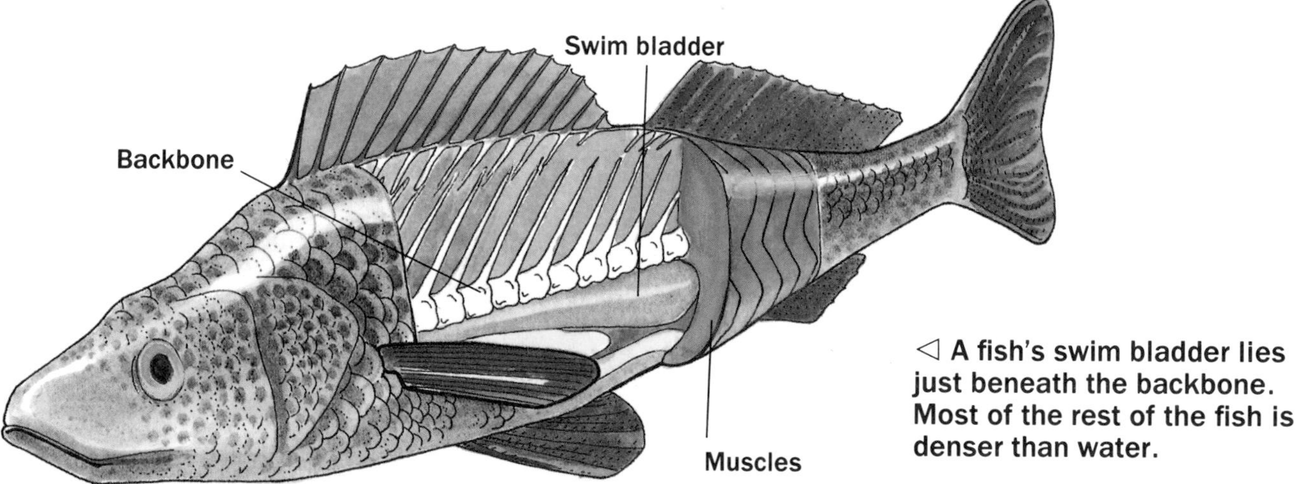

◁ A fish's swim bladder lies just beneath the backbone. Most of the rest of the fish is denser than water.

◁ Sharks and their relations do not have swim bladders. If a shark stops swimming, it sinks. A shark's fins are like small wings that keep it up in the water as it moves along. A few sharks that live in deep sea store a light, waxy substance called squalene in their livers, which helps them to float.

STREAMLINING

An object with a shape that lets water (or air) pass over it easily is streamlined. Streamlining is very important for fish. If they could not move through water easily they would waste a lot of energy and travel much more slowly. In order to be streamlined, most fish have a smooth, curved shape. They are often narrow in one direction, for example, across their bodies. Fins and other parts that stick out slope backward.

As well as having a streamlined shape, fish have skin that allows water to pass over it easily. Scales overlap and point backward rather than forward. And fishes' skin is often covered with slippery mucus, which again helps water to pass over it.

△ Most fish, such as the stickleback, are shaped to let water slide over them easily.

▽ Most fish are well streamlined, but the trunk fish has poor streamlining.

EXPERIMENT

You can find out which shapes are best streamlined. Cut three pieces of cardboard, about 6 by 12 inches. Make them into the shapes shown below. Use paper clips where needed. Move the shapes through water in the directions shown by the arrows. Which shape moves most easily? Which is most like a fish?

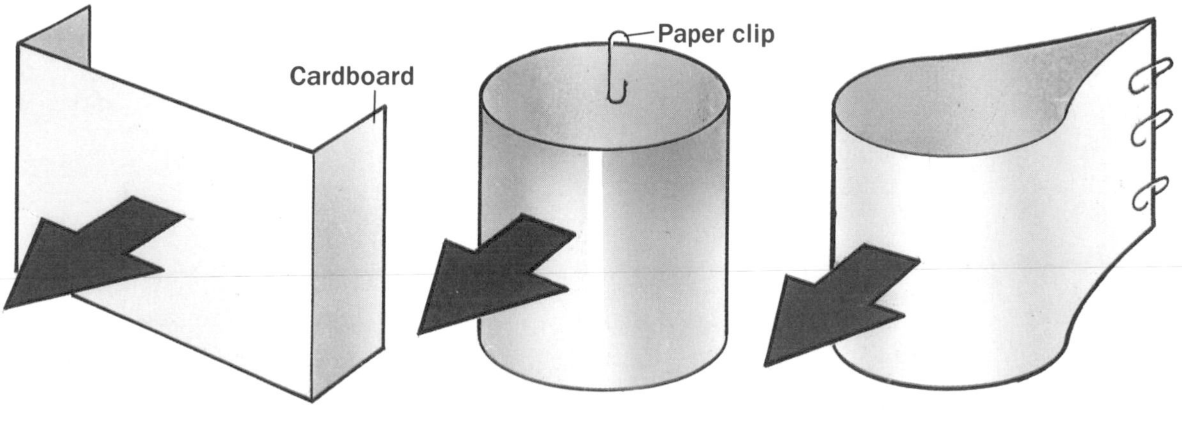

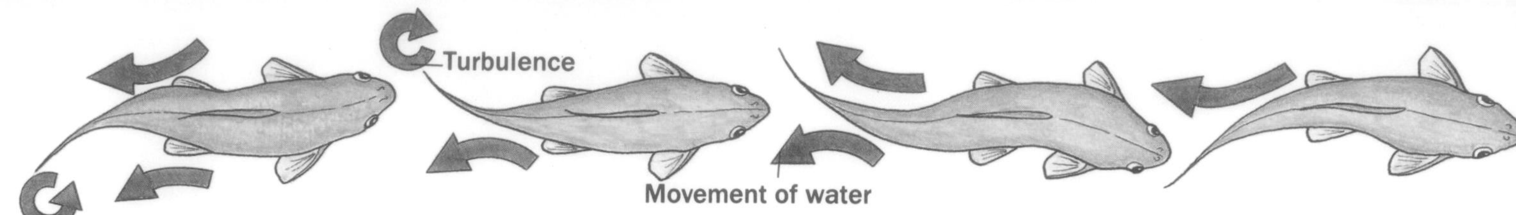

CONTROL AND MOVEMENT

Fish are not only efficient swimmers, but are also very good at controlling their movement in the water. To control movement and to keep themselves stable, fish use their fins.

There are three main ways that a fish can turn in the water. It can "pitch," which is turning up or down; it can "yaw," which is turning to the left or right; and it can "roll," which is turning over sideways.

Different fins are used to control each type of movement. The main functions of the dorsal and anal fins are to control rolling and yawing. The pectoral and pelvic fins are in pairs, with one at each side of the body. Their main function is to control pitch, although in most fish they also help to control rolling and yawing. In fact, the exact functions of each fin vary from one type of fish to another.

The tail fin is also involved in control, but its chief function is in helping with swimming forward. The main method of swimming that most fish use is undulating (waving) their bodies. As a fish undulates its body, water is pushed backward beside the fish, and the fish is pushed forward. The tail helps to increase the effect of the undulations. Some fish move mostly by waving the back ends of their bodies and their tails.

DID YOU KNOW?

Some fish use their fins as legs. Mudskippers live on mudflats and in mangrove swamps in Africa and Asia. When the tide goes out, they use their specially adapted pectoral fins to walk over the mud. Their tails drag along behind them.

▽ The fins on a fish control movement in all directions and keep the fish stable.

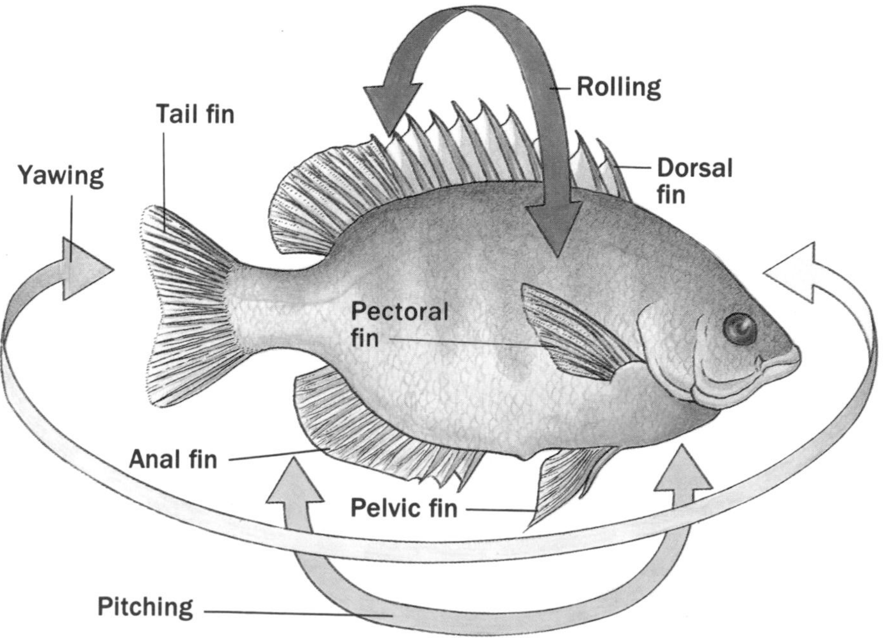

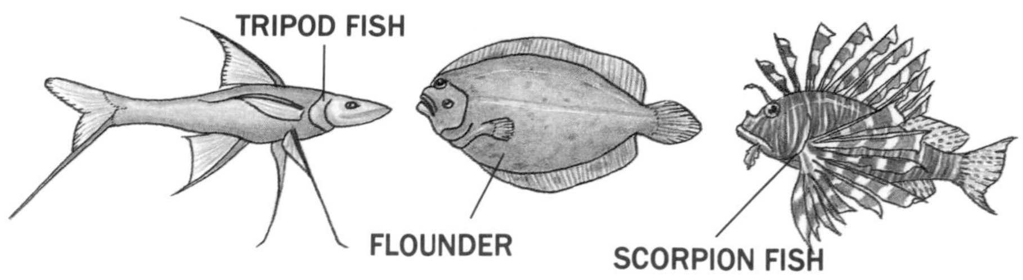

◁ Different fish have very different fins, but all fish use their fins to control movement – even if they use them for other purposes as well, such as camouflage.

◁ As a fish moves, water is pushed backward first on one side and then on the other. The pattern of undulation makes the fish move forward, not sideways.

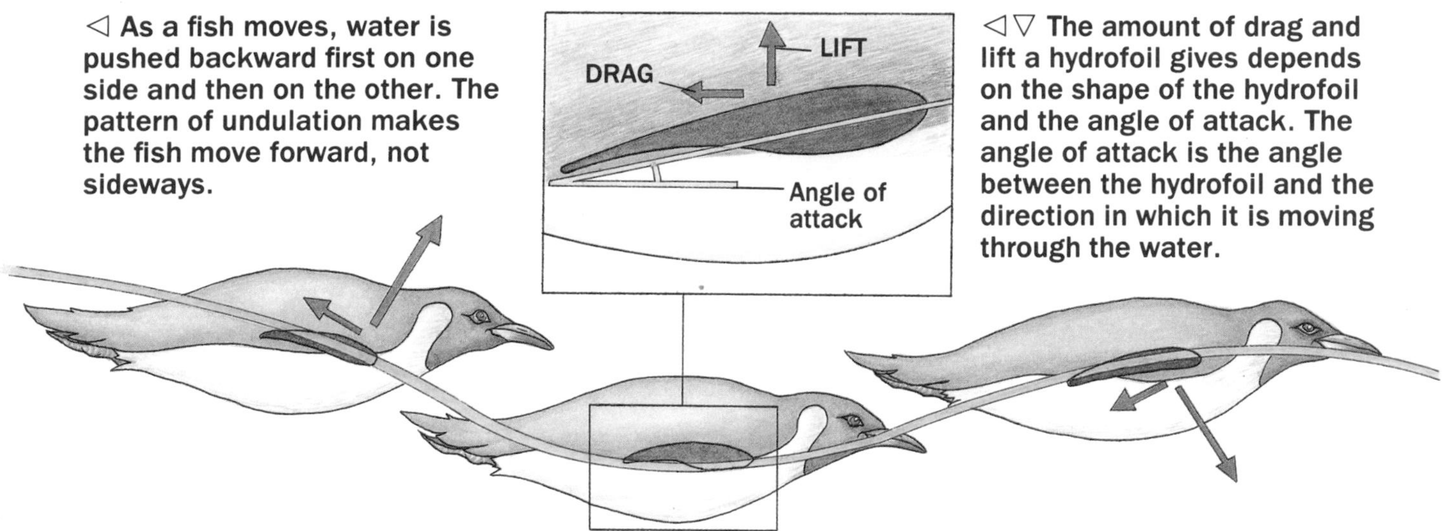

◁▽ The amount of drag and lift a hydrofoil gives depends on the shape of the hydrofoil and the angle of attack. The angle of attack is the angle between the hydrofoil and the direction in which it is moving through the water.

HYDROFOILS

Another way that animals move forward in water is with hydrofoils. A hydrofoil is like a fin, but stronger and moves the animal along in a special way.

An example of an animal that uses hydrofoils to swim is the penguin. As it moves through the water, it flaps its wings up and down (penguins cannot use their wings to fly). The wing works as the hydrofoil. As the wing moves, water passes over it. This causes forces to act on the wing in rather the same way as they do on an aircraft's wing. A small amount of drag slows the penguin down. But the biggest force is lift. Because of the angle at which the wing moves, part of the lift force is forward (the other part is either upward or downward). The combined effects of the overall shape of the penguin, the drag and the forward part of the lift move the penguin forward. A part of the lift is left over, so the penguin tends to move up and down in the water as it swims.

Other examples of animals that swim with hydrofoils include some fast-moving fish (such as tuna and marlins), which use their tails. Whales and dolphins also use their tails as hydrofoils.

△ The water beetle uses one pair of long legs as oars when it is swimming.

OAR PROPULSION

Another way that animals move through water is with an oar action. Many fish swim in this way when they are moving slowly or maneuvering carefully. They use their fins (especially the pectoral fins) as the oars.

The fins move backward, pushing against the water. This movement forces the fish's body forward. The fish then turns its fins sideways so that they can be moved forward without pushing against the water. When in the forward position, the fins are turned once more and are ready to push again.

Animals that live in water are supported by their buoyancy. Animals that live on land do not have this support and so they feel the full force of gravity. This means that land animals need stronger skeletons. If land animals have legs, the legs must be able to support their weight and have strong muscles.

CRAWLING

Many animals crawl on land without using legs. These animals include snakes, slugs and snails, and worms.

Snakes use two methods of crawling. The first method is curving their bodies into S-shaped curves. The back and front parts of each "S" press against the ground while the middle part moves forward. Series of curves pass along the snake's body. The second method is "walking" with the scales on their bellies and ribs. Some scales press against the ground while others move forward.

Slugs and snails move by sliding on a slippery mucus. The mucus becomes firm when it is pressed, so the animal can move by sending waves of muscle contractions along its belly.

Worms have hydrostatic skeletons, so can lengthen and shorten sections of their bodies. Some parts of a worm's body press against the ground while others become narrower and move forward. The parts that have moved then press on the ground, and other parts move. Most worms move in this way.

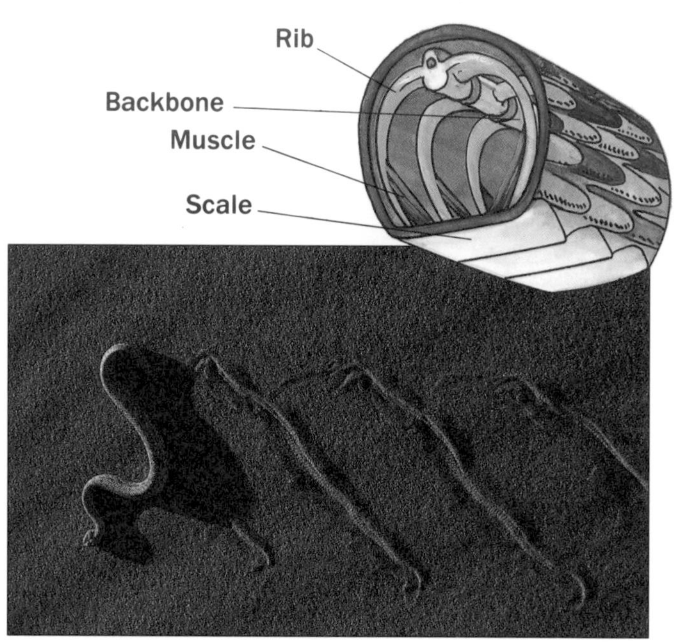

△ Sidewinders move sideways. The head goes forward then the body curves along behind, leaving strange tracks.

WALK

CANTER

DID YOU KNOW?

Millipedes and centipedes have large numbers of legs. Millipedes generally have more than centipedes – the species with the most legs has more than 700! The movement of all the legs is very carefully coordinated so that they do not get muddled up.

PROJECT

Try to observe the different ways that an animal (such as a cat, a dog or a horse) uses its legs when moving at different speeds. Watch especially for the order that it puts its feet down, how it bends its legs, whether the animal moves evenly or up and down, and whether its backbone curves.

▽ Some gaits of a horse, from slowest to fastest, are the walk, trot, canter and gallop.

ON FOUR LEGS

Most mammals have four legs, as do reptiles (except snakes and a few others) and amphibians. There are several advantages to having four legs. It is the smallest even number of legs on which it is easy to balance. An animal can use the whole length of its body to run with by bending its spine (this is very noticeable in the cat family). The weight of the animal is quite evenly supported.

There are many ways of moving four legs. The different ways are known as gaits, and the main difference is in the order in which the feet are put down. Most mammals use more than one gait.

A horse, for example, uses four main gaits, although it can use others. When walking, it lifts its feet in turn and puts them down in the same order. When trotting, it lifts feet at opposite corners, puts them down, then lifts its other two feet. When cantering, one back foot hits the ground, then the other back foot and the front foot on the opposite side together, then the other front foot. When galloping, all four legs hit the ground singly, first the hind then the front legs.

TROT

GALLOP

ON TWO FEET

There is one big advantage in having two feet for animals with four limbs. It means that only two limbs are used for walking, so the other two limbs can be used for something else. Birds use their other pair of limbs as wings. Humans have two legs because their other limbs have hands. Human hands are highly skilled and too delicate to be used for walking.

There are disadvantages in having only two legs. It is generally more difficult to run quickly. Another problem is that all of the animal's weight is on just two legs. But the biggest problem is balance.

Most birds cannot walk, run or hop very well (although some birds that do not fly can run very quickly). Most birds move using their wings, however, so walking well is not very important. It is more important for flying that their legs are light. Birds' feet stick out quite a long way from their legs to help balance.

Human feet also stick out from the legs, but are more complex than birds' feet. They have muscles of their own and take an active part in both balance and walking. Humans have only two normal gaits: walking and running. In both, the feet move in turn – first one moves forward, then the other. In walking, at least one foot is in contact with the ground at all times. In running, neither foot touches the ground between strides.

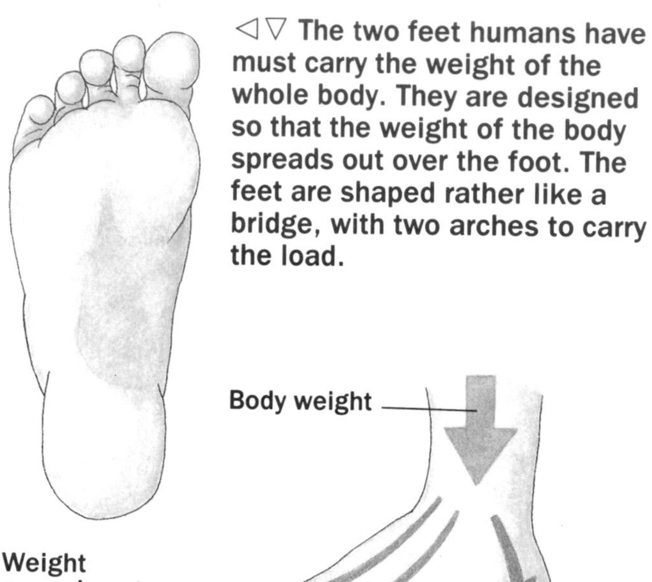

◁▽ The two feet humans have must carry the weight of the whole body. They are designed so that the weight of the body spreads out over the foot. The feet are shaped rather like a bridge, with two arches to carry the load.

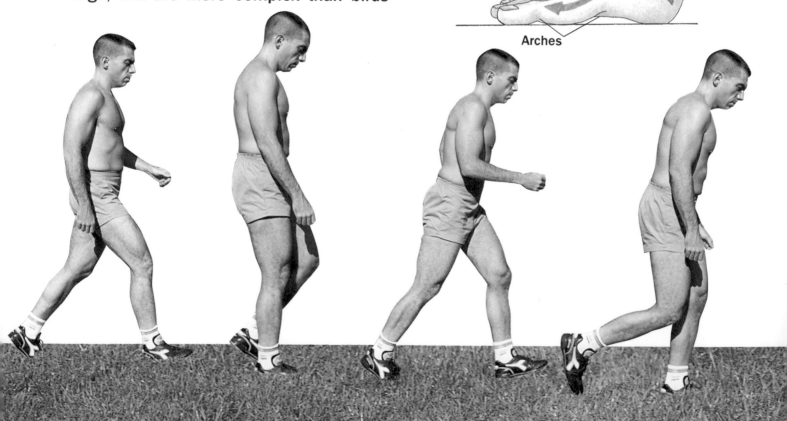

ENERGY

The energy in the body of a walking human is provided by the muscles in the legs. If human legs were perfectly frictionless wheels, one push would keep a person going for a long time. However, as people walk, their legs hit the ground, which loses energy.

The type of energy in a walking person changes during each step. When one leg is straight and vertical, the body has a lot of potential energy. This is because the body is at its highest from the ground. This is like a pendulum at the top of its swing, which has potential energy that will make it swing downward. When one leg is pushing and the other is stretched out in front, the body has more kinetic energy (energy of movement). This is like a pendulum at the bottom of its swing when it is moving fast. Similar changes in energy occur when a person runs.

▽ The amounts of potential and kinetic energy in the body change with each step.

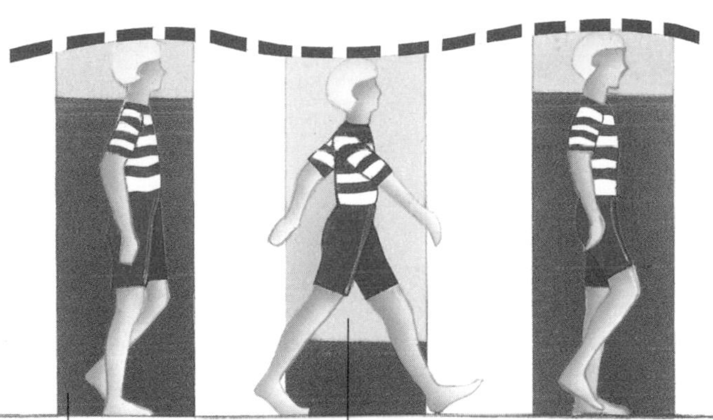

PROJECT

Humans have two normal gaits (walking and running), but how many other ways can you think of for moving along the ground? Try them for yourself. Are some very difficult? Do you find that most ways use a lot of energy for traveling a short distance?

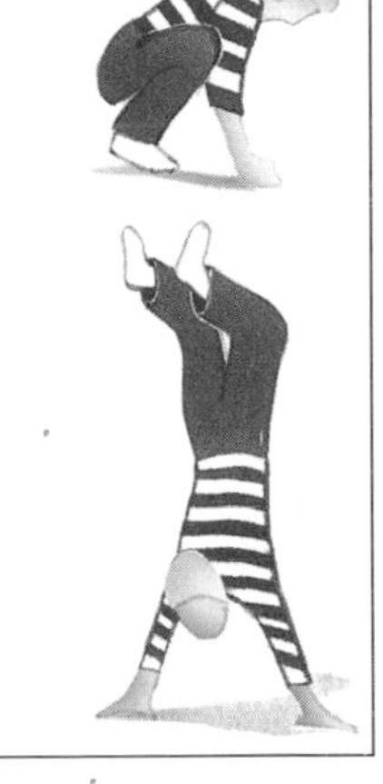

HOPPING

Hopping is moving along by jumping with two legs, and with both legs moving at the same time. Some hopping animals, such as frogs, can also walk on four legs – if not very well. But their main method of moving is by hopping.

Animals that hop need one pair of large, powerful legs – almost always the back legs. The hopping legs must be strong because they provide all the energy for movement. They must be large to carry large muscles, and also to provide long levers to push the animal forward.

Animals hop in different ways and for different reasons. Frogs have long back legs for swimming, which are almost "ready-made" for hopping. Frogs hop in single bounds, stopping between each hop. Frogs land on their short front legs.

Fleas hop to land on an animal from which they will suck blood. They cannot fly, so hopping is the best way to move quickly from one animal to another or from the ground onto an animal.

Kangaroos are very good hoppers. When they are moving fast, they can keep up a steady movement – without stopping between hops in the way that a frog does. Kangaroos use their short front legs to lean on when they are bending down to feed from the ground.

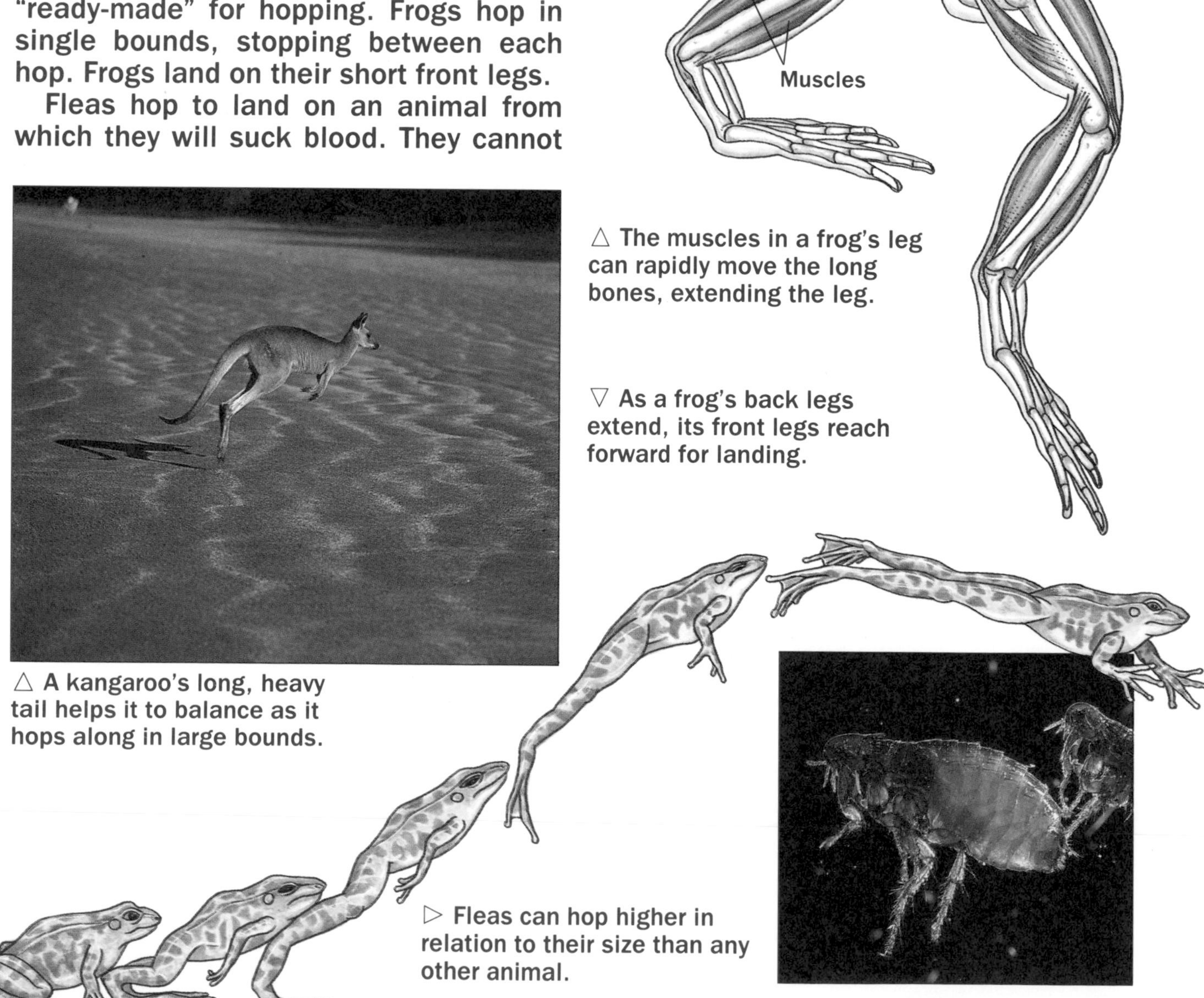

△ The muscles in a frog's leg can rapidly move the long bones, extending the leg.

▽ As a frog's back legs extend, its front legs reach forward for landing.

△ A kangaroo's long, heavy tail helps it to balance as it hops along in large bounds.

▷ Fleas can hop higher in relation to their size than any other animal.

DID YOU KNOW?

Ducks waddle as they walk. The reason is that their legs are arranged for paddling through water more than for walking. To paddle well, the legs are attached far apart on the body. This means that when a duck lifts one leg, it tends to fall over toward that side. To avoid this, ducks rock from side to side as they walk.

▷ A gorilla's foot closely resembles a human foot. Gorillas spend most of their time on the ground and often walk on two feet. A gibbon's foot has a very long "big toe." Gibbons spend most of their time in trees, and this long toe helps them to grip branches. A gibbon's hand has a short thumb. This is because they use the hand like a hook for swinging on branches, and a long thumb would get in the way. Gibbons often use their feet rather than their hands to hold small objects.

ON TWO HANDS!

Many monkeys and apes use their hands for moving. Also, their feet often resemble hands more than feet. The reason is that these animals spend a lot of their lives in trees. Their limbs are designed for gripping onto branches and moving through the branches.

Perhaps the most specialized tree-living ape is the gibbon. Gibbons move rapidly through the trees, swinging from branch to branch. A gibbon's hands are specially adapted for gripping quickly and firmly onto branches. Gibbons have long arms and legs to reach between branches and to give them a long swing. Their bones are quite thin to make their bodies lighter. This gives the hands less weight to support.

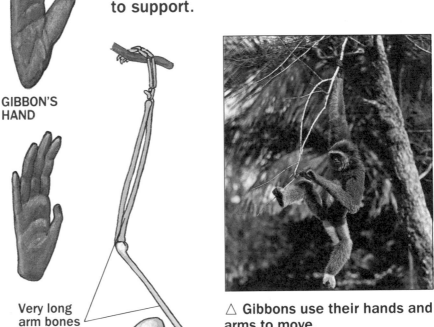

△ Gibbons use their hands and arms to move.

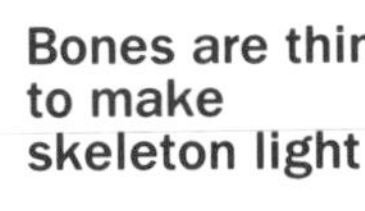

▷ The skeleton of a gibbon in many ways resembles a human skeleton, but the bones of the limbs are much longer to help it swing through the trees.

BIRDS: WINGS AND FLIGHT

Animals that fly have many special characteristics. The most obvious of these is wings, but there are other specializations. Flying animals often have light skeletons and a streamlined shape. Animals that use powered flight have very large and powerful muscles to move their wings.

△ A bird in flight.

WINGS

There are two main types of wing. The wings of bats and insects are made of skin or thin membranes (as are the flaps on gliding animals). Birds have wings made from feathers.

The bones of a bird's wing are basically the same bones as in the front limbs of other animals with a bony skeleton – although specially adapted. There are several types of feather, but a flight feather is made up firstly of a stem. The stem is rigid; one part (the quill) is embedded in the skin around the wing bones; the other part (the rachis) has barbs attached on two sides. The barbs are long, thin and flexible. They are linked together by barbules.

▽ The barbs of a bird's feather are linked with barbules. Some barbules have hooks and some are smooth. Powerful muscles attached to the large breast-bone move the wing.

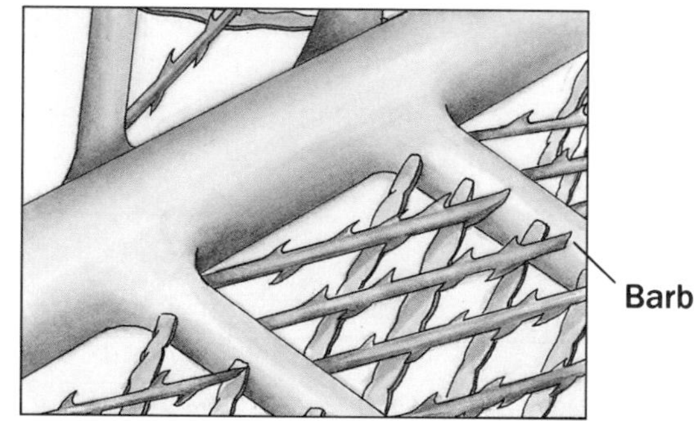

▷ The bones and feathers of a bird's wing form a complex structure.

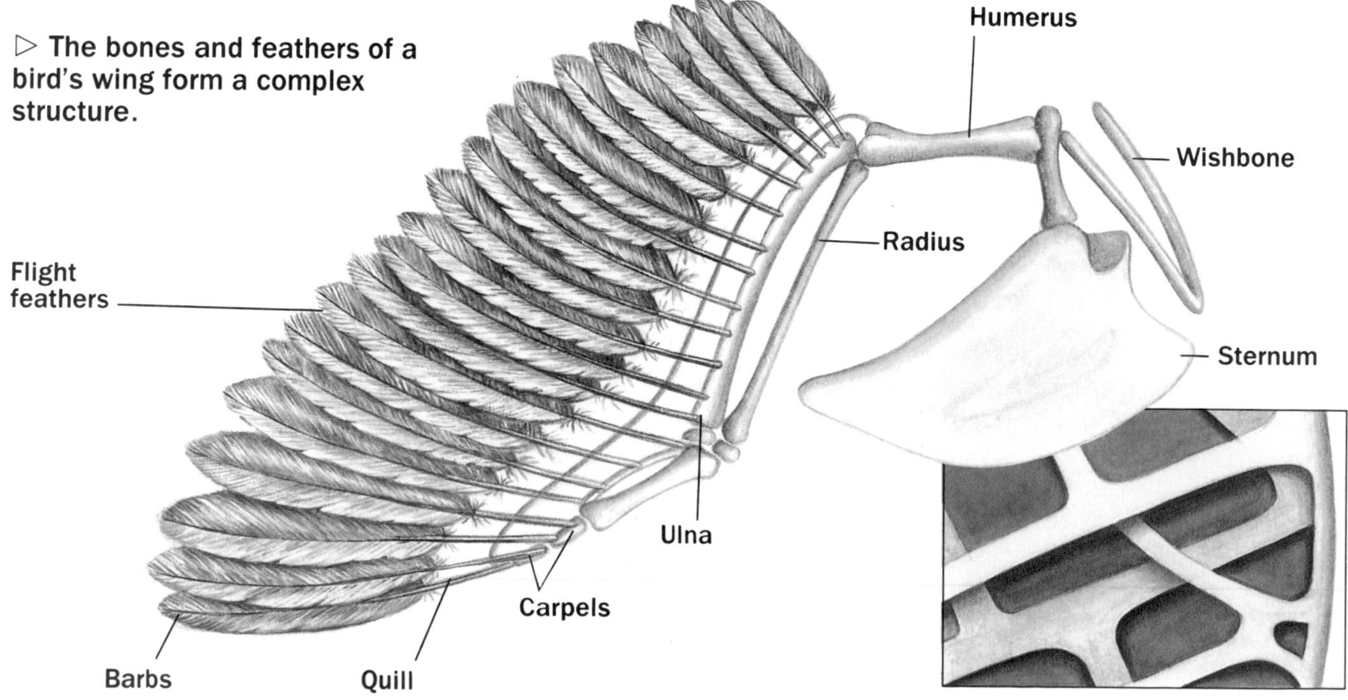

△ The bones of birds are made lighter by air spaces.

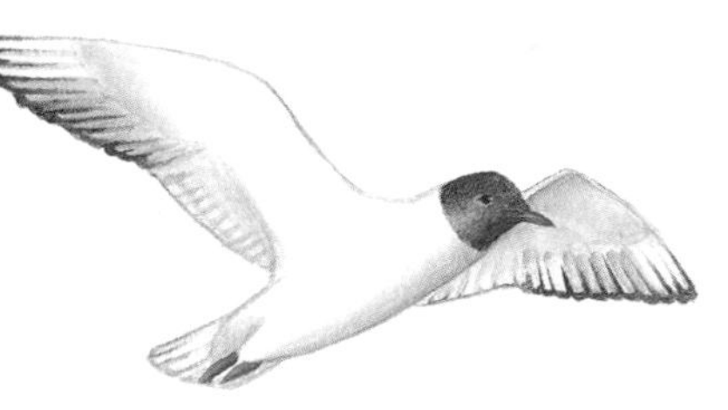

BIRD FLIGHT

There are three main types of flight: gliding, soaring and powered flight. Birds use all three types.

In gliding flight, a bird holds its wings out without moving them. The wings work in the same way as the wings of an aircraft. Because of the wings' shape, air passes more quickly over the top of the wings than underneath. This means that air pressure on top of the wings is less than underneath. The result is an upward force (called lift) on the wings. The bird keeps moving forward because it is dropping under the force of gravity. So the power for the flight comes from the bird's own weight. The problem with gliding is that the bird must start high up and will eventually reach the ground.

△ Large birds can soar for long periods of time.

△ Hummingbirds can hover to sip nectar from flowers.

In soaring flight, a bird's wings work in the same way as in gliding flight. However, the bird places itself in rising currents of air. The rising air lifts the bird, so that it gains height rather than losing it. The rising currents are often known as thermals. Thermals are columns of warm air that have been heated by areas of hot ground. Rising currents of air also occur where wind hits sharply rising ground, such as a cliff. It is mostly large birds with big wings that soar.

Powered flight involves a bird flapping its wings. As the wings flap downward, the feathers close up and overlap. This gives the greatest resistance to the air. The movement of the wings pushes against the air. The way in which the wings move and their shape give a combination of lift and forward thrust. When the wings flap up again, they rotate and bend, and the feathers open up. This gives the least resistance to air so that the bird is not pushed downward again.

INSECT FLIGHT

Insects' wings consist of thin, quite stiff membranes. Insects with wings have either one or two pairs of wings (although many insects have no wings at all). Various insects use their wings in rather different ways. The main difference, however, is between insects that have two pairs of wings. Some – such as dragonflies – move their pairs of wings alternately: as one pair moves up, the other moves down. Others – such as bees – move all four wings together.

Most insects use only powered flight. They are too light for controlled gliding and soaring. An insect's wings work in much the same way as a bird's wings. As the wings flap down, they push against the air, creating lift and forward movement. However, on the upward stroke, there are no feathers that can let air through. As a result, an insect has to turn its wings quite hard to avoid being pushed down. Butterflies, which cannot turn their wings far, fly with a very jagged movement. Most insects move their wings very fast, which creates a buzzing noise as they fly.

△ Bees have two pairs of wings, which move together.

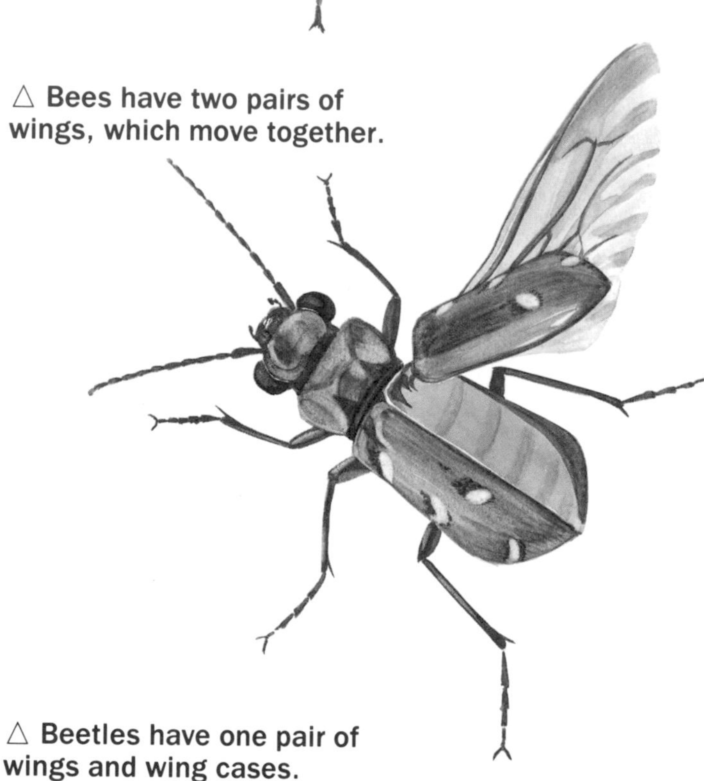

△ Beetles have one pair of wings and wing cases.

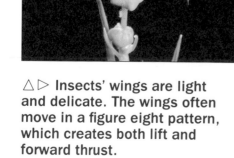

△▷ Insects' wings are light and delicate. The wings often move in a figure eight pattern, which creates both lift and forward thrust.

DID YOU KNOW?

Some very light spiders can drift using their silk. They let out the thread until it becomes caught in the wind.

MAMMALS AND OTHERS

Bats are the only mammals that can use powered flight. They have wings made of skin. The skin is supported by very long, bony fingers. Their wing movements are like those of birds, but they do not have feathers that can let air through. As in birds, bats have powerful flying muscles attached to a large breastbone. Bats fly at night. They find their way by letting out high-pitched squeaks and listening to the echoes. This is why they have large ears and strangely-shaped snouts.

△ A flying squirrel has large flaps of skin and a flat tail.

△ Bats are skillful fliers and hunt for insects at night.

A large number of other animals can glide, but do not have real wings and cannot soar or use powered flight. Flying squirrels have large flaps of skin between their front and back legs. They glide from high up in trees. Flying frogs have large webbed feet that they use to glide – they too glide from trees. Flying snakes and lizards also have flaps of skin along the sides of their bodies. Flying fish have large fins that they can spread out to use as wings. They swim quickly, then shoot out of the water to glide for short distances through the air.

EXPERIMENT

You can find out how flying squirrels jump farther from trees by gliding. Push two empty ballpoint pens or blunt pencils through a cardboard tube from the middle of a toilet paper roll, as shown in the picture. Put a lump of modeling clay in the front. Carefully throw the tube front-first from the top of a flight of stairs – make sure that nobody is at the bottom. Now, using tape and thin cardboard, add flaps between the legs, a wide tail and a head. Try throwing the “squirrel” again.

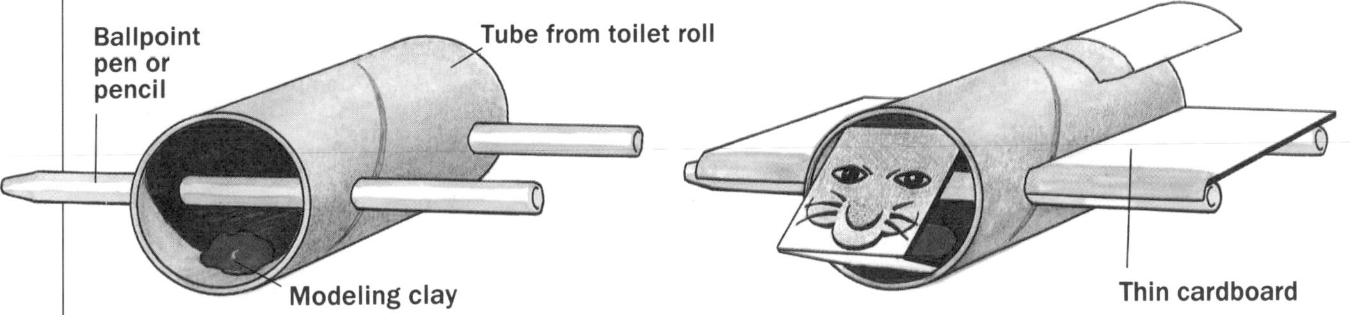

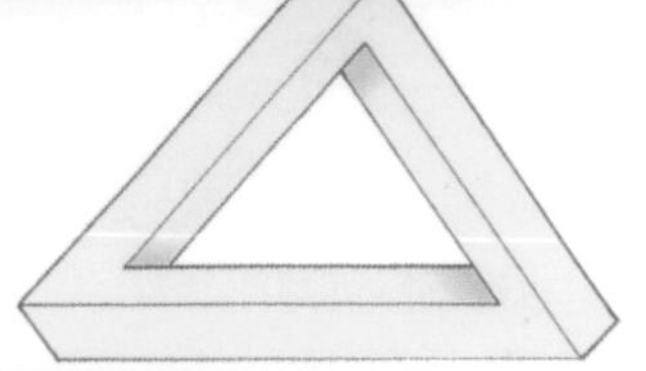

encyclopedia of science

THE SENSES

CONTENTS

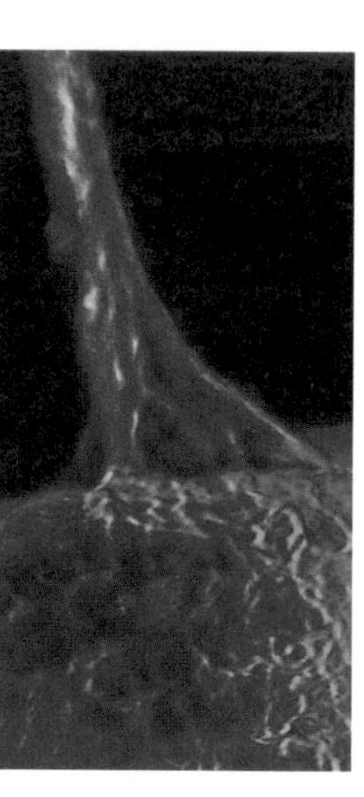

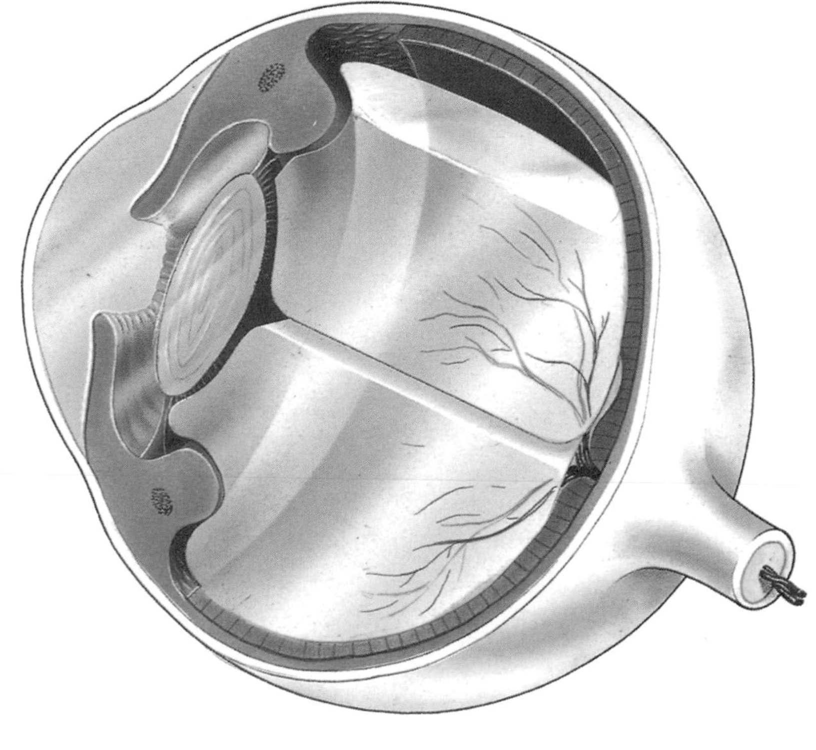

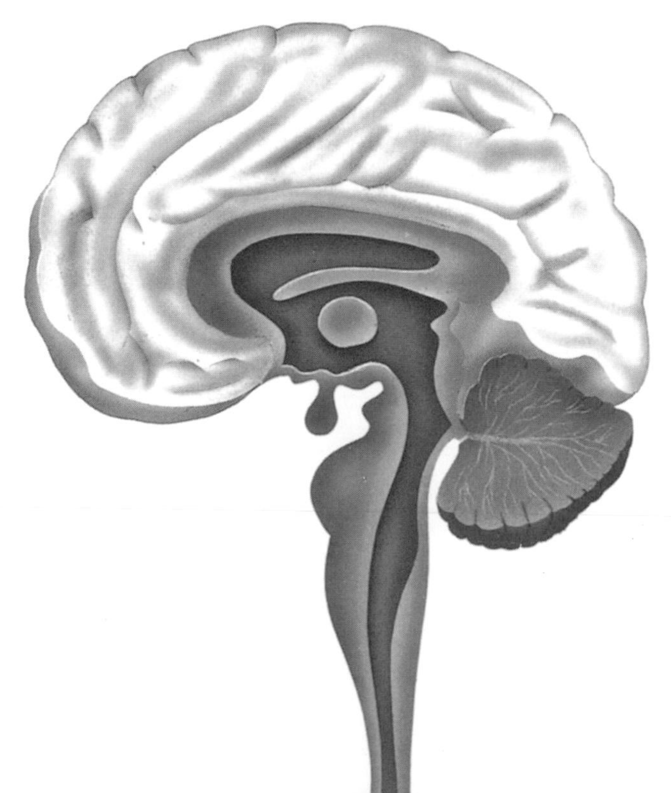

INTRODUCTION

Many types of animals have nerves. Even very simple animals like jellyfish have a basic nervous system. Nerves are the quickest way to send information and instructions around the body of an animal. We think, see, hear, touch and smell using our nerves.

The nervous system of humans is perhaps the thing about us that is most different from other animals. Our ability to think using the brain (which is part of the nervous system) and our skill with our hands (which are controlled by nerves) have shaped the world we live in.

This section describes the human nervous system, and also mentions birds, other mammals and reptiles. But the nervous systems of other animals basically work in the same way as the human system. The biggest difference is usually that their central nervous system, especially the brain, is very much simpler. Sometimes – for example, in jellyfish – there is no brain at all.

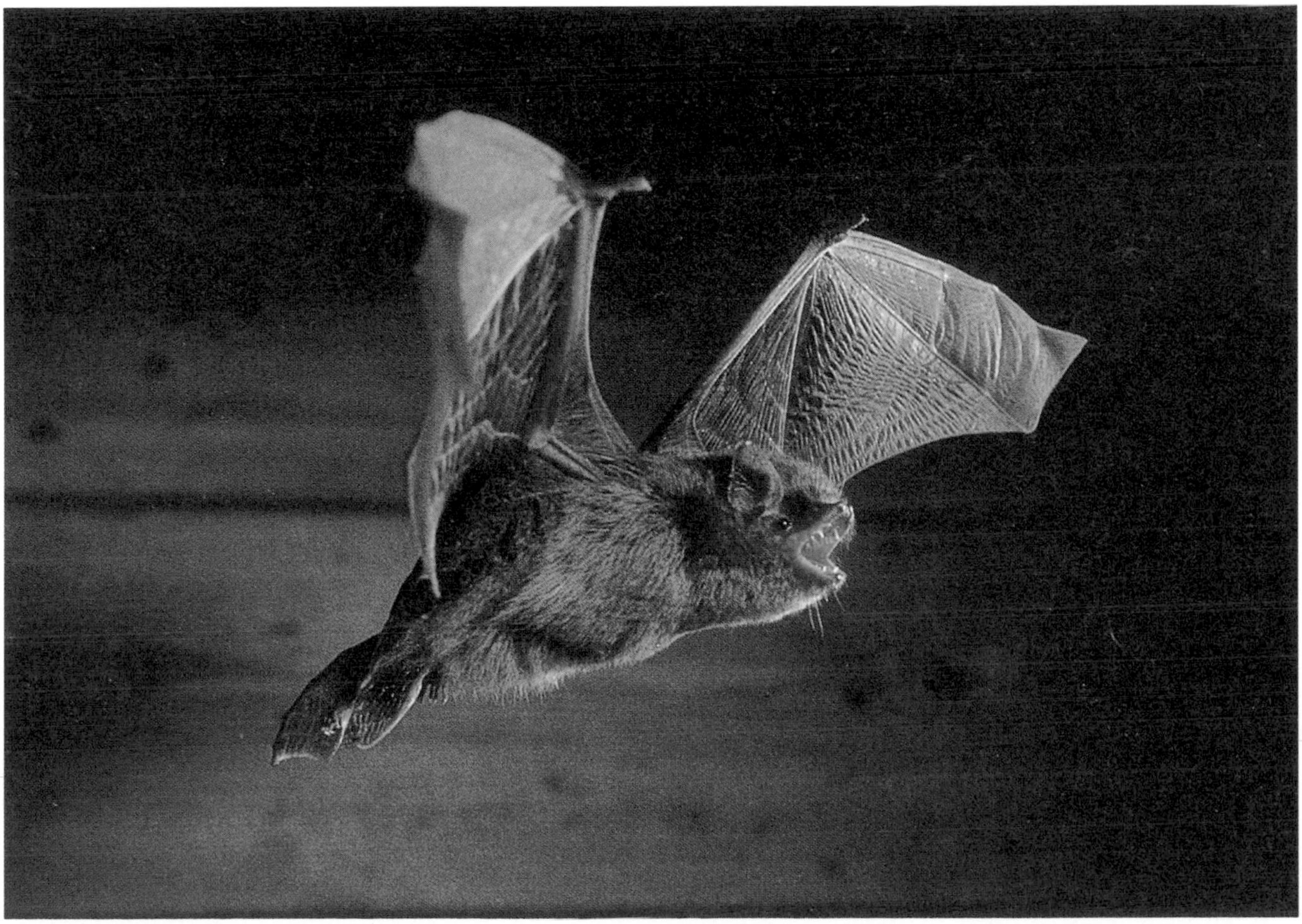

Our senses and nerves let the brain know what is going on, both outside and inside our bodies. The brain can then direct the body to find food when we are hungry, drink water when we are thirsty, sleep when we are tired, keep away from danger, and seek help if we are sick. The nervous system never stops working.

NERVE CELLS

The nervous system works in a similar way to a telephone network. The "wiring" is made up of cells – the microscopic building blocks that form all parts of the body. Nerve cells are called neurons. Like other cells, they have a nucleus and internal cellular parts (organelles). But they cannot reproduce themselves, which most other body cells can, and they have only limited powers of repair if damaged.

Arms extend from a neuron's cell body. Dendrites are thin branching arms that exchange signals with other neurons. Dendrons collect signals from sensory receptors (for example, heat receptors in the skin). Axons carry signals from the cell body to other neurons or to organs such as muscles. Nerve cells connect with each other at junctions called synapses.

The "skin" that covers each nerve cell is called the cell membrane. It is this that carries the tiny electrical signals which make up nerve impulses. As an impulse travels along a cell, electrically charged atoms (ions) of sodium and potassium move in and out of the membrane, causing a change in its electrical charge. Axons are wrapped in a sheath of special insulating material, so that their signals do not get mixed up with signals in neighboring neurons – neurons are often bundled closely together. The insulating material, called myelin, is also made of special cells, called Schwann cells. All the way along the axon, where Schwann cells meet, there are narrow parts called the nodes of Ranvier. Here the signals

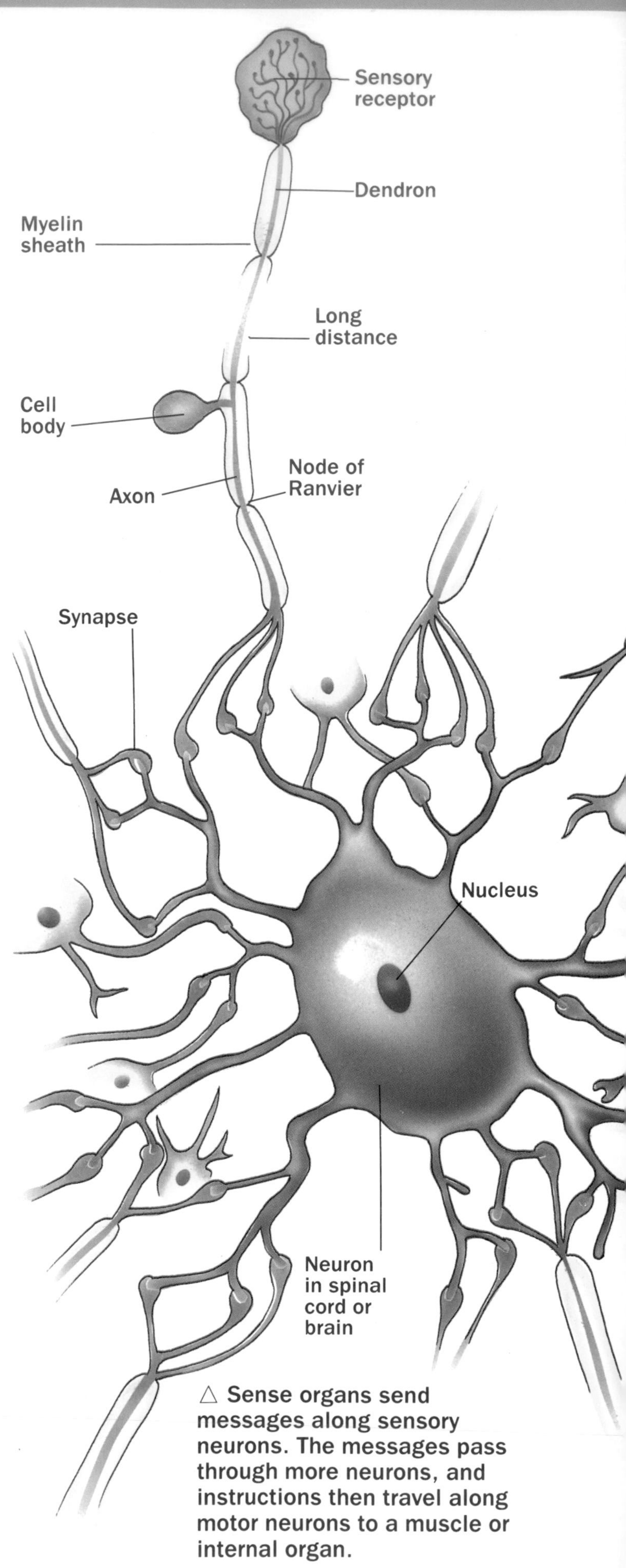

△ Sense organs send messages along sensory neurons. The messages pass through more neurons, and instructions then travel along motor neurons to a muscle or internal organ.

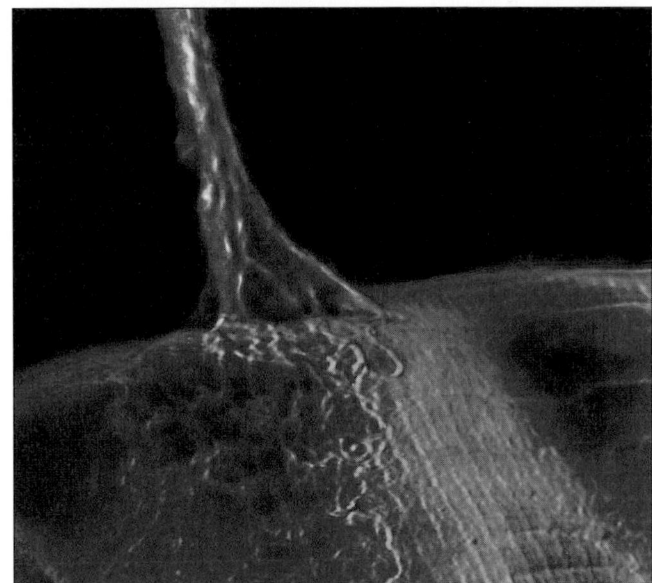

△ Where motor neurons reach a muscle, they branch into several strands. When a nerve message arrives, the strands release chemicals. These chemicals give a signal for the muscle to contract.

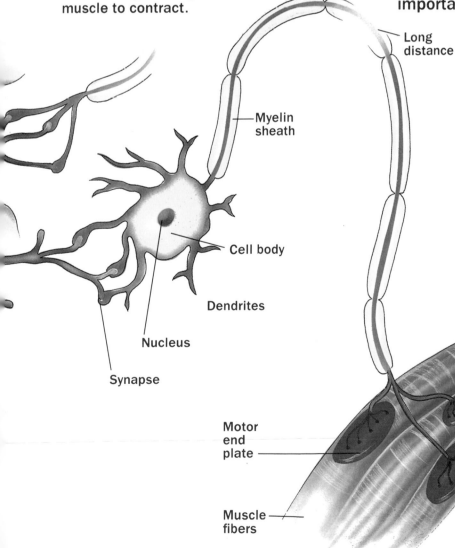

are "boosted" as they jump from node to node.

Nerve cells communicate with each other at the synapses. When an electrical signal arrives at a synapse, it releases special chemicals. The chemicals travel across the microscopic gap between the cells to the next neuron. When the chemicals reach the next neuron, the cell is "fired." The signal then travels on, along its cell membrane. Once a neuron has fired, there is a pause before it recovers and can be fired again.

There are so many neurons and connections in the whole nervous system that it would soon become jammed with messages unless it had some sort of filtering system. Filtering takes place at the synapses. A neuron will transmit a signal only if it receives enough signals from other neurons to suggest it is an important message.

Long distance
Myelin sheath
Cell body
Dendrites
Nucleus
Synapse
Motor end plate
Muscle fibers

A NERVE CIRCUIT

Wire a thumb tack to a flashlight bulb. Connect the bulb to a battery, and wire the battery to another thumb tack. Make a switch from a metal paperclip. When the switch completes the circuit, the bulb lights up. This is rather like a sense organ passing a nerve signal to the brain.

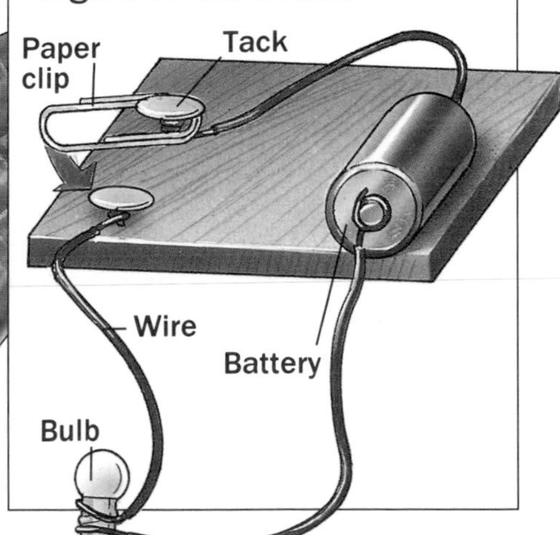

Sensory neurons carry messages from the sense organs to the brain. Motor neurons carry signals from the brain to the muscles. These two make up the peripheral nervous system. The brain and spinal cord form the central nervous system. The autonomic nervous system controls the internal organs.

PERIPHERAL AND CENTRAL

Peripheral nerves travel throughout the body. Sensory neurons carry messages from the skin, eyes, ears and other sense organs to the central nervous system. Motor neurons carry instructions from the central nervous system to the muscles and internal organs. The peripheral nerves are made up of bundles of nerve fibers and their protective sheaths. Usually, both motor and sensory fibers are mixed together in a single nerve.

The peripheral nerves join the spinal cord in pairs. They enter the spine between each of the bones. There are 31 pairs of peripheral nerves. They go to the skin, muscles and most other body organs. Each half of a pair goes to the organs in one half of the body. There are also 12 pairs of cranial nerves in the skull. These are also peripheral nerves. They carry information between the eyes, ears, mouth, nose and skin of the head and the brain.

The spinal cord is a thick bundle of nerves. It passes through a tube formed by the lined-up holes in the backbones, (or vertebrae). At the top end, it passes through a hole at the base of the skull and joins to the brain.

At the spinal cord, the peripheral nerves split so that most sensory neurons enter the cord from the back and the motor neurons enter from the front. Within the H-shaped center of the cord (known as gray matter), the neurons are connected to thousands of other neurons. Some of these neurons travel up and down the cord.

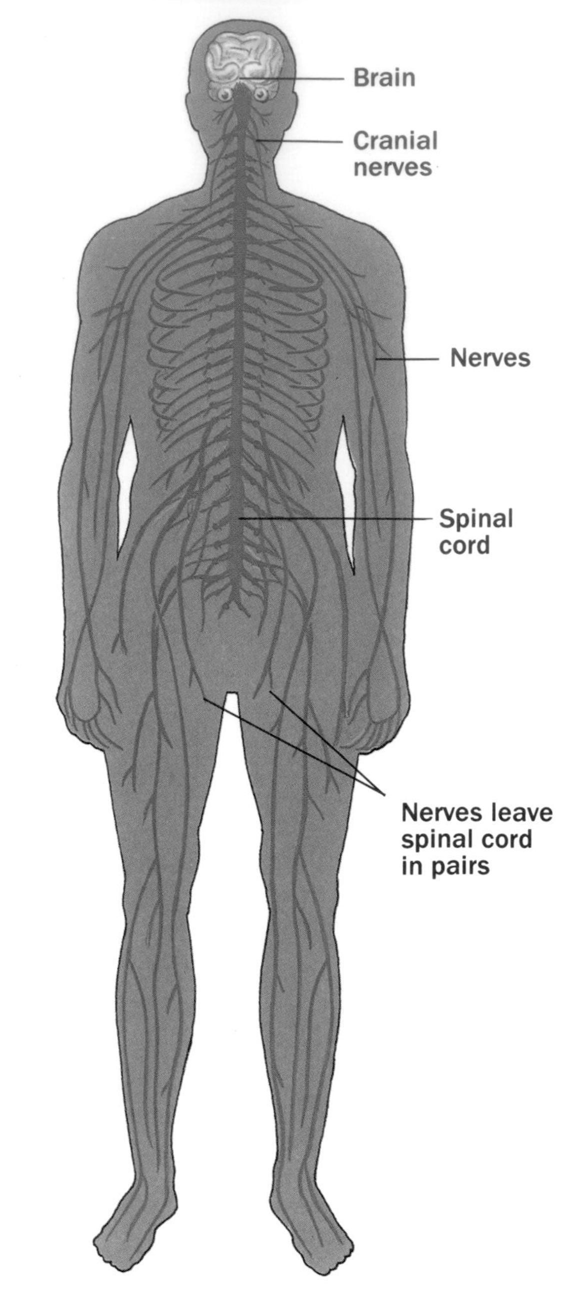

△ The main nerves of the body's nervous system.

DID YOU KNOW?

- Altogether the nerves in the body of an adult human being stretch for 47 miles.
- The average human brain weighs about 3 lbs – but 80 percent of that is water!
- A child's brain is 90 percent of its adult size by the sixth birthday.

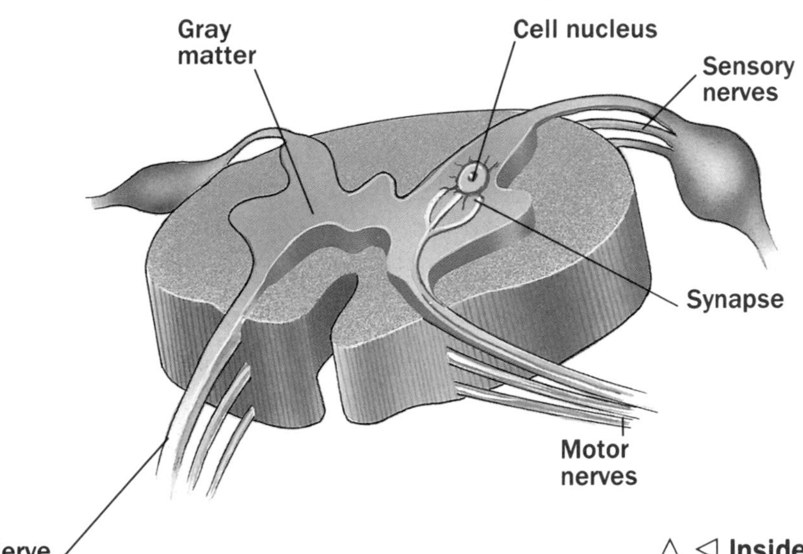

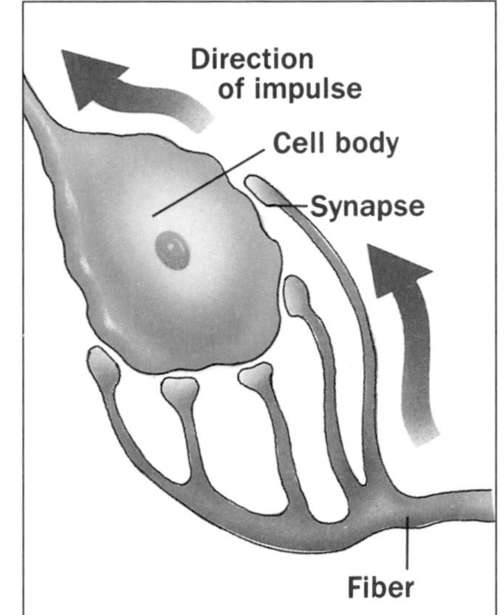

△ ◁ Inside the spinal cord, the white matter is where the nerve fibers pass up and down the cord. Peripheral nerve fibers pass into the gray matter, where they make connections with many other neurons. Nerve signals travel in one direction, from the terminals of the axon to the cell body, then on along the next axon.

REFLEX CONTROL

The body has several types of automatic control system. Some involve chemicals (hormones) that pass around the body. Others involve the autonomic nervous system. Quick changes that involve the peripheral nervous system are called reflex actions.

Reflex actions usually happen in response to a particular stimulus. An example is sneezing, which happens in response to an itch in the nose. Another example is if you put your hand on something very hot, you pull your hand away automatically, without even thinking about it. You have little or no control over most reflex actions, and it is difficult to stop them happening.

The spinal cord is responsible for many reflex actions. There is no time for the brain to be involved because the actions must happen so quickly. Messages from sensory nerves enter the cord. They are sent straight out again through motor nerves to the muscles. The brain is also involved in some reflex actions. These actions mostly concern those parts of the peripheral nervous system that are connected directly to the brain and not to the spinal column.

TEST YOUR REFLEXES

Sit with your legs crossed and ask a friend to tap your knee, just below the kneecap. Your leg will kick. The tendon that attaches your kneecap to your shin bone contains sensors that send a message to the spinal cord. This is part of our automatic walking mechanism. The message comes straight back and tells your foot to move forward quickly.

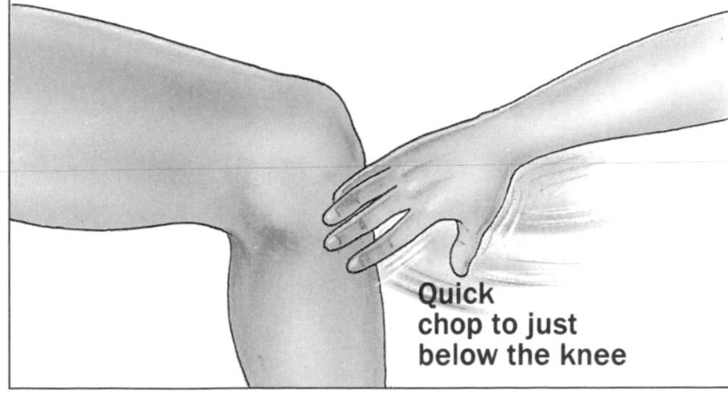

The brain is the central control of the nervous system. It is where information arriving from the sense organs (such as the eyes) is filtered and sorted, decisions are made, and the performance of the organs of the body is monitored and controlled. It is also where our thoughts occur.

STRUCTURE OF THE BRAIN

The brain occupies most of the inside of the skull. It is protected and cushioned by bones and by three layers of tissue called the meninges. The outer of these is the thickest and toughest, the dura mater. The next layer is called the arachnoid layer and is spongy, carrying blood vessels. Within this layer is the cerebrospinal fluid, a clear liquid that nourishes the central nervous system and helps to protect it. The innermost layer is the pia mater, a fine membrane that follows the shape of the brain.

The brain stem, at the base of the brain, is made up of two main parts: the medulla oblongata and the pons. Behind is the wrinkly cerebellum, which is joined to the cerebrum by the midbrain.

The cerebrum at the top is divided into two halves, the cerebral hemispheres. Its surface, the cerebral cortex, is made of gray matter (like that in the spine) and is thrown into walnut-like folds. The two halves of the cerebrum are joined by large bundles of nerve fibers that cross within the corpus callosum. To the sides of the corpus callosum there are spaces that contain the nourishing cerebrospinal fluid. In the center of the brain is the thalamus; most of the information from the senses to the cerebrum passes through this. Also at the center is the hypothalamus, which is concerned with basic urges such as hunger and thirst. Near to the hypothalamus is the pituitary gland. This gland produces many hormones, and these control many different processes in the body.

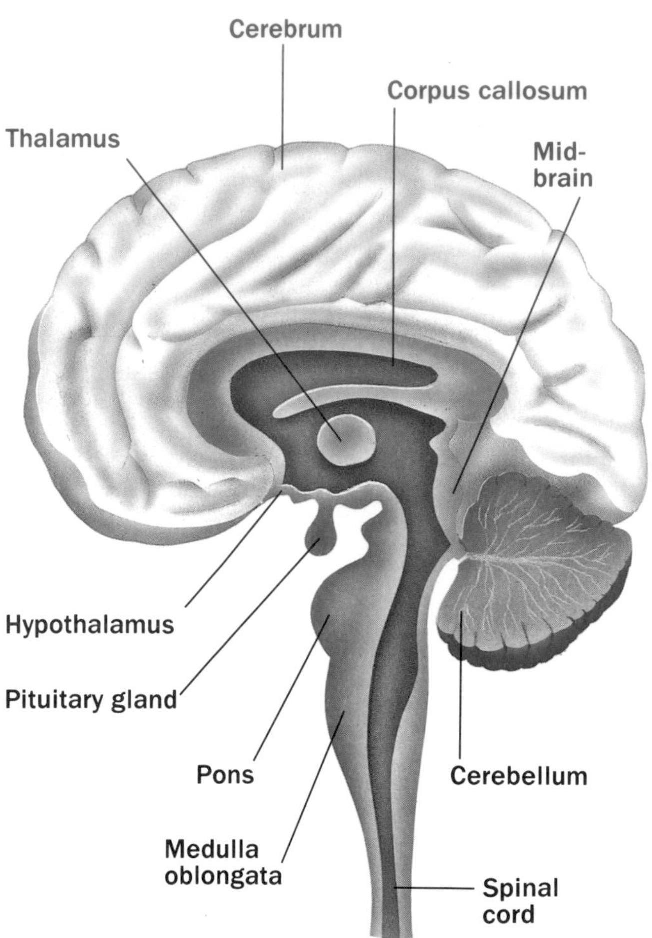

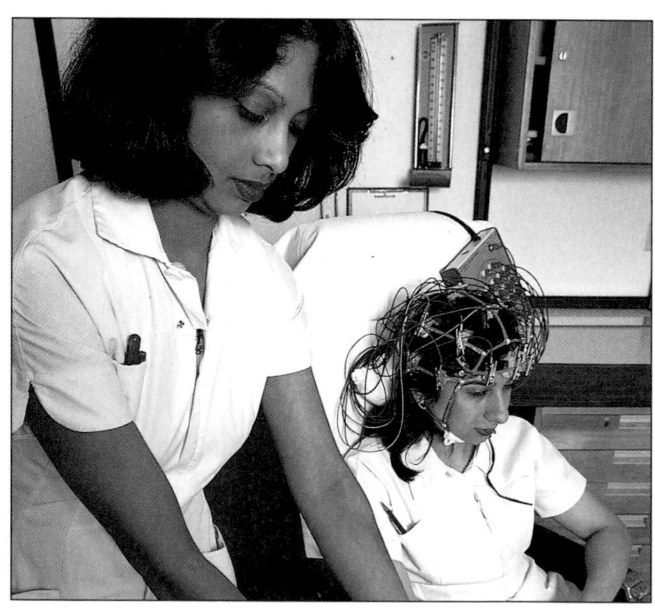

△ The electrical signals of the neurons in the cerebral cortex can be measured and recorded by an EEG (electroencephalography) machine. The wave patterns produced are different when the brain is at rest and when it is thinking.

◁ A human brain has the same parts as the brains of all animals with backbones. But a large cerebrum is found only in mammals. Other parts of the brain control the basic functions that keep an animal alive and well.

▽ The colors show what various parts of the cerebrums of these mammals are used for. They indicate which senses are important to the animal. For example, smell is important to rats, and humans have plenty of nonspecific brain for thinking.

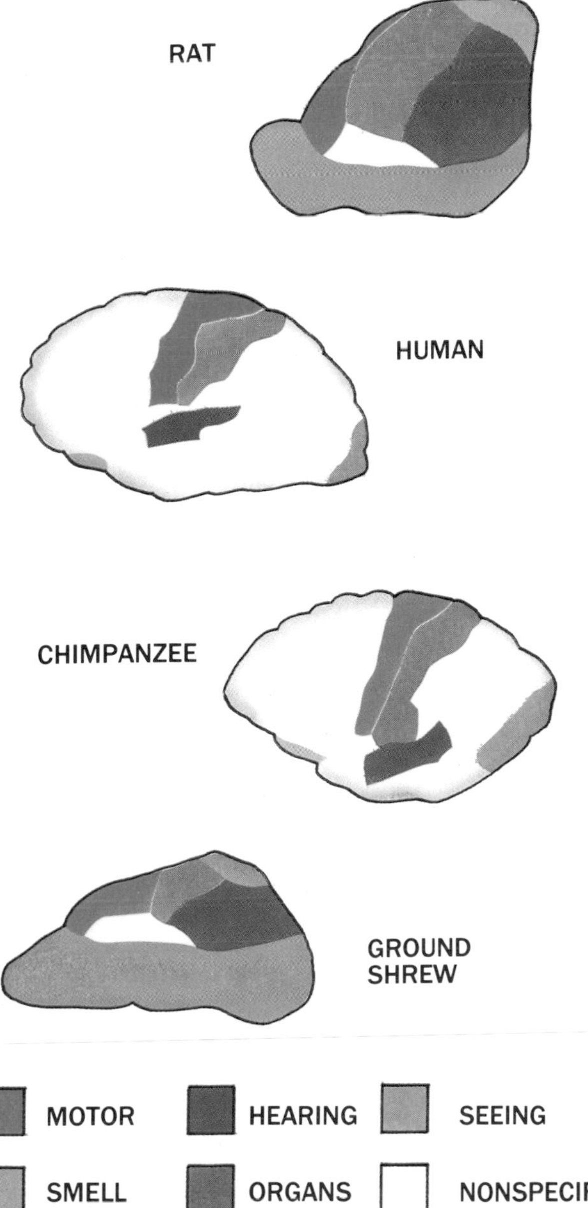

FUNCTIONS OF THE BRAIN

Each part of the brain has a different function. The brain stem – the medulla and pons – are the most "primitive" parts of the brain. They control the basic functions that keep the body alive. They monitor the working of the internal organs such as the heart, lungs and the intestines. Here also the nerve fibers from the body enter the brain from the spinal column.

The cerebellum is responsible for the unconscious control of balance and movements. It coordinates the many muscles that are used in complex patterns of movement, such as walking, running, jumping, playing the piano or riding a bicycle.

The midbrain coordinates movements of the eyes, head and body to follow the sources of sights and sounds.

The cerebral hemispheres are where information from the senses is analyzed, decisions are made, and instructions sent out for all of our conscious activities. Here we calculate, appreciate, make comparisons and memorize our experiences. Thoughts, plans and communications all start here. Each of these functions takes place in a particular area of the folds of the cerebral cortex.

THE CRUMPLED CORTEX

The cerebral cortex is made up of billions of nerve fibers. If they were all arranged on a flat surface, they would cover an area of almost 44 square feet. Stick two large sheets of newspaper together. Crumple them up to see how they could fit inside the skull.

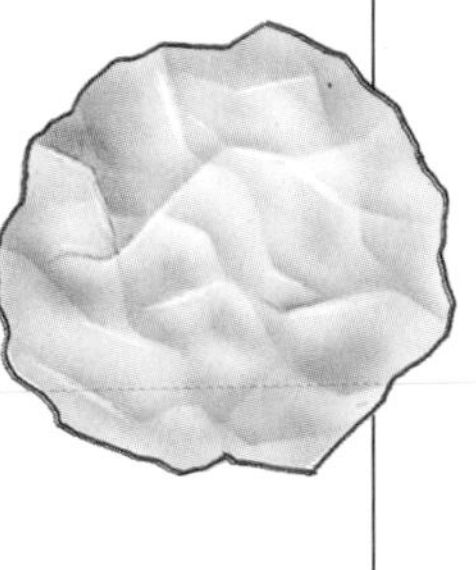

Perception – the way we recognize and understand things – takes place in the cortex of the brain. Scientists know that these processes must involve millions of neurons, all carrying electrical signals and connected together by synapses. But it is still not clear exactly how the mechanism of perception works.

FILTERING INFORMATION

The vast amount of information from the senses that the brain receives is carefully filtered before it comes to our conscious perception. This allows more important signals to be filtered from less important ones. Each neuron has connections to and from many other neurons. Information is filtered at each connection because a neuron will not transmit a new signal unless it receives signals from several other neurons.

When the signals arrive in the correct part of the cerebral cortex, different neurons are fired by different types of information. For example, in the visual part of the cortex some neurons respond only to signals received when the eye sees a vertical line, some only respond to horizontal lines and some only to diagonal lines.

△ The brain monitors all sensory information, but we notice only important things such as hearing our name.

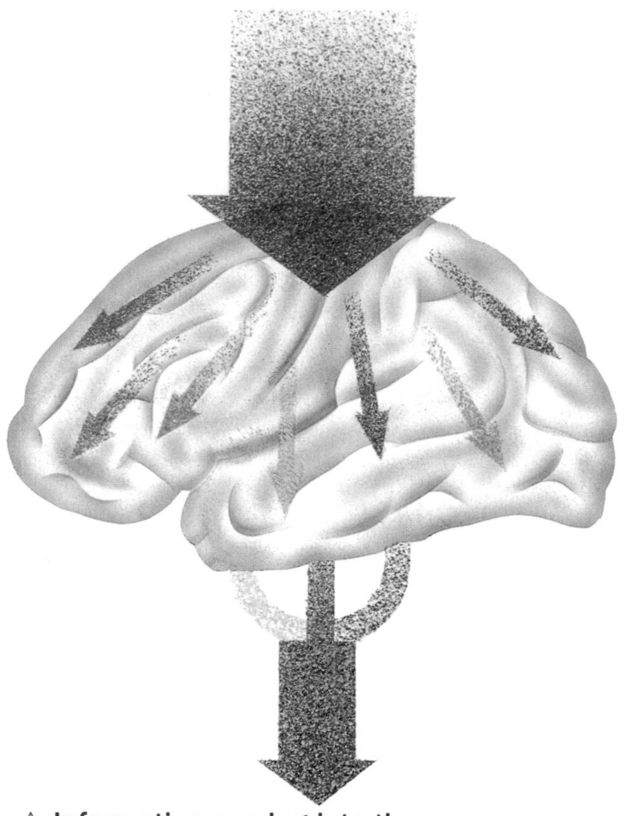

△ Information coming into the brain is filtered and directed to the correct part of the cortex. Here the information is interpreted and directions sent out to the body if any action is needed in response.

INTERPRETING INFORMATION

Interpretation of the meaning of incoming information is done by comparing the pathways that signals have taken and the responses to them of the cortex with experiences in memory. The brain often makes guesses based on previous experience. But because we very quickly learn about the world around us when we are babies, this way of doing things seems to work very well.

We are conscious of normal background sights, sounds and smells. But our attention is drawn particularly to unexpected changes, like a new smell and questions are asked, such as "is it something burning?" When the information has been interpreted, the brain must decide what instructions to send out.

THOUGHTS AND EMOTIONS

The way that we think and feel makes up our individual personalities. We are social animals, that is, much of our time is spent dealing with other people. Our personalities are important to social communication. Conscious thought, which involves reasoning and planning, occurs in a large part of the cortex. It involves both halves (hemispheres) and uses information from all parts of the brain. Thinking involves language, information from the sense organs and memories. Emotions such as fear, anger, pleasure and sorrow also affect the way we think.

Deep within the brain is the limbic system. It is made up of part of the cortex and the hypothalamus. This is the emotional center of the brain. Our emotions are altered by information coming from the sensory organs and also by changes within the body such as hunger or hormonal levels.

The cerebral hemispheres are like two brains, and each can function on its own. But each half has its strengths and weaknesses. They work together to produce the mixture of things that we do well. The left hemisphere is the logical, reasoning side. It is good at calculating and is responsible for language. The right side is more artistic and creative. It is capable of appreciation and imagination. Everyone can do all these things, but the side of the brain that is stronger in us makes us better at some things than at others.

△ The right hemisphere is the more artistic side of the brain and is the stronger side in creative people.

OPTICAL ILLUSIONS

Optical illusions are fun, and they also show how the brain interprets images by comparing them with things it knows and then making guesses. The silhouette can be two faces or one vase. Which of the two flower centers is the largest? Measure them. The triangle is an impossible shape. But when you look at it your brain will try to see a three-dimensional figure.

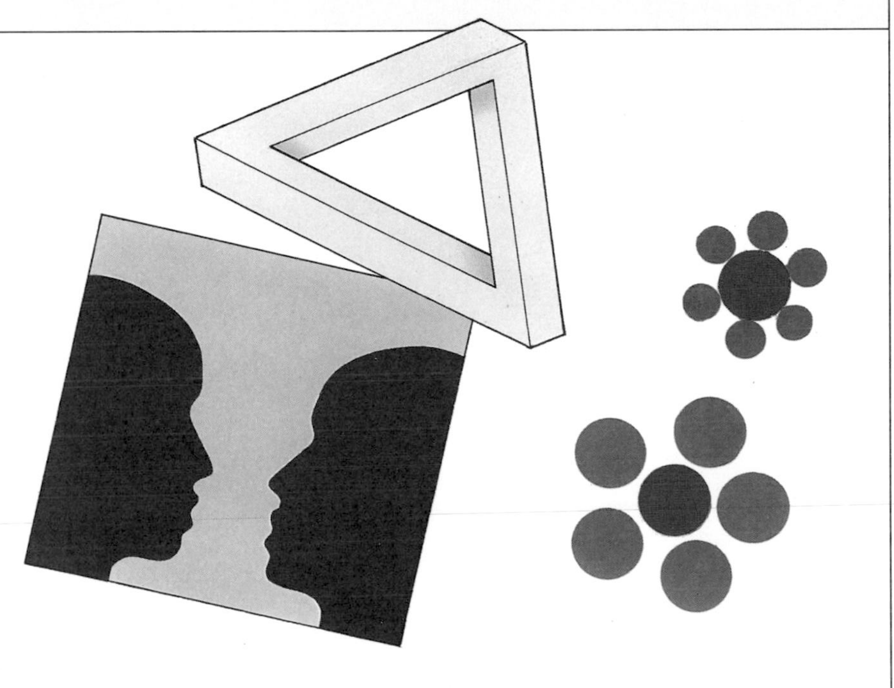

Memory is important because it allows the brain to interpret information. It also allows us to think, speak and reason. The memory is based deep within the brain in regions known as the hippocampus and the amygdala . Scientists are only just beginning to have an understanding of how memory works.

LEARNING

Learning means memorizing information that can alter future behavior. We learn things all the time. Babies start learning about their family and home as soon as they are born. Most children have learned half of everything they will ever know by the time they are six or seven years old. They can talk, walk and use a pencil. They understand thousands of words and are learning to read. After this stage, learning is mainly improving and expanding these abilities.

Learning something new is hard at first. It takes a lot of concentration to set up the nerve pathways involved in a new operation. Each time the pathways are used, they become stronger until the operation is almost automatic. This is how learning works. Practice really does make perfect.

There are also other types of learning. For instance when the school lunch bell rings your mouth waters – you are producing the saliva and other digestive juices that will be needed when your lunch arrives. This is called conditioning. It also happens when we get used to things around us such as bright lights, wearing clothes or hearing a clock ticking. After a while, you stop noticing these things. This type of learning helps to prevent the brain from being overloaded with unimportant information.

△ Learning to ride a bicycle is very difficult to start with. You have to coordinate your muscles with your sense of balance and it takes a lot of practice. But once you have managed to learn it, you will never forget.

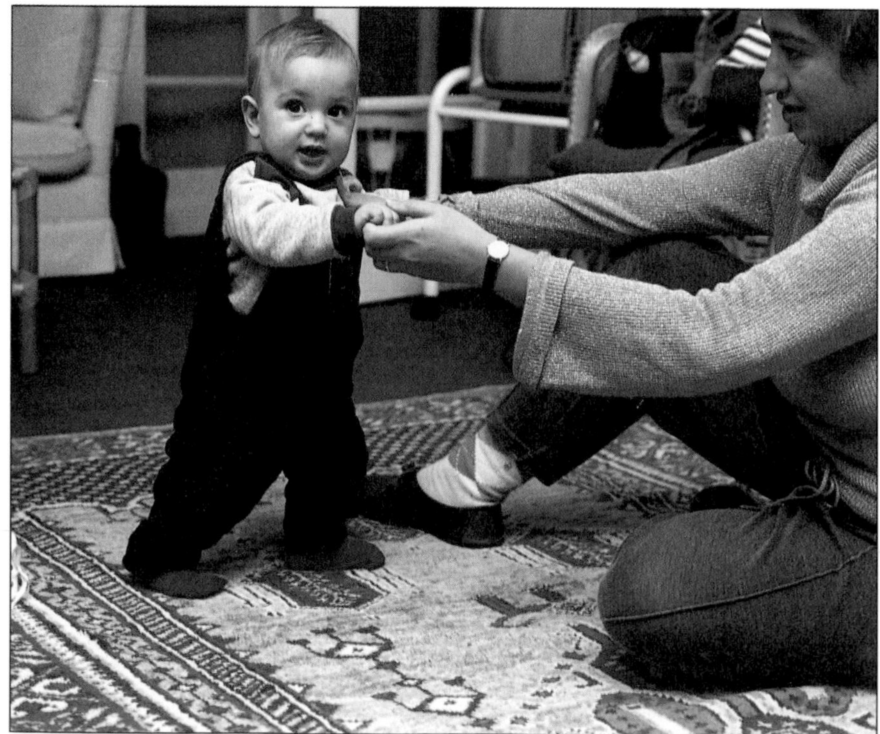

◁ Walking is a built-in skill, but a baby's bones and muscles need to be strong enough before it can start. Practice is needed to improve the balance and coordination that is necessary.

LONG-TERM AND SHORT-TERM

Learning depends on the memory. We use our memories all the time to understand what goes on around us, because most things that happen have happened before. When someone is talking to you, you have to remember the beginning of each sentence so that you can understand it at the end. We can remember not only words but also music, images we have seen, smells, tastes and feelings. When we experience these things again, they often bring back memories which include lots of information about the time we first had the experience.

Memory depends on three stages. The first is the gathering of information, the second is storage and the third is retrieving the information. Information from the senses goes first into the short-term memory, where small amounts of information, such as a telephone number, are stored for about a minute. The short-term memory is very small. Any new information that has to be stored pushes out what is already in it.

If the information in the short-term memory is reinforced often enough by repetition, the information passes into the long-term memory. This memory stores everything we ever learn, consciously or unconsciously. It can hold as much information as the memory banks of a thousand of the biggest computers.

When we forget things, it is either because the memory part of the brain has been damaged or because the recall system is not working properly – perhaps because it has not been used for a while. Techniques to improve peoples' memories are based on improving the recall system. It is often easier to recall information if it is part of a meaningful sequence. So people use sentences such as *Richard Of York Gave Battle In Vain* to make it easy to remember the colors of the rainbow: *Red, Orange, Yellow, Green, Blue, Indigo, Violet.*

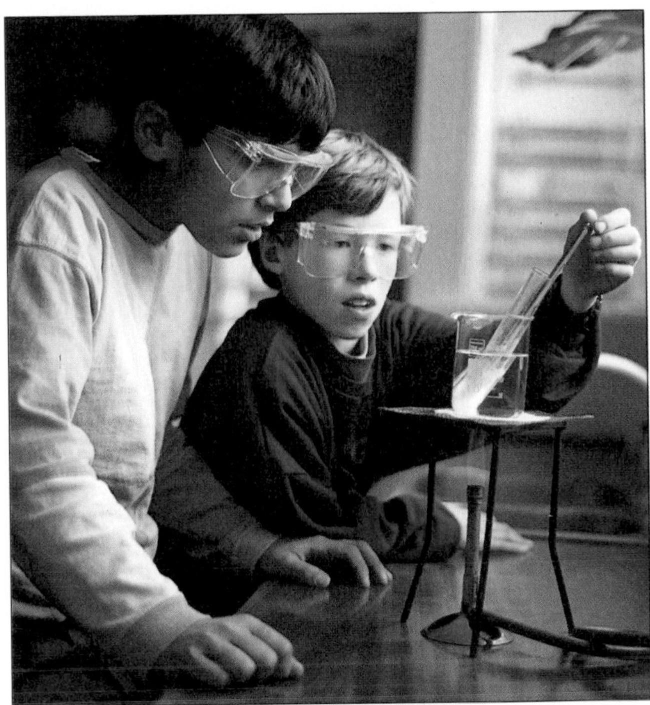

△ It is easier to learn things by doing them and gaining first-hand experience. For example, doing science experiments lets us see what happens for ourselves.

MEMORY TEST

Try this memory game and see how good your memory is. Put several ordinary household articles on a tray and look at them for two minutes. Then get a friend to remove one item while you are not looking. See if you can remember what is missing. To make it harder, put more things on the tray or get your friend to remove more than one item at a time.

The brain sends out motor messages which travel down the spinal cord and along the nerve bundles to all parts of the body. The muscles contract in certain orders and at different levels of power. They are monitored and coordinated by the brain and can carry out the most delicate or the heaviest of jobs.

MOVEMENT

Muscles move the rigid bones that make up the skeleton. Muscles have tendons at each end, which are attached to bones on either side of a joint. When a muscle contracts it becomes shorter and fatter, and pulls the bones toward each other, causing the joint to bend.

Muscles are made of tiny cells shaped like long thin fibers. Several fibers are bundled together and wrapped in a membrane. Several bundles are in turn wrapped in a further membrane to form the muscle. The wrapping membranes continue at each end of the muscle to become the tendons.

Muscle fibers contain long, thin molecules of chemicals called actin and myosin. These molecules are arranged as stacks of actin and stacks of myosin. The stacks are linked together because the ends of the actin molecules lie between the ends of the myosin molecules. When a muscle contracts, the two types of molecule slide along each other using special chemical bonds as "legs." In this way, the stacks of molecules are pulled closer together and the muscle fiber gets shorter. When lots of fibers within a muscle get shorter, the whole muscle contracts.

Each muscle fiber has several plates on its surface that are the ends of motor neurons. These plates are similar to the synapses between neurons, and they release special chemicals (called transmitters). These chemicals start an electrical signal in the muscle fiber which causes it to contract. A muscle often contains both contracting and resting fibers at the same time. The power of the muscle is increased when more fibers are caused to contract.

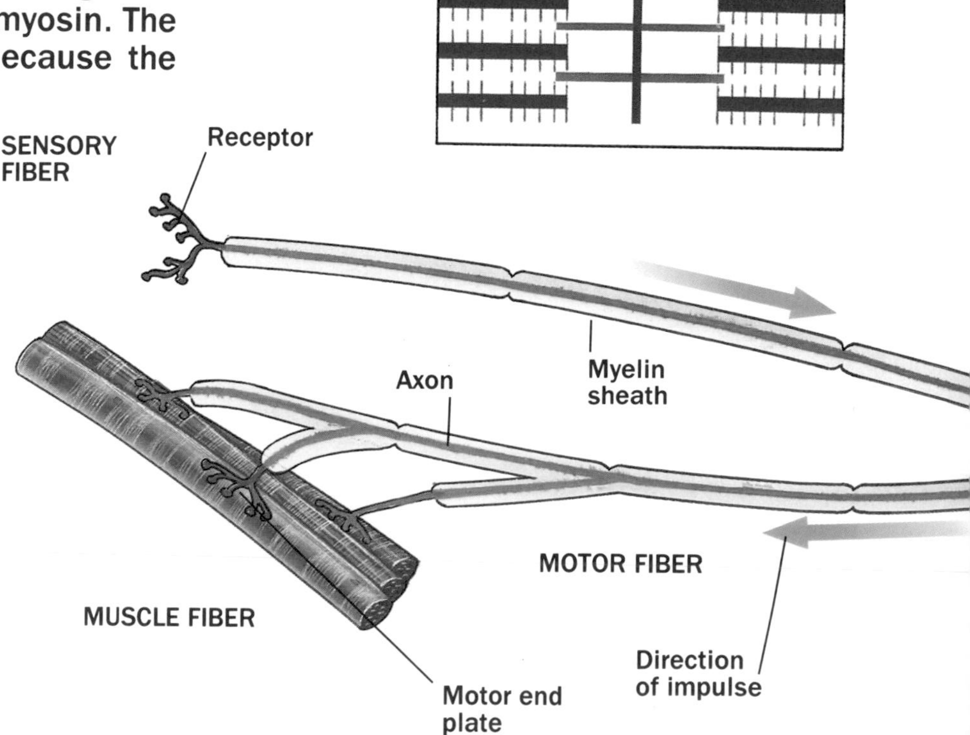

▷ Seen under a microscope, stacks of actin and myosin molecules in a muscle fiber appear as bands. Chemical bonds, acting like "legs," move them together when a muscle contracts (A) and then apart (B).

The contraction is stimulated by the end plates of motor nerves. The signals often come from the brain, traveling through the spinal cord. But in complex actions, such as walking, the signals may be part of reflex actions (see page 9). In this case, signals from sensory nerves travel through the spinal cord and straight out again to a muscle.

CONTROL

Contracting muscles must be finely controlled to perform tasks such as riding a bicycle, writing a word or playing a musical instrument. This control is produced by a system of nerves between the muscles, the sense organs and the brain. For example, walking involves the muscles of the legs, lower back and arms. The brain sends out messages to instruct all these muscles to begin working. But the walking process is controlled by many parts of the body.

Walking is monitored by the organs of balance in the ear to make sure that we are not falling over; by the stretch receptors within the muscles so that we know how hard they are pulling; by the pressure sensors in the skin of the soles of the feet; and by the eyes to see if we are going to crash into anything.

All this sensory information goes to the brain. The brain then modifies the instructions it is sending out to the muscles so that they act in the necessary way. This happens continuously thousands of times every second with hardly any conscious thought. We can even do other things while we are walking, such as unwrapping a piece of candy, talking or even playing an instrument.

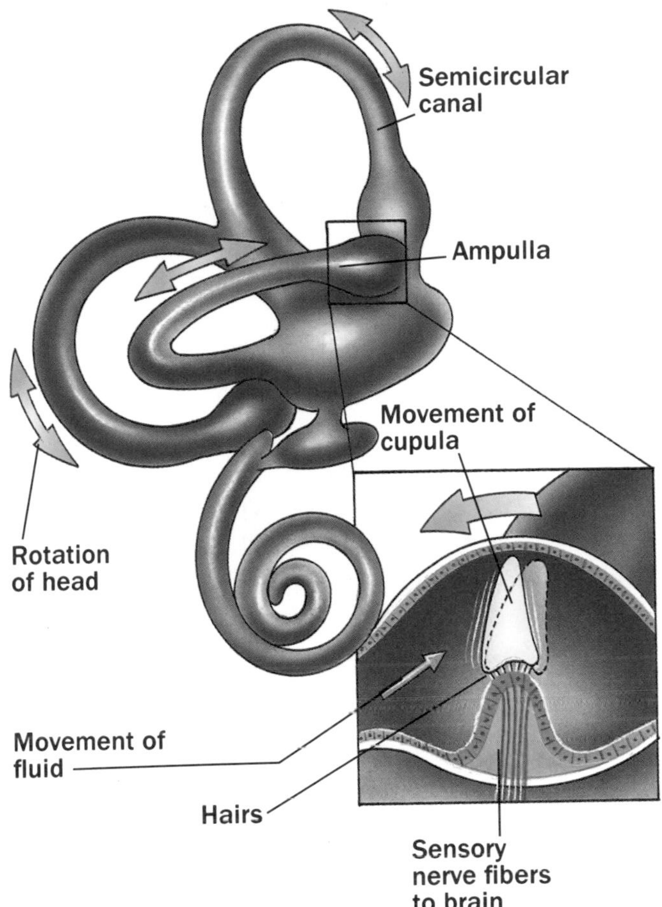

△ The organs of balance are the three semicircular canals in each ear. They contain fluid. Each of the canals has a cupula at one end. When the head moves, the fluid moves, and this in turn moves the cupula. When the cupula moves, it bends tiny hairs that connect to nerve endings.

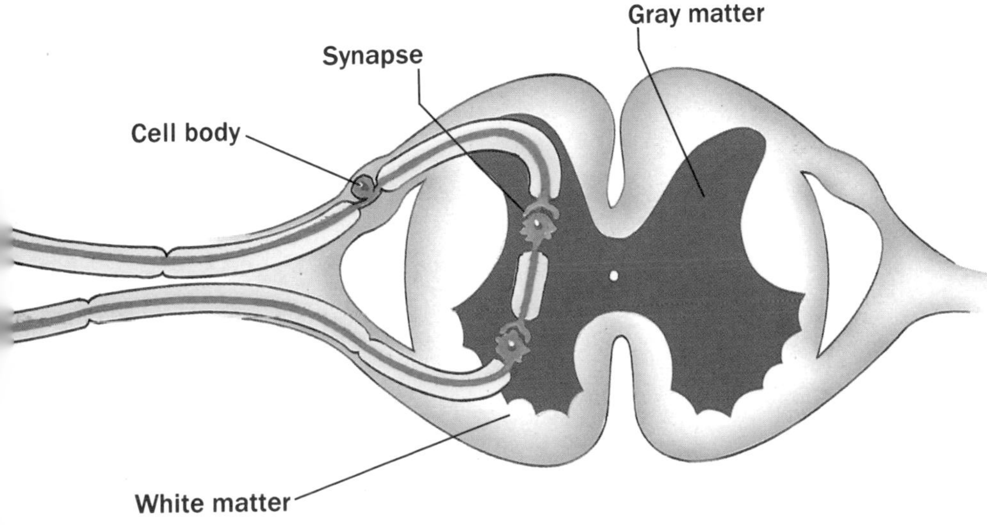

SPINAL CORD

DIZZINESS

Try spinning around and around on one spot in an open space. When we spin, the messages that the brain gets from the eyes do not match up with the messages from the organs of balance in the ears. We feel dizzy, we cannot stand upright properly and we may feel slightly sick.

The brain keeps in touch with what is going on around us by means of the sense organs. The main senses are sight, hearing, touch, taste and smell. Perhaps our best sense is that of sight. We can see in daylight and to some extent at night; we see in color and in three dimensions (width, depth and height).

THE EYE

The eyeball is made up of three layers. The sclera is the outer layer to which the muscles that move the eyeball are attached. At the front of the eye, the sclera becomes the transparent cornea. The cornea is covered by the conjunctiva, a membrane that lubricates and cleans the surface of the eye.

The middle layer is the choroid layer, which contains blood vessels and a pigment to prevent reflection of light. At the front of the eye, behind the cornea, the choroid layer becomes the ciliary muscles, which support and focus the lens of the eye. The muscular iris, which covers most of the lens, also comes from the choroid layer. The hole in the middle of the iris is the pupil.

The third layer, the retina, covers the rear part of the inside of the eye. It contains light sensitive cells – the rods and cones – and the nerve fibers leading from them. The fibers travel to the brain along the optic nerve.

The front of the eye is filled with clear liquid called the aqueous humor, while the main part is filled with a clear jelly called the vitreous humor.

The eye operates on a similar principle to a camera. Light, reflected from the things around us, enters the eye through the pupil. It falls on the retina, forming an upside-down image, focused by the cornea and the lens. The rods and cones are sensory cells which are stimulated by light. The rods are sensitive to light intensity, light and dark. The cones in the fovea respond to color.

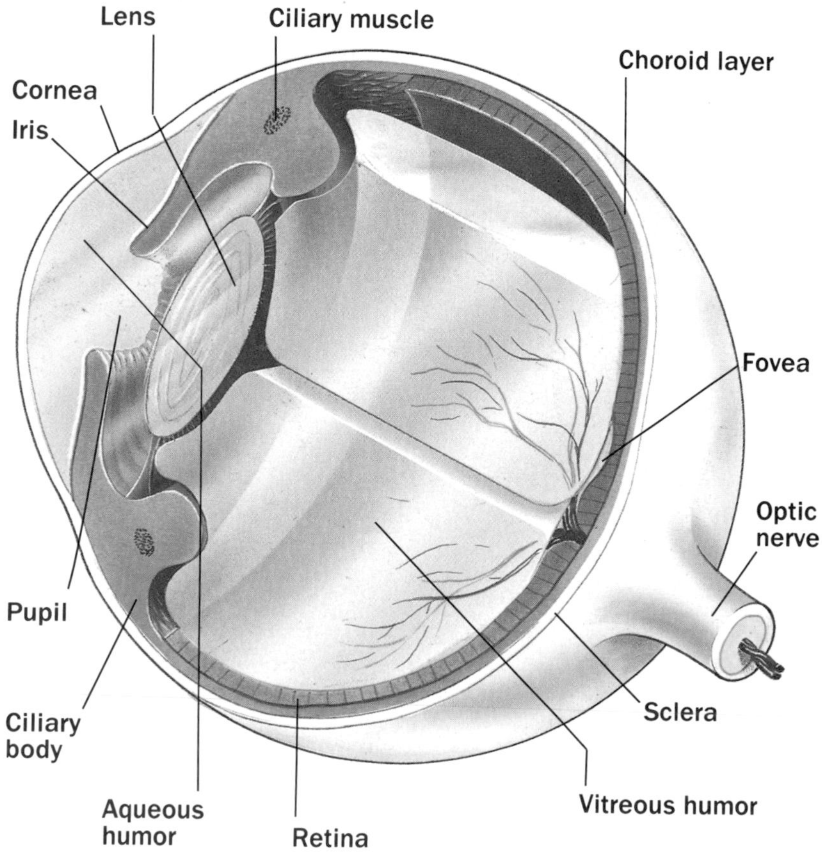

◁ The lens of the eye bulges when the ciliary body contracts. Light from near objects is focused on the retina by a bulging lens, and from distant objects by a thin lens.

DID YOU KNOW?

There is a blind spot at the back of the eye. This is where the nerve fibers leave for the optic nerve and there is no room for rods and cones. You can find your blind spot by closing your left eye and concentrating on the cross. Move the book nearer to you until the dot disappears. We do not usually notice the blind spot because we have two eyes.

+ ●

△ The rods and cones of the retina are arranged so that light must travel through their nerve connections before it reaches them. This seems a strange arrangement. But because the nerves are quite transparent and the brain can fill in any gaps in the image by guesswork, it works well.

COLOR VISION

Human beings have very good color vision, unlike many other animals. We see the sights around us in shades and mixtures of all the colors of the rainbow. Light travels in waves of different lengths and each wavelength is seen as light of a different color. Things appear to be particular colors because of the type of light they reflect or give out.

The cones of the retina are responsible for our ability to see color. There are three types. One type responds to red light, one to blue light and one to yellow light. Everything we see is made up of mixtures of these three colors. The brain analyzes the signals coming from all three types of cone and interprets the color in a similar way to mixing paint. For example, if a lot of yellow- and blue-sensitive cones are firing, but not many red-sensitive cones, in a particular part of the retina, then that part of the image is seen as green.

PROJECT

Find out how the eye produces an image by making a box camera. You will need a shoe box with a lid. Cut a square out of one end and cover it with tracing paper. Make a tiny pin hole at the other end. Point the box at a strongly lit image. The image on the tracing paper will be upside down. This is the same in the eye.

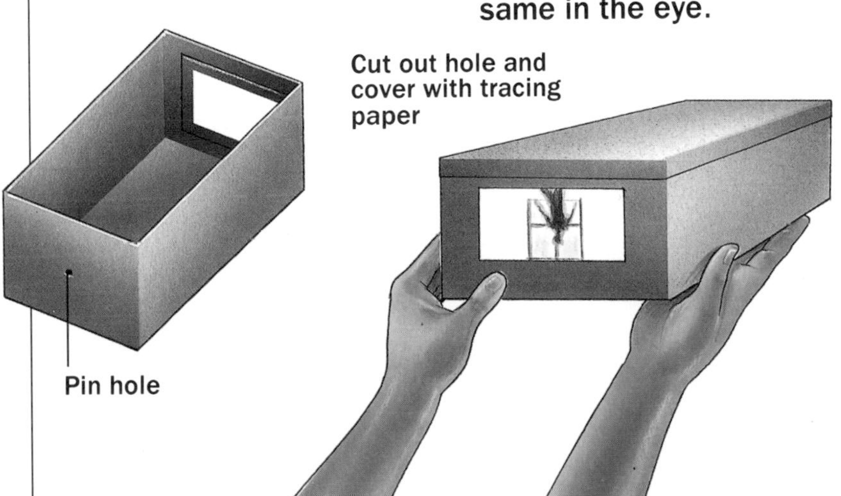

Our sense of hearing, although not as good as that of many animals, serves us very well. Our hearing spans a broad range of sounds, from the gentle patter of rain to a great clap of thunder. We can also hear a wide range of high and low notes. Most importantly, hearing enables us to speak to each other.

△ Many animals have much better hearing than humans. Bat-eared foxes have huge ears that they can swivel in different directions to pick up the sounds of the insects and small animals they hunt. The large ears can "scoop up" a large amount of sound.

THE EAR

The ear flaps act as funnels that direct sound waves into the ear canals. The canals pass into the bone of the skull.

At the end of each canal is an eardrum, which vibrates when sound waves hit it. The vibrations pass along the three tiny bones which are connected to the inside of the eardrum. The last of these bones rests on another membrane which forms an oval window into the inner ear.

The inner ear consists of the semicircular canals (which are concerned with balance) and a coiled cone called the cochlea. It is in the cochlea that the sounds are converted to electrical impulses the brain can understand.

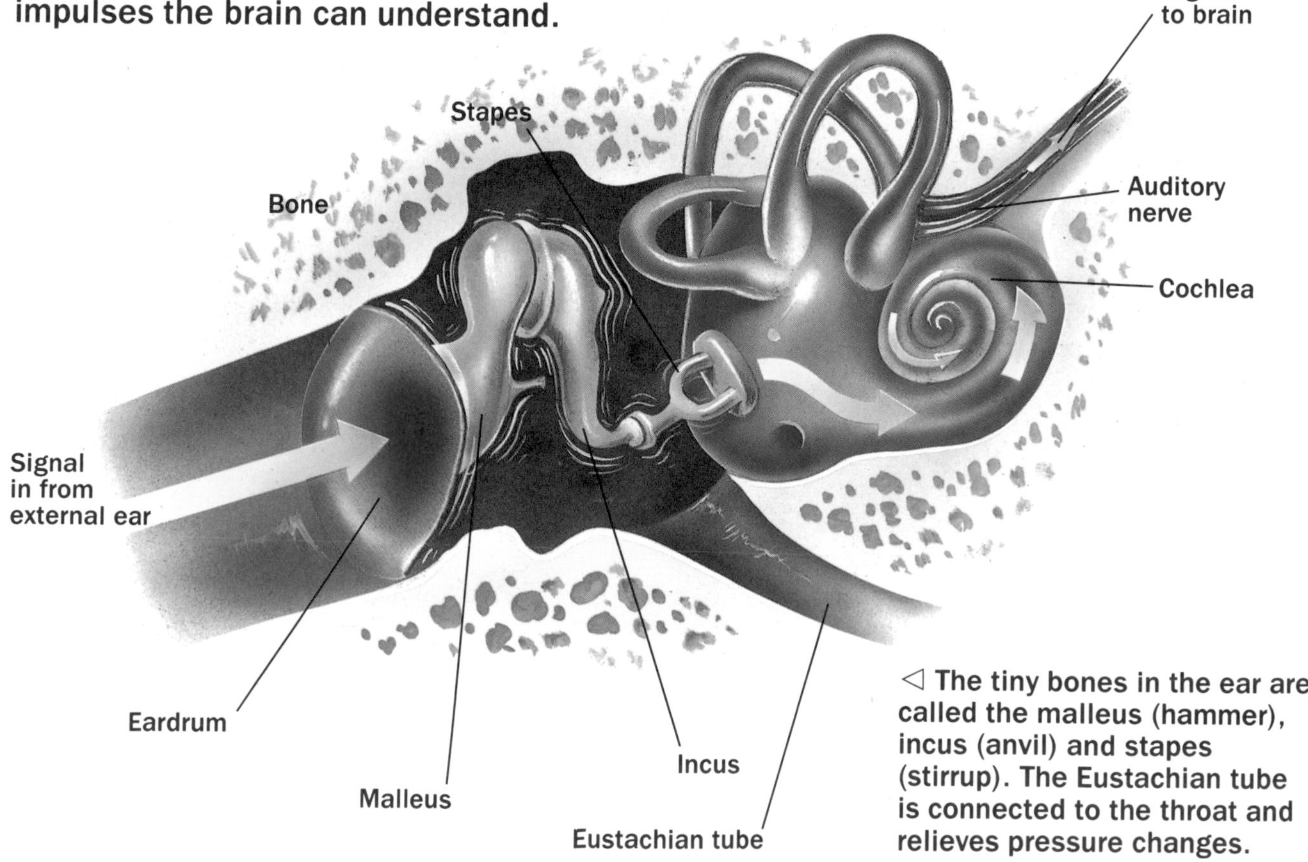

◁ The tiny bones in the ear are called the malleus (hammer), incus (anvil) and stapes (stirrup). The Eustachian tube is connected to the throat and relieves pressure changes.

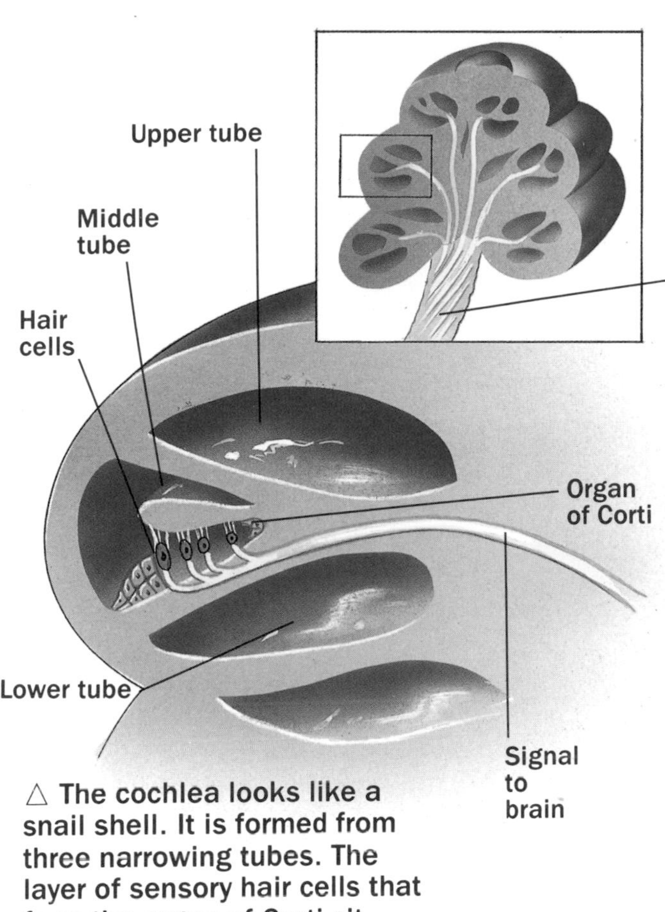

△ The cochlea looks like a snail shell. It is formed from three narrowing tubes. The layer of sensory hair cells that form the organ of Corti sit between two membranes.

PROJECT

Close your eyes and get a friend to move a ticking clock around the room. Can you tell where it is? Our brain works this out by comparing the signals from our two ears.

△ Like ears, microphones turn sounds into electrical signals.

THE SIGNALS

The cochlea is coiled around like a snail's shell. The inside of the cochlea is made up of three parallel tubes. The upper tube runs from the oval window to the point of the cone. The lower tube runs from the point of the cone back to a tiny round window at the wide end. These two tubes are connected at the end point of the cochlea and they contain watery perilymph fluid. The middle tube contains a fluid called endolymph, and is lined on the lower side by the sensory hair cells that form the organ of Corti.

The perilymph fluid carries sound vibrations from the oval window, along the cochlea and back to the round window. As the waves arrive at the round window, it bulges to relieve the pressure. The vibrations then pass on to the endolymph within the middle tube, the cochlea duct. The sensory hair cells respond to the vibrations in the endolymph and produce nerve signals. These travel along the auditory nerve to the brain, where they are interpreted as sounds.

The pitch of a sound is how high or low it sounds. It depends on the frequency of the sound waves (the number of vibrations per second). The ear can tell different pitches apart because different parts of the cochlea duct vibrate more strongly than others at different pitches. The narrow end of the cochlea duct vibrates more with low pitches, and the wide end of the duct vibrates more with high pitches.

The loudness of a sound depends on the amplitude (height) of the sound wave. Loud noises can damage the delicate membranes and sensitive cells in the ear. Amplitude is monitored as the vibrations pass through the tiny bones in the ear. Tiny muscles tighten to reduce the size and strength of the vibrations if the sound passing through is too loud.

Our eyes and ears respond to the physical energy of light and sound. Smell and taste are concerned with the chemical nature of the world around us. The sense organ of smell is within the nose. It detects the chemicals in the air we breathe when they dissolve in the mucus that lines the nasal cavities.

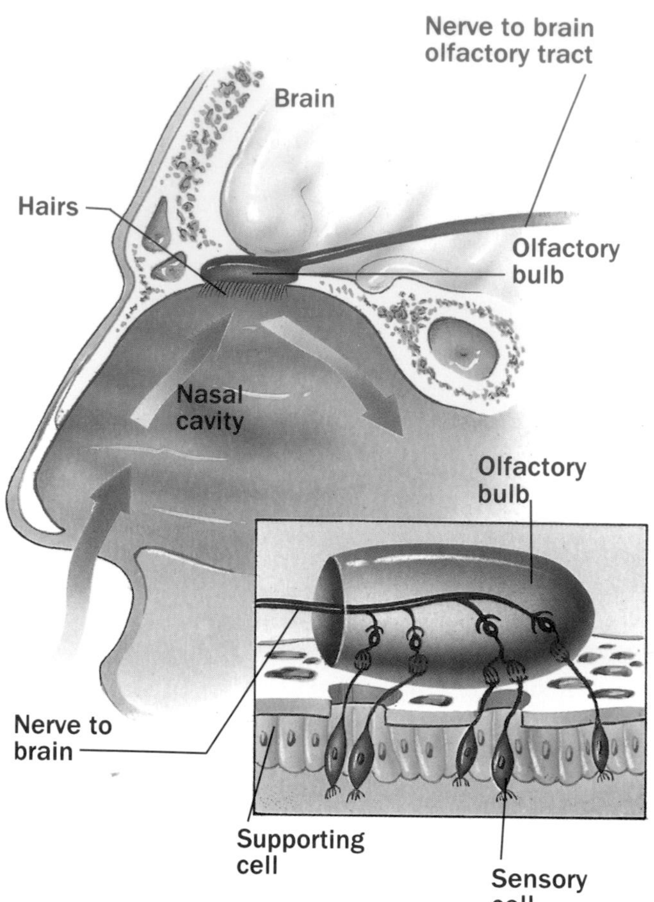

△ Smells are detected in the nasal cavities by the olfactory bulbs, which are extensions of the brain that carry the olfactory nerves.

THE SENSE OF SMELL

The olfactory (smell) organs are in the roof of the nasal cavity. They consist of the two olfactory bulbs. The area of each bulb involved is quite small – about ¾ inch across. The bulbs lie just behind the bridge of the nose. The nasal cavity is lined with skin-covered ridges of bone called the turbinate bones. These help to direct the air we breathe over the olfactory bulbs and down to the back of the throat.

Beneath the olfactory bulbs are cells with tiny hairs. These hairs hang down into the mucus that covers the nasal cavity lining. When the hairs detect molecules of odor in the air, they trigger electrical impulses. The impulses pass to nerve cells in the olfactory bulb and then on to the brain.

Scientists are not exactly sure how we can recognize so many different smells. It is thought that there are at least seven different types of smell receptor cells, and possibly a lot more. The system may work like a "lock-and-key" mechanism. Each odor molecule has a certain shape, so that it only fits into a site on the sensory hairs of the type of cell that detects that particular smell.

The seven or more types of smell occur in different proportions in different smelly substances. The brain can tell by the mixture of signals it receives what the substance is. Everyone can smell as many as 3,000 different smells, but only experts, such as wine tasters and people who make perfume, have trained their brains to remember this many.

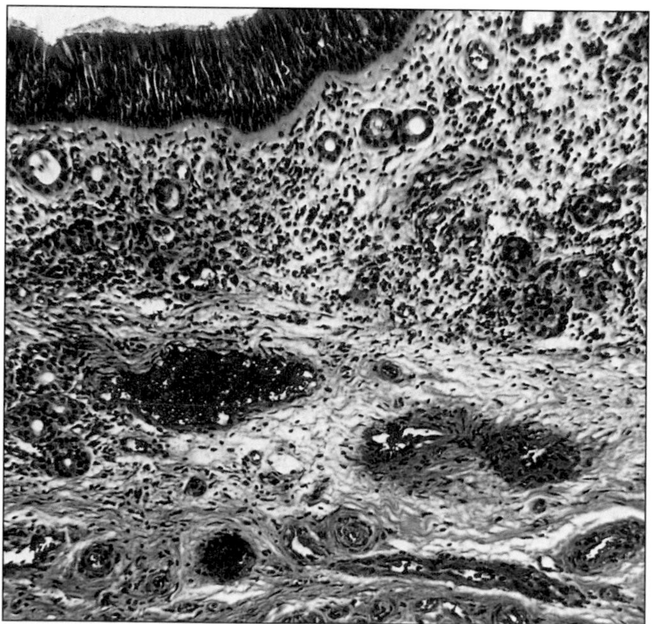

△ Fibers from the olfactory bulb can be seen (top left).

SMELLS

Today we use our sense of smell for pleasure rather than survival. We grow flowers with strong scents and we cook using lots of herbs and spices with mouth-watering smells. We spend a lot of time trying to hide our own body smells and replace them with perfumes. We even wash our clothes and linen in fragrant laundry detergents.

Animals such as dogs still use body smells as a way of recognizing a friend or an enemy. They also leave their scents all around their home territory. Body smells are very important to some animals when they want to reproduce. The smells they produce change when they are ready to mate. These sorts of smells are called pheromones and they carry very powerful messages.

Humans also produce pheromones, but they are much less important than in many animals. Experiments have shown that we are unconsciously aware of them. For example, one experiment showed that people tend to choose a seat in a waiting room if it has had a human pheromone sprayed onto it.

△ Male lions wrinkle their noses when they smell a female pheromone.

△ Humans do not have a good enough sense of smell to use when hunting. So they have trained dogs to point in the direction that the smell of an animal is coming from.

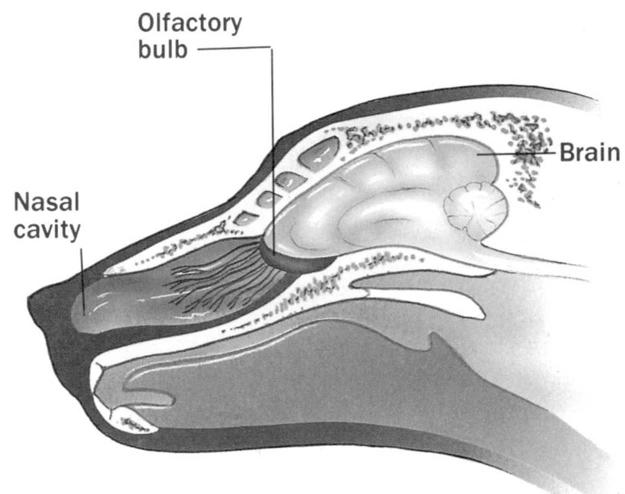

△ A dog's scent apparatus is much larger than ours and employs a much greater part of its brain. A dog's world is as full of smells as ours is full of sights. They recognize other dogs and people by their scents alone. They recognize smells on clothing and footprints, even though the person is long gone. They can also seek out chemical smells such as drugs and explosives.

Our sense of taste is 10,000 times less sensitive than our sense of smell. The two senses work very closely together. Food never tastes quite the same when your nose is blocked up with the mucus of a cold. The tongue is the organ of taste. It can only detect four kinds of taste: sweet, sour, salt and bitter.

THE TONGUE

The tongue is a muscular organ which serves to mix the food in the mouth. It pushes food between the grinding teeth and stirs in the saliva that begins the digestive process. The surface of the tongue is covered with tiny bumps (papillae). In pits between the papillae are groups of special cells. These groups are known as taste buds. The cells detect certain types of chemical when they enter a taste bud. They then send signals along nerve fibers to the brain. Taste buds can only detect chemicals when they are dissolved. One purpose of saliva is to make sure that the chemicals in food that make it taste do dissolve.

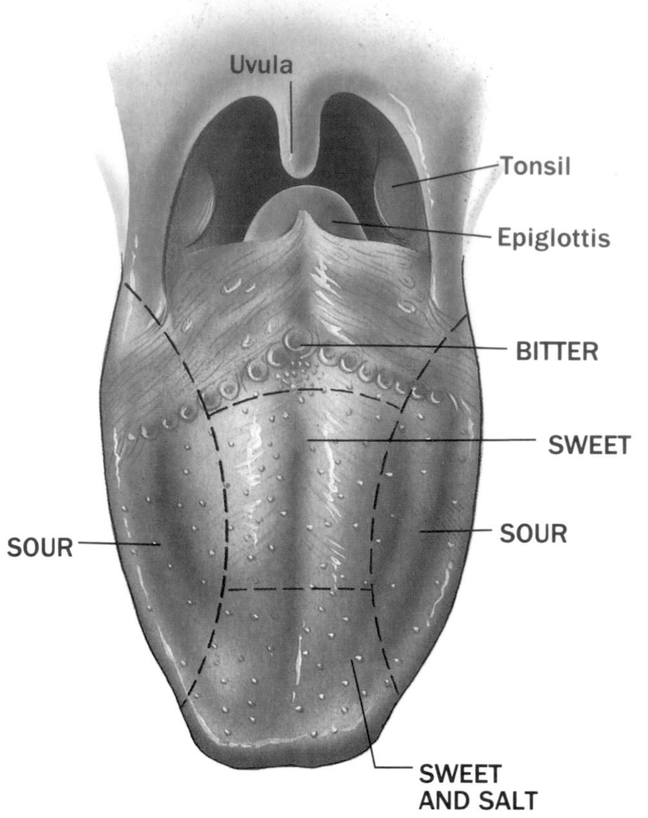

△ Different areas of the tongue have taste buds that respond to different tastes. The tongue is a muscle and can move in all sorts of ways so that food is mixed with saliva and every bit of the mixture touches every taste area.

TASTE AND SMELL

Test your senses of taste and smell and see how they work together. Cover your eyes and taste small amounts of salt and sugar with a clothes pin on your nose. Can you tell the difference? Now try without the clothes pin. Repeat the test with lemon juice and vinegar. Can you taste these tastes all over your tongue? Try placing them on the areas shown in the diagram of the tongue (at the top of the page) with your finger.

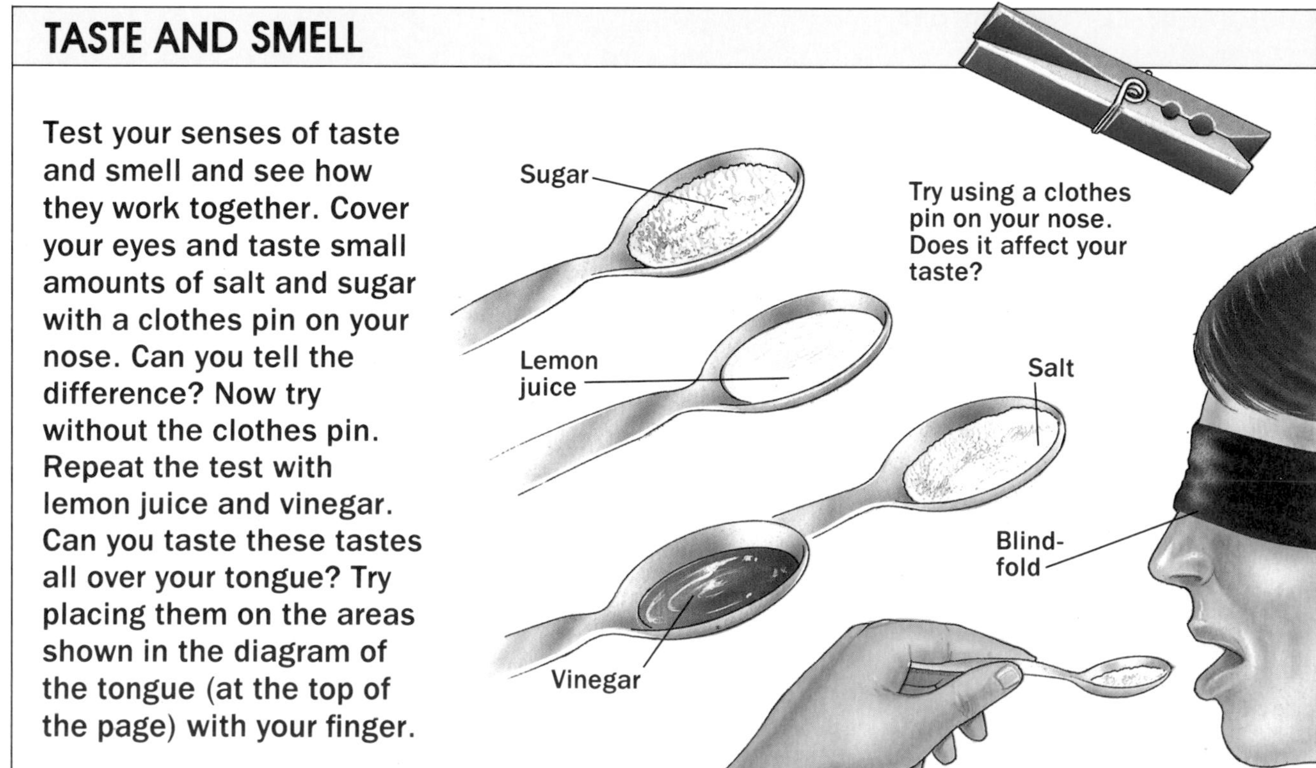

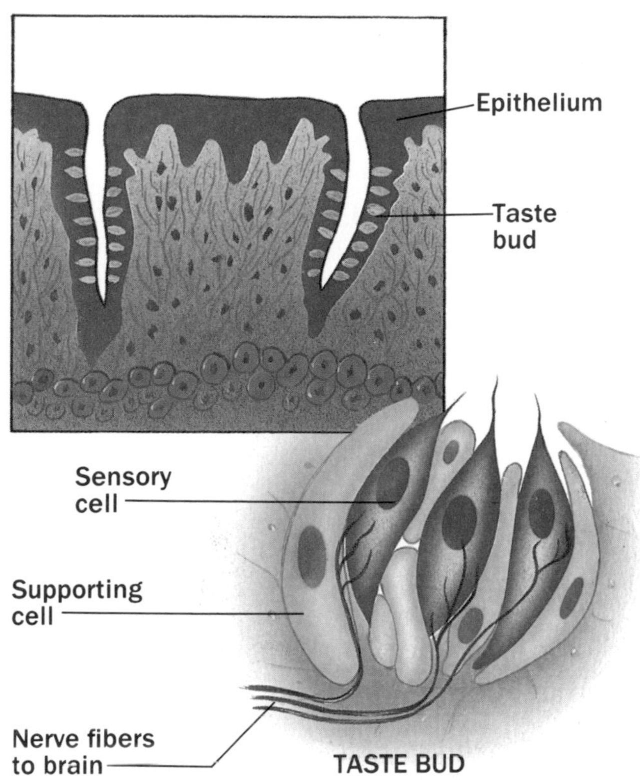

△ Taste buds nestle in pits on the tongue's surface. They are made up of chemical receptor cells which test the solution of food and saliva in the pit. There can be as many as 10,000 taste buds on the surface of the tongue.

△ The tongue is used to move and taste food.

TASTE AND DIGESTION

Mixtures of signals from taste buds in the tongue are sent to the brain. Here they are combined with information from the smell receptors in the nose. The brain analyzes the information and compares it with memorized tastes and smells. We can tell if the food is good or bad, and if we have eaten it before and enjoyed it. We may even suddenly be able to remember all kinds of things about the time and place in which we last experienced a particular taste.

Smell and taste not only serve to monitor our food, but they also get the digestive system going. Mouth-watering smells and tastes cause the salivary glands to produce saliva as soon as food is in our mouths. Chewing creates more taste and causes yet more saliva to be produced. Saliva helps to liquefy and lubricate the food for its journey down the digestive tract. It also contains enzymes – chemicals that begin to break down molecules in the food – and antiseptic substances to kill germs.

Tastes and smells quickly become less noticeable. A meal that tastes delicious for the first few mouthfuls may become quite ordinary by the time the plate is empty. The tastes have not changed, but we have become used to them.

DID YOU KNOW?

Taste buds are not only found on the tongue. They are also found on the soft palate at the back of the roof of the mouth, on the epiglottis and in the membranes lining the throat. There are many more taste buds in the mouth of a child than in an adult, and they continue to disappear as we get older.

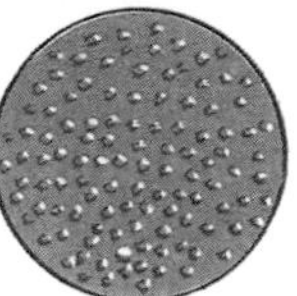

Age 14

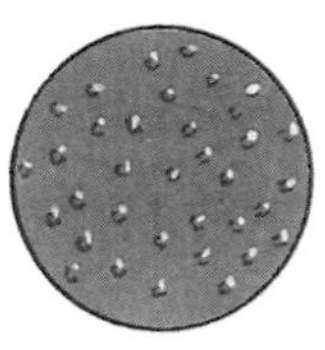

Age 60

We need to have information about things that are in contact with our bodies so that we can walk, hold things, avoid pain and injury, and touch other people. The skin that covers the surface of the body is full of nerve endings which respond to different amounts of pressure, pain and heat.

PRESSURE AND PAIN

The body is covered with about 21 square feet of skin. The skin's functions are to keep germs out and water and other body contents in, to help regulate temperature and to serve as a sense organ.

The skin consists of three layers. The lowest layer is fat. Above it is the dermis, in which blood vessels, nerves and nerve endings, sweat glands, the roots of hairs and oil-producing glands are found. The outer layer is the epidermis. It is constantly renewing itself as its outer dead layers are worn away.

The nerve endings found in the skin are of different types that respond to different stimuli. Those that are sensitive to pain caused by an injury have free ends with no capsule. The ends of light touch receptors are in capsules just under the epidermis. They are mostly in areas of skin which have little or no hair. The capsules of heavy pressure receptors are bigger and deeper in the skin and look like onions. There are many of them on the soles of the feet and palms of the hands. The hairs that cover the skin and scalp also have sensory nerves which respond when the hair is moved by an external force.

All these sensory nerve endings soon become used to the stimulus that initially makes them react. We can feel our clothes when we put them on in the morning, but soon do not notice them unless they are very uncomfortable. We know when our feet first touch the floor but we forget them if we stand still for some time.

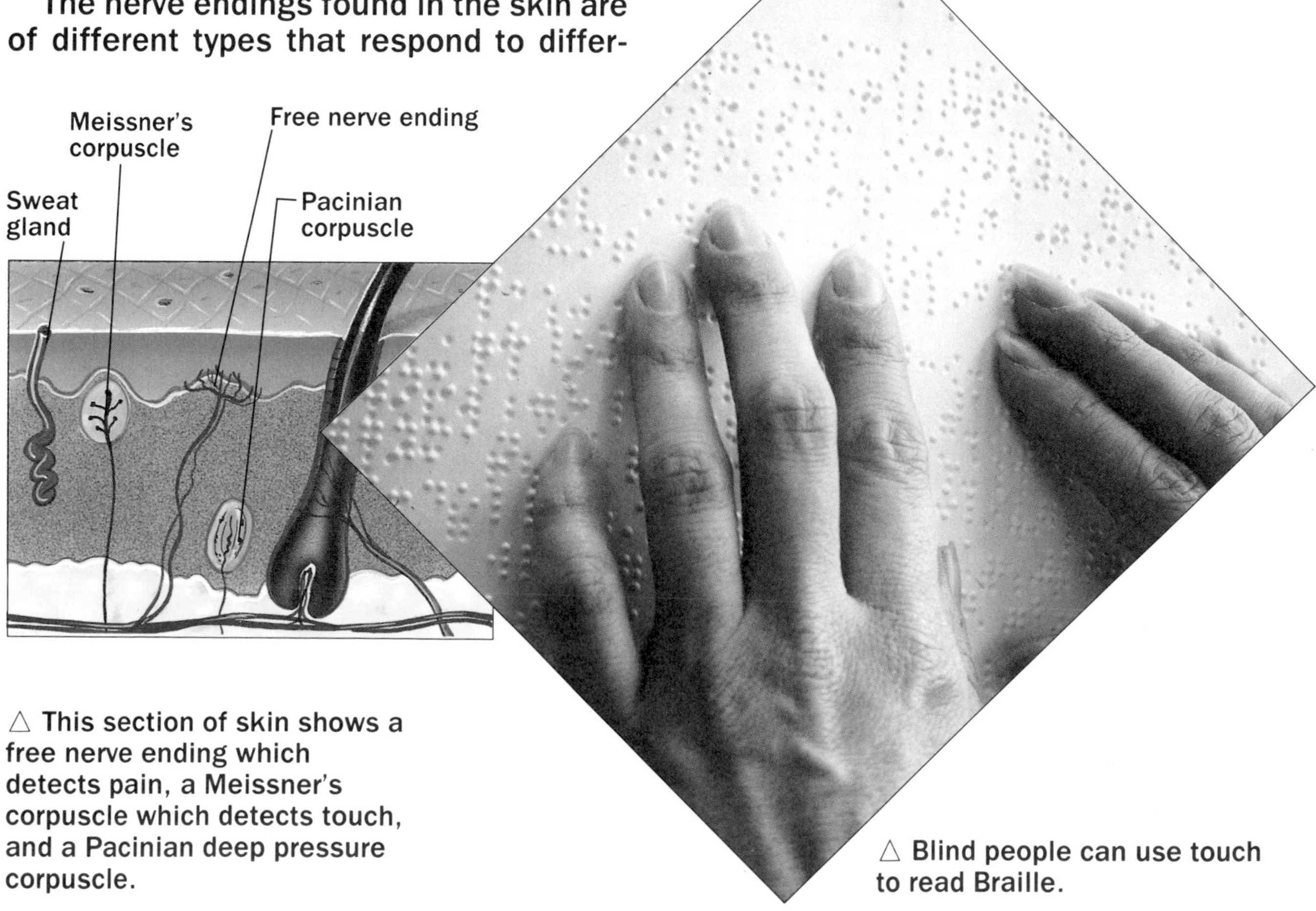

△ This section of skin shows a free nerve ending which detects pain, a Meissner's corpuscle which detects touch, and a Pacinian deep pressure corpuscle.

△ Blind people can use touch to read Braille.

HOT AND COLD

The nerve endings that feel cold are just below the epidermis. They are enclosed by large irregular capsules. The heat receptors are deep in the dermis and are shaped like a squashed sphere. The skin's sensitivity to temperature is very important because it is the main organ that controls body temperature.

When we get too cold, the skin increases its insulation qualities by raising all the little hairs on its surface. The hairs trap a layer of air which reduces heat loss. The blood vessels in the skin also become narrow to decrease the amount of warm blood at the surface; this also reduces heat loss.

If these measures do not produce an increase in the skin temperature and the body is likely to become too cold, instructions go the muscles to shiver or contract and relax very rapidly. Shivering is an involuntary reflex outside our control. We cannot stop it even if we want to. It burns up energy, producing heat within the body in the same way as running or stamping. Our behavior is also influenced by the lowering of skin temperature. We seek warmth by putting on more clothes or turning up the room heating.

△ Touch is one way for people to communicate.

When we get too hot, the hairs on the skin lie flat, increasing the circulation of air around the body. The blood vessels expand to allow more warm blood to flow near the skin's surface. Also, the sweat glands produce quantities of liquid. Sweat is a salty solution which also contains some waste products. We produce it most of the time in greater or lesser quantities. But when we are hot we can lose several quarts of water a day through the skin. As the sweat evaporates, it draws heat from the skin and so causes it to cool down. This cools the blood near the surface.

△ A young orangutan uses its lips to learn by touch.

DID YOU KNOW?

Our fingernails are not just useful for scratching. They also help to push the whole of the fingertip against the object we wish to feel. This increases the sensitivity of the fingertips.

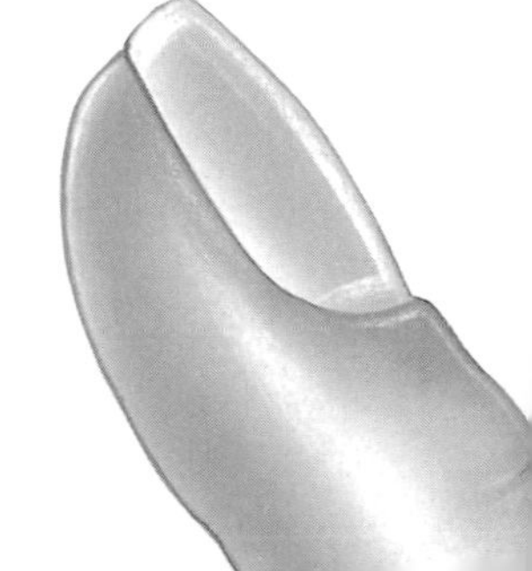

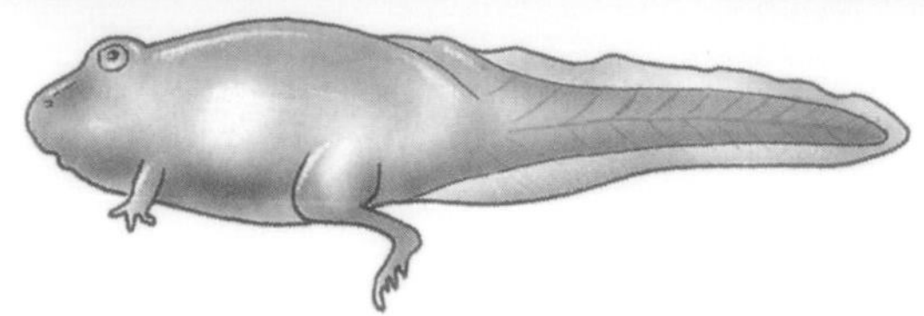

encyclopedia of science

REPRODUCTION

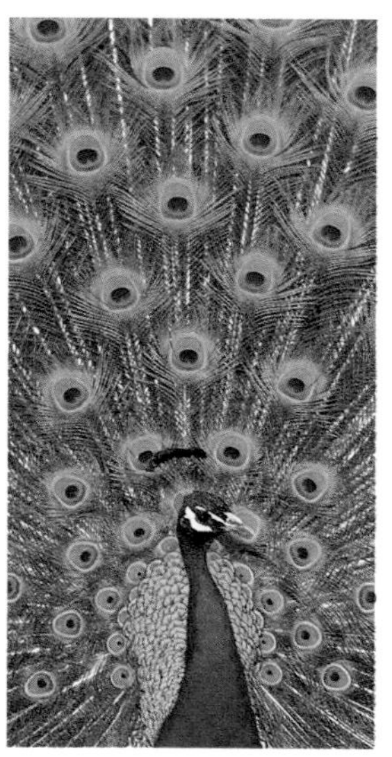

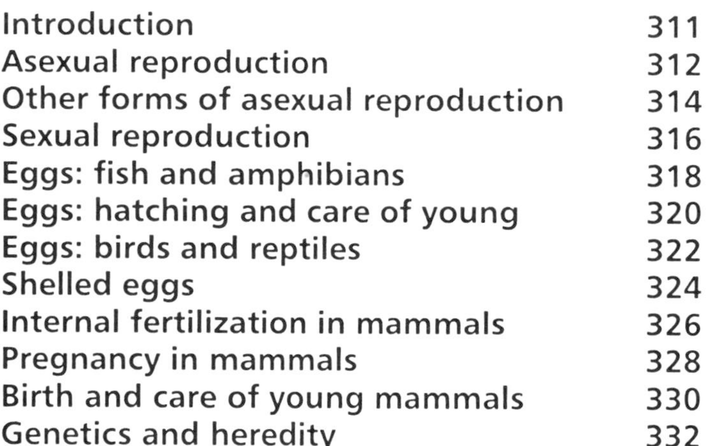

CONTENTS

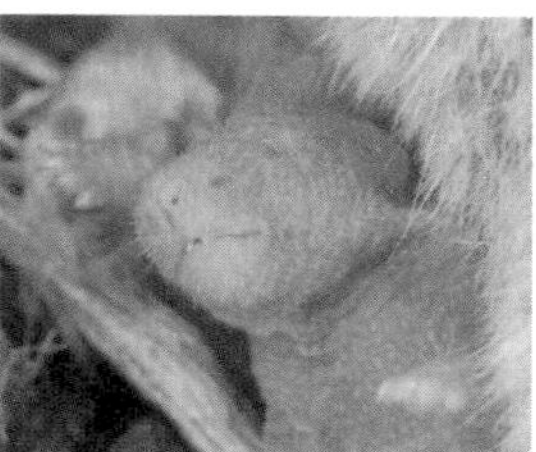

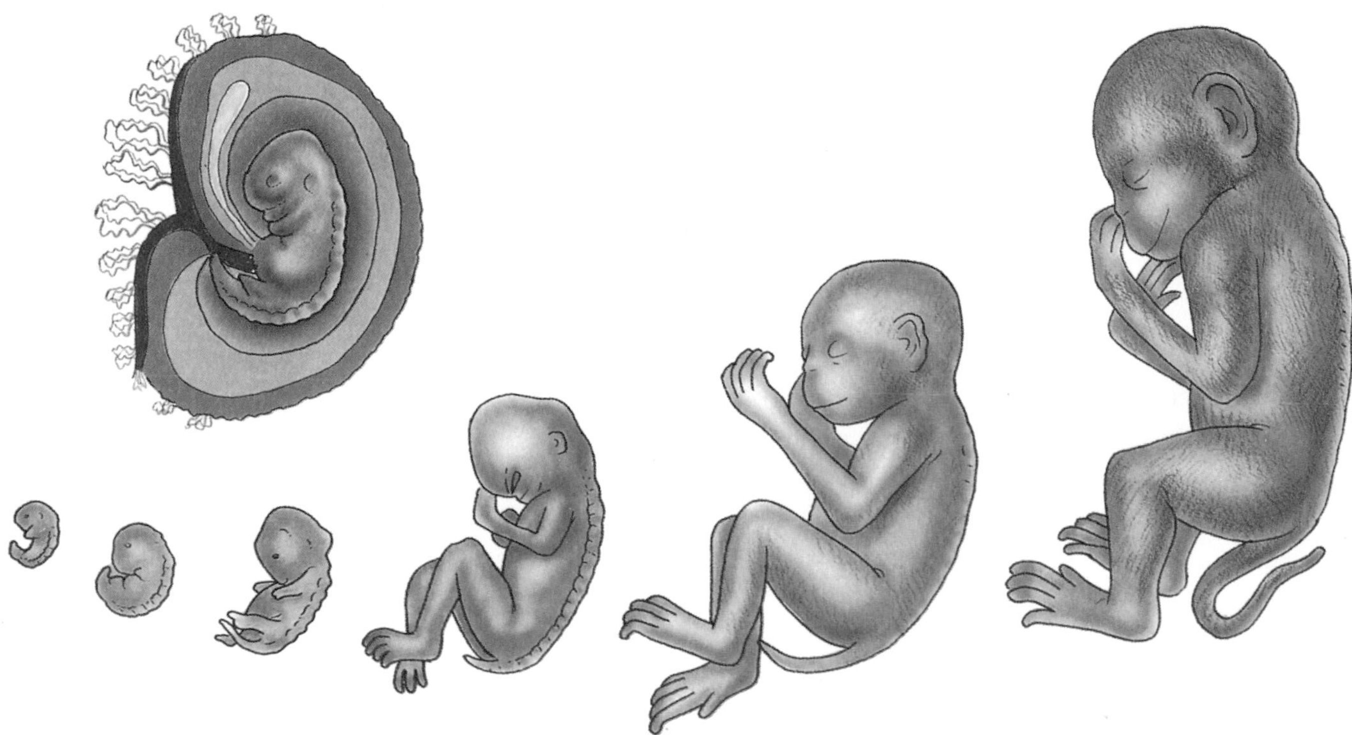

INTRODUCTION

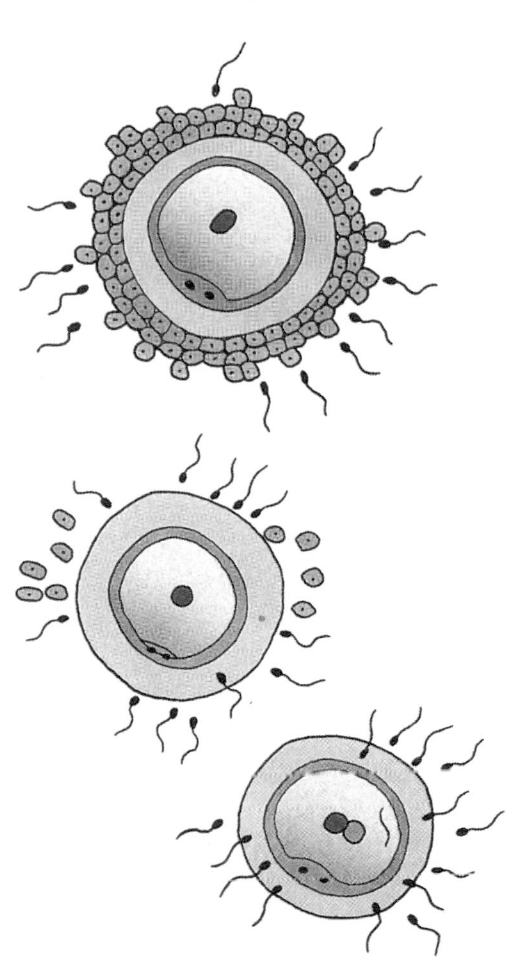

Reproduction is the creation of new individuals from existing members of the population. It is a characteristic of all living species. The members of a species must reproduce if the species as a whole is going to survive. An essential part of this is the passing of information from parents to their offspring on how to develop. This information is stored in a substance called DNA.

Many tiny single-celled animals reproduce asexually. In asexual reproduction, the creation of a new individual requires only a single parent. Offspring created by asexual reproduction are identical copies of their parent.

Larger and more complex animals almost always reproduce sexually. New individuals are created by two parents, one female and one male. The basis of sexual reproduction is the female egg, which needs to be fertilized by a male sperm. The fertilized egg then develops into a new animal.

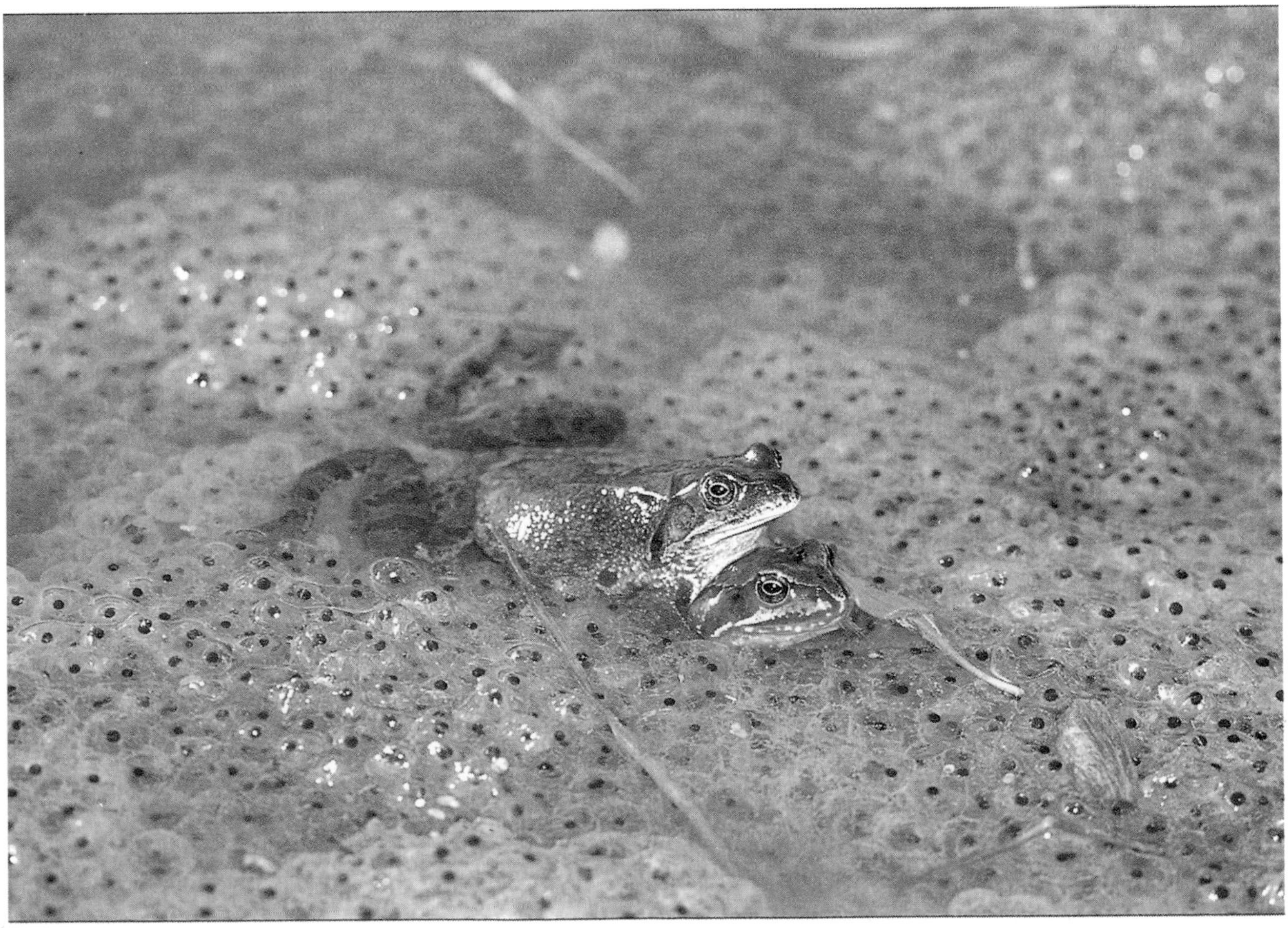

Many of the smaller organisms reproduce asexually. In asexual reproduction, only one parent is necessary in order to produce offspring. One advantage of this is that a large population can be created by just one individual. Some animals only reproduce asexually in conditions when rapid reproduction is useful.

BINARY FISSION

The most basic method of reproduction is binary fission. This is a method of asexual reproduction in which an organism duplicates itself by simply splitting into two. Binary fission happens almost entirely in microscopic organisms that consist of just a single cell, such as amoebas.

After binary fission, each new organism is only half the size of the "parent" organism. When feeding has increased their size, the new organisms can also undergo binary fission. This would produce a total of four organisms. These new organisms in turn can divide. The population can continue to double in size in this way until something stops the increase in numbers, such as the food supply running out.

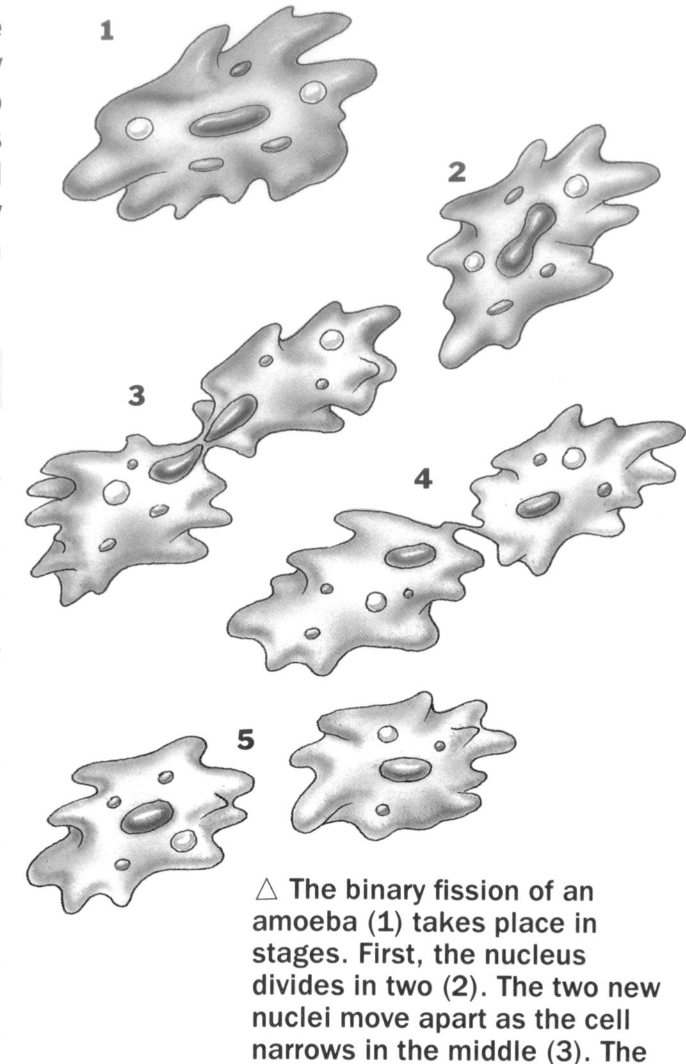

△ The binary fission of an amoeba (1) takes place in stages. First, the nucleus divides in two (2). The two new nuclei move apart as the cell narrows in the middle (3). The narrowing continues (4) until the cell splits into two (5).

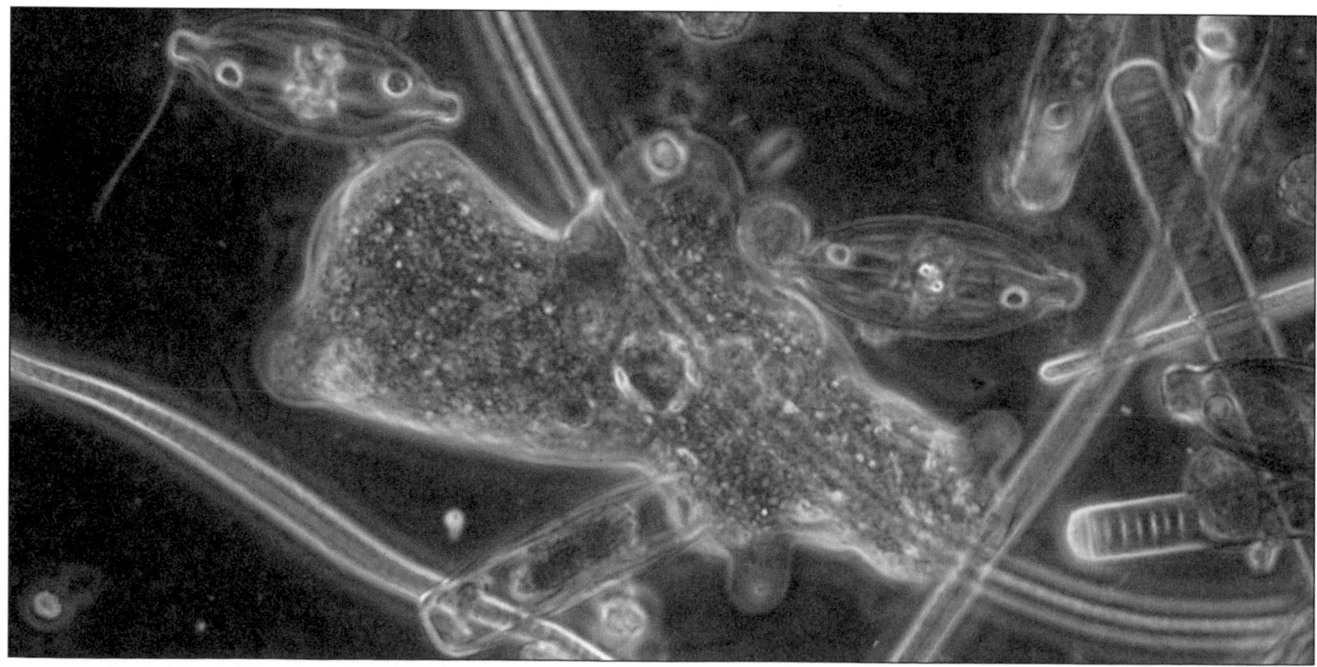

△ Amoebas measure about 0.25 millimeters.

REGENERATION

Larger animals that have simple structures can also reproduce by binary fission. Sea anemones, for example, can divide vertically down the center. The process is much more complicated than in amoebas, because anemones are many-celled animals. After dividing, the two halves of the anemone each grow a new replacement half by a process known as regeneration.

If an anemone is torn from a rock, any portion remaining on the rock can regenerate into a complete individual. Other nonmobile animals, such as sponges and corals, also have the ability to grow a new individual from small pieces that have broken off.

Flatworms are more complex animals. They have brains, eyespots and many internal organs. But they have great powers of regeneration. When cut into pieces, each piece grows into a complete new flatworm. Some species of flatworm can reproduce by deliberately dividing themselves across the middle. This is a quick way of producing new individuals.

Starfish often regrow a missing arm. Sometimes, a detached arm may regenerate the rest of the starfish.

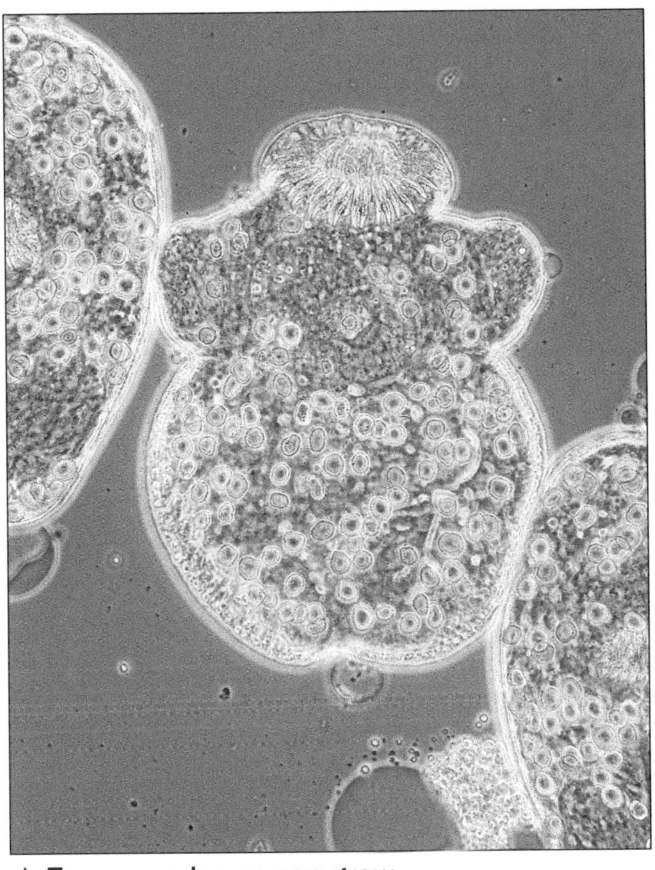

△ Tapeworm larvae can grow many new segments by a process of regeneration.

▽ Planarian flatworms have distinct heads and tails. But if a flatworm is cut into three pieces, even the tail piece will regenerate back into a complete animal.

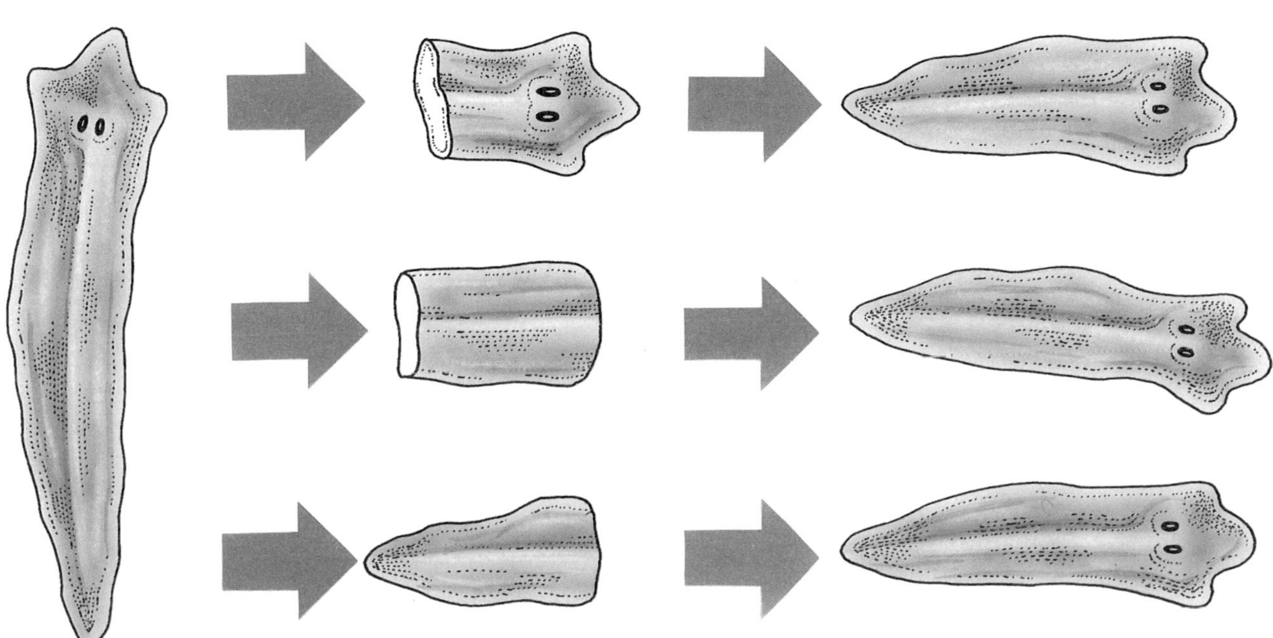

BUDDING

Some organisms reproduce asexually by budding. An example of such an animal is the hydra, which can grow a new individual from a bud on the side of its body. At first, the bud is just a small swelling. It grows into a miniature version of the adult before it breaks off from the parent. Animals that are produced by budding are often referred to as "daughters" of the parent animal.

Sea anemones are closely related to hydras, and can also reproduce by budding. In many species, the buds grow inside the body cavity of the adult. When they have grown large enough to survive on their own, the daughters are ejected through the adult anemone's mouth. They then anchor themselves to rocks.

Some segmented worms can reproduce by a form of budding. The new individual forms from the lower half of the worm, and the two halves then separate.

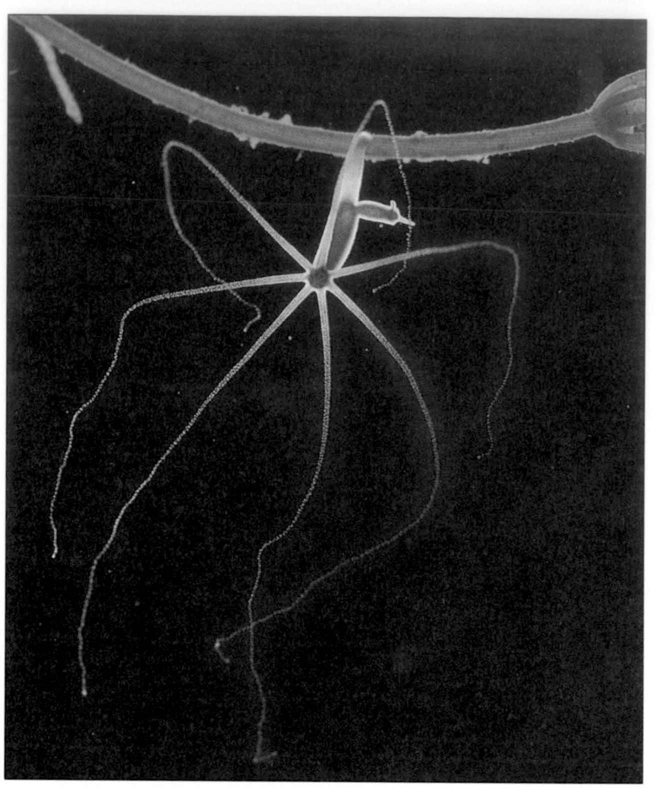

△ Hydras develop buds when food is plentiful. If food is scarce, the parent may absorb the bud back into its body.

INSECTS' EGGS

You can find insects' eggs in many places. The eggs are always very small – usually less than a millimeter across. The easiest place to find insects' eggs is stuck to the bottom of leaves. These are often the eggs of butterflies.

Make notes of all the eggs you can find: how big they are and what color, where you found them and how many there are. See if you can find out what kind of insect laid them. Never take away the eggs: they may belong to a rare species.

As well as insects' eggs, you can also find spiders' eggs quite easily. Many spiders lay their eggs in their webs. The eggs are wrapped in a little package of the silk that the web is made from.

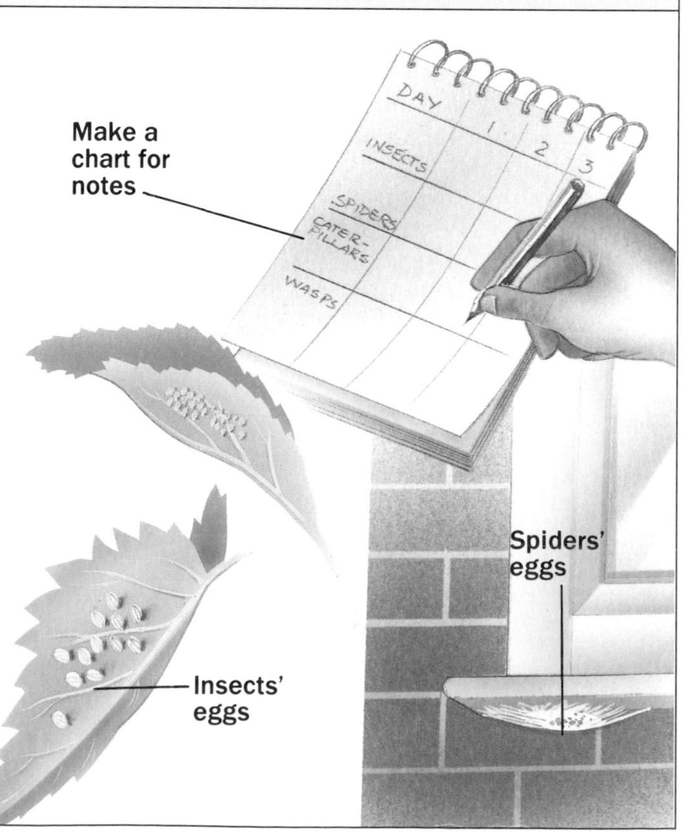

PARTHENOGENESIS

A special form of asexual reproduction called parthenogenesis is found in some more complex types of animal, and especially among insects. Parthenogenesis is the process by which females by themselves produce eggs that develop into new animals. In many ways, parthenogenesis is like sexual reproduction, but it occurs without the need of sperm from the male to fertilize the eggs. Usually, all the eggs develop into female animals. This means that a whole generation of animals may be produced that consists entirely of one sex.

Aphids reproduce by parthenogenesis as part of an annual cycle. In spring, female insects are born that lay eggs without mating. The eggs soon hatch into more females, and during the summer there are several entirely female generations. At the beginning of fall, the females lay some eggs that hatch into males. When they have hatched, mating takes place. The eggs that are laid after mating remain dormant during the winter, and then hatch into females at the beginning of spring.

Daphnia, the water flea, is not in fact an insect, but a crustacean – a relative of such animals as shrimps. Daphnia, which lives in freshwater ponds, often reproduces by parthenogenesis. In some species, the females can produce two sorts of eggs: ones that develop by themselves, and ones that need to be fertilized by sperm.

△ It is possible to see the eggs being held inside the transparent body covering of a female daphnia. The eggs are usually released. But sometimes they are kept inside the body until the animal dies.

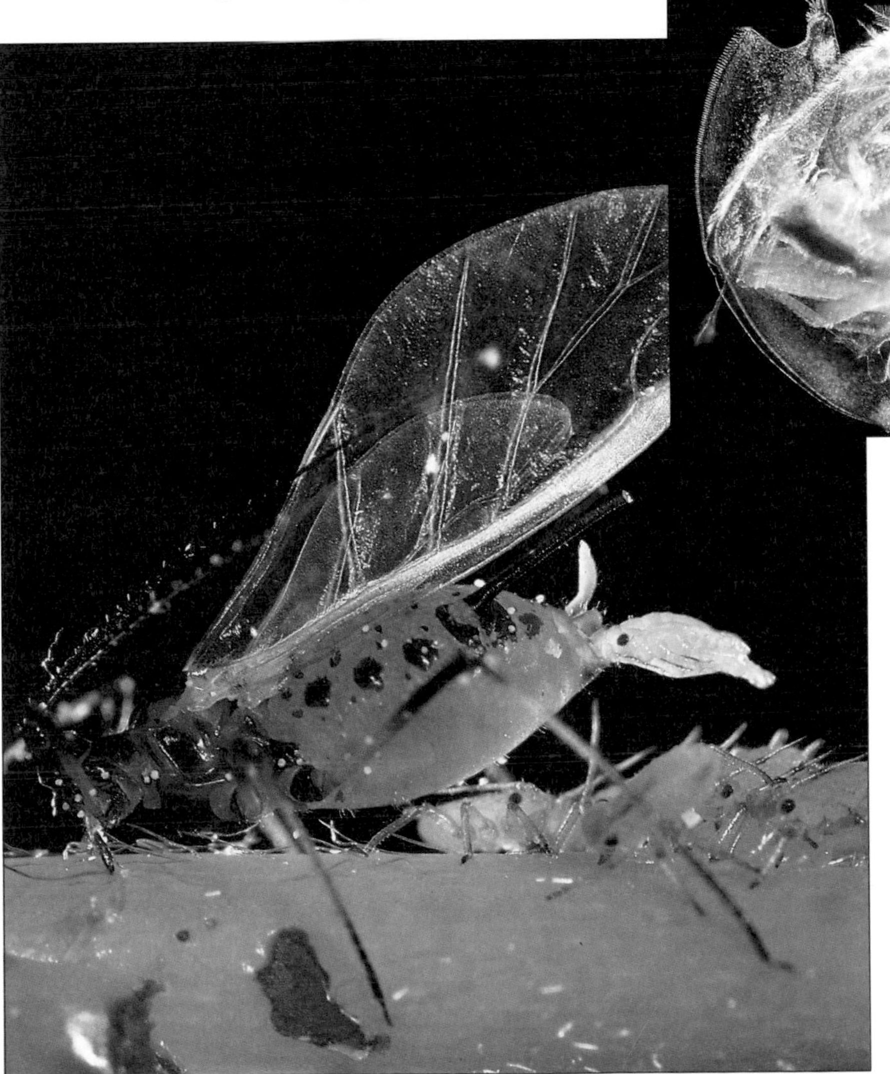

◁ Aphids damage plants by feeding on their sap. A single female aphid can quickly produce a population of many thousands. This is why gardeners and farmers consider aphids to be such a serious pest.

SEXUAL REPRODUCTION

Sexual reproduction takes place by the joining of female and male sex cells after mating. The big advantage of sexual reproduction is that new animals are formed from material provided by two parents. This is important for several reasons, such as good characteristics being spread through the species.

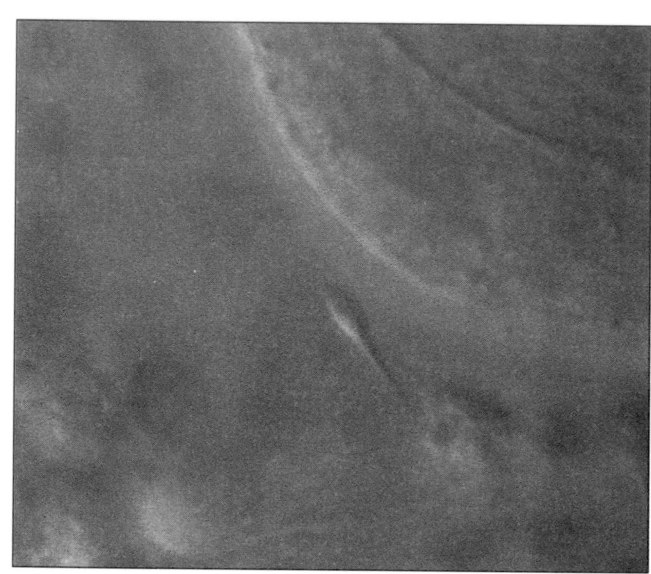

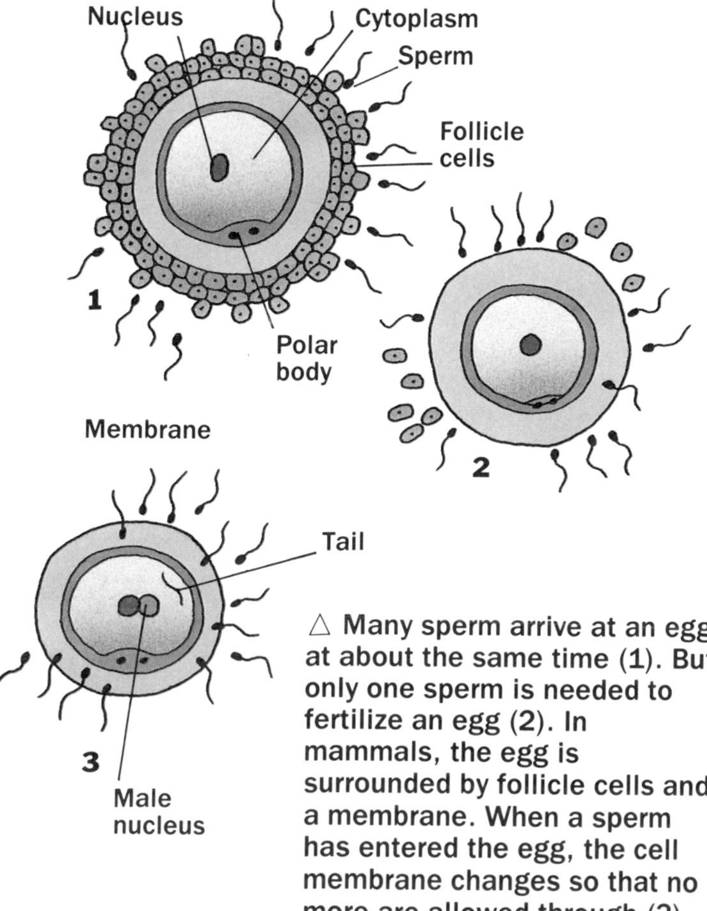

△ Many sperm arrive at an egg at about the same time (1). But only one sperm is needed to fertilize an egg (2). In mammals, the egg is surrounded by follicle cells and a membrane. When a sperm has entered the egg, the cell membrane changes so that no more are allowed through (3).

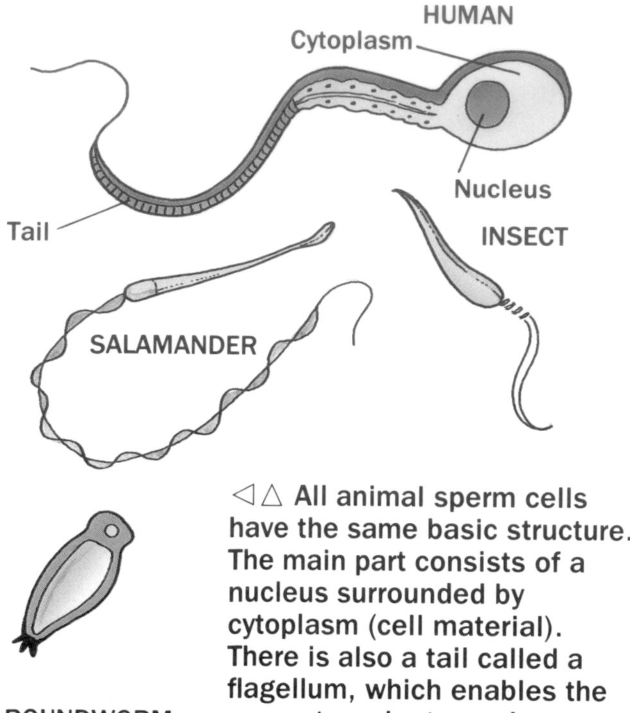

◁△ All animal sperm cells have the same basic structure. The main part consists of a nucleus surrounded by cytoplasm (cell material). There is also a tail called a flagellum, which enables the sperm to swim toward an egg.

EGG AND SPERM

All animals produce special sex cells, which are known as gametes. Female gametes are called eggs, and male gametes are called sperm. These cells are produced by special sex organs: the ovary in females, and the testis in males. Eggs are usually much larger than sperm because they store material needed for when they grow; they are also produced in smaller numbers.

Neither gamete can develop into a new animal by itself (parthenogenesis is a rare exception). A new animal can grow only after fertilization. During fertilization, a sperm breaks through the membrane that surrounds an egg. The nucleus of the sperm then joins with the nucleus of the egg. This creates a cell known as a fertilized egg, or zygote.

The most important feature of sexual reproduction is the fusion (joining) of the nuclei. The nucleus of each gamete contains half of the information needed to make a new individual. In order to understand the process, it is necessary to look more closely at how cells divide.

CELL DIVISION

Cells reproduce themselves by dividing into two new cells. This most commonly occurs when an animal is growing. Each new cell must contain all the information it needs about how it will develop and how it will work. This information is stored in the nucleus of the cell by a substance called DNA (which stands for deoxyribonucleic acid).

The DNA is divided into chromosomes. These only become visible when a cell is about to divide. Different animals have different numbers of chromosomes – for example, humans have 46. A cell that has a full set of chromosomes is known as a diploid cell. The chromosomes of a cell are in pairs. Each one of a pair has information about the same things. The diagrams here show what happens to only one pair of chromosomes.

Normal cell division is known as mitosis. Each chromosome is duplicated, producing two chromatids, which are joined in the middle. The chromatids from each chromosome move to opposite ends of the cell. Then the cell divides in the middle. The chromatids become chromosomes, so each new cell has a pair. The two new cells are just like the old cell, and both are diploid.

When producing gametes, cell division is called meiosis. Chromatids form and the cell divides. But the chromatids of each chromosome stay together, and the cell splits between the chromosomes. This gives two cells with only half the number of chromosomes. These are haploid cells. The new cells divide, splitting the chromatids. In the end there are four gametes, each with one chromosome (each gamete is haploid).

In fertilization, two gametes join together to produce a zygote. The zygote is a diploid cell. This cell will then divide by mitosis. You can now see that in a diploid cell, each chromosome in a pair comes from a different parent.

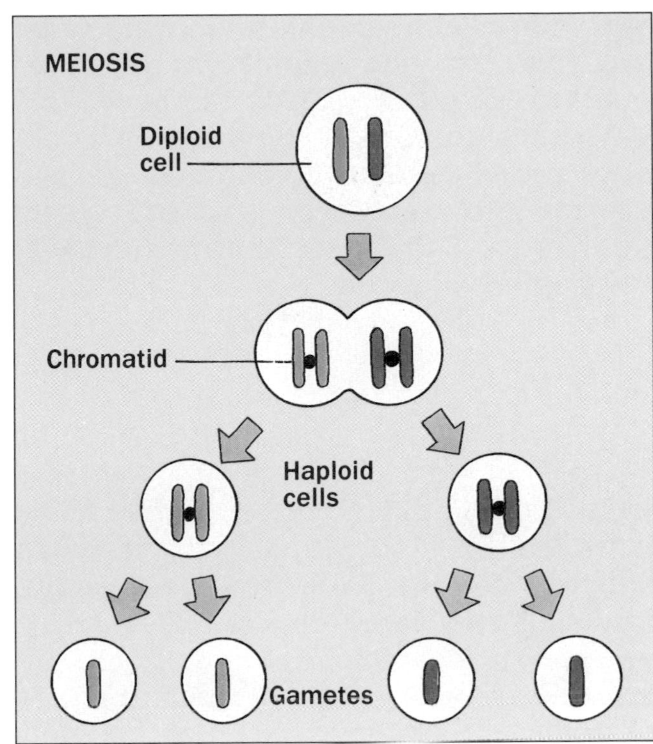

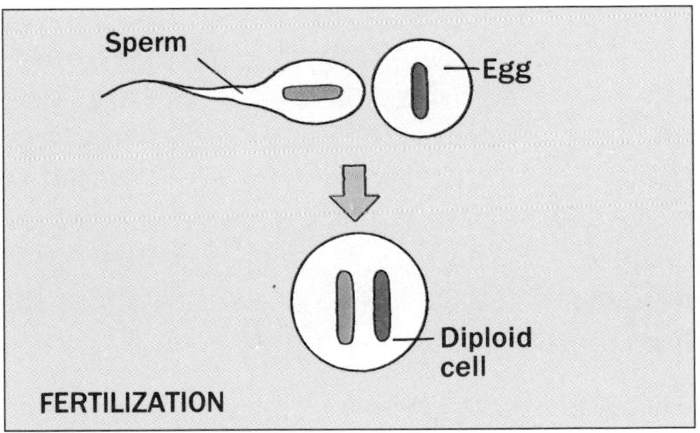

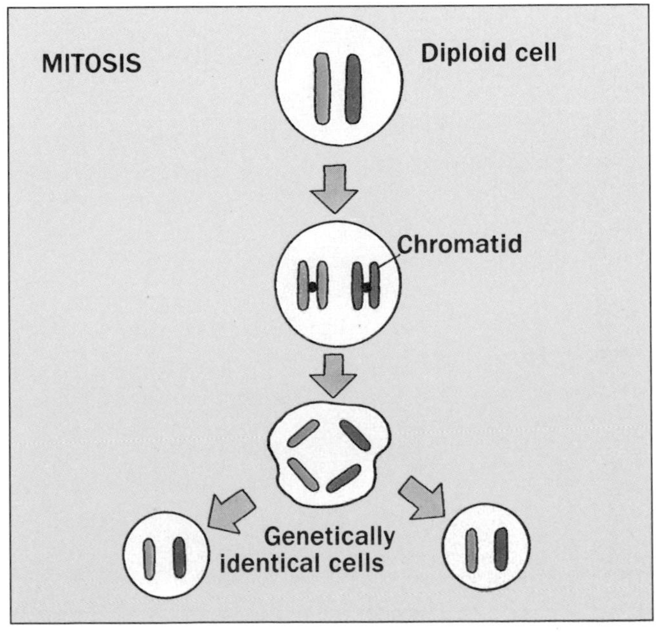

With most animals that live in water – for example, fish and amphibians – fertilization takes place outside the body. This process is known as external fertilization. Both sexes release gametes (eggs and sperm) into the water, and the sperm swim around until they make contact with the floating eggs.

COURTSHIP

Before external fertilization, courtship usually takes place. There are two basic purposes of courtship. First, it helps animals to know that they are opposite sexes of the same species. Second, it allows each animal to know that the other is sexually mature and ready to reproduce. Sexual reproduction can only take place if both parents produce and release gametes at the same time.

Courtship takes many different forms. For example, most species of frog give distinctive cries to show that they are ready to mate; many fish go through a series of special moves, like a sort of dance. There may also be signals from physical changes, such as the color of the animal's skin changing.

NEST BUILDING

Nest building is quite unusual among fish and other animals that live in water. Usually their eggs float freely or are attached to a surface. Some fish do build nests, however, and this is often closely linked with courtship.

Female trout and salmon make shallow scrapes in gravel at the bottom of streams. This attracts males, and means that when the female lays her eggs there is a male nearby to fertilize them. With sticklebacks, it is the male that builds a nest. This attracts females, who lay eggs which the male can fertilize.

△ The stickleback is one of the few fish that builds a nest.

△ The color of these male toads attracts females.

△ When a female jewel fish has laid her eggs, a male releases sperm over them.

RELEASE OF EGGS AND SPERM

In fish and amphibians, the process of laying eggs and fertilization is known as spawning. Some species of fish spawn in shoals (groups), with a large number of individuals releasing clouds of eggs and sperm at the same time. It is just a matter of chance whether a particular egg is fertilized by a particular sperm. Other fish species form definite female-male pairs, which spawn separately.

Among amphibians, such as frogs, forming pairs is the most common method of spawning. Two adults remain in physical contact through the whole process. Being in close contact gives the best chance of eggs and sperm meeting when they are released.

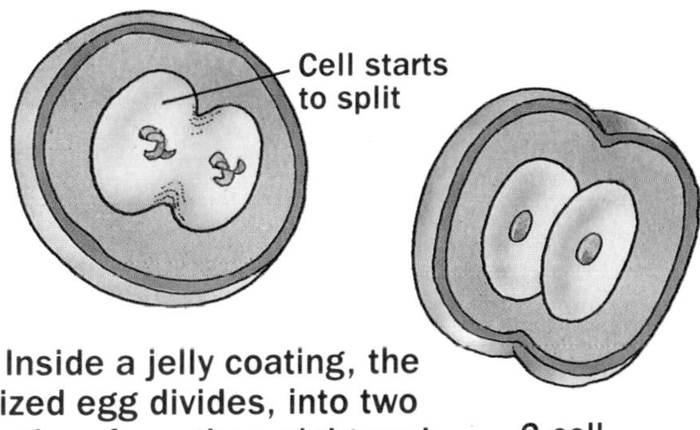

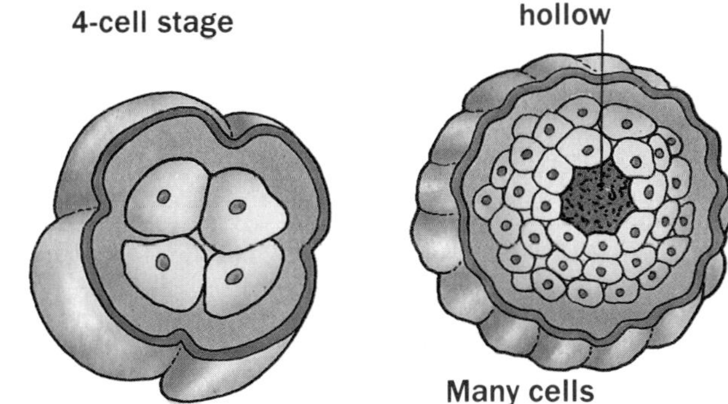

△▷ Inside a jelly coating, the fertilized egg divides, into two cells, then four, then eight and so on to form a hollow ball.

EARLY DEVELOPMENT

Once an egg has been fertilized and becomes a zygote, it begins to develop into a new animal. The zygote grows by dividing into two cells, which themselves then divide and so on (this is a process of mitosis). Each time the cells divide, the number of cells doubles.

During the first stages of the process, the cells multiply evenly until they form a hollow sphere, which is known as a blastocyst. By this stage, the new individual is known as an embryo. The embryo then starts to develop differently. Instead of all the new cells being the same as each other, special cells now start to appear. Each type of cell develops into a different part of the new animal's body.

As development continues, the embryo takes on a definite shape, and internal organs start to form. During the very early stages of development, all animal embryos have a similar appearance. The visible characteristics of different animals only appear later on.

Fish and amphibian eggs often have a jellylike coating. Inside this protective layer, the fertilized egg develops very rapidly. In some frog species, it takes just six hours for the zygote to become a blastocyst containing some 10,000 cells. About 48 hours later, frog embryos have already taken on a distinctive tadpole shape that is clearly visible through the jelly coating.

CARE OF EGGS

In the open sea, fish eggs usually drift in the water. In coastal and fresh waters, the eggs often have a sticky surface which holds them together in clusters or long tapes. These eggs can become attached to a stone or plant.

The only thing an embryo needs from outside an egg is oxygen. In very sheltered water – such as a nest – the amount of oxygen in the water may become quite low. The embryos may then suffocate. Male sticklebacks solve this problem by fanning their fins to sweep fresh water over the eggs.

Only a few other fish, such as the freshwater bass, guard their eggs. A larger number of amphibians take care of their eggs. The most unusual example is the gastric brooding frog of Australia. After fertilization, the female swallows the eggs and they develop and hatch inside her stomach.

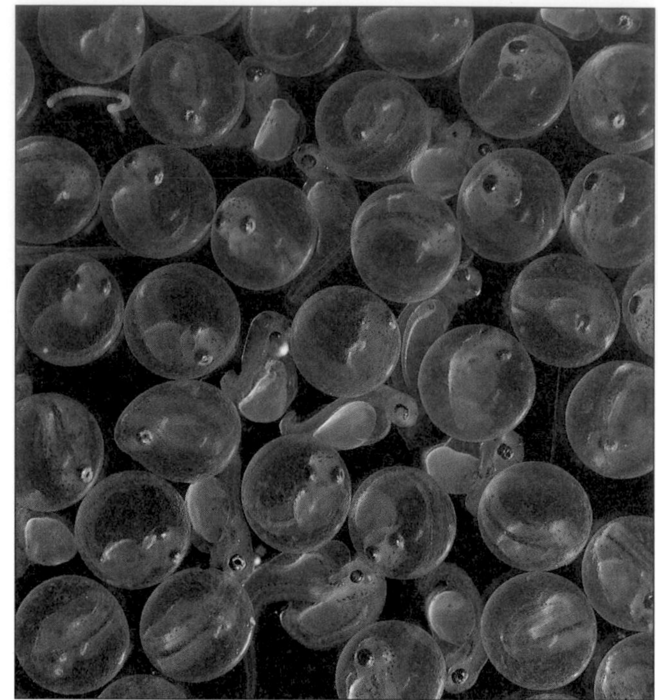

△ It is possible to see the developing embryos inside translucent carp eggs. The eyes are clearly visible. You can also make out the tails that the larvae will swim with.

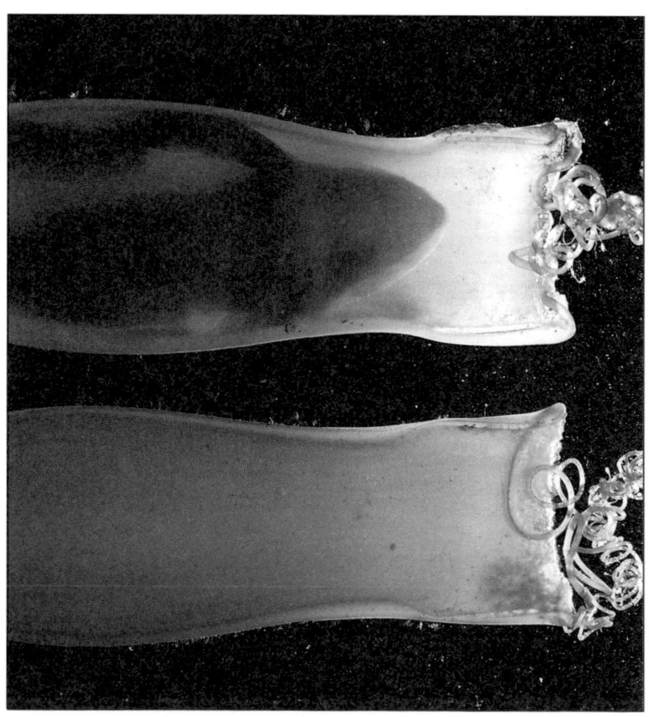

△ The larvae of dogfish can be seen developing in their egg cases, known as mermaid's purses. Here, one has already hatched.

HATCHING

Fish and amphibians lay very large numbers of eggs. For example, large toads can lay more than 20,000 eggs. This is mainly because a great many of these eggs will be eaten by predators.

Inside each egg, the developing embryo is nourished by yolk until it becomes a larva. When it is ready to hatch, the larva produces chemicals that start to dissolve the jelly coating around the egg. It then starts to make swimming movements, which help to free it from the jelly.

Fish eggs usually hatch quite quickly. Eggs in warm water tend to hatch more quickly than those in cold water. The eggs of a few tropical fish hatch in less than 24 hours. Most eggs hatch in two or three weeks. In a few cold-water species, the eggs do not hatch for about four months. Frog and toad eggs usually hatch in under two weeks.

▽ Tadpoles breathe with gills. After a while, the gills disappear and they breathe through spiracles. Finally they start to breathe through their mouths into lungs.

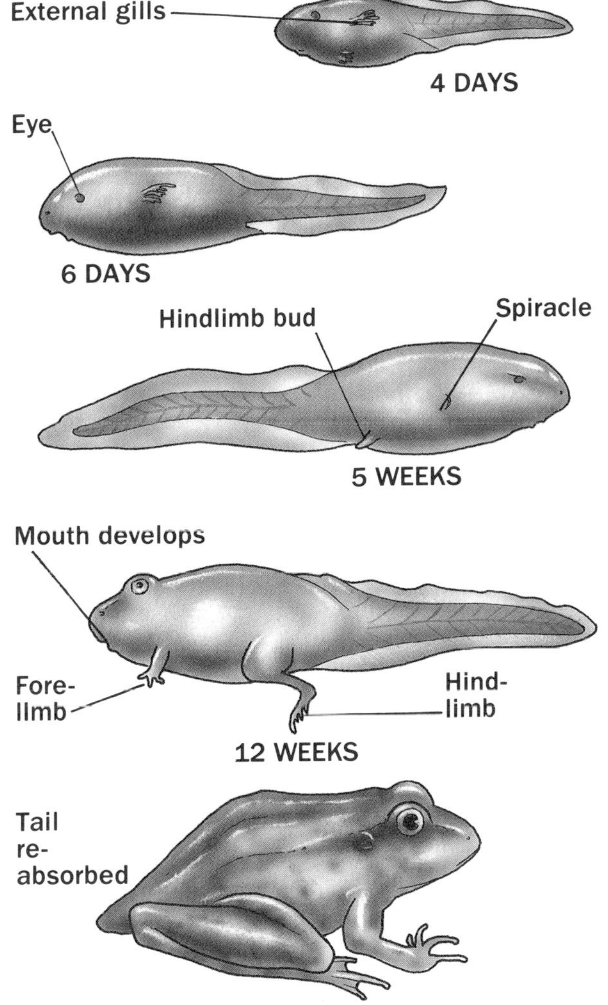

Fish larvae grow directly into adult fish. Amphibian larvae, however, undergo a complete body change, known as metamorphosis. Frog and toad larvae are called tadpoles. Their development takes place gradually over a period of a few weeks.

Some insects also go through metamorphosis. For example, butterfly eggs hatch into caterpillars, which grow but do not change in shape. They then become pupas (cover themselves in hard cases) before emerging as butterflies.

CARE OF YOUNG

The care of eggs and young offspring by the parents is known as brooding. The larvae of fish and amphibians are still in great danger of being eaten after they have hatched. This is another reason why fish and amphibians lay so many eggs – to make sure that at least some of them survive. With fish, looking after larvae is even more unusual than taking care of eggs. A few fish do guard their young. Examples are freshwater bass, some sticklebacks and Siamese fighting fish.

An interesting example of brooding is the several species of mouthbreeder fish. The fertilized eggs hatch and the larvae continue to develop entirely within a parent's mouth.

Care of larvae is more common in amphibians. This is especially true of those whose adults spend most of their time out of water. Examples are salamanders and tree frogs.

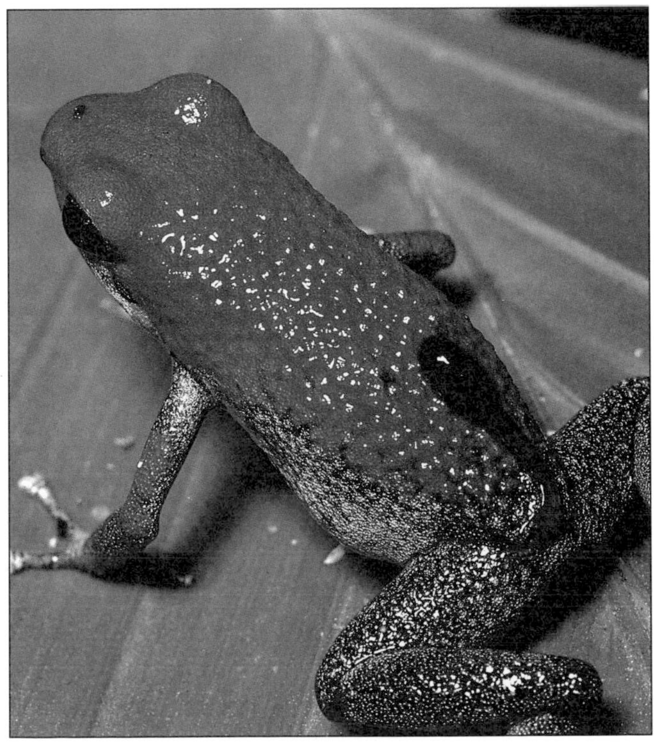

△ The male arrow-poison frog from South America lives on land and carries first eggs and then tadpoles on its back.

Reptiles and birds reproduce by internal fertilization. Their eggs are fertilized while they are still inside the female's body. The female lays the eggs after fertilization. The embryo develops inside the egg, which has a protective shell. Young reptiles and birds hatch out as miniature versions of the adult.

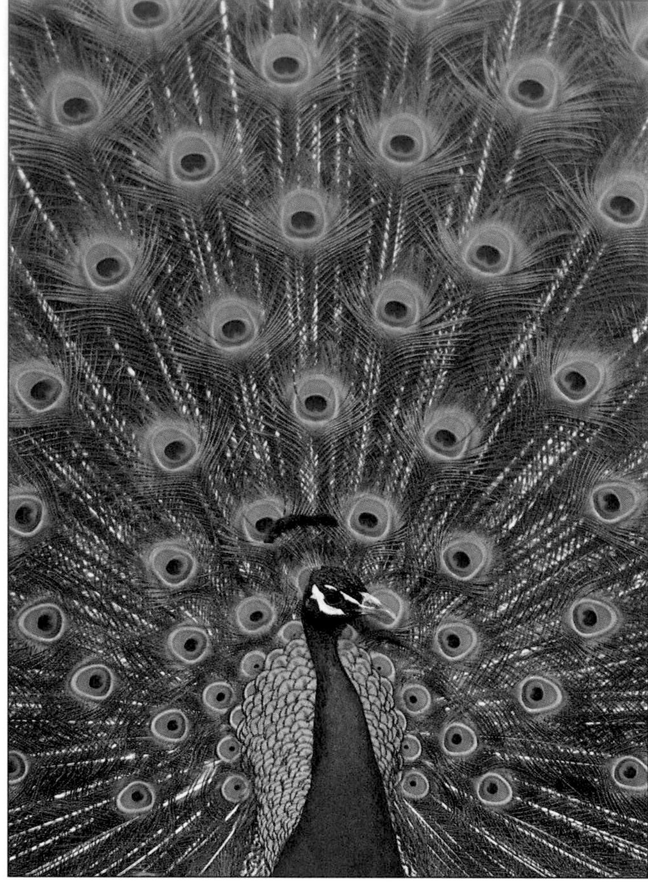

△ Male peacocks display their brightly colored tail feathers as part of courtship rituals.

COURTSHIP

Reptiles and birds form mating pairs. Sometimes the pair will split up as soon as they have mated. But often they stay together for the breeding season.

Male birds often establish their own territories. Their calls are both to attract females and to challenge other males. In the presence of females, the males of many species give complex displays of movement and color.

Courtship is not so complex among reptiles. It is seen most in lizards. Like birds, the males of some lizard species are more brightly colored during the breeding season.

BIRD COURTSHIP

You can quite often see birds courting. Courting usually, but not always, happens in the spring. You can often tell the male and female birds apart because they are different sizes or colors. You may see dancing or strutting, nods of the head, beaks being tapped together and many other sorts of behavior. Make notes of everything you see.

FERTILIZATION

Reptiles and birds have only a single opening (or vent) in the lower part of their bodies. This vent leads to a cavity known as the cloaca, which is used both for excretion and during reproduction.

In birds, sperm produced by the testes pass down a tube to the male cloaca. During mating, the male presses his vent against that of the female, and sperm is transferred from one cloaca to the other. From the female cloaca, the sperm swim up a passageway toward the eggs, which are released from the ovaries. The sperm fertilize the eggs.

The eggs of reptiles and birds need to be fairly large, because miniature adults hatch from them. Birds and reptiles produce many fewer eggs than amphibians and fishes do.

NESTS AND EGGS

Among birds, nest building is sometimes linked to courtship. An example is the African weaverbird. The male weaverbird makes the framework of the nest to attract a mate. With most birds, nest building is done by the female, although the male bird sometimes helps.

Birds' nests are often quite elaborate and take a lot of effort to build. They have to be a safe place for eggs, and also be a nursery for young birds.

The nests made by reptiles are much simpler. They are built by the female just before she lays her eggs. Some reptiles, such as the Florida alligator, heap mud over their eggs. Others, such as turtles, bury their eggs in sand.

▷ An African weaverbird's nest is built by the male. It weaves the nest mostly from grass in a tree where it is fairly safe from predators.

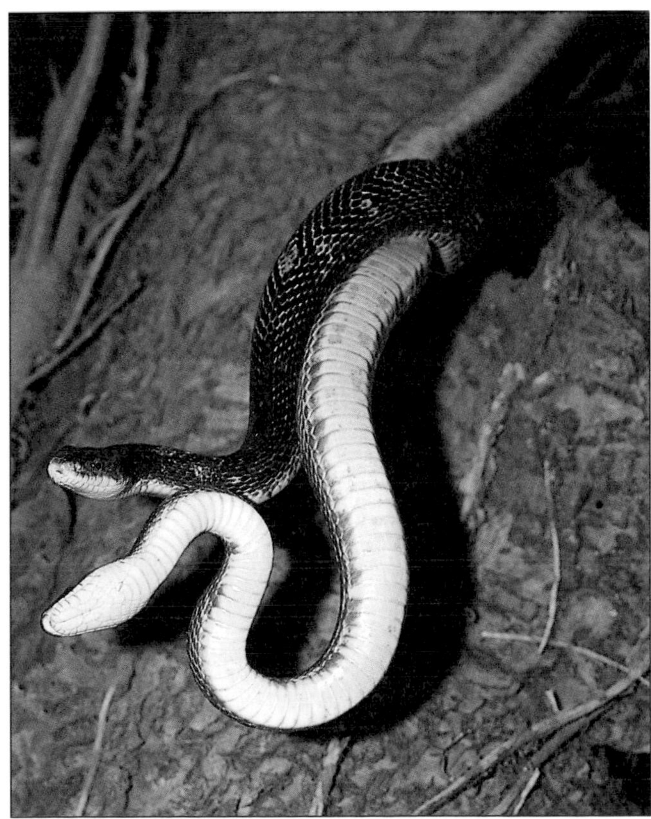

△ Mating black rat snakes twine around each other.

Eggs are produced in an organ called the ovary. They then pass down a tube (the oviduct), in birds to the cloaca. Eggs are usually fertilized just outside the ovary at the top of the oviduct. As an egg travels down the oviduct, it grows its tough outer shell. This creates a sealed environment that stops the embryo from drying out. The eggs of reptiles have a flexible leathery shell. Birds' eggs have a hard, brittle shell. Both types of shell have tiny holes that allow oxygen to pass inside and reach the embryo.

The eggs that are laid by a female at one time are known as a clutch. The number of eggs in the clutch is usually about the same in any particular species of reptile or bird. Reptiles most commonly lay larger clutches than do birds. A crocodile clutch may contain 70 eggs, and that of a turtle 200. Among birds, quails lay the biggest clutches with about 20 eggs. Clutches of five eggs or less are much more common.

INCUBATION

Birds are warm-blooded animals – they can keep themselves warm, even if their environment is cold. Bird's eggs must be kept warm if the embryo is going to continue developing after leaving a bird's body. Keeping eggs warm until they hatch is known as incubation. Birds incubate their eggs by sitting on them. Warmth is transferred to the eggs from an area on the bird's underside known as the brood patch. A layer of insulation that lines the inside of the nest, such as feathers and dry grass, helps to prevent heat from escaping. In most species, both sexes incubate the eggs.

Reptiles are cold-blooded – they obtain body heat from their environment. The warmth of the surrounding air or earth is usually enough to incubate reptile eggs. It is unusual for reptile parents to incubate their eggs.

△ A few species of snake incubate their eggs. For example, some female pythons warm themselves in the sun and then coil around their eggs to transfer the heat.

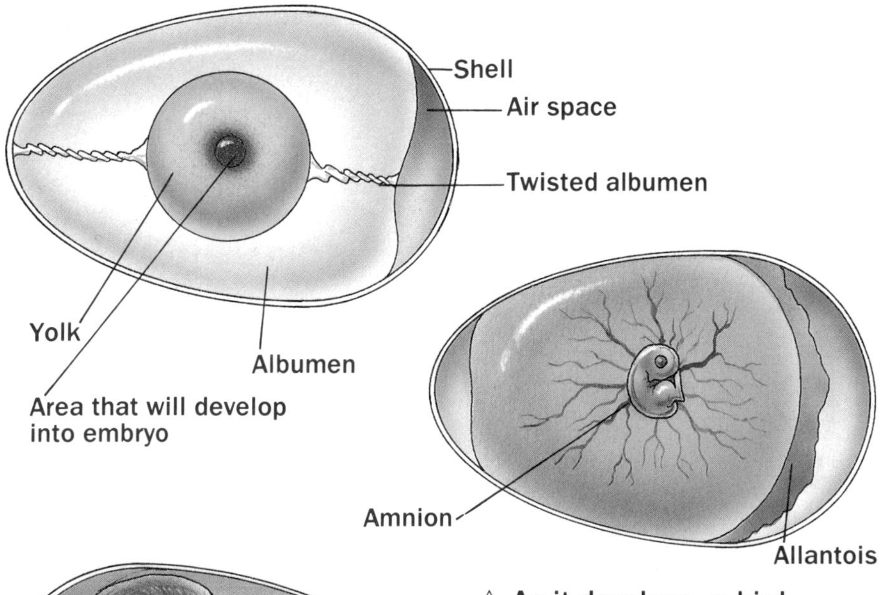

△ As it develops, a bird embryo feeds first off the albumen and then off the yolk. The embryo is surrounded by a membrane called the amnion. Another membrane, the allantois, forms a pocket for waste products. The air space gets bigger as water evaporates through the shell.

DID YOU KNOW?

The sex of some reptiles depends on the temperature at which the eggs were incubated. Alligator eggs kept below a certain temperature will produce females. Above that temperature they will produce males.

HATCHING

When the embryo in an egg is fully developed, it starts to move. In birds, a special hatching muscle at the back of the chick's neck starts to twitch. This twitching action drives the chick's head backward and forward against the inside of the eggshell. A special "egg tooth" growing from the chick's beak makes a small hole in the shell. This process is known as pipping.

The chick can now breathe fresh air using its lungs, and it rests in order to build up strength. A few hours after pipping, the chick starts to cut its way out of the shell using its egg tooth. The parents only help the chick in a very few species, for example, the ostrich.

Reptile eggs hatch in much the same way as bird eggs. The young reptile's egg tooth, which grows from the top of the snout, disappears soon after hatching.

INSIDE AN EGG

Take off a small area of the wide end of the shell of an egg, a tiny piece at a time. Can you see the air space? Then carefully crack the egg onto a plate. Can you see the parts that are labeled in the top picture of an egg on page 18? The egg can be cooked and eaten when you have finished.

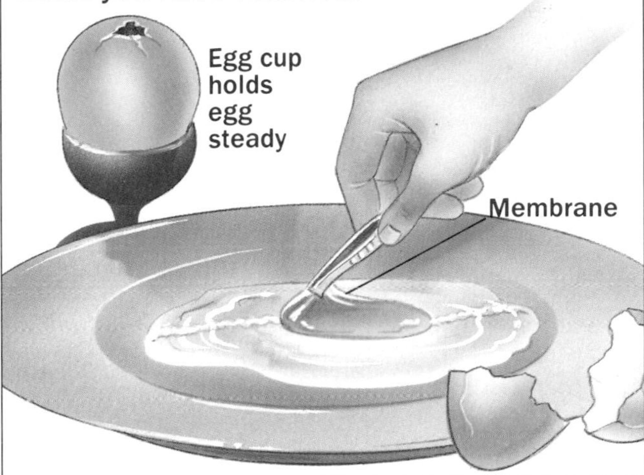

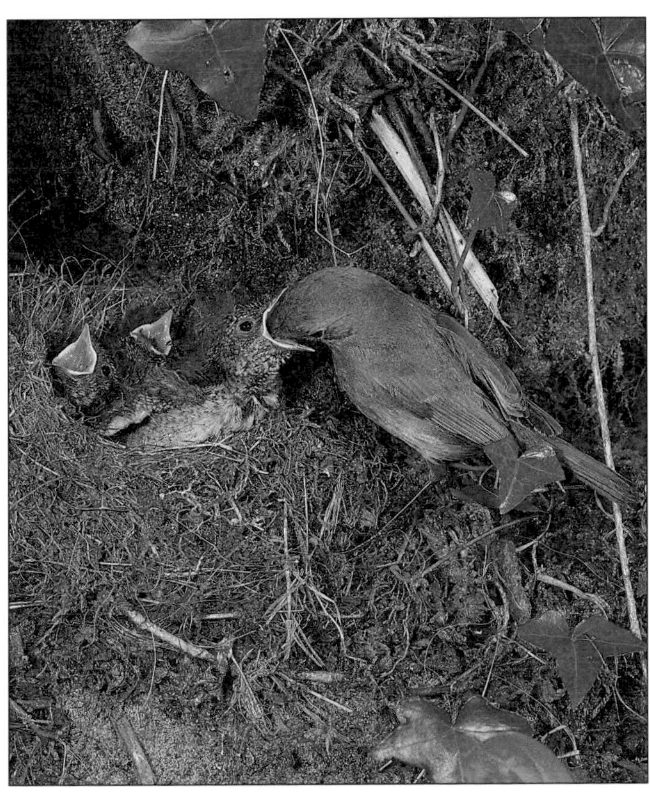

△ The gaping mouths of young robins make sure they are noticed and encourage the parents to bring food.

CARE OF YOUNG

In some bird species, such as ducks and pheasants, the chicks can feed themselves as soon as they have hatched. In most species, however, newly hatched chicks are too small to fend for themselves. They must be fed by the parents. Often, the chicks start by eating food that has already been partly digested by one of the parents. As the chicks grow, they change to solid food.

Among some bird species that lay a pair of eggs, only the first chick to hatch receives any care. The second chick is not fed at all and quickly dies. This is not the parents being cruel. The second egg is just a safeguard in case the first does not hatch out.

Most young reptiles receive no care from their parents. The crocodile is one exception. The female parent picks up the hatchlings in her mouth, and carries them from the nest to the nearest water.

Internal fertilization is most highly developed in mammals. In order to increase the chances of fertilization, sperm is placed inside the female body close to the ovaries. The fertilized eggs then develop inside the female body until they are miniature versions of the adult, and ready for live birth.

COURTSHIP

As with most animals, courtship among mammals is concerned with attracting a mate. It may also stimulate the female to produce eggs. In many animals, the process of producing eggs is largely controlled by chemicals in the female body. These chemicals are hormones (substances that control body functions). In mammals the series of events involved in the production of eggs is known as the estrous cycle, and the time when eggs are produced as estrus. (Primates, including monkeys and humans, go through a rather similar cycle called the menstrual cycle.) In most mammals, estrus takes place regularly through the year. However, some mammals (again like many other animals) have breeding seasons at particular times of year, when courtship and mating take place.

If each female of a group mates with the strongest and healthiest of the available males, it helps to ensure that strong and healthy offspring are produced. For this reason, courtship among mammals sometimes consists of contests between competing males. These contests are simply symbolic in some species; for example, gazelles perform "dances." In other species, however, the contest involves fighting. The winner gains the prize of mating. The loser may even be killed, although this is very rare and only ever happens in a few species.

NESTS

Building nests is not essential in the reproduction of mammals because there is no need to incubate eggs. Some mammals do make a nest of some sort to protect the young and keep them warm. But whether they do depends largely on the overall characteristics of the species.

Many small mammals, such as mice, rabbits and foxes, live in burrows. This is where their young are born. Among larger mammals, the situation is more varied. Some species, such as horses and antelopes, make no preparations for birth. Their young are born out in the open. With other species, such as lions and tigers, the female will seek out a secure and sheltered place where the young can be born in safety.

▷ Competing male giraffes fight by swinging their heads and necks at each other.

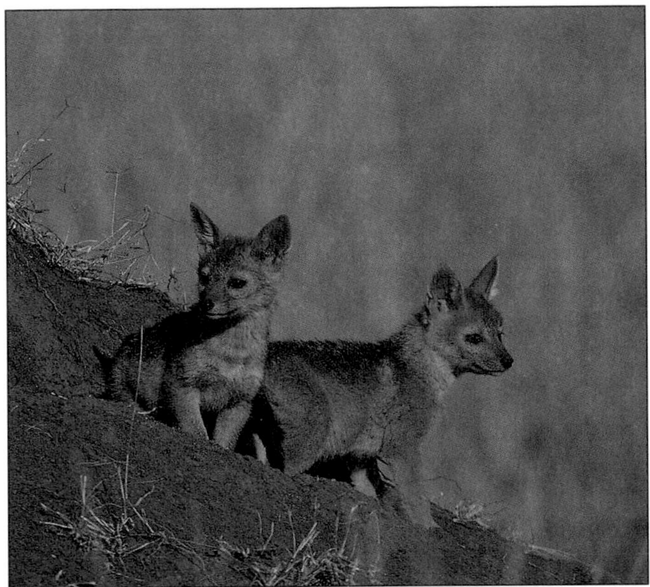

△ Fox cubs are born underground in safety. Only when they are more able to look after themselves do they emerge.

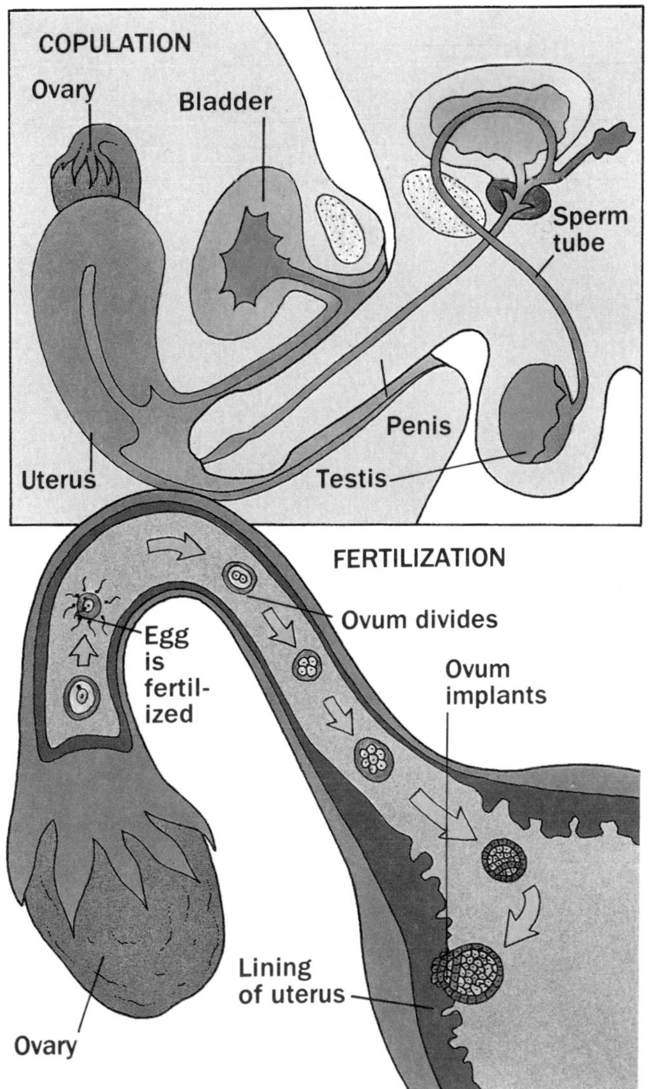

◁ Copulation leaves sperm at the top of the vagina. Sperm travel toward the ovary. One of the sperm fertilizes the egg. The fertilized egg, or zygote, travels toward the uterus. The zygote develops into a ball of cells before implanting in the lining of the uterus.

COPULATION

In mammals, fertilization is achieved by the act of copulation. During copulation, the male penis is placed inside the female vagina. Sperm are transferred to the female by the process of ejaculation. Sperm from the testes passes down the sperm tube and along the penis to the top of the vagina.

Each ejaculation transfers millions of sperm cells. These travel up through the uterus (or womb) toward the ovary. Fertilization occurs some time after copulation has taken place, when one sperm penetrates an egg just outside the ovary. The fertilized egg then passes down into the uterus. When the egg comes into contact with the lining of the uterus, it becomes attached to the surface and continues to develop.

Fertilization can only take place after the release of eggs (ova) by the ovaries – a process known as ovulation. In mammals with an estrous cycle, the female may release several eggs during estrus. There are some variations, for example, rabbits only ovulate after copulation. Primates, which have menstrual cycles, ovulate regularly about once every month. Any eggs that are not fertilized break up inside the uterus.

The number of eggs produced at each ovulation varies between different species. Most mammals produce more than one egg. They give birth to a number of offspring, each developed from a separate egg. Some larger mammals, such as horses and humans, normally produce just one egg at a time.

GESTATION

The development of a new mammal in its mother's uterus is known as gestation (or pregnancy). The length of gestation varies from one species to another. The longest gestation period is that of the Indian elephant at 22 months, while that of the hamster is only 16 days. In humans it is nine months.

In most mammals, the eggs become implanted in the uterus wall about four or five days after fertilization. The egg has by now developed into an embryo. A number of protecting membranes grow around the embryo. The innermost of these, the amnion, forms the amniotic sac. This is filled with fluid in which the embryo floats.

At first, the embryo is nourished by a small yolk sac. During the rest of its development, the embryo receives nourishment from the placenta. This develops from the lining of the uterus and is connected to the mother's blood supply. The embryo is joined to the placenta by the umbilical cord. While the embryo is developing, its blood travels along the cord to the placenta. In the placenta, nourishment and oxygen are absorbed into the embryo's blood and waste products are filtered out.

Quite early on in gestation, an embryo already has the beginnings of a head and four limbs. Then the embryo develops basic forms of all the organs and features that an adult has. This may be, for example, after about one quarter of gestation. From this point on, the new mammal is known as a fetus. At this stage, however, it is still too small and undeveloped to survive outside the parent. It stays inside the uterus until it is ready to be born.

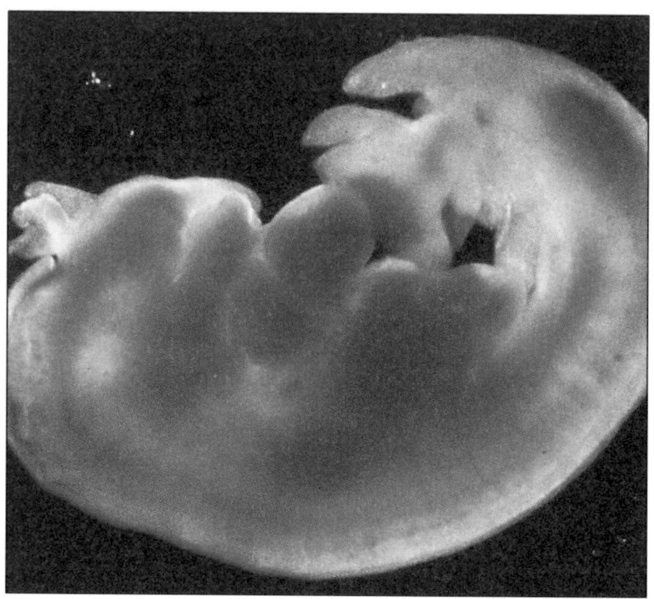

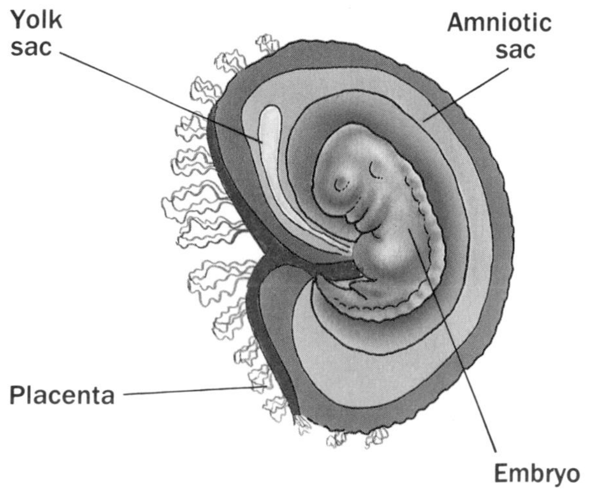

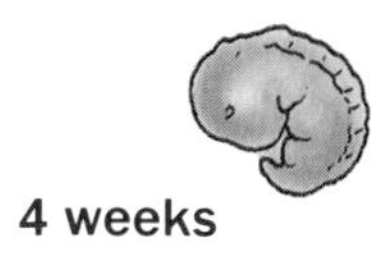

◁▷ Many monkeys have a gestation period of about 26 weeks. After two weeks the yolk supply is nearly used up. But the placenta is already well developed and connected to the embryo by the umbilical cord. Between the fourth and sixth weeks the embryo takes on a definite shape. By the tenth week most features have become visible. By the 18th week the young monkey is complete in most ways.

Mammals with long gestation periods, such as dolphins and apes, can only have about one pregnancy in a year. Species with short gestation periods, such as rats and mice, can have more than one pregnancy a year. The populations of such animals can increase very rapidly.

Some mammals, especially those that experience cold winters, have extended gestation periods. Badgers, for example, mate in July and August. Fertilized eggs develop normally for a few days, and move to the uterus. However, implantation does not take place, and the eggs stop developing. They remain in the uterus until January, when they implant, and continue their development. The young badgers are born in March.

MENSTRUAL CYCLE

Primates (including humans), which have a menstrual cycle, ovulate about once every month. Before each ovulation, the uterus prepares itself to receive a fertilized ovum (egg). This involves the surface layers of the uterus lining becoming thicker. An ovum is then released from an ovary. If the ovum is fertilized, it becomes implanted in the lining of the uterus. If it is not fertilized, after a few days the extra material of the uterus lining starts to break down. Then the ovum, material from the uterus and a certain amount of blood leave the body through the vagina. This is called menstruation.

◁▷ About a tenth of the way through gestation (left), the first features of the developing embryo appear. At this stage it is still difficult to see what anything will become. Halfway through gestation (right) most of the main features of the fetus are visible.

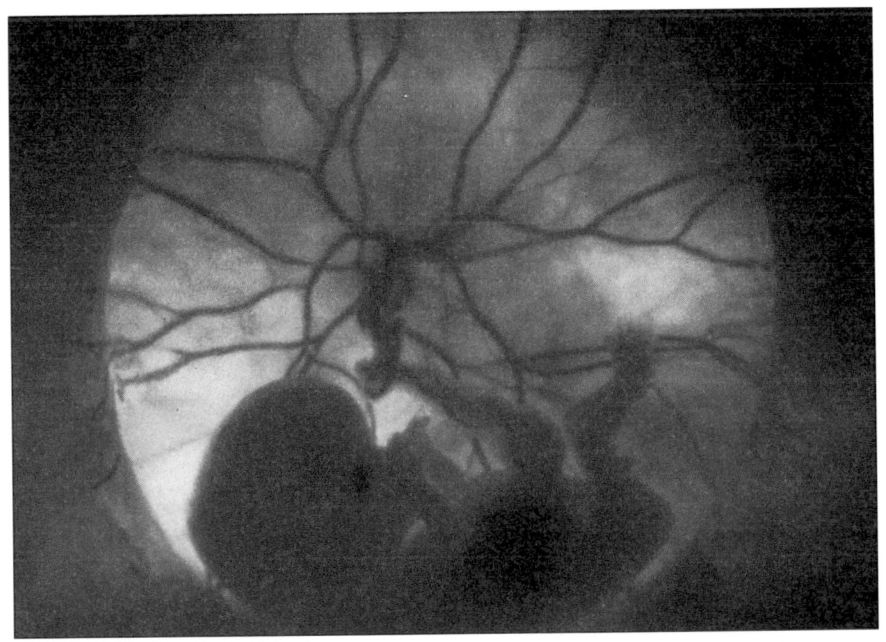

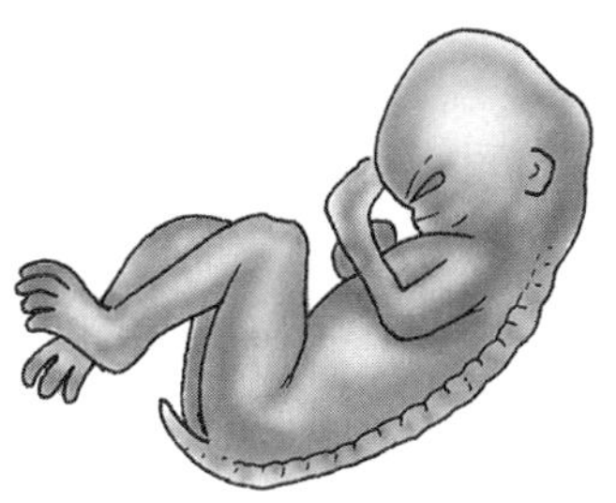

10 weeks

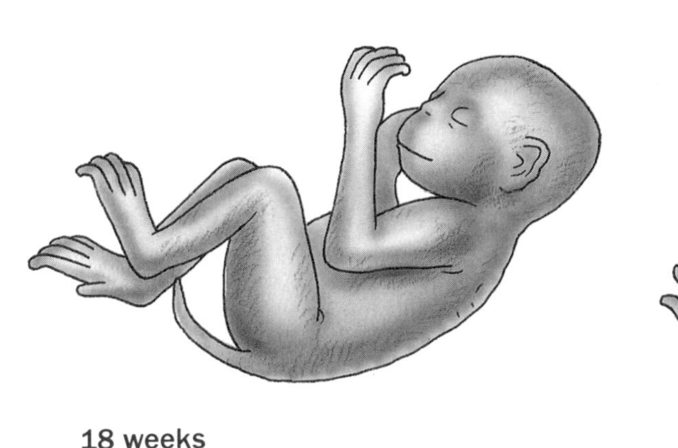

18 weeks

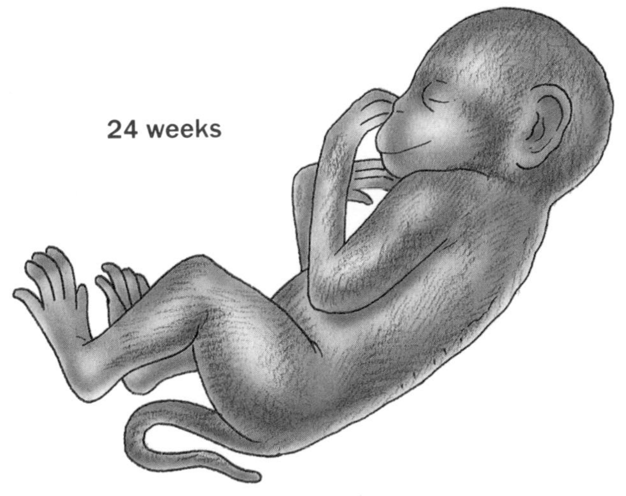

24 weeks

BIRTH

When a mammal fetus is fully developed, it is ready to be born. The birth process is divided into three stages. All stages involve powerful muscle movements in the body of the female parent. For this reason, the birth process is often known as "labor," especially when talking about humans.

During the first stage, the opening at the bottom of the uterus enlarges a great deal. The amniotic sac then bursts, releasing the fluid inside. The second stage is the birth itself. Muscle contractions force the offspring one at a time out of the female's body. As the young animals are forced out, the umbilical cords break, or else the mother bites them through. The new animal must now take its first breath. In the third stage, a final series of contractions forces out the placenta. At this time, the placenta is often called the afterbirth.

△ Newborn hamsters are blind, naked and helpless. Until their fur grows and their eyes open, they are entirely dependent on their mother.

DID YOU KNOW?

Like many young mammals, kittens are blind when they are born. Their eyes do not open for about two weeks. And when they do, kittens' eyes are always blue. Sometimes they stay blue, but in most breeds of cat a different eye color develops after a few weeks.

△ A newborn horse can stand up within minutes of birth, and can run about an hour later. In the wild, animals like the horse are hunted by predators. The young must be able to run away.

CARE OF YOUNG

As soon as a young mammal has been born, its mother usually licks it clean. The movement of the mother's tongue helps to clear out air passages (such as the nose) and may encourage the young animal to start breathing.

After a mammal has been born, it is no longer connected to its mother by the umbilical cord. But it still depends on its mother for food. All young mammals start feeding on milk, whatever they will eat as adults. The milk is made by special glands called mammary glands. It can be sucked from two or more nipples on the mother. Instinct makes newly born mammals suck at any nipple-shaped object.

In some species, such as deer and horses, the young can walk within an hour of birth. Such young animals need little care other than feeding. In other species, the young are helpless for some time, and need warmth and constant attention as well as food. This care is nearly always provided by the female parent. The mothers of most mammals will guard their offspring from danger.

△ As in all mammals, young orangutans feed on milk.

△ Female lions help to look after each other's cubs.

Every living cell contains coded information, known as genetic information. This information describes not only how each individual cell will develop, but also how a whole animal will develop. In animals that use sexual reproduction, the cells of the offspring have genetic information from both parents.

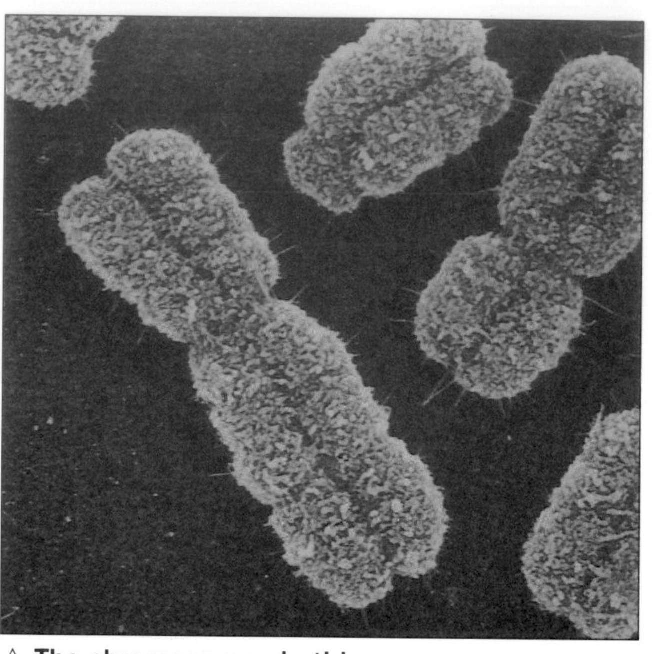

△ The chromosomes in this picture are divided into chromatids, joined at their middles. Each chromatid has exactly the same information. The Y-shaped chromosome is one that carries information for a mammal to be male.

GENES AND CHROMOSOMES

Genetic information is carried by DNA (deoxyribonucleic acid). DNA is an extremely long molecule. It consists of a chain of many pairs of much smaller molecules (there are four types). The order of these pairs makes up the code for information. The chain can be divided into sections called genes. Each gene has the information for the development of one particular characteristic, such as the color of an animal's eyes.

DNA consists of two entwined helixes. The helixes are joined by the pairs of molecules. So DNA is rather like a twisted ladder. This double helix is, in turn, twisted around itself again and again. A huge amount of DNA twisted together can make up a chromosome.

Normally, DNA is spread out through the nucleus of a cell. When cell division is about to take place, the DNA arranges itself into chromosomes. This is so that mitosis or meiosis can take place (these are described on page **317**.

The chromosomes in a cell are divided into pairs. Each pair has genes for the characteristics of the same things (for example, the color of the eyes). But these characteristics may be different (for example, brown eyes or blue eyes). To get more variety in the offspring, pairs of chromosomes exchange some genes in the first stage of meiosis.

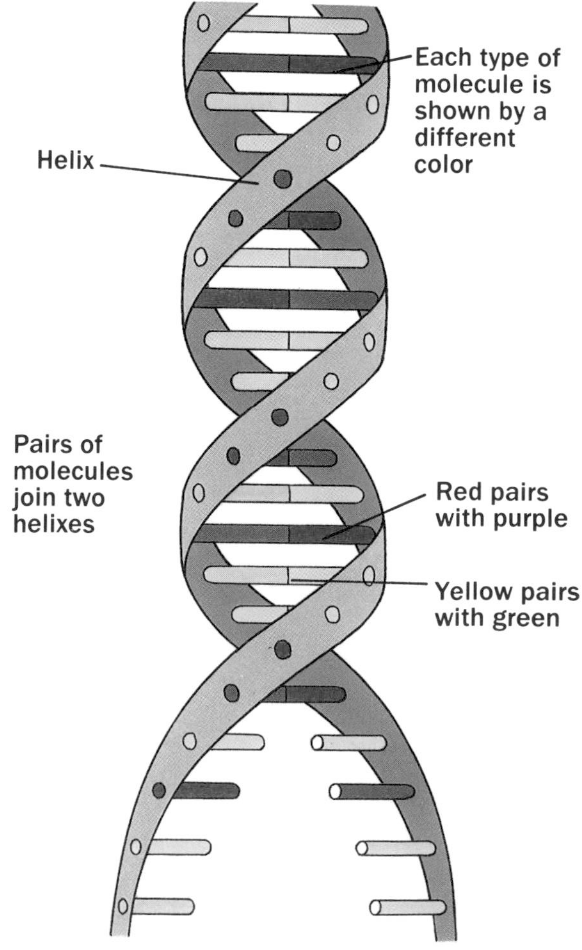

▷ The two halves of a DNA molecule can come apart like a zipper. A new half can "grow" on each original half. This produces two exact copies.

HEREDITY

Most of an animal's genes control the internal organization and working of its body. Most of these genes are the same in all healthy members of a species. Some genes, however, control characteristics that differ between individuals. These can vary because the differences do not significantly affect the health of the animal. Examples of such characteristics are the color of human eyes and the pattern of markings on a leopard's back. The transfer of characteristics from parents to their offspring is called heredity.

Some of the genes that control a particular characteristic have a stronger influence than others. The stronger genes are known as dominant. The weaker genes are called recessive. Understanding heredity involves understanding how genes operate in pairs.

The gene for a particular characteristic, such as the color of fur in cats, is located on both chromosomes of a pair. In a zygote, one half of each pair comes from each parent. If one parent has contributed a dominant black-fur gene, and the other has contributed a recessive white-fur gene, the dominant gene will control development. The zygote will develop into a black cat.

The recessive white-fur gene may be passed on to this black cat's own offspring. If both parents of a cat pass on this gene, the result is a white cat.

▽ This shows what might happen with two generations of cats. The gray gene is dominant and the orange recessive. Compare the colors of the cats to their genes.

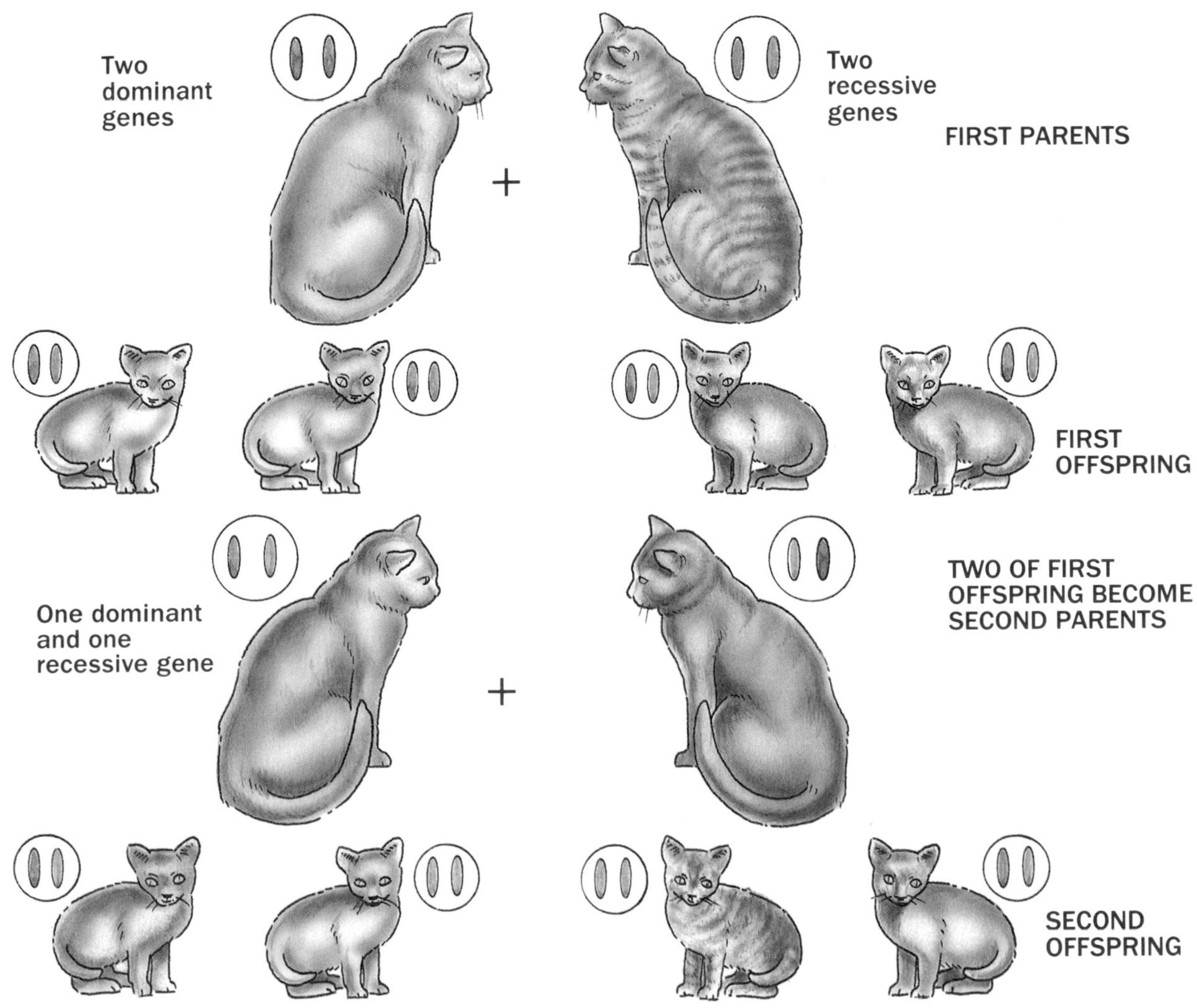

There are more than a million species of animals in the world. Biologists have divided these up into several major groups based on the similarities between them and how they are thought to have evolved. Within the animal kingdom, the most important division is between those animals with backbones, the vertebrates, and those without, the invertebrates, who form the vast majority of animals. The table below shows the many different types of invertebrates living today. New species are being discovered every year. The most primitive of the invertebrates, the Protozoans, represent the first type of animals to evolve on Earth more than 3,000 million years ago.

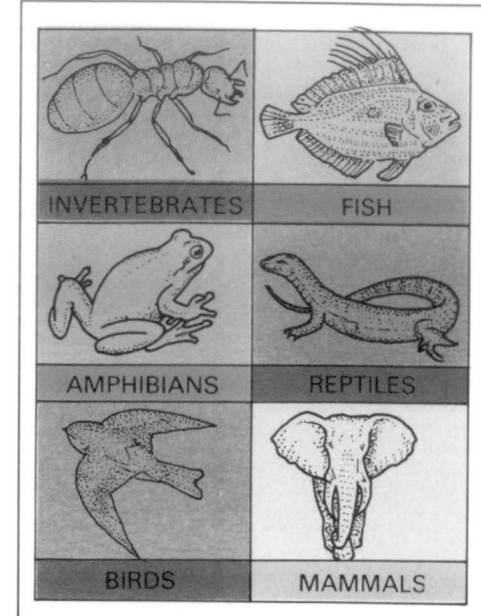

SEGMENTED WORMS		
Bristleworms	Earthworms	Leeches

ARTHROPODS						
Pauropods	Millipedes	Centipedes	Symphylans	Springtails	Two-pronged bristletails	Three-pronged bristletails

ARTHROPODS (continued)					
Insects	Arachnids	Crustaceans	King crabs	Velvet worms	Proturans
Mayflies Dragonflies Notopterans Stoneflies Web-spinners Cockroaches Mantids Termites Zorapterans Grasshoppers Stick-insects Earwigs Book-lice Bird-lice Sucking lice Thrips Bugs Lacewings Alderflies Snakeflies Beetles Strepsipterans Scorpionflies Caddis flies Zeuglopterans Butterflies and moths True flies Fleas Ants, bees, wasps	*Scorpions Pseudoscorpions Camel spiders Micro-whip scorpions Whip scorpions Amblypygids Spiders Ricinuleids Harvestmen Mites and ticks*	*Cephalocarids Branchiopods Mussel shrimps Copepods Mystacocarids Fish lice Barnacles Prawns, crabs, lobsters*			

SPONGES		
Calcareous sponges	Glass sponges	Horny sponges

FLATWORMS		
Free-living	Flukes	Tapeworms

HEMICHORDATES	
Acorn worms	Pterobranchs

COELENTERATES		
Hydrozoans	Jellyfish	Sea anemones and corals

PROTOZOA			
Flagellates	Sarcodines	Spore-formers	Ciliates

ECHNINODERMS				
Starfish	Brittlestars	Sea urchins	Sea cucumbers	Sea lilies

MOLLUSCS					
Monoplacophorans	Chitons	Snails and slugs	Tusk shells	Bivalve molluscs	Squid, cuttlefish, octopuses

ASCHELMINTHES					
Rotifers	Gastrotrichs	Kinorhynchs	Priaulids	Horsehair worms	Roundworms

BEARD BEARERS

SEA SPIDERS

MESOZOANS

COMB JELLIES

RIBBON WORMS

ENTOPROCTS

THORNY-HEADED WORMS

PHORONID WORMS

MOSS ANIMALS

LAMP SHELLS

PEANUT WORMS

ECHIUROID WORMS

TONGUE WORMS

WATER BEARS

ARROW WORMS

N.B. Tunicates such as sea squirts, and lancelets, form a link between vertebrates and invertebrates.

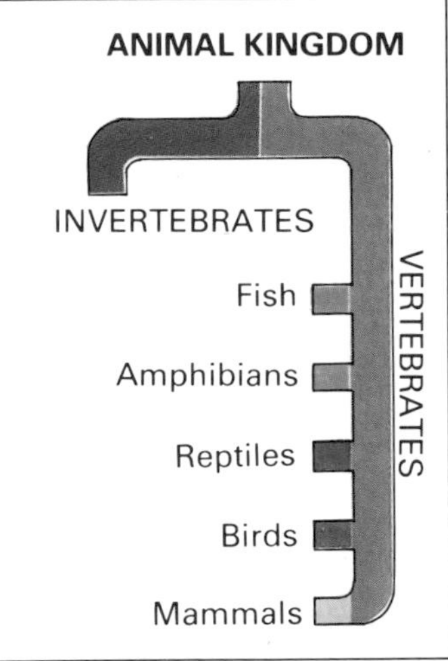

Fish are considered to form the link between vertebrates and invertebrates. There are about 25,000 different species or kinds of fish, (which is more than all the backboned animals put together), and they are divided into cartilaginous fish, bony fish, jawless fish and lungfish. They are cold-blooded, spend all their lives in the water, and breathe through gills. Amphibians evolved from fish. Young amphibians are adapted for life in water, whilst adult ones can walk and spend most of their time on land, but breed in water and dry out if their skin is not kept moist. Reptiles evolved from amphibians about 300 million years ago. Some, like dinosaurs, grew to enormous sizes, others were ancestors of birds and mammals. Reptiles are the most advanced of all cold-blooded vertebrates. They are adapted to living on land, although many species, such as turtles and crocodiles, spend most of the time in water.

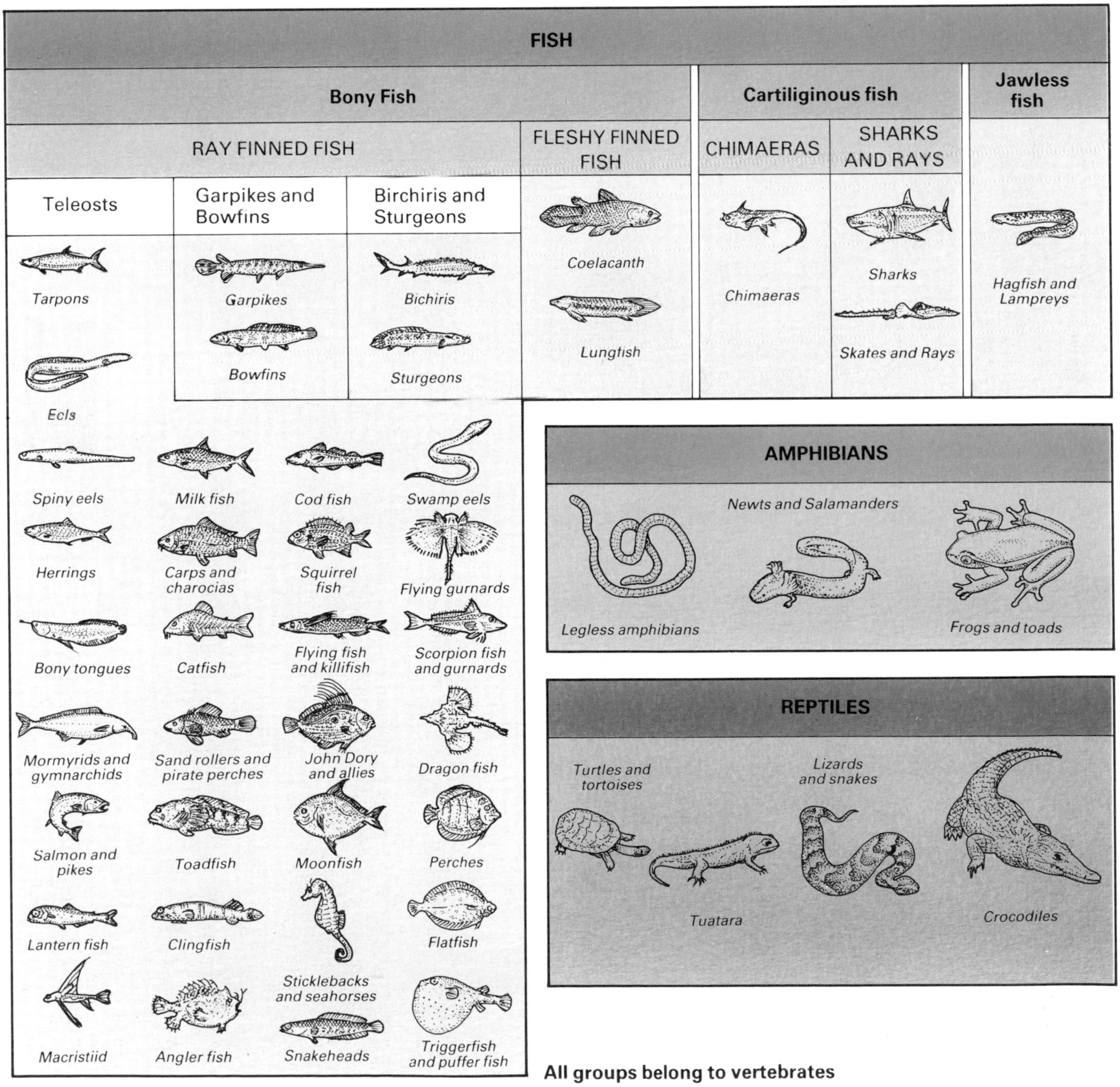

FISH

Bony Fish

RAY FINNED FISH

Teleosts

Tarpons, *Eels*, *Spiny eels*, *Milk fish*, *Cod fish*, *Swamp eels*, *Herrings*, *Carps and charocias*, *Squirrel fish*, *Flying gurnards*, *Bony tongues*, *Catfish*, *Flying fish and killifish*, *Scorpion fish and gurnards*, *Mormyrids and gymnarchids*, *Sand rollers and pirate perches*, *John Dory and allies*, *Dragon fish*, *Salmon and pikes*, *Toadfish*, *Moonfish*, *Perches*, *Lantern fish*, *Clingfish*, *Sticklebacks and seahorses*, *Flatfish*, *Macristiid*, *Angler fish*, *Snakeheads*, *Triggerfish and puffer fish*

Garpikes and Bowfins

Garpikes, *Bowfins*

Birchiris and Sturgeons

Bichiri, *Sturgeons*

FLESHY FINNED FISH

Coelacanth, *Lungfish*

Cartiliginous fish

CHIMAERAS

Chimaeras

SHARKS AND RAYS

Sharks, *Skates and Rays*

Jawless fish

Hagfish and Lampreys

AMPHIBIANS

Legless amphibians, *Newts and Salamanders*, *Frogs and toads*

REPTILES

Turtles and tortoises, *Tuatara*, *Lizards and snakes*, *Crocodiles*

All groups belong to vertebrates

Vertebrates are divided into five main categories, of which birds and mammals are considered to be the most highly evolved. There are about 8,500 different species of birds. They are warm-blooded – that is, they keep their bodies at a constant temperature. Their front legs – legs in most reptiles and mammals – have become modified as wings, and feathers provide the main body covering, with scales on the legs and toes. Feathers trap heat under them and provide large surfaces needed for flight. There are more than 4,000 species of mammals. Mammals are warm-blooded, have a body covering of hair for insulation, and give birth to live young. Mammals have a larger brain than most animals, and are capable of learning much by experience.

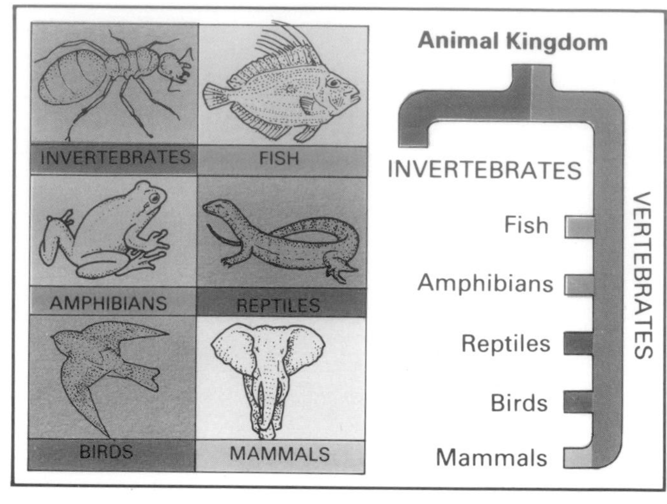

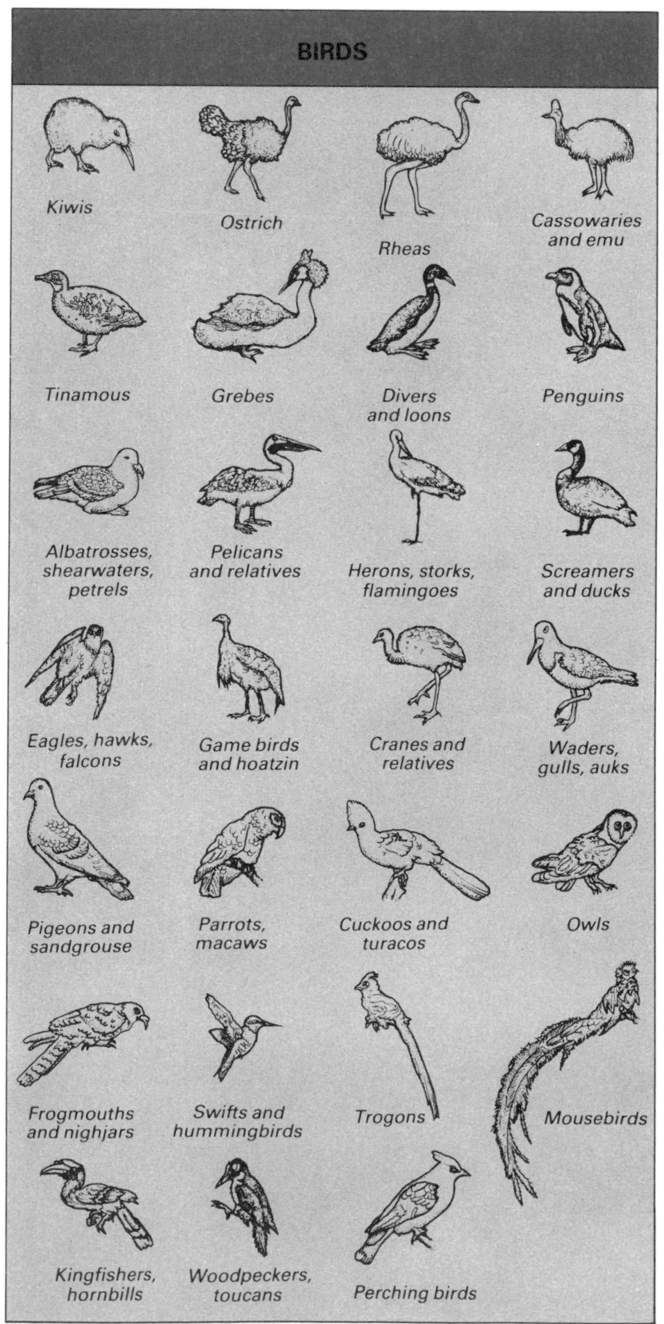

Scientists believe there are more than 350,000 species of plants. The main difference between animals and plants are the ways they feed and the fact that most animals can move around whereas nearly all plants remain in one place. Plants have no sense organs or nervous system.

There is an enormous range of plants from microscopic mosses to conifer trees growing 300ft (100m) tall. Yet all plants photosynthesize (make food from the energy of sunlight, breathing out oxygen as a waste product) and, in terms of internal structure and methods of reproduction, can be grouped into just four main sub-divisions. The most primitive plants are the Bryophytes. These lack true roots, stems or leaves. The next sub-division, the Pteridophytes, includes plants with roots, stems and leaves but which depend on water for their sexual reproduction. Third are the Gymnosperms, the cone-forming plants, and last, the Angiosperms, the flowering plants.

Algae, fungi, lichens and bacteria are often treated as simple types of plants. They have one or more plant characteristic. The first plants were probably single-celled water organisms.

Viruses are considered by some scientists as non-living things and by others as living, so are kept separate.

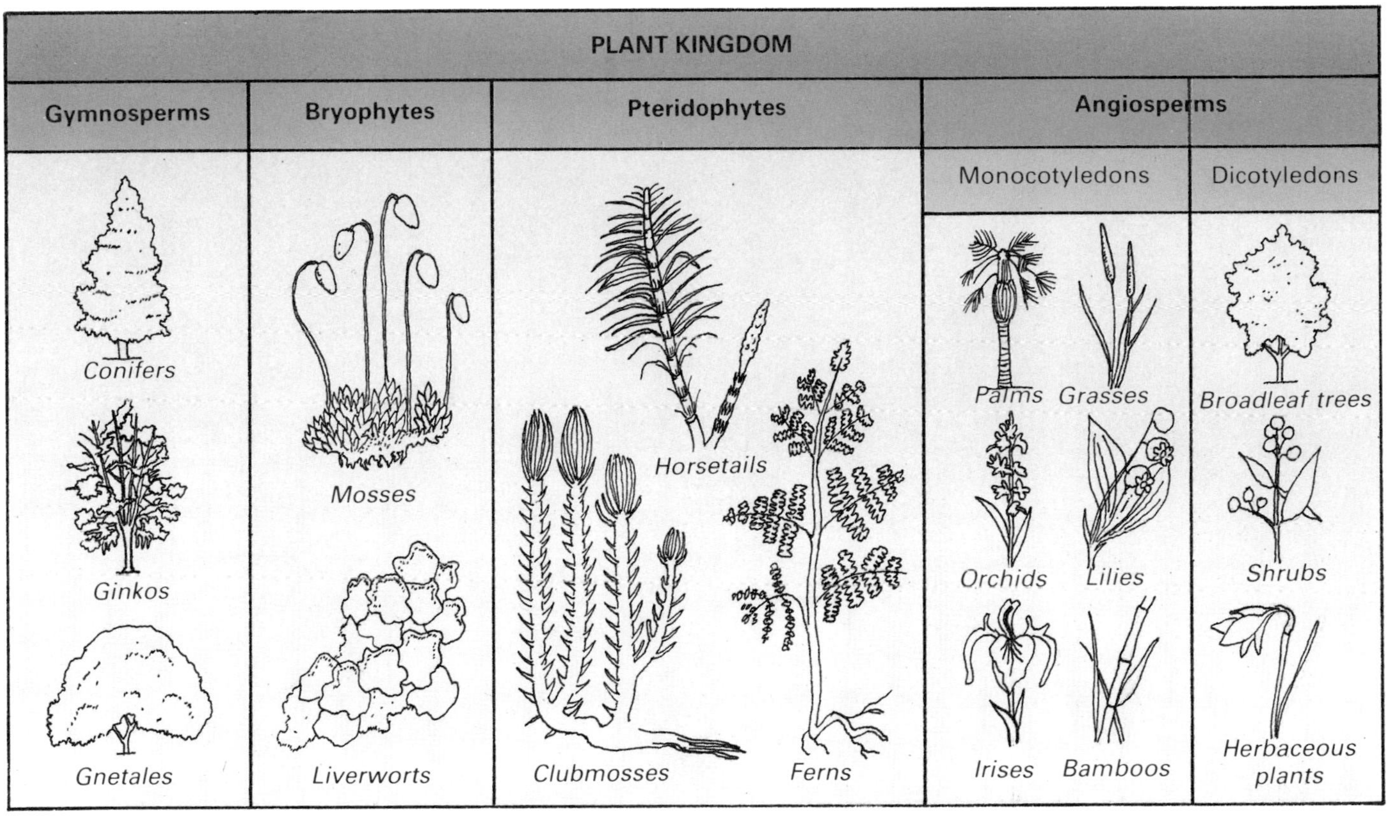

PLANT KINGDOM

Gymnosperms: Conifers, Ginkos, Gnetales

Bryophytes: Mosses, Liverworts

Pteridophytes: Horsetails, Clubmosses, Ferns

Angiosperms
- Monocotyledons: Palms, Grasses, Orchids, Lilies, Irises, Bamboos
- Dicotyledons: Broadleaf trees, Shrubs, Herbaceous plants

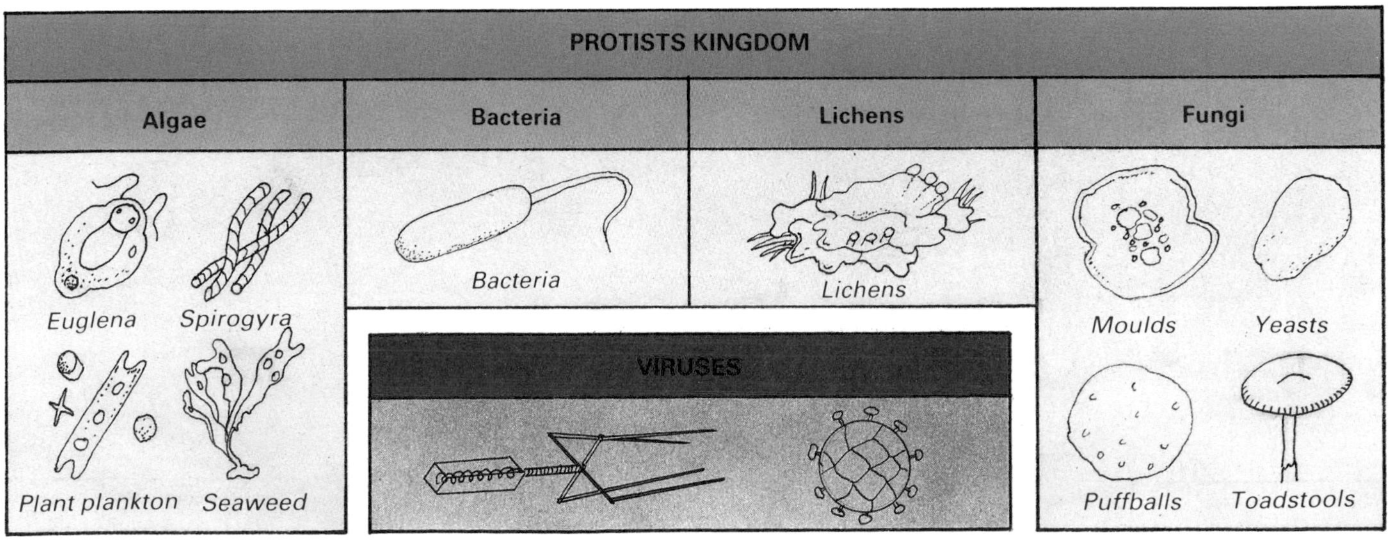

PROTISTS KINGDOM

Algae: Euglena, Spirogyra, Plant plankton, Seaweed

Bacteria: Bacteria

Lichens: Lichens

Fungi: Moulds, Yeasts, Puffballs, Toadstools

VIRUSES

The human body is made up of several systems, each consisting of various tissues and organs. The framework of the body is formed by the skeletal system – the bones and joints. Some bones surround and protect internal organs. Others, with their joints, allow movement. Power for movement comes from the muscles. Muscles and other tissues are provided with oxygen and nutrients by the blood, pumped around the body by the heart in the circulatory system. The action of the muscles, heart and many other organs is stimulated by the nervous system, under the control of the brain. Other nerves carry messages from the sense organs to the brain. Energy and the materials for maintaining the body come from food, processed by the digestive system.

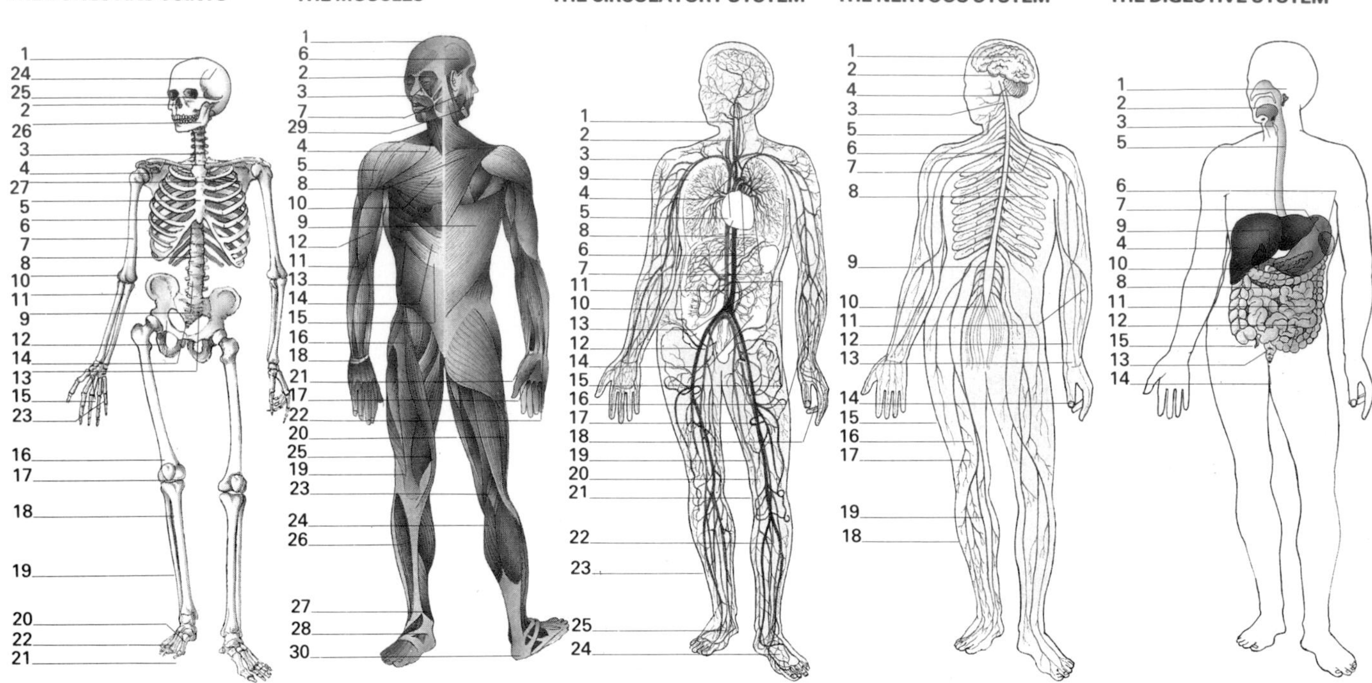

1 Frontal bone of skull
2 Maxilla
3 Cervical vertebrae
4 Clavical (collarbone)
5 Sternum (breastbone)
6 Rib
7 Humerous
8 Thoracic vertebrae
9 Lumbar vertebrae
10 Radius
11 Ulna
12 Pelvis
13 Sacrum
14 Coccyx
15 Carpel bones
16 Femur (thighbone)
17 Patella (kneecap)
18 Tibia (shinbone)
19 Fibula
20 Tarsal bones
21 Phalanges
22 Metatarsals
23 Metacarpels
24 Parietal bone
25 Temporal bone
26 Mandible
27 Scapula

1 Occipitofrontalis
2 Orbicularis oculi
3 Levator labii superior
4 Sternomastoid
5 Deltoid
6 Temporalis
7 Masseter
8 Trapezius
9 Latissimus dorsi
10 Pectoralis major
11 Biceps
12 Triceps
13 Serratus anterior
14 Rectus abdominus abdominis
15 External oblique
16 Abductor muscles
17 Tendons to fingers
18 Extensor retinaculum
19 Quadriceps
20 Gluteus maximus
21 Flexor retinaculum
22 Muscles of wrist and fingers
23 Hamstring muscles
24 Gastrocnemius
25 Sartorius
26 Tibials anterior
27 Soleus
28 Extensor retinaculum
29 Orbicularis oris
30 Achilles tendon

1 Jugular vein
2 Left cartoid artery (supplying head)
3 Subclavian artery and vein
4 Aorta
5 Superior vena cava
6 Pulmonary artery
7 Pulmonary vein
8 Heart
9 Lungs
10 Liver
11 Abdominal aorta
12 Speen with splenic artery and vein
13 Portal vein (from bowel)
14 Kidney with renal artery and vein
15 Inferior vena cava
16 Radial artery
17 Common iliac vessels
18 Digital arteries and veins
19 Femoral artery
20 Femoral vein
21 Great saphenous vein
22 Popliteal artery
23 Anterior tibial artery
24 Dorsalis pedal artery
25 Posterior tibial artery

1 Cerebral cortex
2 Pons
3 Medulla
4 Cerebellum
5 Facial nreve
6 Spinal cord
7 Brachial plexus
8 Thoracic nerves
9 Sacral plexus
10 Cauda equina
11 Ulnar nerve
12 Radial nerve
13 Median nerve
14 Digital nerves
15 Lateral cutaneous nerve of thigh
16 Sciatic nerve
17 Common peroneal nerve
18 Superficial and deep peroneal nerves
19 Tibial nerve

1 Parotid gland
2 Sublingual gland
3 Submandible gland
4 Liver
5 Esophagus
6 Stomach
7 Spleen
8 Pancreas
9 Gall-bladder
10 Duodenum
11 Small intestine (ileum)
12 Large intestine (colon)
13 Rectum
14 Anus
15 Appendix

Scientists use a special table of the elements called the Periodic Table, which is here. Each element has a chemical symbol as well as its name and atomic number.

The elements are organised according to the arrangement of electrons within their electron shells. This puts elements with similar properties into the same column. The main groups are the numbered columns in the table. Group 1 contains the alkali metals, which are highly reactive, while group 7 contains the highly reactive non-metals called the halogens. Group 8 contains the unreactive noble gases.

Between groups 2 and 3 are sets of elements known as the transition elements. These elements are similar to their horizontal neighbors as well as to their vertical neighbors. The lanthanides (58-71) and the actinides (90-103) make up two horizontal sets of similar elements. All the elements above uranium (element 92) are artificial. There are several elements above element 103, which is the highest element normally shown.

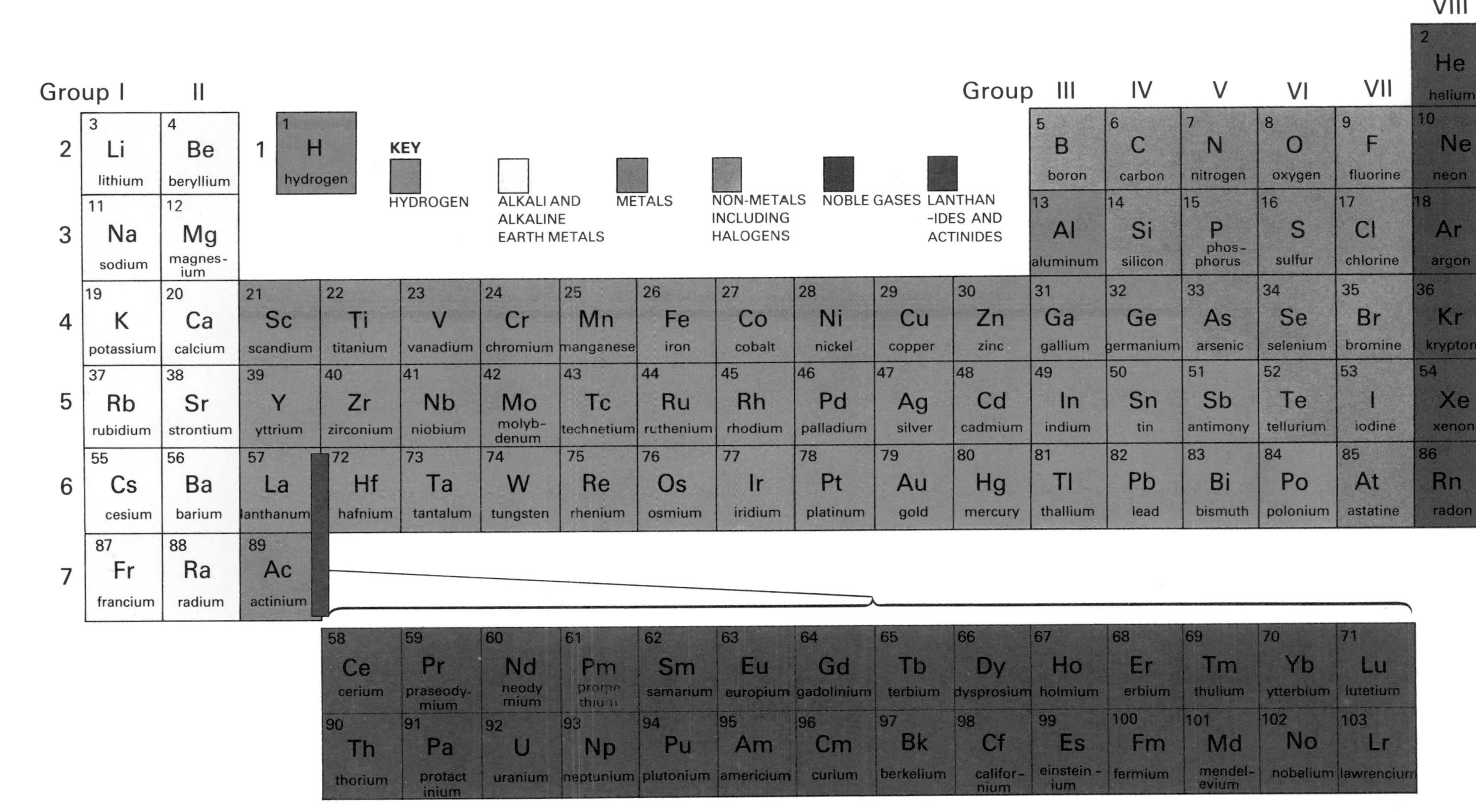

	Group I	II											Group III	IV	V	VI	VII	VIII
1			1 H hydrogen															2 He helium
2	3 Li lithium	4 Be beryllium											5 B boron	6 C carbon	7 N nitrogen	8 O oxygen	9 F fluorine	10 Ne neon
3	11 Na sodium	12 Mg magnes-ium											13 Al aluminum	14 Si silicon	15 P phos-phorus	16 S sulfur	17 Cl chlorine	18 Ar argon
4	19 K potassium	20 Ca calcium	21 Sc scandium	22 Ti titanium	23 V vanadium	24 Cr chromium	25 Mn manganese	26 Fe iron	27 Co cobalt	28 Ni nickel	29 Cu copper	30 Zn zinc	31 Ga gallium	32 Ge germanium	33 As arsenic	34 Se selenium	35 Br bromine	36 Kr krypton
5	37 Rb rubidium	38 Sr strontium	39 Y yttrium	40 Zr zirconium	41 Nb niobium	42 Mo molyb-denum	43 Tc technetium	44 Ru ruthenium	45 Rh rhodium	46 Pd palladium	47 Ag silver	48 Cd cadmium	49 In indium	50 Sn tin	51 Sb antimony	52 Te tellurium	53 I iodine	54 Xe xenon
6	55 Cs cesium	56 Ba barium	57 La lanthanum	72 Hf hafnium	73 Ta tantalum	74 W tungsten	75 Re rhenium	76 Os osmium	77 Ir iridium	78 Pt platinum	79 Au gold	80 Hg mercury	81 Tl thallium	82 Pb lead	83 Bi bismuth	84 Po polonium	85 At astatine	86 Rn radon
7	87 Fr francium	88 Ra radium	89 Ac actinium															

58 Ce cerium	59 Pr praseody-mium	60 Nd neody mium	61 Pm prome thium	62 Sm samarium	63 Eu europium	64 Gd gadolinium	65 Tb terbium	66 Dy dysprosium	67 Ho holmium	68 Er erbium	69 Tm thulium	70 Yb ytterbium	71 Lu lutetium
90 Th thorium	91 Pa protact inium	92 U uranium	93 Np neptunium	94 Pu plutonium	95 Am americium	96 Cm curium	97 Bk berkelium	98 Cf califor-nium	99 Es einstein-ium	100 Fm fermium	101 Md mendel-evium	102 No nobelium	103 Lr lawrencium

KEY

HYDROGEN
ALKALI AND ALKALINE EARTH METALS
METALS
NON-METALS INCLUDING HALOGENS
NOBLE GASES
LANTHAN-IDES AND ACTINIDES

absolute zero lowest possible temperature; it is -459.67^0 F or zero K.

acceleration an increase of speed produced when a force continues to push or pull on an object.

acoustics the study of sound, especially the behavior of sound waves in enclosed spaces, such as concert halls.

aileron a movable flap at the rear edge of an aircraft wing. The aileron controls the rolling movements of the aircraft.

airfoil a surface, such as an aircraft wing, which is shaped to produce lift when air flows over the wing.

air pressure the downward pressure of the atmosphere. It is caused by the weight of the air.

air resistance the slowing force which resists the movement of an object through the air.

amplifier an electronic device that magnifies the strength of a signal, such as a radio signal.

amplitude the strength of a sound wave; loud sounds have a large amplitude. Sound-producing objects that vibrate over a greater distance give sounds with larger amplitude.

anemometer an instrument used for measuring the speed of wind.

anode the place at which negatively charged particles collect during electrolysis.

antenna a long, thin organ that is attached to the head of an animal; it is usually used to detect touch or smell.

anticyclone an area of high pressure, from which winds blow outward.

asexual without sex. Methods of reproduction that involve only one parent.

atmosphere the layer of air that surrounds the Earth. As well as being made up of the gases oxygen, nitrogen and carbon dioxide, it contains water vapor.

atom smallest particle of an element; atoms combine with each other to form molecules. An atom consists of a central nucleus surrounded by negatively charged particles called electrons.

autonomic nervous system the part of the nervous system that controls organs of the body without us being aware of what is happening.

axon the part of a nerve fiber that carries signals toward the main part (the cell body) of a neuron.

backbone row of bones that runs along the back of an animal. The bones surround a bundle of nerves. Animals that have backbones are called vertebrates.

Beaufort scale used to measure the strength of winds. The scale is named after Francis Beaufort, a British commander who developed it.

boiling point temperature at which a liquid changes into a gas or vapor.

buoyancy the ability of an object to float. Buoyancy depends on the density (the weight of a certain volume) of the object.

carnivore an animal that eats only other animals.

catalyst substance that speeds up a chemical reaction but remains unchanged at the end of it.

cathode the place at which positively charged particles collect during electrolysis.

cell the tiny basic unit from which living things are made. Each cell is surrounded by a thin membrane that separates it from other cells. All animals (except protozoans) are made up of many cells.

Celsius temperature scale on which the freezing point of water is zero degrees and the boiling point of water is 100^0. It is the same as the Centigrade temperature scale.

charge inside an atom's nucleus, protons carry a positive charge and electrons, a negative charge. Positive and negative charges attract each other, but like charges, such as two electrons, repel.

chromatography a way of separating different colored substances in a liquid.

chromosome one of a pair of rods into which DNA arranges itself in a dividing cell.

circuit a complete path around which an electric current can flow.

color blind a condition where a person cannot tell the difference between two or more colors.

compass an instrument with a pivoted magnetic needle that always points northwards.

condensation the process by which water vapor turns back to a liquid state as it cools.

copulation the physical union between female and male animals that involves the transfer of sperm from the male to the female, and that allows internal fertilization to take place.

dendron the part of a nerve fiber that carries signals toward the main part (the cell body) of a neuron.

dendrite a small branching dendron that connects to another neuron.

density the ratio between the weight of an object and its volume.

depression an area of low air pressure toward which winds blow. Warm areas tend to have a low pressure.

diaphragm a thin metal or cardboard sheet that vibrates in a loudspeaker or microphone.

digestion the chemical breakdown of food. Digestion breaks down food into substances that can be absorbed and used by an animal's body.

domain a very small region in a magnetic material that behaves like a tiny magnet.

drag the resistance of the air or water to the movement of anything moving through.

egg special cell that is produced by a female animal and is usually covered by a protective case. Fertilized eggs grow into young animals.

electric motor a machine that uses an electric current to produce rotary motion of a coil in a magnetic field.

electrical signal an electric current that changes in strength at the same frequency as a sound wave. It is an electrical copy of the sound wave, used in sound systems.

electromagnet a coil of wire with an iron bar inside it. It becomes a magnet when an electric current flows through the wire.

electronic instrument a musical instrument that produces electrical signals, but no audible sound. The signals can be made audible through a sound system.

electric current a flow of negative charge (electrons) round a circuit.

electromagnetic wave a wave that can travel through empty space. Light and heat rays travel as electromagnetic waves.

elevator a flap on the rear wings of an aircraft that is moved to make the craft climb or dive.

embryo an animal during the early stages of development before hatching or birth.

energy ability to do work, measured in joules.The work might be lifting a heavy object, or it might be a chemical reaction that changes one substance into another.

enzyme a biological catalyst. Many enzymes are involved in digestion.

evaporation the process by which the surface of water is constantly losing molecules of water vapor.

external skeleton a hard covering on the bodies of arthropods. It holds the body in shape and protects it.

Fahrenheit a temperature scale on which the freezing point of water is 32^0 and the boiling point of water is 212^0.

ferrite a type of magnetic tape that can be formed into any shape and then baked hard in an oven.

fertilization the process by which a female gamete (egg, or ovum) and male gamete (sperm) join to form a single cell that will develop into a new plant or animal.

fetus an unborn mammal during the later stages of development in the uterus (womb).

focus adjust to make a clear image.

force an influence that makes an object move or change direction. For example, air pressure on a wing is a force.

freezing point the temperature at which water turns to ice.

frequency the rate of vibration of a sound wave, measured in hertz (Hz), which equals the number of complete vibrations per second. Radio and other frequencies are also measured in hertz.

friction a force that occurs when two surfaces rub against each other. It always slows movement, and brings motion to a stop if no other force is applied to overcome it.

galvanometer an instrument for measuring the strength of an electric current.

gamete a sex cell: an egg (ovum) in a female and a sperm in a male. The joining of female and male gametes is the basis of sexual reproduction.

gene a section of DNA that refers to one particular inheritable characteristic.

genetics the study of heredity and DNA.

generator a machine that uses the rotary motion of a metal coil in a magnetic field to produce an electric current that flows through the wire.

gestation the development of a young animal in the uterus: also called pregnancy.

gill a structure in an animal that absorbs oxygen from water. Most animals that live in water use gills to breathe.

gravity the pulling force of the earth that makes things fall, and gives things weight.

grid the national system that connects electricity generators, such as power stations and users of electricity, such as homes, by cables.

herbivore an animal that eats only plants.

heredity the process of inheritance, by which particular characteristics are passed on from parents to their offspring.

hormone a chemical that is produced by glands in the body. Hormones (together with the autonomic nervous system) control the functions of organs of the body.

host a living plant or animal that a parasite feeds off.

hydroelectricity power produced by using water to drive turbine generators.

image the picture of an object that is produced by a lens or a mirror.

impermeable waterproof.

incubation the keeping of eggs at the right temperature for the embryos inside.

inertia a resistance to any change in movement that is possessed by everything.

internal combustion engine engine in which the fuel is burned inside the engine, such as a petrol engine.

intestine a tube-like passage in an animal's body in which food is digested and absorbed – also known as a gut.

irrigation providing extra water to crops where the rainfall is insufficient.

joule unit that is used to measure amounts of energy.

kelvin temperature scale temperature scale on which absolute zero is 0 and the freezing point of water is 273.15. Degrees on this scale are the same size as those on the Celsius scale.

kinetic energy energy that a moving object has because it is moving.

latent heat amount of heat absorbed when a liquid boils, or a solid melts.

lift an upward force – in animals, usually on a wing or a fin.

line of force a line that shows the magnetic effect around a magnet. They can be seen by spreading fine iron filings around a magnet.

lung a structure in animals that absorbs oxygen from air. Some invertebrates that live on land use lungs to breathe.

magnetic field the area around a magnet where the magnetic effects can be felt.

magnetic material any material that is attracted to a magnet. Iron and steel, and a few other materials are magnetic.

magnetic pole the place on a magnet where the magnetic effect is strongest.

magnify to make an image appear bigger.

mammal an animal that has a backbone, warm blood, gives birth to live young, and feeds its young on milk. Humans, dogs, sheep and whales are all mammals.

melting point temperature at which a solid turns into a liquid.

membrane a thin layer that covers a part of the body, such as the lining of the the nose, or the outer living layer of a cell.

metamorphosis the change from the young form of an animal to the adult form in animals where the young form is very different from the adult.

molecule the smallest whole unit of a substance. Molecules are extremely small, and are held together by powerful forces similar to gravity.

mucus a sticky or slippery substance produced by an animal.

muscle a body tissue made up of bundles of fibers that can shorten to make the muscle contract. Muscles are needed for bodily movement.

nerve a neuron or a bundle of neurons, which carry nerve impulses to and from the central nervous system.

nerve impulse an electrical signal that travels along a neuron.

neuron a special type of cell that carries electrical signals in the body.

non-magnetic material a material that is not attracted by a magnet. Glass, wood and most metals except iron and steel are non-magnetic materials.

north magnetic pole a place in northern Canada towards which a compass needle always points.

nucleus the central part of a cell that stores DNA and controls the cell.

nutrient a substance in an animal's food that is absorbed and used by the animal's body. For example, vitamins and fats are both nutrients.

omnivore an animal that eats both plants and other animals.

optic nerve a long string-like structure which carries messages from the eye to the brain.

organ a part of the body of an animal that has one or more particular functions. Most organs are made up of a number of special kinds of tissue.

organism any living thing, for example, a plant, an amoeba, or an elephant. Most organisms are made up of a number of special kinds of tissue.

ovary the female organ that produces eggs (ova). Most animals have two ovaries.

parasite an animal that feeds off another living thing.

penis the part of a male animal that passes sperm to a female.

perception the process of getting information about the world by using the sense organs.

periscope a device with two mirrors to help you see around corners.

permeable describes a substance that allows water to pass through it.

pitch the highness or lowness of a sound, defined by the frequency or wavelength of its sound wave. Higher frequency and shorter wavelength give a higher pitch.

placenta an organ that develops in the uterus of a pregnant mammal and provides nourishment to the unborn offspring.

potential energy stored energy, such as that in a stretched spring or a weight raised above the ground.

power rate of doing work, measured in watts (joules per second).

precession a movement that occurs when a wheel rotates and its axle is made to swivel.

predator an animal that hunts other animals for its food.

prey an animal that a predator hunts and kills for its food.

primary color a color that cannot be made by mixing other colors. The primary colors of light are red, green and blue.

radiation energy that can pass through empty space. Heat travels through empty space as infra-red radiation.

reasoning thinking that involves the conscious analysis of information; for example, doing a mathematical problem or analyzing the results of an experiment.

reflection when light bounces off a surface we say it is reflected. Everything reflects some light.

reflex action an action that is directly in response to a stimulus, without the brain being involved, for example, blinking at a sudden bright light.

refraction when light passes from one substance to another it usually changes direction.

refrigerant liquid that circulates through the working parts of a refrigerator and evaporates to produce cooling.

repel to push apart. Two similar magnetic poles repel each other.

reservoir an artificial lake for storing water, and often made by building a dam.

respiration process by which living things produce energy from food substances - especially carbohydrates.

sense one of the ways in which an animal gets information about the world; for example, sight or touch.

sense organ a part of an animal that is used to detect things in the animal's surroundings, for example, eyes or ears.

signal information carried as waves which is received by the television.

siphon a device for lifting water out of a container.

solenoid a coil of wire that behaves like a magnet when an electric current passes through it.

solute substance that dissolves in a solvent to form a solution.

solvent substance in which a solute dissolves.

sound wave the form in which sound travels. A sound wave moves through a material such as air carrying vibrations from a vibrating object that is generating the sound. The object sets up alternate compressions and refractions in the air, which are regions of higher and lower pressure.

speed of light light travels at a speed of 186,000 miles per second, almost 984,252 million feet per second.

speed of sound sound travels at a speed of 1,090 feet per second, which is equal to 742 miles per hour, in air at sea level. The speed of sound is slower high in the atmosphere, where the air is thinner and cooler. Sound travels faster in liquids and solids than in air; it moves at about 4,029 feet per second in water and at 17,060 feet per second in steel.

sperm the male sex cell (gamete), produced by the testis.

spinal cord a large bundle of nerves that runs down from the brain through the tube formed by the bones of the spine.

static electricity when certain materials are rubbed together, electrons move from one material to the other. One material becomes positively charged while the other gains a negative charge. The build-up of negative charge on this material does not flow anywhere so it is called static electricity.

stimulus anything that affects the movement, behavior, or control systems (such as the nerves) of a living organism.

streamlining making an object smooth and rounded so that air or water flows easily over it.

sublimation process in which a solid changes directly into a gas without first becoming a liquid.

superconductor a material which does not resist the flow of electric current at all.

superstation electricity leaves the power station in a form which is too powerful for you to use. Before it reaches your home it passes through substations where the power is adjusted.

surface tension an effect of the surface layer of molecules that pulls water into shape.

synapse a place where signals pass from one neuron to another.

terminal the part of a battery to which wires can be joined. A battery has two terminals – one positive and one negative.

terminal speed the constant speed which falling objects reach when falling through a gas or liquid.

testis the male organ that produces sperm. Most animals have two testes.

thrust the force produced by an engine, that drives it forward.

tissue a group of cells of the same type, all of which have a particular function or group of functions. For example, liver tissue or skin tissue.

transmitter apparatus that sends out signals.

turbine a machine that converts the energy of moving water (or steam, or gas) to some other form of energy. Turbines usually generate electricity.

turbulence swirling movement in a gas or a liquid. Turbulence is caused when an object moves through a gas or liquid.

unconscious a word that describes something that happens in the body without us knowing that it is happening. For example, we are unconscious of the autonomic nervous system controlling our digestive processes.

uterus the organ inside female mammals in which the young develop before birth; also called the womb.

vapor a gas that has evaporated from the surface of a liquid.

vibration rapid back and forth movement. Molecules vibrate more rapidly when heated.

water table the level reached by water in the completely soaked part of the ground. This level varies according to factors such as rainfall.

water wheel a wheel that is turned by moving water. The energy of the moving wheel is used to drive machinery.

watt unit used to measure power. One watt equals one joule per second.

wave a way in which energy travels from one place to another.

wavelength the difference between two successive regions of high pressure. Different types of radiation have different wavelengths. Radio waves have the longest wavelength and gamma rays have the shortest.

zygote a fertilized egg (ovum) which will develop into a new individual.

With special thanks to the following picture libraries and photographers:

Professor Allen (University of St Andrews), Allsport, Vanessa Bailey, BMW Motors, Marie-Helene Bradley, Paul Brierley, J Allan Cash Library, Chapel Picture Library, Bruce Coleman Limited, Mary Evans Picture Library, Eye Ubiquitous, Ford Motor Company, Robert Harding Library, Eric and David Hosking, Hutchinson Library, Flick Killerby, Frank Lane Picture Agency, Mansell Collection, Ministry of Defence, Picturepoint, Planet Earth Pictures, Popperfoto, Science Photo Library, Spectrum Colour Library, Frank Spooner Agency, Topham Picture Library, Roger Vlitos, Richard Alan Wood/ Animals/ OSF, Zefa.